APPROACHES TO NATURAL LANGUAGE

PROCEEDINGS OF THE 1970 STANFORD WORKSHOP ON GRAMMAR AND SEMANTICS

Edited by

K. J. J. HINTIKKA

Academy of Finland

and

J. M. E. MORAVCSIK AND P. SUPPES

Stanford University

D. REIDEL PUBLISHING COMPANY

DORDRECHT-HOLLAND / BOSTON-U.S.A.

Library of Congress Catalog Card Number 72–179892

ISBN 90 277 0220 9

Published by D. Reidel Publishing Company,
P.O. Box 17, Dordrecht, Holland

Sold and distributed in the U.S.A., Canada, and Mexico
by D. Reidel Publishing Company, Inc.
306 Dartmouth Street, Boston,
Mass. 02116, U.S.A.

Printed in The Netherlands

APPROACHES TO NATURAL LANGUAGE

SYNTHESE LIBRARY

MONOGRAPHS ON EPISTEMOLOGY,

LOGIC, METHODOLOGY, PHILOSOPHY OF SCIENCE,

SOCIOLOGY OF SCIENCE AND OF KNOWLEDGE,

AND ON THE MATHEMATICAL METHODS OF

SOCIAL AND BEHAVIORAL SCIENCES

PREFACE

The papers and comments published in the present volume represent the proceedings of a research workshop on the grammar and semantics of natural languages held at Stanford University in the fall of 1970. The workshop met first for three days in September and then for a period of two days in November for extended discussion and analysis. The workshop was sponsored by the Committee on Basic Research in Education, which has been funded by the United States Office of Education through a grant to the National Academy of Education and the National Academy of Sciences – National Research Council. We acknowledge with pleasure the sponsorship which made possible a series of lively and stimulating meetings that were both enjoyable and instructive for the three of us, and, we hope, for most of the participants, including a number of local linguists and philosophers who did not contribute papers but actively joined in the discussion.

One of the central participants in the workshop was Richard Montague. We record our sense of loss at his tragic death early in 1971, and we dedicate this volume to his memory.

None of the papers in the present volume discusses explicitly problems of education. In our view such a discussion is neither necessary nor sufficient for a contribution to basic research in education. There are in fact good reasons why the kind of work reported in the present volume constitutes an important aspect of basic research in education. The main reason is easy to state. Talking and listening are two of the most characteristic activities of education, and yet our understanding of either the syntactic or the semantic structure of speech, not to mention problems of phonology, is as yet imperfect. This can also be said for our understanding of the process of reading. These three processes – talking, listening, and reading – are the main methods by which information is transmitted and intellectual skills are learned. The task of providing an adequate fundamental theory of these processes is comparable to the most challenging problems in any domain of systematic inquiry.

We are under no illusion that any of the papers in this volume provide definitive solutions to the problems they pose. It is premature to expect results of such magnitude. Nevertheless we do feel that the papers taken together make a significant contribution to our better understanding of the nature of language. In the past, much research on learning and cognition, especially by psychologists, has proceeded on the simplifying assumption that an analysis of language would not be necessary to obtain a satisfactory theory of these processes. In certain limited cases this simplifying assumption is probably correct. For the kinds of learning of importance in education, it is now widely recognized that it is certainly not true. It seems likely that no adequate theory of complex learning or cognition will be able to ignore the complex structure of language. Most of the papers in the present volume contribute to showing just how complex this structure is, and yet they have as a common thesis, it is fair to say, the view that this structure is discoverable and analyzable in understandable terms.

The diversity of approaches to these complex matters exhibited in the present volume is, it seems to us, a desirable feature. Not only are there many different problems to be studied, as is clear from the three main sections of the volume, one dealing with grammar, one with semantics, and one with a variety of special topics, but the plurality of approaches even within a given section provides evidence that there is still no single royal road to the truth about language.

We want to express our great appreciation to Mrs. Lillian O'Toole for her editorial assistance and to Mrs. Dianne Kanerva and Mrs. Marguerite Shaw for their secretarial services. As staff members of the Institute for Mathematical Studies in the Social Sciences, they have patiently and efficiently handled the many aspects involved in preparing a volume of this size for publication.

Stanford, California   JAAKKO HINTIKKA
January, 1972   JULIUS MORAVCSIK
                                                        PATRICK SUPPES

TABLE OF CONTENTS

III. SPECIAL TOPICS

PART I

GRAMMAR

JOAN W. BRESNAN

SENTENCE STRESS AND SYNTACTIC TRANSFORMATIONS*

ABSTRACT. If the Nuclear Stress Rule of English is ordered within the transformational cycle after all of the syntactic transformations, many apparent exceptions to Chomsky and Halle (1968) are predictable, for the stress patterns of certain syntactically complex constructions reflect those of the simple sentences embedded within them in deep structure. This preservation of basic stress pattern through the syntactic derivation provides a new method for determining underlying grammatical representations and deciding questions of syntax, which is illustrated. The consequences for linguistic theory, in particular the lexical vs. transformational hypotheses (Chomsky, 1970b), are discussed.

1. INTRODUCTION

Apart from the current controversies over what form grammars should take, it remains that generative grammar is a theory which leads to the discovery and explanation of linguistic phenomena. I will present here a case of discovery and explanation in phonology which will also provide an illustration of certain theoretical notions to be referred to later.

Chomsky and Halle's work in English phonology led to the discovery of the following phenomenon. Consider the following table of nouns:

A	B
relaxation	devastation
attestation	orchestration
condensation	compensation
torment	torrent
convict	verdict
export	effort

There is a rather subtle difference between the two columns of examples: in the members of column B the second vowel is reduced, or barely pronounced, while the corresponding vowel in each example of column A has fuller quality. This fact is of little interest in itself, but within the context of generative phonology it was a discovery explained by the principle of the phonological cycle.

To understand the explanation, note first that the rules of vowel reduction (the rules which determine the distribution of the reduced vowel ə)

Hintikka et al. (eds.), Approaches to Natural Language, 3–47. All rights reserved.

are dependent upon stress: vowels having sufficiently low stress lose their distinctive quality. Thus, in the word *telégraphy*, the second *e* retains its quality while in the word *télegraph* the second *e* is pronounced *ə* because it is unstressed.

Secondly, consider how the principle of the phonological cycle affects stress assignment. That principle states that the cyclic phonological rules are applied first to an innermost bracketed domain (one containing no internal brackets) and then the brackets are erased and the rules are re-applied to the next bracketed domain. For example, the word stress rules would apply to the word *theatricality* in the following fashion:

$$[_N [_A [_N \text{theatr}] \text{ic} + \text{al}] \text{i} + \text{ty}]$$

$$\begin{array}{llll} & 1 & & \\ \hline & 21 & & \\ \hline & 32 & & 1 \\ \hline \end{array}$$

On the first cycle, primary stress (indicated by the numeral 1) is placed on the first vowel of the noun *theatre*. The brackets around *theatre* are then erased. On the next cycle, primary stress goes on the second vowel of the adjective *theatrical*. By a general convention, whenever 1-stress is applied, all other stress values within the domain are reduced by one. The process repeats on the third cycle. Intuitively speaking, the cyclic application of the stress rules 'means merely that the stress of the whole is a function of the stress of the parts. Thus the secondary stress on the second vowel of *theatricality* reflects the original assignment of primary stress to the subpart *theatrical*.

Now if we reexamine the table of examples, we observe that there is a short verb corresponding to each member of column A, but none for B:

A′	B′
reláx	*devast
attést	*orchestr
condénse	*compense
tormént	*torrént
convíct	*verdíct
expórt	*effórt

The cyclic operation of the stress rules thus distinguishes between A and B:

$$[_N [_V \text{relax}] \text{ation}] \quad [_N [_V \text{devastate}] \text{ion}]$$
$$[_N [_V \text{torment}]] \quad [_N \text{torrent}]$$

In the A cases, the second vowel receives primary stress on the first cycle and that stress protects the vowel from reduction throughout the derivation; in the B cases, by contrast, the second vowel never receives primary stress and so is fully reduced. (For a much more detailed account of the above, consult Chomsky and Halle, 1968.)

In the absence of a theory, not much could be made of such subtle, almost labile data as A and B. It is significant that the theory of generative phonology provides an insight into the systematic relation of vowel reduction in the nouns of A and B to the verb forms in A′ and B′.

The theoretical devices of generative grammar are therefore not just formal ways of summarizing or representing observed facts, but means of explaining linguistic phenomena. I will give another preparatory example. It has often been observed that English sentences and noun phrases normally tend to have primary stress on the right:

$$\overset{2}{} \quad \overset{3}{} \quad \quad \overset{1}{}$$
$$[_S \text{ Mary teaches engineering}]$$
$$\overset{2}{} \quad \quad \overset{1}{}$$
$$[_{NP} \text{ a happy philosopher}]$$

(I am not speaking of emphatic or contrastive stress.) One way of representing this observation is to write a rule which applies to sentences (S) and noun phrases (NP), marking the rightmost occurrence of primary stress and reducing, by convention, all other occurrences of stress by one. This rule is called the Nuclear Stress Rule (NSR). It is necessary to distinguish the NSR from another rule which applies, not to sentences and noun phrases, but to compound nouns, and marks the leftmost occurrence of primary stress (thus reducing other stress values by one):

$$\overset{1}{} \quad \quad \overset{2}{}$$
$$[_N \text{ defense department}]$$
$$\overset{1}{} \quad \quad \overset{2}{}$$
$$[_N \text{ philosophy teacher}]$$

Some expressions are structurally ambiguous, and are assigned stress

differentially: *an English teacher, an English teacher*. The compound noun

English teacher, meaning 'teacher of English', has the syntactic form $[_N [_N \text{English}] [_N \text{teacher}]]$ and hence receives leftward stress. The compound noun itself can occur in noun phrases, as in *a happy English teacher*, which has the form $[_{NP} \text{Article Adjective Noun}]$. In this case, both rules apply, as follows:

$$[_{NP} \text{ a } [_A \text{ happy}] [_N [_N \text{ English}] [_N \text{ teacher}]]]$$

1	1	1	word stress rules
	1	2	compound rule
2	1	3	NSR
2	1		

The noun phrase *an English teacher*, meaning 'a teacher who is English', has the form $[_{NP} \text{Article Adjective Noun}]$, and like the NP *a happy philosopher* receives rightward primary stress.

The point of this example is that the NSR is not merely a device for representing the observation that English tends to have rightward primary stress. It is rather a phonological rule which interacts with other rules in a systematic way to produce the complex intonation contours of English. If we said merely, "English tends to have rightward primary stress, as in *a happy philosopher*," we would immediately be faced with the question of why we do not normally say *a happy philosophy teacher* rather than *a happy philosophy teacher*. The theory of generative phonology, with its principles of rule ordering, provides an explanation which relates the stress pattern of *a happy philosophy teacher* to that of *philosophy teacher*.

In what follows I will consider a different class of exceptions to the observation that English has rightward primary stress and show how they can be explained. The explanation requires a relatively simple modification of linguistic theory, but one which has interesting and far-reaching consequences. I will argue that the NSR interacts with syntactic transformations in a systematic way. This interaction both extends the predictive power of English phonology and provides a new source of information about the nature of syntactic representation and the existence of deep structure.

2. THE ORDERING HYPOTHESIS

The NSR is a cyclic rule applying after all rules affecting the stress of individual lexical items; it is formulated as follows:[1]

$$\text{NSR} \quad \overset{1}{V} \to 1/[_A \overset{1}{X V Y}\underline{\quad} Z]$$

where Z may contain no V and where A ranges over major categories such as NP, VP, S. Given the convention that any application of 1-stress within a cycle reduces all other stress values by 1, the NSR has the effect shown in Figure 1.

$$[_S [\text{Mary}] [_{VP} [\text{teaches}] [\text{engineering}] _{VP}] _S]$$

1	1	1	(word stress)
	2	1	1st cycle: NSR
2	3	1	2nd cycle: NSR

Fig. 1.

There is a question whether the NSR should be allowed to cycle on VP. Note that if it does not cycle on VP, the stress contour [221] will result in Figure 1. But there is another rule which alters [221] to [231].[2] Thus, instead of the derivation shown in Figure 1, the type of derivation shown in Figure 2 may be correct:

$$[_S [\text{Mary}] [\text{teaches}] [\text{engineering}]_S]$$

1	1	1	(word stress)
2	2	1	NSR
	3		[221] →[231]

Fig. 2.

For the moment I shall ignore this detail in the application of NSR. It is clear that this rule results in primary stress on the rightmost constituent in a sentence. This is, in general, the 'normal' intonation for an English sentence. There are, however, well-known classes of exceptions to this pattern. Final anaphoric pronouns do not normally receive primary stress:

$$\overset{1}{\text{Helen teaches it.}}$$

$$* \overset{1}{\text{Helen teaches it.}}$$

('Normally' means 'excluding emphatic or contrastive stress'.) Nor do final indefinite pronouns receive primary stress normally:

$$\overset{1}{\text{The boy bought some.}}$$

$$* \overset{1}{\text{The boy bought some.}}$$

Other anaphoric items, even when grammatically definite, receive no 1-stress:

$$\text{John knows a woman who excels at karate, and he avoids the} \overset{1}{}$$
woman.

In what follows I will assume that by some means or other anaphoric and indefinite elements are not assigned primary stress, and generally I will ignore the stressing of items which are not relevant to the point at issue.

Now the stress patterns of certain syntactically complex constructions appear to violate the general prediction made by the NSR. There are four cases that I will be concerned with here. The first is the type of contrast observed by Newman (1946):

$$\overset{1}{}$$
(Ia)   George has plans to leave.

$$\overset{1}{}$$
(Ib)   George has plans to leave.

Roughly, the meaning of (Ia) is that George has plans which he intends to leave, while (Ib) means that George is planning to leave. The next pair of examples belongs to the same case:

1
(Ic)   Helen left directions for George to follow.

1
(Id)   Helen left directions for George to follow.

(Ic) means that Helen left directions which George is supposed to follow, while (Id) means that Helen left directions to the effect that George should follow.

The second case I will consider is quite similar:

1
(IIa)   Mary liked the proposal that George left.

1
(IIb)   Mary liked the proposal that George leave.

Here as in case I there is a syntactic difference corresponding to a difference in stress.

A third case involves questions, direct and indirect:

1
(IIIa)   John asked what Helen had written.

1
(IIIb)   John asked what books Helen had written.

1
(IIIc)   What has Helen written?

1
(IIId)   What books has Helen written?

1
(IIIe)   You can't help noticing how he is.

1
(IIIf)   You can't help noticing how serene he is.

1
(IIIg)   Whose have I taken?

1
(IIIh)   Whose umbrella have I taken?

It should be noted here that the interrogative *which* is inherently contrastive; in the sentence

2   1

Which books has John read?

reading is being implicitly contrasted with some other notion:

He has READ SOME books but only SKIMMED OTHERS.

That such sentences with *which* do not have the intonation characteristic of case III is therefore of no concern here.

The fourth case involves relative clauses again:

                                                    1

(IVa)   George found someone he'd like you to meet.

                                1

(IVb)   George found some friends he'd like you to meet.

                                        1

(IVc)   Let me tell you about something I saw.

                                            1

(IVd)   Let me tell you about something strange I saw.

The interesting fact about the above apparent exceptions to the NSR is that they are all predictable without any special modifications in that rule, given one assumption: the NUCLEAR STRESS RULE IS ORDERED AFTER ALL THE SYNTACTIC TRANSFORMATIONS ON EACH TRANSFORMATIONAL CYCLE.

Note first that if transformations cycle on the nodes NP and S (Chomsky, 1970b) but not VP, the above assumption entails that NSR applies not on VP within S, but only on NP and S (and any other transformationally cycled nodes). Secondly, the above assumption entails that the NSR is cyclic. I will now verify the above claim.

First I will derive (Ic) and (Id); (Ia) and (Ib) are similar, but involve an additional deletion. The grammatical representations that follow are only approximate. See Figure 3.

As shown in Figure 3, the stress difference in (Ic) and (Id) is predictable from the fact that in the deep structure of (Ic) *follow* has a direct object, while in (Id) *follow* has no direct object and hence receives primary stress as the rightmost constituent. Case II is parallel: see Figure 4.

[S Helen left [NP directions [S for George to follow directions S] NP] S]

1	1	1	1	1	1	(word stress)
			2	2	1	1st cycle: NSR
				φ		2nd cycle: syntax
2	2	1		3	3	3rd cycle: NSR

Derivation of (Ic)

[S Helen left [NP directions [S for George to follow S] NP] S]

1	1	1	1	(word stress)
		2	1	1st cycle: NSR
	2	3	1	2nd cycle: NSR
2	2	3	4	1	3rd cycle: NSR

Derivation of (Id)

Fig. 3.

JOAN W. BRESNAN

[s Mary liked [NP the proposal [s that George left the proposal s] NP] s]

	Mary	liked	the	proposal	that	George	left	the	proposal	
(word stress)	1	1		1		1	1	1	1	
1st cycle: NSR				2			2		1	
2nd cycle: syntax									ø	
3rd cycle: NSR	2	2		1			3		3	

Derivation of (IIa)

[s Mary liked [NP the proposal [s that George leave s] NP] s]

	Mary	liked	the	proposal	that	George	leave	
(word stress)	1	1		1		1	1	
1st cycle: NSR						2	1	
2nd cycle: NSR				2		3	1	
3rd cycle: NSR	2	2		3		4	1	

Derivation of (IIb)

Fig. 4.

In the derivation of case III, I have bracketed the examples to reflect the phrase structure rule.

$$\bar{S} \rightarrow COMP\ S,$$

where COMP is Q, the interrogative morpheme. This rule is justified in
$+WH$
Bresnan (1970b). I have omitted the corresponding bracketing from the preceding cases because it plays no role there. I shall derive (IIIa) through (IIId).

In Figure 5 the object of *written* is the interrogative pronoun *what* (which I am assuming to be derived from *something*, though this is not a necessary assumption for the point at issue); pronouns, it should be recalled, do not receive primary stress. Thus the verb retains primary stress.

As shown in Figure 6, the full NP object of *written* receives primary stress, causing the stress on *written* to be lowered. The difference in stress between (IIIa) and (IIIb) reflects the stress difference between the simple sentences embedded in them:

$$\overset{1}{\text{Helen had written something.}}$$

$$\overset{1}{\text{Helen had written some books.}}$$

The same is true of (IIIc) and (IIId): see Figure 7.

The analysis given in case III correctly predicts the existence of a stress difference associated with the two readings of sentences like

The parable shows what suffering men can create.

The readings may be indicated as follows:

$$\overset{1}{\text{The parable shows what (suffering men) can create.}}$$

$$\overset{1}{\text{The parable shows (what suffering) men can create.}}$$

These examples are exactly analogous to those of case III: the pronominal object *what* permits the verb to retain primary stress; the full object *what suffering* causes the verbal stress to be lowered. There are many similar examples, e.g., *I forgot how good bread smells.*

In cases I and II, the stress difference depended on whether there had been an underlying object of the verb: if so, the verbal stress was lowered;

[s John asked [s COMP [s Helen had written something s] s] s]
                 +WH   +wh

1 1	1	1	(word stress)
	2	1	1st cycle: NSR
	something	ϕ	
	+wh		
2 2	1		2nd cycle: syntax
	3	1	3rd cycle: NSR

Derivation of (IIIa)

Fig. 5.

[s John asked [s COMP [s Helen had written some books s] s] s]
                 +WH   +wh

1 1	1	1	(word stress)
	2	2	1st cycle: NSR
	some books	ϕ	
	+wh		
2 2	1		2nd cycle: syntax
	3	3	3rd cycle: NSR

Derivation of (IIIb)

Fig. 6.

[s COMP [s Helen has written something s] s]
 +WH   +wh

		1	1	(word stress)
		2	1	1st cycle: NSR

something   has   φ   φ
 +wh
   1
   2   φ

	2	1

2nd cycle: syntax: Question
Formation
Subject-Verb Inversion

What has Helen written?
Derivation of (IIIc)

[s COMP [s Helen has written some books s] s]
 +WH   +wh

	1	1	1
	2	2	1

(word stress)
1st cycle: NSR

some books   has   φ
 +wh
    1

1	2	2

2nd cycle: syntax: Question
Formation
Subject-Verb Inversion

What books has Helen written?
Derivation of (IIId)

Fig. 7.

if not, the verb retained primary stress throughout the derivation. In case
III the crucial factor was what *kind* of object the verb had: if pronominal,
the verb kept primary stress; if a full object, the verbal stress was lowered.
Now in case IV it appears that the kind of object – pronominal or full –
affects the stress contours of relatives just as it does questions: see Figure 8.

This fact would lead one to predict that the difference between *plans to*
$$\overset{1}{leave}$$
leave and *plans to leave* is neutralized when the head is pronominal. In
other words, there should be a stress contrast between the relative clause

construction of case I – *George has* $\overset{1}{plans}$ *to leave* – and the same type of
construction with a pronominal head; this prediction is borne out: *George*

has $\overset{1}{something}$ *to leave.*

   In general, where the simple sentence embedded in a relative would
receive verbal primary stress by itself –

$$\overset{1}{I\ like}\ a\ man\ (like\ that).$$

– the corresponding relative has verbal primary stress:

$$\overset{1}{He's}\ a\ man\ I\ like.$$

In these two examples *a man* is predicative. If *a man* is specific, it can
receive primary stress in the simple sentence:

$$I\ like\ a\ \overset{1}{(certain)}\ man.$$

And correspondingly we find

$$A\ \overset{1}{(certain)}\ man\ I\ like.\ \ldots$$

There are sentences in which just this stress difference decides the reading;
for example

   A man I like believes in women's liberation.

[s George found [NP someone [s he would like you to meet someone s] NP] s]

1 1		1 1		(word stress)
		2	1	1st cycle: NSR
				2nd cycle: syntax
2 2		3	1	3rd cycle: NSR
			φ	

Derivation of (VIa)

[s George found [NP some friends [s he would like you to meet some friends s] NP] s]

1 1		1 1 1		(word stress)
		2 2	1	1st cycle: NSR
		3 3		2nd cycle: syntax
2 2		3 3		3rd cycle: NSR
			φ	

Derivation of (VIb)

Fig. 8.

When *man* has greater stress than *like*, the sentence is understood as being about a certain man; when *like* carries greater stress than *man*, the sentence is, in a sense, about the speaker.[3]

All of the cases discussed involve the movement or deletion of verbal objects rather than subjects. The reason is that since the NSR assigns primary stress to the rightmost element, only cases in which the underlying rightmost element has been affected by transformations can provide crucial evidence. Thus both the ordering hypothesis advanced here and the previously proposed ordering can account for the stress in

$$1$$
I asked whose children bit Fido.

$$1$$
the man whose children bit my dog

$$1$$
a desire to eat

But only the new ordering hypothesis accounts for the stress in

$$1$$
I asked whose children Fido bit.

$$1$$
the man whose children my dog bit

$$1$$
food to eat.

In the latter examples the underlying objects have diverged from their original rightmost position, where they had caused the verbal stress to be lowered during cyclic application of the NSR.

The ordering hypothesis explains the fact that the stress patterns of certain syntactically complex constructions reflect those of the simple sentences embedded within them in deep structure. This preservation of basic stress pattern through the syntactic derivation provides a new method for determining underlying grammatical representations and deciding questions of syntax. To illustrate this method, I will consider the following question. It has been proposed (most recently by Emonds, 1970, but earlier by Lees, 1960) that certain infinitival complements should be derived from deep structure VP's rather than S's. Suppose this proposal is applied to the analysis of certain adjective + complement constructions. The question is whether in a construction like

It is tough for students to solve this problem.

there is an underlying S = [for students to solve this problem] or an underlying PP + VP = [for students] [to solve this problem].[4]

There are several facts which argue against the sentential analysis: first, if there were an underlying sentence, one would normally expect such a sentence-cyclic transformation as *There* Insertion to take place.[5] But though one can say

It will be tough for at least some students to be in class on time.

one cannot say

* It will be tough for there to be at least some students in class on time.

Compare cases which are truly sentential:

The administration is eager for there to be at least some students in class on time.
The commander left directions for there to be a soldier on duty at all times.
It wouldn't surprise me for there to be countless revolutionaries among the secretaries.

Second, the *for* complementizer of a true sentential complement allows many types of objects which the preposition *for* after *hard* does not:

Emmy was eager for that theorem on modules to become known.

* It was tough for that theorem on modules to become known.

It would surprise me for a book on Hittite to please John.

* It would be tough for a book on Hittite to please John.

Third, the complement of *hard*, *tough*, *a bear*, *a breeze*, and similar predicates does not behave as a sentential constituent under S Movement: compare a true sentential complement –

It is surprising [for a woman to act that way $_s$].
[For a woman to act that way $_s$] is surprising.

– with the complement of *hard* or *tough*:

> It is hard for a woman to act that way.
> * For a woman to act that way is hard.
>
> It's tough for students to grasp this concept.
> * For students to grasp this concept is tough.

It is a difficult syntactic problem to determine the correct analyses of *for* constructions.[6] The above ordering hypothesis provides new evidence bearing on this problem, for *tough*, *hard* and the other adjectives of this construction are subject to a transformation which affects the object of the complement to produce such sentences as

> This theorem was a breeze for Emmy to prove.

Given that transformations do not cycle on VP, the hypothesis advanced above results in exactly the right stress contours for these sentences if the complement is represented as PP + VP. To illustrate, suppose that Figure 9 shows a permissible deep structure for *That theorem was tough to prove*, ignoring details:

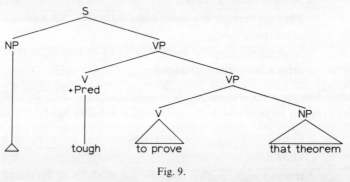

Fig. 9.

As noted, there is no cycle on VP, so not until S will any rules apply. At that point the object of *prove* is shifted, yielding the derived structure shown in Figure 10.

Then NSR will apply, giving the contour [221], which will eventually become [231] by the rule referred to in note 2.

On the other hand, suppose this example came from a deep structure with a sentential complement to *tough*, for example that shown in Figure 11.

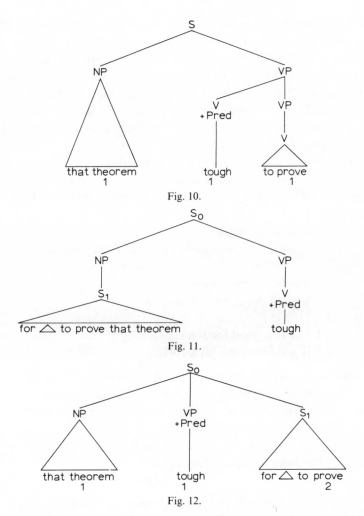

Fig. 10.

Fig. 11.

Fig. 12.

Again, the exact details of the representation are immaterial. The NSR
would apply on the S_1 cycle, producing *prove that theorem*; on the S_0
cycle *that theorem* would be moved into subject position and S_1 extraposed:
see Figure 12.

Again NSR would apply, yielding the incorrect contour *[213].[7]

In this way one is led to conclude from both stress and syntax that VP as well as S must be a possible adjectival complement in deep structure. (See Appendix I for further discussion.) A given adjective may therefore be subcategorized for VP or S (or both). If the Object Shift transformation applies only to adjectives with VP complements, there will be no need to resort to rule features to describe this phenomenon; that is, arbitrariness in the grammar may be reduced by stating Object Shift in such a way that it will apply only to VP complements.[8]

There is in fact a class of adjectives permitting both S and PP + VP complements, namely, the class including *good*, *bad*, *sweet*, *pleasant*, and *appropriate*. The ambiguity in such cases was noticed by Lees (1960). The sentence

> It is good for John to leave.

may mean either

> For John to leave is good.
> = It is good (for John to leave).

or

> To leave is good for John.
> = It is good for John (to leave).

Lees maintains a clear distinction between the ambiguous class (*good*; his type 7) and the unambiguous class (*hard*, *tough*; his type 8), but some speakers may class certain of the latter with the former, permitting sentences like[9]

$$\text{For John to please Mary is} \begin{Bmatrix} \text{hard} \\ \text{easy} \\ \text{difficult} \end{Bmatrix}.$$

The possibility of both VP and S complements for these adjectives accounts for the following paradigm:

(Xa)   * Such things are not $\begin{Bmatrix} \text{good} \\ \text{appropriate} \end{Bmatrix}$ for there to be children involved in.

(Xb)   It is not $\begin{Bmatrix} \text{good} \\ \text{appropriate} \end{Bmatrix}$ for there to be children involved in such things.

(Xc)   Such things are not $\left\{ \begin{matrix} \text{good} \\ \text{appropriate} \end{matrix} \right\}$ for children to be involved in.

(Xd)   It is not $\left\{ \begin{matrix} \text{good} \\ \text{appropriate} \end{matrix} \right\}$ for children to be involved in such things.

The fact that (Xa) is ungrammatical is precisely what is predicted from the analysis given here. For *good* and *appropriate* may take both S and VP complements. Object Shift can apply only to VP complements, as shown in note 9, and *There* Insertion can apply only to S complements. The presence of *there* in (Xa) and (Xb) forces the 'S interpretation' of the complement in both (Xa) and (Xb) and hence the shifted object in (Xa) is ungrammatical.[10]

I have discussed adjectives which, like *tough*, take only (PP) + VP complements as well as adjectives which, like *good*, take both (PP) + VP and S. It should not be surprising to discover adjectives taking (PP) + S, and indeed that is just what we would expect if VP is, with S, a possible complement generated in phrase structure: the phrase structure rules will specify VP as an alternative choice wherever S is specified, as in the rule

$$VP \rightarrow \ldots (PP) \left(\left\{ \begin{matrix} VP \\ S \end{matrix} \right\} \right).$$

One adjective which displays the possibility PP + S is *good*:

> For Mary to learn karate would be good for her.
> It would be good for Mary for her to learn karate.

In fact, one would predict that Object Shift cannot apply to these examples, since a full S follows *for Mary*, and this prediction is borne out:

> * Karate would be good [for Mary$_{PP}$] [for her to learn$_S$].
> Karate would be good [for Mary$_{PP}$] [to learn$_{VP}$].

The ungrammaticality of * *Karate would be good for Mary for her to learn* is another crucial test in favor of the formulation of Object Shift given here.

To conclude, it is because both the *tough to prove* and the passive construction have rightward primary stress that I have ordered the NSR after all transformations on each cycle. This ordering guarantees that on a given cycle Object Shift or Passive may apply before the NSR:

1

John was seen by Mary.

1

John was hard to see.

Note that the same applies to Noun Phrases: the passivization of nominals (Chomsky, 1970b) also precedes the NSR:

1

the enemy's destruction of the city.

1

the city's destruction by the enemy.

On the other hand, within a derivation Question Formation and Relative Clause Formation must apply after the NSR has affected the simple S's embedded in interrogative and relative structures:

1

What books has Helen written?

1

I wonder what books Helen has written.

1

Here's a book for you to read.

This ordering follows automatically from the principle of the transformational cycle and the analysis of syntactic structures given, in which there is a simple S embedded within interrogatives as well as relatives (Bresnan, 1970b). That Question Formation and Relative Clause Formation actually do apply on the transformational cycle is shown in Appendix II by independent syntactic arguments.

3. SOME CONSEQUENCES

The ordering of the NSR proposed here has interesting consequences for linguistic theory. The most immediate consequence is, of course, the inadequacy of a basic assumption of generative phonology (Chomsky and Halle, 1968, p. 15):

It is well known that English has complex prosodic contours involving many levels of stress. . . . It is clear even from a superficial examination that these contours are determined in some manner by the surface structure of the utterance.

Instead it appears that the stress contours of English sentences are determined in a simple and regular way by their underlying syntactic structures. Further, because prosodic stress rules like the NSR require prior assignment of word stress, the latter must occur either on deep structure or in the lexicon.[11] But if word stress is assigned prior to the syntactic transformations, then it follows automatically that transformationally attached affixes are stress-neutral.[12] For example, the primary stress on the verb *derive* is unchanged by the affix *ing* but shifts when *ation* is affixed:

$$1$$
deriving
$$1$$
derivation.

This would follow if *ing*, but not *ation*, were attached to *derive* by a syntactic transformation. But this is exactly what Chomsky (1970b) argues on independent syntactic and semantic grounds: his lexicalist hypothesis states that gerundive nominals like

Wanda's deriving the answer

– which are productive and sentence-like – are created by syntactic transformation, while derived nominals like

Wanda's derivation of the answer

– which are restricted and noun-like – are created by lexical rules. Because the NSR may apply on the first syntactic cycle, and because word-stress assignment precedes prosodic stress assignment, all lexical insertion must occur on or before the first transformational cycle. If there is some level in derivations at which all lexical insertion converges, then deep structure, in the sense of Chomsky (1965), exists. Now the assignment of word stress prior to prosodic stress simply follows from the principle of the phonological cycle (Chomsky and Halle, 1968): in other words, the stress of the whole is a function of the stress of the parts. Therefore, IT IS A CONSEQUENCE OF THE ORDERING HYPOTHESIS PRESENTED HERE TOGETHER WITH THE PRINCIPLE OF THE PHONOLOGICAL CYCLE THAT THE LEXICAL HYPOTHESIS (CHOMSKY, 1970b) IS CORRECT AND THAT DEEP STRUCTURE EXISTS.[13]

Those grammarians who accept the transformational hypothesis (see Chomsky, 1970b, for references) must either reject the stress ordering hypothesis presented here or the principle of the phonological cycle. Let us see what is entailed in the latter course. One concrete way of rejecting the phonological cycle is to claim that the NSR assigns stress to non-terminal symbols only and that word stress occurs subsequently.[14] This proposal implies that prosodic stress does not depend in any way on lexical information, but only on syntactic configurations. Yet, as we have seen, the NSR must 'know' whether it is applying to a pronoun or to a fully specified lexical noun phrase in order for the systematic difference between such pairs of examples as these to be explained:

$$1$$
Helen detests misogynists.

$$1$$
Helen detests them.

$$1$$
The parable shows (what suffering) men can create.

$$1$$
The parable shows what (suffering men) can create.

(Because the ordering hypothesis entails that pronouns are in deep structure, it is interesting to observe that recent work has shown independently that they are present in deep structure and not created transformationally: see, for example, Bresnan, 1970a; Dougherty, 1969; and Jackendoff, 1969.) The same is true of semipronouns like *people*, *things*:

$$1$$
I like people.

$$1$$
There are many people I like.

Similarly, the derived stress contours of sentences containing anaphoric and nonanaphoric noun phrases differ:

> 2   3   1
> John knows a woman.
> 2   1   3
> John avoids the woman.

Different stress contours are produced by the NSR as a function of the difference in stress between anaphoric and nonanaphoric lexical items. It is hard to see how this dependency of stress contour on the stress level of individual lexical items can be explained if the phonological cycle is given up.

Another interesting consequence of the ordering hypothesis is this: English is not a VSO (Verb Subject Object) language in the sense of McCawley (1970).[15] The reason is just this: McCawley proposes that English has underlying VSO word order throughout the transformational cycle and converts to SVO (Subject Verb Object) only by a postcyclic verb-second rule. In McCawley's system intransitive verbs would precede their subjects throughout the cycle, and thus get reduced stress by the cyclic application of the NSR. Instead of

> 1
> They said that Jesus wept.

the incorrect contour

> 1
> * They said that Jesus wept.

would result as the normal English intonation. On the other hand, if McCawley's verb-second rule were cyclic, his arguments for underlying VSO order in English would disappear.

We see that the stress ordering hypothesis provides a kind of 'naturalness condition' on syntactic derivations: the formal properties of surface structures cannot diverge too greatly from those of deep structures without destroying the relation between syntax and prosodic stress. In a sense, it is natural that a close relation should exist between sound and syntactic structure; after all, languages, unlike the countless logics and 'logical languages' invented by philosophers, are spoken. It is not surprising that McCawley's system, explicitly modeled on one kind of notation used in symbolic logic, proves to be an inadequate syntactic basis for a description of English stress contours.

Having sketched these consequences for linguistic theory, I would finally like to consider three problems for further research.

The first problem concerns sentences like

> This theory was believed by George to have been thought by Paul to have been refuted by Jim.

It is possible that such sentences derive from an underlying form close to

> [s George believed [s that Paul thought [s that Jim refuted this theory s] s] s]

by a sequence of operations indicated in Figure 13; note the derived stress contour.

Evidently, these syntactic processes can be repeated indefinitely:

> This theory was expected by Dave to have been believed by George to have been thought by Paul to have been refuted by Jim.
> This theory was said by John to have been expected by Dave to have been believed by George to have been thought by Paul to have been refuted by Jim.

In such a way the derived subject *this theory* may receive stress indefinitely weak compared with the verb. This result is clearly wrong. Therefore, if the syntactic derivation of such sentences is correct, it appears that some convention limiting iterated stress reduction is needed. Just this conclusion is argued independently in Bierwisch (1968). Further research on the form and scope of the stress reduction convention is necessary; if stress reduction is limited, the observed variation can be effected by 'rhythm' rules, e.g., [2221] →[2321].

A second problem may lie in the formulation of the Nuclear Stress Rule itself. The problem is seen when there is more material than one Noun

[George believed [Paul thought [Jim refuted this theory]]]   (word stress)
   1   1   1   1

this theory was refuted by J.   Passive
            1   1
         2   1   NSR

Paul thought this theory [φ to have been refuted by J.]   Subject Raising
 1   1   2   2   1
                   2   1   Passive
                3   1   NSR

this theory was thought by P. to have been refuted by J.
 2   1   2   2   1   Passive
 3   2   3   1   NSR

George believed this theory [φ to have been thought by P. to have been refuted by J.]   Subject Raising
  1   3   2   2   2   3   1
                  2   2   3   1   Passive

this theory was believed by G. to have been thought by P. to have been refuted by J.   Passive
 3   1   2   2   2   3   1
 4   2   3   3   4   1   NSR

Fig. 13.

Phrase to the right of the verb. Compare these examples

$$\overset{1}{\text{Peter used a knife.}}$$

Peter used a knife.

$$\overset{1}{\text{Whose}}$$

Whose knife did Peter use?

with these

Peter sliced the salami with a knife.

Whose knife did Peter slice the salami with?

The first pair, but not the second, is explicable from what I have proposed so far. Here are further examples like the second pair:

Mary found a car on Thursday evening.

On what evening did Mary find a car?

Mary gave a book to Peter's children.

Whose children did Mary give a book to?

What book did Mary give Peter's children?[16]

Recall that the effect of the NSR is to lower stress on every element to the left of the rightmost primary stress within the appropriate contexts. The above examples suggest that perhaps all primary-stressed items to the right of the verb – and not just the rightmost – should retain primary stress until the late application of a rhythm rule. This conjecture is illustrated in Figure 14.

The third problem[17] is to account for the following contrast:

(A)   Peter had plans for dinner.

(B)   Peter had clams for dinner.

[s Peter sliced the salami with a knife]

1	1	1	1	(word stress)
2	2		1	revised NSR
2	3		2	1	rhythm rule

[s COMP [s Peter sliced the salami with someone's knife]]
+WH   +wh

1	1	1	(word stress)
2	2	1	revised NSR

Question Formation

someone's knife   φ   φ   φ
+wh

Subject-Verb Inversion

did Peter slice

whose knife did Peter slice the salami with

1	2	2	1	revised NSR
2	3	3	1	

Fig. 14.

As it stands, *plans for dinner* is the predicted stress contour; the problem lies with (B). Note that when a pronoun is used for *clams*, the stress shifts rightward:

1

Peter had them for dinner.

Further, *plans for dinner* but not *clams for dinner* is a constituent:

Plans for dinner were suggested by Peter.

* Clams for dinner were suggested by Peter.

It appears that the formulation of the NSR may have to take into account certain kinds of prepositional phrases.

Although the problem posed by (B) is still unsolved, the basic principle that stress patterns are preserved through syntactic derivation still holds: compare (A) and (B) with (C) and (D):

2   1

(C)   The plans Peter had for dinner didn't come off.

2   1

(D)   The clams Peter had for dinner didn't come off.

Therefore, as in the preceding cases, this problem concerns the proper formulation of the NSR rather than the ordering hypothesis: once the principle for applying stress to (B) is found, the ordering hypothesis will predict (D).

ACKNOWLEDGMENTS

For suggestions for improving several earlier versions of this paper I am very grateful to Noam Chomsky, Morris Halle, and James D. McCawley, who of course are not responsible for the remaining defects.

APPENDIX I

The existence of VP complements in deep structure is not a *necessary* consequence of the ordering hypothesis presented here. It is possible to 'preserve sentences', so to speak, by deriving *John is tough to please* from

$John_i$ is tough [$_S$ . . . to please him_i].

The presence of the pronominal object of *please* will allow the verb to retain primary stress on the innermost S-cycle and the presence of a specified subject *John* would prohibit a sentential subject: * *For Mary to please John is tough.* However, this solution leaves unexplained several of the other nonsentential properties of such constructions:

(1)   the absence of *There* Insertion;
(2)   the selectional properties of *for*;
(3)   the generalization that Object Shift does not cross S-brackets.

Further, it would require some sort of special constraint to guarantee the presence of a pronominal object in the complement which would have the subject of *tough* as antecedent.

It is possible to amend the above solution to take account of (1)–(3), though the proposed amendment is ad hoc. Suppose that *Mary is tough for John to please* were derived from

(Y) Mary$_i$ is tough [$_{PP}$ for John$_j$] [$_S$ he$_j$ please her$_i$]

by two obligatory deletions – Object Deletion, affecting *her$_i$*, and Equi-NP Deletion, affecting *he$_j$*. See Postal (1968a) on the latter transformation. Object Deletion will be written almost exactly as Object Shift is stated in note 8:

$$[_S \text{ NP Pred (PP) } [V^* \text{ NP }_{VP}]] \rightarrow 1\ 2\ 3\ 4\ \phi$$
$$1\quad 2\quad 3\quad 4\quad 5$$

The PP in (Y) would account for (2); a new constraint that the subject of the complement take the object of the preposition as antecedent will take care of (1), since *there* cannot be an underlying subject and cannot replace anaphoric pronouns; and (3) will follow from the pruning of the embedded S after Equi-NP Deletion. This solution requires, of course, that Equi-NP Deletion be cyclic (contra Postal, 1968b): in order to derive *Mary is believed by everyone to be tough for John to please*, Object Deletion must take place before the cyclic Passive rule; and Equi-NP Deletion must precede Object Deletion so that S will prune to VP.

It is quite striking that this method of preserving a sentential complement for adjectives like *tough* uses only the bare verbal skeleton of the sentence: subject and object are obligatorily deleted pronouns, so that the postulated underlying S has no trace in any surface form derived from the proposed deep structure (Y).

APPENDIX II

I have shown that it is possible for the NSR to be ordered within the transformational cycle, but I have not actually shown that it is necessary. For I
have assumed without explicit justification that Relative Clause Formation and Question Formation are cyclic transformations. If these transformations were not cyclic one might think of ordering the NSR after the
entire transformational cycle but before the postcyclic transformations,
taking the latter to include Relative Clause Formation and Question
Formation.[18] There are two kinds of evidence against this alternative.
First, all of the stress evidence indicates that the NSR does not precede
known postcyclic transformations; for example, we do not have

1   2

* Away ran Fido.

but rather

2   1

Away ran Fido.

The former would result if the NSR preceded the postcyclic transformation which preposes *away*. Likewise, we do not have

1   2   3

* Seldom does John sing.

but rather

2   3   1

Seldom does John sing.

Yet the former would result if the NSR preceded the postcyclic transformation which fronts *seldom*.[19] (See Emonds, 1970, on both of these
transformations, Directional Adverb Preposing and Negative Adverb
Preposing.)

Second, there is syntactic evidence that Relative Clause Formation and
Question Formation are indeed cyclic transformations. Because of the
consequences for linguistic theory of the cyclicity of the NSR, I will
demonstrate here that Question Formation (QF) and Relative Clause
Formation (RCF) are cyclic transformations. The matter is of some intrinsic interest as well.[20] From this demonstration and the fact that the

NSR precedes these transformations while following other cyclic transformations, it can be concluded that the NSR is indeed cyclic, applying
after all the transformations applying to each cycle.

As preparation, observe that there is a transformation which performs
operations like the following:

> Mary has studied little and yet Mary has accomplished a
> great deal. →
> Mary has studied little and yet accomplished a great deal.

This transformation, which I will refer to as Right Conjunct Reduction,
may be thought of as deleting material in the right conjunct which repeats
that in the left.[21] The conjuncts may be full sentences, as above, or noun
phrases:

> The trees in Northern California and the trees in Oregon are
> similar. →
> The trees in Northern California and (in) Oregon are similar.

The argument I will give consists in showing that there are derivations in
which Right Conjunct Reduction may follow an application of QF and
derivations in which it may precede an application of QF. To show the
latter it will be necessary to use a transformation which I shall call Postposing. This is an optional rule which postposes certain complements to
noun phrases, relating pairs like these:

> The news from Italy was the same. →
> The news was the same from Italy.
> The results on the virus were parallel. →
> The results were parallel on the virus.
> The stories about her are similar. →
> The stories are similar about her.

Such a transformation is needed to explain certain peculiarities in the
distribution of prepositional phrases. For example, the impossibility of

> * That was the same from Italy.

is explained by the ungrammaticality of its source under Postposing:

> * That from Italy was the same.

Prepositional phrases which *can* be generated to the right of predicates are not excluded by such pronominal subjects:

> That is the same in France.
> They were similar during the occupation.

Postposing preserves structure (Emonds, 1970), so that if a prepositional phrase already occupies immediate postpredicate position, the rule does not apply (i.e., since a node is moved by a structure preserving rule only into a place where the same node can be generated by the base, the transformation does not apply if the place is already filled):

> Some things about France are quite similar to those you mention about England.
> * Some things are quite similar to those you mention about England about France.
> * Some things are quite similar about France to those you mention about England.
> Cf. Some things are quite similar about France.

(The last sentence should be imagined in a conversational context, e.g., *Concerning what you have just observed about England, I can add that some things are quite similar about France.*)

> Their results on that virus were parallel to ours on the phage.
> * Their results were parallel to ours on the phage on that virus.
> * Their results were parallel on that virus to ours on the phage.

A second useful fact about Postposing may be inferred using the fact that it is structure preserving. We have seen that the sentence

> Their results on that virus are similar to our results on the phage.

cannot undergo Postposing, because there is already a prepositional phrase in immediate postpredicate position:

> * Their results are similar to our results on the phage on that virus.

Now suppose that the postpredicate phrase is removed by QF:

> To whose results on the phage are their results on that virus similar?

If it were in general possible for Postposing to follow QF, then these ungrammatical strings would result:

> * To whose results on the phage are their results similar on that phage?
> * To whose results are their results on that virus similar on the virus?

The conclusion is that Postposing precedes QF on any cycle.

A final fact needed for the ensuing argument is that Right Conjunct Reduction precedes Postposing on any cycle. Consider the following derivations, in which Right Conjunct Reduction precedes Postposing:

> The facts about him and the facts about her were virtually identical, but he got the job. →
> The facts about him and (about) her were virtually identical, but he got the job. →
> The facts were virtually identical about him and (about) her, but he got the job.
> The wines from the eastern regions of France and the wines from the western regions of Germany are quite similar. →
> The wines from the eastern regions of France and (from) the western regions of Germany are quite similar. →
> The wines are quite similar from the eastern regions of France and (from) the western regions of Germany.

For Postposing to precede Right Conjunct Reduction in such cases, there would have to be a step like this in the derivation:

> The facts about him and the facts about her were virtually identical, but he got the job. →
> * The facts and the facts were virtually identical about him and (about) her, but he got the job.

As shown, Postposing would have to separate the prepositional phrases from their conjoined subjects; but this operation is in general impossible:

> The rumors about Adele and the gossip concerning Jean were
> similar. →
> * The rumors and the gossip were similar about Adele and
> concerning Jean.

Therefore, taking the second and third facts together, we have this ordering on any cycle:

> Right Conjunct Reduction
> Postposing
> Question Formation (QF).

But note that there are two relevant situations that may arise in deep
structure: there may be a single interrogative S containing conjoined
nodes embedded within it, or there may be two interrogative S's contained
within a conjoined structure. In the latter case we would expect Right
Conjunct Reduction to follow QF, if QF were cyclic, and this is just what
happens. To proceed with the argument, note that Right Conjunct Reduction must apply after QF in this derivation:

(a)   I wonder what strange sights yòu'll see in mý country and
        what strange sights Ì'll see in yóur country. →
(b)   I wonder what strange sights yòu'll see in mý country and Ì'll
        see in yóur country.

QF has already applied to (a). If Right Conjunct Reduction only preceded
QF in derivations, (b) would not be generable. For to apply prior to QF,
Right Conjunct Reduction would have to delete the material between the
verb and the prepositional phrase which has not yet been fronted by QF:
but this operation is in general impossible, producing ungrammatical
strings:

> * You'll hit some great spots in my country and I'll hit in your
> country.

Conjunct Reduction may only delete repeated material at the extreme of
the conjunct. This establishes that Right Conjunct Reduction must follow
QF to derive (b).

On the other hand, Conjunct Reduction must also be able to precede

QF within a derivation. Consider the following assertion and question:

(y)   He said that some things about France and some things about Italy were similar.

(z)   What things did he say were similar about France and (about) Italy?

Sentence (z) cannot be taken as a base form for the same reasons that show Postposing to be a transformation. For example, this sentence certainly has no reading like (y)'s:

> * He said that they are similar about France and (about) Italy.

Therefore, (z) must have an application of Postposing in its derivation. Now we already know that Postposing cannot follow QF, so it must precede QF in the derivation of (z). Right Conjunct Reduction must in turn precede Postposing in the derivation of (z), for otherwise Postposing would have to detach prepositional phrases from conjoined subjects, an operation which has been shown to be impossible:

> He said that what things about France and what things about Italy were similar? →
> * He said that what things and what things were similar about France and about Italy?

But this means that Right Conjunct Reduction must precede QF in the derivation of (z):

> He said that what things about France and what things about Italy were similar? →
> He said that what things about France and (about) Italy were similar? →
> He said that what things were similar about France and (about) Italy? →
> What things did he say were similar about France and (about) Italy?

We see that both sentence (z) and the sentence

> What things about France and (about) Italy did he say were similar?

are derived by applying Right Conjunct Reduction and then QF; the only difference is that in (z) the optional Postposing rule intervenes after Right Conjunct Reduction and before QF. We used Postposing merely as a means of 'forcing' Right Conjunct Reduction to apply before QF in this derivation.

From the demonstration that there is a derivation in which Right Conjunct Reduction must precede and a derivation in which it must follow QF, I conclude that both are cyclic transformations.

Let us turn now to Relative Clause Formation (RCF). We see at once that an argument exactly parallel to the last can be formulated using a sentence analogous to (z) to show that Conjunct Reduction can precede RCF –

> The things that he said were quite similar about France and (about) Italy were these.

– and a sentence analogous to (b) to show that Conjunct Reduction may follow RCF –

> There are many strange sights that yòu'll see in mý country and (that) Ì'll see in yoúr country.

Observe that RCF is not only cyclic, it is NP-cyclic. That is, its domain of application is NP rather than S, just as I have assumed in the stress derivation. This formulation is syntactically necessary to derive 'double relatives', such as

> The men she has met that she likes are all artists.
> The only solution I've found that satisfies me is this.

Each example contains two relatives but only one head. For the first there would be an underlying representation (roughly) like that shown in Figure 15. (I take no stand here on whether relatives come from the Determiner in deep structure; if so, then the transformation which shifts them to the right of the head must be NP-cyclic to produce the configuration in Figure 15.) If RCF applies to NP, the derivation is easily accomplished by first applying RCF to NP_1 and then NP. Otherwise the sentence cannot be derived without letting cyclic transformations reapply on the same cycle.

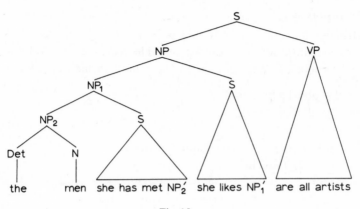

Fig. 15.

The stress contours of the relative clause construction pose a set of problems which are compounded by the fact that an adequate syntactic analysis of that construction has not yet been given. For example, in Figures 3 and 4 I give derivations in which a full noun phrase appears as the underlying object: *diréctions for George to follow* and *the propósal that George left* are assumed to derive from underlying representations similar to [direction [for George to follow directions]] and [the proposal [that George left the proposal]]. One problem that arises immediately concerns the nature of the determiner of the underlying object; it clearly cannot in general be identical to the determiner of the head, both for semantic and prosodic

$$\overset{2}{}\quad\overset{3}{}$$

reasons. For semantically the embedded underlying sentence *George left*

$$\overset{1}{}$$

the proposal does not indicate that it is the same proposal that Mary liked; on the other hand, if *the proposal* is understood as bearing an anaphoric

$$\overset{2}{}\quad\overset{1}{}\quad\overset{3}{}$$

relation to the head, it should be destressed – *George left the proposal* – and then the verb should retain primary stress throughout the derivation, leading to the wrong contour. One possible solution is that the underlying object is a nondestressable anaphoric noun phrase, such as *that proposal*.

The problems are more general, however. Consider the relative clause construction *all I could dó*. It cannot be derived from [all [I could do all]], both for semantic and prosodic reasons. The correct analysis of this type of example must also explain a set of related facts, including the following:

> * all which I could do
> all that I could do
>
> all $\left\{ \begin{array}{l} \phi \\ \text{that} \\ \text{* which} \end{array} \right\}$ you wànted of the wíne
>
> (all of the wine) $\left\{ \begin{array}{l} \phi \\ \text{that} \\ \text{* which} \end{array} \right\}$ you wánted
>
> all of (the wíne $\left\{ \begin{array}{l} \phi \\ \text{that} \\ \text{which} \end{array} \right\}$ you wanted)

Certain determiners always result in final primary stress when they have a quantifier-like reading. Compare

> what(ever) foods the general áte
> what(ever) the general áte
>
> What foóds the general ate!
> What the general áte!
>
> anything he wánted
> any dishes he wánted
>
> something he wánted
> some díshes he wanted
>
> (those dishes) he wánted
> those (díshes he wanted)

The definite determiner *the* has both a specific and a quantifier-like reading, corresponding to a difference in stress:

> The Norwégian John wants to marry must be táll.
> (= That Norwegian must be tall.)

The Norwegian John wants to márry must be táll.

(= Any such Norwegian must be tall.)

A fuller discussion of the syntactic and prosodic properties of such constructions is given in Bresnan (in preparation).

Massachusetts Institute of Technology

NOTES

* Also appeared in a slightly different form in *Language* **47** (1971) 257–297. This work was
supported in part by the National Institutes of Mental Health (Grant MH-13390) and the
Institutes of Health (Grant 5 TO1 HD00111).
[1] This is the preliminary formulation given by Chomsky and Halle (1968, p. 17), though later
they collapse the NSR with another rule. If the proposal of this paper is correct, the NSR
should remain as first formulated. The statement of the rule in Chomsky and Halle (1968)
omits the condition on Z which guarantees that only the rightmost primary-stressed vowel
receives l-stress by the NSR.
[2] This rule is tentatively stated in Chomsky and Halle (1968, pp. 115 – 117) as a word-stress
rule; they note that it could be generalized to such cases as I am considering here. I am
assuming that the NSR may apply to any phrase node, including VP, in isolation.
[3] Under the latter reading the sentence is generic, and may be paraphrased (approximately)
as

$$A \, [= \text{any}] \text{ man I like} \begin{Bmatrix} \text{must} \\ \text{would} \end{Bmatrix} \text{believe.} \ldots$$

Some examples of the general types I have been discussing are given in Bolinger (1968) as
counterexamples to the óbservations in Newman (1946). As I have shown, these are only
apparent counterexamples to the theory of generative phonology. A very few of Bolinger's
examples – mostly idiomatic, e.g., *money to búrn* – remain unexplained.
[4] This is not an exhaustive alternative in that, if VP and S are both available as underlying
complements, one would expect a full range of possible subcategorizations for Adjectives:
VP, S, PP + VP, PP + S, etc. These possibilities are compactly expressed in the rule

$$\text{VP} \rightarrow \ldots (\text{PP}) (\begin{Bmatrix} \text{VP} \\ \text{S} \end{Bmatrix}).$$

In fact, as will become clear, all of these possibilities are realized with various adjectives. But
there do exist predicates which clearly resist S complements, including PP + S complements:

    * For John to accept this view would be tough (for him).

    * It would be tough for John for him to accept this view.

    * For us to solve that problem was a bear (for us).

    * It was a bear for us for us to solve that problem.

    Cf. That problem was a bear for us to solve.

In Appendix I the possibility of 'preserving' an S analysis for *tough, a bear*, and other predicates by deriving their PP + VP complements from PP + S is discussed.

    Note that it is immaterial here whether the complement is conceived as originating in
subject position or at the rightmost position in VP. See Emonds (1970) for a general argument
in favor of the latter view.

[5] *There* Insertion places the expletive *there* in subject position before certain indefinites:

> There will be a son of the nobility present.

There Insertion is cyclic, since it may both follow and precede Passive in a derivation. It follows Passive in this derivation:

> While you watch, a pig will be roasted. →
> While you watch, there will be a pig roasted.

(The latter sentence must be carefully distinguished from

> ? While you watch, there will be a roasted pig.
> ? While you watch, there will be a pig that is roasted.

In these examples, Passive has not applied to the main sentence.)

There Insertion precedes Passive in this derivation:

> Δ proved that mercury was in the bottle. →
> Δ proved that there was mercury in the bottle. →
> There was proved to be mercury in the bottle.

[6] The problem lies in determining the correct criteria to distinguish among the many possible analyses. The S-Movement criterion is probably the best type for determining simple sentencehood.

[7] The connection between this type of construction and the ordering hypothesis advanced here was brought to my attention by Joan Maling.

[8] Object Shift may be (tentatively) stated as follows:

$$[_s \Delta \text{Pred (PP)} [_{VP} V^* \text{(P) NP}]]$$

where V^* represents an arbitrarily long string of Verbs. This formulation would permit derivation of

> John is easy for Bill to please.
> John is hard for Bill to even try to please.
> John is hard for Bill to even begin to try to please.

but not

> * You are tough for me to believe that Harry hates. (Postal 1968a, p. 103.)
> * Harriet is tough for me to stop Bill's looking at. (Postal, 1968a, p. 109.)

Postal (1968a, p. 102) states that Object Shift (his 'Tough Movement') transports an NP into subject position only from an 'immediately lower clause'. This statement leads him to both awkward complications of the rule and ad hoc theoretical elaborations. While Postal's version states that Object Shift may not occur across MORE THAN ONE S-bracket, the version of the rule given here states, in effect, that Object Shift may not occur across ANY S-brackets. There is therefore an empirical difference between these two versions, and the crucial evidence is presented in paradigm (X) of this paper. The evidence there, as the reader will note, crucially favors an 'intra-sentence' version of the rule over any 'cross-sentence' version; that is, any version like Postal's will incorrectly predict that (Xa) is a grammatical sentence.

[9]   One such speaker is Postal (1968a, p. 25) who writes:
one must observe that the whole construction involves a subtle structural ambiguity of a not understood type. A string like:

3.(8)   It was difficult for Tony to rob the store

has two different Surface Structures:

  3.(9) *a* it was difficult for Tony (to rob the store)
        b it was difficult (for Tony to rob the store).

The difference in meaning is real though subtle. The first seems to associate the difficulty directly with Tony personally. The second allows for a more generic attribution of difficulty. The difference shows up clearly in two variant pronunciations.

[10] The sentence *John was good to leave* is itself ambiguous: John may be understood as the one leaving (*It was good of John to leave*) or the one left (*It was good to leave John*). Corresponding to these readings is a difference in stress:

$$\overset{3}{}\qquad\overset{2}{}\qquad\overset{1}{}$$
John was good to leave (*John* is subject of *leave*).

$$\overset{2}{}\qquad\overset{3}{}\qquad\overset{1}{}$$
John was good to leave (*John* is object of *leave*).

The former is probably transformationally derived from

$$\qquad\overset{2}{}\qquad\overset{3}{}\quad\overset{1}{}$$
It was good of John to leave.

$$\hspace{8cm}\overset{1}{}\qquad\overset{3}{}$$
Of John is probably a PP complement to *good*: the stress on *good of John* in isolation suggests that it is the Compound Rule which is applying. The Compound Rule (Chomsky and Halle,

$$\hspace{8cm}\overset{1}{}\quad\overset{3}{}$$
1968, p. 17) results in the characteristic initial stress of English compounds: *blackbird* is

$$\hspace{4cm}\overset{2}{}\quad\overset{1}{}$$
produced by the Compound Rule while *black bird* is produced by the NSR. Thus we would have a derivation like

[It was [good [of John]] [to leave]]				
1	1	1	1	(word stress)
				1st cycle: NSR
	2	1		
				2nd cycle: Compound Rule
	1	3	2	
				3rd cycle:
2				syntax
John	φ	φ		NSR
3	2		1	

Notice that to avoid the derivation of **Mary was good of John to leave* by Object Shift from *It was good of John to leave Mary*, either the prepositional phrase *for NP* must be distinguishable by the rule from *of NP*, or else the infinitive must in these cases be an unreduced sentence at the point where Object Shift would apply.

[11] Since the ordering hypothesis entails that some phonological rules apply in deep structure or the lexicon, it is natural to ask whether all phonological rules so apply. It is clear that the rules of 'external sandhi' in some languages, affecting segments across word boundaries, must apply on surface structure, for two words which have separate locations in deep structure may be contiguous in surface structure and undergo sandhi. Such rules of 'external' phonological phenomena are analogous to the postcyclic or last-cyclic syntactic rules, in that both apply after the cyclic rules. Prosodic rules, such as the NSR, are analogous to cyclic transformations in a way that the ordering hypothesis makes clear. Word-internal rules affecting stress or segmental phonology (see Chomsky and Halle, 1968) are analogous

to rules of derivational morphology and doubtless interact with them. Further research pursuing the parallel articulation of phonological and syntactic rules and their interactions may prove interesting.

[12] Arlene Berman first pointed this consequence out to me, and Noam Chomsky called the further consequence for the lexicalist hypothesis to my attention.

Needless to say, it does not follow that stress-neutral affixes are transformationally attached, but only that a nonstress-neutral affix is not transformationally attached. This consequence raises a number of problems for further research. For example, inflectional morphology often involves radical phonological changes, yet the context for a passive vs. active verb or a nominative vs. accusative noun is determined transformationally. Since it is still an open question whether passive and active deep structures differ in some way (see Hasegawa, 1968), it is possible that passive verbs are lexically inserted as such. Case-marking and number/gender agreement rules operate on derived structures. It is possible that these rules apply to already inflected items, that is, that they are 'feature-checking' rather than 'feature-changing', in an obvious sense.

[13] Deep structure is definable as the phrase marker P_i of a derivation $\Sigma = (P_1, \ldots, P_n)$ s.t. (a) for $j < i P_j$ is formed from P_{j-1} by a lexical transformation and (b) for $j > i P_j$ is formed from P_{j-1} by a nonlexical, or syntactic, transformation. A lexical transformation inserts a lexical item into a phrase marker. (See Chomsky, 1970a, for further exposition.)

Strictly speaking, the phonological cycle and the ordering hypothesis imply that all lexical insertion *within the domain of cycle C* must occur on or before any transformation on C. But in this case, all lexical insertion transformations can be reordered before all cyclic and post-cyclic syntactic transformations without loss of any linguistically significant generality. To see this, consider a hypothetical cyclic syntactic transformation which precedes a lexical insertion transformation L. Our hypotheses imply that on a cycle C at which T applies, all lexical insertion into the domain of C had taken place prior to T's application. Therefore L must occur on the 'next higher' cycle C'. But now on C' L cannot insert into the domain of the previous cycle C without inserting a lexical item *for other lexical items*, which is impossible. Therefore L must insert into some subphrase-marker of the domain of C' not in the domain of C. Thus, L is independent of the output of T and can be reordered prior to any application of T.

Concerning L, I am making the generally accepted assumptions (i) that lexical items are not strictly subcategorized for syntactically transformed structures and (ii) that lexical items are not in general substitutable for lexical items. Assumption (i) is necessary since, otherwise, any L which inserted into C'-C a lexical item subcategorized for a derived structure in C which is the output of T obviously could not be reordered before T.

If one could display a well-motivated precyclic syntactic transformation which preceded an L, then the above definition of deep structure would have to be given up. However, a slightly weaker notion of deep structure would still be definable by omitting (a) from the definition.

[14] This formulation was suggested to me by James D. McCawley.

[15] This consequence was called to my attention by James D. McCawley.

[16] The problem posed by the dative was pointed out to me by Frank Heny.

[17] This problem was pointed out to me by Peter Culicover.

[18] This alternative was suggested to me by James McCawley.

[19] I have excluded the transformation Topicalization from discussion because topicalized sentences seem inherently emphatic or contrastive: *Jóhn I like*; *John I like*. It is likely that many postcyclic transformations, because they create so-called stylistic inversions, are closely connected with contrast and emphasis.

[20] Because relative and interrogative clauses have special properties which prevent certain kinds of interactions with many of the better known cyclic transformations, it is difficult to prove from rule-ordering arguments that RCF and QF are cyclic. (See Ross, 1967, for an exposition of some of these properties and a proposed explanation.) In Postal (1968b, pp. 26 – 27) an argument is presented that 'WH Q Movement' is not cyclic. Postal's argument is actually addressed to a version of QF unlike that assumed here. Here, QF is a Complementizer-Substitution Transformation in the sense of Bresnan (1970b): QF scans an S on every S-cycle, but only applies when its structural description is met – that is, when the S is complementized by WH [= Q] – and then QF substitutes the first eligible question word for WH. (See Bresnan, in preparation.) For example, the structural description of QF is met only at S_2 in the following example, and so QF actually applies only on that cycle:

$[_{S_3}$ John asked me $[_{S_2}$ WH $[_{S_1}$ you thought $[_{S_0}$ he liked what]]]].

The derived sentence is *John asked me what you thought he liked*. Now the version of QF which Postal assumes permits the following kind of derivations:

John asked me WH you thought he liked what. →
John asked me WH you thought what he liked. →
John asked me what you thought he liked.

The question word (in this case, *what*) is brought to the front of every S until it reaches WH, or 'Q'. Postal notes that since QF optionally preposes prepositional phrases –

Who did you speak to?
To whom did you speak?

– this version of QF would allow prepositions to be 'stranded', producing ungrammatical strings; for example, in addition to the grammatical sentences

Who did she think you spoke to?
To whom did she think you spoke?

an ungrammatical string like this would result optionally

* Who did she think to you spoke?

by fronting the entire phrase *to whom* on the first cycle, but fronting only *who* on the next cycle. Because QF, under the version I am assuming, moves question words only into (and never from) WH complementizers, Postal's 'stranding' argument does not apply. But even the version of QF Postal assumes is not refuted by his argument, since the feature [+ wh] could be assigned either to NP or to PP (Prepositional Phrase), and whichever node carried the feature would be shifted by QF throughout the derivation. (This possibility was mentioned to me by Noam Chomsky.)

[21] If Right Conjunct Reduction MERELY deleted material, the derived constituent structure would be wrong, for when *the news from France and the news from Italy* is reduced, *from France and from Italy* behaves as a prepositional phrase constituent under the Postposing rule, which will be discussed:

* The news from France is similar and from Italy.
The news is similar from France and from Italy.

For discussion distinguishing various kinds of conjunct reduction rules see Kuno (to appear) and the references cited there.

ARLENE I. MOSKOWITZ

THE ACQUISITION OF PHONOLOGY AND SYNTAX:
A PRELIMINARY STUDY*

1. INTRODUCTION

Several aspects of the study of language acquisition are very intriguing for
their potential application to other studies. As language acquisition is one
of the very few primary, nonmediated forms of human learning, it should
contribute significantly to the psychological study of learning. As it is also
one of the few bodies of data on the English language from nonliterate
informants, it cannot be ignored in the formulation of linguistic theories.
This paper discusses a new approach to the study of language acquisition
data and draws some conclusions relevant to the fields of learning and
linguistics. It is an attempt to draw together the previously distinct fields of
syntax acquisition and phonology acquisition: the *concepts* which the
child must discover in order to assimilate primary linguistic data are shown
to be more relevant to the process of language acquisition than are postulated 'innate' structures. The acquisition process is shown to be one of
language creation rather than one of learning (imitation); i.e., the child
learns (discovers) the relevant concepts and then applies them to create a
language. This process occurs repeatedly, and with each new occurrence
the created language is a bit closer to the adult language (in a sense which
will be discussed later).

Linguistic science has always dealt with units in the investigation of
language structure: phonemes, distinctive features, words, sentences, to
name a few. Such units are static entities used to describe (systematically
and economically) the language of adult speakers. The economy of a
child's linguistic system is of a different nature from that of the adult
system – it must be economical not only from the point of view of a speaker
but also from that of a learner (possibly opposing points of view) – and is
thus subject to different constraints entirely. The child's linguistic system
is also not static, but instead is very dynamic. Thus we must remain open
to the possibility that units different from those of the adult grammar may

be necessary in the description of child grammar. Such units idea
revealed by the data itself and their utilization in a linguistic descr.
should enable us to see more clearly the actual processes by which lang
is acquired.

A 'unit' is the smallest section of the speech chain which the child uses
distinctively. It is not defined by the investigator's recognition of distinction, but rather by the child's evidencing in some significant way that he
has achieved an ability to organize his grammar on the basis of that unit.

Previous studies of language acquisition have clearly distinguished
production from perception. That distinction is certainly a valid one, but is
perhaps less useful than might be thought. Production has been shown in
many cases to follow perception by a short and varying time period. However, productive ability is not always reflected in accurate production: in
some cases far more subtle factors can evidence a child's productive
abilities and reveal that production and perception are more closely in
keeping than we suspected at first. This is most obvious in the case of
phonology, where the inability to articulate a sound (phonetic lack) may
obscure an acquired phonological (systematic[1]) distinction, but it is equally
true of syntax, where a length limitation on sentences (or any one of many
other factors) may obscure syntactic knowledge which the child has.
Whether or not the child yet produces a particular linguistic entity or
construction, he perceives it *only if* it is part of his system, and is thus
eligible for production. Rather than emphasizing a production-perception
dichotomy, we must recognize the conflict between the child's system and
those factors which interfere with its accurate display. Among such factors
are progressive and regressive idioms – units of production which belong
to later or earlier systematic stages.

Most child language studies of the last several years have utilized the
framework and the methodology of generative grammar to trace the
expanding language of the child. Although the framework here is quite
different, it is not in opposition: different approaches to data always reveal
different aspects of their potential. This approach is complementary to
others and is worth pursuing for the unique conclusions it offers.

2. PHONOLOGY ACQUISITION

Jakobson, in his extremely important work, *Child Language, Aphasia, and*

Phonological Universals (1968), made four important points which were summarized by Charles A. Ferguson as follows:

(1) At any given synchronic stage during the process of language acquisition, the child's speech has a structure of its own.

(2) In addition to this central, systematic, structural core of speech there are some marginal (extra-systematic) elements.

(3) At any given stage, the child's speech will exhibit systematic correspondences to the adult model.

(4) Across all children and all languages, there is a regular order in the acquisition of phonological distinctions.

These four points must form the basis of any theory of phonology acquisition. Jakobson's work is devoted largely to an exposition of the fourth point: many diary studies have indicated the accuracy of the third. Most of Section 2 of this paper is devoted to a description of the structure mentioned in (1). At the end of the section, (2), which has until now been largely overlooked, is discussed: it is an extremely important aspect of the study of language acquisition.

Much of the earlier literature makes a distinction between a 'pre-linguistic stage' and a 'linguistic stage', the separation occurring at the point when the child acquires his first word. The evidence for that acquisition may be either the production of that first word, or the contrastive production of the first two words. This distinction between two stages is arbitrarily based on the criterion of the adult's recognition of an overt manifestation which happens to be explainable in terms of adult speech, and is thus not necessarily justifiable in terms of the child's linguistic capacity at any one point and may be extremely misleading, in that it implies that this is the one major step he makes in linguistic knowledge. The theory presented here assumes that a large number of interrelated stages, representing various degrees of sophistication, cannot be strictly isolated from one another in any such neat manner. It also assumes that the child, from fairly soon after birth, begins his linguistic development, and therefore manifests no prelinguistic stage as such. The preverbal stage is very short and is followed by babbling, the significance of which has just been guessed at prior to this time.

The babbling period begins with the production of short utterances and progresses eventually to include production of quite long utterances which can be characterized as sounding subjectively very much more language-like than their predecessors. Early in this period the child is aware of the difference between human and nonhuman sounds in his environment, an innate endowment: during the babbling stage he additionally develops a linguistic identity of his own, i.e., the closer he can match his sound productions to his perceptions of human sound, the more he can identify himself as a member of the species community. He is surrounded, moreover, by an incredible diversity of sound, for he is able to hear phonetic distinctions with great accuracy (although there is no reason to assume consistency), but he has no concept of the potentiality of a system underlying that array of sounds – the system is a deduction he will make much later on the basis of his own speech behavior. Therefore those perceptions which his production is compelled to match are fairly random.

The first of the child's endeavors which we notice is the increase in the length of the strings he produces: together with this goes an increase in the total amount of verbal output per time segment. The increase in output is probably in part a maturational result and in part behavioral evidence of the child's increasing awareness that the speech of the adults in his environment consists of longish but finite strings of random sound: the child's earlier short utterances have given him the practice necessary for these longer outputs, which are more rewarding precisely because they more closely approximate what he hears as language, namely, long random strings. In other words, within the child's world, he is beginning to satisfactorily participate in the process of linguistic exchange known as communication. This constitutes a first major step in socialization (or, the learning of semantics) by its suggestion of a unit which can carry meaning, namely, a long finite string of sound separated by pauses, known as 'sentence'. In fact the sentence in this way becomes the first linguistic unit for the child.

A significant thing which is occurring during this time is the initiation of a process which is described in detail by Braine (1971). Briefly summarized, this process involves the operation of a series of storage devices within the brain. These storage devices, or black boxes, are ordered with respect to the strength of the learning they represent. All linguistic data enter the first black box, and all data which cannot be shifted fairly soon to

the next box are eliminated from the first box by forgetting; data shifted to
the second box last a little longer before they must be shifted to the third
box – where they will last even longer – or else are returned to the first box
where they are subject to the same time restrictions as any new data
entering that box. In very simplified terms, data are shifted to a higher box
when enough instances of a particular type of data are collected in a
particular box to warrant such a shift; they are shifted to a lower box if
additional occurrences are not found. This model is proposed by Braine to
account for grammar learning, but it works just as well for the sound
system. The process requires no negative feedback whatsoever (and indeed
there is strong evidence that negative feedback about either pronunciation
or syntax is not utilized by the child). It provides us with a picture whose
implication is that that which occurs most generally in the input will be
sorted out first by the child and will therefore occur first in the output; that
which is more limited in detail can be given attention by the child when he
has mastered the control of the more general aspects of grammar or
phonology.

This manner in which this process works during the late babbling stage
is quite simple. The child is still listening to a vast amount of phonetic
input which sounds reasonably random. But the grossest features of the
input – namely, the supersegmental features which we call intonation –
move rapidly from box to box and are learned before any other aspects of
the sound system. In conjunction with the increasing length of his babbling
utterances, we would expect the child to make use of this new knowledge of
intonational structure by imposing a small number of recognized patterns
on his babbling utterances to make them sound once more like his perceptions of the utterances of adults – longish strings of random sounds with
superimposed intonational structure. There is some evidence that children
do exhibit intonation patterns characteristic of the adult language in their
late babbling, although the evidence is certainly inconclusive as yet and the
matter needs more investigation.[2]

The preoccupation with intonation which the child exhibits in his late
babbling stage has distinct ramifications in the subsequent step in phonology acquisition. Before we can examine this we must backtrack slightly
to examine two concepts which the child has developed. The first is the
concept of unit, which has so far had its only manifestation (in production)

as the sentence-unit. The only relevant phonetic feature of the sentence-unit is the intonation which it carries. We may therefore suspect that when the child begins to look for a unit smaller than the sentence, he will be predisposed toward finding one which is still a carrier of intonation. The second concept as yet exists only in the child's perception; his overt behavioral evidence of this concept is purely nonlinguistic. Specifically, he is able to recognize the name of a game (such as 'patty-cake') or other similar label which obviously elicits from him a fixed behavior pattern. He may not be reacting to the exact words *in toto* which the adults use to label the game, but he can recognize some part of it. Labelled games of this type apparently exist in a large variety of cultures and are usually aimed at the 'preverbal' child. When the child is able to react consistently to such a stimulus, we may conclude that he has learned that a particular subsequence of the sentence-unit may have meaning by itself and, in particular, that a linguistic string may have 'meaning'. Whether this represents the acquisition of the concept of 'word' is an open question; certainly this is at least a precursor of that concept, but the amount of generalization necessary from this pattern to the concept of 'word' is significant, and may still be in the future. Unquestionably, however, this step represents the child's new awareness that some of the vast number of phonetic differences in the sounds around him are inconsequential. His tolerance of the small differences in subsequent adult productions of that label indicates that he has made the first giant step in the acquisition of phonetics – the realization that some, but not all, sound differences are inconsequential, and particularly that certain slight phonetic variations are 'free'. It is probably often true that a game name or other such label will typically be offered to the child in a higher-than-normal pitch or with an exclamation intonation, thus making the child's job of recognition somewhat easier than it might otherwise be. In addition, acquisition is facilitated by the many repetitions of the word or phrase, often in isolation, and by the fact that it is one of the few bits of linguistic input which is directed at the child in particular.

As we have said, this focus on intonation has important ramifications. Following Braine's model, we see that once the child has mastered some of the salient aspects of intonation he is free to turn his attention to the phonetic qualities of sentences once again. The child who has operated with a sentence-unit for a while is ready to abstract from the model a more

salient unit: his experience has taught him that a limited number of contrasting sentence-intonations do not suffice to express all possible meanings that his verbal environment seems to offer, and so he knows that he
still has a job to do. There are two significant factors which determine the
precise nature of the next linguistic concepts he will master: (1) he still can
hear a huge variety of phonetic differences, and he has no possible way of
sorting out from this mass which differences are inconsequential – indeed
he does not yet realize in any pervasive way that most of the differences are
inconsequential (and certainly has no suspicion of the variety of ways in
which a difference may be inconsequential) – and he has no semantic or
syntactic clues which will aid him in developing a relevant discovery
procedure; and (2) he has previously worked with only one type of unit,
and that unit has significantly been one which carries intonation. Thus his
search for a smaller unit than the sentence is, in effect, a narrowing-down
process which should produce for the child a unit smaller than the sentence,
but which can carry intonation; there is absolutely no reason to suspect
that the child would be able to achieve the understanding of a unit as small
as the segment, and all of the evidence presented so far indicates that this
next significant unit is the syllable.

Once this notion of the syllable has been arrived at, further babbling
may or may not continue; if it does continue, its function is not entirely
clear – it may just be a remnant of 'fun' vocal activity; if it does not continue, it may be that the child has realized the magnitude (partially) of the
job before him, and he is embarking on the activity of devoting much of his
attention to the solution.

The initial syllables are all CV types; this phenomenon, together with
the fact that almost all languages have CV syllables, and that CV syllables
are statistically the most prevalent among the different syllables of a given
language, are all due to the same cause: that they are phonetically the
simplest.[3] (Since we have no evaluative way of defining 'phonetic simplicity'
in linguistics, we have avoided using the notion for a long time now, which
has actually been a good step in the direction of not over-using and mis-
using the notion. We see in child language data, however, a good criterion
for defining this notion; though, again we must not over-use the argument,
because the facts of phonetic simplicity are interfered with by the concurrent phonological learning.)

The phonetic realizations of these first syllables may be extremely varied, except that they all have features of stress and/or pitch. At about this same time, with the help of both his newly found shorter unit and the labelling activity of the adults around him, and also with the aid of other devices which we know nothing about, the child develops the semantic notion of the 'word', a linguistic concept of great consequence. The word and the unit become equated, and the child's perception of the minor phonetic variations of the words of his environment leads him to the conclusion that a certain amount of phonetic variation is permissible within the definition of a word (syllable) which still retains its identity as opposed to all of the other words of his vocabulary. He may ascribe too much leeway to this phonetic variation, and will have to correct that later through counternotions of phonetic invariance.

One of the most interesting and important aspects of the progress of syllable acquisition is the reduplication stage. The significance of reduplication has not been explained until now, although its pervasiveness is indisputable. Table I lists the syllable structures in the vocabulary of Hildegard Leopold[4] (Leopold, 1939) at age 2. Out of 51 words of the form CV*CV* (where $V^* = V$ or $V\underset{\smile}{V}$), 16 – more than 31 percent – are reduplications. Since Hildegard has 33 CV words and 24 $C V \underset{\smile}{V}$ words, a random juxtaposing of any two CV* syllables would produce 57^2 possible CV*CV* words, of which 57 – less than 2 percent – would be reduplications. By any statistical measure of significance, the presence of 31 percent reduplication is a purposeful and important phonological device.

TABLE I

Syllable structures of Hildegard, age 2
[$V\underset{\smile}{V}$ indicates diphthong]

One-syllable words	Miscellaneous
CV 33/$CV\underset{\smile}{V}$ 24	$VCVCV\underset{\smile}{V}$ 1
CVC 50/$CV\underset{\smile}{V}C$ 15	Others 3 [include only CV and CVC syllables]

Two-syllable words

CVCV (redup. CV) 14/CVCV (3 phonèmes) 6/CVCV (4 phonemes) 18
$CVCV\underset{\smile}{V}$ and $CV\underset{\smile}{V}CV$ 11/$CV\underset{\smile}{V}CV\underset{\smile}{V}$ (redup. $CV\underset{\smile}{V}$) 2
$CV\underset{\smile}{V}V$ 5/$V\underset{\smile}{V}CV$ 1
CVCVC 3/$CVCV\underset{\smile}{V}C$ 1
CVCCVC 2

The phonological process which allows the child to reduplicate syllables (and, in fact, pretty much demands that he do so) has an extremely simple explanation. Once the child has encoded a small syllabary (most or all of which is not yet further analyzed), he faces the need to produce words longer than CV; by now the concept of 'word' is strongly entrenched in his linguistic cognizance and he has begun or is beginning to recognize that words are often longer than one syllable. Absolutely the simplest manner in which he can produce a longer word is to utilize one unit – a single CV – twice, and the result is reduplication, a phonological phenomenon which embodies several significant precursors to the adult phonological structure. First, where the child previously had only an *equation*

(1) $W = S$

(where W stands for 'word' and S for 'syllable') which involved no directionality, he now has a *rule*

(2) $W \rightarrow \begin{Bmatrix} S \\ S_i + S_i \end{Bmatrix}$

and, in particular, one which involves directionality; no longer is he confined to simply filling in a word slot with a single unit from his syllabary: he is now able to generate items to fill the word slot by imposing a structure, namely, reduplication, on any of those elementary units of his inventory. We have no way of knowing that at the earlier stage he did not, in fact, have the rule

(3) $W \rightarrow S$

rather than the equation given above. There does not seem to be any way to test the psychological difference between the two. Purely in terms of linguistic description, there is no reason to infer structure where it is not needed, and where that might be tantamount to imputing structure where it does not exist. The first combination of two elementary units into a word presents an adequate behavioral criterion that the undifferentiated syllable and the word are no longer identical concepts, and therefore form the first linguistic evidence that rule (3) is a better description than Equation (1); rule (3) is incorporated as part of rule (2), the entirety of which succeeds and replaces Equation (1). The emergence of the first reduplicated word then reveals the acquisition of the basic ideas of linguistic rule, of the directionality which a rule involves, and of the formal separation of the phonological inventory (syllabary) from the word list (lexicon).

The second significant precursor which is embodied in this monumental achievement of the initial reduplicated word is the recognition by the child that there is a formal phonotactics which governs the construction of words. (In an even larger sense, this could be viewed as a recognition of syntax in general, although the syntax of word combination, as opposed to word formation, cannot be behaviorally displayed until later.) This phonotactics is extremely limited, allowing only the occurrence of either a single elementary unit or of two identical elementary units; but even such a rudimentary phonotactics as rule (2) already incorporates a generalization which will remain true throughout the entire development of phonology, namely, the larger the number of elementary units in a string which comprises a word the greater the restrictions on those elementary units: note that the second part of rule (2) requires indices while the first part does not. (It is of course not true that there is one-to-one correspondence in the adult phonology between the length of a word and the total number of restrictions relevant for the selection of the elementary units which comprise it, but the relationship does hold as a generalization: i.e., if we plotted word length against total number of restrictions over the entire adult lexicon, and then smoothed the curve out a bit, we would expect the result to be an increasing function.) We note that the phonotactics operates at the level of elementary units but does not reveal any information about the units themselves. At this stage, the internal composition of the syllable is a phonetic, not phonological, matter; when the child begins to recognize other elementary units, such as segments and distinctive features, he will immediately formulate phonotactic rules governing their combinatorial possibilities within words, and at that point the internal composition of the syllable will become phonologically relevant and interesting.

At least one more significant precursor is inherent at this point in development – that of phonetic invariance – although for some children it may have occurred even earlier, as evidenced by the near-identity of the phonetic composition of different tokens (across time) of some words. For those learners, however, who displayed disparate phonetic representations of the same words, the advent of words involving reduplication is the first occasion which necessitates a consistency in the phonetic production of the same syllable, at least across the time span required for the two-syllable word – although subsequent productions of that word, each being internally consistent, may still be different from each other.

After the landmark of reduplicated-syllable words has been achieved, the next step is the production of a CVCV word which, in terms of adult phonology, consists of only three different segments, i.e., either the onsets or the vocalic portions of the syllables are identical. These partial re-duplications seem to be an intermediate stage, followed naturally by the CVCV word composed of four unlike segments. Some of the CVCV words of this final complexity may still be encoded and stored in syllabic form, but many will consist only of those most basic segments which have by now been reanalyzed and re-encoded as segments through their more extensive utilization in the syllabary. Thus this final stage no longer belongs strictly to the developmental sequence of syllable acquisition. The stage of partial reduplication, however, is extremely interesting, primarily because it falls into what is currently – through lack of data – the very hazy area of transi-tion from syllables to segments and distinctive features. When the child is beginning to formulate words of the patterns C_iVC_iV and CV_iCV_i, he is still operating primarily within the framework of his syllabary, utilizing primarily units which are therefore already existent. It is the interaction between phonetic fact and phonological rule which is here most inter-esting: does the child's mental comparisons of the units in his syllabary resulting in a partial reanalysis of some items into component segments allow him to recombine them more randomly than was permitted before, based on the new rules which his deductions added to his phonotactics? Or is quite the opposite the explanation – that the child's phonetic capacity is outstripping his phonological one, and although words still occur in the phonological form CVCV, the phonetic practice which has been an inherent by-product of phonological reduplication has resulted in a more sophisticated concept of identity which permits a partial phonetic identity (e.g., same onsets) to qualify two phonologically still unanalyzed syllables as elementary units in what is still phonologically a syllable-reduplication word pattern?

In terms of other things we do know about with regard to phonology acquisition, the second explanation seems more plausible. It seems that for every patterned step of the process we have discussed so far, there is a linguistically logical motivation, and each step has contributed to the complex set of concepts which underlies the organization of phonology. The first explanation offers a deviation from this pattern: it assumes a complex mental process, the linguistic necessity of which is not apparent, that is then implemented in a rather limited way phonetically. (Would this phonological reanalysis result directly in a word with four different segments?) Later we will examine some scattered evidence indicating that phonetic ability (with a few exceptions) is at all stages more advanced than phonological production and is obscured by that production so that it seems to be more limited than it actually is. If this is true, the second explanation – that phonetic advances cause changes in the phonology – is more plausible in terms of patterned, motivated progress and provides adequate justification for the existence of partially reduplicated words as an intermediate stage.

Although the data quoted in Burling's (1959) diary article do not, unfortunately, comprise a complete lexicon, together with Burling's comments they are sufficient to allow a very nice picture of the development of the CVCV word. At 1.4, the child has 'twelve or so' words, all of them CV or reduplicated CVCV types (e.g., *ma, kiki, tu*). At 1.5, he 'learned *suddenly and decisively*[5] to use two different syllables in the same word, including either different vowels or different consonants' as exemplified by *kiti* (< *kiki*) and *babi*. Within the theory of phonology with which Burling was working, this development at 1.5 revealed no increase in the child's knowledge whatsoever: the lexicon at 1.4 evidenced that the child 'knew' the 'phonemes' /ptkmnaiu/, and this decisive step on Stephen's part at 1.5 involved no new phonemes. (Precisely that this step did not utilize new phonemes is immensely significant.) Realizing the philosophy of phonemic theory in which this case history presents the data, the quotation above is unusual; in fact it does not fit the tone of the rest of the paper at all. We can only conclude that something about Stephen's behavior must have been extremely striking in order to motivate the father's observation. Could it have been that Stephen was quite pleased with himself for what he recognized as a significant breakthrough? Near the end of the month, Burling tells us, his son 'acquired' the phoneme /l/; he used it for the name of his Garo nurse, Emula. He produced it as *lala*, a fact which Burling does not question. Since the article basically discusses the order of acquisition of taxonomic phonemes, we have the right to wonder why Stephen did not pronounce this name as *mula*: he already had 'acquired' the phonemes /m/, /u/, and /a/. The answer is that he was not acquiring /l/, but rather the syllable *la*. At this very early stage of verbal behavior, this radically new syllable had to be utilized in the earlier practice frame of the reduplicated CVCV word, a frame whose function (partially) is to provide ideal conditions for the stabilization of the phonetic realization of the new syllable by timewise juxtaposing two occurrences for the sake of comparison. To have chosen instead the pronunciation *lula* would have been to choose a structure at the very limits of his phonological capacity, introducing a conflict with the need for phonetic practice: perhaps the child at 1.5 is sensible enough to attack only one 'linguistic front' at a time with each new word. The pronunciation *mula* is obviously far beyond the child's capabilities at this point. The word *lala* is for Stephen a by-product of an extremely adaptive mechanism which balances the phonological and phonetic complexities in such an intricate way that a new lexical item makes only a limited contribution to the advancement of the sound system and also makes only limited demands on the expanding productive capacity: the child cannot utilize just one lexical item as a source of considerable achievement both phonologically and phonetically.

Since syllables are not learned in isolation, but along with many other aspects of the sound system, the actual data rarely look quite so neat as those offered by Burling. (The neatness is an example of the artificiality which is imposed on data of this type when they are presented in terms of one basic unit which is assumed to remain at the base of phonology throughout the learner's life: some phonetic detail is omitted because it has been analyzed out as 'allophonic' – a good example of the way in which significant aspects of the development of the sound system can be obscured by the obsessive desire for an analysis which utilizes the same criteria as would an analysis of an adult sound system – and some phonetic detail is overanalyzed and labeled 'phonemic' despite the fact that for the child it is a phonetic manifestation but not yet an independent part of functional phonology.)

The data of Table II, which are given in more complete detail and therefore present a picture of many things which are occurring simultaneously,

TABLE II

Hildegard's vocabulary to age 1.3, with changes which words later underwent.
[Forms in parentheses occurred only once or twice.]

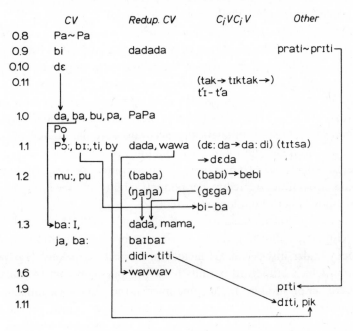

	CV	Redup. CV	$C_i V C_i V$	Other
0.8	Pa~Pa			
0.9	bi	dadada		prati~prɪti
0.10	dɛ			
0.11			(tak→tɪktak→) t'ɪ-t'a	
1.0	da, ba, bu, pa, Po	PaPa		
1.1	Pɔ:, bɪ:, ti, by	dada, wawa	(dɛ: da→da: di) (tɪtsa) →dɛda	
1.2	mu:, pu	(baba) (ŋaŋa)	(babi)→bebi (gɛga) →bi-ba	
1.3	ba: I, ja, ba:	dada, mama, baɪbaɪ didi~titi		
1.6		wavwav		
1.9				pɪti
1.11				dɪti, pik

are far less neat. The progression of structure within the two-syllable word
in Hildegard's early speech nevertheless conforms quite well to the pattern
which has been outlined so far. The earliest words are CV, and the reduplicated form appears soon after; up to 1.4, words of these forms are the
greatly dominant part of her vocabulary. The first multisyllabic word is
aberrant in that it consists of three rather than two identical syllables; that
this is a phonetic experiment, and not a phonological possibility, is evidenced by the subsequent stability of bisyllabic reduplicated forms.

Just before the end of her first year, actually earlier than we would
normally expect it, the first partial reduplication appears. That t'ɪ-t'a is
not instead a conforming simple reduplication may be related to the
complex psychological factors involved in the motivations which determine what particular lexical items the child chooses to add to his vocabulary. Interestingly, Leopold (1939) transcribes this word with a hyphen

separating the syllables indicating that some kind of pause occurs between the syllables, and that the word is not CVCV at all but is instead a concatenation of two separate syllables. The same notation is also used for the partial reduplication *bi-ba* which occurs at 1.2.

From Leopold's notes we find that Hildegard was extremely fascinated by clocks and devoted a good deal of her time and attention to them, and so perhaps she was highly motivated to match as accurately as possible the phonetic sound of the label which her father offered – 'tick-tock' – which, incidentally, may have been an additionally appealing word because of its onomatopoetic value. Her first attempt at the word was *tak*, and her second rendition was *tiktak*, a phonetically accurate and phonologically impressive achievement, but one which could not be maintained. The word became stabilized as *t'ı-t'a*, a sort of compromise between the more elaborate possibilities offered by her phonetic ability and the more restrictive demands of her phonological system.

If we ignore for the moment the fourth column of Table II, we can follow the developments shown in the table, then, as being highly supportive of the theory under discussion. Of incidental interest is the kind of experimentation which Hildegard permits herself to pursue within the narrow confines of her phonology. In the same spirit as the sequence leading to the stabilization of *t'ı-t'a*, we observe the compromises which reduce the complexities of *dɛda* and *dada* (< *gɛga*); the first of these evidences the limitation of phonetic long vowels, an experimentation which is immediately pushed back to the level of the CV syllable, where it is nurtured and leads further to the advent of the diphthong, in which form it later returns to the multisyllabic word (a reduplicated one, of course, parallel to Stephen Burling's *lala*). A different type of change of a lexical item occurs over a longer time span: what is for a while a perfectly stable word is later changed to another, related, stable form, one which reflects a more advanced phonological stage. Because such words did not *have* to be changed, they indicate the stability and mastery of their new phonological representations (as opposed to the first occurrence of those representations which, like *t'ı-t'a*, may be compromises which indicate the absolute extreme limits of phonological possibility and are the precursors of new forms rather than the manifestations of them). Examples of this situation are *ba* > *ba:ı* at 1.3, which indicates the solid status of long vowels in

CV; *wawa* > *wauwau* at 1.6, diphthongs; *didi* ~ *titi* > *dɪti* at 1.11, the four segment CVCV; and *by* > *pik* at 1.11, the CVC syllable.

Now that we have tacitly returned to column 4, we must deal with the one glaring exception it presents, the extreme deviation from an otherwise completely explainable pattern. The existence of *prɪti* in the lexicon is not a counterexample to the theory, it simply is a glaring exception; it is a very nice example of what Jakobson meant when he said that there are often some extra-systematic phenomena in children's speech. In contrast to the examples in Hildegard's lexicon where the limitations of the phonology held back the exuberancies of an elaborate phonetic capacity, this one word utilizes that capacity to as great an extent as possible. It remains outside of the system in a very real sense; not only does it avoid conforming to the constraints of the phonological system, but its deviance exempts it from benefiting as a result of subsequent refinements and advances of the phonological system.

As an isolated, memorized item, its encoding is incommensurable with that of any other part of the system; in particular, as long as it continues to remain outside of the system, it is nothing more than a phonetic idiom and it cannot incorporate additional appropriate phonetic complexities as the phonological system makes such complexities available to the other lexical items. Exactly what the encoding of this item could be – as a single-word unit or as two syllables – is neither knowable nor important. What is important is that it is a representative of a phenomenon which occurs more frequently in children's vocabularies than we recognize, primarily because most of the other examples do not happen to be so glaringly different from the rest of the lexicon and can be either described within the system itself, or within a slight modification which is a distortion of the child's actual grammar, but a distortion sufficiently minor that we cannot recognize it as such. In the case of Hildegard's 'pretty', it is too obvious to be ignored: she has no other consonant clusters, and even no other examples of either *p* or *r* in any other syllables. After a long tenure, the isolated *prɪti* gives way to *pɪti*, which seems superficially to be simpler but is actually far more complex, precisely because this new item is a concession to the system and is governed by the same restrictions on phonetics which operate throughout the lexicon, and is generatable by the same phonological rules which operate everywhere else. Words of this deviant type do not always get re-encoded so efficiently and so early; many of those which remain in their phonetic encoding, particularly when their form is much simplified from the adult model, show up as 'residue words' when their production does not improve correspondent to other lexical items when the advancing phonological system would allow a more complex representation. (There are other sources of extra-systematicity which also result in 'residue words', such as the failure to re-encode an item from one organizational level to another – e.g., from syllables to segments – so that the item remains in a form to which the revised rules of the phonology are inapplicable.

In his early inventory of syllables (which constitutes both the syllabary – the phonological inventory – and the lexicon – the vocabulary inventory) the child will of necessity utilize some distinctions to keep these words apart. They are not always successful distinctions, and the result is that it is often difficult for adults to tell when the 'first words' have been introduced into the child's language. If they are successful, and the child will soon find a way of making them so, they may depend on distinct intonations[6] or may depend on the embodiment of a phonetic distinction which happens to be incorporated phonemically into the adult language, such as *pa* vs. *ka*. This second type of distinction will eventually be added, if not immediately, and it is this which is most interesting for our purpose. The child's strategy is quite simply to select and use a variety of different syllables, the repetitions of which enable the practice of two necessary types of learning: by practicing different syllables, the child begins to grasp the notion of phonetic contrast, and, particularly, consistent contrast: by practicing different repetitions of the same syllable at different times, the child begins to grasp the notion of phonetic similarity and identity, together with the limits of the absolute free variation which is an inherent part of any phonetic series of like phonetic manifestations. Through the necessary processes which result from the syllable's place as the elementary unit of speech, the child develops notions of rules in phonology, directionality of rules, and elementary phonotactics.

Through his practice of syllables, the child develops the specific motor-coordinations and brain directions to the muscles which will be an unconscious part of his language-use for the rest of his life. Through this process he *suppresses* all those extremely similar but not exactly the same possible sets of neural commands which would produce slightly different acoustic results, and this may be the reason why correct pronunciation in second-language learning is so difficult: in fact, it predicts that such learning will be more difficult if it involves neural command patterns which had to be explicitly suppressed, as opposed to those which were irrelevant and therefore neither practiced nor necessarily suppressed. To give a concrete example, suppose that the child incorporates into his syllabary *ka* and *ki*. Let us look closely at what the child both learns and suppresses in the process.

First he learns the correct front vs. back productions of /k/ not as allophonic variants of the same phoneme, but as the distinctly different onsets which these two phones represent before the two different vowels; it will not be until much later that he 'realizes' that these two different *k*'s are variants of the same phoneme, a fact which will come considerably after the understanding of 'complementary distribution'. For now, he is simply learning a set of neural commands which determine the salient features of an entire syllable *ka* and an entire syllable *ki*, including the specific changes in formants which determine the connections between *k* and *a*, between *k* and *i*, as well as the targets for formants at the onset of the syllable and at its end (the latter also including a portion of time before the end), as well as the time relationships which connect these targets in an acceptable pattern. In the process he learns the amount of variation which may be tolerated for the result to be a correct production, while he suppresses those configurations which result in productions which are just beyond the limits. He need not suppress those possibilities which are sufficiently beyond the limits to be excluded automatically once the limiting possibilities have been excluded. In addition, he must learn to produce these syllables with aspiration on the initial part, or onset; he learns to produce the 'correct' amount of aspiration by suppressing the slightly different possibilities of too much or too little aspiration, but he does not have to suppress the extremely different possibilities of lack of aspiration or extreme plosion. It is later, when he must learn to control both the unaspirated *k*'s of other syllable positions and the unreleased *k*'s of still others, that he will have to suppress those as possibilities for the allophones of /k/ which occur in the environment /_V. We would suspect that since he does not ever have to suppress extreme release, he would be able to learn a distinction of $/k_1/$ with the degree of aspiration acceptable in English vs. $/k_2/$ with an extreme explosion with reasonable ease in a foreign language. The presentation of this paragraph is, of course, oversimplified, omitting both detail of the processes mentioned and also additional processes involved in the same picture, but the idea is that the child learns the constraints of phonetic representation automatically as part of the practice of the syllable acquisition stage, and long before those constraints play any part in the phonological aspect of language. Thus we can conclude that those phonetic details rightly do not belong to the structure of language in any way, and allophonic statements have no place in a linguistic description of phonology.

In relation to the concept of unit, it is important to notice that, although the syllable will be replaced by more sophisticated units as the basis of phonology, the fact that it was at one time the basic unit of phonological organization leaves its imprint forever on the adult system. The neural encodings which are developed at this early stage impose the articulatory restraints, which cannot be accounted for in any other systematic way.

Inherent in the syllabic function of sound learning are the two opposing and complementary processes of 'grouping' several phonetically similar manifestations into one unit (i.e., building up units by means of losing distinctions) and of 'degrouping' (i.e., extracting from a vast number of different sounds some distinctions which 'work'). These learned distinctions, we must remember, are at the level of the syllable, the only significant unit the child has so far. All such distinctions, throughout the entire process of acquisition of sound system, will continue to be learned at the level of the syllable. Once the child has begun the process of deducing segments and distinctive features from their syllable context that process will slowly transfer the function of phonological elementary unit from the syllable to the segment and/or distinctive feature. As the transfer process becomes more rapid, and its results therefore more pervasive, information about distinctions, acquired at the syllable level, is rapidly subject to the transfer process.

We can now view the child who has a reasonably large syllabary and has begun the deductive process of judging some small phonetic differences to be nondistinctive and certain other gross phonetic differences to be distinctive, and can view him in the light of the acquisition model which we have proposed. As he sorts this data of his syllabary through the black boxes of

THE ACQUISITION OF PHONOLOGY AND SYNTAX

memory, he slowly but surely discovers the significant generalization of the processes of judgment of phonetic sameness and phonetic difference, that generalization being that the judgment need not be confined to individual syllables. Although on the level of neural and motor control, and thereby production, the exact phonetic qualities of segments are still controlled by earlier syllable learning, on the level of segmental encoding the differences between the several different t's before distinct vowels become insignificant. The child 'realizes' that these are in some sense the same t (because the transfer of the more miniscule phonetic differences to higher boxes has left the lower ones free to deal with these larger differences), and thus the concept of a phonological unit smaller than the syllable is discovered.

At the very beginning of this process, just one or a very few segments are thus extracted from the data of the syllabary. But there is a chain-reaction through the syllabary which insures that eventually all (or almost all) of it will be reanalyzed this way. Suppose, for example, that consonant X is first discovered as a segment in this manner; that implies that there are in the syllabary several syllables in which consonant X occurs, and the new status of consonant X leaves all of these syllables in an unusual position, partially devoid of their earlier integrity. The vowels A, B, C, . . . of these syllables which involve X as onset will then be *subject* to immediate reanalysis as segments, too. Those which occur with reasonable frequency in the syllabary will in turn *realize* this potential reanalysis (while a few may not) and will therefore instigate reanalysis of other consonants, Y, Z, . . . with which they occur in syllables. Through this process, then, a large number of segments will eventually be developed as independent units of the phonology[7].

(It is important to interpose here a brief explanation of the precise meaning of 'segment' in this context. The notion is only vaguely similar to the idea of the taxonomic 'phoneme'. The segment is limited to only one possible position with respect to other consonant or vowel segments and word (syllable) boundaries. In the above example, consonant X is limited to the environment __V. In other words, the segment is limited to the environment from which it is extracted. In addition, the segment does not necessarily include all of the reflexes of a particular 'phoneme' – the child might, for example, have two different k segments, for obvious reasons.)

It is now apparent that a child will have a larger repertoire of distinctions among consonants in word-initial position than in word-final position throughout most of the acquisition period precisely because segments first are discovered through their occurrences in CV syllables, and later in CVC syllables – the chain-reaction takes much longer to affect final segments.

The order in which individual segments are acquired varies greatly from child to child. The order in which distinctive features are acquired, however, is regular, as has already been pointed out by Jakobson; and the expected regularities are precisely those which Jakobson has described as properties of the nature of language.

Soon after the child begins extracting segments from his syllables, he is in a position to compare these segments and derive from them a still more elementary unit. This unit is the distinctive feature, and its earliest occurrences will be of a general nature, e.g., consonantal vs. vocalic. Later, refinements such as the division of one feature into two – consonantal vs. nonconsonantal and vocalic vs. nonvocalic – will take place. As these features represent the ultimate units for which the child has been searching, no further learning beyond the refinement of this system itself (except for the insignificant further generalization of segments previously discussed) is predicated upon it.

One further generalization will eventually occur in this process of extending notions of phonetic sameness and phonetic difference. This last step requires even greater tolerance for phonetic diversity than the previous one, and it is reserved probably for a much later stage since it is not a necessary step in the sense of being a prerequisite for the development of a linguistic concept, nor is it an ordinary step in the series of reanalysis that the child experiences. In fact, it is nothing more than a logical *conclusion* to the distinctive feature acquisition process which is bound up with the segmental recoding. This generalization is that which identifies some segments as being 'same' and lumps them together, resulting in a limited inventory of segments which is close to the inventory of the systematic phonetic level as proposed by Chomsky and Halle (1968). By means of this generalization, the child is able to lump together the contextually conditioned variants of a segment, such as t-/ __ V, -t-/V__V, -t/V__, and the several segments t which occur in various positions in various clusters. In addition the child, if he has not already done so, is now able to group together 'allophones' which are conditioned by specific and more limited qualities of the context – an example being k before front vowels, and k before back vowels.

The child's attention is focused on discovering the complete system upon which is based the structure of phonology. Shvachkin's experiment (to appear) with Russian children indicates that there is evidence in perception that this ordering is both neat and explicit. Evidence in production is not nearly so neat, indicating interference from phonetics and possibly also from that property of language which we designate by the term 'marking'.

The interference of phonetics is a two-fold one, and is deeply embedded in the pervasive conflict between phonetics and phonology which the child has spent so much effort resolving. At early stages, phonetic ability is considerably greater than can be displayed through the structural sieve of phonology – thus we can often find that the child's very first production of a particular word is phonetically quite accurate, while subsequent productions are mediated by the existent phonology and seem therefore to be phonetically much less sophisticated. (This fact, incidentally, indicates that all child sound-system data which have been collected in 'imitation' situations are probably unreliable and even misleading.) At later stages – when phonetic suppressions may have been falsely overgeneralized, when phonetically 'difficult' segments such as θ are being encountered, or when segments are sufficiently infrequent to make the appropriate feature generalizations less than obvious – interference from phonetics has precisely the opposite effect: namely, certain phonological distinctions which have been acquired may be inobvious with respect to certain segments because there is no phonetic distinction by means of which the child is able to show us that he does in fact control the relevant phonological distinction. A good example of this situation is the status of the fricative consonants in the speech of two of the children discussed in Moskowitz (1970).

Mackie and Erica had acquired all of the relevant features for the complete set of English fricatives, as evidenced by the operation of those features in other parts of their systems. Their treatment of those fricatives which they partially or completely lacked (phonetically), in terms of the patterns of substitutions and omissions which we observe for those segments, indicates that their phonological systems had 'slots' reserved for these segments. To give one example, Erica correctly pronounced [ð] when it occurred in an extremely limited environment – immediately after a segment marked + [nasal]: in all other environments, [ð] was either omitted entirely or [d] substituted for it – these two possibilities each occurred approximately 50 percent of the time. As this pattern was quite different from that of any of her other segments, we can conclude that she acquired an /ð/ which is distinctive from other segments; phonetic interference prevented the consistent phonological evidence of her learning. In the limiting case, we can imagine a situation in which a relevant piece of phonological learning is completely obscured in production data by even more substantial phonetic interference.

The data in Table III, a composite of the evidence of fricative acquisition for six children at different stages, illustrates well the interference of phonetics and phonology in the child's acquisition. Superficially we could draw from it the following conclusions:

(1)   f, s, š seem to be acquired first and θ last of the eight consonants
(2)   z, ð, ž, v seem to appear in that order, although ž stabilizes first.

There is no obvious order to this acquisition until we examine it in the light of the interference between phonetics and phonology. Correct control of voicing occurs late in the acquisition schedule so we would expect f, s, š, θ to all occur before their voiced counterparts. Since s and t and f are learned very early and are phonetically quite stable, we can predict that θ, which falls in the *intersection* of the articulatory suppression by s and t, and the acoustic suppression by f, will be well suppressed. Thus θ, unlike the other voiceless fricatives, must be relearned as a phonetic entity later, and such phonetic learning is apparently put off until the phonological system is quite well mastered. Although v is not phonetically stable until quite late, the evidence indicates that it is learned as a phonological entity not long after f. Similarly its unique phonetic patterning indicates that the phonological establishment of z soon after s is relatively stable. The evidence also indicates that phonological ð occurs considerably before it is phonetically stable. Since neither d nor z is phonetically stable as early as are t and s, it seems that ð begins to appear before it is phonetically suppressed by d and z (and also v). It even seems that this earlier occurrence of ð contributes to the instability of v: the incorrect productions of v show a marked tendency toward bilabial articulation, which cannot be a result of

TABLE III

Acquisition of fricatives

Inventory — Substitutions for:	f	v	s	z	š	ž	θ	ð
A. Withe[a] 2.2 f, (s) (x)	f ~ p		d, (x)	d, (s)	b		p	ð
B. Hildegard[b] 2.0 š, x, (ž)	w		š, (t)	š	š, (ž)		š, t	d
C. Mackie[c] 2.2 f, s, š, (z) (ð)	f	v, β, vf, b, d, p	s	s ~ z	š		t, s, θ	d, ð
D. Stanford[a] 1.11 f, s, š, (v) (z) (ð)	f	—β— b-, -v-, -f —b—	s ~ š,[d]	š,[d](z)	š	š	f, x	ð, d
E. Erica[c] 2.0 f, s, š, ž, (v) (z) (θ) (ð)	f	b-, -v-, -f	s ~ š,[d]	s ~ š,[d] z ~ ž,[d]	~ š	ž	f	ð, d
F. Erica[a] 2.6 f, s, z, š, ž, ð, (v) (θ)	f	b-, -v-, -f	s	s ~ z	š	ž	f	ð, (d)
G. Steven[a] 3.5 f, v, s, z, š, ž, ð	f	v	s	z	š	ž	f	ð

[a] unpublished data.
[b] from Leopold (1939).
[c] from Moskowitz (1970).
[d] ş and z̧ are palatal blade fricatives.

articulatory difficulty (since f is stable) but instead seems to be an attempt to more maximally differentiate v from $\eth$. Thus we can postulate an ideal ordering for the acquisition of phonological fricatives as follows:

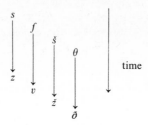

The theory as outlined so far indicates a path from babbling to a stage where phonological organization involves segments roughly of the systematic phonetic level that can be designated at least in part by distinctive features. It remains to be shown how the systematic phonological level is reached from this stage. Data relevant to this last step are not really to be found in free-speech data of preschool children, and in the future it will be necessary to carry out controlled experiments with children ages 4 to 10. A detailed study of the processes in the syllable stage provides evidence for the child's developing the concept of rule directly from the data he has; evidence from the systematic phonetic stage (Moskowitz, 1970) indicates that children experiment with a variety of rules in their efforts to find correct, usable ones. On the evidence of Gleitman and Gleitman's (1971) study of noun-compounding in English, we may assume that some but not all speakers of English learn a complete set of systematic phonological rules, and the majority learn those rules to some degree.

An interesting (and unique) prediction of this theory is that of idiomaticity. Several types of idioms arise during the acquisition process, some of them temporary and others permanent.

(1) The most short-lived idioms are the phonetic idioms which arise during the early syllabic stage. Frequently a child will pronounce a word with great accuracy on his first attempt, and subsequently reduce it to a CV syllable which complies with the constraints of his system.

(2) Phonetic idioms also arise, early in the acquisition process, which retain their idiomatic form for a long period. Preliminary evidence suggests that these idioms may be semantically favored, but exactly why they exist

is still unknown. They are 'memorized' as entities and much later are brought back into the constraints of the system – i.e., are later analyzed. Considerably more common than has been suspected, these idioms are frequently overlooked because either (a) they can be analyzed as a part of the system without modifying the system at all or (b) they are of sufficiently small deviation from the system that they can be accounted for by slight modifications incorporated into the system. (Notice that the second alternative in practice means that the investigator, by not being able to identify the idioms, has done some injustice to the child's system in his description of it.)

A clear example of this type of idiom is Hildegard's 'pretty', discussed earlier.

(3) The two idiom types described above are *progressive* idioms. More interesting are the *regressive* idioms, those which account for elements of language that do not 'catch up' with the rest of the system – i.e., those which remain encoded in a form which utilizes a unit of an earlier stage than that utilized by the remainder of the utterances.

At the point when the child begins to use a new unit, the vast majority of his utterances will then be idioms until they are reanalyzed into the new framework. (For example, the child who continues to babble after using a few syllabic words with reasonably consistent meaning can be viewed as having a repertoire of idioms in the sentence unit.) More interesting are those few idioms which remain unreanalyzed when everything else has been incorporated into the new system. Some of these idioms may never be reanalyzed and thus will remain as phonological idioms in the adult system. They are pieces of data which cannot and should not be analyzed in the same manner as the rest of the data.

There are two types of phonological idioms: those which are culturally shared and those which are idiosyncratic. Examples of the first are syllabic idioms such as [ʔəʔ–ʔəʔ] and [m:ʔm:], 'no' and 'yes', which are learned early by children and not reanalyzed. The stylized hissing noise of a tea-kettle and other sounds produced by protracted fricatives come under this category too. Idiosyncratic idioms are less easy to cite for obvious reasons. In my own speech I find imitations of animal noises (which differ from phonemicized versions like 'bow-wow'), a variety of isolated foreign-language words, and some baby-talk items (which can be used only with a

unique pitch pattern) as some examples: doubtless there are many more,
some of which will be very difficult to discover because of their seeming
compliance with the rules of my system. For those people who learn a
second dialect well, the few revealing words which show distinct signs of the
first dialect probably come under this category also. The description of
idioms in adult speech may prove to have a significant effect on our formulation of phonology.

3. INTEGRITY OF LANGUAGE

The language acquisition process consists of the discovery of relevant
concepts (rule, sentence-unit, syllable, etc.) and the gradual creation of
language on the basis of them. The created language, while not identical
to that of the adult model which serves as input data, is very close to it, and
that fact must be accounted for if we are to believe that language is created
and not learned.

From soon after birth the child is aware of the human language around
him. He is able to differentiate it from the other sounds of his environment
and even though he makes no effort to discover its system he is 'absorbing'
something of the language. He learns in effect the salient features which
characterize a sound sequence as being part of that language. It has been
noticed that the child of about two years who is transferred from one
language environment to another ceases speaking for a time before com-
mencing the job of acquiring the new language. All that is happening is
that the child must pause for a while and allow himself the opportunity to
absorb the salient aspects of the new language, 'to get a feel for it'. Also it
has been noticed that the child in a bilingual environment from birth has
relatively little difficulty keeping the two languages apart; this too is due
to his knowledge of the salient characteristics which distinguish them even
on the grossest level.

That which is salient about the language is what I would like to characterize by a notion suggested by Robert H. Whitman[8] which he calls the
integrity of a language.

The notion of integrity is still a very vague one and should be further
explicated, although that is difficult to do at this early stage of thinking. A
language cannot be assumed to be logically systematic apart from its
integrity – the underlying aspects which unify that language and allow its

diverse features to interrelate in specific ways. Thus integrity is related to the way in which we view language as a synchronic system. (Notice, by the way, that integrity can apply to some extent to a subsystem of a language, such as its phonology, but it more importantly applies to a language as a whole. In this sense it predicts that the separation of levels is an artificial construct and that an interrelation of levels is more to be expected. Recent work on the unified treatment of syntax and semantics as well as Bresnan (this vol. pp. 3–47), is a step in the direction of such a wholistic treatment of language.) In this synchronic sense of integrity, too, we may suppose that the deviance of a language from the requirements of an absolute universal has to be accounted for in a manner significant to the remainder of the system of that language, i.e., is related to the peculiar integrity of that language. Universals are therefore seen as occurrences whose probabilities are very high because they are almost essential to an integral language system. In a diachronic sense, any change which a language undergoes must first of all preserve that language's integrity, and second, result directly from that integrity. With respect to language acquisition, we must certainly say that a synchronic analysis of a child's speech at any point reveals an integrity to the system, but each successive stage possesses an integrity which more closely approximates that of the model language. Just as the changes of a language are integrity-preserving, so are the changes of a child's language; each such change transforms the integrity in ways that are specific and that characterize all children. No change should directly violate prior integrity, but should expand it in accommodating ways.

It is important to emphasize the diachronic aspect mentioned above. Any change which occurs in a language must preserve the integrity of that language, and this is accomplished in two ways. (1) The particular change which occurs should not violate the language's integrity, i.e., must not result in a system which is antithetical to the original one. Thus we take very special notice of those changes which seem to us to be 'strange' in their introduction of elements which a system seems inconducive to or in their changing the basic nature of the system. (2) Any change which occurs grows out of the integrity of the language, i.e., the potential for its occurrence, is itself a part of the integrity. Another way of saying this is to focus on the knowledge that the child has gained about the abstract nature of his language and to focus on the limitation which the adult's knowledge therefore places on possible changes in the system once it has been learned.

As a brief, informal example, we can view Whitman's theory of the process of palatalization in Slavic languages. The change which we call 'palatalization' was predicated upon something integral to the nature of all Slavic languages, or alternatively, to the nature of the shared ancestor language. Thus such a change has occurred in all of these languages. But each language has carried the change to a different extent (phonetically, at least) and these differences are predicated upon the specific differences in the integrities of the various languages.

Even during the early babbling stage the child is learning the integrity of his model language. All of his attempts at language creation are consistent with that integrity although not until the end of the acquisition process are they wholly consistent with the integrity in all its finest details. But there are always loose ends of the language, aspects which are neither consistent with nor inconsistent with the integrity, and these change most easily and rapidly from generation to generation. Changes in more salient aspects occur more slowly, and those changes must preserve integrity to a large degree. Over a long period of time the accumulation of such changes may have the effect of altering integrity significantly – resulting in a 'new' language.

4. SYNTAX ACQUISITION

We cannot conceive of the child learning either the phonology or the syntax of a language in isolation. A language basically hangs together in non-arbitrary ways: it is one integrated system, complete with inherent tendencies. Just as it is truly artificial to attempt to describe the phonology and syntax of a language without relating them, it would not be sufficient to describe the acquisition process as having two distinct subparts. Both systems increase in size and complexity simultaneously. Both are created on the basis of a single integrity.

The child discovers concepts which are relevant to language and in his unique version of efficiency he utilizes them whenever possible in his creation of language. Hopefully, when we can finally describe all of these basic concepts accurately, the acquisition of each should entail a certain amount of language creation as a natural, elegant, and not very complex outgrowth of that concept.

First, the child must discover the *unit*. He must discover that all the sound around him is actually built up of units. The first manifestation of the unit is the sentence-unit: that long string of nondiscrete sound which occurs between pauses. Later on, through various processes, other units emerge, some phonological (such as the segment), others syntactic-semantic (such as the phrase), and still others obviously relevant to both levels (such as the word). It is significant that all are just extensions of the basic concept, requiring less creativity and effort for their formulation than was initially necessary.

Connected with this search for units is another basic notion of linguistic structure which the child must develop: that of *discreteness*. This is most obvious in terms of phonology, but just as valid for syntax. Evidence for the sentence-unit is often attributed to babbling data; in that context, the unit is both a rudimentary phonological and syntactic notion. The search for the smaller unit leads the child next to the syllable – a phonological unit in its own right, but also a syntactic one, as the syllable is initially identical with the word. On both the phonological and syntactic levels the child has had to make an elementary discovery of discreteness, since he has rarely been presented with a syllable isolated from the running stream of speech. We can imagine a variety of relevant acoustic cues which allow this elementary notion of discreteness to emerge with little difficulty: it is in the case where discreteness must be created – in terms of segments – on the basis of acoustic data where discreteness is not an obvious aspect at all that it becomes a relevant concept for dealing with the data. However, its earlier partial manifestation with respect to syllables is probably a tremendous advantage to the child, who would be hard put to create such a notion without at least that little bit of prior help.

From the initial emergence of *rules* the child has within his grasp what is probably the most essential of all language-related concepts. The earliest rule describes simply the way two syllables may be put together to form a word, but inherent in it are such significant possibilities as *directionality* of a rule and *limitation* of subparts of a rule. Predicated upon this may be the later discovery of *rule ordering* and *cyclic application*. From the form of his first rule the child can deduce that two things (in the first case, single syllables which had functioned as words) can be put together to form a third, unique thing (a distinct word). This leads directly to the discovery of *concatenation*.

The earliest stage of syntactic development is that of holophrastic sentences, when the child utilizes a single syllable as the basic unit on all levels and equates it as a sound, a syllable, a phrase, a sentence, and an idea, as Jakobson has pointed out. When the child leaves the holophrastic stage, he enters a two-word stage which has been described by several investigators as obeying the rules of a pivot grammar. The two-word stage is significant in many respects, and the process of concatenation inherent in it is in some ways one of the most crucial the child will undertake during the entire acquisition process. During this stage the child practices the putting together of two words (in a sense, two holophrastic sentences) to form a third, distinct semantic entity: the rules must obey certain extremely limited conditions, namely, that pivot words are not free to occur in either position. There is no three-word stage. (Analogously, the child who puts great effort into the production of reduplicated forms does not undertake at any time the consistent production of triduplicated forms.) The two-word stage satisfies the need to practice putting together distinct things to form a new entity, or a basic kind of relation. In the adult grammar most of the significant relationships are bipartite – actor:action, action:object, possessor:possessed, etc. And we find most of these relationships practiced semantically during the two-word stage. Thus in the two-word stage, by practicing within this limited framework which can be accounted for so easily, the child can develop many of the important grammatical relationships for which he will have to work out the details later – conjunction, possession, etc. Even after the child progresses beyond the two-word stage to produce multiword sentences, he still utilizes this basic framework of combining two units as a first step in the development of new grammatical concepts. Thus concatenation serves as a basis for chunking information into longer sentences; e.g., if the child uses a sentence A + B during the two-word stage, he may use X + (A + B) or (A + X) + B or (X + A) + B later. In this way he can increase sentence length without any longer limiting himself to a specific length as an upper limit for all sentences.

For example, Klima and Bellugi's (1966) data on the acquisition of negation indicate that the first step is to combine the word 'no' (one unit) with any sentence which the child's grammar could otherwise generate (another unit). Still working within this two-unit framework, the child develops the negative 'no' into a few more possibilities – 'don't', 'not' –

which are limited in their distributions in the same way. Only later can the child progress to a multiword framework. Just as before he was able to extend his sentence structure to incorporate additional units [(action + object) + (actor + action)] → [actor + action + object] now he can do the same with negatives [(neg + S) + (actor + action)] → [actor + neg + action].

At age 2.0 the majority of Erica's utterances were still one- or two-word sentences. A few sentences were longer. Those which were answers to questions were among the longest samples because they utilized repetitions from the questions. We might suppose then that a sequence repeated from a question constitutes no more than one unit. The two-word sentences cannot be described by a pivot grammar: Erica had a very large vocabulary, talked a lot, and incorporated into her sentences a large variety of syntactic combinations. For example:

"Fall down."	"I'm finish."
"On knee."	"The leaf."
"My frog."	"Whole banana."
"Eye big."	"See grandma."
"Put on."	"Fly allgone."
"Got eyes."	"Need help."
"There eyes."	"Erica's stockings."
"Shoes off."	"Going night-night."

In other words, despite the apparent short length of most of her sentences, a fairly simple grammar could not account for Erica's speech during this time. The following guidelines were used as constraints on a grammar of Erica's speech during this time.

(1) Most of the rules of this grammar describe the internal structure of the unit, the two-word sequence. For example,

$$U \rightarrow V + N_{obj}$$

which accounts for such sentences as "Got eyes," "See grandma," and "Need help." A rule of this type is expected to later expand to permit other two-word sequences to occur in either the V or N_{obj} positions.

(2) A few of the two-word sequences still accounted for a single unit, along with all other one-word utterances. "Fall down," for example, also occurred in the two-word sentence. "I fall down." Neither "fall" nor

"down" occurred without the other. Later we would expect one of these words to begin combining with still other words; when the second does so also there is absolute evidence that they are distinct items, although even then in the sequence "fall down" they *may* still constitute an idiom.

(3) Some two-word sequences may not be describable by a rule such as proposed under (1) because they are semantically unique – a general rule would in fact account for only one utterance. "On knee," for example, was obviously the prototype for a large number of two-word sequences which would appear later, but here it was the only such phrase. By accounting for it as a progressive idiom, we also prepare in the grammar the path of development we expect to account for in the future.

(4) One-word sentences can be considered as idioms (regressive) and do not have to be accounted for by the grammar *per se* as long as the grammar is considered to be a reflection of the child's current linguistic knowledge rather than a description of all utterances.

(5) Longer sentences, which seem to call for complex grammatical description, can be handled as progressive idioms, in part, and can largely be explained as extensions of Erica's two-word combinations. Some examples are

"I don't want want the clothes on."
"Come see choo-choo train."
"Watch him, let's watch."
"I catch a fly."
"He going home for breakfast."

The first example is particularly interesting in light of experimental data from Slobin and Welsh (1968), which indicate that when asked to repeat sentences children delete unnecessary word repetitions which occur in sample sentences. The voluntary inclusion of such a repetition here seems to indicate that the sentence "I don't want the clothes on" would be too much for Erica to handle grammatically; the two shorter utterances "I don't want" and "want the clothes on" were more reasonable in terms of her grammatical ability at the time and they can be concatenated together as if each were a unit. Neither of the two shorter sentences could be used alone without the word 'want': therefore each must include it. "I don't want" follows the pattern of Erica's other negative sentences, where "don't" plus verb seems to act as a single unit, a negative verb. "Want the clothes on" was a response to the mother's prior question "Do you want to put the clothes on?", an idiom of immediate repetition. In the second example, "Come see" functions as a single word. The third sentence is an even clearer example of the explanation given above for the first sentence. The fourth is probably representative of the extreme limits of the capacity of Erica's grammar at this time. The fifth is unusual and difficult to explain. Its occurrence was preceded by "He going home" but the entire sentence is reasonably thought of as a progressive idiom, particularly since "for breakfast" is unique, both semantically and syntactically, in the corpus.

When Erica was 2.6 we began a 20-hour tape series which covered a short period of time and provided us with a large corpus for a fairly uniform period. At this time Erica's grammar was considerably more complex than six months earlier.

Mother: What do you want for lunch?
Erica: Peanut butter and jelly.
Mother: What do you want to drink?
Erica: I want to drink peanut butter.
Mother: You want to drink peanut butter?
Erica: No.
Mother: That's pretty silly, isn't it?
Erica: Uh huh. I'm gonna eat orange juice.
Mother: Orange juice?
Erica: Uh huh. Not gonna spill it.

Erica was trying to say something quite distinct from her culinary preferences – that she no longer knew two words ('eat' and 'drink'), each of which occurred idiomatically with a subset of ingestable objects, but instead knew two words and a semantic rule which determined appropriateness. In effect, she had had before a large set of semantic idioms. At some point, probably shortly before the above conversation, the rule developed which eliminated all of those idioms.

From the several examples given so far emerges a pattern involving the child's use first of progressive idioms, then of generalized rules based on particular units of grammar and finally of regressive idioms which have not been reanalyzed and which need not be accounted for in a more specific way when the grammar is described in a more sophisticated form.

5. CONCLUSION

The units which occur during the different stages of language acquisition are surface structure phenomena which are relevant to the organization of language. While much information eventually is re-encoded on a more abstract level, some remains idiomatically encoded in the earlier forms. A grammar of a language must account for such surface idiomatic data. In addition a grammar must account for the possibility that some information is encoded in several ways simultaneously. For example, while most phonological knowledge is probably eventually re-encoded in the form described by a generative phonology, the physical act of pronunciation is governed by encodings which remain throughout life in syllable form. This, plus the evidence for the importance of syllables in early speech, as well as several recent studies in phonology (for example, Bell, 1971, and Fromkin, 1971) indicates that the syllable must be accorded theoretical status in a grammar of phonology. Some distinctive features may operate across whole syllables or across that part of a syllable which was at one time in the speaker's life a unit (e.g., the CV part of an adult CVC syllable). Many sound changes are best described as a redistribution of the status of distinctiveness and redundancy of a feature within the confines of a syllable. Similarly, it is possible that some aspects of syntax are really idiomatic (in the broad sense of 'idiom' used in this paper) and can best be described in terms of surface structure.

The learning process exemplified in language acquisition is unique among the learning situations which have been investigated. The few attempts which have been made to develop a psychological theory of learning which can account for language acquisition have been encumbered by the frameworks of stimulus-response and various traditionally recognized 'drives'. If language learning does satisfy some innate human drives, they are probably ones such as exploration, curiosity, and self-fulfilment, needs for variety, and an antithesis to boredom. The theory outlined here indicates that learning in its primary form is really a process of creation within a defined area, with the learner setting his own goals according to the current state of his progress. Under the conditions of no pressure (or at least no sensitivity to pressure) and no long-term goals, the learner does a far better job with language than he will probably ever again do in his life with almost anything else. Early language learning, like many other forms of early human activity, presents great possibilities for discovery.

It is possible that the more closely we can adapt teaching situations to duplicate this natural learning the easier will be the job of teaching. The learning outlined above requires no previous knowledge, no innate intuitions; there is not even the need to assume that the child has any idea of the enormity of the job he has undertaken or of the complexity of the end product. He proceeds step by step, allowing each step to grow out of precisely that which he has mastered to date, never knowing that the next step will not be his last. All of the concepts necessary for final mastery grow out of the learning process itself.

A feature of this form of learning is the stable system of development which is shared by all children; the order of steps and the essential character of each step is dictated by the nature of the data. Within this framework, however, there is much room for vast idiosyncratic differences which in no way interfere with the attainment of the final goal. Perhaps the teaching of such broad frameworks is the only goal which education can usefully attain. Machine teaching programs which allow students to deduce their own generalizations after large numbers of instances of data are a step in the direction of this type of education.

University of California, Berkeley

NOTES

* Since I wrote this paper in 1969–70, many of the points brought up herein have been revised and expanded upon considerably. I would like to refer readers to my *The acquisition of phonology*, Project on Linguistic Analysis Reports, Phonology Laboratory, Berkeley, 1972. This more recent account includes a fuller discussion of some important issues only touched on here, e.g., the function of partial reduplication, acquisition of segments and distinctive features, phonological idioms, the role of babbling in language acquisition, and others; the theory is there exemplified with more data.

[1] 'Systematic' is used here in the sense of being a part of the language system, not in the sense used in generative phonology.

[2] A study of the acquisition of intonation by infants in English-, Chinese-, and Russian-speaking homes is currently being conducted.

[3] Jakobson ('Why Mama and Papa') speaks of this tendency: "During the babbling period in the infant's development, many of the uttered syllables consist of a vocalic sound succeeded by a consonantal articulation. The most natural order of sound production is an opening of the mouth followed by its closure . . .. As soon as the child moves from his babbling activities to the first acquisition of conventional speech, he at once clings to the model

'consonant plus vowel'. The sounds assume a phonemic value and thus need to be correctly identified by the listener, and since the best graspable clue in discerning consonants is their transition to the following vowels, the sequence 'consonant plus vowel' proves to be the optimal sequence . . . ."

[4] If we look only at CV syllables where the vowel is simple, we would expect 33^2 possibilities, of which 3 percent would be reduplications if random; in actuality, we find 37 percent reduplicated words among the CVCV types, and an additional 15 percent 'partial reduplications'.

[5] Italics added.

[6] For example, Leopold reports that Hildegard's first distinction was that of ?əↆ with ?əↈ.

[7] This explanation of the role of partial reduplication in the development of distinctive features and segments is inaccurate and misleading. For a discussion of this complex and important aspect of phonological acquisition, see the reference given in footnote 1.

[8] Personal communication, 1970.

ELIZABETH M. GAMMON

A SYNTACTICAL ANALYSIS OF SOME
FIRST-GRADE READERS*

1. INTRODUCTION

An important consideration in teaching children to read is the appropriate matching of the reading material to the child. In the past the appropriateness of materials has been discussed in relation to their content, their format and organization, and their difficulty level as expressed by their vocabulary load, sentence structure, and level of human interest (Chall, 1958). In the revision of primary readers, in particular, the concern has been with finding the appropriate level of difficulty as measured by the frequency of new vocabulary words and the number of repetitions of a new word (Becker, 1936; Gates, 1930; Hockett, 1938; Mehl, 1931; Spache, 1941). But recent evidence (Bormuth, 1966; Ruddell, 1964, 1965; Strickland, 1962) has indicated that there is another concept of appropriateness which must be considered: How does the sentence structure found in the readers compare with the sentence structure of the child's speech?

As a first step toward making a comparison of first-grade readers to first-grade speech, I have attempted to provide a syntactical analysis of some widely used first-grade basal readers. I have written probabilistic grammars according to the method developed in Suppes (1970). Basal readers have often been derided for their simplicity, and a casual reading leads one to expect a few stereotypic grammatical forms to dominate the corpus with a high frequency of occurrence. As this paper will show, the facts were quite different. Syntactical analysis revealed that first-grade readers have a wider variety of grammatical forms than vocabulary and that no form has a high frequency of occurrence.

2. PRELIMINARY STEPS OF ANALYSIS

The corpus for this study is the Ginn first-grade reading series and the Scott-Foresman first-grade reading series.[1] These texts are widely used and appeared to be similar in terms of format, content, and sentence structure. My hope was that the data from the two series would combine

Hintikka et al. (eds.), Approaches to Natural Language, 85–133. All rights reserved.
Copyright © 1973 by D. Reidel Publishing Company, Dordrecht-Holland.

to form large frequencies for all sentence types; although, as will be seen later, this did not prove to be precisely the case. Each first-grade series is divided into a set of preprimers, a set of primers, and a set of first readers which are read by all students; all of these have been included in the analysis.

The texts are divided into short stories consisting mainly of conversations between persons or animals, so many sentences contain an identification of the speaker. Typical examples are: "*I like this kitten,*" *said Betty*, and *Susan said*, "*Toy Mouse wants a ride.*" Neither the titles of the stories nor the speaker identifiers (*Betty said, he said,* etc.) were included in the analysis. The titles consisted mainly of short noun phrases and were clearly not indicative of the grammar used for sentences within the stories. Speaker identifiers, too, had a structure of their own, and it seemed appropriate to consider them merely as labels. To consider *Susan said,* "*Toy Mouse wants a ride*" as the sentence for analysis rather than simply *Toy Mouse wants a ride* would distinguish sentence types in a way which would not emphasize the most interesting characteristics of the grammar. In that case, *Susan said,* "*Toy Mouse wants a ride,*" "*Toy Mouse wants a ride,*" *said Susan,* and "*Toy Mouse*", *said Susan,* "*wants a ride*" would have to be considered as separate sentence types; while this is a meaningful distinction, it was not considered essential for a first syntactical analysis.

Structures which were included in the analysis will from here on be called 'utterances'. An utterance is a string of words which begins with a capital letter and ends with one of the following terminal punctuation marks: '.', '?', '!', or a ',' followed by a speaker identifier and a '.'. (The symbol '.' used to indicate abbreviations was not considered terminal.) Speaker identifiers found at the beginning or the middle of an utterance were ignored, and all punctuation was ignored except for the purpose of distinguishing utterances. Thus, the sentence, "*I want it,*" *said Bill,* "*but I can't eat it*" includes one utterance: *I want it but I can't eat it*; whereas the sentences, "*I want it,*" *said Bill. "But I can't eat it*" include two utterances: *I want it* and *But I can't eat it*.

All of the utterances in both first-grade reading series were included in the analysis. The number of utterances in each text is shown in Table I.

The table indicates that the number of utterances in each division were roughly the same for each series, although the number of utterances in the Ginn series was consistently greater.

TABLE I

Utterance count

Text	Preprimer	Primer	Reader	Total
Ginn	858	1343	1925	4126
Scott-Foresman	638	1040	1450	3128
Totals	1496	2383	3375	7254

The first step in the analysis was the coding of each utterance according to type. Each utterance was coded as an ordered n-tuple consisting of the part of speech of each word in the order of occurrence. The part of speech was determined according to rules commonly used for English grammars. Table II lists all parts of speech found in the corpus along with the abbreviations used in coding (and throughout this paper), typical examples, and examples of any phrases of two or more words which were considered to be a unit and coded as only one part of speech.

TABLE II

Parts of speech in corpus

Part of speech	Abbreviation	Example	Examples of types containing more than 1 word
adjective	A	pretty	
adverb	ADV	fast	
article	T	the	
common noun	N	house	ice cream
conjunction	C	and	
copulative verb	CV	is	
interjection	I	oh	
interrogative adjective	IADJ	which	
interrogative adverb	IADV	how	
interrogative pronoun, objective case	IP(2)	whom	
interrogative pronoun, subjective case	IP(1)	who	

Table II (Continued)

Part of speech	Abbreviation	Example	Examples of types containing more than 1 word
intransitive verb	IV	go	
locative	L	here	
modal	M	can	
negation	–	not	
number used in counting	NBR	one	
preposition	J	into	
pronoun, objective case	P(2)	him	
pronoun, subjective case	P(1)	he	
proper noun	G	Betty	Mr. Green, Frisky Kitten
rejoinder	R	yes	all right, thank you
relative pronoun, objective case	RP(2)	whom	
relative pronoun, subjective case	RP(1)	who	
salutation	S	hello	Good day, Happy birthday
sound	Z	zoom	
subordinate conjunction	CON	that	
'to' used with infinitives	O	to	
transitive verb	TV	want	
vocative	K	Betty	Mr. Green, Frisky Kitten

Clearly, a given word could be assigned to different parts of speech depending on its usage in a particular utterance. In *I saw the boy who hit Mary,* *who* is a relative pronoun, whereas in *Who is he, who* is an interrogative pronoun. Similarly the coding of phrases such as *Frisky Kitten* depended on usage. The phrase, *Frisky Kitten* was usually used as the name of a cat in which case the phrase was coded as a proper noun (G, not G + G); however, in the sentence, *My pet is a frisky kitten, frisky kitten* would be coded as an adjective followed by a common noun.

A comment must be made about the classification of verbs. Verbs were put into one of three categories according to their position in the utterance.

Verbs which were followed by a noun phrase were labeled transitive verbs; verbs which were not followed by a noun phrase or an adjective phrase were labeled intransitive verbs, and verbs which were followed by an adjective phrase were labeled copulative verbs. (Nouns used as adverbs as in *He goes home* were classified as such so that in this sentence *goes* is intransitive. Passive constructions were not used.) Under this classification scheme 'to be' verbs can be in any of the three categories depending on usage; the verb is transitive in *He is a very good boy*, intransitive in *Sally is here with me*, and copulative in *Your new dress is very pretty*. If 'to be' verbs had been placed in a category of their own as is often done, a fourth category would have been required for verbs such as *look* and *get* in *She looks beautiful* and *She is getting more beautiful every day*. As will be seen, a problem of too many types and small frequencies within types was already present and to add a fourth category for verbs would only increase this problem.

The utterances were then sorted according to type. This original classification scheme produced a very large number of types with relatively small frequencies of occurrence as is illustrated in Table III.

TABLE III

Statistics for utterance types under original classification

Text	Total number of types	% of types with frequency > 5	% of types with frequency > 1
Ginn preprimer	250	10.4	45.2
Scott-Foresman preprimer	277	8.3	28.9
Preprimers combined	454	10.1	39.9
Ginn primer	664	5.0	28.8
Scott-Foresman primer	666	3.3	19.1
Primers combined	1185	4.6	26.3
Ginn reader	1099	3.3	25.8
Scott-Foresman reader	1096	1.6	12.8
Readers combined	2015	2.9	21.3

Table III shows that contrary to expectation the Ginn and Scott-Foresman series do not in general contain the same utterance types. The Ginn reader, for example, contains 1099 utterance types and the Scott-Foresman reader contains 1096 types; thus if the readers had no types in common, the readers combined would contain 2195 types. In fact, the readers combined contain 2015 types indicating that only 180 or about 16 percent of the utterance types in each reader are common to both readers. Further study indicates that the types common to both readers are those with the greatest frequencies in the individual readers, and that the types with small frequencies in one reader do not usually find a match in the other reader.

It is interesting to note that the number of utterance types in each section of each series is nearly the same; the number of types in the two preprimers differs by 27 and the number of types in the primers and readers differs by 2 and 3, respectively. In each case the Scott-Foresman series contains the greater number of utterance types which was unexpected because the Ginn series contains the greater number of utterances (Table I).

To construct a probabilistic grammar for the corpus and to apply the chi-square statistic as a test of fit, a smaller number of utterance types is desirable and greater frequencies within types are required. Elimination of all types with frequency less than or equal to five, for example, was not feasible at this point because only a small percentage of the corpus would then be described by the grammar (55.5 percent of the preprimers combined, 33.5 percent of the primers combined, and 24.3 percent of the readers combined). In order to obtain a smaller number of types and greater frequencies within types, a method for meaningfully collapsing the types was developed. This involved the combining of certain groups of letters (parts of speech) into one category whenever they occurred. One grammar would then be written to represent each set of rules for combination, and another grammar would be written for the utterance types containing the collapsed categories.

The first attempt involved the use of noun phrases and verb phrases. Pronouns and strings of articles, adjectives, and nouns were replaced by NP for 'noun phrase', and strings of modals, negatives, and verbs were replaced by VP for 'verb phrase'. For example the sentences, *Betty does not want the pretty red ball* of type (G + M + − + TV + T + A + A + N) and *The puppy likes me* of type (T + N + TV + P (2)) would both be of type (NP + VP + NP) under noun-phrase and verb-phrase collapsing. This made a substantial reduction in the number of types, but a large number of types with low frequencies remained.

The final collapsing involves the use of a category called 'verbal modifiers' (VM) as well as the noun-phrase and verb-phrase categories. In the verbal modifier category are strings of adverbs, prepositional phrases, locatives, and noun phrases used as adverbs. The utterances *He runs fast* (P (1) + IV + ADV), *He runs very fast* (P (1) + IV + ADV + ADV), and *He runs to the house* (P (1) + IV + J + T + N) would all be of type (NP + VP + VM) under the final collapsing. Complete details of the noun-phrase, verb-phrase, and verbal-modifier classifications systems are given by the phrase-structure grammars. The noun-phrase grammar appears in the next section; the verb-phrase and verbal-modifier grammars may be found in Gammon (1969).

This final collapsing greatly reduced the number of types as is shown in Table IV.

TABLE IV

Statistics for utterance types under final classification

Text	Total number of types	% of types with frequency > 5	% of types with frequency > 1
Ginn preprimer	90	30.0	56.7
Scott-Foresman preprimer	116	16.4	54.3
Preprimers combined	153	24.2	57.5
Ginn primer	204	23.5	49.0
Scott-Foresman primer	262	12.6	40.5
Primers combined	364	17.3	46.2
Ginn reader	325	14.8	44.3
Scott-Foresman reader	511	9.2	28.2
Readers combined	689	11.6	35.3
All combined	882	14.7	42.0

While the percentage of types with frequencies greater than five remains low, the percentage of the corpus which can now be accounted for by types with frequencies greater than five has substantially increased. Eighty-four percent of the corpus can now be described by types with frequency greater than five. In general the trends apparent under the original classification system (Table III) have continued. Each section of the Scott-Foresman series contains a greater number of types but a smaller percentage of types with frequency greater than 5 (and greater than 1) than the corresponding Ginn section. This implies that the Scott-Foresman books contain a greater variety of sentence types than the Ginn books and in this sense are more difficult. The total number of types for the combined sections still indicates a large number of types present in only one reader, but the percentage of common types is now much greater than in the previous classification system. Again, it is generally the small frequency types which are present in only one series.

3. THE PHRASE-STRUCTURE GRAMMARS

Three probabilistic grammars corresponding to the collapsed categories were written for parts of utterances: a noun-phrase grammar, a verb-phrase grammar, and a verbal-modifier grammar; these grammars were then utilized in the grammar for complete utterances. The grammar for utterances will generate such types as $(NP + VP + NP)$, but will not generate such types as $(T + A + N + TV + A + A + N)$. To generate a form of the latter type, first the utterance grammar, and then the noun-phrase, verb-phrase, and verbal-modifier grammars must be used.

The grammar for complete utterances was written as three separate grammars, a grammar for statements with verbs, a grammar for statements without verbs, and a grammar for interrogatives. Only the noun-phrase grammar and the grammar for statements with verbs (sometimes called simply 'the statement grammar') will be discussed in this paper; a complete discussion of the remaining grammars may be found in Gammon (1969).

The grammars were evaluated according to the method explained in Suppes (1970). Since details may also be found in Gammon (1969), the explanation given here will be brief. Parameters assigned to each of the choice points of the grammar are used to state the theoretical probability of any syntactical type derivable from the grammar. If optional transformations are included in the grammar, parameters must be assigned to the options and incorporated into the theoretical probabilities. Obligatory transformations require no parameters.

Using the theoretical probabilities and the observed type frequencies, the parameters are estimated according to the method of maximum likelihood. This method is workable as long as the grammar is unambiguous; that is, as long as each syntactical type can be generated in only one way. If more than one derivation is possible for a syntactical type, the theoretical probability of that type consists of a sum of products and the maximum-likelihood calculations are extremely difficult.

Once the parameters have been estimated, the estimated frequencies of each syntactical type are calculated. Chi-square tests are then used to determine the goodness of fit of the model (the grammar) to the observed type frequencies.

3.1. *The Noun-Phrase Grammar*

The noun-phrase grammar is given in Table V.

TABLE V

The noun-phrase grammar

| | Parameters | |
Rewrite rules	Rule-choice probabilities	Within-rule-choice probabilities
$NP \rightarrow P$	A_1	
$NP \rightarrow G$	A_2	
$NP \rightarrow (T) + \left(\left\{ \begin{matrix} A \\ A+A \end{matrix} \right\} \right) + N$	A_3	$B1_1$ $\quad$ $\begin{matrix} B2_1 \\ B2_2 \\ B2_3 \end{matrix}$ $B1_2$
$NP \rightarrow A + A + A + N$	A_4	

Obligatory transformations:
(a) If N is 'something', $A + N \rightarrow N + A$.
(b) If A is 'what' or 'all', $T + A + N \rightarrow A + T + N$.
(c) If A_1 is 'what' or 'all', $T + A_1 + A_2 + N \rightarrow A_1 + T + A_2 + N$.

Note that for this grammar and the statement grammar, the generation ends with a nonterminal vocabulary of words describing parts of speech rather than a terminal vocabulary of words such as *the, girl, pretty*.

Throughout this paper variables which must sum to 1 have the same name and different subscripts. Thus in the noun-phrase grammar, $A_1 + A_2 + A_3 + A_4 = 1$, $B1_1 + B1_2 = 1$, and $B2_1 + B2_2 + B2_3 = 1$. The parameters indicated in Table V represent the following probabilities:

A_1: Probability of choosing the first noun-phrase rule.

A_2: Probability of choosing the second noun-phrase rule.

A_3: Probability of choosing the third noun-phrase rule.

A_4: Probability of choosing the fourth noun-phrase rule.

$B1_1$: Probability of choosing T.

$B1_2$: Probability of deleting T.

$B2_1$: Probability of choosing A.

$B2_2$: Probability of choosing 'A + A'.

$B2_3$: Probability of deleting either choice.

Note that while nine parameters have been indicated for this model, only six of the parameters are free to vary; the remaining three will be determined because of the three sets of parameters which must sum to 1. Nine types of noun phrases are derivable from the model, so the original model allows two degrees of freedom. The number of degrees of freedom for this grammar and for the statement grammar is sometimes decreased because of low predicted frequencies; whenever the predicted frequency of a type was less than five, the observed and predicted frequencies of that type were combined with those of the following types until the total predicted frequency was greater than five. (The number '5' is not sacred; it provides a good practical rule. When the theoretical frequency is too small, e.g., 1, 2, or 3, the assumptions on which the goodness-of-fit test is based are violated.) One degree of freedom was lost each time one cell was combined with another.

The transformations shown in Table V are obligatory and as such require no parameters. Transformation (a) is necessary to transform a phrase like *red something* (A + N) into *something red* (N + A); transformations (b) and (c) change phrases like *the all children* (T + A + N) and *a what big ball* (T + A + A + N) to *all the children* (A + T + N) and *what a big ball* (A + T + A + N).

For the noun-phrase grammar the analysis described above was run on the individual sections of the corpus – the Ginn preprimer, the Scott-Foresman preprimer, the preprimers combined, the Ginn primer, the Scott-Foresman primer, the primers combined, the Ginn reader, the Scott-Foresman reader, and the readers combined – as well as on the entire corpus. Tables VI–IX summarize the results of the noun-phrase analysis.

Table VI shows the percentage of each section of the corpus accounted for by the grammar (that is, the percentage of noun phrases in the corpus whose syntactical types are derivable from the grammar); Table VII gives the maximum-likelihood estimates; Table VIII provides a comparison of the total chi-squares for each section; and Table IX shows for each section the observed and theoretical frequencies and corresponding chi-square

TABLE VI

Percentage of each section of the corpus accounted for by the noun-phrase grammar

Ginn preprimer	S-F preprimer	Preprimers combined	Ginn primer	S-F primer	Primers combined	Ginn reader	S-F reader	Readers combined	All combined
99.0	98.1	98.6	98.6	97.8	98.2	98.7	97.3	98.0	98.2

TABLE VII

Maximum-likelihood estimates for each section of the corpus for the noun-phrase grammar

Parameter	Ginn preprimer	S-F preprimer	Preprimers combined	Ginn primer	S-F primer	Primers combined	Ginn reader	S-F reader	Readers combined	All combined
A_1	.2979	.6309	.4529	.4369	.5290	.4803	.3710	.3761	.3733	.4171
A_2	.3290	.1964	.2673	.1719	.1484	.1608	.1535	.1218	.1389	.1635
A_3	.3718	.1726	.2791	.3810	.3205	.3525	.4677	.4960	.4808	.4135
A_4	.0013	.0000	.0007	.0102	.0020	.0064	.0078	.0060	.0070	.0059
$B1_1$	.6272	.4741	.5831	.5820	.5453	.5663	.6142	.4631	.5421	.5522
$B1_2$	.3728	.5259	.4169	.4180	.4547	.4337	.3858	.5369	.4579	.4477
$B2_1$	.2265	.3276	.2556	.3502	.3958	.3697	.3338	.3939	.3625	.3543
$B2_2$	.0871	.0776	.0844	.1561	.1495	.1533	.1312	.0973	.1150	.1221
$B2_3$	.6864	.5948	.6600	.4937	.4547	.4770	.5350	.5087	.5225	.5237

TABLE VIII

Comparison of total chi-squares for noun-phrase grammar

Text	No. of phrases accounted for	Total chi-square	Degrees of freedom
Ginn preprimer	772	.5	1
Scott-Foresman preprimer	672	2.3	0
Preprimers combined	1444	1.3	1
Ginn primer	1664	52.2	2
Scott-Foresman primer	1482	42.6	1
Primers combined	3146	95.3	2
Ginn reader	3081	81.5	2
Scott-Foresman reader	2651	177.5	2
Readers combined	5732	247.6	2
All combined	10322	316.8	2

TABLE IX

Observed and expected frequencies, chi-square contributions, and
total chi-squares for each section of the corpus for the
noun-phrase grammar

		Ginn preprimer	
Observ.	Expect.	Chi-Sq.	Source
230	230.0	.0	P
254	254.0	.0	G
76	73.4	.1	N
23	24.2	.1	A + N
8	9.3	.2	A + A + N
121	123.6	.1	T + N
42	40.8	.0	T + A + N
17	15.7	.1	T + A + A + N
1	1.0		A + A + A + N
1	1.0		Residual
772	772.0	.5	Total
		1	Degrees of freedom

		Scott-Foresman preprimer	
Observ.	Expect.	Chi-Sq.	Source
424	424.0	.0	P
132	132.0	.0	G
33	36.3	.3	N
24	20.0	.8	A + N

Table IX (Continued)

Scott-Foresman preprimer			
Observ.	Expect.	Chi-Sq.	Source
4	4.7		A + A + N
36	32.7	.3	T + N
14	18.0	.9	T + A + N
5	4.3		T + A + A + N
9	9.0	.0	Expected freq. less than 5.0
0	.0		A + A + A + N
0	.0		Residual
672	672.0	2.3	Total
		0	Degrees of freedom

Preprimers combined			
Observ.	Expect.	Chi-Sq.	Source
654	654.0	.0	P
386	386.0	.0	G
109	110.9	.0	N
47	42.9	.4	A + N
12	14.2	.3	A + A + N
157	155.1	.0	T + N
56	60.1	.3	T + A + N
22	19.8	.2	T + A + A + N
1	1.0		A + A + A + N
1	1.0		Residual
1444	1444.0	1.3	Total
		1	Degrees of freedom

Ginn primer			
Observ.	Expect.	Chi-Sq.	Source
727	727.0	.0	P
286	286.0	.0	G
86	130.8	15.4	N
123	92.8	9.8	A + N
56	41.4	5.2	A + A + N
227	182.2	11.0	T + N
99	129.2	7.1	T + A + N
43	57.6	3.7	T + A + A + N
17	17.0	.0	A + A + A + N
0	.0		Residual
1664	1664.0	52.2	Total
		2	Degrees of freedom

Table IX (Continued)

Observ.	Expect.	Chi-Sq.	Source
		Scott-Foresman primer	
784	784.0	.0	P
220	220.0	.0	G
63	98.2	12.6	N
110	85.5	7.0	A + N
43	32.3	3.6	A + A + N
153	117.8	10.5	T + N
78	102.5	5.9	T + A + N
28	38.7	3.0	T + A + A + N
3	3.0		A + A + A + N
3	3.0		Residual
1482	1482.0	42.6	Total
		1	Degrees of freedom

Observ.	Expect.	Chi-Sq.	Source
		Primers combined	
1511	1511.0	.0	P
506	506.0	.0	G
149	229.4	28.2	N
233	177.8	17.1	A + N
99	73.7	8.7	A + A + N
380	299.6	21.6	T + N
177	232.2	13.1	T + A + N
71	96.3	6.6	T + A + A + N
20	20.0	.0	A + A + A + N
0	.0		Residual
3146	3146.0	95.3	Total
		2	Degrees of freedom

Observ.	Expect.	Chi-Sq.	Source
		Ginn reader	
1143	1143.0	.0	P
473	473.0	.0	G
215	297.5	22.9	N
238	185.6	14.8	A + N
103	72.9	12.4	A + A + N
556	473.5	14.4	T + N
243	295.4	9.3	T + A + N
86	116.1	7.8	T + A + A + N
24	24.0	.0	A + A + A + N
0	.0		Residual
3081	3081.0	81.5	Total
		2	Degrees of freedom

Table IX (Continued)

| | Scott-Foresman reader | | |
Observ.	Expect.	Chi-Sq.	Source
997	997.0	.0	P
323	323.0	.0	G
239	359.2	40.2	N
370	278.1	30.4	A + N
97	68.7	11.6	A + A + N
430	309.8	46.6	T + N
148	239.9	35.2	T + A + N
31	59.3	13.5	T + A + A + N
16	16.0	.0	A + A + A + N
0	.0		Residual
2651	2651.0	177.5	Total
		2	Degrees of freedom

| | Readers combined | | |
Observ.	Expect.	Chi-Sq.	Source
2140	2140.0	.0	P
796	796.0	.0	G
454	659.4	64.0	N
608	457.5	49.5	A + N
200	145.2	20.7	A + A + N
986	780.6	54.0	T + N
391	541.5	41.9	T + A + N
117	171.8	17.5	T + A + A + N
40	40.0	.0	A + A + A + N
0	.0		Residual
5732	5732.0	247.6	Total
		2	Degrees of freedom

| | All combined | | |
Observ.	Expect.	Chi-Sq.	Source
4305	4305.0	.0	P
1688	1688.0	.0	G
712	1000.7	83.3	N
888	677.0	65.8	A + N
311	233.3	25.9	A + A + N
1523	1234.3	67.5	T + N
624	835.0	53.3	T + A + N
210	287.7	21.0	T + A + A + N
61	61.0	.0	A + A + A + N
0	.1		Residual
10322	10322	316.8	Total
		2	Degrees of freedom

100ELIZABETH M. GAMMON

contributions of each syntactical type. All computations for Tables VI–IX and other tables of a similar nature were carried out with five decimal digits; the resulting values were rounded off at the time of output to those shown in the tables.

The second section of Table IX, the section concerning the Scott-Foresman preprimer, illustrates all of the notation used in this table and in the corresponding tables for the statement grammar. The source designated 'Expected Freq. Less Than 5.0' is the total from categories which have been combined because of low expected frequencies; it occurs whenever the expected frequency has accumulated to 5.0. For the Scott-Foresman preprimer, the observed and expected values of this source are the sums of the corresponding values of types (A + A + N) and (T + A + A + N); the chi-square is obtained from the total values. Here two categories were combined into one, and so one degree of freedom was lost at this point. A second degree of freedom was lost because for the last type, (A + A + A + N), the expected frequency was again less than five. The line labeled 'Residual' contains types such as (A + A + A + N) whose individual predicted frequencies were less than 5 and whose total predicted frequency was less than 5; that is, the residual contains all types whose predicted frequencies were less than 5 and which fell below the last 'Expected Freq. Less Than 5.0' line. The residual also contains round-off errors causing some negative values. Due to the two degrees of freedom lost through collapsing, the noun-phrase grammar for the Scott-Foresman preprimer has zero degrees of freedom. The chi-square for this part of the corpus must be studied for descriptive purposes only and must not be used to determine significance levels.

As Table VI indicates, the noun-phrase grammar accounts for a very high percentage (98.2 percent) of the noun phrases in the entire corpus, and for a nearly equivalent percentage of each section of the corpus. Only types that appear in the corpus can be generated; in fact, all derivable types occur at least sixty times in the corpus as a whole. Thus according to the criteria of generating all types, and only those, appearing in the corpus, this grammar is very good.

The chi-square tables (Tables VIII and IX) indicate the 'goodness' of the grammar with regard to type frequency. In discussions of the chi-square values the term 'comparative chi-square value' is used to indicate that any differences in degrees of freedom have been considered and the effects incorporated into the comparisons. When differences in degrees of freedom made comparisons difficult, an F test of significance was used. For the noun-phrase grammar the comparative chi-square values increase significantly from the preprimers to the primers and from the primers to the readers, indicating that with regard to frequency the grammar is much more representative of the preprimers than the primers and readers. For the preprimers and primers the comparative chi-squares for the Ginn and Scott-Foresman books are roughly equivalent, but for the readers the Scott-Foresman chi-square is considerably greater. With respect to type frequency, the grammar is a much better representation of the Ginn reader than the Scott-Foresman reader.

With the exception of the preprimers the comparative chi-square values are higher for the combined volumes than for either volume separately, and the comparative chi-square for the total corpus is the largest of all. This trend indicates the difference in noun-phrase type-frequency patterns for the two reading series and for the different sections within each series. The difference is apparent in the observed frequencies and is most obvious in the readers. The Scott-Foresman reader, for example, has more phrases of type (N) than of any other type containing N, while in the Ginn reader phrases of types (A + N), (T + N), and (T + A + N) all have greater frequencies than phrases of type (N).

Table IX gives further details regarding the chi-square values. The first, second, and last noun-phrase types, (P), (G), and (A + A + A + N), contributed nothing to the chi-square value because the theoretical probabilities of each of these types consist of only one parameter. For the preprimers and the preprimers combined the comparative chi-square values are consistently low. For the remaining sections consistently high contributers to the total chi-square are the (N), (A + N), and (T + N) types, with predictions for type (N) being consistently high and predictions for types (A + N) and (T + N) being consistently low. For the readers individually and combined the predictions for the (T + A + N) types are high yielding additionally large chi-square contributions. The table also shows that the great difference in total chi-square between the Ginn and Scott-Foresman readers is caused by higher contributions for all types in the Scott-Foresman book rather than one extremely large contribution from one or a few types.

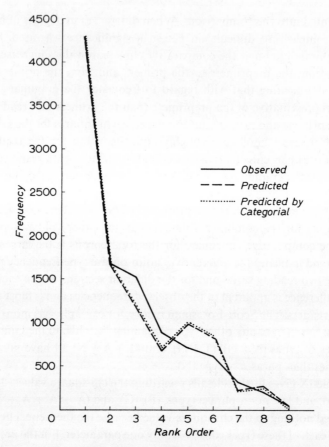

Fig. 1. Comparison of observed and predicted frequencies for noun phrases (entire corpus).

Figure 1 shows the fit of the noun-phrase grammar to the entire corpus. The observed frequencies were arranged in rank order and plotted accordingly; the predicted frequencies were plotted at the rank of their corresponding observed value.

The figure shows an extremely good fit. With the exception of types (A + N) and (A + A + N), the predicted rank order is the same as the observed, and the two curves are nearly identical. However, in view of the large number of parameters which have been used and the small number of degrees of freedom, it is not surprising that some sort of fit has been obtained. It is hoped that in a later stage of investigation the number of parameters can be reduced.

3.2. *The Statement Grammar*

As would be expected this grammar was the most complicated of the six grammars; it generates 131 utterance types and uses 43 parameters. This would allow 87 degrees of freedom if no collapsing due to low predicted frequencies were necessary. The grammar is presented in Table X; it contains 24 rewrite rules and 5 obligatory transformations.

The rewrite rules for the statement grammar have been divided into three categories for reading convenience: (1) statements with simple subjects and predicates and without embedding, (2) statements with compound subjects or compound predicates and without embedding, and (3) statements with embedding. The rules for embedding generate three basic utterance types: embedded statements without adverbial or subordinate connectives such as *I can help mother do this* (rules 14–16), statements with infinitive phrases such as *I can help mother to do this* (rules 17–22), and statements with subordinate conjunctions such as *He did not know that Sally was ready* and *Tom did not know how to dance* (rules 23 and 24).

Subscripts have been used to insure that subjective noun phrases and verbs agree in number and person and to indicate the case (subjective or objective) of noun phrases. Of course, the person and case subscripts cause a change in terminal vocabulary only in case the noun phrase is a pronoun. Number and person subscripts have been attached to the noun phrases in the objective position even though there is no verb with which they must agree; these subscripts were needed for transformation 5 as well as to avoid confusion of subscript meaning. In the tables showing the statistical analysis of this grammar, only the case subscripts have been indicated; these are necessary to clarify the type involved, but the other subscripts should be apparent as they are specifically dictated by the grammar.

Any choices which involved the same subphrases and occurred in relatively the same position in different rewrite rules were assigned the same parameters. For example, whenever the choice (VM) occurred after the main verb (rules 2, 4, 11, 12, 13, 14, 15, 17, 18, 22, and 24), the parameters $B4_1$ (probability of accepting) and $B4_2$ (probability of deleting) were assigned; whenever the choice (VM) occurred before the main verb (rules 3,

TABLE X

The grammar for statements with verbs

I. Statements with single subject, single predicate, and no embedding:

Rewrite rules	Rule-choice probabilities	Within-rule-choice probabilities		
1. $S \rightarrow \left(\left\{\begin{smallmatrix} C \\ VM \end{smallmatrix}\right\}\right) + NP_{i,j,1} + VP_{i,j} + NP_{k,\ell,2} + \left(\left\{\begin{smallmatrix} K \\ VM \end{smallmatrix}\right\}\right)$	A_1		$B1_1$ $B1_2$ $B1_3$	$B2_1$ $B2_2$ $B2_3$
2. $S \rightarrow \left(\left\{\begin{smallmatrix} R \\ C \\ VM \end{smallmatrix}\right\}\right) + NP_{i,j,1} + VP_{i,j} + (VM) + (K)$	A_2	$B3_1$ $B3_2$ $B3_3$ $B3_4$	$B4_1$ $B4_2$	$B5_1$ $B5_2$
3. $S \rightarrow (VM) + VP_{i,2} + NP_{k,\ell,2} + \left(\left\{\begin{smallmatrix} K \\ VM \end{smallmatrix}\right\}\right)$	A_3		$B6_1$ $B6_2$	$B2_1$ $B2_2$ $B2_3$
4. $S \rightarrow (VM) + VP_{i,2} + (VM) + (K)$	A_4	$B6_1$ $B6_2$	$B4_1$ $B4_2$	$B5_1$ $B5_2$
5. $S \rightarrow NP_{i,j,1} + VM + NP_{k,\ell,2}$	A_5			
6. $S \rightarrow NP_{i,j,1} + VM + VP_{i,j} + VM$	A_6			
7. $S \rightarrow C + VM + NP_{i,j,1} + VP_{i,j}$	A_7			
8. $S \rightarrow NP_{i,j,1} + VP_{i,j} + (VM) + A + \left(\left\{\begin{smallmatrix} K \\ VM \end{smallmatrix}\right\}\right)$	A_{12}		$B9_1$ $B9_2$	$B2_1$ $B2_2$ $B2_3$

9. $S \rightarrow VP_{i,2} + VM + A + K$ — A_{13}

II. Statements with compound subjects or compound predicates:

10. $S \rightarrow VP_{i,2} + C + VP_{i,2} + (NP_{k,\ell,2}) + \left(\left\{ \begin{array}{c} K \\ VM \end{array} \right\} \right)$ — A_8

11. $S \rightarrow NP_{i,j,1} + VP_{i,j} + C + VP_{i,j} + (NP_{k,\ell,2}) + (VM)$ — A_9

12. $S \rightarrow (VM) + NP_{i,j,1} + C + NP_{k,\ell,1} + VP_{2,\ell} + (NP_{m,n,2}) + (VM)$ — A_{10}

13. $S \rightarrow (VM) + (NP_{i,j,1}) + VP_{i,j} + NP_{k,\ell,2} + C + NP_{m,n,2} + (VM)$
where $j = 2$ if $NP_{i,j,1}$ is deleted — A_{11}

III. Statements with embedding:

14. $S \rightarrow (VM) + (NP_{i,j,1}) + VP_{i,j} + NP_{k,\ell,2} + VP_3 + (VM)$
where $j = 2$ if $NP_{i,j,1}$ is deleted — A_{15}

15. $S \rightarrow (NP_{i,j,1}) + VP_{i,j} + NP_{k,\ell,2} + VP_3 + NP_{m,n,2} + (VM)$
where $j = 2$ if $NP_{i,j,1}$ is deleted — A_{16}

16. $S \rightarrow (NP_{i,j,1}) + VP_{i,j} + \left\{ \begin{array}{c} RP_{k,\ell,2} \\ NP_{k,\ell,2} \end{array} \right\} + NP_{m,n,1} + VP_{m,n} + \left(\left\{ \begin{array}{c} O + VP_3 \\ VM \end{array} \right\} \right)$
where $j = 2$ if $NP_{i,j,1}$ is deleted — A_{17}

17. $S \rightarrow (VM) + NP_{i,j,1} + VP_{i,j} + O + VP_3 + (NP_{k,\ell,2}) + (VM)$ — A_{18}

Label	Column I	Column II	Column III
A_{13}			
A_8	$B7_1$, $B7_2$		$B2_1$, $B2_3$, $B2_3$
A_9	$B7_1$, $B7_2$		$B4_1$, $B4_2$
A_{10}	$B6_1$, $B6_2$	$B7_1$, $B7_2$	$B4_1$, $B4_2$
A_{11}	$B6_1$, $B6_2$	$B8_1$, $B8_2$	$B4_1$, $B4_2$
A_{15}	$B6_1$, $B6_2$	$B8_1$, $B8_2$	$B4_1$, $B4_2$
A_{16}		$B8_1$, $B8_2$	$B4_1$, $B4_2$
A_{17}	$B8_1$, $B8_2$	$B10_1$, $B10_2$	$B11_1$, $B11_2$, $B11_3$
A_{18}	$B6_1$, $B6_2$	$B7_1$, $B7_2$	$B4_1$, $B4_2$

Table X (Continued)

	Rewrite rules	Parameters	
		Rule-choice probabilities	Within-rule-choice probabilities
18.	$S \rightarrow NP_{i,j,1} + VP_{i,j} + NP_{i,\ell,2} + O + VP_3 + \left(\begin{Bmatrix} NP_{m,n,2} \\ NP_{m,n,2} + VP_3 \end{Bmatrix}\right) + (VM)$	A_{19}	$B12_1$, $B12_2$, $B12_3$ $B4_1$, $B4_2$
19.	$S \rightarrow NP_{i,j,1} + C + NP_{k,\ell,1} + VP_{2,\ell} + O + VP_3 + VM$	A_{20}	
20.	$S \rightarrow NP_{i,j,1} + VP_{i,j} + VM + O + VP_3$	A_{21}	
21.	$S \rightarrow NP_{i,j,1} + VP_{i,j} + O + VP_3 + NP_{k,\ell,2} + VP_3$	A_{22}	
22.	$S \rightarrow NP_{i,j,1} + VP_{i,j} + A + O + VP_3 + (VM)$	A_{14}	$B4_1$, $B4_2$
23.	$S \rightarrow NP_{i,j,1} + VP_{i,j} + CON + O + VP_3$	A_{23}	
24.	$S \rightarrow NP_{i,j,1} + VP_{i,j} + (NP_{k,\ell,2}) + (VM) + CON + NP_{m,n,1} + \begin{Bmatrix} VP_{m,n} \\ VP_{m,n} + VM \end{Bmatrix}$	A_{24} $B7_1$, $B7_2$	$B4_1$, $B4_2$ $B13_1$, $B13_2$, $B13_3$

in $NP_{i,j,k}$: $i = 1,2$ = number; $j = 1,2,3$ = person; $k = 1,2$ = case

in $VP_{i,j}$: $i = 1,2$ = number; $j = 1,2,3$ = person

VP_3 = infinitive form (verbs lacking infinitive form may not be used)

Obligatory transformations:

1. If VM is an adverbial phrase of location or direction (for example: here, up, away, then up, off to the store), *or if* VM is one of these descriptions: 'hippity-hop', 'faster and faster', 'swish', 'swish, swish', 'hop, hop', 'splash, splash', 'left foot first', 'right foot first', *and if* $VP_{i,j}$ is a form of 'to be' or one of these verbs of locomotion: 'walk', 'jump', 'go', 'run', 'come', 'roll', 'buzz', *and if* $NP_{i,j,1} \neq P$, then

$$(C) + VM + NP_{i,j,1} + VP_{i,j} + \cdots \longrightarrow (C) + VM + VP_{i,j} + NP_{i,j,1} + \cdots$$

2. If VM is 'so' and $VP_{i,j}$ is a form of 'to be' or 'to do', or is: 'can', 'could', 'may', 'will', 'shall', or 'must', then

$$VM + NP_{i,j,1} + VP_{i,j} \rightarrow VM + VP_{i,j} + NP_{i,j,1}$$

3. If $VP_{i,j}$ is a form of 'to be', then

$$\cdots + VP_{i,j} + NP_{k,\ell,2} + \cdots \rightarrow \cdots + VP_{i,j} + NP_{k,\ell,1} + \cdots$$

4. If $NP_{k,\ell,2}$ is 'what + NP', then

$$\cdots + NP_{i,j,1} + VP_{i,j,1} + NP_{k,\ell,2} + \cdots \rightarrow \cdots + NP_{k,\ell,2} + NP_{i,j,1} + VP_{i,j} + \cdots$$

5. If $VP_{i,j}$ is a form of 'to wish', 'to think', 'to say', 'to guess', or 'to know', then

$$\cdots + NP_{i,j,1} + VP_{i,j} + NP_{k,\ell,2} + VP_3 + \cdots \rightarrow \cdots + NP_{i,j,1} + VP_{i,j} + NP_{k,\ell,1} + VP_{k,\ell} + \cdots$$

4, 12, 13, 14, and 17), the parameters $B6_1$ (probability of accepting) and $B6_2$ (probability of deleting) were assigned. Parameter notation in Table X is the same as has been used previously. The A_i parameters always denote a rule-choice probability, and the Bj_i parameters denote probabilities of choices within a given rule. In a column of Bj_i parameters the first member indicates the probability of the first (the top) choice within the parentheses, the second member the second choice, and so on; the last member of the column indicates the probability of choosing nothing from that set of parentheses. If two or more sets of parameters which sum to 1 are necessary for the same rule, the first vertical column of within-choice parameters contains probabilities for the first (left-most) set of choices in the rule, the second column contains probabilities for the second set of choices, etc.

In certain instances inversions of the form specified by the rules regularly occurred. For example *Here comes Sally* was used instead of *Here Sally comes*, and *Away ran Dick* was used instead of *Away Dick ran*. The first transformation specifies exactly when these inversions occur; the adverbial phrase is usually one of location or direction (here, up, off to the store), the verb is a form of 'to be' or a verb of locomotion (run, come), and the noun phrase is something other than a pronoun. The structure *Here he comes* is always used rather than *Here comes he*. The second transformation handles a second type of inversion; it changes expressions like *So I can* into *So can I*.

The third transformation changes the noun in the objective case following a form of 'to be' into the subjective case; for example, it would change *That is him* into *That is he*. The fourth transformation would change an utterance like *That is what a pretty dress* into *What a pretty dress that is*. Note that a noun phrase of the form 'what + NP' was derivable from the noun-phrase grammar by deriving $(T + A + \cdots + N)$, choosing the first A to be 'what', and applying an obligatory transformation. The last transformation changes the verb of an embedded utterance following a verb of thought or observation from the infinitive form to a form which agrees in number and person with the subject of the embedded clause. For example, it would change *I think he want to come* into *I think he wants to come*.

The statistics for this grammar are presented in Tables XI–XIV. The Ginn preprimer and the Scott-Foresman preprimer contained many zero and low frequency types making a chi-square analysis for these individual

TABLE XI

Percentage of each section of the corpus accounted for by the grammar for statements with verbs

Ginn preprimer	S-F preprimer	Preprimers combined	Ginn primer	S-F primer	Primers combined	Ginn reader	S-F reader	Readers combined	All combined
93.9	87.4	91.2	90.6	83.5	87.5	88.5	72.6	81.8	85.5

TABLE XII

Maximum-likelihood estimates for sections of the corpus included in the analysis for the grammar for statements with verbs

Parameter	Preprimers combined	Ginn primer	S-F primer	Primers combined	Ginn reader	S-F reader	Readers combined	All combined
A[1]	.1875	.2735	.2579	.2670	.2913	.2778	.2862	.2582
A[2]	.1884	.2724	.2453	.2611	.3562	.3102	.3389	.2808
A[3]	.1082	.0291	.0425	.0347	.0216	.0240	.0225	.0454
A[4]	.2743	.1637	.1541	.1597	.1110	.0802	.0995	.1574
A[5]	.0000	.0000	.0000	.0000	.0029	.0108	.0059	.0027
A[6]	.0000	.0011	.0016	.0013	.0022	.0024	.0023	.0015
A[7]	.0009	.0011	.0000	.0007	.0043	.0012	.0032	.0019
A[8]	.0821	.0191	.0157	.0177	.0151	.0072	.0122	.0294
A[9]	.0028	.0135	.0126	.0131	.0115	.0132	.0122	.0104
A[10]	.0103	.0213	.0330	.0262	.0231	.0395	.0293	.0241
A[11]	.0196	.0045	.0142	.0085	.0130	.0108	.0122	.0127
A[12]	.0084	.0392	.0314	.0360	.0260	.0251	.0257	.0251
A[13]	.0000	.0000	.0000	.0000	.0029	.0012	.0023	.0010
A[14]	.0000	.0123	.0031	.0085	.0036	.0024	.0032	.0041
A[15]	.0280	.0314	.0236	.0281	.0187	.0311	.0234	.0259
A[16]	.0084	.0078	.0142	.0105	.0115	.0251	.0167	.0129

Table XII (Continued)

Maximum-likelihood estimates for sections of the corpus included in the analysis for the grammar for statements with verbs

Parameter	Preprimers combined	Ginn primer	S-F primer	Primers combined	Ginn reader	S-F reader	Readers combined	All combined
A[17]	.0196	.0314	.0283	.0301	.0130	.0108	.0122	.0195
A[18]	.0504	.0617	.0865	.0720	.0433	.0826	.0581	.0608
A[19]	.0112	.0135	.0267	.0190	.0079	.0216	.0131	.0145
A[20]	.0000	.0000	.0000	.0000	.0000	.0060	.0023	.0010
A[21]	.0000	.0000	.0000	.0000	.0036	.0000	.0023	.0010
A[22]	.0000	.0034	.0047	.0039	.0022	.0000	.0014	.0019
A[23]	.0000	.0000	.0000	.0000	.0036	.0000	.0023	.0010
A[24]	.0000	.0000	.0047	.0020	.0115	.0168	.0135	.0068
B1[1]	.0448	.0123	.0427	.0245	.0668	.1078	.0818	.0570
B1[2]	.0000	.0533	.1159	.0784	.1436	.1595	.1494	.1020
B1[3]	.9552	.9344	.8415	.8971	.7896	.7328	.7689	.8410
B2[1]	.0845	.0280	.0588	.0405	.0285	.0681	.0429	.0521
B2[2]	.1739	.2609	.3620	.3020	.3788	.4050	.3883	.3098
B2[3]	.7415	.7112	.5792	.6575	.5927	.5269	.5688	.6381
B3[1]	.0000	.0000	.0577	.0226	.0061	.0347	.0159	.0155
B3[2]	.0149	.0905	.0321	.0677	.0931	.0425	.0757	.0643
B3[3]	.4307	.3621	.3590	.3609	.3704	.4363	.3931	.3892
B3[4]	.5545	.5473	.5513	.5489	.5304	.4865	.5153	.5310
B4[1]	.5000	.5736	.6336	.5989	.6887	.6503	.6739	.6126
B4[2]	.5000	.4264	.3664	.4011	.3113	.3497	.3261	.3874

B5[1]	.3891	.1825	.1968	.1882	.1142	.0828	.1037	.1964
B5[2]	.6109	.8175	.8031	.8118	.8858	.9172	.8963	.8036
B6[1]	.0114	.0612	.1422	.0974	.1219	.2277	.1654	.0922
B6[2]	.9886	.9389	.8578	.9026	.8781	.7723	.8346	.9078
B7[1]	.4679	.4078	.4330	.4200	.4069	.3835	.3957	.4211
B7[2]	.5321	.5922	.5670	.5800	.5931	.6165	.6043	.5789
B8[1]	.3333	.5373	.4706	.5085	.6410	.7077	.6713	.5351
B8[2]	.6667	.4627	.5294	.4915	.3590	.2923	.3287	.4649
B9[1]	.0000	.0000	.3000	.1091	.3333	.1905	.2807	.1818
B9[2]	1.0000	.0000	.7000	.8909	.6667	.8095	.7193	.8182
B10[1]	.0000	.2143	.1111	.1739	.7222	.4444	.6296	.2660
B10[2]	1.0000	.7857	.8889	.8261	.2778	.5556	.3704	.7340
B11[1]	.0000	.0714	.0556	.0652	.1111	.1111	.1111	.0638
B11[2]	.1429	.1786	.1111	.1522	.1667	.3333	.2222	.1702
B11[3]	.8571	.7500	.8333	.7826	.7222	.5556	.6667	.7660
B12[1]	.4167	.5000	.4118	.4483	.1818	.3333	.2759	.3714
B12[2]	.0000	.0000	.0000	.0000	.0000	.0000	.0000	.0000
B12[3]	.5833	.5000	.5882	.5517	.8182	.6667	.7241	.6286
B13[1]	.0000	.0000	.6667	.6667	.4375	.2857	.3667	.3939
B13[2]	.0000	.0000	.3333	.3333	.0625	.3571	.2000	.2121
B13[3]	.0000	.0000	.0000	.0000	.5000	.3571	.4333	.3939

TABLE XIII

Comparison of total chi-squares for the grammar for statements with verbs

Text	No. of statements accounted for	Total chi-square	Degrees of freedom
Preprimers combined	1072	364.7	2
Ginn primer	892	249.6	8
Scott-Foresman primer	636	254.2	7
Primers combined	1528	478.3	26
Ginn reader	1387	406.3	25
Scott-Foresman reader	835	206.0	15
Readers combined	2222	729.2	44
All combined	4822	1644.0	61

TABLE XIV

Observed and expected frequencies, chi-square contributions, and total chi-squares for the statement grammar for the entire corpus

Observ.	Expect.	Chi-Sq.	Source
653	668.1	.3	NP(1) + VP + NP(2)
31	54.6	10.2	NP(1) + VP + NP(2) + K
363	324.3	4.6	NP(1) + VP + NP(2) + VM
47	45.3	.1	C + NP(1) + VP + NP(2)
1	3.7		C + NP(1) + VP + NP(2) + K
23	22.0	.0	C + NP(1) + VP + NP(2) + VM
88	81.0	.6	VM + NP(1) + VP + NP(2)
1	6.6	4.8	VM + NP(1) + VP + NP(2) + K
38	39.3	.0	VM + NP(1) + VP + NP(2) + VM
108	223.8	59.9	NP(1) + VP
601	354.0	172.4	NP(1) + VP + VM
3	54.7	48.9	NP(1) + VP + K
7	86.5	73.1	NP(1) + VP + VM + K
20	6.5	27.7	R + NP(1) + VP
1	10.3	8.4	R + NP(1) + VP + VM
0	1.6		R + NP(1) + VP + K
1	5.3	3.5	Expected freq. less than 5.0
0	2.5		R + NP(1) + VP + VM + K
26	27.1	.0	C + NP(1) + VP
59	42.8	6.1	C + NP(1) + VP + VM
0	6.6	6.6	C + NP(1) + VP + K
2	10.5	6.9	C + NP(1) + VP + VM + K
268	164.0	65.9	VM + NP(1) + VP
240	259.5	1.5	VM + NP(1) + VP + VM
17	40.1	13.3	VM + NP(1) + VP + K
2	63.4	59.5	VM + NP(1) + VP + VM + K

Table XIV (Continued)

Observ.	Expect.	Chi-Sq.	Source
124	126.9	.1	VP + NP(2)
34	10.4	53.9	VP + NP(2) + K
27	61.6	19.4	VP + NP(2) + VM
18	12.9	2.0	VM + VP NP(2)
3	1.1		VM + VP + NP(2) + K
13	6.3	7.3	VM + VP + NP(2) + VM
95	214.5	66.6	VP
253	339.2	21.9	VP + VM
221	82.9	230.0	VP + VM + K
3	8.4	3.5	VM + VP + VM + K
156	52.4	204.7	VP + K
4	5.3	.3	VM + VP + K
4	21.8	14.5	VM + VP
23	34.4	3.8	VM + VP + VM
13	13.0	.0	NP(1) + VP + VM + NP(2)
7	7.0	.0	NP(1) + VM + VP + VM
9	9.0	.0	C + VM + NP(1) + VP
28	52.5	11.4	VP + C + VP
72	38.2	30.0	VP + C + VP + NP(2)
25	25.5	.0	VP + C + VP + VM
8	4.3		VP + C + VP + K
11	7.9	1.3	Expected freq. less than 5.0
3	18.5	13.0	VP + C + VP + NP(2) + VM
6	3.1		VP + C + VP + NP(2) + K
23	11.2	12.4	NP(1) + VP + C + VP
13	8.2	2.9	NP(1) + VP + C + VP + NP(2)
13	17.7	1.3	VP(1) + VP + C + VP + VM
1	12.9	11.0	NP(1) + VP + C + VP + NP(2) + VM
10	23.6	7.8	NP(1) + C + NP(1) + VP
19	17.2	.2	NP(1) + C + NP(1) + VP + NP(2)
12	27.2	8.5	NP(1) + C + NP(1) + VP + NP(2) + VM
39	37.3	.1	NP(1) + C + NP(1) + VP + VM
21	2.4		VM + NP(1) + C + NP(1) + VP
27	5.5	83.7	Expected freq. less than 5.0
4	1.7		VM + NP(1) + C + NP(1) + VP + NP(2)
2	2.8		VM + NP(1) + C + NP(1) + VP + NP(2) + VM
9	3.8		· VM + NP(1) + C + NP(1) + VP + VM
15	8.3	5.4	Expected freq. less than 5.0
15	10.0	2.5	VP + NP(2) + C + NP(2)
0	15.8	15.8	VP + NP(2) + C + NP(2) + VM
33	11.5	40.4	NP(1) + VP + NP(2) + C + NP(2)
6	18.2	8.1	NP(1) + VP + NP(2) + C + NP(2) + VM
0	1.0		VM + VP + NP(2) + C + NP(2)
1	1.6		VM + VP + NP(2) + C + NP(2) + VM
6	1.2		VM + NP(1) + VP + NP(2) + C + NP(2)

Table XIV (Continued)

Observ.	Expect.	Chi-Sq.	Source
0	1.8		VM + NP(1) + VP + NP(2) + C + NP(2) + VM
7	5.6	.3	Expected freq. less than 5.0
62	63.2	.0	NP(1) + VP + A
10	14.0	1.2	NP(1) + VP + VM + A
6	5.2	.1	NP(1) + VP + A + K
0	1.1		NP(1) + VP + VM + A + K
31	30.7	.0	NP(1) + VP + A + VM
12	6.8	3.9	NP(1) + VP + VM + A + VM
5	5.0	.0	VP + VM + A + K
7	7.7	.1	NP(1) + VP + A + O + VP
13	12.3	.0	NP(1) + VP + A + O + VP + VM
42	20.4	22.8	VP + NP(2) + VP
32	32.3	.0	VP + NP(2) + VP + VM
15	23.5	3.1	NP(1) + VP + NP(2) + VP
29	37.2	1.8	NP(1) + VP + NP(2) + VP + VM
0	2.1		VM + VP + NP(2) + VP
0	3.3		VM + VP + NP(2) + VP + VM
0	6.5	6.5	Expected freq. less than 5.0
0	2.4		VM + NP(1) + VP + NP(2) + VP
7	3.8		VM + NP(1) + VP + NP(2) + VP + VM
7	6.2	.1	Expected freq. less than 5.0
18	11.2	4.2	VP + NP(2) + VP + NP(2)
15	17.7	.4	VP + NP(2) + VP + NP(2) + VM
15	12.9	.4	NP(1) + VP + NP(2) + VP + NP(2)
14	20.3	2.0	NP(1) + VP + NP(2) + VP + NP(2) + VM
21	24.6	.5	VP + NP(2) + NP(1) + VP
2	5.5	2.2	VP + NP(2) + NP(1) + VP + VM
0	2.0		VP + NP(2) + NP(1) + VP + O + VP
39	28.3	4.1	NP(1) + VP + NP(2) + NP(1) + VP
5	6.3	.3	NP(1) + VP + NP(2) + NP(1) + VP + VM
2	2.4		NP(1) + VP + NP(2) + NP(1) + VP + O + VP
5	8.9	1.7	VP + RP(2) + NP(1) + VP
8	2.0		VP + RP(2) + NP(1) + VP + VM
10	6.4	2.1	Expected freq. less than 5.0
0	.7		VP + RP(2) + NP(1) + VP + O + VP
7	10.2	1.0	NP(1) + VP + RP(2) + NP(1) + VP
1	2.3		NP(1) + VP + RP(2) + NP(1) + VP + VM
4	.9		NP(1) + VP + RP(2) + NP(1) + VP + O + VP
33	59.6	11.9	NP(1) + VP + O + VP
92	43.4	54.5	NP(1) + VP + O + VP + NP(2)
31	68.6	20.6	NP(1) + VP + O + VP + NP(2) + VM
110	94.3	2.6	NP(1) + VP + O + VP + VM
9	6.1	1.4	VM + NP(1) + VP + O + VP
7	4.4		VM + NP(1) + VP + O + VP + NP(2)
12	8.3	1.7	Expected freq. less than 5.0

Table XIV (Continued)

Observ.	Expect.	Chi-Sq.	Source
0	7.0	7.0	VM + NP(1) + VP + O + VP + NP(2) + VM
11	9.6	.2	VM + NP(1) + VP + O + VP + VM
25	17.0	3.7	NP(1) + VP + NP(2) + O + VP
21	10.1	11.9	NP(1) + VP + NP(2) + O + VP + NP(2)
0	.0		NP(1) + VP + NP(2) + O + VP + NP(2) + VP
19	27.0	2.3	NP(1) + VP + NP(2) + O + VP + VM
5	15.9	7.5	NP(1) + VP + NP(2) + O + VP + NP(2) + VM
0	.0		NP(1) + VP + NP(2) + O + VP + NP(2) + VP + VM
5	5.0	.0	NP(1) + C + NP(1) + VP + O + VP + VM
5	5.0	.0	NP(1) + VP + VM + O + VP
9	9.0	.0	NP(1) + VP + O + VP + NP(2) + VP
5	5.0	.0	NP(1) + VP + CON + O + VP
0	2.9		NP(1) + VP + CON + NP(1)
5	2.9		NP(1) + VP + CON + NP(1) + VP
5	5.8	.1	Expected freq. less than 5.0
6	1.6		NP(1) + VP + CON + NP(1) + VP + VM
0	2.1		NP(1) + VP + NP(2) + CON + NP(1)
0	2.1		NP(1) + VP + NP(2) + CON + NP(1) + VP
6	5.8	.0	Expected freq. less than 5.0
0	1.1		NP(1) + VP + NP(2) + CON + NP(1) + VP + VM
8	4.6		NP(1) + VP + VM + CON + NP(1)
8	5.8	.9	Expected freq. less than 5.0
8	4.6		NP(1) + VP + VM + CON + NP(1) + VP
1	2.5		NP(1) + VP + VM + CON + NP(1) + VP + VM
9	7.1	.5	Expected freq. less than 5.0
5	3.4		NP(1) + VP + NP(2) + VM + CON + NP(1)
0	3.4		NP(1) + VP + NP(2) + VM + CON + NP(1) + VP
5	6.7	.4	Expected freq. less than 5.0
0	1.8		NP(1) + VP + NP(2) + VM + CON + NP(1) + VP + VM
0	2.0		Residual
4822	4822.0	1644.0	Total
		61	Degrees of freedom

sections invalid, but all other sections of the corpus including the preprimers combined were analyzed.

The grammar accounts for 85.5 percent of all statements with verbs in the corpus as a whole. In each of the three major sections (the preprimers, the primers, and the readers) a greater percentage of the Ginn utterances than the Scott-Foresman utterances were derivable from the grammar. The Scott-Foresman books contain a greater variety of utterance types and display more irregularity of syntactic pattern than the Ginn books.

This grammar generated some types which did not appear in the corpus as can be seen from the observed frequencies in Table XIV. (Table XIV displays only the statistics for the entire corpus; the corresponding statistics for the individual sections of the corpus can be found in Gammon (1969). However the probabilities of such types are low (the largest is .003), and from a probabilistic viewpoint this is completely acceptable. In a probabilistic grammar the criterion that the grammar not generate utterances not found in the corpus is not as important as the criterion that the probabilities of such utterances be low. If the theoretical grammar includes but is not identical to the grammar (the actual grammatical types) of the corpus, a good probabilistic fit could be obtained, and there is no real need for the two grammars to be identical.

The degrees of freedom available for each section of the corpus were sufficiently different to require F tests for purposes of comparison. These tests showed no significant differences in fit among sections with the exception of the preprimers combined which had a significantly poorer fit than the other sections. Neither was there any significant difference between the fit of the grammar to the Ginn series nor the fit to the Scott-Foresman series.

Table XIV (and the corresponding statistics for the individual sections of the corpus) indicates that a large percentage of the total chi-square is due to a few types which contribute very large chi-square values, rather than to many types with rather large chi-square contributions. Subtraction of the ten largest chi-square contributions yields a total chi-square of 573.7, a reduction of 1070.3 or 65.1 percent. Thus, in general, the grammar provided a good fit; again, however, the number of degrees of freedom is relatively small, and some sort of fit would be expected. Only one type, $(NP_{i,j,l} + VP_{i,j} + VM)$, was a large contributer for all sections of the corpus; predictions for this type were always too low. This type can be derived from the second rewrite rule; removing this possibility from the rule and forming instead a new rule in hopes of changing the parameters and providing a better fit for this type would involve changing the whole structure of the rule and including several more rules. This in turn might change some of the good predicted frequencies of other types derivable from the rule and in this way again increase the total chi-square value. Thus it seemed best to make no change in the grammar.

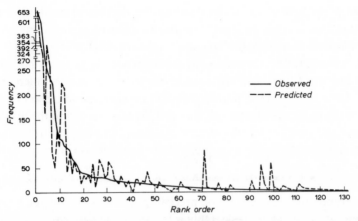

Fig. 2.   Comparison of observed and predicted values for statements (entire corpus).

Figure 2 shows the fit of the grammar to the observed frequencies and their rank order. It too indicates a fit which is in general quite good, although it has a few major discrepancies.

TABLE XV

Comparison of total chi-squares for the noun-phrase and statement grammars

Text	Noun-phrase grammar			Statement grammar		
	Chi-sq.	DF	Average chi-sq.	Chi-sq.	DF	Average chi-sq.
Ginn preprimer	.5	1	.5	–	–	–
Scott-Foresman preprimer	2.3	0	–	–	–	–
Preprimers combined	1.3	1	1.3	364.7	2	182.4
Ginn primer	52.2	2	26.1	249.6	8	31.2
Scott-Foresman primer	42.6	1	42.6	254.2	7	36.3
Primers combined	95.3	2	47.7	478.3	26	18.4
Ginn reader	81.5	2	40.8	406.3	25	16.3
Scott-Foresman reader	177.5	2	88.8	206.0	15	13.7
Readers combined	247.6	2	123.8	729.2	44	16.6
All combined	316.8	2	158.4	1644.0	61	27.0

Table XV summarizes the total chi-squares and the respective degrees of freedom for the noun phrase and statement grammars for every section of the corpus in which the statistic was applicable. It also shows the average chi-squares found by dividing the degrees of freedom into the total chi-square; these values form the numerators and denominators of the F tests and make pairwise comparisons somewhat easier.

The fits given by the statement grammar for the primers individually and combined and for the Ginn reader were not significantly different from those given by the noun-phrase grammar for corresponding sections. The fit for the preprimers combined was significantly worse and the fits for the Scott-Foresman reader, the readers combined, and the corpus as a whole were significantly better than those of the noun-phrase grammar.

4. A CATEGORIAL GRAMMAR FOR NOUN PHRASES

The grammars presented in the preceding section were written to fit the corpus as nearly as possible. Only a few syntactic patterns which do not appear in the corpus can be generated by the grammars, and no provision was made for unbounded embedding. In later uses, for example, in making comparisons with oral speech, more general grammars might be preferable; in that case the same grammar would be used for both corpora but different parameters would be estimated. Although more general constructions and unbounded embedding are possible in phrase-structure grammars, they are somewhat easier to conceptualize in categorial grammars. With this in mind, a categorial grammar was written for the noun phrases for purposes of comparison.

It has been shown (Bar-Hillel *et al.*, 1960) that phrase-structure grammars and categorial grammars are equivalent in the range of languages they are capable of characterizing. Categorial grammars, while less easy to interpret than phrase-structure grammars, are more easily adapted to fit other corpora because they contain at most two rewrite rules. To adapt a categorial grammar to a new corpus the parameters must be reestimated and sometimes a few new categories must be added, but no new rewrite rules are needed.

The two rewrite rules for standard categorial grammars are:

(1) $\alpha \rightarrow \alpha/\beta, \beta$

(2) $\alpha \rightarrow \beta, \beta\backslash\alpha$

where α and β are categories. In writing a categorial grammar a finite number of primitive categories is selected; the primitive categories are usually taken to be s for sentence and n for noun. All primitive categories are categories, and when α and β are categories, $[\alpha/\beta]$ and $[\alpha\backslash\beta]$ are categories – these are called derived categories. All words in the terminal vocabulary are classified into one or more of these categories.

A premise (s in standard categorial grammars) is chosen, and all grammatical types of utterances must be derivable from the premise, the rewrite rules, and the categories. The following example illustrates the method of derivation in a categorial grammar. Let n be the category for nouns and $[n\backslash s]/n$ be the category for transitive verbs. Then the categorial symbolism for the syntactical type (N + TV + N) is $(n, [n\backslash s]/n, n)$, and this can be generated as follows:

$$s \rightarrow n, n\backslash s \qquad \text{Rule 2, } s \text{ for } \alpha, n \text{ for } \beta$$
$$n, n\backslash s \rightarrow n, [n\backslash s]/n, n \quad \text{Rule 1, } [n\backslash s] \text{ for } \alpha, n \text{ for } \beta.$$

Corresponding to the phrase-structure grammars, parameters may be assigned to each choice point of the derivations, and the same statistical procedures for evaluating the grammars may be followed. In general four types of parameters are necessary for categorial grammars: a stopping parameter, a parameter for the choice of rule used, parameters denoting substitutions for β, and parameters denoting substitutions for α.

The first three parameter types represent unconditional probabilities and present no problem. The parameters for the choice of α, however, are conditional probabilities; they are conditional on the choices available from the previous application of the rule. In the example above, when rule 2 is applied, the only choice for α is s so the probability of that choice is one, when rule 1 is applied in the next step, there are two choices available for α, n and $n\backslash s$, and the probability of choosing s at this point is zero. In this example three parameters for α are needed: $P[s$ for α given $s]$, $P[n$ for α given $n, n\backslash s]$, and $P[n\backslash s$ for α given $n, n\backslash s]$; clearly the first probability is one and the sum of the last two probabilities is one. Under this system, a new set of α parameters is required each time a new set of choices is available. Some simplification can be achieved by considering the number of the choice instead of the choice itself. In the example above the required parameters would be: $P[$first choice given one choice$]$, $P[$first choice given two choices$]$, and $P[$second choice given two choices$]$; again the first probability is equal to one and the sum of the last two is one. When the number of the choice is the basis for parameter assignment, the number of necessary sets of α parameters is equal to the maximum number of times the rule is applied in any derivation of the grammar. If the grammar provides for an infinite number of rule applications, a decision could be made to stop when the probability of syntactical patterns reached a certain level close to zero; the maximum number of rule applications would then be finite. In the noun-phrase grammar no choice of α is available, so the problem of conditional parameters does not arise.

The categorial grammar for noun phrases is summarized in Table XVI,

TABLE XVI
The categorial grammar for noun phrases

Rewrite rule: $\alpha \to \alpha/\beta, \beta$
Premises from which derivations are possible: n
Premises from which no derivations are possible: p, g
Primitive categories: n
Categories:
    n (noun)
    g (proper noun)
    p (pronoun)
    t (article)
    n/n (adjective)
Obligatory transformations:
  (a) If n is 'something', $n/n, n \to n, n/n$
  (b) If n/n is 'what' or 'all', $t, n/n, n \to n/n, t, n$
  (c) If n/n_1 is 'what' or 'all', $t, n/n_1, n/n_2, n \to n/n_1, t, n/n_2, n$
Optional transformation: Any statement derivable from n may begin with an article, t.
Parameters: A_1-A_3, premise choice parameters
              S_1-S_2, stopping parameter
              T_1-T_2, optional transformation parameter

TABLE XVII
Derivations from the categorial grammar for noun phrases

Type	Derivation	Theoretical probability
P	g	A_2
G	g	A_3
N	n	$A_1\binom{N}{0}S_1{}^0S_2{}^N T_2$
$A + N$	$n \to n/n, n$	$A_1\binom{N}{1}S_1{}^1S_2{}^{N-1} T_2$
$A + A + N$	$n \to n/n, n \to n/n, n/n, n$	$A_1\binom{N}{2}S_1{}^2S_2{}^{N-}$
$T + N$	n + transformation	$A_1\binom{N}{0}S_1{}^0S_2{}^N T_1$
$T + A + N$	$n \to n/n, n$ + transformation	$A_1\binom{N}{1}S_1{}^1S_2{}^{N-1} T_1$
$T + A + A + N$	$n \to n/n, n \to n/n, n/n, n$ + transformation	$A_1\binom{N}{2}S_1{}^2S_2{}^{N-2} T_1$
$A + A + A + N$	$n \to n/n, n \to n/n, n/n, n \to n/n, n/n, n/n, n$	$A_1\binom{N}{3}S_1{}^3S_2{}^{N-3} T_2$

and the derivations and theoretical probabilities are given in Table XVII.

As can be seen from the derivations, only one rewrite rule is required for the noun-phrase grammar, so no parameter is necessary for the choice of the rewrite rule. The only choice made for α and β is n, so no parameters are required for these choices either.

Three premises have been selected, n, p, and g, but derivations are permitted from only the first of these. This is a deviation from standard categorial grammars in which only one premise is chosen and all derivations are made from the one premise. But such a deviation was necessary to correspond to the phrase-structure grammar in not allowing adjectives and articles to precede pronouns and proper nouns. Three parameters were required for the three premises; A_1 is the probability of choosing n for the premise, A_2 is the probability of choosing p, and A_3 is the probability of choosing g.

The optional transformation requires one (free) parameter; T_1 is the probability of choosing an article and $T_2 = 1 - T_1$ is the probability of not choosing an article. This method of generating types such as $(T + A + N)$ as well as $(A + N)$ was the simplest which could be found. Other means, such as classifying articles as adjectives, generated phrases with the article between the adjective(s) and noun (for example, *red the ball* instead of *the red ball*) as well as the desired syntactical types. As Table XVI shows, the same obligatory transformations used for the phrase-structure grammars are used here.

The variable S_1 was chosen for the stopping parameter; this is a binomial parameter, $\binom{N}{x} S_1^x (1 - S_1)^{N-x}$, where x is the number of times the rewrite rule was applied and N is chosen to be some number greater than the maximum number of times the rule must be applied to generate all observed syntactical types. This a priori choice of N is not entirely satisfactory, but as will be seen in a later discussion of chi-square contributions and total chi-squares, the choice does not have a significant effect on the parameter estimation. If S_1 is estimated separately for types formed according to the number of times the rule was applied, S_1 is a maximum-likelihood estimate as shown in the following derivation for $N = 6$, the value used in the application of the maximum-likelihood procedures as explained in Section 3.

Type	Frequency	Probability
1	$K_1 = f_N + f_{T+N}$	$(1 - S_1)^6$
2	$K_2 = f_{A+N} + f_{T+A+N}$	$6(1 - S_1)^5(S_1)$
3	$K_3 = f_{A+A+N} + f_{T+A+A+N}$	$15(1 - S_1)^4(S_1)^2$
4	$K_4 = f_{A+A+A+N}$	$20(1 - S_1)^3(S_1)^3$
5	$K_5 = 0$	$15(1 - S_1)^2(S_1)^4$
6	$K_6 = 0$	$6(1 - S_1)(S_1)^5$
7	$K_7 = 0$	S_1^6

$$L = [(1 - S_1)^6]^{K_1}[6(1 - S_1)^5 S_1]^{K_2}[15(1 - S_1)^4 S_1^2]^{K_3} \times$$
$$\times [20(1 - S_1)^3 S_1^3]^{K_4}$$
$$\log L = K_1 \log[(1 - S_1)^6] + K_2 \log[6(1 - S_1)^5 S_1] +$$
$$+ K_3 \log[15(1 - S_1)^4 S_1^2] + K_4 \log[20(1 - S_1)^3 S_1^3]$$
$$\frac{\partial \log L}{f S_1} = \frac{-6K_1}{1 - S_1} + \frac{K_2}{S_1} - \frac{5K_2}{1 - S_1} + \frac{2K_3}{S_1} - \frac{4K_3}{1 - S_1} + \frac{3K_4}{S_1} - \frac{3K_4}{1 - S_1}.$$

Setting the derivative equal to zero and solving:
$$S_1 = \frac{K_2 + 2K_3 + 3K_4}{6K_1 + 6K_2 + 6K_3 + 6K_4}$$

Using the observed frequencies for the corpus as a whole (Table XIX), $S_1 = .1054$. And this is the estimate obtained when the maximum-likelihood estimation procedures explained in Section 3 are applied. (Table XVIII.)

If S_1 had been chosen to be a geometric distribution, no a priori choices would have been necessary. This distribution was effective in Suppes (1970), but it would provide a poor fit in this case. If the geometric distribution had been used here, the parameter S_1 would have appeared in every theoretical probability involving N, and whenever one or more adjectives were included, a corresponding number of $S_2 = 1 - S_1$ terms would have appeared in the probability. The probability of type (N), for example, would have been: $(A_1) (S_1) (1 - T_1)$ and the probability of type $(A + N)$ would have been: $(A_1) (1 - S_1) (S_1) (1 - T_1)$. Thus the grammar would always predict a greater number of (N) types than $(A + N)$ types, a greater number of $(A + N)$ types than $(A + A + N)$ types, etc. But the observed data did not show this trend. The poisson distribution would have fit the stopping data in a manner similar to the binomial distribution and would

TABLE XVIII

Maximum-likelihood estimates for each section of the corpus for the categorial grammar for noun phrases

Parameter	Ginn preprimer	S-F preprimer	Preprimers combined	Ginn primer	S-F primer	Primers combined	Ginn reader	S-F reader	Readers combined	All combined	All combined N = 5	All combined N = 7	All combined N = 8
A_1	.3731	.1726	.2798	.3912	.3225	.3589	.4755	.5021	.4878	.4194	.4194	.4194	.4194
A_2	.2979	.6309	.4529	.4369	.5290	.4803	.3710	.3761	.3733	.4171	.4171	.4171	.4171
A_3	.3290	.1964	.2673	.1719	.1484	.1608	.1535	.1218	.1389	.1635	.1635	.1635	.1635
S_1	.0683	.0805	.0718	.1206	.1182	.1196	.1059	.1029	.1045	.1054	.1264	.0903	.0790
S_2	.9317	.9195	.9282	.8794	.8818	.8804	.8941	.8971	.8955	.8946	.8736	.9097	.9210
T_1	.6250	.4741	.5817	.5668	.5418	.5562	.6041	.4575	.5343	.5445	.5445	.5445	.5445
T_2	.3750	.5259	.4183	.4332	.4582	.4438	.3959	.5425	.4657	.4555	.4555	.4555	.4555

TABLE XIX

Observed and expected frequencies, chi-square contributions,
and total chi-squares for each section of the corpus for the
categorial grammar for noun phrases

		Ginn preprimer	
Observ.	Expect.	Chi-Sq.	Source
230	230.0	.0	P
254	254.0	.0	G
76	70.6	.4	N
23	31.1	2.1	A + N
8	5.7	.9	A + A + N
121	117.7	.1	T + N
42	51.8	1.8	T + A + N
17	9.5	5.9	T + A + A + N
1	.6		A + A + A + N
1	1.6		Residual
772	772.0	11.3	Total
		3	Degrees of freedom

		Scott-Foresman preprimer	
Observ.	Expect.	Chi-Sq.	Source
424	424.0	.0	P
132	132.0	.0	G
33	36.9	.4	N
24	19.4	1.1	A + N
4	4.2		A + A + N
36	33.2	.2	T + N
14	17.5	.7	T + A + N
5	3.8		T + A + A + N
9	8.1	.1	Expected freq. less than 5.0
0	.5		A + A + A + N
0	1.0		Residual
672	672.0	2.5	Total
		2	Degrees of freedom

Table XIX (Continued)

Observ.	Expect.	Preprimers combined Chi-Sq.	Source
654	654.0	.0	P
386	386.0	.0	G
109	108.1	.0	N
47	50.2	.2	A + N
12	9.7	.5	A + A + N
157	150.3	.3	T + N
56	69.7	2.7	T + A + N
22	13.5	5.4	T + A + A + N
1	1.0		A + A + A + N
1	2.5		Residual
1444	1444.0	9.1	Total
		3	Degrees of freedom

Observ.	Expect.	Ginn primer Chi-Sq.	Source
727	727.0	.0	P
286	286.0	.0	G
86	130.4	15.1	N
123	107.3	2.3	A + N
56	36.8	10.0	A + A + N
227	170.7	18.6	T + N
99	140.4	12.2	T + A + N
43	48.1	.5	T + A + A + N
17	6.7	15.7	A + A + A + N
0	10.5	10.5	Residual
1664	1664.0	85.0	Total
		5	Degrees of freedom

Table XIX (Continued)

Observ.	Expect.	Chi-Sq.	Source
		Scott-Foresman primer	
784	784.0	.0	P
220	220.0	.0	G
63	103.0	15.5	N
110	82.8	8.9	A + N
43	27.7	8.4	A + A + N
153	121.8	8.0	T + N
78	97.9	4.1	T + A + N
28	32.8	.7	T + A + A + N
3	5.0		A + A + A + N
3	12.0	6.7	Residual
1482	1482.0	52.3	Total
		4	Degrees of freedom

Observ.	Expect.	Chi-Sq.	Source
		Primers combined	
1511	1511.0	.0	P
506	506.0	.0	G
149	233.3	30.5	N
233	190.1	9.7	A + N
99	64.6	18.4	A + A + N
380	292.5	26.2	T + N
177	238.3	15.8	T + A + N
71	80.9	1.2	T + A + A + N
20	11.7	5.9	A + A + A + N
0	17.5	17.5	Residual
3146	3146.0	125.1	Total
		5	Degrees of freedom

Table XIX (Continued)

Observ.	Expect.	Ginn reader Chi-Sq.	Source
1143	1143.0	.0	P
473	473.0	.0	G
215	296.3	22.3	N
238	210.6	3.6	A + N
103	62.4	26.5	A + A + N
556	452.1	23.9	T + N
243	321.3	19.1	T + A + N
86	95.2	.9	T + A + A + N
24	9.9	20.3	A + A + A + N
0	17.4	17.4	Residual
3081	3081.0	133.9	Total
		5	Degrees of freedom

Observ.	Expect.	Scott-Foresman reader Chi-Sq.	Source
997	997.0	.0	P
323	323.0	.0	G
239	376.3	50.1	N
370	259.0	47.5	A + N
97	74.3	6.9	A + A + N
430	317.4	40.0	T + N
148	218.5	22.7	T + A + N
31	62.7	16.0	T + A + A + N
16	11.4	1.9	A + A + A + N
0	11.4	11.4	Residual
2651	2651.0	196.6	Total
		5	Degrees of freedom

Table XIX (*Continued*)

Observ.	Expect.	Readers combined Chi-Sq.	Source
2140	2140.0	.0	P
796	796.0	.0	G
454	671.5	70.4	N
608	470.1	40.4	A + N
200	137.1	28.8	A + A + N
986	770.5	60.3	T + N
391	539.4	40.8	T + A + N
117	157.4	10.4	T + A + A + N
40	21.3	16.3	A + A + A + N
0	28.6	28.6	Residual
5732	5732.0	296.1	Total
		5	Degrees of freedom

Observ.	Expect.	All combined Chi-Sq.	Source
4305	4305.0	.0	P
1688	1688.0	.0	G
712	1011.0	88.4	N
888	714.5	42.1	A + N
311	210.4	48.1	A + A + N
1523	1208.4	81.9	T + N
624	854.0	61.9	T + A + N
210	251.5	6.8	T + A + A + N
61	33.0	23.7	A + A + A + N
0	46.2	46.2	Residual
10322	10322	399.3	Total
		5	Degrees of freedom

Table XIX (Continued)

Observ.	Expect.	All combined (N = 5) Chi-Sq.	Source
4305	4305.0	.0	P
1688	1688.0	.0	G
712	1003.1	84.5	N
888	726.0	36.1	A + N
311	210.2	48.4	A + A + N
1523	1198.9	87.6	T + N
624	867.7	68.5	T + A + N
210	251.2	6.8	T + A + A + N
61	30.4	30.7	A + A + A + N
0	41.4	41.4	Residual
10322	10322	403.9	Total
		5	Degrees of freedom

Observ.	Expect.	All combined (N = 7) Chi-Sq.	Source
4305	4305.0	.0	P
1688	1688.0	.0	G
712	1016.5	91.2	N
888	706.5	46.6	A + N
311	210.5	48.0	A + A + N
1523	1215.0	78.1	T + N
624	844.4	57.5	T + A + N
210	251.5	6.9	T + A + A + N
61	34.8	19.7	A + A + A + N
0	49.6	49.6	Residual
10322	10322	397.7	Total
		5	Degrees of freedom

Table XIX (Continued)

| | All combined (N = 8) | | |
Observ.	Expect.	Chi-Sq.	Source
4305	4305.0	.0	P
1688	1688.0	.0	G
712	1020.6	93.3	N
888	700.6	50.1	A + N
311	210.4	48.1	A + A + N
1523	1219.9	75.3	T + N
624	837.4	54.4	T + A + N
210	251.5	6.9	T + A + A + N
61	36.1	17.1	A + A + A + N
0	52.2	52.2	Residual
10322	10322	397.5	Total
		5	Degrees of freedom

not have involved an a priori choice; but the remaining statistical calculations would have been more complicated, and for a first approximation this was not deemed necessary.

The categorial grammar for noun phrases generates the same types as the phrase-structure grammar, so the percentages of the corpus accounted for by the categorial grammar are the same as those shown in Table VI. However, the stopping parameter allows the categorial grammar to generate seven types which are not found in the corpus. The stopping parameter allows the rule to be applied six times; thus all types from (N) to $(A + A + A + A + A + A + N)$ and from $(T + N)$ to $(T + A + A + A + A + A + A + N)$ are possible, although the probabilities of the longer types are small. The grammar generates nine observed types and the seven unobserved types which are placed in one cell; four parameters are used so without further collapsing due to low predicted frequencies, the model allows five degrees of freedom.

Tables XVIII and XIX show the maximum-likelihood estimates and the chi-square analysis for this grammar; in the maximum-likelihood calculations 6 was used for N unless otherwise stated. In Table XIX the column labeled 'residual' includes the expected frequencies for types generated but not listed as well as any remaining uncollapsed types and round-off errors. When the expected frequency of the residual was greater than 5, the chi-square was evaluated and one degree of freedom was added; otherwise it was not. The contributions from unlisted types were substantial, but never as large as the largest contribution from the observed types.

Table XIX shows that for different sections of the corpus the source of the large chi-square contributions varies. The contribution from type (N) is usually, but not always, the largest, and no other pattern is evident. For the phrase-structure grammar, on the other hand, the contributions from types (N), $(A + N)$, and $(T + N)$ were consistently the greatest.

The last three sections of Table XIX show the chi-squares for the entire corpus for different choices of N, the number chosen in connection with the stopping parameter. It is apparent that the choice has little effect on the total chi-square or on the individual contributions; for N equal to 5, 6, 7, and 8, the total chi-square values are 403.9, 399.3, 397.7, and 397.5, respectively.

Table XX presents a comparison of total chi-squares for each section of the corpus for the phrase-structure and categorial grammars.

TABLE XX

Comparison of total chi-squares for the phrase-structure and
categorial grammars for noun phrases

Text	No. of phrases accounted for	Phrase-structure grammar		Categorial grammar	
		Total chi-square	Degrees of freedom	Total chi-square	Degrees of freedom
Ginn preprimer	772	.5	1	11.3	3
Scott-Foresman preprimer	672	2.3	0	2.5	2
Preprimers combined	1444	1.3	1	9.1	3
Ginn primer	1664	52.2	2	85.0	5
Scott-Foresman primer	1482	42.6	1	52.3	4
Primers combined	3146	95.3	2	125.1	5
Ginn reader	3081	81.5	2	133.9	5
Scott-Foresman reader	2651	177.5	2	196.6	5
Readers combined	5732	247.6	2	296.1	5
All combined	10322	316.8	2	399.3	5

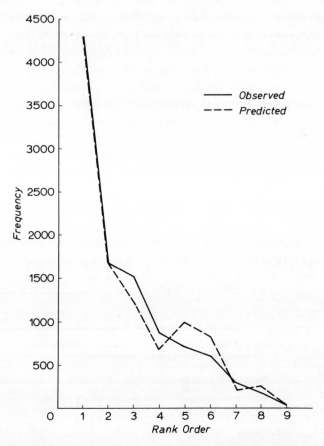

Fig. 3. Comparison of observed and predicted frequencies for phrase-structure and categorial grammars for noun phrases (entire corpus).

Because of the differing degrees of freedom, F tests were used to compare the chi-squares; in this situation the independence assumption is violated, so the results must be considered only as approximations. However, no significant differences were apparent. While the grammars differ in their ability to predict particular phrase types, the overall fit provided by each grammar is approximately the same. The similarity of the fit is further demonstrated by Figure 3 which shows the observed frequencies plotted against their rank order and the frequencies predicted by the phrase-structure and categorial grammars plotted at the rank of the corresponding observed frequencies.

Table XX shows that the rank order of the total comparative chi-squares ('comparative chi-square' indicates that differences in degrees of freedom have been considered) from the Ginn primer to the entire corpus is the same for the phrase-structure and categorial grammars. In both the trend of increasing chi-squares from the preprimers to the primers and from the primers to the readers is apparent. For both, the total comparative chi-square for the primers and readers combined is greater than the total comparative chi-square for either of the individual volumes, and the comparative chi-square for the entire corpus is the largest of all. It is interesting that for both grammars the preprimers showed an exception to the rule of chi-squares for combinations being greater than chi-squares for individual volumes. For the phrase-structure grammar the comparative chi-square for the Scott-Foresman preprimer is larger than that for the preprimers combined, and for the categorial grammar the Ginn preprimer has a larger comparative chi-square than the preprimers combined.

The job of analyzing the syntax of first-grade readers was much more complicated than I had expected. Instead of a few stereotypic grammatical forms occurring with high frequencies, I found an extremely large number of grammatical forms all occurring with relatively low frequencies. The resulting analysis was far from perfect in that the size of many of the chi-square values was large compared to the number of parameters. Speculation on how better results can be obtained in the future will not be attempted here.

Instructional Services, Riverside County Schools Office

NOTES

* This paper was drawn from my dissertation which is on file in the Stanford University library. The work reported here has been supported by the National Science Foundation (Grant G-18709), Office of Education Contract OEC-4-6-061493-2089 and the Ravenswood Subcontract to Stanford under Office of Education Grant OEG 0041.
[1] These texts are listed in the references according to the authors: Ousley and Russell (1957, 1961), Robinson *et al.* (1962a), and Russell and Ousley (1957). Throughout this paper these texts will be referred to by their reading level and publisher; this is the clearest and most widely used procedure.

JOYCE FRIEDMAN

A COMPUTATIONAL TREATMENT OF
CASE GRAMMAR*

1. INTRODUCTION

In this paper I am concerned with the attempted application of a computer
model of transformational grammar (based on Chomsky, 1965) to a
grammar based in part on more recent theories, in particular the lexicalist
and case theories. The computer system is one written at Stanford and
described in Friedman (1969) and Friedman *et al.* (1971). The grammar is
the UCLA English Syntax Project grammar and is described in a two-
volume unpublished report (Stockwell *et al.*, 1969), and in a forthcoming
publication.

The main part of the paper describes an attempt to mesh these two
projects. First, I comment on why this seemed to be an interesting thing to
do.

1.1. *Historical Background*

The design and programming of our computer system for transformational
grammar was carried out at Stanford in the two years September 1966 –
August 1968. At UCLA, for a period slightly longer at both ends, the same
sponsor (The Air Force Electronic Systems Division) supported the
project on the Integration of Transformational Theories on English
Syntax. One idea in having the two concurrent projects was that the
linguistics project would write a grammar, and that our computer science
project would construct some programs which would be in some way
useful as aids to the linguistics project (and hence, to other projects in
which grammars were being written).

As it turned out, there was some interaction between the two projects.
We exchanged memoranda and working papers, and in the spring of 1968,
when our programs were essentially complete, one of the members of the
UCLA group visited on two occasions and ran some simple grammars.
These grammars were small and preliminary, and while they embodied

Hintikka et al. (eds.), *Approaches to Natural Language,* 134–152. *All rights reserved.*
Copyright © 1973 *by D. Reidel Publishing Company, Dordrecht-Holland.*

some of the ideas which were to be the basis of the final version, they were not convincing evidence that we could in fact accept the kinds of grammars we had set out to work with.

Notice that there is an obvious problem in writing computer programs to accept grammars – that is, the notion of what a grammar is can change more rapidly than computer programs can be written. A good recent example of this occurs in Bresnan (this vol., pp. 3–47); if her elegant argument about the nuclear stress rule in phonology in fact influences the way in which people write phonological rules, then of the current phonological rule- and grammar-tester programs, those which do not also handle syntax are immediately unable to treat stress, and those which currently handle syntax and phonology in serial may be subject to major revision. This will depend of course on the details of the particular program – the Bresnan suggestion might, in some possible worlds, be handled with no program changes. In view of this history, it is not unnatural to be curious about whether the final UCLA grammar could be accepted by our programs.

Another reason for the attempt to translate and run the UCLA grammar is that it is the largest formal transformational grammar of English available. This immediately makes it important, and would justify trying to put it into computer form. The computer form makes it much more accessible for purposes of teaching and experimentation.

So much for reasons for wanting to put the UCLA grammar into our computer system. I will now describe very briefly the form of the UCLA grammar, and then give a quick sketch of what a computer system for grammar looks like. Then I will discuss in detail two specific aspects of the computer system which directly affect the way we implemented the UCLA grammar.

1.2. *The UCLA Grammar*

The UCLA grammar (Stockwell *et al.*, 1969) is a large (62 transformations), relatively formal grammar, accompanied by a two-volume defense. It draws linguistic insights from a variety of sources and unifies them by presentation in a lexicalist-case framework. It is not the purpose of this paper to comment on the adequacy of the grammar as a grammar of English, nor to criticize it in any way.[1] We take the grammar as given and use it as an example in an investigation of how to represent case.

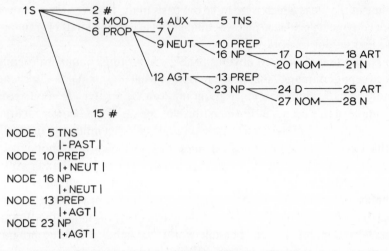

Fig. 1.   Phrase structure.

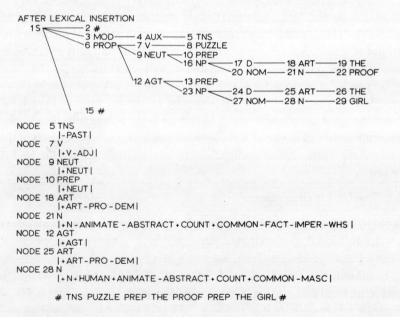

Fig. 2.   After lexical insertion.

As a brief introduction to the UCLA grammar, we give a short sample derivation. The derivation begins by phrase-structure generation of the tree[2] of Figure 1.

Points to notice about the base tree are first the case structure, and second the somewhat unusual generation of feature specifications in the phrase-structure component.

After lexical insertion, with verbs inserted before nouns, a possible result for this base tree is the tree of Figure 2.

The first transformation which applies to this tree is PREP-SPREAD, which moves the preposition *over* onto the first preposition from the complex symbol of the V dominating *puzzle* (no such feature is shown in Figure 2 because, as we shall see later, in the computer system it was implemented differently).

The case placement transformations then apply. UOBJ (Unmarked Object) selects *the proof* as the object and adjoins it as right sister of the verb *puzzle*. The corresponding preposition *over* is chomsky-adjoined to

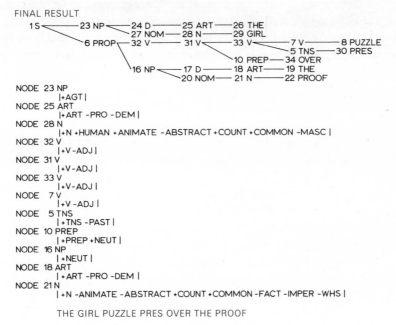

Fig. 3.   Final result.

the right of *puzzle*. ACTSUBJ (Active Subject) selects *the girl* as subject and
adjoins it as left sister of MOD. The corresponding preposition (node 13)
is erased.

The final step in completing the derivation is AFFIXSHF (Affix Shift),
which chomsky-adjoins the tense marker to the verb.

The resulting tree is given in Figure 3. Its terminal string is *The girl
puzzle* PRES *over the proof.*

1.3. *The Computer System and Its Uses*

We have treated the UCLA grammar within a computer system designed
to accept transformational grammars and to generate sentences according
to the rules of the grammar. The computer program runs on several
different computers, including both IBM and CDC machines. The user
of the program prepares a computer readable version of a grammar,
according to specifications provided. He also provides as input to the
program information about the types of output which he wants. He may ask
to see completely random trees, or, at the other extreme, to see the result
of transforming a particular base tree which is already provided with its
lexical items. Within this wide range, the system makes it possible for the
user to obtain trees which relate to any particular aspect of the grammar of
his current concern, be it a particular transformation, or a particular
lexical construct. The user also specifies to the program the amount of
output desired, both the number of runs for each input specification and
the amount of intermediate output in a derivation.

The program assists the linguist by providing examples of derivations
within the grammar. It is not an exhaustive tester, nor are probabilities
attached to the rules.

The system is definitely not intended to be used for evaluation of a
grammar written by someone else; it is meant to help the writer of a
grammar. In completing the formalization of a grammar to the point
where it is comprehensible to a computer program, there are inevitable
decisions which will affect how the grammar works, so that it is no longer
entirely the responsibility of its original authors. The translation process,
if done independently of the authors, may well distort their intentions.
(For example, there is more than one interpretation of the instruction
'Attach node 2 to node 4' – is this as sister, daughter?)

Examination of computer-generated derivations is bound to turn up problems both in individual transformations and in interactions of rules. The similarity between a large grammar and a large computer program suggests that it is unlikely that a consistent grammar can be written (particularly with more than one author) without extensive computer testing. (We computer programmers cannot do it – how could they do it?) There will be bugs. It is reasonable only to ask whether the bugs can be repaired without doing violence to the structure of the grammar – to ask that a grammar be initially bug-free is asking far too much.

2. THE COMPUTER MODEL

We turn now to a more detailed examination of the model which underlies the computer program. After some brief comments on the model as a whole, we will examine the process of lexical insertion and the use of n-ary features in the phonological component. Once these two aspects of the model are understood, it will be easy to see how the case grammar was implemented.

The model includes lexical insertion, phrase-structure generation, and transformation. The computer model is based on an interpretation of the model in Chomsky (1965). However, it does not follow Chomsky in all his decisions. In a number of cases we have offered broader alternatives, and allowed the user to agree with Chomsky as one possible choice.

An example of this freedom is in the order of lexical insertion. We did not want to turn away users who wanted to insert verbs first and serve only noun-first linguists ... indeed, it seemed that one might want to be able to try either alternative. So we required the user to specify as an input to the program (that is, as part of the grammar) the order of lexical insertion. He may agree with Chomsky if he likes. (Actually, it is hard to construct an example where it matters.)

A recent major modification to the model is its extension to include a phonological component, based in part on the system given in Chomsky and Halle (1968). The program changes needed for phonology, n-ary features and variables over feature values, were extremely convenient in our translation of the UCLA grammar.

2.1. *Lexical Insertion*

After the generation of a phrase-structure tree, the next step in the generative process is the insertion of lexical items into the tree. Each lexical item is characterized by various unanalyzable explicit features and also by contextual features, which are analyzable as structural descriptions. These structural descriptions are matched against the tree to determine if the lexical item is suitable for insertion at a particular point. If so, certain side effects of the insertion, indicated by the contextual feature, are performed as the item is inserted.

To illustrate the use of contextual features, we give as Figure 4 a simple lexical component. The illustration, which is not to be taken too seriously, shows how inserting a verb such as *drink*, which requires a liquid object, constrains the later[3] selection of the object noun to one which is not marked −LIQUID, while selection of *break* constrains the object to one which is not marked +LIQUID. At the same time the object noun takes the appropriate value of the feature LIQUID. In Figure 6 we show the complex symbols associated with the object noun after lexical insertion is complete. The example uses the vague noun *stuff*, which is marked in the lexicon as +N and +COMMON only. The underlying phrase structure for the sentence is given in Figure 5.

PHRASESTRUCTURE
  S = # NP VP #.
  VP = V (NP).
  NP = (DET) N.
  $ENDPSG
LEXICON
  CATEGORY V N DET.
    INHERENT
      ABSTRACT ANIMATE COUNT HUMAN LIQUID.
    CONTEXTUAL
      V1 = ⟨VP/⟨ — % N|+LIQUID|⟩⟩,
      V2 = ⟨VP/⟨ — % N|−LIQUID|⟩⟩,
      TRANS = ⟨VP⟨ — NP⟩⟩,
      COMMON = ⟨NP⟨DET — ⟩⟩,
      ANIMSUBJ = ⟨S⟨ # NP⟨% N|+ANIMATE|⟩VP⟨ — %⟩#⟩⟩,
      NANIMSUBJ = ⟨S⟨ # NP⟨% N|−ANIMATE|⟩VP⟨ — %⟩#⟩⟩,

ANIMOBJ = ⟨VP⟨ — NP⟨% N|+ANIMATE|⟩⟩⟩,
NANIMOBJ = ⟨VP⟨ — NP⟨% N|−ANIMATE|⟩⟩⟩,
NABSTOBJ = ⟨VP⟨ — NP⟨% N|−ABSTRACT|⟩⟩⟩.
RULES
  |+COUNT| =⟩ |+COMMON|,
  |+ABSTRACT| =⟩ |+COMMON −ANIMATE|,
  |+HUMAN| =⟩ |+ANIMATE|,
  |+LIQUID| =⟩ |−ANIMATE −ABSTRACT|⟩⟩⟩,
  |+ANIMATE| =⟩ |−ABSTRACT|.
ENTRIES
  SINCERITY VIRTUE |+N −COUNT +ABSTRACT|
  BOY |+N +COUNT +HUMAN|
  GEORGE BILL |+N −COMMON −COUNT +HUMAN|
  THE |+DET|
  EAT |+V +V2 +TRANS +ANIMSUBJ +NABSTOBJ|
     |+V −TRANS +ANIMSUBJ|
  FRIGHTEN |+V +TRANS +ANIMOBJ|
  BOOK |+N −LIQUID −ANIMATE +COUNT|
  STUFF |+N +COMMON|
  BEER |+N +COMMON +LIQUID|
  DRINK |+V +V1 +ANIMSUBJ|
  BREAK |+V +V2 +ANIMSUBJ +NANIMOBJ +NABSTOBJ|

Fig. 4. Illustration of lexical component.

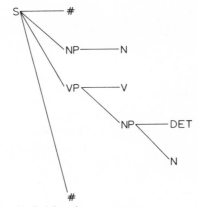

Fig. 5. Underlying phrase structure.

In sentence (1), the verb *drink* is selected. *Drink* is marked in the lexicon as |+V +V1 +ANIMSUBJ|. V1 and ANIMSUBJ are both contextual features. The definition of the first of these is V1 = ⟨ VP/ ⟨ − %N| + LIQUID|⟩⟩. It specifies that a word with this feature must be inserted only in a VP, which must have at the far right an N which is compatible with the feature +LIQUID. Since the verb is inserted before the noun, the feature +LIQUID is added to the otherwise initially empty complex symbol for the N, as a side effect of inserting the verb *drink*. The feature +LIQUID is added at the time *drink* is inserted, and will thus force the subsequent choice of a noun to be compatible with the feature +LIQUID. (Had a noun already been present, say by being specified on input, the selection of *drink* would be possible only if the noun were compatible with +LIQUID.) Once the feature specification +LIQUID is inserted, the specifications −ANIMATE and −ABSTRACT follow automatically by a redundancy rule in the lexicon. Insertion of the verb *drink* also has a side effect on the subject noun: the contextual feature specification +ANIM-SUBJ forces the subject noun to be +ANIMATE.

In contrast to sentence (1), sentences (2) and (3) give different sets of features for the object *stuff*.

(1) George drinks the stuff
   |+N −ABSTRACT −ANIMATE +LIQUID +COMMON|
(2) Bill breaks the stuff
   |+N −ABSTRACT −ANIMATE −LIQUID +COMMON|
(3) George frightens the stuff
   |+N −ABSTRACT +ANIMATE + COMMON|

Fig. 6.   Complex symbols after lexical insertion.

The use of contextual features and side effects suggests itself as a way of handling prepositions in case grammar without a PREP-SPREAD transformation and without adding any new mechanism to the system. Just as *drink* marks its subject as +ANIMATE and its object as +LIQUID, so might a verb, say *rely*, mark its neutral preposition with a feature selecting uniquely the preposition 'on'.

2.2. *Features in Phonology*

The fact that there is a small number of cases immediately suggests that case be treated as an *n*-ary feature, like stress in phonology. In the UCLA grammar there are seven different case features, + ESS, + DAT, . . . , + PART, and presumably also some implicit redundancy rules to guarantee that no node is marked for two different cases. An *n*-ary feature expresses just this situation: if CASE is an *n*-ary feature with seven possible values, then, by very basic conventions, no node can be marked for two different cases, since that would be to have two values for the same feature.

As the treatment of the UCLA grammar developed, we found the *n*-ary features to be extremely valuable in this and other ways. To show how this came about we first describe the parts of the system which we used.

(i) *n-ary features*. In the purely syntactic versions of our computer system, there are only three values for features: + and −, and the unspecified value (roughly ±) indicated by *. Phonology rules require the use of numerical feature values and of variables over those values. These are the '*n*-ary features' to which we refer. To handle *n*-ary features, the syntax of transformational grammar was modified,[4] so that (1) values may be either signs or integers, (2) there are variables over feature values, and (3) restrictions allow numerical comparisons of feature values.

Numerical values are most important for the stress rules. A good example of the notation of the system is the auxiliary reduction rule, here somewhat simplified:

TRANS AUXRED "AUXILIARY REDUCTION".
SD % 1'|(ALPHA)STRESS| ('C) '| (BETA)STRESS|%,
    WHERE (ALPHA > BETA) & (BETA < 4).
SC |−STRESS| MERGEF 1.

This rule applies whenever there are two stressed elements, possibly separated by a consonant ('C). If the stress value of the first is greater than that of the second, and the second is less than 4, then the first becomes unstressed.

(ii) *Variables over feature values*. The AUXRED transformation illustrates also the use of variables over feature values. ALPHA and BETA are used as the variables. We see that they can be compared with one another and with integers. Simple arithmetic is also possible. For example, in one stress adjustment rule we find the change |(ALPHA + 1)STRESS|

MERGEF 2. This will add one to the value of ALPHA and then store the result as the STRESS value of node 2.[5]

PHONEMES
O. = |−CONS +VOC −HIGH +BACK −LOW −ANT
      +ROUND|,
O, = |−CONS +VOC −HIGH +BACK +LOW −ANT
      +ROUND|,
@ = |−CONS +VOC −HIGH −BACK +LOW −ANT
      +ROUND|,
A = |−CONS +VOC −HIGH +BACK +LOW +ANT
      −ROUND|,
E = |−CONS +VOC −HIGH −BACK −LOW −ANT
      −ROUND|,
UH = |−CONS +VOC −HIGH +BACK −LOW −ANT
      −ROUND|,
EH = |−CONS +VOC −HIGH −BACK −LOW −ANT
      −ROUND|,
R = |+CONS +VOC −ANT +COR +VOICED −STRID
      +CONT|,
S = |+CONS −VOC +ANT +COR −VOICED +STRID
      +CONT|,
J = |+CONS −VOC −ANT +COR +VOICED +STRID
      −CONT|,
K = |+CONS −VOC −ANT −COR −VOICED −STRID
      −CONT|,
G = |+CONS −VOC −ANT −COR +VOICED −STRID
      −CONT|.

Fig. 7.   Phoneme definitions.

(iii) *Phonological abbreviations*. The phonological component of a grammar contains a set of phoneme definitions, illustrated in Figure 7. These phoneme definitions are used in printing a tree in which the phonemes are represented internally only in terms of features. The internal representation, needed for the phonological rules, is fully expanded. However, when a tree is printed out, only the abbreviation is seen. For

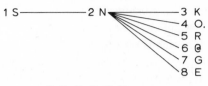

```
K O. R @ G E
```

```
4 O.    |-TENSE -STRESS |
6 @    |-TENSE -STRESS |
7 G    |+DER |
8 E    |-TENSE -STRESS |
```

Fig. 8.   Output tree for *courage*.

example, Figure 8, the output form of the tree for *courage*, displays for node 8 only the letter E with the feature specifications −TENSE and −STRESS that are not part of the complex symbol that E abbreviates.

3. APPLICATION TO CASE GRAMMAR

At this point we have sufficient background to explore the use of the aspects of the system described above to the representation of case grammar.

3.1. *Case Nodes and the CASE Feature*

Following UCLA, we introduce case nodes in the expansion of the nodes PROP and NOM; the rules are:

"4"   PROP = V (ESS) (NEUT) (DAT) (LOC) (INS) (AGT).
"7"   NOM = (NOM (S), N (NEUT) (DAT) (LOC) (INS) (AGT)).
"5"   ESS = PREP NP.
        NEUT = PREP NP.

        . . .

        AGT = PREP NP.

The first representational problem arises with rule 5, which UCLA states not simply as above but as:

$$\text{ESS} \to \text{PREP} \quad \text{NP}$$
$$[+\text{ESS}] \quad [+\text{ESS}]$$
$$\text{NEUT} \to \text{PREP} \quad \text{NP}$$
$$[+\text{NEUT}] \quad [+\text{NEUT}]$$

        . . .

This rule cannot be transformed directly into our phrase-structure notation. Instead, we introduce the contextual features VCASE and NCASE which will put case features on the case nodes, and the transformation FPLACE (which is the first transformation) which moves the case feature to PREP and NP appropriately. Thus in the list of inherent features, under *n*-ary features, we have a feature CASE. In the contextual definitions we define

$$VCASE = \langle PROP\langle \; - \; (ESS|1CASE|)(NEUT|2CASE|) \ldots$$
$$(AGT|6CASE|)\rangle\rangle$$
$$NCASE = \langle NOM\langle \; - \; (ESS|1CASE|)(NEUT|2CASE|) \ldots$$
$$(AGT|6CASE|)\rangle\rangle$$

and we add the redundancy rules

$$|+V| = |+VCASE|$$
$$|+N| = |+NCASE|$$

which will mark every verb for VCASE, at the time of lexical insertion. Consequently as soon as the verb has been inserted in the tree, the case nodes will contain the CASE feature with the correct value.

The CASE feature is moved onto PREP and NP by the transformation FPLACE:

"FEATURE TRANSFORMATION"
TRANS FPLACE I AACC.
SD % * |⟨ALPHA⟩CASE| ⟨1PREP 2NP⟩ %.
SC |⟨ALPHA⟩CASE| MERGEF 1, |⟨ALPHA⟩CASE|
MERGEF 2.

This transformation is the only one in group I and is applied through the base tree before any other transformations are applied. It matches an arbitrary node (*) which has a specification for the feature CASE and has the daughters PREP and NP. The structural change marks the PREP and NP with the same CASE specification as the parent node.

In the UCLA grammar the value of the feature CASE is represented as a subscript on C:

$$\text{S.I. } X \begin{Bmatrix} V \\ N \end{Bmatrix}_{+C_j \to OBJ} c_i[\text{PREP NP}] \, X \, c_j[\text{PREP NP}] \, X \qquad \text{(p. 864)}$$

The CASE feature allows us to state this structural description as

SD % *|⟨ALPHA⟩OBJ| *|⟨GAMMA⟩CASE|
⟨PREP NP⟩ % *|⟨ALPHA⟩CASE| ⟨PREP NP⟩ %.

3.2. N-ary Features for Object and Subject Selection

The SD above also illustrates the *n*-ary feature OBJ which selects the correct case for Object (an *n*-ary feature SUBJ also exists). The feature specification written by UCLA as $+C_j \rightarrow$ OBJ is for us the feature specification *j*OBJ, where *j* is an integer. (This appears to be a true *n*-ary feature because UCLA never uses $-C_j \rightarrow$ OBJ.)

In the LEXICON entries are marked for OBJ and SUBJ. For example, *accuse*, which makes DATIVE the object, is 3OBJ; *contain*, which takes locative subject, is 4SUBJ.

3.3. Features for Prepositions

As we interpret the UCLA grammar, there are four distinguishable types of occurrences of prepositions. Certain occurrences (1) are 'real' and 'meaning-bearing'. These are selected from the lexicon. Other occurrences (2) are predictable from the verb and case. For example, *laugh* takes *at* for the NEUT case, and *puzzle* takes *over* for NEUT. Some occurrences (3) of *of, for* and *by* are inserted by transformations (other than PREP-SPREAD). Finally, other occurrences (4) are predictable from CASE alone, unless the default choice has been overridden earlier in the derivation.

In the UCLA grammar a transformation PREP-SPREAD inserts the prepositions in the second group above. It is argued that PREP-SPREAD must occur after GERNFACT (gerundive, nonfactive) because type (2) prepositions must not be selected by that rule. We have restated GERN-FACT to distinguish between 'real' and other prepositions, and thus do not need PREP-SPREAD. The choice of preposition for a particular case can be stated as part of the case frame feature, and the PREP will at lexical insertion time be marked with the correct specification *i* PRP. For example, *laugh* has the contextual feature $+\langle$PROP $\langle$ — (NEUT $\langle$PREP|1PRP|%$\rangle$)AGT$\rangle\rangle$. This specifies that its case frame requires an AGT and may optionally contain a NEUT. If it contains a NEUT, the corresponding PREP will be marked 1PRP.[6]

The *n*-ary feature PRP has one value for each word which can occur as a preposition of type (2), (3), or (4) above. In the course of a derivation, prepositions (2) and (3) do not explicitly appear as terminal symbols but are carried as the PRP feature on PREP.

A final transformation PREPINS, given in Figure 9, creates corresponding terminal nodes for PREP's which remain. If PRP occurs (type (2) or (3)), its value determines the preposition; otherwise the value of the CASE feature decides (type (4)).

TRANS PREPINS V OB AACC.
SD % 1PREP %, WHERE TRM 1.
SC F ⟨1 INC1 |(ALPHA)PRP|⟩
  THEN ⟨'|(ALPHA)PRP|) AFIDE 1⟩
  ELSE ⟨IF ⟨1 INC1 |(BETA)CASE|⟩
    THEN ⟨'|(BETA)PRP|) AFIDE 1⟩⟩.

Fig. 9.   Creation of prepositions.

PHONEMES
  AT   = |1PRP|,
  OF   = |2PRP|,
  TO   = |3PRP|,
  FROM = |4PRP|,
  WITH = |5PRP|,
  BY   = |6PRP|,
  OVER = |7PRP|.

Fig. 10.   Prepositions as phonemes.

After PREPINS the terminal preposition nodes have the feature PRP but do not have the decoding of it as an actual preposition. But this is supplied from Figure 10 by the same process as that which supplies letters in place of phonological complex symbols. Thus the tree may remain

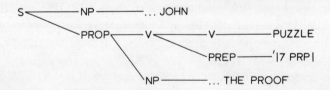

but whenever it or the corresponding sentence is printed, *over* is substituted for '|7PRP| by a decoding process.

4. REPRESENTATION OF LEXICALIST THEORY

The UCLA grammar is a lexicalist-case grammar. We have discussed our implementation of the grammar in the computer system from the point-of-view of case. It remains to discuss the formal implications of the lexicalist hypothesis. Here, in contrast to case, we did not really make a serious attempt to capture the lexicalist aspects of the grammar. Nonetheless we did consider those points which would need to be handled in a thorough treatment. We present them here, as a possible basis for later work.

4.1. *Choice Between V and N in Transformations*

Many of the UCLA transformations have structural descriptions of the form

$$\left\{ \begin{matrix} V \\ N \end{matrix} \right\} [\ldots]$$

where what is meant is that there is either an N or a V which has the sub-analysis given in the square brackets. In our notation this cannot be so simply stated since the obvious translation

$$(V, N) \langle \ldots \rangle$$

is not syntactically well formed. In the system, a *structure* cannot have a *choice* as head *element*. Thus, the above must be stated in the equivalent form

$$\langle V \langle \ldots \rangle, N \langle \ldots \rangle \rangle$$

It should be noted however that the UCLA statements of the form above point to a somewhat spurious generalization, since they are generally accompanied by rather strong conditions to distinguish cases acceptable for V from those acceptable by N. The need for these conditions makes our required form seem less offensive.

4.2. *Distinguished Role of the Sentence Symbol*

In the system the *sentence-symbol* S is distinguished in several ways: (i) it is the only recursive symbol in the phrase-structure, (ii) the phrase-structure generation routine will not introduce an S unless it is explicitly called for by the skeleton, (iii) the analysis routine will not search below an S unless the S is explicitly given in the structural description.

   The parallelism in a case grammar between S and NOM suggests that they should be treated alike in all three respects. (i) In stating the phrase structure for the UCLA grammar it was necessary to repeat several times the expansion rules for NOM. This would be unnecessary if NOM as well as S were recursive. If this were true, then (ii) would also need to be extended to NOM to avoid oversize generations. (iii) A technical error in the UCLA grammar arose from the failure to notice that one of the implications of the lexicalist-class hypothesis is that a case node following a V may not be the case for that V, but rather a case node associated with a NOM under some other case node. For example, in the tree below, the structural description

$$ X \quad \begin{Bmatrix} N \\ V \end{Bmatrix} \quad NP \ X \ AGT \ X $$
$$ | + PASS| $$

selects the AGT under the first NOM, not the (intended) one immediately under the PROP.

(C_i is either DAT or LOC.) This would cause trouble were it not ruled out by extra-grammatical arguments. (The documentation of the grammar indicates that every +PASS verb requires an AGT.) However, there are transformations of the grammar which do fail for this reason.

4.3. *Cycling in the Control Program*

The system is designed so that the traffic rules need not be limited to cycles on S only. At least one computer-tested grammar has also employed cycles based on NP. The UCLA document does not consider cycling at all, but the form of the lexicalist theory suggests that the standard transformational cycle on the 'lowest S' should probably be reconsidered in favor of cycling on both S and NP.

4.4. $\overline{\overline{X}}$, $\overline{X}$, *and* X.

The use of PROP, NOM, etc., in the UCLA grammar is designed as a representation for Chomsky's $\overline{\overline{X}}$, $\overline{X}$, and X, where X is a variable taking the values V and N. The present notation does not automatically display the relationship between PROP and V as $\overline{\overline{V}}$ and V. A feature representation could do this: V|2 BAR|, V|1 BAR|, V|0 BAR|. It would be interesting to see how this change of notation would affect the statement of the transformations.

ACKNOWLEDGMENT

I would like to acknowledge the assistance of Paul Myslenski, who did much of the work of translating the UCLA grammar into computer-acceptable form, and Yves Ch. Morin, who is responsible for the special features of the phonology component of the system.

The University of Michigan, Ann Arbor, Michigan

NOTES

* An earlier version of part of this paper was presented to the Seminar on Construction of Complex Grammars, Cambridge, Massachusetts, June 1970. The research was supported in part by the National Science Foundation under Grant GS-2771 to the University of Michigan.
¹ For a critical study of parts of the UCLA grammar, see Friedman and Myslenski (1970).
² In the tree representation used throughout this paper, daughters of a node are written to the right with left-most daughters in the highest position. Numbers indicate internal node numbers in the computer representation.
³ For this grammar the class of possible sentences is independent of the order of insertion of V and N. We insert verbs first because it is more efficient to do so.
⁴ The new syntax rules for *value* are:

    4.08   *value* :: = *sign* [] *integer* []∗ [] − [] (*prefix*)
    4.09   *prefix* :: = *sign-prefix* [] *integer-prefix*
    4.10   *sign-prefix* :: = opt[−] *variable*
    4.11   *integer-prefix* :: = *variable* opt[*sign integer*]

[5] More precisely, the node corresponding to the term numbered 2 in the structural description of the rule.

[6] In discussion of an earlier version of this paper, David Bennett pointed out that this view of prepositions may be somewhat simplistic, as there seems to be a continuum from verbs which take only one NEUT preposition (*rely on*), to verbs which have a small class of possibilities (*laugh at, laugh over*), to verbs which are free to take any 'real' preposition. Several possibilities suggest themselves as solutions to this problem: one might provide several complex symbols for *laugh*, each with a different preposition selection. Or, one might use a feature, say DURA- TIVE, to distinguish between the two, assigning *laugh* the specification *DURATIVE in the lexicon, so that the system will select either + or − at the time of lexical insertion, and including redundancy rules which imply that if *laugh* is +DURATIVE, *over* is selected, if − DURATIVE then *at* is selected.

HENRY HAMBURGER AND KENNETH N. WEXLER

IDENTIFIABILITY OF A CLASS OF
TRANSFORMATIONAL
GRAMMARS

This paper extends a formal theory of language learning to transformational components. Learning procedures which are psychologically more suggestive than those previously studied are shown to yield positive results under formally specified conditions. Part 1 introduces the general class of problems to be studied; Part 2 states and discusses various possible assumptions; and Part 3 sketches the proof for a particular case of interest. For a complete proof, see Hamburger (1971).

1. INTRODUCTION

A formal theory of language learning has been proposed (Gold, 1967), in which the learner is presented with a sequence of data and must guess, after each datum, what language of a given class he is encountering. He is never told whether his guess is correct but if his guessing sequence converges, he is said to succeed. More specifically, if his procedure must in all cases lead to a correct guess sooner or later, and then stay correct, then the procedure 'identifies-in-the-limit' that class of languages.

Note that the problem facing the learner (child, program-plus-computer, or Turing machine) is to *select* a language from a *class* of languages. If the class consists of a single language, then the learner can, trivially, succeed instantly simply by always guessing that language, even though the language itself is exceedingly complex. Thus it is meaningless to ask whether a particular language is identifiable; we ask only about classes.

If the data are only the correct sentences, then Gold shows that there is no learning procedure for any of the classes of languages commonly studied in connection with natural language. That is, the context-sensitive, context-free and even the finite-state grammars all of which have been proposed as models of the base for transformational grammar correspond

Hintikka et al. (eds.), Approaches to Natural Language, 153–166. All rights reserved.

to language classes which are not learnable in this sense. On the other hand, for the so-called 'informant' presentation scheme which also includes all possible instances of nonsentences, labeled as such, the above classes and even the class of primitive recursive languages is identifiable in the limit.

In view of the prominent role of transformational grammar in current linguistic research we have investigated the identifiability of a certain class of transformational mappings. It is necessary in this context to speak of mappings, not languages, in order to indicate precisely what the learner is required to accomplish. If we ask only that he select a language from a class, then we must be satisfied if he gives us a correct representation of the set of surface strings, with no indication of which of them goes with which base phrase-marker. For example, the learner might provide a 'surface grammar' which generates all and only the surface strings. To accept such a result is to ignore a tenet of transformational theory that the mapping of particular deep structures to particular utterances is part of linguistic competence.

In this connection we introduce the notion of *moderate equivalence*. Two transformational components are moderately equivalent with respect to a given base grammar if for each phrase-marker of the base the two respective derived structures (obtained by transforming the base phrase-marker with the two components, respectively) have the same terminal string. This definition differs from strong equivalence in that the two derived pm's need not be identical, and it differs from weak equivalence in that the mapping and not just the surface language is preserved, as discussed in the preceding paragraph.

To select the correct member of a class of T mappings it is sufficient to specify one member of the set of moderately equivalent T components which accomplish that mapping, just as, in the case of, say, *cfl*'s it is sufficient to specify one of the weakly equivalent *cfg*'s that generate it. We shall deal only with procedures in which the learner guesses at the mappings by guessing a T component, and therefore use the terms grammar-class and mapping-class interchangeably.

No mention has been made of the learning of the base. It is of course possible to seek conditions under which both the base and the T component can be found, but attention is here restricted to the T component. That is, we make the assumption, discussed in the next section, that the base is known to the learner from the outset.

Let T be a class of transformational mappings, I a scheme of information presentation, C a criterion of convergence or learning, and P a learning procedure. We seek quadruples $\langle T,I,C,P \rangle$ such that T is learnable in sense C by applying P to information about T of form I.

A vast array of positive and negative results can be obtained along these lines, some of which are trivial and others of which are nontrivial but uninteresting. Interestingness of the results depends on adequacy of T as a model of natural language; the strength of C; and the plausibility of P and I, judged by implications for human development, simplicity, efficiency, or as a starting point, subjective reasonableness.

P is of particular interest since it can be regarded as a theory of learning, though it is premature to seriously suggest any of the P's looked at so far as such. Certain results can be obtained using enumeration procedures, but if taken as models of human language learning, they have bizarre implications, discussed in the next section.

2. DISCUSSION OF ASSUMPTIONS

In the preceding section we noted that our interest would be in quadruples consisting of a grammar (or mapping) class, a presentation scheme, a learning criterion and a procedure. The results cited from Gold show that learnability depends crucially on the data presented as well as on language class. We note in 2.2 below that even a change in the kind of data *sequence*, with no change in the *class* of data, can have a striking effect on what procedure may be used.[1] Such differences in procedure are not of importance in proofs of Turing machine capability, but may bear importantly on the plausibility of a model for human language acquisition. Learnability may also hinge on what criteria are used. Some preliminary studies in that area have been made by Feldman (1969), but it is not one of our principal concerns here. The four subsections which follow deal respectively with the four aspects mentioned in the first sentence of this section.

2.1. *The Class of Transformational Grammar*

The base grammar is taken from the class, called *eCFG*, of context-free grammars in which the start symbol, S, is an essential recursive element.

That is, recursion occurs only through S, so that any two occurrences of a nonterminal symbol on the same path of a base phrase-marker must be separated by an S.

The transformational component is first applied to subtrees dominated by bottommost S's in the base phrase-marker. Other S-dominated subtrees are transformed only after all those within them have been transformed. A singulary transformation is one which refers only to nodes dominated by no S other than the root-S of the subtree being transformed. A binary transformation may refer to nodes dominated by at most one S other than that root S, in the subtree being transformed. Only singulary and binary transformations are allowed. When a binary transformation takes nodes out from under an S those nodes must, under certain conditions, be marked as ineligible for future transforming. The particular conditions are motivated by specific studies of English and are also used in the proof of identifiability.

All transformations are obligatory. Only one transformation may apply at any given level. That is, in order to transform an S-dominated subtree, check whether there is some proper analysis of that subtree, consisting only of currently eligible nodes, which fits the structural description of one of the transformations in the T component. If so then the structural change indicated by the transformation is carried out; if not, no change is made. In the principal theorem it is assumed that there will never be two transformations which both are applicable at the same point and which give conflicting results. The same result can also be shown in the case where there is a precedence ordering over transformations so that whichever applicable transformation comes earlier in the ordering is the one used. A slightly more complex learning procedure is used in the latter case.[2]

Sequential application of more than one transformation at the same level is not allowed. Formally this requirement is a restriction on the class of T components since it has been shown (Ginsburg and Partee, 1969) that there are sequences of transformations which achieve structural changes unattainable by a single transformation. Still one might put forth an empirical claim that such situations do not occur in natural language. But if we are going to bring in linguistic considerations then it must be admitted that descriptions of natural language will be complicated enormously by this assumption. For example, suppose in some language there is a passive transformation, T_p, and a question transformation, T_q. Further imagine that there are passive questions which can be formulated by applying both T_p and T_q successively at the same level. Although it may be formally possible to create a new transformation by composition of T_p and T_q, such a move would be counter to the aim of economy of description. In fact, it has been argued that passivization itself is appropriately described as a composite of two simpler transformations (Chomsky, 1970b).

Some parts of the foregoing description of the class of grammars are based on properties suggested by transformational linguists in other contexts; some are not. Of particular interest are the restrictions on node-raising noted above and made precise in Section 3. These have not been mentioned in previous work but appear to be true at least for English. If our observation is substantiated it will mean that the formal study of acquisition has provided an insight into the acquired language structure.

2.2. *The Information Presentation Scheme*

Learning transformational grammar appears intuitively to be a formidable task, one requiring a rich information source. Moreover, to restrict the learner to working only with surface strings or even with sentential and nonsentential strings distinctively labeled (Gold's 'informant') is to deprive him of resources available to children and linguists. The fact that a child's first words refer to the objects and scenarios ('bye-bye,' 'allgone') of his experience is ample proof that he attends not merely to utterance but to meaning as well. As for the linguist, there is a reason why the Rosetta Stone was such a big find. That is, even if one is equipped with distributional analysis, it is helpful to have meaning available.

On the formal side, since the class of transformational grammars includes the class of *fsg*'s, identifiability from surface strings alone is impossible. Furthermore, Peters and Ritchie (this volume, pp. 180–93) have shown that the addition of a certain class of transformations to even a simple finite state base yields the power of a Turing machine. This result, together with Gold's, shows that this class of T grammars is not learnable even from an informant. It is thus necessary either to decrease the power of T component or to increase the richness of the information source, or both, if T grammar is to be learnable according to our criteria. We have done both: the restrictions on the T component are described in the preceding subsection; here we describe the enriched information.

We assume that the base grammar is known to the learner at the outset. The universal base hypothesis will not be defended here; we only note that it is consistent with our assumption. Another interpretation of this assumption might be that although the base is not present at the start, a particular transformation is learned only after the related portion of the base is learned. Certainly kernel sentences, which are 'closer' to the base, seem to be learned before nonkernel sentences.

The information presentation consists of a sequence of ordered pairs. The first element of each pair is a base phrase-marker, while the second is a surface string. If one believes in generative semantics, then such information is meaning-plus-utterance. It seems doubtful that the child receives as input the precise meaning of each sentence as it is spoken, independently of the utterance.

We may alternatively suppose that the child learns from responses to his own output. To make this notion clearer, suppose that in order to communicate a child first formulates an idea and then translates it into an utterance. If the idea constitutes a base phrase-marker and the translation is accomplished by using a not-yet perfect transformational component, then the resulting utterance may be close enough to the correct one (which would have resulted from using a correct T component) so that an adult can figure out what is intended and supply the correct utterance. This adult utterance would then be second member of the ordered pair making up a datum; the first being the base pm.

A possible objection to the idea of correction by adults is the contention by observers of children that corrections are ignored. Evidence cited for this position is typically that children repeat errors soon after being corrected. This objection can be answered in several ways. If the error is the result of using a wrong transformation (arising from, say, a previous overgeneralization) then our procedure can result in the rejection of *any* transformation used. If the child picks the wrong one to throw out, then he will still err on that sentence, though in a different way. Also, unless the repetition is a sentence identical to the first, the child may have acted on the correction but has done so by hypothesizing a transformation of too limited generality. Thus 'repeated errors' may not really be repetitious from the viewpoint of the child's developing grammar.

A more fundamental objection to the idea of correction by adults is that, if taken seriously, a theory of correction must be precisely stated. That is, we must specify just how it is that adults convert a child-sentence into the appropriate adult-sentence. In a way this proposal converts the problem of how a child learns adult language into the complementary problem of how an adult learns a child language. We may escape this circular reasoning by supposing that the latter problem, which is easier than the former, is done at least partly by the 'input' method described above. In this way, adult and child share the computational burden.

The presentation scheme consists of choosing a datum pair from the set of all correct datum pairs according to a fixed probability distribution. Each pair has a fixed nonzero probability of occurrence regardless of how often it has appeared previously. This kind of scheme appears to run counter to the notion of corrected output, discussed above, in which the learner determines what datum comes next by picking a base phrase-marker. However, if the learner requires a particular datum, he can use the strategy of waiting until it appears again. For each datum the probability of this strategy failing forever is zero. Conversely if he is allowed to determine the order of presentation he may choose to do so randomly.

A probabilistic information source insures that any particular datum will always appear again, so it is unnecessary to save all previous data. This is certainly a desirable consequence for a model of human learning. Although a child may retain *some* data in raw form for a while, it would certainly be unjustified to require retention of all data throughout learning.

2.3. *Criterion*

Probabilistic presentation requires a probabilistic criterion of learning. A language class is identifiable-in-the-limit-with-probability-1 with respect to a probabilistic presentation scheme if there exists a learning procedure such that for any member of the class there is a subset, of measure 1, of the set of presentation sequences, for which the procedure identifies-in-the-limit the language.

2.4. *Procedure*

2.4.1. *Comparison with enumeration.* The learning procedure introduced

here differs from enumeration in at least three ways, all of which are related to its plausibility as a model of human learning. First it does not require storage of all previous data; this aspect was discussed at the end of 2.2.

Second and most importantly, it does not engage in the wholesale rejection of T components. With the advent of each new datum, there is a computation based solely on that datum together with the currently hypothesized set of transformations. The result of that computation is to reject a single transformation from the hypothesized set, to add a new one to it or to leave the set unaltered. ('New' here simply means 'not currently a member'; the added transformation may have been hypothesized and discarded previously.) The procedure actually specifies several candidates for hypothesization (adding to the currently guessed set) and several for rejection, the choice among alternatives to be made probabilistically. Since the probabilities may be assigned in a variety of ways we actually have a family of procedures; so different allowable methods of assigning probabilities may be thought of as heuristics, any of which will yield identifiability, some being more efficient than others in certain situations. Whatever the probabilistic scheme, we emphasize that a datum can affect only a single rule, not as with enumeration, reject an entire component only to examine a new component chosen arbitrarily from an a priori enumeration scheme unrelated to any of the data presented.

A third objection to enumeration which is overcome by the procedure used here has to do with a discovery of inserted morphemes. A learner, even if he has the base grammar, has no knowledge of the set of inserted morphemes at the outset. Thus he cannot actually construct an enumeration of T components unless he makes some assumption about what that set is. Since the set varies for different natural languages, it is not reasonable to suppose that knowledge of the exact set is part of the learner's initial information.

Two alternative assumptions suggest themselves, both of them unsatisfactory though for different reasons. First we might assume initial knowledge of the class of all morphemes which could possibly be inserted in any language. This would amount to knowledge of a universal discrete phonological alphabet, assuming one exists. The enumeration would then include all components consisting of transformations calling for insertion in all possible ways of all possible combinations of morphemes, each morpheme consisting of any possible sequence of phonemes taken from the universal phonological alphabet. The reader may judge the plausibility of this procedure for himself.

Another possible solution to the morpheme discovery problem for an enumeration procedure is to begin by using an enumeration with the set of inserted morphemes assumed to be empty. Thereafter, each time a new morpheme is encountered in the data, that morpheme is added to the set of inserted morphemes and a new enumeration of T components is begun with this augmented morpheme class assumed to be correct. It can be seen that this procedure makes no use of any information gleaned from data prior to the presentation of the last morpheme, except to extract the correct set of morphemes. (Note that its computation load during this period is no lighter than normal since it never knows whether the period is over.)

The procedure used here incorporates new morphemes into transformations in the same way that it handles permutation, deletion and copying. Any transformation which is hypothesized must be applicable to the current datum, and we will see that eventually data appear for which some possible hypotheses insert that morpheme. The identifiability proof of course shows more than that morphemes find their way into the T component. But that aspect is emphasized in this connection to compare our method to enumeration. The point is that we handle morphemes in a straightforward integrated part of the procedure, without making a special list for them and restarting the procedure each time a new one appears.

2.4.2. *Description of procedure.* The procedure operates on each successive datum to produce a set of transformations which may be hypothesized and a set which may be rejected. It then chooses one set randomly from among them and adds it to or removes it from the current component. The 'current component', which constitutes the current guess, is the set of all current transformations, together with a fixed (a priori correct) set of meta-rules concerning application.

The base phrase-marker which constitutes the first half of each datum is transformed according to the current T component. If the resulting derived phrase-marker has a terminal string identical to the correct surface string given as the second half of the input datum, then no change is made in the current component. This insures that when the correct mapping (that is, the correct T component or any component moderately equivalent to it) is found, no further changes will be made. It will then be necessary only to show that the expected value of the time at which the correct mapping is found is finite.

If on the other hand the current component assigns to the input base phrase-marker a wrong surface string or if the component is ambiguous[3] in its treatment of that phrase-marker, then the operation of the component up to the point of error discovery is examined. Error in this connection is said to be discovered at the lowest point in the pm where ambiguous application is encountered or else, in the case of a wrong derived string, at the top of the phrase-marker. Each application (up to that point) of the current component to an S-dominated subtree consists either of no transforming or else the application of a single transformation. Any transformation which has been applied is a candidate for rejection. For each S-dominated subtree where no transformation was applied, create candidate hypotheses by using the hypothesizer $H(p,t)$ where p is that S-dominated subtree, t is a terminal string and $H(p,t)$ consists of all possible transformations which transform p into a phrase-marker with terminal string t. The terminal string t to be used is the correct surface string, s, given as part of input, whenever p is the subtree which is the entire derived phrase-marker (that is, when working at the top level). Otherwise, a 'string-preserving' transformation is hypothesized; that is, t is taken to be the terminal string of p.

The particular specifications of this procedure, though reasonable, are not obvious or more natural than many others one could envision. They are not motivated by any direct attempt to model what might be human procedures. What is claimed for them, rather, is that taken together they achieve formal learning without exhibiting the undesirable characteristics cited for enumeration.

3. SKETCH OF PROOF

The various possible current components are regarded as states of a Markov chain and the various probabilities of moving from one state to another are investigated with a view to putting lower bounds on some of them. It was noted earlier that once an acceptable component (one moderately equivalent to the correct one) becomes the current component it is always guessed thereafter. In the proof this is rephrased as the statement that any acceptable component corresponds to an absorbing state. It is then shown that there is a path from any possible current component to some acceptable component, such that the path is shorter than some pre-assigned upper bound and such that each step of the path has probability greater than some preassigned lower bound. We now state this formally. Let Q be the set of states corresponding to possible current components. Let A be the set of states corresponding to acceptable components. Then

$$(\exists p)\,(\exists k)\,(\forall q \in Q)\,(\exists a \in A)\,(\exists r \leq k)$$
$$(\exists q_1, q_2, \ldots, q_{r-1} \in Q)\,(p(q_{i+1}|q_i) \geq p,$$
$$\text{for } 0 \leq i \leq r\text{-}1, \text{ where } q_0 = q \text{ and } q_r = a).$$

Not all sets of allowable transformations constitute possible current components. According to the meta-rules we are imposing on transformational components, if two transformations have the same structural description then either there is a datum for which they conflict or else one of them is superfluous. It is thus a desirable[4] trait that the procedure used here can never have two such transformations. This follows from the fact that hypothesizations are always based on (partially transformed) phrase-markers to which no current transformation applies.

The use of only singulary and binary transformations, together with the restrictions on raising, results in a bound on the number of operationally distinguishable proper analyses of phrase-markers even though there are infinitely many base- and derived-phrase-markers. It follows that there is also a bound on the number of structural descriptions which fit these proper analyses. This latter fact together with the considerations of the preceding paragraph gives a bound on the size of the current component.

A crucial and complicated piece of the argument is to show that any component which makes some mistake must make one on some datum of degree less than some preassigned value. The details of the proof of this point appear to provide no particular linguistic insight. We conclude from it that any nonacceptable component will be revealed as such by one of a finite set of data, hence with lower-bounded probability. That finite set of data is the set of all data with base phrase-marker of degree less than a particular preassigned value which is determined solely by the given base component.

We have been speaking up to this point of acceptable components. At this point we arbitrarily single out some particular acceptable component and henceforth[5] call it the 'correct component'. At an arbitrary point in time let the current component be any possible nonacceptable component. Then, as asserted above, there is a lower bound on the probability that the next datum is both incompatible with the current component and of degree less than some upper bound.

From boundedness of degree it is shown that the number of transformations which the learning procedure puts forth as candidates for rejection or hypothesization is bounded. Among the candidates for rejection and hypothesization there may be one (or more) which is a candidate to move the 'right' way with respect to the component we have singled out as 'correct'. That is, perhaps (a) one of the candidates for rejection is not in the correct component or (b) one of the candidates for hypothesization is in the correct component. Working up from the bottom of the phrase-marker, the *first*[6] S-dominated subphrase-marker which is handled incorrectly gives rise to the first mistaken structure (partially derived phrase-marker). On the one hand if this first mistaken structure arises from application of a transformation then that transformation is a candidate for rejection (so are all other transformations used on the datum). On the other hand if the first mistaken structure is a result omission, there being no applicable transformation even though the correct component contains an applicable transformation, T, then there are two possibilities: either T is string-preserving with respect to the particular subphrase-marker or it is not. If it is, then T is a candidate hypothesis, according to the procedure; if not then there is another datum, of lower degree than the one being considered (hence also with probability exceeding the lower bound), which is also incompatible with the current component. This lower-degree datum is the one whose base phrase-marker is formed from that of the original datum (which we have been dealing with up to this point) by taking the S-node being considered together with all the nodes it dominates. This new datum is handled correctly by the current component right up to but not including the top cycle, at which point the correct component applies T, thereby altering the terminal string whereas the current component has no applicable transformation and hence must give an incorrect surface string. The hypothesization operator is applied to give as candidate hypotheses all transformations which give the same string that T gives at this point. T must be one of these, so T is a candidate hypothesis. As noted above, the number of all candidate alterations of both types will be shown bounded. Thus if candidates are equiprobable,[7] there is a lower bound for their individual probabilities.

In summary to this point, there are lower bounds on the following probabilities: (a) that a datum will occur which reveals the unacceptability of the current component (if indeed it is unacceptable), (b) that any particular alteration specified as a possibility by the procedure will be made, and (c) that for some datum as described in (a) some alteration in the right direction will be among the specified alterations. Taken together these imply a lower bound on the probability that the next datum results in a step toward the designated correct component.

As noted earlier, there is a bound on the size of current components. At an arbitrary point in time let the current component be C and let the fixed correct component be C^t (t for 'true'). What we have argued is that, with lower-bounded probability either a member of $C^t - C$ (set-difference) is hypothesized or a member of $C - C^t$ is rejected. This continues to be the case until either C^t or some other acceptable component is reached. The time to reach C^t in the event that no other acceptable component is reached first is equal to the size of $(C^t - C) \cup (C - C^t)$, and is therefore bounded by the sum of the size of C^t and the bound on the size of possible current components. The statement (*) has thus been established and it follows that we can put a bound on the expected value of the total time taken to 'converge', that is, reach an acceptable state. Finally, the probability of identifiability-in-the-limit must be 1 for if there were nonzero probability of nonidentifiability then the expected 'convergence' time would be infinite.

University of California, Irvine

NOTES

[1] Gold also shows such a result, but the restriction he places on the data sequence is severe and the result is therefore of diminished interest. Gold recognizes this in referring to that presentation scheme as 'anomalous text'. When citing Gold's results we implicitly exclude this case.

[2] See Hamburger (1971).

166   HENRY HAMBURGER AND KENNETH N. WEXLER

³ This is not the allowable ambiguity of many phrase-markers mapping to a single surface string, but rather its converse, which for obligatory T's is not allowable.

⁴ Desirable with respect to the class of T components as defined.

⁵ We could just as well have singled it out at the outset, by phrasing the problem as one of finding either *the* correct component or one moderately equivalent to it, instead of saying we would look for a mapping. The locutions are equivalent.

⁶ If there are mistakes in several nonoverlapping subphrase-markers then none is uniquely first but any of them will do for this argument.

⁷ It is not necessary to assume equiprobability.

KENNETH N. WEXLER AND HENRY HAMBURGER

ON THE INSUFFICIENCY OF SURFACE DATA
FOR THE LEARNING OF TRANSFORMATIONAL
LANGUAGES

ABSTRACT. Identifiability in the limit is studied, with special reference to transformational languages on a given base. First a theorem is proved which gives necessary conditions for a class of languages to be identifiable in the limit. With added assumptions, these conditions become sufficient for identifiability. The question of whether the class of transformational languages on a fixed context-free base is identifiable is studied. Counterexamples, that is, context-free grammars for which the set of transformational languages is not identifiable, are exhibited. One of these examples involves no deletion, the use of the transformational cycle and only binary transformations.

If one claims to understand a particular phenomenon, then, in order to check that claim, we must decide what it is to understand that phenomenon. Another way of saying this is that we must decide for what the claimant is accountable.

Note that what the theorizer says about his accountability is not necessarily a criterion. For if he says that he is explaining this but not that, it may nevertheless be the case that we cannot understand this without understanding that.

In particular, suppose a claim is made that one understands language competence. That is, one puts forth a theory of linguistic competence. We can then ask whether this theory is accountable for an explanation of the acquisition of language.

We do not argue that a theory of linguistic competence must include a theory of language acquisition. It does seem possible that one can understand language and its use by humans without understanding how it was acquired.

But matters are not so simple. Suppose we agree that language competence is acquired. That is, early in a child's life he cannot speak and later on he can. Suppose, in addition, that we have a theory of mechanism which we believe is as powerful as anything the human mind could be. Then, if this mechanism can be shown incapable of acquiring language as conceived by the theory of linguistic competence, there is a lapse in our understanding for which we must account. The present work is undertaken in the spirit of demonstrating and illustrating this gap in our understanding.

1. IDENTIFIABILITY IN THE LIMIT

A *grammar* is a general rewriting system (see, for example, Hopcroft and Ullman, 1969). If G is a grammar, then $L(G)$ is the language generated by G.

Gold (1967) defined a notion of learnability of language in the following way. Suppose time is discrete and at each time the learner receives a piece of information about the language which he is learning. At each time the learner guesses the identity of the language. A class of languages is said to be *identifiable in the limit* if there is an algorithm such that, given any language in the class, there is a finite time after which the guesses will all be correct.

Gold considered various methods of information presentation. In text presentation, only positive instances of sentences in a language are allowed. In informant presentation, negative instances (identified as such) are allowed. Gold showed that informant presentation allowed a far wider class of languages to be identified. However, there is some reason to consider text presentation as a better model of the actual situation faced by the child as he acquires language. At first sight, at least, there appears to be a far larger number of positive instances given to a child. Also, what little empirical evidence there is (Brown and Hanlon, 1970) supports this view.

The definitions we present follow, with some modification, those found in Feldman (1969) and Feldman *et al.* (1969). An *information sequence* $I(L)$ of a language L is a sequence of sentences of L such that every sentence of the language appears in the sequence. Let $I(L) = a_1, a_2, \ldots$ be an information sequence. Then a sample (to time t) of I is $S_t(I) = \{a_1, \ldots, a_t\}$. Thus a sample is an unordered set.

A *learning device* D is a function from the set of samples (that is, the set of finite subsets of Σ^*) into the set of grammars in some class C. We conceive of $D(S_t(I))$ as being the guess that D makes at time t when presented with the information sequence I.

We say that the class of languages $L(C)$ is *identifiable in the limit* if there is an effective function D such that for any $G \in C$ and any information sequence $I(L(G))$ there exists a τ such that $t > \tau$ implies both

(a) $D(S_t(I)) = D(S_r(I))$, and

(b) $L(D(S_r(I))) = L(G)$.

Gold has shown that none of the usual classes of languages are identifiable in the limit. This includes the finite-state and context-free grammars. In fact, any class of languages which includes all the finite languages and at least one infinite language is not identifiable.

This result leaves us in the following dilemma. If none of the classes of languages normally taken as models for natural languages can be identified, how then is language learned? Before attempting an answer to this question, we will first find it useful to characterize some identifiable languages in the following way. We assume that a class of languages only includes recursive languages.

THEOREM. If a class of languages K is identifiable in the limit then K does not contain an infinite subset of languages $K' = \{L_0, L_1, L_2, \ldots\}$ such that

(1) $L_0 = \bigcup_{i=1}^{\infty} L_i$, and

(2)   for every finite subset F of L_0, there are an infinite number of $L_i \in K'$ such that $F \subseteq L_i$.

PROOF. We show that if K contains such a K' then K is not identifiable. Since it is well known that a superset of a nonidentifiable class is not identifiable, it will be sufficient to show that K' is not identifiable.

We construct an information sequence $I(L) = a_1, a_2, \ldots$ of elements of L_0 such that an infinite number of changes will be made in the guessed language. Let D be a function from samples into a class of grammars such that K' is identified in the limit by D. (We suppress $I(L)$ when the information sequence is fixed.)

To construct the sequence $I(L)$, first present a finite sequence $T_1 = a_1, a_2, \ldots, a_{t_1}$ such that $L(D(S_{t_1})) = L_1$, where $L_1, L_2, \ldots$ is an enumeration of $K' - \{L_0\}$. That is, after this sequence the learning device guesses a grammar for L_1. We know that such a sequence exists because D identifies K'. We next want to present a sequence that will make D guess another language. But we have to make sure that every sentence in L_0 appears in the information sequence. We can effectively enumerate the sentences of L_0, obtaining $b_1, b_2, \ldots$. After each of the sequences which causes D to change its guess we will add the next sentence of this enumeration, thus assuring that every sentence in L_0 appears at least once in the information sequence. Thus $I(L)$ starts with T_1, b_1. Let $i_1 = 1$.

By assumption 2, S_{t_1+1} is a subset of infinitely many L_i. Let i_2 be the smallest $i \neq 1$ such that $S_{t_1+1} \subseteq L_i$. Since S_{t_1+1} is finite and each L_i is recursive, there is an effective procedure for calculating i_2. Now let $T_2 = a_{t_1+2}, \ldots, a_{t_2}$ be a sequence of strings from L_{i_2} such that $L(D(S_{t_2})) = L_{i_2}$. Next we list b_2. Thus the information sequence up to $t_2 + 1$ is T_1, b_1, T_2, b_2.

We continue in this manner. The general rule is: after the sequence has been constructed up to time $t_j + 1$, add a sequence of strings from $L_{i_{j+1}}$ such that a grammar of L_{i_j} is guessed after that sequence, where $L_{i_{j+1}}$ is the first language in the enumeration of the L_i which contains the sample up to time $t_j + 1$ and such that for $1 \leq k \leq j, L_{i_k} \neq L_{i_{j+1}}$, that is, the guessed language is not one of those guessed at an earlier time i_k. The reason we can always choose a new language which contains the sample is that property 2 holds. Then add b_{j+1}.

In this manner we construct the sequence

$$I(L) = T_1, b_1, T_2, b_2, \ldots, T_i, b_i, \ldots.$$

At each time t_i a grammar is guessed which is different from the grammar guessed at all earlier $t_j, j \leq i$. Thus by definition D does not identify K'. We have shown that if K is identifiable, no such K' exists. This proves the theorem.

As far as we know, this theorem is new. The following examples illustrate the theorem.

EXAMPLE 1. (Feldman *et al.*, 1969). Let $L_0 = a^*b^*$.

For each $i > 0$, let

$$L_i = \bigcup_{j=1}^{i} a^j b^*,$$

where a^j means a sequence of j a's and $a^j b^* = \{a^j b, a^j bb, a^j bbb, \ldots\}$, as in regular language terminology.

Then $K = \{L_0, L_1, \ldots\}$ meets conditions 1 and 2 of the theorem and thus K is not identifiable in the limit.

EXAMPLE 2. Let $K = \{L_1, L_2, \ldots\}$ where L_i is as in the preceding example. In other words, L_0 is excluded. Then K has no subset which satisfies the conditions of the theorem. This does not, of course, prove that K is identifiable, but it turns out that it is. A successful algorithm is the following: Guess a grammar which generates the first language in the enumeration $L_1, L_2, \ldots$ which is compatible with (i.e., includes) the sample to date. Eventually this will be the correct grammar.

EXAMPLE 3. This example shows that a nested infinite sequence of languages $L_1 \subseteq L_2 \subseteq \ldots$ is not necessary for nonidentifiability. For any vocabulary T, enumerate the strings in T^*, obtaining $a_1, a_2, \ldots$. Let $L_i = \{T^* - a_i\}$ for $i > 0$ and let $L_0 = T^*$. Then $K = \{L_0, L_1, \ldots\}$ is not identifiable since it meets the conditions of the theorem. But there is no infinite nested sequence of languages in K.

EXAMPLE 4. If $L_0 = T^*$ is left out of K in the preceding example, K becomes identifiable. Enumerate the grammars and at each time pick the first compatible grammar.

EXAMPLE 5. To see that condition 1 of the theorem may not be omitted, consider the languages $L_i, i > 0$, of example 1 and add a string c to each of them, obtaining $L_i' = L_i \bigcup \{c\}$. Since c is not in L_0, the union of the L_1 is not equal to L_0. Thus $K = \{L_0, L_1', L_2', \ldots\}$ does not meet condition 1. In fact, K is identifiable. Guess a grammar for L_0 until c appears and then guess a grammar for the first compatible language in the enumeration $L_1', L_2', \ldots$.

EXAMPLE 6. To see that condition 2 of the theorem may not be omitted, let $L_0 = a^*b^*$ and let $L_i = a^i b^*$. Then $K = \{L_0, L_1, \ldots\}$ does not meet condition 2 of the theorem, since, for example, $\{abb, aab\}$ is a finite subset of L_0 which is not a subset of infinitely many of the L_i. In fact it is a subset only of L_0. K is identifiable by guessing a grammar for L_i if the first string presented is $a^i b^j$ and changing the guess to a grammar for L_0 whenever a string of the form $a^k b^g, i \neq k$, is encountered.

The reason we have gone over so many examples is to motivate the conjecture that, in fact, the conditions of the theorem are not only sufficient, but necessary, that is, if $K' \subseteq K$ meeting conditions 1 and 2 does not exist, then K is identifiable. In all our examples where K' failed to meet conditions 1 and 2, it turned out to be identifiable. All the examples we have found in the literature conform to this hypothesis. In fact, we have proved the following, weaker, theorem.

THEOREM. If K is a class of recursive languages such that there is an effective procedure for enumerating the grammars for the languages in K, and if there is an effective procedure for deciding, for any two grammars G_i, G_j of languages in K, whether $L(G_i) \subseteq L(G_j)$, then K is identifiable in the limit if it does not contain an infinite subset $K' = \{L_0, L_1, \ldots\}$ such that

(1) $L_0 = \bigcup_{i=1}^{\infty} L_i$, and

(2)   for every finite subset F of L_0, there are an infinite number of $L_i \in K'$ such that $F \subseteq L_i$.

SKETCH OF PROOF. We construct an algorithm D which will identify any language in K. Enumerate the grammars for K, obtaining G_1, G_2, ... The information sequence is a_1, a_2, ... At time t, D guesses a grammar from $A_t = \{G_1, \ldots, G_t\}$. First form the set $C_t \subseteq A_t$ of compatible grammars, that is, grammars which generate the strings $a_1, \ldots, a_t$. Next, form the set $M_t \subseteq C_t$ of minimal grammars, that is, $G_i \in C_t$ is minimal if there is no $G_j \subseteq C_t$ such that $L(G_j) \subseteq L(G_i)$. Then D guesses that grammar in M_t which is first in the enumeration, that is, which has the smallest i.

Our assumption makes D effective. We show that eventually G_i is guessed when $L(G_i)$ is presented. Suppose that $L(G_i)$ does not contain an infinite number of subsets in K. Then there is some time t' such that for all $t > t'$, no grammar for a subset of $L(G_i)$ is in C_t. Thus, for $t > t'$, $G_i \in M_t$. Also, there is a time t'' such that for each $G_j, j < i, G_j$ will be eliminated from C_t for $t > t''$, as long as $L(G_j)$ is not a superset of $L(G_j)$. Thus for $t > \max(t', t'')$, D guesses G_i. Thus we consider only L_0 such that L_0 contains an infinite number of languages $L_1, L_2, \ldots$.

Clearly, $L_0 \supseteq \bigcup_{i=1}^{\infty} L_i$. Suppose $a \in L_0$ but $a \notin L_i$ for any L_i. But then when a appears, at time t, only grammars for L_0 will be in C_t. Thus D will guess a grammar for L_0. Thus we can consider only cases where $L_0 = \bigcup_{i=1}^{\infty} L_i$.

Suppose condition 2 does not hold, that is, there is a subset F of L_0 such that F is contained in only a finite number of the L_i. But then once F has been presented, there are only a finite number of grammars G_i which are compatible with the sample. Each of these (except for grammars for supersets of the correct language) is eventually eliminated from C_t, and thus M_t contains only the correct grammar, and D identifies the grammar. This proves the theorem.

The 'recursive' and 'enumeration' conditions will perhaps be necessary to prove the theorem, and are not very restrictive from our point of view, since they are met for example by the set of context-sensitive languages. The condition we hope to eliminate is the one which requires decidability of the subset problem. Our current proof requires this condition because the algorithm D must determine what languages in a finite set are minimal. It is an open problem whether this condition can be eliminated.

2. TRANSFORMATIONAL GRAMMARS ON A UNIVERSAL BASE

It has been known since Gold's original formulation that the classes of languages which are usually studied are not identifiable in the limit. This is true of the finite-state, context-free and context-sensitive languages. This result is an immediate corollary of our first theorem applied to the class of languages defined in example 1 of the preceding section.

This result leads to an attempt to restrict the class of possible languages in such a way that the class is identifiable. It would be particularly insightful if this restriction could be done in a linguistically interesting way. A strong interpretation of one version of linguistic theory (Chomsky, 1965) is that there is a single universal context-free base, and every natural language is defined by a transformational grammar on that base. At first sight it might appear that if we fixed the base and considered the class of languages to be the set of transformational languages on the base, then, since all the languages were related by virtue of having a common base, this class of languages might be identifiable in the limit.

It is important to realize that we are suggesting the class of transformational languages on a given base, not the set of all transformational languages. That is, let B be a context-free grammar and T_i a finite set of transformations. Then we are considering the class of languages $K = \bigcup_i T_i(B)$, and not the class $\bigcup_B \bigcup_i T_i(B)$. This latter class is clearly not identifiable since it includes all the context-free languages, which may be obtained by taking the identity transformation on each base language.

Peters and Ritchie (1972) have shown that the set of transformational languages on a fixed base is equal to the set of recursively enumerable languages. Thus this set is not identifiable. However, it is still interesting to see whether we obtain identifiable classes of languages when we use only transformational models of limited power. For example, what happens when we do not allow deletion?

In the following examples we will have to use some notation from transformational theory. When the transformations get a little complex and we want to be precise, we will use notation from the transformational model developed by Ginsburg and Partee (1969). The reader unfamiliar with these notions is referred to this paper. Here we only recall that a transformational rule is a pair consisting of an 'analysis' or a 'domain statement' and a 'structural change' on that domain statement.

3. A NONIDENTIFIABLE CLASS OF TRANSFORMATIONAL LANGUAGES

If B is a context-free grammar, let $T(B)$ be the set of transformational languages on B. We will exhibit a context-free grammar B such that $T(B)$ contains all the finite languages on a vocabulary and an infinite language. Gold showed that such a 'superfinite' class was not identifiable and such a result follows easily from our first theorem.

We take as the base the grammar B which has the following rules:

$$S \to cS'$$
$$S' \to aS'$$
$$S' \to bS'$$
$$S' \to a$$
$$S' \to b$$

where S is the starting symbol and $\{a,b,c\}$ is the terminal vocabulary. Thus the generated language $L(B) = c(a,b)^*$. Now, to show that any finite language on $\{a,b\}$ may be generated from B by a finite set of transformations, we will define the transformations.

Suppose $F = \{s_1, \ldots, s_n\}$ is a finite set of strings on $(a,b)^*$ and suppose $s_i = cx_{i1}x_{i2} \ldots x_{in_i}$ where $x_{ij} = a$ or b. Then for each s_i we define the transformation T_i in the following way.

T_i: domain statement $D = c,x_{i1},\ldots,x_{in_i}$
    structural change $C = \phi, 1, \ldots, n_i$.

Note that ϕ is the symbol for the empty string. The effect of T_i is to erase the c from s_i, and to leave all other sentences untouched. Define the transformation

T_0 : domain statement $D = c,S'$

structural change $C = \phi,\phi$.

T_0 deletes any string in $L(B)$ which has a c in it. Now to generate F we simply take the $n + 1$ transformations $T_1, T_2, \ldots, T_n, T_0$ in that order, i.e., in particular, T_0 must apply last. Then the effect of $T_1, \ldots, T_n$ is to delete the c from each s_i in F. T_0 then deletes all strings except those in F. Thus F is the generated language.

Now, $(a,b)^*$ is also a transformational language on B since we can define a transformation T with domain statement c,S' and structural change $\phi,2$, which simply deletes c from each string. The grammar consisting only of T thus generates $(a,b)^*$. Thus every finite language on $\{a,b\}$ and at least one infinite language is in $T(B)$, which is thus not identifiable in the limit.

4. A MORE SATISFYING NONIDENTIFIABLE CLASS OF TRANSFORMATIONAL LANGUAGES

One reason why we are not happy with the preceding example is because it depends so heavily on deletion, and, in fact, filtering, that is, base sentences which never reach the surface. In our search for nonidentifiable classes of transformational languages, we can use the first theorem which we proved. If we require that each base sentence correspond to only one surface sentence, then the base grammar must generate an infinite language (or else all languages in $T(B)$ would be finite and thus the class would be identifiable). But if we do not want to use filtering of sentences, then an infinite base language will yield an infinite transformed language. Thus we need classes of languages in which each language is infinite. The theorem tells us that if we find a class with certain properties then it is not identifiable in the limit.

The class of languages we will generate from a universal base is $K = \{L_0, L_1, \ldots\}$, where

$$L_0 = \{a^j cb^j | j = 1,2,\ldots\} \bigcup \{b^j a^{j+1} cb | j = 1,2,\ldots\},$$

and for $i > 0$,

$$L_i = \{a^j cb^j | j = 1,2,\ldots\} \bigcup \{b^j a^{j+1} cb | j = 1,2,\ldots,i\}.$$

Clearly conditions 1 and 2 of the theorem hold, and K is not identifiable in the limit.

The base grammar B is defined by the following rules:

$$S \rightarrow aSb$$
$$S \rightarrow acb$$
$$S \rightarrow abc.$$

Note that the strings in $L(B)$ can be classified according to whether the last rule applied yielded acb or abc. The former will yield all strings of the form $a^j cb^j$. No transformations will apply to these strings and thus they will account for the first part of each L_i. The other kind of string ends with a rule yielding abc. For the language L_0, every string of the form $a^{j+1} bcb^j$ will be mapped into the string $b^j a^{j+1} cb$, thus yielding the other strings in L_0. For the language L_i every string of the form $a^{j+1} bcb^j$ will be mapped into $b^j a^{j+1} cb$ if $j \leq i$, but if $j > i$ then the string will be mapped into $a^{j+1} cb^{+1}$ which is already in L_i and thus nothing new will be added to the language. Thus for each $L_i, i > 0$, a finite number of the 'noncentral c' strings will be mapped into a new string, and all the rest will be mapped into strings which were already directly generated by B. Note that the grammar for $L_i, i > 0$, is ambiguous since L_i contains strings which have two derivations.

We assume in this example the principle of the transformational cycle, that is, transformations first apply to the most deeply embedded S, then the next highest, and so on. Ginsburg and Partee (1969) write this ordering restriction into the definition of each transformation, but for simplicity we will take it as a meta-rule.

The transformations will operate in the following manner. Suppose we want to generate language L_i. First T_0 operates by bringing b in the most deeply embedded S up front in the next highest S-dominated subtree. Then T_1 brings this b and another b from the rear to the front in the next highest subtree. In other words, with each new transformation applied, an additional b is added to the front of the new (transformed) terminal string. Thus the ability to generate these kinds of strings in L_i. But if the phrase-marker on which the transformations are working has more than i S's, i.e., more than i a's and b's, then if this process continues a string with more than i b's in front will be in the language, contrary to its definition. And if the transformations just stop applying, a sentence with a number of a's, then a number of b's, then more a's will be generated. This sentence is also not in L_i. Thus we apply the transformations $\bar{T}_i$. This transformation counts the number of b's at the front of the string, and as soon as this number becomes greater than i, the entire string of beginning b's is shifted to the end of the sentence, thus producing a sentence already in the language (directly from the base) and not allowing any more transformations to apply.

The language L_i will be generated by a grammar with $i + 2$ obligatory transformations, $T_0, T_1 \ldots, T_i, \bar{T}_i$. Before we define these transformations, consider L_1 as an example. Let D be the domain statement and C the structural change.

$T_0.\ D = aabcb.\ C = $ ③ ① $-$ ② $-$ ϕ $-$ ④ $-$ ⑤.
$T_1.\ D = abaSbb.\ C = $ ② ⑤ ① $-$ ϕ $-$ ③ $-$ ④ $-$ ϕ $-$ ⑥.
$\bar{T}_1.\ D = abbaSbb.\ C = $ ① $-$ ϕ $-$ ϕ $-$ ④ $-$ ⑤ $-$ ⑥ $-$ ⑦ ② ③.

The operation of these transformations on the base phrase-marker P is shown in Figure 1. P_0, P_1 and $\bar{P}_1$ are the resulting phrase-markers after the application of T_0, T_1 and $\bar{T}_1$, respectively. Figure 2 attempts to diagram the example in another way.

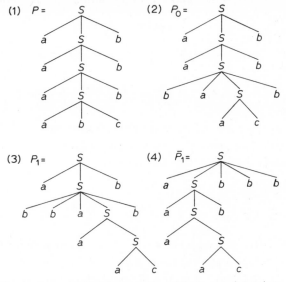

Fig. 1.   An example of the operation of the L_1 transformations.

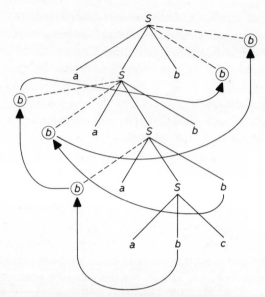

Fig. 2.   The same operations as in Figure 1.

The definitions of the needed transformations are as follows.

T_0. As above. For $i > 0$,

T_i. $D = ab^i aSbb$. $C =$

$$② \quad ③ \quad \dots \quad ⓘ_{(i+1)} \quad ⓘ_{(i+4)} \quad ① \quad - \quad \underbrace{\phi \quad - \quad \dots \quad - \quad \phi}_{i} \quad - \quad ⓘ_{(i+2)} \quad - \quad ⓘ_{(i+3)} \quad - \quad \phi \quad - \quad ⓘ_{(i+5)}.$$

$\overline{T}_i$. $D = ab^{i+1} aSbb$. $C =$

$$① \quad - \quad \underbrace{\phi \quad - \quad \dots \quad - \quad \phi}_{i+1} \quad - \quad ⓘ_{(i+3)} \quad - \quad ⓘ_{(i+4)} \quad - \quad ⓘ_{(i+5)} \quad - \quad ⓘ_{(i+6)} \quad ② \quad ③ \quad \dots \quad ⓘ_{(i+2)}.$$

The language L_i, then, is generated by the transformations $T_0, T_1, \dots, T_i, \overline{T}_i$. It remains only to define the transformations for L_0. L_0 is generated by the previously defined T_0 together with T.

T. $D = aXaSbb$. $C =$

$$② \quad ⑤ \quad ① \quad - \quad \phi \quad - \quad ③ \quad - \quad ④ \quad - \quad \phi \quad - \quad ⑥$$

T accomplishes the same operation as T_i does, but without bound. That is, T raises the string of b's at the beginning of the string and adds to them one from the end, and it does this no matter how long the string of b's. A variable (X) was used for the first time in the definition of T. This is also the first place in which we have departed from the Ginsburg and Partee model, because X was moved to a different position in the structural change, contrary to the Ginsburg and Partee assumption.

These grammars, then, generate the class K, which is thus a subset of the class of transformational languages on the fixed base B. But K is not identifiable in the limit. Thus $L(B)$, the set of transformational languages on B, is not identifiable.

The properties of our grammar are interesting. First, we have not used deletion at all, and yet have obtained nonidentifiability. Also, we have applied the transformational cycle. All transformations are binary, that is, they analyze only two depths (of S's) down. Only one transformation applies to each S-dominated subtree.

Hamburger and Wexler (this volume, pp. 153–66) investigated the possibility of identifying the transformational mapping when (base, surface) pairs were presented. With transformations of exactly the above properties (with one exception, to be discussed below), a positive answer was obtained; the mapping is identifiable. Thus, with very similar grammars we have found in one case that the languages are not identifiable with only surface information presented, but they are identifiable when pairs of base and surface were presented.

The one exception involves restrictions on 'raising' (Hamburger and Wexler, this volume, pp. 153–66) which are not made here, and on which, in fact, our grammars fail. If we could find an example of nonidentifiable (in our sense, from surface information) languages which also meet the raising restriction, or equivalently, if we could eliminate the raising restriction from the set of assumptions in the base, surface pair case, then we could conclude formally that base information is necessary for the class of transformational languages on a universal base to be identifiable.

University of California, Irvine

P. STANLEY PETERS, JR. AND R. W. RITCHIE

NONFILTERING AND LOCAL-FILTERING TRANSFORMATIONAL GRAMMARS*

1. INTRODUCTION

A transformational grammar delimits a set of grammatical sentences by virtue of containing (a) a base component which generates a set of base Phrase-markers (labeled trees or labeled bracketings), (b) a transformational component which maps these into derived Phrase-markers and (c) filter predicates which pose a further admissibility condition on the latter Phrase-markers. A string x is grammatical according to such a grammar if there is a Phrase-marker generated by the base component which is mapped by the transformational component to a Phrase-marker satisfying all the filter predicates and having x as its terminal string. Thus all these three parts of a grammar play a role in specifying what strings are grammatical – the base component by determining what Phrase-markers will be available for transformations to operate on, the transformational component by converting these inputs into derived Phrase-markers, the filter predicates by excluding certain of these outputs as inadmissible.

It is known (Peters and Ritchie, 1972) that every transformationally generable language is generated by a grammar with no filter predicates. In obtaining this result, we permitted the base component to be any context-sensitive grammar; we can then have the base generate all output tapes of a Turing machine and the transformational component delete 'blank' symbols from these strings. As we showed, one can insure deletion of all 'blanks' without using filter predicates, so every recursively enumerable language is generated without filtering (and only these languages are generated by arbitrary transformational grammars). Thus no generative power is lost if we restrict transformational grammars to not utilizing filter predicates. We have also shown (Peters and Ritchie, 1971) that every recursively enumerable language is generated by a transformational grammar with a context-free base component. Therefore, the base can be restricted in this way without loss of weak generative power. In proving

Hintikka et al. (eds.), Approaches to Natural Language, 180–194. All rights reserved.
Copyright © 1973 by D. Reidel Publishing Company, Dordrecht-Holland.

the latter result we made heavy use of filtering, however.

Thus we are led to the question whether simultaneously outlawing use of filter predicates and restricting the base component to context-free diminishes the class of languages that are generated. Before tackling this question, we sketch a few more details of transformational grammars that will play a role in later proofs. For complete definitions, the reader may consult Sections 2–4 of Peters and Ritchie (1972). The base component performs three essential functions in a transformational grammar. (1) It provides a set of Phrase-markers (labeled bracketings) as inputs to the transformational component. (2) It controls cycling in transformational derivations by distinguishing one of the phrase types (labels which appear on brackets) as the category of sentences. (3) It distinguishes a terminal symbol as the 'sentence boundary' symbol for reference by filter predicates.

The transformational component is a finite, linearly ordered sequence of grammatical transformations. Each transformation T consists of a structural condition – specifying what Phrase-markers T is applicable to – and a set of elementary transformations – specifying what modification T effects on each Phrase-marker to which it is applicable. The transformations are applied in cycles to form a sequence of Phrase-markers beginning with any base Phrase-marker; each cycle of transformations operates on a sub-Phrase-marker belonging to the category of sentences (a 'subsentence'). At the onset of each cycle, one chooses as the subsentence to be operated on the leftmost one such that all subsentences it properly contains have already been operated on by the transformational cycle. After selection of the appropriate subsentence φ, the cycle operates as follows. Let $\tau = (T_1, \ldots, T_n)$ be the transformational component. Examine each transformation $T_1, T_2 \ldots$ in turn until the first one T_i is reached which is applicable to φ. Form φ' from φ by carrying out the deletions, substitutions and adjunctions indicated in T_i. Now examine $T_{i+1}, T_{i+2}, \ldots$ until the first subsequent transformation T_j is reached which is applicable to φ'. Form φ'' from φ' by applying T_j. Continue this process until the end of the sequence $(T_1, \ldots, T_n)$ is reached. The sequence $\varphi, \varphi', \varphi'', \ldots, \varphi^{(k)}$ of (sub-)Phrase-markers thereby obtained constitutes one cycle of the derivation. Transformational cycles operate in this fashion, beginning with a base Phrase-marker and continuing until every subsentence has been operated upon. The result is a sequence of Phrase-markers called a transformational derivation, the final member of which is a derived Phrase-marker.

Following Chomsky (1965), we require that a derived Phrase-marker φ satisfy a filter predicate specifying that it contain no occurrences of the sentence boundary symbol distinguished by the base component if φ is to be generated by the transformational grammar. Perlmutter (1970a, b) has convincingly argued that empirically adequate transformational grammars must contain other sorts of filter predicates stating admissibility conditions on derived Phrase-markers. We do not attempt to formalize his 'surface structure constraints' here since the present paper is concerned with grammars in which filtering is heavily restricted, but such formalization is clearly of importance for future studies dealing with the general form of transformational grammar.

2. BASIC CONCEPTS

Given a transformational grammar containing filter predicates, one may begin with a base Phrase-marker and construct a lengthy transformational derivation only to discover at the last step that it is filtered out by an admissibility condition on surface structures. With a nonfiltering grammar this situation could never arise, of course. So intuitively it might seem that enumerating the language generated by a grammar with filtering is inherently less efficient than enumerating the language of a nonfiltering grammar provided that one can enumerate the set of base Phrase-markers efficiently. This notion is worthy of further exploration since Marsh and Ritchie (to appear) have shown that if a set can be enumerated efficiently enough, then it belongs to a proper subclass of the class of all recursively enumerable sets. This suggests that we might be able to show that the languages generated by context-free based nonfiltering transformational grammars can be enumerated efficiently enough to be in this restricted subclass.

In order to make this precise, we repeat here Marsh and Ritchie's crucial definition.

DEFINITION 1: A language L is *predictably enumerable* if it is finite or if there are both a Turing machine Z and an elementary recursive function[1] a such that

(i) L is the language enumerated by Z and

(ii) Z enumerates at least $n + 1$ distinct members of L in computations using at most $a(n)$ squares of tape for every natural number n.

For a predictably enumerable language, the amount of storage required to enumerate an arbitrary number of its members is predictably computable.[2] Marsh and Ritchie prove that the predictably enumerable languages are precisely the finite sets together with the ranges of one-to-one elementary recursive functions. In proving many of our statements, the following result of Marsh and Ritchie (to appear, Theorem 1), stated here without proof, will be useful.

LEMMA 1: If L is a recursively enumerable language with an infinite predictably enumerable subset, then L is predictably enumerable.

The same arguments which show that nonfiltering transformational grammars generate easily enumerated languages also apply in the presence of restricted filtering of a sort which we now define.

DEFINITION 2: A transformational grammar G is *local-filtering* if every transformational derivation D of G satisfies the following condition: if the output of any cycle of D contains a sentence boundary symbol, then D's last line contains a sentence boundary; i.e., if there is a $j \leq p$ such that ψ_{j,i_j} contains $\#$, then $\sigma_p \psi_{p,i_p} \tau_p$ contains $\#$ in Definition 4.2 in Peters and Ritchie (1972). The class C of languages is defined to contain just those languages generated by context-free based local-filtering transformational grammars.

Any transformational grammar which has no filter predicates satisfies Definition 2. The linguistic interpretation of local-filtering in the presence of a context-free base is that subordinate clauses are transformed versions of sentences. We shall show in Lemma 3 that for such grammars transformations, in effect, operate on surface structures.

The class C obviously contains all context-free languages. It also contains some noncontext-free languages, for example, $L_{e_1} = \{a^n | n = 2^m, m \geq 0\}$, as we show by constructing a context-free based local-filtering transformational grammar G_{e_1} which generates L_{e_1}.

EXAMPLE: Let the base component of G_{e_1} be the context-free grammar $\langle V_T, V_N, S, \#, \rightarrow \rangle$, where $V_T = \{a, \#\}$, $V_N = \{S\}$, and $S \rightarrow aS$ and $S \rightarrow a$. Since these base rules do not introduce $\#$ into any generated string, a transformational grammar containing this base component is nonfiltering. Let the transformational component of G_{e_1} contain the single transformation specified in the usual informal linguistic notation as:

$$a - S$$
$$1 \quad 2$$
$$\Rightarrow 2 \quad 2$$

i.e., the transformation which applies to a subsentence if it consists of a followed by any subsentence φ and replaces the occurrence of a by φ. Each cycle of a transformational derivation doubles the number of a's produced as output of the preceding cycle, so the base Phrase-marker

$$[_S a[_S a \cdots [_S a]_S \cdots]_S]_S,$$
$$\underbrace{\qquad\qquad\qquad}_{m}$$

which has 'S-depth' m, underlies the sentence containing 2^m occurrences of a.

3. RESULTS

We are now able to state the following theorem, the proof of which will be deferred to Section IV.

THEOREM 1: If L is in C, then

(i) L is predictably enumerable and

(ii) if L is infinite, then there is a constant K such that for every natural number n some $x \, \varepsilon \, L$ satisfies $K^n \leq \ell(x) < K^{n+1}$.

COROLLARY 1: The language $L_{e_2} = \{a^n | n = 2^{2^m}, m \geq 0\}$ is not in C.

PROOF: Note that the string containing $2^{2^{m+1}}$ symbols is 2^{2^m} times as long as the next shorter string in L_{e_2}, violating condition (ii) of Theorem 1.

REMARK 1: Since L_{e_2} is the range of a one-to-one elementary function it is predictably enumerable. Therefore, the containment of C in the class of predictably enumerable languages is proper.

REMARK 2: Clearly L_{e_2} is a context-sensitive language, since it is accepted by a linear bounded automaton. Therefore, there is a context-sensitive language not in C.

These remarks settle the question we raised in Section I. Restricting transformational grammars by jointly requiring the base component to be a context-free grammar and limiting the use of filtering as we have here turns out to have a major effect on weak generative power. Some relatively simple (i.e., context-sensitive) languages are not generated by transformational grammars restricted in this way. This restriction is not as strong as one might at first think though. We will show this by means of Theorem 2.

THEOREM 2: For every recursively enumerable language L there are a regular language L_1 and a language L_2 in C such that $L = L_1 \cap L_2$. In fact, L_2 can be chosen so that it is generated by a context-free based transformational grammar whose base rules do not introduce the sentence boundary symbol at all.

PROOF: In proving that every recursively enumerable language is generated by a context-free based transformational grammar, we made use of the following filter predicate: Phrase-marker φ does not contain the sentence boundary symbol (Peters and Ritchie, 1971, Theorem 1). The proof of that theorem can be modified to yield our present theorem in the following way. Let L be any recursively enumerable language over alphabet A. We showed how to construct a context-free based transformational grammar G which generates L. G has as its terminal vocabulary $A \cup \{b, \#\}$, where b and $\#$ are distinct symbols not in A, $\#$ being the boundary symbol. We can now construct G_2 from G by adding a new symbol c to G's terminal vocabulary and replacing all occurrences of $\#$ by c in the *rules*, both base and transformational. Grammar G_2 makes no use of the filter predicate stated above, since its base component still distinguishes $\#$ as the boundary symbol but no Phrase-markers generated by either base or transformational rules of G_2 contain $\#$. Uniform replacement of $\#$ by c in G's rules still permits generation of every string which is generated by G, since the derivations of G_2 are exactly those of G except that $\#$ is replaced in every Phrase-marker by c. Putting $L_2 = L(G_2)$, we have $L = L(G) \subseteq L(G_2) = L_2$. Let $L_1 = A^*$, the set of all finite strings over A. We wish to show that $L = L_1 \cap L_2$. Note first that any string in L is in both L_1 (trivially) and L_2 (since $L \subseteq L_2$), hence $L \subseteq L_1 \cap L_2$. Now letting x be any string in $L_1 \cap L_2$, observe that a derivation of x by G_2 yields a derivation of x by G if we replace c by $\#$. Furthermore $x \varepsilon L_1$ insures that this derivation will not be filtered out in G since x, the terminal string of the derived Phrase-marker, contains no c (to be replaced by $\#$) or $\#$. Hence $L_1 \cap L_2 \subseteq L(G) = L$. We observe that L_1 is a regular language and note that L_2 is not only in C but is generated without filtering to complete the proof.

COROLLARY 2: C contains a nonrecursive language.

PROOF: (Due to Frank W. Heny). Let L be any nonrecursive but recursively enumerable language. By Theorem 2, there are a regular language L_1 and a language L_2 in C such that $L = L_1 \cap L_2$. Now L_1 is recursive and the set of all recursive languages is closed under intersection. Hence L_2 is not recursive.

Theorem 2 also allows us to settle a question raised by Kimball (1967, p. 181). He asks whether nonfiltering context-free based languages are closed under intersection with regular languages.

COROLLARY 3: C is not closed under intersection with regular languages. In fact, the class of languages generated by context-free based transformational grammars whose base rules do not introduce sentence boundaries is not closed under intersection with regular languages.

PROOF: Let L be any recursively enumerable language which is not in C, e.g., L_{e_2} of Corollary 1. Theorem 2 guarantees the existence of a regular language L_1 and a language L_2 in C such that $L = L_1 \cap L_2$. If C were closed under intersection with regular languages, then L would be in C. Theorem 2, in fact, guarantees that L_2 may be chosen so as to be generable without any use of the boundary symbol.

COROLLARY 4: C is not closed under intersection.

PROOF: By Corollary 4, since trivially every regular language is in C.

Remark 2 and Corollary 2 show that C, although it contains all context-free languages, is incomparable with any class containing the context-sensitive languages and contained in the recursive languages. Hence C does not fit into well-known hierarchies of languages.

Although unrestricted use of filtering is not justified by empirical evidence, some filtering is an empirical necessity in the description of natural languages. It is interesting that even if we generalize local-filtering somewhat, allow certain uses of Perlmutter's surface structure constraints and redefine C as the languages generated by a class of grammars that employ filtering in this way, then all our results would remain true as stated. Thus, it appears that the ability of context-free based transformational grammars to generate arbitrary recursively enumerable languages involves use of filtering in a way that is empirically unjustified and linguistically unnatural.

4. SUPPORTING ARGUMENTS

We present in this section a series of results culminating in a proof of

Theorem 1. A detailed understanding of this part presupposes familiarity with the definitions given in Peters and Ritchie (1972). Our next lemma reduces the problem of proving that a transformational grammar generates a predictably enumerable language to the corresponding problem for surface structures, those derived Phrase-markers which satisfy all filter predicates. As we defined them, Phrase-markers are reduced terminal labeled bracketings; the terminal string of a Phrase-marker is its de-bracketization, the string obtained by erasing all brackets and their labels.

LEMMA 2: If f is a one-to-one elementary recursive function whose range is a set of reduced labeled bracketings for which there is a constant K such that $\ell(f(n)) \leq K \cdot \max_{i < n} \ell(f(i))$, then,

(i) the range of $d \circ f$ is predictably enumerable and[3]

(ii) there is a constant K such that for every natural number n some $x \varepsilon$ Range $(d \circ f)$ satisfies $K^n \leq \ell(x) < K^{n+1}$.

PROOF: Since $f(i)$ is a reduced labeled bracketing, $\ell(f(i)) \leq (4q + 1)\ell(d(f(i)))$, where q is the cardinality of V_N (Peters and Ritchie, 1972, Lemma 2.4) and hence Range $(d \circ f)$ is infinite. Furthermore

$$(1) \qquad \ell(d(f(n))) \leq \ell(f(n)) \leq K(4q + 1) \cdot \max_{i < n} \ell(d(f(i))).$$

To establish (ii), put $K = K(4q + 1) + \ell(d(f(0)))$. Assume that for some $n \geq 0$, there is no $x \varepsilon$ Range $(d \circ f)$ such that $K^n \leq \ell(x) < K^{n+1}$. Since Range $(d \circ f)$ is infinite there is a least j such that $\ell(d(f(j))) \geq K^{n+1}$. From the assumption it follows that no $i < j$ satisfies $\ell(d(f(j))) \leq K \cdot \ell(d(f(i)))$, hence $j = 0$ by Equation (1). But $\ell(d(f(0))) < K$, which contradicts our choice of j to be the least producing a debracketization whose length is greater than or equal to K^{n+1}.

To establish (i), we appeal to the observation in Marsh and Ritchie (to appear) that the range of an elementary recursive function φ is predictably enumerable if there is an elementary recursive ψ such that $\{\varphi(0), \ldots, \varphi(\psi(n))\}$ contains at least $n + 1$ elements. The function $d \circ f$ is elementary recursive and to show that its range is predictably enumerable we show that in $\{d(f(0)), \ldots, d(f(K_1^{K_2^n}))\}$ there are at least $n + 1$ elements, where K_1 and K_2 are defined below. For every n, let m_n be the least number such that $\{d(f(0)), \ldots, d(f(m_n))\}$ contains $n + 1$ elements. From inequality (1) by induction on n, we obtain $\ell(d(f(m_n))) \leq (K(4q + 1))^n \ell(d(f(0)))$. Thus for no $i \leq m_n$ is it possible that $\ell(f(i)) > (4q + 1)(K(4q + 1))^n \ell(d(f(0)))$ or else $d(f(i))$ would be longer than $d(f(0))$, $d(f(m_1))$, ..., $d(f(m_n))$. There are only $(p + 3q + 1)^{(4q+1)(K(4q+1))^n \ell(d(f(0)))}$ labeled bracketings of this length at most, since any labeled bracketings of length ℓ or less can be regarded as a string of length exactly ℓ on an alphabet containing p terminal symbols, q nonterminals, $2q$ labeled brackets and one 'blank' symbol. Setting $K_1 = p + 3q + 1$ and $K_2 = K(4q + 1)^2 \ell(d(f(0)))$, we note that m_n must be less than or equal to $K_1^{K_2^n}$ to complete the proof of the lemma.

In order to use Lemma 2 in proving Theorem 1 we must show that there is a predictable enumeration of surface structures which is appropriately 'dense'. To this end, we construct an ascending chain of base Phrase-markers and a corresponding chain of surface structures, which can be enumerated in such a fashion. The ascending chain $\Delta_1, \Delta_2, \Delta_3, \ldots$ of base Phrase-markers is constructed so that Δ_i contains just those of S-depth at most i. The S-depth of a Phrase-marker φ is intuitively the maximum depth of nesting of subsentences of φ. The set Σ_i of surface structures in the corresponding chain contains just those surface structures transformationally derived from elements of Δ_i. From the intuitive description of Δ_i in terms of S-depth, it is apparent that Δ_i consists of all Phrase-markers formed by substituting elements of Δ_{i-1} for S's in the set of labeled bracketings of S-depth precisely one generated by the base component.

DEFINITION 3: Let $B = \langle V_T, V_N, S, \#, \rightarrow \rangle$ be a context-free grammar. We define Γ to be the language weakly generated by the context-free grammar $\langle V_T', V_N', S', \#, \Rightarrow \rangle$, where $V_T' = V_T \cup \{S\} \cup L \cup R$, $V_N' = (V_N \cup \{S'\}) - \{S\}$, and $A \Rightarrow [_A \varphi]_A$ if $A \rightarrow \varphi$ and $A \neq S$ while $S' \Rightarrow [_S \varphi]_S$ if $S \rightarrow \varphi$. Here L and R are respectively the sets of left $[_A$ and right $]_A$ brackets labeled by symbols of V_N, and S' is a new symbol.

There is a constant K_b such that for any string φ in Γ except those with least number of symbols in V_T, some $\psi \varepsilon \Gamma$ contains a number of symbols in V_T which is at most K_b fewer than the number φ contains (cf. Hopcroft and Ullman, 1969, Theorem 4.7, p. 57).

DEFINITION 4: Let $G = (B, \tau)$ be a transformational grammar with context-free base component B and transformational component τ. Set $\Delta_1 = \Gamma \cap (V_T \cup L \cup R)^*$, and define, for each $i \geq 1$, Δ_{i+1} to be the union of the complete substitutions of Δ_i into elements of Γ, where by the *complete substitution* of a set Δ of labeled bracketings into a labeled bracketing γ we mean the smallest set Δ' such that if $\gamma = \gamma_1 S \gamma_2 \cdots \gamma_{K-1} S \gamma_K$ where $\gamma_i \varepsilon (V_T \cup L \cup R)^*$ and if $\delta_1, \ldots, \delta_{K-1}$ are elements of Δ, then $\gamma_1 \delta_1 \gamma_2 \cdots \gamma_{K-1} \delta_{K-1} \gamma_K$ is in Δ'. If $K = 1$, then $\Delta' = \{\gamma\}$ by this definition. For each $i \geq 1$, let Σ_i be the set of labeled bracketings φ such that there is a transformational derivation $\psi_1, \ldots, \psi_n$ with respect to τ such that ψ_1 $\varepsilon \Delta_i$, $\psi_n = \varphi$, and ψ_n does not contain $\#$.

For any context-free based transformational grammar, each Δ_i is contained in Δ_{i+1} and the set of all base Phrase-markers is clearly just $\bigcup_{i=1}^{\infty} \Delta_i$, hence $\Sigma_i \subseteq \Sigma_{i+1}$ and the set of surface structures is precisely $\bigcup_{i=1}^{\infty} \Sigma_i$.

To illustrate these definitions, refer back to the grammar G_{e_1} of the example. For this grammar, $\Gamma = \{[_S a]_S, [_S a S]_S\}$, $\Delta_i = \{[_S a]_S, [_S a [_S a]_S]_S, \cdots, [_S a [_S a \cdots [_S a]_S \cdots]_S]_S\}$, and Σ_i contains just the i distinct surface structures which underlie the strings $a, aa, \ldots, \underbrace{a \ldots a}_{2^i}$.

In order to show that these definitions do yield an appropriately 'dense' predictable enumeration of surface structures, we now exhibit an efficient means of generating the Σ_i's.

LEMMA 3: Given a context-free based local-filtering transformational grammar (B, τ), the set Σ_{i+1} of surface structures contains just those labeled bracketings φ such that there is a transformational cycle $\psi_1, \ldots, \psi_m$ with respect to τ such that ψ_1 is the reduction of a member of the complete substitution of Σ_i into a member of Γ, $\varphi = \psi_m$ and ψ_m does not contain $\#$.

PROOF: If φ is a member of Σ_{i+1}, then there are a $\delta \varepsilon \Delta_{i+1}$ and a transformational derivation D with respect to τ such that δ is the first line of D, φ is the last line of D and furthermore does not contain $\#$. By definition of Δ_{i+1}, there are $\gamma = \gamma_1 S \gamma_2 \cdots \gamma_{n-1} S \gamma_n$ in Γ and $\delta_1, \ldots, \delta_{n-1} \varepsilon \Delta_i$ such that $\delta = \gamma_1 \delta_1 \gamma_2 \cdots \gamma_{n-1} \delta_{n-1} \gamma_n$. If $n = 1$, then D consists of a single transformational cycle and is the desired transformational cycle since the complete substitution of Σ_i into γ is $\{\gamma\}$. If $n > 1$, then it follows from the definition of transformational derivation that $D = \omega_1, \ldots, \omega_{K_1}, \omega_{K_1+1}, \ldots, \omega_{K_2}, \ldots, \omega_{K_{n-2}+1}, \ldots, \omega_{K_{n-1}}, \omega_{K_{n-1}+1}, \ldots, \omega_{K_n}$ is divided into successive sequences of labeled bracketings such that[4] $\omega_{K_j+1} = \rho(\gamma_1 \sigma_1 \gamma_2 \cdots \gamma_j \sigma_j \gamma_{j+1} \delta_{j+1} \cdots \gamma_{n-1} \delta_{n-1} \gamma_n)$ and ω_{K_j+1} is the result of substituting σ_{j+1} for δ_{j+1} in ω_{K_j+1} $(j < n - 1)$. Further, each $\sigma_j (1 \leq j \leq n - 1)$ is a surface structure in Σ_i since

σ_j does not contain $\#$ and the sequence $\omega_{K_{j-1}+1}, \ldots, \omega_{K_j}$ of labeled bracketings induces a transformational derivation of σ_j from δ_j, which is in Δ_i. Thus, $\omega_{K_{n-1}+1} = \rho(\gamma_1 \sigma_1 \gamma_2 \cdots \gamma_{n-1} \sigma_{n-1} \gamma_n)$ and hence is the reduction of a member of the complete substitution of Σ_i into γ. Furthermore, $\omega_{K_{n-1}+1}, \ldots, \omega_{K_n}$ is a single transformational cycle, $\varphi = \omega_{K_n}$ and ω_{K_n} does not contain $\#$.

To show conversely that the $\#$-free output of a single transformational cycle applied to $\rho(\gamma_1 \sigma_1 \gamma_2 \cdots \gamma_{n-1} \sigma_{n-1} \gamma_n)$ leads to a member of Σ_{i+1} if $\sigma_1, \ldots, \sigma_{n-1} \ \varepsilon \Sigma_i$ and $\gamma_1 S \gamma_2 \cdots \gamma_{n-1} S \gamma_n \varepsilon \Gamma$, an entirely similar argument suffices.

Lemma 3 makes precise what we meant by saying that transformations in effect operate on surface structure in local-filtering grammars with context-free bases. This lemma also has the following corollary about the chain $\Sigma_1, \Sigma_2, \ldots$.

COROLLARY 5: Given a context-free based local-filtering transformational grammar, if $\Sigma_i = \Sigma_{i+1}$, then $\Sigma_j = \Sigma_i$ for all $j \geq i$.

PROOF: Assume the corollary is false and $\Sigma_i = \Sigma_{i+1} = \cdots = \Sigma_{j-1} \neq \Sigma_j$. Let φ be any member of Σ_j. By Lemma 3, φ is derived in a single transformational cycle from $\rho(\gamma_1 \sigma_1 \gamma_2 \cdots \gamma_{n-1} \sigma_{n-1} \gamma_n)$, where $\gamma_1 S \gamma_2 \cdots \gamma_{n-1} S \gamma_n$ is in Γ and $\sigma_1, \ldots, \sigma_{n-1} \varepsilon \Sigma_{j-1}$. But since $\Sigma_{j-1} = \Sigma_i$, Lemma 3 indicates that φ is in $\Sigma_{i+1} = \Sigma_i$. Thus $\Sigma_i = \Sigma_j$ (because $\Sigma_i \subseteq \Sigma_j$), which is a contradiction.

We now have all the machinery available to prove Theorem 1 by describing an appropriate enumeration of surface structures.

PROOF OF THEOREM 1: Given any language L in C, if L is finite, then both (i) and (ii) are immediate. So assume that L is infinite and let G be a context-free based local-filtering transformational grammar which generates L. Enumerate an infinite set of surface structures as follows. Generate all members of Δ_1 in lexicographic order and as each one is obtained perform on it the finitely many transformational derivations, each one cycle long. As each surface structure is produced, compare it with the stored set of previously produced surface structures and, in case it is not in the list, output it and store it. This subprocedure terminates if and only if Σ_1 has been enumerated. Assume that Σ_i has been enumerated and enumerate the rest of Σ_{i+1} as follows. Generate all members of Γ in lexicographic order; as each one is obtained perform all complete substitutions of Σ_i, apply the reduction mapping ρ and carry out all one cycle derivations to obtain surface structures. As before, store and output each new surface structure obtained. This subprocedure is entered just in case Σ_i is finite and it terminates just when it completes the enumeration of Σ_{i+1}, since Lemma 3 guarantees that all members of Σ_{i+1} are obtainable in this fashion and that only members of Σ_{i+1} are obtainable. The storage required to enumerate σ_n, the $n + 1$st distinct surface structure obtained, is just the space required to store $\sigma_0, \ldots, \sigma_{n-1}$ plus the maximum for $0 \leq i \leq n$ of the space required to perform one transformational cycle on whatever input led to σ_i.

We wish to show that there is a constant K^* such that σ_n contains at most $K^* \cdot \max_{i < n} \ell(d(\sigma_i))$ terminal symbols. In establishing this, we shall make use of three constants associated with the transformational grammar G: 'base constant' K_b, whose existence was noted after Definition 3, 'transformational expansion constant' K_e and 'transformational contraction constant' K_c. Note that each transformation T of the grammar G factors each labeled bracketing to which it applies into a specific number n(fixed for T) of factors. Since each terminal symbol in the output of T must be a copy of a symbol in the input, the maximum number of terminal symbols in an output φ of T is $n + 1$ times the number in an input from which T produces φ. This increase can be achieved if each factor of the input is operated on by an elementary transformation which adjoins a copy of the entire input to the factor in question. The grammar G contains just a finite number of transformations, each applied at most once per transformational cycle. Hence there is a constant K_e with the property that the output of any transformational cycle contains at most K_e times as many terminal symbols as the input of that cycle. For the contraction constant K_c, one may take the constant K_3 of Lemma 6.3 (Peters and Ritchie, 1972). In fact, from the proof of that lemma it can be seen that $(n(c + 1))^{(k-1)}$ is sufficiently large to bound the ratio of number-of-terminal-symbols-in-the-input to number-in-the-output of a single transformational cycle (where n, c and k are as in that proof) and hence we may take K_c as this number.

Returning to the problem of showing that the constant K^* of the preceding paragraph exists, we consider three cases: (a) Δ_1 is infinite, (b) Δ_1 is finite but Γ is infinite and (c) Γ (hence also Δ_1) is finite. In case (a), the above procedure enumerates precisely Σ_1. Consider σ_n and the Phrase-marker $\delta \varepsilon \Delta_1$ from which it was transformationally derived. The length of $d(\sigma_n)$ is at most $K_e \ell(d(\delta))$. Output σ_{n-1} is transformationally derived either from δ itself or from the $\delta' \varepsilon \Delta_1$ which immediately precedes δ in the enumeration of Δ_1, so that $\ell(d(\delta)) \leq \ell(d(\delta')) + K_b$. If σ_{n-1} is derived from δ, then $\ell(d(\delta)) \leq K_c \ell(d(\sigma_{n-1}))$; so $\ell(d(\sigma_n)) \leq K_e K_c \ell(d(\sigma_{n-1}))$. If σ_{n-1} is derived from δ', then $\ell(d(\delta')) \leq K_c \ell(d(\sigma_{n-1}))$, so $\ell(d(\delta')) + K_b \leq K_c \ell(d(\sigma_{n-1})) + K_b$ and $\ell(d(\sigma_n)) \leq K_e \ell(d(\delta)) \leq K_e(K_c \ell(d(\sigma_{n-1})) + K_b)$. Therefore, $\ell(d(\sigma_n)) \leq K_e(K_c + K_b)\ell(d(\sigma_{n-1}))$.

Turning now to case (b), observe that there are only finitely many σ_i's enumerated by substituting into the first member of Γ and carrying out one transformational cycle, since Δ_1 is finite. Let K_1 be $\max(\ell(d(\sigma_n))/(\ell(d(\sigma_0))))$, for σ_n among this finite set of outputs. If σ_n is derived by substituting into some subsequent member of Γ, then let γ be that member and ε be the reduction of the result of substituting into γ. We have $\ell(d(\sigma_n)) \leq K_e \ell(d(\varepsilon))$. Let γ' be the member of Γ preceding γ in the enumeration, let ε' be the result of substituting σ_0 for each occurrence of S in γ' and consider any σ_m which is transformationally derivable from ε'. Because of the order of enumeration, we know that $m < n$. Furthermore $\ell(d(\gamma)) \leq \ell(d(\gamma')) + K_b$ and $\ell(d(\gamma')) \leq \ell(d(\varepsilon')) \leq K_c \ell(d(\sigma_m))$. Putting $K_2 = \max\limits_{\sigma_i \varepsilon \Sigma_1} \ell(d(\sigma_i))$, we note that $\ell(d(\varepsilon)) \leq K_2 \ell(d(\gamma))$ since $d(\varepsilon)$ is obtained from $d(\gamma)$ by replacing each S by a terminal string of length at most K_2. But then $\ell(d(\sigma_n)) \leq K_e \ell(d(\varepsilon)) \leq K_e K_2 \ell(d(\gamma)) \leq K_e K_2 (K_c \ell(d(\sigma_m)) + K_b$. Therefore $\max(K_1, K_e K_2(K_c + K_b))$ is the desired constant.

Finally for case (c), consider any σ_n not among the finite number derived from members of Δ_1. Such a σ_n is obtained by substituting some previously enumerated $\sigma_{i_1}, \ldots, \sigma_{i_p}$ into a γ in Γ, reducing to obtain ε and performing one cycle of transformations. Now $\ell(d(\varepsilon)) \leq \ell(d(\gamma)) + \ell(d(\sigma_{i_1})) + \cdots + \ell(d(\sigma_{i_p}))$ and $\ell(d(\sigma_n)) \leq K_e \ell(d(\varepsilon))$. Putting $K_2 = \max\limits_{\gamma \in \Gamma} \ell(d(\gamma))$, we have

$$\ell(d(\sigma_n)) \leq K_e(K_2 + \ell(d(\sigma_{i_1})) + \cdots + \ell(d(\sigma_{i_p}))) \leq K_e(K_2 + K_2 \cdot \max\limits_{m < n} \ell$$

$(d(\sigma_m)))$ since p is at most K_2. Letting $K_1 = \max\limits_{\sigma_i \varepsilon \Sigma_1} (\ell(d(\sigma_i))/(\ell(d(\sigma_0)))$ it is clear that $\max(K_1, 2K_e K_2)$ may be taken as the desired constant.

Now we define a function f by putting $f(n) = \sigma_n$ and note that f is one-to-one. In order that we may apply Lemma 2, we show that f is elementary recursive and that the constant K of that lemma exists. As we remarked earlier, the amount of storage required to compute $f(n)$ is just enough to store $f(0), \ldots, f(n-1)$ plus the maximum amount (over i) required to perform one transformational cycle on the input which leads to $f(i)$, $0 \leq i \leq n$. We have seen that there is a constant K^* such that $\ell(d(f(n))) \leq K^* \max_{i < n} \ell(d(f(i)))$, so $\ell(f(n)) \leq (4q+1) K^* \max_{i < n} \ell(d(f(i)))$, where $2q$ is the number of labeled brackets in the alphabet, since $f(n)$ is a reduced labeled bracketing. But $\ell(d(f(i))) \leq \ell(f(i))$, so we may take K of Lemma 2 as $(4q+1) K^*$. Clearly then $\ell(f(n)) \leq K^n \ell(f(0))$, so the space required to store all earlier outputs is $\sum_{i=0}^{n-1} \ell(f(i)) \leq \ell(f(0)) \sum_{i=0}^{n-1} K^i \leq K^n \ell(f(0))$. Furthermore, the single transformational cycle leading to $f(i)$ consists of at most $K_1 + 1$ labeled bracketings (where K_1 is the number of transformations in G) each of which has length at most $K_c \ell(f(i)) \leq K_c K^n \ell(f(0))$ and no more space is required to execute the transformational cycle than to store these labeled bracketings. Hence $f(n)$ can be computed in at most $(K_c(K_1 + 1) + 1)$ $K^n \ell(f(0))$ tape squares. Since any function which can be computed in space bounded by an elementary recursive function is itself elementary and this expression is an elementary function of n, f is elementary recursive.

We can now apply Lemma 2 to infer that Range $(d \circ f)$ is predictably enumerable. But Range (f) is a set of surface structures of G, hence Range $(d \circ f)$ is an infinite predictably enumerable subset of $L(G)$. Therefore, $L(G)$ is predictably enumerable, by Lemma 1, since it is recursively enumerable. To complete the proof, we need only note that Range $(d \circ f)$ is an infinite subset of $L = L(G)$ satisfying (ii) of Theorem 1, so clearly L satisfies that clause.

The University of Texas at Austin and
The University of Washington

NOTES

* This work was supported in part by the 1969 Advanced Research Seminar in Mathematical Linguistics, sponsored by the Center for Advanced Study in the Behavioral Sciences, Stanford, California. The first author also received support from National Science Foundation Grant GS 2468.
[1] In the sense of Csillag-Kalmár; see Kleene (1952; Ex. 1, Sec. 57, p. 285ff.) for a definition.

[2] Predictably computable functions are defined and investigated in Ritchie (1963).

[3] For the remainder of the paper we will make frequent use of the functions ℓ and d. The value of ℓ on any string is the length of that string and the value of d on any labeled bracketing is the string which results by deleting all brackets and labels.

[4] The function ρ is the 'reduction mapping' of Definition 2.9 of Peters and Ritchie (1972).

PART II

SEMANTICS

JAAKKO HINTIKKA

GRAMMAR AND LOGIC:
SOME BORDERLINE PROBLEMS

Recently it has been claimed by generative semanticists that "the rules of grammar are identical to the rules relating surface forms to their corresponding logical forms" (Lakoff, 1970b, p. 11). Even apart from such sweeping claims, a certain convergence of interest is unmistakable among logically minded linguists and linguistically minded logicians. Examples are offered by much of the recent work by several participants of the present meeting.

Much of this convergence of interest has taken place in the area which logicians know as modal logic (in the wide sense of the word in which it includes, e.g., the logic of propositional attitudes) and in the study of the behavior of these modal terms in ordinary language. Thus Lakoff writes: "It seems to me that recent developments in modal logic, together with recent developments in linguistics, make the serious study of natural logic possible" (*op. cit.*, p. 124), 'natural logic' being for Lakoff tantamount to "the empirical study of the nature of human language and human reasoning" (*op. cit.*, p. 126).

It seems to me that in modal logic and its applications we indeed have a promising field for the interaction of logical and linguistic viewpoints. A major reason for this promise is precisely the one Lakoff mentions, viz. recent developments in modal logic, especially the development of a satisfactory semantical theory of modality (in logicians' sense of semantics, of course). At the same time, it seems to me that much remains to be done and even changed in this area. Some of the logicians' insights have apparently been partly overlooked by linguists. Some of these insights may even serve to disprove certain claims by linguists or at least to bring to light major difficulties in them. In particular, in this direction we may perhaps discover serious difficulties in some of the more sweeping theses of such linguists as Lakoff.

Hintikka et al. (eds.), Approaches to Natural Language, 197–214. All rights reserved.
Copyright © 1973 by D. Reidel Publishing Company, Dordrecht-Holland.

In the present paper, I shall try to illustrate these points by discussing somewhat tentatively a couple of problems arising from those aspects of natural languages which correspond – in some rough sense – to the phenomena modal logicians have studied.

First, it seems to me that the most germane idea in the last fifteen years' work in modal logic, viz. the use of 'possible worlds' to elucidate the semantics of modality, has not been brought to bear by the linguists on their problems in its full strength. This idea is as simple as it is fruitful.[1] According to it, to understand a modal notion is to understand a certain relation – we may call it an alternativeness relation – on a set of possible worlds. In the case of propositional attitudes, this relation is relative to a person. For instance, in the case of necessity, the alternatives to a world W may be thought of as those possible worlds which could be realized instead of W. Then a necessary truth in W means truth *simpliciter* in all these alternatives. Likewise, alternatives to W arising in considering what a person a believes – we may call them doxastic a-alternatives to W – are possible worlds compatible with what a believes, they have tried to construe in W that a believes that p if and only if p is true in all these alternatives.[2]

These examples show how we may obtain truth-conditions for modal statements. Putting the main point very briefly and somewhat crudely, by stepping from a world to its alternatives, we can reduce the truth-conditions of modal statements to truth-conditions of nonmodal statements. And in view of the importance of such truth-conditions it is only to be expected that on their basis we can easily explicate a good deal of the behavior of modal notions.

The advantages of this approach are nowhere more clearly in evidence than in dealing with questions of reference. If all nonredundant use of modal notions entails the consideration, however tacit, of several possible worlds, then for each singular term – linguists might prefer speaking of nouns and noun phrases here – we *ipso facto* have to consider its several references in these different worlds. This shows at once that there is nothing strange in the failure of such so-called laws of logic as the substitutivity of identity in modal contexts. Clearly two singular terms 'a', 'b' which in the actual world pick out the same individual and hence make the identity '$a = b$' true *de facto* may fail to do so in alternative worlds, and hence fail to admit of interchange *salva veritate* in a context containing modal terms.

Likewise, the law known as existential generalization can only be expected to fail, for a singular term '*a*' may very well make a statement – say '*F(a)*' – true and yet fail to allow any foothold for maintaining that '*(Ex)F(x)*' is true, i.e., that '*F(x)*' is true of some definite individual *x*. This may happen when '*a*' picks out different individuals in the different possible worlds which we are considering in '*F(a)*', assuming that it contains nonredundant modal notions.

All this is old hat to most logicians and to some linguists. It can all be given an explicit logico-semantical formulation, which nevertheless would neither add much to nor detract much from the central theoretical ideas just adumbrated.

An informal remark might illustrate further the naturalness of this approach. Some of those linguists who have in fact seen the advantages of the idea of considering several 'possible worlds' have occasionally tried to get away with a simpler scheme. Instead of considering, say, all the possible worlds compatible with what *a* believes, they have tried to consider *a*'s 'belief world', that is, the world as *a* believes it to be. The only thing wrong here is that unless *a* is supremely opinionated, his beliefs do not specify completely any particular world, but rather a disjunction (as it were – usually it would have to be infinite) of descriptions of several such worlds. To specify 'the world as it is believed by *a* to be' is not to describe any one possible world, but rather a set of possible worlds. However, these are precisely the doxastic *a*-alternatives to the actual world. Hence to specify these *is* to specify what *a* (actually) believes.

Now assuming that our possible-worlds semantics is something like the true story of the 'logical form' of our modal statements, some interesting conclusions are immediately suggested by it.

For instance, consider the role of what has been called by grammarians coreferentiality. It is exemplified by the dependence of the admissibility of a derivation of

    (1)   John lost *a black pen* yesterday and Bill found *it* today

from

    (2)   John lost *a black pen* yesterday and Bill found *a black pen* today,

possibly by way of

(3)   John lost *a black pen* yesterday and Bill found *the black pen* today.

(I am stealing these examples, and others, from Partee, 1970b.) Consideration of more complicated examples already led Postal (1968a) to realize that the reference (or coreference) in question cannot be one that obtains in the actual world. However, it is not very easy to tell precisely what else it could be. For instance, it is sometimes said that what counts here is some kind of identity relative to the "speaker's mental picture of the world." Apart from the vagueness of such characterizations, this particular formulation is demonstrably insufficient, for what matters is in some cases the 'mental picture' – whatever it may look like – not of the speaker, but of some other person. A simple case in point is offered by

(4)   John lost a black pen yesterday and Bill believes that he has found it today.

One reason why (4) cannot be dealt with in terms of coreferentiality in the actual world or in the kind of world the speaker is assuming is that the speaker may know that Bill is mistaken in his belief and has not found John's pen – and perhaps has not found anything at all.

Yet all these troubles are predictable – and solvable – as soon as it is acknowledged that in modal contexts more than one possible world is inevitably at issue. For then we cannot even speak meaningfully of coreferentiality except relative to the specification of some particular possible world or class of possible worlds. For instance, what makes the difference in (4) is the identity (or the coreferentiality of the corresponding terms) of the black pen John lost yesterday with the one Bill has found today in Bill's doxastic alternatives to the world (4) is dealing with. By systematically using the possible-worlds idea, the theory of coreferentiality can be freed from the looseness of 'mental pictures' and other similar largely metaphorical paraphernalia.

Likewise, we can at once appreciate a fact which *prima facie* can be fitted into the coreferentiality framework only by mild violence, viz. the fact that "coreferentiality may hold independently of referentiality." By this paradoxical-sounding statement I mean such things as, e.g., the fact that we can say

(5)   John wants to catch *a fish* and eat *it* for supper.

even when John is not assumed to be angling for any particular piece of seafood. (According to the coreferentiality theory, the occurrence of "it" in (5) presupposes coreference.) *Prima facie*, all talk of coreference is here vacuous, for "a fish" in (5) does not (on the so-called nonreferential interpretation of (5)) refer to any particular submarine beast rather than another, and hence apparently cannot be said to refer to the same (or a different) fish as any other term. Yet the sense in which the coreferentiality idea applies here is transparently clear on the possible-world approach: in each possible world compatible with John's wants he catches a fish and eats *that fish* for supper. The fact that in different possible worlds different specimens of fish undergo this fate does not spoil this coreference in each world, considered alone.

There remains the problem, however, of formulating the precise rules for this kind of coreferentiality in English. Part of the difficulty here is due to the fact that the account just given presupposes, logically speaking, that in such pairs of sentences as

(5a)   John was trying to catch a fish. He wanted to eat it for supper.

"it" is within the scope of the operator tacitly introduced by "was trying." This does not seem to be the case in any grammatically natural sense of 'scope'. Here it is very hard to see the connection between 'logical form' and 'grammatical form' of the sentences in question.

This difficulty seems to be due to the way in which quantifying expressions operate in ordinary language. What goes on there is *prima facie* quite unlike ordinary quantification theory, where the scopes of the several quantifiers are the main determinants of logical structure. What happens is, rather, that ordinary language uses – for reasons that are likely to be quite deep – for the purposes of quantification scopeless ('free') terms not completely unlike Hilbert's ε-terms (Hilbert and Bernays, 1934, 1939).[3] What matters here is not the respective scopes of these terms, for they are typically maximal (comprising as much discourse as belongs to one and the same occasion), but rather the order in which they are thought of as being introduced. There seems to be a fair amount of data concerning in effect the grammatical indicators of this order. However, the study of 'natural logic' seems to have been hampered here by the absence of an appropriate logical framework. Linguists and linguistically oriented logicians should here pay much more attention to such unconventional reformulations of quantification theory or Hilbert's ε-theory.

One of the indicators sometimes used in ordinary language for this purpose is simply the order in which the complex terms appear in ordinary language. Since this is affected by the passive transformation, this transformation affects in an important way the meaning of the sentence in question. Chomsky's example (1965, p. 224) "every one in this room knows at least two languages" vs. "two languages are known by everyone in the room" illustrates this point. I do not see any evidence for Chomsky's claim that an ambiguity between these is latent in the former (or in its 'deep structure').

Here we are already approaching a group of problems which has recently exercised both philosophical logicians and linguists, viz. the ambiguity between what have been called by Donnellan (1966) the referential and the attributive uses of certain singular terms, especially definite descriptions. It is exemplified by the ambiguity of

(6)   John wants to marry a girl who is both pretty and rich.

Here it may be that beauty and wealth are among John's *desiderata* for a wife in general, or it may be that John is keen on marrying some particular girl who happens to have these desirable qualities. The former is the attributive reading of (6), the latter the referential reading. For the historically minded, it may be pointed out that the distinction between the two readings belongs to the older stock of a logician's trade. In the Middle Ages, the referential reading would have been said to yield a statement *de re*, the attributive a statement *de dicto*.

The possible-worlds semantics at once shows what the distinction amounts to under any name. Consider a statement which contains a singular term – say '*b*' – and also some modal notions. These notions imply that we are in effect considering several possible worlds over and above the actual one. Now such a statement can often be understood in two different ways. It may be taken to be about the individuals – typically different ones – which the term '*b*' picks out from the several possible worlds we are considering. This yields the *de dicto* statement. However, it can also be taken to be about that particular individual – considered of course as a citizen of several possible worlds – whom the term '*b*' picks out in the actual one. This results in the *de re* statement. For instance,

(7)   John believes that the richest man in town is a Republican

may mean that in each possible world compatible with John's beliefs the description "the richest man in town" picks out a Republican. It may also mean that John has a belief about a particular person, who as a matter of fact is the richest man in town, viz. the belief that he is Republican.

Letting bound variables range over (well-defined) individuals (in the logical sense of the word), as Quine and others have persuasively argued that we had better do, we may symbolize the two statements as follows:

(8) $F(a)$ (*de dicto*)

(9) $(Ex)(x = a \,\&\, F(x))$ or alternatively
         $(x)(x = a \supset F(x))$ (*de re*).

Some philosophers of language, e.g., Quine (1956, 1960), have described the ambiguity as a contrast between two interpretations of the verb in question, an opaque and a transparent one. The former is supposed to yield the attributive and the latter the referential reading. Our analysis of the situation shows that these cannot be considered as two unanalyzable senses of the verbs in question. In fact, in (9) the so-called transparent sense is analyzed in terms of the opaque one (plus quantifiers). As to the assumption of the ambiguity of the verb in question, we just do not need that hypothesis. Later it will be seen that speaking of two senses of the verb in question is misleading for another reason, too.

Likewise, the contrast between two apparently irreducible uses of definite descriptions postulated by Donnellan seems to me completely unnecessary, for an analysis can be given of the two uses which does not presuppose any irreducible ambiguities or irreducible conflicts between different ways of using the expressions in question.

This account of the ambiguity at once suggests several conclusions which do not all agree with what the linguists have said of the subject.

First, the *de dicto-de re* ambiguity (if it may be so called) is unlike many other types of ambiguity in that the two senses coalesce in the presence of simple kinds of further information. What this information is, is shown by our semantics. The difference between a statement about the several

references of a term 'b' in certain possible worlds and a statement about
the individual actually referred to by this term 'b' disappears as soon as
'b' picks out one and the same reference in all these worlds. Depending
on what the worlds are, this may amount to a simple factual assumption
concerning the people in question. For instance, the two readings of (7)
collapse if the phrase "the richest man in town" picks out one and the
same man in all of John's doxastic alternatives to the actual world.
But this, obviously, means nothing but John's having a belief as to who the
richest man in town is. And of course it is obvious that if John has such an
opinion, the difference between the two interpretations of (7) indeed does
not matter.

This power of simple factual assumptions (which of course usually
cannot be made) to dissolve the *de dicto-de re* ambiguity by making the two
senses coincide seems to me an interesting phenomenon which distinguishes this type of ambiguity from many others. (No factual assumption
can apparently eliminate, say, the ambiguity of "flying planes can be
dangerous" without ruling out one of its two senses.) It is beautifully
accounted for, it seems to me, by the possible-worlds semantics.

Secondly, our semantical theory shows that the *de dicto-de re* ambiguity
is present only in a context where we have to consider several possible
worlds (including the actual one). Typically, but perhaps not quite
exclusively, these are contexts involving (nonredundant) modal notions
in our wide sense of the word.

Now it has recently been claimed that, on the contrary, the *de dicto-de re*
contrast can be present in nonmodal contexts. Since a couple of interesting
methodological points are involved in this question, I shall comment
briefly on it. Partee (1970b) claims that such sentences as the following:

(10)   John married a girl his parents didn't approve of.

(11)   Bill caught a snipe.

(12)   The man who murdered Smith is insane.

exhibit the same ambiguity as (6) or (7).

For instance, (12) is said to be ambiguous because "either the speaker is
asserting of a particular individual, referred to by the definite noun
phrase, that that individual is insane; or the speaker is asserting that who-

ever it is that murdered Smith is insane – i.e., the definite noun phrase gives a characterization of an individual not necessarily otherwise known, and the sentence asserts that whatever individual is so characterized is insane." However, there is no reason, it seems to me, why the speaker should be asserting one of these things as distinguished from the other. Whoever utters (12) is merely claiming that the person who as a matter of fact murdered Smith is insane, and the question whether the speaker has in mind some particular candidate for that role need not be as much as raised.[4] The fallacy involved here seems to be the following. From the fact that a sentence can be split into a disjunction of several sentences by evoking some further feature of the speech-situation in questions, it does not follow that it is ambiguous. Or, to put the same point in more linguistic terms, from the fact that an expression exhibits an ambiguity when imbedded in a certain kind of context it does not follow that it is ambiguous when considered alone.[5]

To illustrate this claim, let me point out that the same fallacy is exhibited by George Lakoff's recent claim (1970b, pp. 12–14) that the sentence

(13)   That archaeologist discovered nine tablets . . .

is ambiguous in that it can 'mean' that the archaeologist discovered a group of nine tablets or that the tablets he discovered totalled nine in number. The trouble here is brought out by asking: Why should such possibility of a further description of the feats of one archaeologist make (13) ambiguous? Any sentence could be shown ambiguous by parallel arguments, it seems to me. The point Lakoff is trying to make is presumably that if someone's beliefs concerning one archaeologist are explicitly evoked, a distinction has to be made. Thus Lakoff may perhaps be right in thinking that another example of his, viz.

(14)   Sam believed that that archaeologist discovered nine tablets.

is ambiguous between what he calls the group-reading and the quantifier-reading. However, this does not in the least go to show that (13) is ambiguous. Lakoff's claim is merely another instance of the same fallacy as Mrs. Partee's.[6]

The further reason Mrs. Partee gives for the alleged ambiguity of such sentences as (10–(12) is that when they are imbedded in an opaque context, they exhibit the referential-attributive ambiguity. Hence, the argument seems to go, they cannot on their own be partial to one reading (presumably to the referential one). This mistake involved here is again demonstrated by our possible-worlds semantics. It shows that it is not the case that such nonmodal sentences as (10)–(12) for some reason have to be given the referential rather than attributive reading. Rather, the very distinction referential vs. attributive does not apply to nonmodal contexts. Hence Mrs. Partee's argument presupposes that her opponents are assuming the referential reading of nonmodal sentences, whereas the true moot point is whether the distinction applies to such sentences in the first place.

Another point which the possible-worlds semantics serves to bring out is that the referential-attributive contrast has much less to do than people commonly assume with the relative emphasis on the naming of a particular object in contrast to describing it. Rather, the importance of the descriptive element in the *de dicto* interpretation is secondary, derived from a deeper feature of the situation. According to the *de dicto* interpretation, the statement in question deals with the several individuals which a noun or noun phrase picks out in several different possible worlds. Since they are not (manifestations of) the *same* individual, we often – but not always – have to rely on their descriptive characteristics to pick them out from among the members of the world in question. They are not automatically picked out by the general criteria we have for identity of one and the same individual in different worlds.

Although the descriptive element is therefore often quite important, it is not uniformly so. As soon as it can be assumed for any reason whatsoever that a singular term picks out a definite individual from each of the worlds we are considering, however different these individuals may be, we have an opening for the attributive reading, even though the singular term in question has little descriptive content. It has been claimed (Partee, 1970b) that "names are almost always used referentially, since they have virtually no descriptive content." Questions of frequency aside, there nevertheless is no difficulty whatsoever in finding examples of the attributive use of names. For instance, consider the following:

(15)   Sherlock Holmes believes that the murder was committed by
         Mr. Hyde, although he does not know who Mr. Hyde is.

Here a *de dicto* reading is the only natural one. Since Sherlock Holmes is assumed not to know who Mr. Hyde is, his belief can scarcely be said to be about any particular person. (In different worlds compatible with his knowledge and presumably even with his beliefs, Mr. Hyde will be a different person.)

Notice, moreover, that (15) does not amount to saying that Sherlock Holmes is looking for *a man called* Mr. Hyde, for he is not at all interested, say, in Hyde's namesake in Manchester with a perfect alibi. Hence, we cannot in this way give "Mr. Hyde" in (15) a normal descriptive content.

By the same token, a wide class of sentences in terms of names admit of a *de dicto* reading, assuming that they contain words for knowledge, belief, memory, wishing, hoping, wanting, etc.

Such observations strongly suggest, incidentally, that much of the terminology in this area is misleading. This is the case with the terms 'referential' and 'attributive' as well as (though to a lesser degree) *'de re'* and *'de dicto'*.

Mistaken emphasis on the descriptive element in the attributive (*de dicto*) use of nouns and noun phrases has apparently led to a misclassification of some interesting examples. For instance, we read that the following sentence "seems unambiguously non-referential":

(16)   Since I heard that from a doctor, I'm inclined to take it seriously.

Insofar as the *de dicto-de re* distinction is here applicable at all, the presumption seems to me to be that a *de re* (referential) reading is being presupposed here rather than the *de dicto* (nonreferential) one. For whoever utters (16) is surely likely to have in mind some definite person from whom he heard whatever he is there said to have heard. In other words, (16) is naturally taken to be equivalent to something like

(17)   Since the man from whom I heard that is a doctor,
        I am inclined to take it seriously.

which shows that we are dealing with a *de re* reading here.

A point which I can raise but not answer here concerns a possible moral of the *de dicto-de re* ambiguity for such claims as Lakoff's concerning the near-identity of grammar and 'natural logic'. This claim is trivial if it only extends to the identity of *some* grammatical and logical phenomena. Moreover, there are surely features of grammar (in any reasonable sense of the word) which have little logical interest. Hence Lakoff's thesis has a bite only if it is taken to claim that all or at the very least all really interesting features of the logical behavior of ordinary language can be turned into "rules relating surface forms to their corresponding logical forms."

Another restraint that is needed to make Lakoff's claim relevant is the following. The thesis must presuppose some idea what the rules of grammar are independently of the requirement that they match (or can be interpreted as) rules of logic. For if there is no such independent criterion, Lakoff's thesis can be satisfied trivially, simply by taking some suitable formulation (if any) of the relevant aspects of logic and postulating grammatical relations and rules to match these. The real question, it seems to me, is not whether this is possible, but whether such an attempt to satisfy Lakoff's thesis is likely to produce results that have some independent grammatical significance.

My modest proposal here is to use the *de dicto-de re* ambiguity as a test for such theses as Lakoff's. If they are correct, this ambiguity must be possible to account for in the usual way in grammatical terms. If my diagnosis of the situation is correct, we have here a widespread and clear-cut phenomenon whose explanation in grammatical terms would be of considerable interest. Because from a logical point of view we can see the unity of the different manifestations of the ambiguity, according to Lakoff's thesis we presumably ought to be able to give to it a unified grammatical treatment.

I have no proof that such a treatment is impossible. As far as I can see – and here I may very well be mistaken – there nevertheless are some definite difficulties confronting any attempt to account for the ambiguity in a satisfactory manner in ordinary grammatical terms. In an old-fashioned terminology, we might say that here linguistic form perhaps does not match logical form.

As I said, I have no strict impossibility proof here, and I do not believe that such a proof is possible until some explicit restraints are imposed on the grammar which is supposed to account for the ambiguity. However, some indications of the nature of the problem can be given. Part of the aim would have to be to derive all sentences of the form

(18)   *a* knows (believes, remembers, hopes, wishes, intends, etc.)
        that *p*

where nouns or noun phrases occur in *p* in more than one way. One
way is presumably some more or less straightforward imbedding of *p* in
the "knows that" context. However, it is far from clear what the other
derivation might look like. Moreover, it does not suffice to provide just
one alternative derivation, for when several nouns or noun phrases occur
in *p*, we often face (*ceteris paribus*) a choice, for each of them, whether to
interpret it *de dicto* or *de re*. (Thus *n* nouns or noun phrases occurring in
p may create 2^n-fold ambiguity.)

Incidentally, this suggests that it is misleading to attribute (as Quine
among others has done) the ambiguity in question to the verb which
serves to express the propositional attitude in question, unless we are
prepared to countenance such strange consequences as, e.g., that the
number of readings of the verb in question depends on the number of
nouns and noun phrases in the imbedded clause. Hence Quine's analysis
of the situation appears very suspect.

A fairly obvious candidate for the role of an intermediate stage of the
desired derivation would be something of the form

(19)   *a* knows (believes, etc.) of *b* that – he –.

or of one of the similar parallel or more complicated forms. It is in fact
true that (19) is prejudiced in favor of the *de re* interpretation much more
firmly than the corresponding construction

(20)   *a* knows (believes, etc.) that – *b* –.

Hence the choice of (19) rather than (20) may very well serve to signal that
the speaker is opting for the *de re* interpretation.

However, it is not clear whether (19) itself is ambiguous in the same
way as (20). An example of the attributive reading of a sentence of the
form (19) is perhaps offered by the following:

(21)   It is believed of Jack the Ripper that he killed more than
        thirty women.

thought of as being uttered in a context where complete ignorance of – and
complete doxastic disinterest in – the identity of Jack the Ripper is being
presupposed. (Would anyone find (21) at all strange if uttered in such

circumstances? I doubt it very much.) If so, the alleged possibility of deriving (20) from (19) scarcely serves to explain why (20) is ambiguous.

The fact, registered above, that the two senses involved in a *de dicto-de re* ambiguity will coalesce as soon as a simple factual assumption is satisfied also seems to militate against any simple-minded attempt to account for it in terms of two different derivations of the ambiguous sentence. It is hard to see how this latter type of duality can be made to disappear by changing certain facts about the world.

The problem is thus to account in grammatical terms for the two features which distinguish the *de dicto-de re* ambiguity from typical structural ambiguities. These features are (i) the collapse of the different senses into one wherever certain simple kinds of factual information are present and (ii) the dependency of the number of sense on the number of singular terms (nouns and noun phrases) in the sentence in question or in some part of it.

It is perfectly possible to account for these interesting phenomena in a sufficiently sophisticated logical and/or grammatical theory. For instance, there is no difficulty in explaining (ii) in Montague's formal grammars. However, in such cases the question of independent grammatical interest of the account can perhaps be raised.

Moreover, certain widely accepted grammatical theories do not seem to admit of an adequate account of (i)–(ii). For instance, if ambiguities of this kind are to be explained by reference to pretransformation (i.e., deep structure) base components and if this base component is to be obtained in the simple way assumed, e.g., by Chomsky (1965, pp. 67–68, 120–123, 128), I cannot see any hope for explaining (ii) by means of alternative ways of obtaining the base component. Furthermore, it is even unclear what an account of (i) would look like in terms of typical contemporary grammatical theories.

What is likely to even be more important here is that there does not seem to be any independent grammatical reason for postulating a derivation of (20) from (19). Yet we saw that such reasons are needed to prevent Lakoff's thesis from degenerating into a triviality. I cannot help finding it very unnatural to think of (20) as being derived by so circuitous a route as (19). Of course, this may be merely due to my ignorance of grammatical theory. But even if this should turn out to be the case, the onus of proof is very much on the generative semanticists. If they cannot supply one, or some alternative account of the situation, we have here a counterexample to their claims.

A final word of warning is perhaps needed here concerning the further complications into which the possible-worlds semantics leads us. Or per-haps – hopefully – we rather ought to speak of the complexities it helps to unravel. I have spoken rather casually of this or that individual's making his or its appearance in the different possible worlds we are considering. In reality, the criteria by means of which we actually do this – that is, cross-identify or tell of members of different possible worlds whether these are the same or different – are not unproblematic, at least not for philosophical purposes. Although luckily our possible-worlds semantics enables us to pose some very interesting questions here, it is not even com-pletely clear what structural properties the 'world lines' have that connect the different 'manifestations' of 'roles' of or 'counterparts' to or one and the same individual with each other. One such structural question is of a particular concern to the subject matter of this paper. This is the question whether a 'world line' may split when we move from a world to its alterna-tives. If this question is answered affirmatively, we can no longer speak light-heartedly of *the* individual (considered as a member of a number of alternative worlds several 'manifestations of' or 'counterparts to' to this actual world. For if splitting is admissible, there may be in some of the alternative worlds several 'manifestations of' or 'counterparts to' to this individual. What that would mean is that the whole *de dicto-de re* contrast becomes messier. Or, more accurately speaking, the *de re* reading becomes considerably less sharp.

Can we rule out splitting of world lines (of the kind just mentioned)? This question is of considerable importance to many philosophers of logic and of language, but unfortunately there is nothing remotely like a con-sensus concerning the answer. Rather plausible arguments both *pro* and *con* can in fact be found in the literature.

Here I cannot survey these arguments. It may nevertheless be worth-while to recall the fact – which I have pointed out elsewhere (Hintikka, 1969a, pp. 112–147) – that a prohibition against splitting is essentially tantamount to the most plausible version of the famous principle of the substitutivity of identity which Quine and others have made the corner-

stone of their interpretation of the logic of modal notions. If the prohibition against splitting cannot be upheld, Quine is in serious trouble even
on a relatively charitable interpretation of his views on modality and
reference.

In contrast, allowing world lines to split would not tell in the least against
the possible-world semantics as such. It would merely show that some of
the phenomena that can be studied by its means exhibit complications that
at first do not meet the eye.

The only constructive suggestion I want to offer here is that what looks
like splitting is often an indication of something quite different. It often
indicates that more than one overall principle of cross-identification is at
work.

Elsewhere (Hintikka, 1969a, pp. 112–147; 1970c, 1971a) I have studied
some such contrasts between different methods of cross-identification in
some detail. I do not think that I exaggerate if I say that they turn out to
have a tremendous philosophical interest. The reason why I mention them
here is that recognizing the frequent presence of different principles of
cross-identification is highly relevant to the theory of reference as it has
been employed by linguists, especially to some of the puzzle examples that
have been bandied around in the literature. Suffice it here to point out that
the logic of McCawley's well-known example becomes crystal clear from
this point of view. I mean of course the sentence

(22)   I dreamt that I was Brigitte Bardot and that I kissed me.

Here it is abundantly clear that in the speaker's dream-worlds (worlds
compatible with what he dreams) there were two counterparts of him. It
is also clear that they are counterparts in a different sense. What precisely
the two respective senses are is not specified by the example and may be
difficult to spell out in detail. It is fairly clear, nonetheless, that the distinction participant-observer, employed by some analysts, does not give us
much mileage here, although it perhaps points to the right direction.
However, the outlines of the two cross-identification principles used in the
example are clear enough. One of the speaker's counterparts is the person
whose experiences he has in the dream-world, the other is the one who is
like him by some less exciting criteria.

Much work remains to be done concerning different kinds of principles of cross-identification. For one thing, it has not been worked out what consequences the presence of the methods of cross-identification has grammatically. I believe that the contrast is not expressed in English very systematically, although in a somewhat smaller scale it has some clear-cut linguistic counterparts. (See my analysis of the direct-object construction in the papers mentioned in note 3.) These counterparts largely remain to be further investigated. It may be the case, as Lakoff has urged, that for this purpose the usual simple-minded method of referential indices, first proposed by Chomsky, is insufficient, though no hard proof to this effect has been given. (Lakoff's analysis seems to me misleading in any case in that he speaks of a person's splitting into several in another possible world. The presence of two different methods of cross-identification is nevertheless a phenomenon which ought to be sharply distinguished from the splitting of individuals under one and the same method.) However, they do not reflect in the least on the possible-worlds semantics, which on the contrary gives us excellent methods of analyzing the situation. And since the possible-worlds semantics which I have informally sketched here can easily be turned into an explicit treatment of this part of logic by means of an explicit axiomatization, I cannot agree with Lakoff's claim that "symbolic logic ... is of no help here" (1968, p. 5), though Lakoff may provide a way out for himself by speaking of "symbolic logic of the traditional sort." Traditional or not, a satisfactory logical account here does not fall with the use of referential indices.

Since I have been criticizing many of the specific things logically minded linguists have recently said, let me end by reiterating that I find their direction of interest not only worthwhile but also distinctly promising. The corrections I have tried to offer to their claims are calculated to illustrate this promise rather than to detract from it. I am especially deeply indebted to the authors whose detailed remarks I appear to be criticizing most, viz. to George Lakoff and Barbara Hall Partee.

Academy of Finland and Stanford University

NOTES

[1] Probably the best brief account of this approach is still to be found in the original papers by Saul Kripke (1963a, 1963b, 1965). Cf. also my *Models for Modalities* (1969a), Kanger (1957), Kaplan (1969) and the writings of Montague.

[2] This account is in need of a major qualification, however, for as it stands it implies that we all believe all the logical consequences of what we believe, that having inconsistent beliefs entails believing everything, plus all the awkward parallel conclusions for other propositional attitudes. The problem arising here is discussed by Barbara Hall Partee in her contribution to the present meeting (this vol., pp. 309–336). I have outlined a solution to the problem in other papers, especially Hintikka (1970a, 1970b).

[3] I recall that Paul Ziff used to make the same – or at least closely related – point in discussion already some twelve years ago.

[4] Notice that there is no ambiguity in the truth-conditions of (10)–(12). For instance, (10) is true if and only if John's bride actually was not approved of by his parents, quite independently of the specificity of the speaker's knowledge of who that girl is.

Notice also the interesting difference between what is claimed by Partee about (10) and what in fact happens in (6). Here, it is suggested, it makes a difference whether *the speaker* has in mind a particular girl or not. This is entirely different from *John's* having a specific girl in mind in the state of affairs described by (6). The ambiguity that is claimed to reside in (10) is not the same one that surfaces in (6).

[5] Another, supplementary mistake may also be operative here, viz. a tacit assumption that the sentences in question, e.g., (10)–(12) are to be thought of as *asserted* by the speaker. If so, their logical force will in fact be tantamount to the following:

(10)   * I assert that John married a girl his parents didn't approve of.

(11)   * I assert that Bill caught a snipe.

(12)   * I assert that the man who murdered Smith is insane.

Since 'assert' is a modal verb, (10)*–(12)* are indeed ambiguous. However, there is no reason for thinking that the logic of (10)–(12) must be brought out by considering them as asserted sentences. Hence the tacit assumption is likely to be illicit.

[6] What has probably misled many people here is the very fact illustrated by Lakoff's claim, viz. the fact that surprisingly often modal notions are tacitly being considered in apparently nonmodal contexts. This important fact would deserve some further attention, and it partly excuses the kind of mistake I have been criticizing.

COMMENTS ON HINTIKKA'S PAPER

1

Professor Hintikka in his highly suggestive paper made a good case for the possible fruitful application of modal logic and semantics of possible worlds to contemporary linguists' studies of language. Hintikka made his point by offering a clear critique of linguists' claims and then providing ways of dealing with issues at hand from the point of view of logical semantical theory. Now the purpose of my comments here is not intended to make a defense of any linguists' view or to advance their views in a better context, but on the contrary, to lay bare certain fundamental problems in the interpretation of the possible-worlds semantical approach and to suggest possible lines of solution.

2

It seems that one basic assumption of the possible-worlds semantics is that we can reduce truth conditions of modal statements and statements of propositional attitudes to truth conditions of nonmodal statements and statements without reference to propositional attitudes. The questions are how this reduction is to be achieved and what philosophical justification can be provided. Hintikka's answer to the *how* question is found in his suggestion of alternativeness relation. On the basis of this relation, possible worlds as alternative worlds to a given world *simpliciter* or to a world depicted by one's beliefs or one's knowledge or one's wants can be introduced for the definition of truth conditions of modal statements and statements of propositional attitude. In the case of the necessary statement, this is fairly easy to understand: A necessary statement P is true in the given world W iff P is true in all the possible worlds alternative to W. The more difficult question is how does one say about the truth condition of a statement of belief: A believes that P? Hintikka's suggestion is ingenious: A

Hintikka et al. (eds.), Approaches to Natural Language, 215–220. All rights reserved.
Copyright © 1973 by D. Reidel Publishing Company, Dordrecht-Holland.

believes that P [in W] iff P is true in all possible worlds alternative to W, but compatible with A's beliefs in W.

3

Now two primitive concepts in this construction need to be made explicit. First, there is the primitive concept that P is true in a possible world. Second, there is the primitive concept that the alternative worlds for a belief of A in W are possible worlds which are compatible with the world as characterized by all A's beliefs in W.

These two primitive concepts are implicit in any definition of possible worlds based on an alternativeness relation. A close look at the second primitive concept in the definition of any set of possible worlds indicates that in the metalanguage of the semantics of possible worlds one has to assume that the worlds as characterized by one's beliefs or wants can be always given. This means that in order to determine the truth conditions of a belief or a want one has to assume the feasibility of a well-defined world as determined by all one's beliefs or all one's wants which of course have to be also assumed to be consistent. If this condition is satisfied, we may simply say that A's belief or A's want P is true relative to all A's beliefs or relative to all A's wants. To say this is to say that all A's beliefs or all A's wants give rise to a set of possible worlds which are compatible with all A's beliefs or all A's wants and P is true in each of these possible worlds.

4

Even though "P is true in a possible world" and "A's beliefs or wants determine or characterize a world" are primitive notions, for the purpose of philosophical understanding we have to make some important observations on the explication of these primitive notions. In the first place, when we refer to all possible worlds compatible with *everything* that A believes in the actual world W, or equivalently when we refer to all A's beliefs, the *everything* that A believes in W or *all* A's belief should not a priori include the belief P which is being attributed to A and which may be said to be true in the possible worlds compatible with all A's beliefs. For if *everything* which A believes in W or *all* A's beliefs include all beliefs in an absolutely universal sense of *everything* or *all*, then there is no point of making the explication of "*A* believes that *P*" in terms of "*P*'s being true in the possible worlds compatible with all *A*'s beliefs." This would amount to an impredicative definition of *A*'s believing that *P*. In our explication of beliefs, we should permit the possibility that "*A* believes that *P*" is false: this possibility would mean that *P* is false (or not true) in all the possible worlds compatible with all *A*'s beliefs. Perhaps we should regard the reference to *everything* that *A* believes in *W* or to *all A*'s beliefs as a reference to *everything* that *A* is *known* to believe in *W* or *all A*'s known beliefs, for the proper restriction of the range of the implicit universal quantification.

5

To facilitate adequate understanding of the possible-worlds semantics, I think we need also an explication of the notion of "true in a possible world compatible with one's (known) beliefs (call this one's belief set)." For the statement that "*P* is true in the possible world compatible with *A*'s belief set *S*," there would be two ways of construing the truth of *P* in the possible world *W* as determined by the belief set *S*.[1]

A.   The first is a deductive construal: '*P* is true in *W*' if *P* is derivable from *S*. This *amounts* to a reversal of a minimal requirement of belief sentence: Whoever believes that *D* believes that *D'* where *D'* is a logical consequence of *D*. This means whoever believes that *D* believes that *D'*, where *D'* are premises of *D*. Even though this way of construal may have many imperfections, it is capable of being used to explain the failure of substitutibility of identity, for the same belief could have different *belief sets* as premises of its derivation.

B.   The second way of construal is an inductive one. *P* is a member of the belief set *S*, if *P* is established on the same inductive ground on which *S* is established. This construal is empirical in spirit and has the same capacity of explaining failure of substitutibility of identity.

6

The 'possible worlds' idea certainly provides a clear illustration of the nonidentity of *referents* in belief contexts such as sentence (4) in Hintikka's paper. But it seems that (4) can be accounted for by interpreting the embedded sentence of belief as established by all the beliefs of Bill, but a corresponding sentence that "Bill has found the black pen today" cannot be so established.

7

Sentence (6) "John wants to catch a sea animal and eat it for supper," does not follow from sentence (5) "John wants to catch a fish and eat it for supper," even though a fish is a sea animal.

Why does the substitution fail to preserve the truth value of (5)? Can we say that "John catches a fish" is true in all possible worlds compatible with John's wants, while "John catches a sea animal" is not true in these possible worlds, but instead in another set of possible worlds? Can we also express this by saying that "John catches a fish" and "John eats the fish" are both related to John's wants, but "John catches a sea animal" and "John eats the sea animal" are not? Is this form of speech necessarily vague or more obscure than the speech on possible worlds?

8

Concerning showing the ambiguity between the referential and the attributive use of certain singular terms, the reference to possible worlds seems to be most helpful. But we may also say that in the opaque sense of belief "The nicest man in town" in (7) refers to an object as conceived in John's beliefs, but in the transparent sense of belief the same phrase refers to an object without being conceived in John's beliefs. Thus substitution may fail in the former case, while it succeeds in the latter. Given the factual assumption that "the richest man in town" as described by John's beliefs is in fact the richest man in town, it is clear that the distinction between transparent sense and opaque sense of belief collapses. But I do not see how the transparent sense of belief $(Ex)(x = a \& F(x))$ or $(x)(x = a \supset F(x))$ was to be *analyzed* in terms of the opaque sense of belief $F(a)$.

9

Now regarding the question whether *de re-de dicto* ambiguity extends to nonmodal contexts like sentences (10), (11), and (12) in Hintikka's paper, I am sympathetic with Hintikka's criticism of Partee. The unembedded sentence (12) "The man who murdered Smith is insane" is not ambiguous as (12) is clearly a direct statement without indirect reference. On Russell's theory of description, (12) is an existential quantified sentence which is either true or false. There is no reason to bring in consideration of speaker's conception of reference of the subject of the sentence. But in the case of sentence (13) "That archaeologist discovered nine tablets," the *de re-de dicto* ambiguity does seem to pertain because of the intentionality of the verb 'discover'. Thus it may be suggested that (13) can be rendered in some cases as meaning the same as (13') "That archaeologist believed to discover nine tablets." The ambiguity in (13') becomes conspicuously clear. Similarly, sentence (11) "Bill caught a snipe" may be interpreted as meaning the same as (11') "Bill believed to have caught a snipe," and (10) "John married a girl his parents did not approve of" may be interpreted as (10') "John married a girl he believed his parents didn't approve of." Of course, this way of interpreting (13), (11), and (10) does not share Lakoff's or Partee's argument to the same effect. My point is exclusively that certain verbs may carry modal significance and hence are open to a possible-worlds interpretation of ambiguity of the *de re-de dicto* type. In fact, Hintikka seemed to recognize this possible construal when he referred to the failure of existential generalization independent of a modal context.

10

I agree that no linguistic form has been discovered to match logical form. But I disagree that Hintikka has disproved the validity of Quine's suggestion on making a syntactical distinction between referential reading and attributive reading of belief contexts. It can be pointed out that if a referring term in (21) has occurred in the scope of a propositional attitude, its later occurrence in direct speech will inherit the ambiguity of the original occurrence of the term. Thus (21) does not constitute a *counterexample* that (20) may independently of any prior occurrence of *b* in the scope of a propositional attitude imply a *de re* interpretation. On the other hand, it is also true that if a term occurs in a direct speech and later occurs in the scope of a propositional attitude, there can be strong reason to believe that it should be given a *de re* interpretation in a later modal context. This of course, does not show that we can represent any logical distinction, say, as based on the possible-worlds semantics, in grammatical terms. I think that there is a great challenge for linguists in general to meet. One way they perhaps can meet the challenge is to incorporate logical insights of possible-worlds semantics and other logically significant explanations into a generative theory of deep structure semantics.

University of Hawaii

NOTE

[1] *Editors' note:* As shown by his other writings, Hintikka interprets truth-in-a-world in the usual sense, codified by a suitable truth-definition of the Tarski-Carnap type, without any reference to anyone's beliefs. Contrary to Cheng's interpretation, truth-in-a-world-compatible-with-someone's-beliefs is not an unanalyzable notion for Hintikka.

RICHARD MONTAGUE

THE PROPER TREATMENT OF QUANTIFICATION
IN ORDINARY ENGLISH*

1. INTRODUCTION

The aim of this paper is to present in a rigorous way the syntax and semantics of a certain fragment of a certain dialect of English. For expository
purposes the fragment has been made as simple and restricted as it can
be while accommodating all the more puzzling cases of quantification and
reference with which I am acquainted.[1]

Suppes (1971) claims, in a paper prepared for the present workshop,
that "at the present time the semantics of natural languages are less
satisfactorily formulated than the grammars . . . [and] a complete grammar
for any significant fragment of natural language is yet to be written." This
claim would of course be accurate if restricted in its application to the
attempts emanating from the Massachusetts Institute of Technology, but
fails to take into account the syntactic and semantic treatments proposed
in Montague (1970a and 1971). Thus the present paper cannot claim
to present the *first* complete syntax (or grammar, in Suppes' terminology)
and semantics for a significant fragment of natural language; and it is
perhaps appropriate to sketch relations between the earlier proposals and
the one given below.

Montague (1971) contains a general theory of languages, their interpretations, and the inducing of interpretations by translation. The
treatment given below, as well as that in Montague (1970a) and the
treatment of a fragment of English proposed at the end of Montague
(1971), can all easily be construed as special cases of that general theory.
The fragment in Montague (1970a) was considerably more restricted
in scope than that in Montague (1971) or the present paper, in that
although it admitted indirect discourse, it failed to accommodate a number
of more complex intensional locutions, for instance, those involving *intensional verbs* (that is, verbs like **seeks, worships, conceives**). The fragment
in Montague (1971) did indeed include intensional verbs but excluded

Hintikka et al. (eds.), Approaches to Natural Language, 221–242. All rights reserved.
Copyright © 1973 by D. Reidel Publishing Company, Dordrecht-Holland.

certain intensional locutions involving pronouns (for instance, the
sentence **John wishes to catch a fish and eat it**, to which a number of
linguists have recently drawn attention). The present treatment is capable
of accounting for such examples, as well as a number of other heretofore
unattempted puzzles, for instance, Professor Partee's **the temperature is
ninety but it is rising** and the problem of intensional prepositions. On
the other hand, the present treatment, unlike that in Montague (1971),
will not directly accommodate such sentences as Moravcsik's **a unicorn
appears to be approaching**, in which an indefinite term *in subject position*
would have a nonreferential reading, but must treat them indirectly as
paraphrases (of, in this case, **it appears that a unicorn is approaching** or
that a unicorn is approaching appears to be true).

On their common domain of applicability the three treatments essentially
agree in the truth and entailment conditions imposed on sentences.[2]
Further, when only *declarative* sentences come into consideration, it is the
construction of such conditions that (Suppes notwithstanding) should
count as the central concern of syntax and semantics.[3] Nevertheless, the
details of the present development possess certain aesthetic merits, of
coherence and conceptual simplicity, not to be found in the treatment of
English in Montague (1971). (It is in order to preserve these merits that
I here forego a direct account of such sentences as Moravcsik's.)

2. THE SYNTAX OF A FRAGMENT OF ENGLISH

Let e and t be two fixed objects (0 and 1, say) that are distinct and neither
ordered pairs nor ordered triples. Then *Cat*, or the set of *categories* of
English, is to be the smallest set X such that (1) e and t are in X, and (2)
whenever A and B are in X, A/B and $A/\!\!/B$ (that is, $\langle 0, A, B \rangle$ and $\langle 1, A, B \rangle$,
respectively) are also in X.

It should be pointed out that our categories are not sets of expressions
but will instead serve as *indices* of such sets. We regard e and t as the
categories of entity expressions (or individual expressions) and truth value
expressions (or declarative sentences), respectively. We shall regard the
categories A/B and $A/\!\!/B$ as playing the same semantical but different
syntactical roles. An expression of either category is to be such that when
it is combined (in some as yet unspecified way, and indeed in different ways

for the two categories) with an expression of category B, an expression of category A is produced. (The precise character of the categories A/B and $A//B$ is unimportant; we require only two different kinds of ordered pair.)

It will be observed that our syntactic categories diverge from those of Ajdukiewicz (1960) only in our introduction of two compound categories (A/B and $A//B$) where Ajdukiewicz would have had just one. The fact that we need only two copies is merely an accident of English or perhaps of our limited fragment; in connection with other languages it is quite conceivable that a larger number would be required.[4]

Keeping in mind the intuitive roles described above, we may single out as follows certain traditional syntactic categories.

IV, or the category of intransitive verb phrases, is to be t/e.

T, or the category of terms, is to be t/IV.

TV, or the category of transitive verb phrases, is to be IV/T.

IAV, or the category of *IV*-modifying adverbs, is to be IV/IV.

CN, or the category of common noun phrases, is to be $t//e$.

The following categories will also be exemplified in our fragment although no special symbol will be introduced for them.

t/t is the category of sentence-modifying adverbs.

IAV/*T* is the category of *IAV*-making prepositions.

IV/t is the category of sentence-taking verb phrases.

IV//*IV* is the category of *IV*-taking verb phrases.

By B_A is understood the set of *basic expressions* of the category A; the notion is characterized as follows.

$B_{IV} = \{$**run, walk, talk, rise, change**$\}$

$B_T = \{$**John, Mary, Bill, ninety, he$_0$, he$_1$, he$_2$, . . .**$\}$

$B_{TV} = \{$**find, lose, eat, love, date, be, seek, conceive**$\}$

$B_{IAV} = \{$**rapidly, slowly, voluntarily, allegedly**$\}$

$B_{CN} = \{$**man, woman, park, fish, pen, unicorn, price, temperature**$\}$

$B_{t/t} = \{$**necessarily**$\}$

$B_{IAV/T} = \{$**in, about**$\}$

$B_{IV/t} = \{$**believe that, assert that**$\}$

$B_{IV//IV} = \{$**try to, wish to**$\}$

$B_A = \Lambda$ (that is, the empty set) if A is any category other than those mentioned above. (In particular, the sets B_e of basic entity expressions and B_t of basic declarative sentences are empty.)

By a *basic expression* of the present fragment is understood a member of $\bigcup_{A \in Cat} B_A$.

By P_A is understood the set of *phrases* of the category A. (We may read "P_{CN}," "P_{TV}," and the like as 'the set of common noun phrases', 'the set of transitive verb phrases', and so on.) These sets are introduced, in a sense to be made precise below, by the following rules, S1–S17.

2.1. *Syntactic Rules*

2.1.1. *Basic rules*

S1. $B_A \subseteq P_A$ for every category A.

S2.   If $\zeta \in P_{CN}$, then $F_0(\zeta)$, $F_1(\zeta)$, $F_2(\zeta) \in P_T$,
where $F_0(\zeta) =$ **every** ζ,
$\qquad F_1(\zeta) =$ **the** ζ,
$\qquad F_2(\zeta)$ is **a** ζ or **an** ζ according as the first word in ζ
$\qquad\qquad$ takes **a** or **an**.

S3.   If $\zeta \in P_{CN}$ and $\phi \in P_t$, then $F_{3,n}(\zeta, \phi) \in P_{CN}$, where $F_{3,n}(\zeta, \phi)$ $= \zeta$ **such that** ϕ', and ϕ' comes from ϕ by replacing each occurrence of $\mathbf{he}_n$ or $\mathbf{him}_n$ by

$\begin{Bmatrix} \mathbf{he} \\ \mathbf{she} \\ \mathbf{it} \end{Bmatrix}$ or $\begin{Bmatrix} \mathbf{him} \\ \mathbf{her} \\ \mathbf{it} \end{Bmatrix}$, respectively, according as the first B_{CN} in ζ is of $\begin{Bmatrix} \text{masc.} \\ \text{fem.} \\ \text{neuter} \end{Bmatrix}$

gender.

2.1.2. *Rules of functional application*

S4.   If $\alpha \in P_{t/IV}$ and $\delta \in P_{IV}$, then $F_4(\alpha, \delta) \in P_t$, where $F_4(\alpha, \delta) = \alpha\delta'$ and δ' is the result of replacing the first *verb* (i.e., number of B_{IV}, B_{TV}, $B_{IV/t}$, or $B_{IV//IV}$) in δ by its third person singular present.

S5.   If $\delta \in P_{IV/T}$ and $\beta \in P_T$, then $F_5(\delta, \beta) \in P_{IV}$, where $F_5(\delta, \beta) = \delta\beta$ if β does not have the form $\mathbf{he}_n$ and $F_5(\delta, \mathbf{he}_n) = \delta$ $\mathbf{him}_n$.

S6.   If $\delta \in P_{IAV/T}$ and $\beta \in P_T$, then $F_5(\delta, \beta) \in P_{IAV}$.

S7.   If $\delta \in P_{IV/t}$ and $\beta \in P_t$, then $F_6(\delta, \beta) \in P_{IV}$, where $F_6(\delta, \beta) = \delta\beta$.

S8.   If $\delta\in P_{IV//IV}$ and $\beta\in P_{IV}$, then $F_6(\delta,\beta)\in P_{IV}$.

S9.   If $\delta\in P_{t/t}$ and $\beta\in P_t$, then $F_6(\delta,\beta)\in P_t$.

S10.   If $\delta\in P_{IV/IV}$ and $\beta\in P_{IV}$, then $F_7(\delta,\beta)\in P_{IV}$, where $F_7(\delta,\beta)$ $=\beta\delta$.

2.1.3. *Rules of conjunction and disjunction*

S11.   If ϕ, $\psi\in P_t$, then $F_8(\phi,\psi)$, $F_9(\phi,\psi)\in P_t$, where $F_8(\phi,\psi)$ $=\phi$ **and** ψ, $F_9(\phi,\psi)=\phi$ **or** ψ.

S12.   If γ, $\delta\in P_{IV}$, then $F_8(\gamma,\delta)$, $F_9(\gamma,\delta)\in P_{IV}$.

S13.   If α, $\beta\in P_T$, then $F_9(\alpha,\beta)\in P_T$.

2.1.4. *Rules of quantification*

S14.   If $\alpha\in P_T$ and $\phi\in P_t$, then $F_{10,n}(\alpha,\phi)\in P_t$, where either (i) α does not have the form $\mathbf{he}_k$, and $F_{10,n}(\alpha,\phi)$ comes from ϕ by replacing the first occurrence of $\mathbf{he}_n$ or $\mathbf{him}_n$ by α and all other occurrences of $\mathbf{he}_n$ or $\mathbf{him}_n$ by

$\begin{Bmatrix} \text{he} \\ \text{she} \\ \text{it} \end{Bmatrix}$ or $\begin{Bmatrix} \text{him} \\ \text{her} \\ \text{it} \end{Bmatrix}$, respectively, according as the gender of the first B_{CN} or

B_T in α is $\begin{Bmatrix} \text{masc.} \\ \text{fem.} \\ \text{neuter} \end{Bmatrix}$, or (ii) $\alpha=\mathbf{he}_k$, and $F_{10,n}(\alpha,\phi)$ comes from ϕ by replac-

ing all occurrences of $\mathbf{he}_n$ or $\mathbf{him}_n$ by $\mathbf{he}_k$, or $\mathbf{him}_k$, respectively.

S15.   If $\alpha\in P_T$ and $\zeta\in P_{CN}$, then $F_{10,n}(\alpha,\zeta)\in P_{CN}$.

S16.   If $\alpha\in P_T$ and $\delta\in P_{IV}$, then $F_{10,n}(\alpha,\delta)\in P_{IV}$.

2.1.5. *Rules of tense and sign*

S17.   If $\alpha\in P_T$ and $\delta\in P_{IV}$, then $F_{11}(\alpha,\delta)$, $F_{12}(\alpha,\delta)$, $F_{13}(\alpha,\delta)$, $F_{14}(\alpha,\delta)$, $F_{15}(\alpha,\delta)\in P_t$, where $F_{11}(\alpha,\delta)=\alpha\delta'$ and δ' is the result of replacing the first verb in δ by its negative third person singular present, $F_{12}(\alpha,\delta)=\alpha\delta''$ and δ'' is the result of replacing the first verb in δ by its third person singular future, $F_{13}(\alpha,\delta)=\alpha\delta'''$ and δ''' is the result of replacing the first verb in δ by its negative third person singular future, $F_{14}(\alpha,\delta)$ $=\alpha\,\delta''''$ and δ'''' is the result of replacing the first verb in δ by its third person singular present perfect, $F_{15}(\alpha,\delta)=\alpha\delta'''''$ and δ''''' is the result of replacing the first verb in δ by its negative third person singular present perfect.

The precise characterization of the sets P_A, for A a category, is accomplished as follows. We first define the auxiliary notions occurring in the rules above in an obvious and traditional way: the *gender* of an arbitrary member of $B_T \cup B_{CN}$, the *indefinite article taken* by an arbitrary basic expression, and the *third person singular present*, the *negative third person singular present*, the *third person singular future*, the *negative third person singular future*, the *third person singular present perfect*, and the *negative third person singular present perfect* of an arbitrary verb. Then we may regard S1–S17 as constituting a simultaneous inductive definition of the sets P_A. Since, however, inductive definitions of this form are somewhat unusual, it is perhaps in order to state a corresponding explicit definition: the sets P_A (for $A \in Cat$) are the smallest sets satisfying S1–S17; that is to say, $\langle P_A \rangle_{A \in Cat}$ is the unique family of sets indexed by Cat such that (1) $\langle P_A \rangle_{A \in Cat}$ satisfies S1–S17, and (2) whenever $\langle P'_A \rangle_{A \in Cat}$ is a family of sets indexed by Cat, if $\langle P'_A \rangle_{A \in Cat}$ satisfies S1–S17, then $P_A \subseteq P'_A$ for all $A \in Cat$. (It is easily shown, using an idea I believe to have originated with Dr. Perry Smith, that there is exactly one family of sets satisfying these conditions.)

By a *meaningful expression* of the present fragment of English we may understand a member of any of the sets P_A for $A \in Cat$.

As an example, let us show that

every man loves a woman such that she loves him

is a declarative sentence (that is, member of P_t). By S1, $love \in P_{TV}$ and $he_0 \in P_T$. Hence, by S5, **love him$_0 \in P_{IV}$**. Therefore, by S1 and S4, **he$_1$ loves him$_0 \in P_t$**. Thus, by S1 and S3, **woman such that she loves him$_0 \in P_{CN}$**. Therefore, by S2, **a woman such that she loves him$_0 \in P_T$**. Hence, by S1 and S5, **love a woman such that she loves him$_0 \in P_{IV}$**. Therefore, by S1 and S4, **he$_0$ loves a woman such that she loves him$_0 \in P_t$**. Also, by S1 and S2, **every man $\in P_T$**; and hence, by S14, **every man loves a woman such that she loves him $\in P_t$**.

We may indicate the way in which this sentence has just been constructed by means of the following *analysis tree* (p. 227).

To each node we attach a meaningful expression, together, in case that

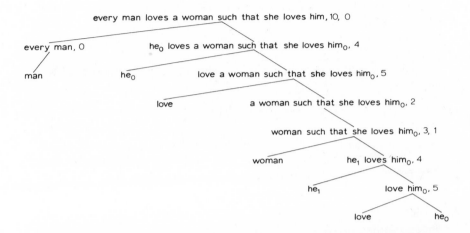

expression is not basic, with the index of that structural operation among F_0–F_2, $F_{3,0}$, $F_{3,1}$, ..., F_4–F_9, $F_{10,0}$, $F_{10,1}$, ..., F_{11}–F_{15} (as characterized above), within S1–S17) which we understand as having been applied in obtaining the expression in question; the nodes dominated by any node are to be occupied by the expressions to which the structural operation is understood as having been applied in obtaining the expression occupying the superior node. (For example, the numbers 10, 0 attached to the top node of the tree above indicate that the expression attached to that node is regarded as the value of the operation $F_{10,0}$ as applied to certain arguments; and the nodes beneath indicate that those arguments are understood to be the expressions **every man** and **he₀ loves a woman such that she loves him₀**.) A precise characterization of an *analysis tree* in the sense of these remarks would be routine and will not be given here; for such a characterization in an analogous content the reader might consult Montague (1970a).

Now there are other ways of constructing the sentence under consideration, and hence other analysis trees for it; indeed, it can be shown that every declarative sentence of our fragment has infinitely many analysis trees. But in the case considered, the various analyses will differ only inessentially; that is to say, they will all lead to the same semantical results.

There are other cases, however, of which this cannot be said. For instance, the sentence

John seeks a unicorn

has two essentially different analyses, represented by the following two trees:

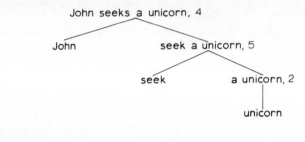

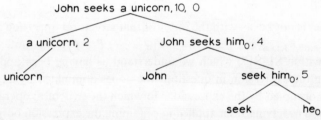

As we shall see, the first of these trees corresponds to the *de dicto* (or nonreferential) reading of the sentence, and the second to the *de re* (or referential) reading.

Thus our fragment admits genuinely (that is, semantically) ambiguous sentences. If it were desired to construct a corresponding unambiguous language, it would be convenient to take the analysis trees themselves as the expressions of that language; it would then be obvious how to characterize (in keeping with Montague, 1971) the structural operations of that language and the correspondence relation between its expressions and those of ordinary English.[5] For present purposes, however, no such construction is necessary.

3. INTENSIONAL LOGIC

We could (as in Montague, 1970a) introduce the semantics of our fragment directly; but it is probably more perspicuous to proceed indirectly, by (1) setting up a certain simple artificial language, that of tensed intensional logic, (2) giving the semantics of that language, and (3) interpreting English indirectly by showing in a rigorous way how to translate it into the artificial language. This is the procedure we shall adopt; accordingly, I shall now present the syntax and semantics of a tensed variant of the intensional logic I have discussed on earlier occasions.[6]

Let s be a fixed object (2, say) distinct from e and t and not an ordered pair or triple. The *Type*, or the set of *types*, is the smallest set Y such that (1) $e, t \in Y$, (2) whenever $a, b \in Y$, $\langle a, b \rangle \in Y$, and (3) whenever $a \in Y$, $\langle s, a \rangle \in Y$.

We shall employ denumerably many variables and infinitely many constants of each type. In particular, if n is any natural number and $a \in Type$, we understand by $v_{n,a}$ the nth variable of type a, and by Con_a the set of constants of type a. (The precise cardinality of Con_a need not concern us, provided only that it be infinite.)

By ME_a is understood the set of *meaningful expressions* of type a; this notion has the following recursive definition:

(1)   Every variable and constant of type a is in ME_a.

(2)   If $\alpha \in ME_a$ and u is a variable of type b, then $\lambda u \alpha \in ME_{\langle b,a \rangle}$.

(3)   If $\alpha \in ME_{\langle a,b \rangle}$ and $\beta \in ME_a$, then $\alpha(\beta) \in ME_b$.

(4)   If $\alpha, \beta \in ME_a$, then $\alpha = \beta \in ME_t$.

(5)   If $\phi, \psi \in ME_t$ and u is a variable, then $\neg\phi$, $[\phi \wedge \psi]$, $[\phi \vee \psi]$, $[\phi \to \psi]$, $[\phi \leftrightarrow \psi]$, $\bigvee u\phi$, $\bigwedge u\phi$, $\Box\phi$, $W\phi$, $H\phi \in ME_t$.

(6)   If $\alpha \in ME_a$, then $[\hat{\ }\alpha] \in ME_{\langle s,a \rangle}$.

(7)   If $\alpha \in ME_{\langle s,a \rangle}$, then $[\check{\ }\alpha] \in ME_a$.

(8)   Nothing is in any set ME_a except as required by (1)–(7).[7]

By a *meaningful expression* of intensional logic is understood a member of $\cup_{a \in Type} ME_a$.

If u is a variable of type a, then $\lambda u \alpha$ is understood as denoting that function from objects of type a which takes as value, for any such object x, the object denoted by α when u is understood as denoting x. The expression $\alpha(\beta)$ is as usual understood as denoting the value of the function denoted by α for the argument denoted by β. The equality symbol $=$, the negation symbol $\neg$, the conjunction symbol $\wedge$, the disjunction symbol $\vee$, the conditional symbol $\to$, the biconditional symbol $\leftrightarrow$, the existential quantifier $\bigvee$, and the universal quantifier $\bigwedge$ are all understood in the usual way. The symbols $\square$, W, H may be read 'it is necessary that', 'it will be the case that', 'it has been the case that', respectively. The expression $[\hat{\ }\alpha]$ is regarded as denoting (or having as its *extension*) the *intension* of the expression α. The expression $[\check{\ }\alpha]$ is meaningful only if α is an expression that denotes an intension or sense; in such a case $[\check{\ }\alpha]$ denotes the corresponding extension.

We could have done with a much smaller stock of primitive symbols, as in Montague (1971); but there is no point in considering here the relevant reductions.

In the presentation of actual expressions of intensional logic square brackets will sometimes for perspicuity be omitted, and sometimes gratuitously inserted.

Let A, I, J be any sets, which we may for the moment regard as the set of entities (or individuals[8]), the set of possible worlds, and the set of moments of time, respectively. In addition, let a be a type. Then $D_{a,A,I,J}$, or the set of *possible denotations* of type a corresponding to A, I, J, may be introduced by the following recursive definition. (If X and Y are any sets, then as usual we understand by X^Y the set of all functions with domain Y and values in X, and by $X \times Y$ the *Cartesian product* of X and Y (that is, the set of all ordered pairs $\langle x, y \rangle$ such that $x \in X$ and $y \in Y$). Further, we identify the truth values falsehood and truth with the numbers 0 and 1, respectively.)

$$D_{e,A,I,J} = A,$$
$$D_{t,A,I,J} = \{0,1\},$$
$$D_{\langle a,b \rangle,A,I,J} = D_{b,A,I,J}{}^{D_{a,A,I,J}},$$
$$D_{\langle s,a \rangle,A,I,J} = D_{a,A,I,J}{}^{I \times J}.$$

By $S_{a,A,I,J}$, or the set of *senses* of type a corresponding to A,I,J, is understood $D_{\langle s,a \rangle,A,I,J}$, that is, $D_{a,A,I,J}{}^{I \times J}$.

By an *interpretation* (or intensional model) is understood a quintuple $\langle A,I,J, \leq, F \rangle$ such that (1) A,I,J are nonempty sets, (2) $\leq$ is a simple (that is, linear) ordering having J as its field, (3) F is a function having as its domain the set of all constants, and (4) whenever $a \in Type$ and $\alpha \in Con_a$, $F(\alpha) \in S_{a,A,I,J}$.

Suppose that $\mathfrak{A}$ is an interpretation having the form $\langle A,I,J, \leq, F \rangle$. Suppose also that g is an $\mathfrak{A}$-*assignment* (of values to variables), that is, a function having as its domain the set of all variables and such that $g(u) \in D_{a,A,I,J}$ whenever u is a variable of type a. If α is a meaningful expression, we shall understand by $\alpha^{\mathfrak{A},g}$ the *intension* of α with respect to $\mathfrak{A}$ and g; and if $\langle i,j \rangle \in I \times J$ then $\alpha^{\mathfrak{A},i,j,g}$ is to be the *extension* of α with respect to $\mathfrak{A}, i, j$, and g – that is, $\alpha^{\mathfrak{A},g}(\langle i,j \rangle)$ or the function value of the intension of α when applied to the point of reference $\langle i,j \rangle$. These notions may be introduced by the following recursive definition.

(1)   If α is a constant, then $\alpha^{\mathfrak{A},g}$ is $F(\alpha)$.

(2)   If α is a variable, then $\alpha^{\mathfrak{A},i,j,g}$ is $g(\alpha)$.

(3)   If $\alpha \in ME_a$ and u is a variable of type b, then $[\lambda u \alpha]^{\mathfrak{A},i,j,g}$ is that function h with domain $D_{b,A,I,J}$ such that whenever x is in that domain, $h(x)$ is $\alpha^{\mathfrak{A},i,j,g'}$, where g' is the $\mathfrak{A}$-assignment like g except for the possible difference that $g'(u)$ is x.

(4)   If $\alpha \in ME_{\langle a,b \rangle}$ and $\beta \in ME_a$, then $[\alpha(\beta)]^{\mathfrak{A},i,j,g}$ is $\alpha^{\mathfrak{A},i,j,g}(\beta^{\mathfrak{A},i,j,g})$ (that is, the value of the function $\alpha^{\mathfrak{A},i,j,g}$ for the argument $\beta^{\mathfrak{A},i,j,g}$).

(5)   If $\alpha, \beta \in ME_a$, then $[\alpha = \beta]^{\mathfrak{A},i,j,g}$ is 1 if and only if $\alpha^{\mathfrak{A},i,j,g}$ is $\beta^{\mathfrak{A},i,j,g}$.

(6)   If $\phi \in ME_t$, then $[\neg \phi]^{\mathfrak{A},i,j,g}$ is 1 if and only if $\phi^{\mathfrak{A},i,j,g}$ is 0; and similarly for $\wedge, \vee, \rightarrow, \leftrightarrow$.

(7)   If $\phi \in ME_t$ and u is a variable of type a, then $[\vee u \phi]^{\mathfrak{A},i,j,g}$ is 1 if and only if there exists $x \in D_{a,A,I,J}$ such that $\phi^{\mathfrak{A},i,j,g'}$ is 1, where g' is as in (3); and similarly for $\wedge u \phi$.

(8)   If $\phi \in ME_t$, then $[\Box \phi]^{\mathfrak{A},i,j,g}$ is 1 if and only if $\phi^{\mathfrak{A},i',j',g}$ is 1 for all $i' \in I$ and $j' \in J$; $[W\phi]^{\mathfrak{A},i,j,g}$ is 1 if and only if $\phi^{\mathfrak{A},i,j',g}$ is 1 for some j' such that $j \leq j'$ and $j \neq j'$; and $[H\phi]^{\mathfrak{A},i,j,g}$ is 1 if and only if $\phi^{\mathfrak{A},i,j',g}$ is 1 for some j' such that $j' \leq j$ and $j' \neq j$.

(9)   If $\alpha \in ME_t$, then $[\hat{\ }\alpha]^{\mathfrak{A},i,j,g}$ is $\alpha^{\mathfrak{A},g}$.

(10)   If $\alpha \in ME_{\langle s,a \rangle}$, then $[\check{\ }\alpha]^{\mathfrak{A},i,j,g}$ is $\alpha^{\mathfrak{A},i,j,g}(\langle i,j \rangle)$.

If ϕ is a *formula* (that is, member of ME_t), then ϕ is *true* with respect to $\mathfrak{A}, i, j$ if and only if $\phi^{\mathfrak{A},i,j,g}$ is 1 for every $\mathfrak{A}$-assignment g.

It will be useful to call attention to some particular meaningful expressions of intensional logic. If $\gamma \in ME_{\langle a,t \rangle}$ and $\alpha \in ME_a$, then γ denotes (that is, has as its extension) a set (or really the characteristic function of a set) of objects of type a, and we may regard the formula $\gamma(\alpha)$, which denotes truth exactly in case the object denoted by α is a member of that set, as *asserting* that the object denoted by α is a member of the set denoted by γ.

If $\gamma \in ME_{\langle a,\langle b,t\rangle\rangle}$, $\alpha \in ME_a$, and $\beta \in ME_b$, then γ may be regarded as denoting a (2-place) *relation*, and $\check{\gamma}(\beta,\alpha)$ is to be the expression $\gamma(\alpha)(\beta)$, which asserts that the objects denoted by β and α stand in that relation. If $\gamma \in ME_{\langle s,\langle a,t\rangle\rangle}$ and $\alpha \in ME_a$; then γ denotes a *property*, and $\gamma\{\alpha\}$ is to be the expression $[\check{\ }\gamma](\alpha)$, which asserts that the object denoted by α has that property. If $\gamma \in ME_{\langle s,\langle a,\langle b,t\rangle\rangle\rangle}$, $\alpha \in ME_a$, and $\beta \in ME_b$, then γ may ·be regarded as denoting a *relation-in-intension*, and $\gamma\{\beta,\alpha\}$ is to be the expression $[\check{\ }\gamma](\beta,\alpha)$, which asserts that the objects denoted by β and α stand in that relation-in-intension. If u is a variable of type a and ϕ a formula, then $\hat{u}\phi$ is to be $\lambda u\phi$, which denotes the set of all objects of type a that satisfy ϕ (with respect to the place marked by u), and $\hat{u}\phi$ is to be $[^\wedge\hat{u}\phi]$, which denotes the property of objects of type a expressed by ϕ. If $\alpha \in ME_e$, then α^* is to be $\hat{P}[P\{\check{\ }\alpha\}]$, where P is $v_{0,\langle s,\langle\langle s,e\rangle,t\rangle\rangle}$.

4. TRANSLATING ENGLISH INTO INTENSIONAL LOGIC

We first introduce a mapping f from the categories of English to the types of intensional logic. Accordingly, f is to be a function having *Cat* as its domain and such that

$$f(e) = e,$$
$$f(t) = t,$$
$$f(A/B) = f(A//B) = \langle\langle s, f(B)\rangle, f(A)\rangle \text{ whenever } A, B \in Cat.$$

The intention is that English expressions of any category A are to translate into expressions of type $f(A)$.[9]

In all that follows let g be a fixed biunique function such that (1) the domain of g is the set of basic expressions of our fragment of English other than **be**, **necessarily**, and the members of B_T, and (2) whenever $A \in Cat$, $\alpha \in B_A$, and α is in the domain of g, $g(\alpha) \in Con_{f(A)}$. Let j, m, b, n be particular distinct members of Con_e. (If we had introduced a definite well-ordering of the constants of intensional logic, we could at this point have explicitly defined g, j, m, b, and n. Such details would, however, be irrelevant to our present concerns.) Let u, v be the particular individual variables $v_{0,e}$, $v_{1,e}$, respectively; x, y, x_n be the particular individual-concept variables $v_{1,\langle s,e\rangle}$, $v_{3,\langle s,e\rangle}$, $v_{2n,\langle s,e\rangle}$, respectively, (for any natural number n); p be the proposition variable $v_{0,\langle s,t\rangle}$; P, Q be the variables $v_{0,\langle s,\langle\langle s,e\rangle,t\rangle\rangle}$, $v_{1,\langle s,\langle\langle s,e\rangle,t\rangle\rangle}$, which range over properties of individual concepts; $\mathscr{P}$ be the variable $v_{0,\langle s,\langle\langle s,\langle\langle s,e\rangle,t\rangle\rangle,t\rangle\rangle}$, which ranges over properties of properties of individual concepts; M be the variable $v_{0,\langle s,\langle e,t\rangle\rangle}$, which ranges over properties of individuals; S be the variable $v_{0,\langle s,\langle e,\langle e,t\rangle\rangle\rangle}$, which ranges over two-place relations-in-intension between individuals; and G be the variable $v_{0,\langle s,\langle e,f(IAV)\rangle\rangle}$.

We shall now consider some rules of translation, T1–T17, which will be seen to correspond to the syntactic rules S1–S17, respectively, and to constitute, in a sense to be made precise below, a definition of the translation relation.

4.1. *Translation Rules*

4.1.1. *Basic rules*

T1. (a) If α is in the domain of g, then α translates into $g(\alpha)$.

(b) **be** translates into $\lambda\mathscr{P}\,\lambda x\,\mathscr{P}\{\hat{y}[\check{}\,x = \check{}\,y]\}$.

(c) **necessarily** translates into $p[\Box p]$.

(d) **John, Mary, Bill, ninety** translate into j^*, m^*, b^*, n^*, respectively.

(e) **he**$_n$ translates $\hat{P}P\{x_n\}$.

T2. If $\zeta \in P_{CN}$ and ζ translates into ζ', then **every** ζ translates into $\hat{P}\wedge x[\zeta'(x) \to P\{x\}]$, **the** ζ translates into $\hat{P}\,\vee y[\wedge x[\zeta'(x)\leftrightarrow x=y]\wedge P\{y\}]$, $F_2(\zeta)$ translates into $\hat{P}\vee x\,[\zeta'(x) \wedge P\{x\}]$.

T3. If $\zeta \in P_{CN}$, $\phi \in P_t$, and ζ, ϕ translate into ζ', ϕ', respectively, then $F_{3,n}(\zeta, \phi)$ translates into $\hat{x}_n[\zeta'(x_n) \wedge \phi']$.

4.1.2. *Rules of functional application*

T4. If $\delta \in P_{t/IV}$, $\beta \in P_{IV}$, and δ, β translate into δ', β', respectively, then $F_4(\delta, \beta)$ translates into $\delta'(\hat{}\,\beta')$.

T5. If $\delta \in P_{IV/T}$, $\beta \in P_T$, and δ, β translate into δ', β', respectively, then $F_5(\delta, \beta)$ translates into $\delta'(\hat{}\,\beta')$.

T6. If $\delta \in P_{IAV/T}$, $\beta \in P_T$, and δ, β translate into δ', β', respectively, then $F_5(\delta, \beta)$ translates into $\delta'(\hat{}\,\beta')$.

T7. If $\delta \in P_{IV/t}$, $\beta \in P_t$, and δ, β translate into δ', β', respectively, then $F_6(\delta, \beta)$ translates into $\delta'(\hat{}\,\beta')$.

T8. If $\delta \in P_{IV//IV}$, $\beta \in P_{IV}$, and δ, β translate into δ', β', respectively, then $F_6(\delta, \beta)$ translates into $\delta'(\hat{}\,\beta')$.

T9.   If $\delta \in P_{t/t}$, $\beta \in P_t$, and δ, β translate into δ', β', respectively, then $F_6(\delta, \beta)$ translates into $\delta'(\hat{\ } \beta')$.

T10.   If $\delta \in P_{IV/IV}$, $\beta \in P_{IV}$, and δ, β translate into δ', β', respectively, then $F_7(\delta, \beta)$ translates into $\delta'(\hat{\ } \beta')$.

4.1.3. *Rules of conjunction and disjunction*

T11.   If ϕ, $\psi \in P_t$ and ϕ, ψ translate into ϕ', ψ', respectively, then ϕ **and** ψ translates into $[\phi \wedge \psi]$, ϕ **or** ψ translates into $[\phi \vee \psi]$.

T12.   If $\gamma, \delta \in P_{IV}$ and γ, δ translate into γ', δ', respectively, then γ **and** δ translates into $\hat{x}[\gamma'(x) \wedge \delta'(x)]$, γ **or** δ translates into $\hat{x}[\gamma'(x) \vee \delta'(x)]$.

T13.   If $\alpha, \beta \in P_T$ and α, β translate into α', β', respectively, then α **or** β translates into $\hat{P}[\alpha'(P) \vee \beta'(P)]$.

4.1.4. *Rules of quantification*

T14.   If $\alpha \in P_T$, $\phi \in P_t$, and α, ϕ translate into α', ϕ', respectively, then $F_{10,n}(\alpha, \phi)$ translates into $\alpha'(\hat{x}_n \phi')$.

T15.   If $\alpha \in P_T$, $\zeta \in P_{CN}$, and α, ζ translate into α', ζ', respectively, then $F_{10,n}(\alpha, \zeta)$ translates into $\hat{y}\alpha'(\hat{x}_n[\zeta'(y)])$.

T16.   If $\alpha \in P_T$, $\delta \in P_{IV}$, and α, δ translate into α', δ', respectively, then $F_{10,n}(\alpha, \delta)$ translates into $\hat{y}\alpha'(\hat{x}_n[\delta'(y)])$.

4.1.5. *Rules of tense and sign*

T17.   If $\alpha \in P_T$, $\delta \in P_{IV}$, and α, δ translate into α', δ', respectively, then $F_{11}(\alpha, \delta)$ translates into $\neg\alpha'(\hat{\ } \delta')$, $F_{12}(\alpha, \delta)$ translates into $W\alpha'(\hat{\ } \delta')$, $F_{13}(\alpha, \delta)$ translates into $\neg W\alpha'(\hat{\ } \delta')$, $F_{14}(\alpha, \delta)$ translates into $H\alpha'(\hat{\ } \delta')$, $F_{15}(\alpha, \delta)$ translates into $\neg H\alpha'(\hat{\ } \delta')$.

The precise import of the rules T1–T17 is that the translation relation may be defined as the smallest binary relation satisfying them; that is to say, an expression ϕ is characterized as *translating into* an expression ϕ' if the pair $\langle \phi, \phi' \rangle$ is a member of every binary relation R such that T1–T17 hold (with the condition that one expression translates into another replaced by the condition that the relation R holds between the two expressions).

The translation relation is of course not a function; a meaningful expression of English may translate into several different expressions of intensional logic. We could, however, speak of *the translation* of a given meaningful expression of English corresponding to any given analysis tree for that expression; the rather obvious definition of this notion will be omitted here. The interpretations of intensional logic may, by way of the translation relation, be made to play a second role as interpretations of English.[10] Not all interpretations of intensional logic, however, would be reasonable candidates for interpretations of English. In particular, it would be reasonable in this context to restrict attention to those interpretations of intensional logic in which the following formulas are true (with respect to all, or equivalently some, worlds and moments of time):

(1) $\quad \vee u \,\square[u = \alpha]$, where α is j, m, b, or n,

(2) $\quad \square[\delta(x) \rightarrow \vee u \; x = \,^\wedge u]$, where δ translates any member of B_{CN} other than **price** or **temperature**,

(3) $\quad \vee M \wedge x \,\square[\delta(x) \leftrightarrow M\{\,^\vee x\}]$, where δ translates any member of B_{IV} other than **rise** or **change**,

(4) $\quad \vee S \wedge x \wedge \mathscr{P} \,\square[\delta(x, \mathscr{P}) \leftrightarrow \mathscr{P}\{\hat{y}S\{\,^\vee x, \,^\vee y\}\}]$, where δ translates **find**, **lose**, **eat**, **love**, or **date**,

(5) $\quad \wedge \mathscr{P} \vee M \wedge x \,\square[\delta(x, \mathscr{P}) \leftrightarrow M\{\,^\vee x\}]$, where δ translates **seek** or **conceive**,

(6) $\quad \wedge p \vee M \wedge x \,\square[\delta(x, p) \leftrightarrow M\{\,^\vee x\}]$, where δ translates **believe that** or **assert that**,

$\quad \wedge P \vee M \wedge x \,\square[\delta(x, P) \leftrightarrow M\{\,^\vee x\}]$, where δ translates **try to** or **wish to**,

(8) $\quad \vee G \wedge \mathscr{P} \wedge Q \wedge x \,\square[\delta(\mathscr{P})(Q)(x) \leftrightarrow \mathscr{P}\{\hat{y}[[\,^\vee G](\,^\vee y)(Q)(x)]\}]$, where δ translates **in**,

(9) $\quad \square[\mathbf{seek'}(x, \mathscr{P}) \leftrightarrow \mathbf{try\text{-}to'}(x, \,^\wedge[\mathbf{find'}(\mathscr{P})])]$, where **seek'**, **try-to'**, **find'** translate **seek**, **try to**, **find**, respectively.

The truth of (1) guarantees that proper nouns will be 'logically determinate' according to the interpretations under consideration, that is, they will have extensions invariant with respect to possible worlds and moments of time. In view of (2), 'ordinary' common nouns (for example, **horse**) will denote sets of *constant* individual concepts (for example, the set of constant functions on worlds and moments having horses as their values; from an intuitive viewpoint, this is no different from the set of horses). It would be unacceptable to impose this condition on such 'extraordinary' common nouns as **price** or **temperature**; the individual concepts in their extensions would in the most natural cases be functions whose values vary with their temporal arguments. The truth of (3) is the natural requirement of *extensionality* for intransitive verbs, that of (4) the condition of extensionality (or extensional first-order reducibility) for transitive verbs, and that of (8) the condition of extensionality (or extensional first-order reducibility) for prepositions. The *intensional* (or nonextensional) transitive verbs **seek** and **conceive**, as well as the verbs **believe that, assert that, try to, wish to** of other categories, are nevertheless *extensional with respect to subject position*, and this is expressed by imposing conditions (5)–(7). Condition (9) is the natural definition of **seek** as **try to find**.

Several notions of a logically possible interpretation may reasonably come into consideration, depending on whether, and if so how many, conditions analogous to (1)–(9), stemming from our intended system of translation, are to be imposed. For present purposes we may perhaps resolve the matter as follows: by a *logically possible interpretation* understand an interpretation of intensional logic in which formulas (1)–(9) are true (with respect to all worlds and moments of time). Logical truth, logical consequence, and logical equivalence, for formulas of intensional logic, are to be characterized accordingly. For instance, a formula ϕ of intensional logic is construed as *logically true* if it is true in every logically possible interpretation, with respect to all worlds and moments of time of that interpretation; and two formulas ϕ and ψ of intensional logic are *logically equivalent* if and only if the biconditional $[\phi \leftrightarrow \psi]$ is logically true.

If δ is an expression of intensional logic of such type as to translate a transitive or intransitive verb, then δ_* is to be an expression designating the set of individuals or relation between individuals that naturally corresponds to the set or relation designated by δ. In particular, if $\delta \in ME_{f(IV)}$, then δ_* is to be the expression $u\delta([\,^\vee u])$; and if $\delta \in ME_{f(TV)}$, then δ_* is to be $\lambda v \widehat{u} \delta([\,^\vee u],[\,^\vee v^*])$. Notice that since $f(CN) = f(TV)$, this characterization is also applicable in the case in which δ translates a common noun.

It is a consequence of principles (2), (3), (4) that if δ is among the constants involved in those principles (that is, constants translating 'ordinary' common nouns or 'extensional' transitive or intransitive verbs), then δ is definable in terms of δ_*. More exactly, the following formulas are logically true:

$\square\,[\delta(x)\leftrightarrow\delta_*(\,\check{}\,x)]$, if δ translates any member of B_{CN} or B_{IV} other than **price, temperature, rise**, or **change**;

$\square\,[\delta(x,\mathscr{P})\leftrightarrow\mathscr{P}\{\hat{y}\delta_*(\,\check{}\,x,\,\check{}\,y)\}]$, if δ translates any member of B_{TV} other than **seek** or **conceive**.

Notice that although the verb **be** (or its translation) is not covered by principle (4), it is by the last principle above. The reason why the extensionality of **be** was not explicitly assumed is that it can be proved. (More precisely, the analogue of (4) in which δ is the expression translating **be** is true in all interpretations (with respect to all worlds and moments).)

5. EXAMPLES

The virtues of the present treatment can perhaps best be appreciated by considering particular English sentences and the precisely interpreted sentences of intensional logic that translate them. I shall give a list of such examples. It is understood that each English sentence listed below translates into some formula logically equivalent to each of the one or more formulas of intensional logic listed with it, and that every formula into which the English sentence translates is logically equivalent to one of those formulas. It should be emphasized that this is not a matter of vague intuition, as in elementary logic courses, but an assertion to which we have assigned exact significance in preceding sections and which can be rigorously proved. (The constants of intensional logic that translate various basic expressions of English are designated below by primed variants of those expressions.)

The first five examples indicate that in simple extensional cases symbolizations of the expected forms are obtained.

Bill walks: $\mathbf{walk'}_*(b)$

a man walks: $\vee u[\mathbf{man'}_*(u) \wedge \mathbf{walk'}_*(u)]$

every man walks: $\wedge u[\mathbf{man'}_*(u) \to \mathbf{walk'}_*(u)]$

the man walks: $\vee v \wedge u[[\mathbf{man'}_*(u)\leftrightarrow u=v] \wedge \mathbf{walk'}_*(v)]$

John finds a unicorn: $\vee u[\mathbf{unicorn'}_*(u) \wedge \mathbf{find'}_*(j,u)]$

The next sentence, though superficially like the last, is ambiguous and has two essentially different symbolizations corresponding to the two analysis trees presented above; the first gives the *de dicto* reading; and the second the *de re*.

John seeks a unicorn:
$$\begin{cases} \textbf{seek}'(\hat{\ }j, \hat{P} \; \lor u[\textbf{unicorn}'_*(u) \land P\{\hat{\ }u\}]) \\ \lor u[\textbf{unicorn}'_*(u) \land \textbf{seek}'_*(j, u)] \end{cases}$$

The source of the ambiguity of **John seeks a unicorn** will perhaps be clarified if we compare that sentence with the intuitively synonymous **John tries to find a unicorn**, which contains no intensional verbs but only the extensional verb **find** and the 'higher-order' verb **try to**. Here, though perhaps not in **John seeks a unicorn**, the ambiguity is clearly a matter of scope, and indeed depends on the possibility of regarding either the component **find a unicorn** or the whole sentence as the scope of the existential quantification indicated by **a unicorn**.

John tries to
find a unicorn:
$$\begin{cases} \textbf{try-to}'(\hat{\ }j, \hat{y}\lor u[\textbf{unicorn}'_*(u) \land \textbf{find}'_*(\check{\ }y, u)]) \\ \lor u[\textbf{unicorn}'_*(u) \land \textbf{try-to}'(\hat{\ }j, \hat{y}\;\textbf{find}'_*(\check{\ }y, u))] \end{cases}$$

It might be suggested, as in Quine (1960) or Montague (1969), that intensional verbs be allowed only as paraphrases of more tractable locutions (such as **try to find**).[11] Such a proposal, however, would not be naturally applicable, for want of a paraphrase, to such intensional verbs as **conceive** and such intensional prepositions as **about**; and I regard it as one of the principal virtues of the present treatment, as well as the one in Montague (1971), that it enables us to deal directly with intensional locutions. The next example accordingly concerns **about** and gives us, as intuition demands, one reading of **John talks about a unicorn** that does not entail that there are unicorns.

John talks about
a unicorn
$$\begin{cases} \textbf{about}'(\hat{P} \; \lor u[\textbf{unicorn}'_*(u) \land P\{\hat{\ }u\}]) \\ (\hat{\ }\textbf{talk}')(\hat{\ }j) \\ \lor u[\textbf{unicorn}'_*(u) \\ \land \textbf{about}'(\hat{\ }u^*)(\hat{\ }\textbf{talk}')(\hat{\ }j)] \end{cases}$$

The next two examples indicate that our uniform symbolization of **be** will adequately cover both the **is** of identity and the **is** of predication; views along this line, though not the rather complicated analysis of **be** given here, may be found in Quine (1960).

Bill is Mary: $b = m$
Bill is a man: $\textbf{man}'_*(b)$

The next few examples concern an interesting puzzle due to Barbara Hall Partee involving a kind of intensionality not previously observed by philosophers. From the premises **the temperature is ninety** and **the temperature rises**, the conclusion **ninety rises** would appear to follow by normal principles of logic; yet there are occasions on which both premises are true, but none on which the conclusion is. According to the following symbolizations, however, the argument in question turns out not to be valid. (The reason, speaking very loosely, is this. **The temperature** 'denotes' an individual concept, not an individual; and **rise**, unlike most verbs, depends for its applicability on the full behavior of individual concepts, not just on their extensions with respect to the actual world and (what is more relevant here) moment of time. Yet the sentence **the temperature is ninety** asserts the identity not of two individual concepts but only of their extensions.)

the temperature is ninety: $\vee y[\wedge x[\textbf{temperature}'(x) \leftrightarrow x = y]$
$\wedge\ [\ ^{\vee}y] = n]$
the temperature rises: $\quad \vee y[\wedge x[\textbf{temperature}'(x) \leftrightarrow x = y]$
$\wedge\ \textbf{rise}'(y)]$
ninety rises: $\textbf{rise}'(^{\frown}n)$

We thus see the virtue of having intransitive verbs and common nouns denote sets of individual concepts rather than sets of individuals – a consequence of our general development that might at first appear awkward and unnatural. It would be possible to treat the Partee argument itself without introducing this feature, but not certain analogous arguments involving indefinite rather than definite terms. Notice, for instance, that **a price rises** and **every price is a number** must not be allowed to entail **a number rises**. Indeed they do not according to our treatment; to see this, perhaps it is enough to consider the first premise, which, unlike **a man walks,** requires individual-concept variables (and not simply individual variables) for its symbolization.

a price rises: $\quad \vee x[\textbf{price}'(x) \wedge \textbf{rise}'(x)]$

The next example shows that ambiguity can arise even when there is no element of intensionality, simply because quantifying terms may be introduced in more than one order.

a woman loves every man:
$$\begin{cases} \vee u[\mathbf{woman'}_*(u) \wedge \wedge v[\mathbf{man'}_*(v) \\ \to \mathbf{love'}_*(u, v)]] \\ \wedge v[\mathbf{man'}_*(v) \to \vee u[\mathbf{woman'}_*(u) \\ \wedge \mathbf{love'}_*(u, v)]] \end{cases}$$

The next example indicates the necessity of allowing verb phrases as well as sentences to be conjoined and quantified. Without such provisions the sentence **John wishes to find a unicorn and eat it** would (unacceptably, as several linguists have pointed out in connection with parallel examples) have only a 'referential' reading, that is, one that entails that there are unicorns.

John wishes to find a unicorn and eat it:
$$\begin{cases} \vee u[\mathbf{unicorn'}_*(u) \wedge \mathbf{wish\text{-}to'}(\hat{\,}j, \\ \hat{y}[\mathbf{find'}_*(\check{\,}y, u) \wedge \mathbf{eat'}_*(\check{\,}y, u)])] \\ \mathbf{wish\text{-}to'}(\hat{\,}j, \hat{y} \vee u[\mathbf{unicorn'}_*(u) \\ \wedge \mathbf{find'}_*(\check{\,}y, u) \wedge \mathbf{eat'}_*(\check{\,}y, u)]) \end{cases}$$

The next example is somewhat simpler, in that it does not involve conjoining or quantifying verb phrases; but it also illustrates the possibility of a nonreferential reading in the presence of a pronoun.

Mary believes that John finds a unicorn and he eats it:
$$\vee u[\mathbf{unicorn'}_*(u) \wedge \mathbf{believe\text{-}that'}(\hat{\,}m, \hat{\,}[\mathbf{find'}_*(j, u)$$
$$\wedge \mathbf{eat'}_*(j, u))]]$$
$$\vee u[\mathbf{unicorn'}_*(u) \wedge \mathbf{believe\text{-}that'}(\hat{\,}m, \hat{\,}[\mathbf{find'}_*(j, u)])$$
$$\wedge \mathbf{eat'}_*(j, u)]$$
$$\mathbf{believe\text{-}that'}(\hat{\,}m, \hat{\,} \vee u[\mathbf{unicorn'}_*(u) \wedge \mathbf{find'}_*(j, u)$$
$$\wedge \mathbf{eat'}_*(j, u)])$$

On the other hand, in each of the following examples only one reading is possible, and that the referential:

(1)   **John seeks a unicorn and Mary seeks it**,

(2)   **John tries to find a unicorn and wishes to eat it**.

This is, according to my intuitions (and, if I guess correctly from remarks in Partee, 1970b, those of Barbara Partee as well), as it should be; but David Kaplan would differ, at least as to (2). Let him, however, and those who might sympathize with him consider the following variant of (2) and attempt to make nonreferential sense of it:

(2')   **John wishes to find a unicorn and tries to eat it.**

Of course there are other uses of pronouns than the ones treated in this paper – for instance, their use as what have been called in Geach (1962, and 1967a) and Partee (1970b) *pronouns of laziness*, that is, as 'standing for' longer terms bearing a somewhat indefinite relation to other expressions in the sentence in question (or preceding sentences within the discourse in question). For instance, it is not impossible to construe **it** in (2) as standing for **the unicorn he finds** (that is, **the unicorn such that he finds it**), **a unicorn he finds**, or **every unicorn he finds**, and in this way to obtain a nonreferential reading of that sentence; but this is not a reading with which David Kaplan would be content.

University of California, Los Angeles

NOTES

* Much of the research reported here was supported by United States National Science Foundation Grant GS-2785. I am indebted to Mr. Michael Bennett, Mr. Harry Deutsch, and Mr. Daniel Gallin for helpful comments.
[1] The medieval and twentieth-century philosophical literature has pointed out a number of such difficulties, most of them involving so-called intensional contexts. I am indebted to Barbara Hall Partee for pointing out others, both in conversation and in her provocative paper (Partee, 1970b). (This remark should not, however, be taken as implying agreement with any of Professor Partee's conclusions.)
[2] With the exception that in Montague (1971) a number of intuitively plausible ambiguities were for simplicity ruled out.
[3] In connection with imperatives and interrogatives truth and entailment conditions are of course inappropriate, and would be replaced by fulfillment conditions and a characterization of the semantic content of a correct answer.
[4] It was perhaps the failure to pursue the possibility of syntactically splitting categories originally conceived in semantic terms that accounts for the fact that Ajdukiewicz's proposals have not previously led to a successful syntax. They have, however, been employed semantically in Montague (1970a) and, in a modified version, in Lewis (1972).
[5] This way of constructing an underlying unambiguous language, though convenient here, would be unsuitable in connection with fragments of natural language exhibiting greater syntactical complexities of certain sorts.
[6] In particular, in talks before the Southern California Logic Colloquium and the Association for Symbolic Logic in April and May of 1969, and in the paper by Montague (1971). The addition of tenses is rather routine in the light of the discussion in Montague (1968); and it would be possible to replace the tense operators by predicates, thus preserving exactly the language in Montague (1971), in the manner indicated in Montague (1970b).
[7] Clause (8) is of course vague but can be eliminated in a familiar way. To be exact, the recursive definition given above can be replaced by the following explicit definition: ME_a is

the set of all objects α such that αRa, where R is the smallest relation such that clauses (1)–(7) hold (with all parts of the form $\beta \in ME_a$ replaced by βRa).

[8] Or possible individuals. If there are individuals that are only possible but not actual, A is to contain them; but this is an issue on which it would be unethical for me as a logician (or linguist or grammarian or semanticist, for that matter) to take a stand.

[9] The simplicity and uniformity of the present correspondence stands in remarkable contrast to the *ad hoc* character of the type assignment in Montague (1971).

[10] Alternatives are possible. For instance, we could instead consider *direct* interpretations of English induced by interpretations of intensional logic in conjunction with our translation procedure; the precise general construction is given in Montague (1971). Though this would probably be the best approach from a general viewpoint, it would introduce slight complications that need not be considered in the present paper.

[11] Strictly speaking, this would mean, within the framework of the present paper, introducing a syntactic operation F such that, for example, F (**John tries to find a unicorn**) = **John seeks a unicorn**, a syntactic rule to the effect that $F(\phi) \in P_t$ whenever $\phi \in P_t$, and a corresponding translation rule that whenever $\phi \in P_t$ and ϕ translates into ϕ', $F(\phi)$ translates into ϕ'.

BARBARA HALL PARTEE

COMMENTS ON MONTAGUE'S PAPER

1. FIRST APPROXIMATION

I would like to try to relate Montague's theory of grammar (henceforth, M grammar) to transformational grammar (T grammar). It seems to me that the T grammar approach has led to the discovery of many highly specific and interesting principles of syntactic organization in natural language. The attempt to incorporate semantics into T grammar has not been without difficulties, however, and has been in part responsible for a number of proposals for far-reaching changes in the theory. Since one of the prime features of M grammar is the elegant manner in which syntax and semantics are related, M grammar is potentially of great interest to linguists.

The first problem to which most of these comments are directed is the terminology barrier. Linguists working with T grammar have evolved a rather specialized terminology which is often obscure to philosophers; and Montague's highly condensed logical notation presents considerable difficulty to the linguist. I will attempt to describe M grammar in terms linguists will understand; it is possible that philosophers may glean some insights into T grammar therefrom.

In order that points of comparison not lead to too hasty value judgments on either side, it is worth emphasizing the different motivations behind M grammar and T grammar. The goal of T grammar is the characterization of all and only the possible human languages, in hopes of developing hypotheses about structural properties of the brain. Every aspect of a T grammar is supposed to have 'psychological reality', in some sufficiently abstract sense. The goal of M grammar is a theory of syntax and semantics of all languages, with no special priority given to human ones. Success is defined in terms of formal elegance rather than psychological reality. There may not be a theory that can satisfy both kinds of requirements; but neither are they necessarily incompatible. The framework of M grammar

Hintikka et al. (eds.), Approaches to Natural Language, 243–258. All rights reserved.
Copyright © 1973 by D. Reidel Publishing Company, Dordrecht-Holland.

will necessarily be broader, but it is possible that the class of human languages will be characterizable by restrictions statable in natural ways within that framework.

With these generalities out of the way, I will begin an exposition of M grammar (in particular, of the grammar in the paper under discussion), at first misrepresenting it somewhat to try to make it look as much like T grammar as possible, and then showing how and why it differs.

	Categories	
M grammar	M grammar abbreviated name	Nearest T grammar equivalent
t		S
e		no such category
t/e	IV	VP [S/e]
$t//e$	CN	NOM [S//e]
t/IV	T	NP [S/VP]
IV/T	TV	V_t [VP/NP]
IV/t		V_s [VP/s]
$\text{IV}//\text{IV}$		V_{vp} [VP//VP]
t/t		ADV_s [S/S]
IV/IV	IAV	ADV_{vp} [VP/VP]
IAV/T	PREP	$\text{ADV}_{vp}/\text{NP}$]

The specification of the categories is derived in part from categorial grammar, as the notation suggests, but this is not a categorial grammar, as will be made clear below.

Many of the above categories can occur either as 'terminal' or 'non-terminal', as is in general the case with categorial grammars. Thus for instance the category IV, which I translated VP, corresponds both to the lexical category 'intransitive verb' and to the nonterminal category VP. A garden-variety CF grammar would include a rule VP → V, and the V's generated by that rule would be the intransitive verbs. In general, all categories relatable by nonbranching *PS* rules are conflated – e.g., NP and proper nouns and pronouns. A distinction is subsequently drawn between phrases of category A, i.e., P_A, and basic, or lexical, expressions of category A, i.e. B_A.

This is not a categorial grammar because the syntactic rules in an M grammar are not determinable simply from the names of the categories. In a categorial grammar there is, for every category A/B, a syntactic rule $A \to A/B + B$. In an M grammar one can infer from a category name A/B (or $A//B$) only that there will be *some* syntactic operation which will combine a B phrase and an A/B phrase to form an A phrase (and that there will be a corresponding semantic function from meanings of the component phrases to a meaning for the result).

For some categories, the M grammar does contain exactly the rules that a categorial grammar would contain, in particular:

S4 : $S \to NP + VP$
S5 : $VP \to V_t + NP$
S6 : $ADV_{vp} \to PREP + NP$
S7 : $VP \to V_s + S$
S8 : $VP \to V_{vp} + VP$
S9 : $S \to ADV_s + S$
S10: $VP \to VP + ADV_{vp}$

(Actually only S7, S8, and S9 are quite this simple; the function F_6 which they share is the simple concatenation function. The function F_7 of S10 is 'concatenation in reverse order'. The function F_4 of S4 includes concatenation, number and person agreement, and present-tense formation. The function F_5 of S5 and S6 is concatenation plus accusative-marking in case NP is a pronoun.

Other rules which look more or less like *PS* rules, but less like rules of a categorial grammar include the following:

S2: $NP \to every + NOM$ $(F_0(NOM))$
    $NP \to the + NOM$ $(F_1(NOM))$
    $NP \to AN + NOM$ $(F_2(NOM))$.

S2, in particular F_2, also contains a statement of the morphophonemic alternation of $AN : a/an$. The function F_0 can be described as that function which takes a NOM and makes it into an NP by adding *every*; similarly for F_1, F_2.

S11: $S \to S$ and S
    $S \to S$ or S.

S12: VP → VP and VP

  VP → VP or VP.

S13: NP → NP or NP

  (*and* omitted simply to avoid having to introduce plural NP's in this sample grammar.)

The rule S1 can be interpreted as a rule schema, roughly:

  A phrase → *A* word.

It applies to all categories which include lexical as well as phrasal representatives.

The remaining rules, S3 and S14–S17, resemble transformations more than they do *PS* rules. In this first approximation, I will write them as transformations, although I will thereby introduce some distortions.

S3: Relative clause rule schema $(F_{3,n}(\text{NOM,S}))$

This is a transformation which, like those in *Syntactic Structures*, deforms and combines two independently generated structures. Unlike Chomsky's transformations, however, these *M* rules do not use sentences as the sole 'building blocks'. This transformation, for instance, combines a NOM and an S to make a NOM.

I will present the rule first grossly oversimplified, and then translate the details as well.

Oversimplified: SD: (1) NOM

  1

  (2) S

  2

  SC: $_{\text{NOM}}[1 - \text{such that} - 2]$.

In greater detail:

  SD: (1) $_{\text{NOM}}[\text{NOM-word} - X]$

  [α gender]

  1   2

  (2) $_S[X - (\text{PRO}_n) - X - (\text{PRO}_n)^i - X]$

  [β accus]   [γ accus]

  3   4   5   6   7

  SC: $_{\text{NOM}}[\,1 - 2 - \text{such that} - 3 - 4 - 5 - 6 - 7]$

                [α gender]   [α gender]

S14: Quantification. The relative clause rule took a NOM and an S and made a new NOM. This rule, which is for quantifying over a sentence, takes an S and an NP and makes a new S. There are various unexciting ways it can apply, including vacuously; the important cases are when the NP itself was formed by rule S2, i.e., includes a quantifier.

$$\text{Case 1: SD: } _{NP}[X - \left\{ \begin{array}{c} \text{NOM-word} \\ \text{NP-word} \end{array} \right\} - X]$$

$$\begin{array}{ccc} 1 & 2 & 3 \end{array}$$

$$_S[X - PRO_n - X - (PRO_n)^i - X]$$

$$\begin{array}{ccccc} 4 & 5 & 6 & 7 & 8 \end{array}$$

Conditions: $1 - 2 - 3 \neq$ PRO. 1 does not contain a NOM-word or NP-word. SC: $_S[4 - 1 + 2 + 3 - 6 - 7 - 8]$ (with instructions about the gender of 7).

Case 2: NP $= PRO_k$: substitute PRO_k for PRO_n in S.

S15: Same rule, but second part is NOM and result is NOM.

S16: Same rule, but second part is VP and result is VP.

S17: Negative, future, and present perfect. This rule, with its five sub-rules, subsumes functions which would probably be handled by a combination of *PS* rules and *T* rules in a modern *T* grammar; the negation rule in particular is like that of *Syntactic Structures* in this respect, introducing the negative morpheme and simultaneously transforming the result. There is some obvious lack of syntactic economy in stating the five subrules separately.

(1)   S → NP + NEG + VP
plus specification of formation of negative 3rd person singular present

(2)   S → NP + FUT + VP plus specification of future

(3)   S → NP + NEG + FUT + VP (plus ...)

(4)   S → NP + PERF + VP (plus ...)

(5)   S → NP + NEG + PERF + VP (plus ...).

2. RULES AND FUNCTIONS

The above translations are misleading in that the formal similarities among the rules in Montague's own terms are completely obscured. Each *rule*, in Montague's terms, defines one or more *functions*. Each *function* is single valued and takes a given number of arguments. The *rule* tells what categories the arguments are to be taken from and what the category of the result is. The *function* describes the operations involved – concatenation in the cases where I have translated it into a *PS* rule, more complicated operations where I have made it look more like a *T* rule.

The same *function* may appear in more than one rule.

Examples: Rules S5, S6 both use the function which is defined as concatenation plus accusative-marking. Rules S7, S8, and S9 all use the simple concatenation function. S11 and S12 each use the same *two* functions. S14, S15, and S16 all use the same (2-case) function: only the categories involved differ. In transformational terms, this is somewhat akin to having a single rule containing a bracketed constituent whose label is given as a disjunction:

$$\left[\ldots \begin{Bmatrix} S \\ NOM \\ VP \end{Bmatrix} \right.$$

The things called *rules* are partly arbitrary. Any rule that specifies two functions could just as well be two rules. But the rules are not dispensable, because the functions do not contain intrinsically any specification of the categories of their domains and ranges.

Consider McCawley's question "Where Do Noun Phrases Come From?" The answer, for the cases he was thinking about, is "either S4 (F_4) or S14-15-16 ($F_{10,n}$)." The two trees Montague gives for "John seeks a unicorn" illustrate the difference. For a McCawley sentence like "John believes that a unicorn loves Mary," the two sources for "a unicorn" might be described informally as follows:

(i)   "a unicorn" is primitively part of the sentence to which "believes" is applied to make a VP. (This gives the *de dicto* or opaque sense.)

(ii)   Starting with a sentence form containing a variable over entities, roughly "John believes that X loves Mary," we substitute "a unicorn" for X_i. (*De re*, or transparent, sense.)

If the question is pushed further, "where does that NP in case (ii) come from?" it must simply be answered "it's pulled out of a hat." The situation is entirely analogous to two-sentence transformations back in *Syntactic Structures* days. In that framework, a sentence was just "pulled out of a hat" to add to another sentence as a relative clause.

Another way of making a comparison:

In *Syntactic Structures*, there are just two types of functions:

(i)   concatenation (the *PS* rules)

(ii)   functions which map one or two arguments of the category S onto new members of the category S.

But in the relative clause rule, for instance, the only relevant part of the matrix S is the NP to which the relative clause is being attached. So instead of thinking of that as a rule which maps two S's onto a new S, we could think of it as mapping an NP and an S onto a new NP (or NOM and S onto a new NOM).

E.g.,

$$_{\text{NOM}}[\text{a boy}] + {}_S[\text{I saw } x_0 \text{ hurting } x_0\text{-self}] \Rightarrow$$
$$_{\text{NOM}}[\text{a boy whom I saw hurting himself}].$$

3. RULE ORDERING AND TREES

In a typical *T* grammar, the rules are largely extrinsically ordered. In particular, all *PS* rules (concatenation-rules) precede all lexical-insertion rules, which in turn precede all *T* rules. There are no cases where a difference only in the order of application of rules makes any semantic difference. For instance, in a sentence with two quantifiers, it is not meaningful to inquire which quantifier was introduced first.

In an *M* grammar, however, the only rule-ordering is intrinsic. (This is typical of inductive definitions in general.) And the rules that look like *PS* rules can intersperse freely with the rules that look like *T* rules. Since it is the lexical rule schema (VP includes the intransitive verbs, etc.) that ties the inductive definition to explicitly given elements, lexical insertion in a sense must apply first; the rules then allow larger units to be constructed, sometimes by plain concatenation, sometimes with accompanying 'transformations'.

Both *T* grammars and *M* grammars use trees to display syntactic structure, but the resemblance is superficial. The *T* grammar tree is simply a hierarchical structuring of the elements which are linearly concatenated to form the actual sentence. When T rules map trees onto new trees, they are (i) mapping sentences, or terminal strings, onto new sentences, and (ii) specifying the hierarchical structuring of the new sentences in terms of that of the old. Decisions of type (ii) are sometimes very hard to make and are often left inexplicit.

In Katz and Postal (1964) another kind of tree, called a T marker, was suggested: its function was to display the 'transformational history' of a sentence. Trees in M grammars are much more like these than they are like ordinary phrase-marker trees. The *root* of an M tree is labelled with the surface sentence, and the branching structure below it is its derivational history.

Each 'nonterminal' node of an M tree is labelled with an ordered pair (α, β), where α is a string of morphemes[1] or words and β is the index of a *function*. The branches then go down to the argument(s) of the given functions, i.e., to nodes labelled (α_i, β_i) where α_i is one of the arguments of the given function and β_i is the index of the function used to form α_i. The bottom nodes are labelled with basic expressions, i.e., proper lexical items, but their left-to-right order need not correspond to that in the actual sentence.

4. COMMENTS ON THE RELATIVE CLAUSE RULE AND THE QUANTIFIER RULES

In the transformational literature, there is a lot of discussion about the relative clause rule and the notion of 'shared NP'. The earliest statements of the rule said roughly, "Take two sentences which share an NP, replace the NP in one of them by a relative pronoun, and embed that sentence into the shared NP of the other sentence." Thus,

$$\left.\begin{array}{l} \text{I saw a boy} \\ \\ \text{A boy was on a bicycle} \end{array}\right\} \Rightarrow \text{I saw a boy who was on a bicycle.}$$

When semantic questions were brought in, more care was taken to distinguish the determiner from the rest of the NP and exempt the determiners from the identity conditions, claiming typically that the embedded-sentence determiner should just be *a*. (This is gross over-simplification – there were and are many arguments.) Thus,

$$\left.\begin{array}{l} \text{I saw} \left\{\begin{array}{l} \text{a} \\ \text{the} \\ \text{some} \\ \dots \end{array}\right\} \text{boy} \\ \text{A boy was on a bicycle} \end{array}\right\} \Rightarrow \text{I saw} \left\{\begin{array}{l} \text{a} \\ \text{the} \\ \text{some} \\ \dots \end{array}\right\} \begin{array}{l} \text{boy who was on a} \\ \text{bicycle} \end{array}$$

But even that did not give a satisfactory underlying form for quantified cases:

$$\left.\begin{array}{l} \text{Every pacifist is crazy} \\ \text{A pacifist supports the war} \end{array}\right\} \Rightarrow \begin{array}{l} \text{Every pacifist who supports} \\ \text{the war is crazy.} \end{array}$$

So linguists began to appreciate a need for variables of some sort in order to represent relative clauses in a semantically reasonable way. But in a kind of baby-with-the-bath-water move, McCawley and Bach and others following suit have thrown away the head noun of the relative clause, too: identity of NP's or NOM's is now replaced by identity of variables, and the head noun has to be introduced by a relative clause of its own or by some sort of 'restricted quantification'. So the deep structure of the example above might be given as something like:

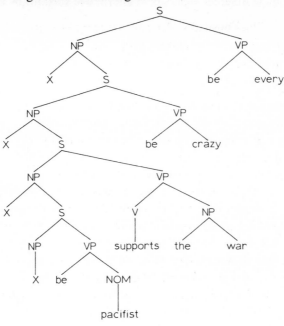

Now let me lay out for the benefit of the linguists what the *M* tree would be. A crucial difference is that the head noun is generated in the matrix NOM, and the relative clause (and only the relative clause) starts out with variables in the corresponding NP positions.

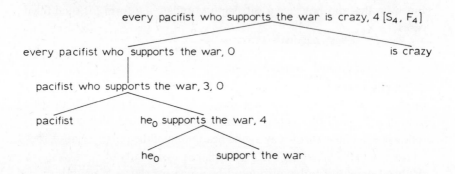

The pronouns he_i in *M* grammar have interesting points of similarity with three quite different elements in alternative versions of *T* grammar:

(i) the variables posited in deep structure by McCawley *et al.*
(ii) the deep structure pronouns proposed by Jackendoff
(iii) the unspecified or dummy NP's of Chomsky or Katz and Postal (1964).

Like the variables of (i), they are indexed to indicate referential sameness or difference and thus are semantically unambiguous in a way that (ii) and (iii) are not. Like the deep structure pronouns, (ii), they are subject to accusative-marking (as ordinary nouns are not). Furthermore, like (ii), they need not be transformationally replaced at all, but can stand as deictic pronouns. Like both (ii) and (iii), they always occur as full NP's – they do not allow modifiers, determiners, or the like. In this respect they differ from (i), since McCawley apparently allows variables to be introduced in rules like NP → *x* S, thus apparently allowing variables sometimes to occur as common nouns. (See more on this point below.) They are like (iii) in that lexical material can be substituted for them.

Suppose we tried to incorporate these *M* pronouns into a deep structure tree, e.g., as follows:

This is not equivalent to the M tree above because there is no indication that he_0 is the pronoun to be relativized on; if the embedded sentence were he_0 *voted for* he_1 such a structure could yield both of the following:

> Every pacifist who voted for him is crazy.
> Every pacifist for whom he voted is crazy.

I can imagine it being suggested that *pacifist* should carry an index to resolve such indeterminacy; but that would be to miss the distinction between NOM (i.e., common noun phrase; including N) and NP (including pronouns). NOM and N are predicates; NP is a referring expression. Hence referential indices are appropriate only to the latter. Looked at in this way, it is not surprising that the statement of 'identity conditions' for relative clauses has always caused difficulty: the two constituents involved are a NOM in the matrix and an NP in the embedded sentence, and a NOM and an NP cannot possibly be identical. On the other hand, to try to analyze the embedded NP as some determiner plus a NOM, picking some particular determiner like *a*, so as to be able to require NOM identity, leads to bad semantic results because it treats the embedded sentence as a 'closed formula' rather than as an 'open formula'.

I can also imagine it being suggested that the word *pacifist* ought somehow to be included in the deep structure of the embedded sentence, and if this were done, it would be clear which NP in the embedded sentence was to be relativized. But that would not solve the problem because it would not provide distinct deep structures for a pair of sentences like the following:

> Every pacifist who attacks a pacifist suffers.
> Every pacifist whom a pacifist attacks suffers.

It therefore seems that the only way to mirror the *M* grammar structure in *T* grammar terms is to abandon the principle of deep structure semantics and revert to the earlier notion of a *T* marker with corresponding "Type 2 projection rules" – semantic rules corresponding to transformational operations. Further requirements would be that derivations need not start with S, that trees can be built from bottom to top as well as top to bottom, that *T* rules can be interspersed among *PS* rules, and that NP can be rewritten as a variable (he_0, etc.), which may later be replaced. A derivation for the example above would then look as follows:

(1)   apply S $\rightarrow$ NP VP, VP $\rightarrow$ V$_t$ NP, etc., to generate $_S[he_0$ *supports the war*]

(2)   apply NOM $\rightarrow$ N to generate $_{NOM}$[pacifist]

(3)   apply Rel Clause rule to outputs of (1) and (2), on he_0, to produce $_{NOM}$[pacifist who supports the war]

(4)   apply NP $\rightarrow$ every + NOM, using as NOM the output of (3), to produce $_{NP}$[every pacifist who supports the war]

(5)   apply S $\rightarrow$ NP VP; take the output of (4) for the NP, and generate by *PS* rules the VP *is crazy*.

For each of the rules applied, there is a corresponding semantic interpretation rule. The semantic rules are to be applied in the same order as the syntactic ones. The basic claim made in *M* grammar about the relation of semantics and syntax is that semantics is not determined by any configurational properties of *P* markers, either deep or surface, but by the rules applied and their order of application.

For another example, consider the sentence, "Every woman who supports herself respects herself." Its derivation could begin with the construction of the three following 'kernels':

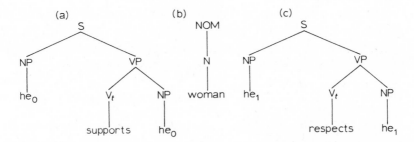

Reflexivization (a rule not included by Montague) would presumably apply in (a) and (c) to add *-self*. Then REL will combine (a) and (b) to form

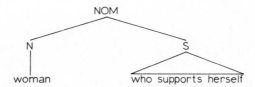

To this structure, the rule $NP \rightarrow every + NOM$ can be applied. The result can then be substituted for the first he_1 in (c) by the Quantifier rule with an accompanying gender specification of the second he_1.

The *M* tree for the above example would be (assuming a rule of reflexivization):

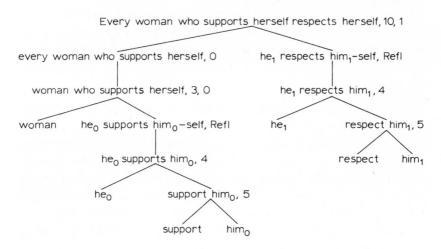

Note that such a structural representation stays much closer to English surface structure than does either the traditional logical notation (which would require an 'if-then' construction in place of the relative clause) or the Lakoff-McCawley abstract structures already illustrated.

5. A NOTE ON MCCAWLEY'S VARIABLES

McCawley's use of variables in essentially common noun positions did not strike me as peculiar until I compared it with Montague's use of variables. It occurs to me that the reason a rule like $NP \rightarrow x\ S$ could occur to McCawley and seem natural to other logic-oriented linguists is that logic teachers have unwittingly set a trap for us by teaching us to translate the existential quantifier with the locution "There is an x such that," i.e., using x as a common noun modified by a relative clause. Such locutions are neither proper English nor proper logic, and simply serve as pedagogic devices (of limited usefulness) to help students bridge the gap.

McCawley's abstract structures have been put forward as 'semantic representations' and therefore he and his colleagues have made no attempt to define semantics for them; I think this position has resulted from an erroneous belief that the semantics of ordinary logic would operate on these representations, and can therefore be left unstated (probably being assumed as universal). It seems to me highly dubious that a coherent semantics could be defined on the kind of structures McCawley proposes, even for sentences comfortably handled within first-order predicate calculus, because of the ambivalent treatment of variables as common and proper nouns and the treatment of quantifiers like *every* as predicates.

6. A NOTE ON SUBJECT-PREDICATE STRUCTURE

Both the sample M grammar and classical T grammars include the rule $S \rightarrow NP\ VP$, but there is an important difference in how the rule is used. For a sentence like "Every boy ate an apple," T grammar (excluding generative semantics) would have to treat as the major constituents "every boy," "ate an apple." If semantic interpretation rules are to operate on the syntactic structure, this means that the semantics should somehow end up predicating the property "ate an apple" of the entity referred to by "every boy." It is one of the fundamental insights of modern logic that the primary constituent break of such sentences, as far as their logical form goes, is *not* the subject-predicate split, but the quantification and the sentence form quantified over.

In M grammar, the $S \rightarrow NP\ VP$ rule applies in the derivation of every sentence, but in a sentence containing a quantified subject, the 'kernel' NP will be a variable, and the quantified NP will substitute for it by a transformation-like rule, for which there is a corresponding semantic interpretation rule. The order of the semantic rules follows the order of the syntactic derivation, not the hierarchical order of a constituent structure tree.

7. A NOTE ON S-RECURSION

In post-1964 T grammar, all embedded S's are generated in their embedded position; in the earlier *Syntactic Structures* model, none were. In this M grammar, there is a rule $VP \rightarrow V_s + S$ for verbal complements, but no phrase structure rule for relative clauses. I would predict that complements of all sorts (for nouns like *fact*, adjectives like *afraid that*, etc.) would follow the verb-complement pattern; it is interesting to note that in *Syntactic Structures*, *Comp* was one of the few abstract symbols that could appear in kernel sentences. I expect that comparative clauses, like relative clauses, would be built up "transformationally." I am not certain what to expect for nominalizations and other sentence embeddings.

8. PRONOUNS OF LAZINESS

Within the M grammar, there is no derivation for the following notorious type of sentence:

> The man who deserves it will get the prize he wants.

This can be seen by attempting to derive an M tree for it.

> The man who deserves it will get the prize he wants.
> I.e., The man such that he deserves it will get the prize such that he wants it.

Must relativization be the first rule invoked? No, in fact it cannot be; either $S \rightarrow NP\ VP$ or quantification (either of the NP's) must precede. We do not want NP VP first or there could not be cross-reference between the pronouns.

the man such that he deserves (it)   he₀ will get the prize such that he₀ wants (it)

Dead End: the circled *it's* will never be related.

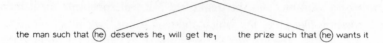

the man such that (he) deserves he₁ will get he₁   the prize such that (he) wants it

Dead End: circled *he's* will never be related.

Conclusion: at least one of the pronouns must be a pronoun of laziness. As long as we do not claim that they all are, this should not seem paradoxical.

E.g.,

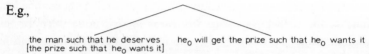

the man such that he deserves
[the prize such that he₀ wants it]   he₀ will get the prize such that he₀ wants it

I suspect that the he_0 in the left constituent could have a different index and still count as identical for pronominalization (pronoun of laziness type), and that this is relevant to what Grinder and Postal and others call "sense anaphora."

9. FINAL REMARKS

I think it is clear that M grammar is of interest to linguists who are concerned with semantics as well as syntax. I have said little about M semantics; insofar as I can understand it, I see nothing to disagree with. The ways in which the syntax in this fragment differs from T grammar seem to me potentially to be improvements (except perhaps for some of the attempts to handle morphology – but that could easily be changed). More severe syntactic tests will arise as the fragment is expanded, but it does not seem impossible that many T rules could be included in something very much like their familiar forms. It will probably be necessary, however, to introduce derived constituent structure more systematically at some point.

University of California, Los Angeles

NOTE

[1] There are two sorts of morphemes (or words) here, as there are in T grammars. There are the lexical morphemes, or basic expressions, and the grammatical morphemes, those morphemes which are introduced directly by grammatical rules.

PATRICK SUPPES

COMMENTS ON
MONTAGUE'S PAPER*

Because Montague's efforts at analyzing the semantics and syntax of natural language have probably been developed more extensively than any other now available, it is natural to raise some questions, not so much about the paper itself, but about his own perspective on the future of the kind of analysis he has presented.

Let me begin with a general question about the empirical character of his analysis. From listening to the present paper and reading related papers by Montague I am not sure that Montague regards the problem of providing a semantics and syntax of natural language as an empirical one. Since this question is at the heart of my remarks, let me try to expand upon it.

In asking whether the analysis of formal language in his sense is meant to be empirical, I do not have in mind some subtle and obscure distinction between empirical and logical inquiries. Rather, I have in mind a somewhat crude distinction, one that we cannot always apply, but one that we can recognize in many applications. It is the kind of thing that separates ancient geometry as set forth by Euclid from ancient astronomy as set forth by Ptolemy. In one clear sense, it seems to me, Euclid intends to be mathematical and not empirical while Ptolemy intends to be empirical, although of course he uses mathematical methods in an extraordinarily successful way. For Euclid the criterion of success is primarily the proofs of theorems; for Ptolemy it is fundamentally the fit of theory to data.

I ask Montague whether he feels a closer affinity to the methods and implicit criteria of Euclid or of Ptolemy? I would like to assume that Montague would accept as appropriate for his kind of enterprise neo-Ptolemaic questions about the fit of theory to data, and I would like to set forth several theses, some that I am certain he will reject and others that he will probably accept. I am asking him to clarify his position on these

Hintikka et al. (eds.), Approaches to Natural Language, 259–262. *All rights reserved.*
Copyright © 1973 by D. Reidel Publishing Company, Dordrecht-Holland.

theses, and I will not reveal my own guesses about his answers.

THESIS 1. The Montague semantics and syntax of ordinary English as set forth in his current paper, as well as in earlier ones, can be extended by a reasonably small number of additional rules that include additional basic sets of expressions, etc. With this extension, substantial texts or substantial corpuses of spoken speech can be analyzed. In this formulation it is understood that, although the general sort of text might be known in advance, the text itself is not consulted in setting forth the full set of rules. In other words, a machinery of analysis is established that can be applied without change to any of a wide variety of texts.

I cannot resist asking a probabilistic sort of question in this connection. In terms of my own approach to these matters I would like to introduce generative probabilities into Montague's rules, so that an estimate could be given of how well the model of the theory fits the data of the text. Since I doubt that Montague would accept this kind of approach, I ask him what kind of criterion he would use for goodness of fit.

THESIS 2. The weaker thesis is that the text or corpus must be examined in order to specify the new basic sets of expressions, some new syntactic rules, some new rules of functional application, and so forth, but that relative to a very large corpus, for example, one of a million utterances, a comparatively small number of additional rules may be added to provide an analysis of the text. My work on probabilistic grammars falls under this weaker thesis. The grammars were not written without examining the corpus, and the probabilistic parameters were estimated only by analyzing the corpus. The scientific respectability of the enterprise was preserved, as in other such applications of probabilistic models, by the relatively small number of parameters estimated from the data in relation to the number of utterances considered. Again, however, I doubt that Montague would be satisfied with such a probabilistic criterion, and I ask what his criterion would be.

Criterion of successful analysis of individual sentences. In connection with my remarks thus far, I also am not clear what Montague's methodology is for analyzing a given sentence in natural language. Put another way, how is agreement to be reached on the correct semantic analysis? First let me say that I am dissatisfied with my own methodology as reflected in my own paper on this matter. I feel satisfied with the objectivity of the grammatical analysis; I do not feel nearly as satisfied with the objectivity of the semantic analysis. It seems to me that my analysis of the semantics of Adam I, whatever its other defects, suffers from the defect of depending upon my own rough and ready intuitions about what Adam meant to say in uttering the phrases he did. It does not seem to me that in my own work I have specified a really good criterion for making the semantic analysis objective. In stating the above theses I have talked about the analysis of sentences or of utterances, but again I have deliberately omitted spelling out what is to be regarded as an analysis. I have in mind here of course not the kind of model that Montague stated, but rather the criterion for deciding whether or not the model correctly accounted for the structure of a given sentence. From an ordinary methodological standpoint, characterization of how individual sentences are to be analyzed and the results judged as correct or incorrect is even more fundamental than selection of an overall goodness-of-fit criterion.

Possible evidence against Montague's theory. The problem of making objective the criterion is related to the problem of understanding what evidence Montague would accept as proof that his conception of the proper way to analyze the semantics and syntax of natural language is wrong. Of course, this question is not one with a simple answer. In my own work I would distinguish between giving evidence to refute the general theory and giving evidence that counts against a particular model with particular probabilistic parameters. In the latter case the characterization of evidence that can count decisively or strongly against the correctness of a particular model is easy to give. The corresponding problem for the general theory is more difficult. Hearing how Montague feels about this standard and ubiquitous problem for the case of his own theory would be interesting.

Machine language translation. Most linguists and computer scientists are discouraged about the prospects for mechanical language translation in any immediate future. Many people feel that the early, overly sanguine and optimistic predictions and claims in this field fell through precisely because of the absence of any serious theoretical foundations for the premature attempts that were made. Although Montague, as far as I know, has indicated no special interest in the problems and prospects of mechanical language translation, because of his extensive technical analysis of fragments of natural language, it is natural to ask him to express his views in these areas. I suppose the real point of my asking for his views is that I feel his answer may provide a further perspective on the extent to which he views his theoretical analyses as empirical or quasi-empirical in character.

Stanford University

NOTE

* These comments were written at the time of the Workshop and thus before Montague's death. To preserve the sense of interaction at the Workshop they have been left unchanged.

JULIUS MORAVCSIK

MASS TERMS IN ENGLISH

1

The nest of problems dealt with in this paper has its origins in Aristotle's distinction between form and matter. Aristotle noticed that terms like 'bronze', 'water', 'air', etc., differ in fundamental ways from terms like 'statue', 'man', 'house', etc. These fundamental differences play crucial roles in Aristotle's metaphysics and philosophy of science. In this paper it will be argued that they play also fundamental roles in the semantics and syntax of a natural language like English.

On the contemporary scene one can find four distinct successors to Aristotle's speculations on this topic. Some of these problems are pursued by linguists and some by philosophers, though all of the relevant issues should be of interest to both. Following Jespersen (Quine, 1960, p. 91) we shall designate terms like 'water', 'iron', etc., as mass terms. The first of the four problems is the most narrow in scope. It consists of the task to distinguish syntactically and semantically concrete mass-nouns from concrete count-nouns. The expression 'mass term' has its clearest intuitive force in the context of this problem. Work on this problem, however, led people to notice that concrete mass terms have a lot in common syntactically and semantically with certain nonconcrete nouns such as 'speed', 'vagueness', etc. Thus the second problem can be viewed as an extension of the first. It calls for a distinction between mass- and count-nouns, regardless of whether their ranges of denotation cover concrete or non-concrete entities. At this stage calling the noncount nouns mass terms might seem somewhat forced, and the terminology of count+ or − recommends itself. Still, for the sake of uniformity we shall continue to use the expression 'mass term' in this wider sense.

If one concentrates on semantic analysis alone, and considers nouns, adjectives, and verbs as denoting expressions on the same level, on the ground that the same class can be denoted by an expression in one language

Hintikka et al. (eds.), Approaches to Natural Language, 263–285. All rights reserved.
Copyright © 1973 by D. Reidel Publishing Company, Dordrecht-Holland.

and another expression in another language, even though the two expressions belong to different syntactic categories, then the problem of mass terms gains again in scope – as well as in difficulty. For viewing matters in this context, the task becomes one of giving a general characterization of the semantic representation of all mass terms, regardless of the syntactic categories of natural languages to which any given mass term might belong. In the context of this problem 'red', 'blue', 'sweet', 'loud', etc., also count as mass terms; and at this stage the locution 'mass term' loses most of its intuitive force. We shall retain it for the sake of convenience, allowing us to move freely between the four problems outlined in this introductory section. An adequate solution to the third problem would present us with a grand dichotomy separating terms that somehow individuate their ranges of application from those denoting terms that do not. This, in turn, leads some of us to speculate about the extent to which the existence of mass terms is a prerequisite to grafting unto a natural language the terms and concepts involved in quantitative analysis – without which science is impossible. This last point presents the fourth of the problems connected to mass terms, and deserves some elaboration. A language with count-terms only would not present us with terms that designate what can be compared and measured with respect to magnitudes. If we have only terms like 'man', 'star', or 'house' available, then questions concerning ordering with respect to more or less, and comparisons in terms of magnitude cannot be expressed. This becomes possible only when a vocabulary is added that expresses concepts such as length, weight, etc., on the one hand, and concepts such as flesh, iron, etc., on the other, where the latter are regarded as concepts capturing the material of which men, stars, etc., consist. In other words we can state facts for science to explain once we can describe not only objects but also their aspects of weight, length, etc., and their material constituents in terms of a list of elements. It is an empirical question whether these concepts are likely to be expressed by one or the other of the main syntactic categories such as noun, verb, etc. (e.g., 'weight', vs. 'weighs more', or 'length' vs. 'long'), and the extent to which such distribution remains invariant across natural languages.

The concepts introduced by mass terms (or 'noncount-terms', in a more cumbersome terminology) serve only to state facts that require scientific explanation. Once the right questions are asked and the right problems posed, science proceeds by analyzing the mass constituents into a variety of elements captured by count-terms (such as molecule, atom, etc.) and by introducing count-terms to mark units of measurement that allow us to construct scales and to apply mathematics to the ordering of quantities with different magnitudes. Thus most of the time the final framework and vocabulary of a science has room for mass terms as designating that which is to be analyzed rather than the refined tools of analysis that are captured mostly by count-terms. But it is important to remember that without mass terms scientific investigation cannot get started. These considerations need spelling out for they are not always adequately grasped. For example, Quine (1960, p. 95) seems to suggest that mass term is an "archaic category," not very suitable for more sophisticated discourse, and it mirrors the semantics of the child's early vocabulary. Quine makes an important point when he calls attention to the similarity between the ways in which mass terms and some of the first terms used by a child fail to individuate their ranges of denotation. But this similarity should not keep us from seeing also the important differences; the differences that account for the fact that the child's early vocabulary does not invite the formation of scientific hypotheses, while the vocabulary of mass terms used by mature competent speakers does. The child's early vocabulary, as well as the anthropomorphic and mass-termless vocabulary of a possible primitive language equally, doesn't provide for the expression of quantitative analysis.

These considerations at least provide the background for understanding the choice made in this paper, namely, to pursue the distinction in the third, and thus widest, of ways specified. A brief review of the characterizations proposed so far is in order, since such a review would bring out what kind of work is most needed in order to arrive at an adequate general characterization.

In Chomsky's (1965, p. 82ff.) subcategorization-system the equivalent to what we called 'mass term' is count minus. Only nouns are thus classified, and the schema presented must be interpreted as either classifying all abstract terms together with what we called mass terms as count minus, or as restricting the notion of a mass term to concrete count-minus nouns. In short, it presents a classification that captures the distinction as drawn by the first of the ways surveyed above. Though Chomsky points to the problem of trying to define the various features such as count + −, he

266   JULIUS MORAVCSIK

does not add much that would count towards the solution of this problem. In another paper, by Parsons (1970, pp. 363–88), it is explicitly acknowledged that there are nonconcrete mass nouns, though not much is said about how we should treat these. As syntactic criteria Parsons suggested the fact that mass terms do not admit of pluralization, and that when used in their characteristic sense, they can be preceded by 'much'. These criteria apply to such nonconcrete terms as 'speed' or 'information' as well as to the standard ones like 'air', 'fire', etc. There are exceptions, however, as Parsons notes. For example, in the context: "What did you have for lunch?" "Potatoes," 'potatoes' functions as a mass term in spite of the plural. It can be easily seen that Parsons' characterization corresponds to the second of the ways surveyed above.

The only treatment that provides at least potential answers to the problem of adequate characterization as required by the third way of viewing the problem is furnished by Quine.[1] To be sure, the syntactic conditions that he mentions apply only to nouns – for Quine likens mass terms to singular terms insofar as they resist pluralization and the articles. This proposal, of course, would not divide adjectives into count+ and −, or, to use Quine's terminology, terms that divide their reference and terms that do not. The characterization that takes Quine beyond the confines of syntactic categories is purely semantic. It is the condition that Quine sums up as cumulative reference, e.g., any sum of parts that are water is itself water. In general terms,

> *Quine's condition*: '*w*' is a mass term iff any sum of parts that are *w*, is itself *w*.

It is easy to find examples of adjectives that justify Quine's extension (1960, p. 96) of the distinction to this category, for adjectives like 'red', 'blue', 'sweet', 'bitter', etc., will turn out to be – on the basis of the condition mentioned above – mass terms, while an adjective like 'Spherical' (Quine's own example), will turn out not to be a mass term.

The extension of the count+ − distinction to cover nonconcrete nouns as well is one of the proposals of the subcategorization system developed by Moravcsik (1970). Abstract count-nouns like 'virtue' and 'number' are contrasted with abstract count− terms like 'vagueness', 'nonsense', etc. In addition to the syntactic criteria already mentioned, certain co-occurrence restrictions are explored. For example, adjectives like 'numerous' are said to modify count+ and not count− nouns. A verb like 'count' is said to take as object only count+ nouns, while 'walk' and 'think' must take count+ subjects. It is also pointed out that some verbs like 'flow' or 'melt' can take either count+ or − subjects.

Recently a proposal has been made by Leech (1969, p. 134ff.) according to which even verbs can be divided into count+ or −, depending on whether the verb denotes events or a state. Thus 'fall', 'kick', and 'break' would be count+, while 'enjoy' would be count−.

This survey gives rise to the following observations. There is a need for investigating the possibility of giving a general syntactic characterization of mass terms. It is not clear that syntactic characterizations of the required sort that cut across categories, such as N, V, and Adj, can be made available. In that case, we must rest content that at least this grand division is basically a semantic one. Turning to the semantic characterization, Quine's condition seems promising, provided that a few difficulties can be eliminated. One such difficulty is the question of applicability to a certain class of adjectives. For while 'heavy' and 'large' meet Quine's condition for mass terms, the correlated terms 'light' and 'small' do not seem to do so. Similar considerations apply to such compounds as 'smaller than a breadbasket'. All sums of parts that are heavy are themselves heavy, but not all such sums of parts that are light are so. One remedy might be to rule out adjectives that admit of the comparative form. But it is not clear that color terms would not also meet this condition and besides, we would lose 'heavy', 'large', etc. It has been suggested by Mrs. E. Traugott that perhaps the marked-unmarked and polar+ − distinctions could be utilized to explain the situation since in terms of these distinctions 'light' and 'small' could be shown to be negative. Further work along these lines depends partly on the availability of rigorous definitions for the distinctions referred to (Lyons, 1968, p. 79 and passim).

Another difficulty emerges when one tries to apply Quine's condition to nonconcrete mass terms. This is not Quine's difficulty, since he presumably would not want to allow a class of terms such as abstract mass terms. However, within the project as envisaged in this paper, such application is imperative. The difficulty is posed by the fact that the key notions of Quine's condition are stated in mereological terms, and it is not clear how 'part', 'sum', and 'overlap' apply to abstract entities like numbers, points, and attributes or classes. On the one hand it is intuitively clear that 'sum' in 'sum of water-parts' is different from 'sum' in 'sum of numbers' or from 'the union of sets', but on the other hand, it is not at all clear what rigorous account would give us the required interpretations and delineations.

With regard to the investigation of co-occurrence relations, the following questions need further study. What is the class of verbs that requires count+ subjects where these need not be animate? 'Think' and 'believe' are not beyond controversy; perhaps 'write', 'work', or 'function' are better examples. Second, what is the class of verbs that requires count− subjects? With regard to the examples given above, ice melts but so do statues, and water flows but so do rivers.

So far we talked of the distinction between two classes of expressions. This is, however, an oversimplification. It has been pointed out by Quine (1960, pp. 191–92), Cartwright (1970), and Parsons (1970, p. 362) that many terms have both a count+ and a count− sense of type of application, e.g., 'I drank some water' contrasted with '. . . from the land of sky-blue waters', or 'I ate some chicken' as contrasted with 'I chased a chicken'. This phenomenon raises some questions about the structure of the lexicon that are of interest both to the philosopher and to the linguist. For the difference discussed here cannot be assimilated either to ambiguity or to difference in sense, as e.g., between 'my brother' and 'my fraternity brother'. On the other hand, one can hardly list the pairs as independent and unrelated entities in the dictionary. The situation is analogous to the one holding between abstract singular terms and the corresponding general terms (e.g., 'justice' and 'just'.)

Finally, although it is assumed in this paper that it is worth trying to draw the count/mass dichotomy in the broad sense indicated by our third statement of the problem, there may be independent reasons for wanting to restrict mass terms to nouns. Such motivations emerge, for example, from Montague's work on English as a formal language. One of the interesting features of that system is the attempt to find interesting correlations between the main lexical categories of a natural language, such as noun, adjective, and verb, and types of semantic representations. Thus if a revealing way is found in which nouns and adjectives can be contrasted semantically, then this provides a justification for restricting the class of mass terms to nouns. However, this issue is empirical. It may or may not be the case that semantically interesting distinctions within natural languages correspond to syntactic delineations. In an artificial language this would be obvious, since the syntax is 'tailor-made', so to say, for the semantics. Within natural languages, however, there may be good reasons for certain universal syntactic demarcations even if these do not correspond to semantic distinctions. Syntactic organization may be partly dependent on the fact that natural languages are spoken languages, or on some features of the mental processing operations, etc. A syntax for natural languages that is not based on semantics need not be arbitrary. In any case, the issues here are sufficiently unsettled so as to encourage explorations in several divergent directions.

2

Proposals for the semantics of mass terms. Before we consider some published proposals for the semantics of mass terms, we should consider what the aims of these proposals should be. As an initial characterization one could hardly find fault with Parsons' (1970, p. 363) saying that his aim is to translate sentences containing mass terms into a "logically perspicuous notation." There is room, however, for disagreement on what a logically perspicuous logical notation is. In general, one would want to have a notation in terms of which one can show how complex mass terms are formed out of simples, and how one could specify the conditions of truth of sentences containing mass terms in various positions. One would also want to know how to interpret semantically a complex, a part of which is a mass term. Finally, one would want to know what is unique about mass terms. The previous section has hopefully supplied considerations to support the claim that the count + − distinction is important, and that terms having one or the other of these features behave semantically in different ways. Thus an adequate analysis should supply the tools for exhibiting the differences. It is not clear that Parsons' conception of an adequate program is consistent with these demands, for he goes on to say that his task is "to paraphrase mass nouns in terms of names and count nouns − not because the latter are more basic, but rather because their logic, embodied in the predicate calculus, is better understood than that

of mass nouns." This suggests that an adequate analysis must be reductionistic; its task is to eliminate mass terms in favor of other elements
that fit better with first-order predicate logic. There is no room within the
confines of this paper to discuss in depth all of the issues raised by this
program. It will have to suffice to state simply that the approach adopted
in this paper does not take the first-order predicate calculus to be sacro-
sanct, and above all does not assume that the only adequate analysis of
mass terms is a reductionistic one. After all, if all we want is reduction,
very simple tools are at our disposal; e.g., to introduce a primitive count-
noun, or a set of such primitives, and paraphrase mass terms with the help
of these. Far from being successful, the methodological assumptions of
this paper would lead one to regard such an analysis as unilluminating. To
sum up, effective semantics is desirable, but so is the ability to show what
is unique and characteristic of mass terms; and the choice between intensional and extensional logic should not be prejudged.

The first proposal to be surveyed is that of Quine. As we saw Quine
takes the unique function of mass terms to be that they refer cumulatively.
He ascribes, however, a dual role to mass terms. When they appear before
the 'is' of predication, as in 'water is a liquid', then Quine assimilates them
to singular terms, while in their role behind the 'is' of predication, as in
'that puddle is water', he construes them as having the function of general
terms. Thus, for example, in subject position the mass term 'water' refers
to that individual that is scattered through time and place, and whose
parts are all the water that ever was, is, and will be. The reference, or
denotation, of all mass terms is to be understood in the same way. The
objects referred to are to be interpreted according to the calculus of
individuals, as explained, e.g., by Goodman (1951). The distinctness and
various relations of individuals can be rigorously defined in that calculus
in terms of the primitive 'overlap' and defined notions. This allows us to
generate the reference of complex mass terms from the references of their
constituents. For example, the reference of 'wood furniture' is the
individual, the parts of which are the overlapping parts of the individual
wood and the individual *furniture*, while the reference of 'water and iron'
will be the sum of the individual *water* and the individual *iron*.

Having explained Quine's (1960, p. 97) account of mass terms when
these occur in subject position, we shall turn to what Quine calls the

"simplest plan," i.e., to treat the mass terms as general terms when these occur in predicate position. Quine's actual account is not detailed enough to spare us from problems of interpretation. If we are to treat a mass term like 'water' as a general term in predicate position, what are the entities of which 'water' is true? There seem to be two possible interpretations of Quine's proposal. One of these is supported by the paragraph that follows. According to this interpretation Quine (1960, pp. 97–98) construes mass terms in predicate position as elliptical. For he suggests that 'is sugar' and 'is furniture' (as, e.g., in 'the white part is sugar', and 'the rest of the cargo is furniture') should be read as 'is a bit of sugar' and 'is a batch of furniture', respectively. According to this interpretation Quine does not really mean that, e.g., 'water' can be both a singular and a general term in different contexts, but rather that when in predicate position a mass term is always part of some complex predicate expression such as 'bit of . . .', 'batch of . . .', etc. Thus in fully analyzed form a mass term is really a part of a series of complex general terms when in predicate position. Unfortunately, it is not clear that this interpretation is consistent with everything that Quine says about mass terms. For in the same paragraph he also writes: ". . . in general a mass term in predicative position may be viewed as a general term which is true of each portion of the stuff in question . . . ." This does not sound as if Quine construed mass terms as elliptical when in predicate position. It is not clear, however, how one would interpret Quine in detail when one does not take the interpretation that makes mass terms elliptical. What are the 'portions' of which the term 't' is true? Do portions form mereological or set-theoretical complexes? What is their criterion of individuation? Perhaps one can construe this remark as shorthand for saying that in predicate position a mass term is elliptical for 'is a portion of w', in which case we are back to the first interpretation.

Finding out what Quine means by "treating a mass term as a general term" is not a trivial task since it figures crucially in several parts of Quine's proposal. For example, when he turns to the consideration of complexes formed by the demonstrative 'this' and a mass term Quine (1960, p. 101) again recommends treating the mass term as a general term. Again, however, we are given a paraphrase. 'Water' as used in that context is equivalent to the general term 'body of water'. Thus apparently according to Quine in the combination of demonstrative + mass term, the latter is elliptical, and is to be read in fully analyzed form as a part of a complex general term. (Bodies of water – unlike portions – have relatively clear criteria of individuation through time and space; the reason for this being that 'body', unlike 'portion', is count +.)

We noted already that Quine treats some adjectives also as mass terms. The treatment is uniform. Thus 'red' in subject position refers to that scattered individual whose parts are all that was, is, or ever will be red. The computation of the semantics of complexes parallels the computation of complexes made of nouns. Presumably the analogy carries over also as to the dual role, depending on grammatical position. Thus it seems that in 'some black bears are brown' 'brown' should be treated as a general term, since it comes after the 'is' of predication. According to our previous interpretation this would require that 'brown' should be here elliptical. It is difficult, however, to find the appropriate general term. Would 'bit of brown', or 'patch of brown' do here?

The most interesting part of Quine's (1960, p. 104) treatment of adjectives – and presumably a part of the rationale of the proposal – is his construal of the semantics of complex noun phrases made up of noun and adjective. In a complex in which the noun is count + such as 'red house', Quine proposes to treat the adjective – in this case 'red' – as a general term, and thus the whole NP as count +. In cases where the adjective modifies a noun that is a mass term, Quine proposes to treat the adjective also as a mass term, and thus the whole NP is count –. Quine assumes that adjectives such as 'spherical' that are count + will never modify a noun that is a mass term. To summarize this part of the proposal, in computing the semantics of an NP that is made up of N + Adj, the noun dominates with respect to count + or –, and determines the semantic character of the whole NP.

It remains to explain why Quine can characterize this as the "simplest plan." One possibility would be to give a unified treatment of mass terms by construing these as referring cumulatively regardless of grammatical position. This would involve treating the 'is' of predication as having two interpretations; in a count + context such as 'this object is a statue' the 'is' would stand for class membership, while in 'the white part is sugar' the copula would stand for the 'is a part of' relation as explained by mereological principles. Quine (1960, p. 99) thinks, however, that the mereo-

logical interpretation fails since not all parts of water, sugar, etc., are
themselves water, sugar, etc.; furthermore, Quine sees that there is no
general rule for all mass terms that would determine which parts of a
substance *s* are too small to count as *s*. For example, consider the parts
that are no longer water, the parts that are no longer snow, the parts that
are no longer brown, etc. On the basis of these considerations Quine
concludes that no general limitation could be worked into the relevant
definition of 'is a part of'. Thus the "simplest plan": treat mass terms as
general terms in predicative role and thus save a unitary interpretation of
the copula as class membership, while capturing the uniqueness of mass
terms in interpreting these mereologically when they occur in subject
position.

Thus Quine can show what is unique about mass terms while still
translating English into what he calls canonical notation – essentially the
first-order predicate calculus.

In order to survey Quine's proposal and to allow schematic comparisons
with other proposals, as well as indicating how Quine's suggestion can be
merged with transformational grammar, the proposal will be presented
within the scheme developed below. In the scheme 'NP', 'V', etc., stand
for the corresponding syntactic categories as noted in any standard transformational grammar; except that 'N' will always stand for 'noun that
could be interpreted mereologically'. Mass nouns and count nouns are
indicated by 'Nmass' and 'Ncount', with 'mass' and 'count' attached also
to other category symbols as well.

(1)   NP (N) + VP = Nmass. (Mass noun in subject position is
        interpreted mereologically.)

(2)   ... + VP (... + N) = Ncount (elliptical?). (If the mass noun
        is in predicate position, it is interpreted as a general term, or as
        part of a complex general term.)

(3)   ... + VP (... + Adj) = Adjcount. (Mass adjectives in predi-
        cate position are interpreted as general terms or parts of
        complex general terms.)

(4)   NP (Demonstr. + N) = Ncount. (A mass noun with a
        demonstrative is interpreted as a general term or a part of a
        complex general term.)

(5)   NP (Ncount + Adj) = NPcount (Ncount + Adjcount). (If

what could be a mass adjective modifies a count noun, then
it is treated as a general term or part of a complex general
term.)

(6)   NP (N + Adjcount) = NPcount (Ncount + Adjcount). (There
cannot be a combination of a mass noun and a count adjective
into a well-formed noun phrase.)

(7)   NP (Nmass + Adj) = NPmass (Nmass + Adjmass). (An adjective modifying a mass noun is interpreted as a mass term.)

(8)   Quantifier + N = Ncount. (A mass noun with a quantifier is
interpreted as a general term or a part of a complex general
term.)

(9)   Proper name + Adjmass = NPmass? (It seems that the combination of a proper name with a mass adjective could be
interpreted as referring cumulatively.)

(10)   Def. Descr. (the + Nmass) = NPcount? (It seems that a
definite description containing a mass noun would have to be
interpreted as the uniqueness operator and the mass noun as a
general term or a part of a complex general term.)

(11)   The 'is' of predication always stands for class-membership.
(Or class-subsumption.)

The interpretations of (9) and (10) are conjectural since there is no
direct evidence in Quine with regard to these issues. It follows from these
rules that any noun phrase that occurs in the predicate position will have
to have its components as well as itself interpreted as count. It also follows
that for certain noun phrases no semantic interpretation can be attached
until one sees what higher node dominates these. We shall return to this
point later.

The other proposal under consideration is that of Parsons. Parsons
(1970, pp. 374, 376–77) too construes mass terms when in subject position
as singular terms. He thinks, however, that mass terms name substances,
and that these have to be treated Platonistically, since no mereological
interpretation is possible. The reason he gives for thinking the cumulative
reference to be impossible is that if two substances are contained in the
actual world in the same region of space and time, this does not guarantee
identity. As an example he gives the hypothetical case of all the wood in the
world and all of the furniture in the world contained in the same region

of space and time, and concludes that the two substances would not be identical since some parts of chairs might be wood without counting as furniture (Parsons, 1970, p. 377). On this view, then, mass terms in subject position function in effect as abstract singular terms.

The cases in which a mass noun is in predicative position, such as '. . . is gold' are interpreted by Parsons as elliptical general terms. The general term in question is relational between what Parsons calls "bits of matter" and substances. The relational term is introduced as a primitive, named 'quantity of'. Thus, e.g., to consider an example cited already, 'the white part is sugar' becomes on this interpretation 'the white part is a bit of matter that is a quantity of sugar'. Bits of matter are construed as entities governed by the calculus of individuals (Parsons, 1970, pp. 367–68). The same interpretation is given when mass terms are preceded by demonstratives or quantifiers. Thus, e.g., 'some ink' becomes 'some quantity of ink'. Given this analysis the copula remains always equivalent to the sign designating class membership.

As we turn to Parsons' analysis of complex noun phrases, we must remember that he does not extend the count vs. mass distinction to cover adjectives. Thus if we have as the subject the name of a substance modified by an adjective we have in effect an adjective modifying an abstract singular term, and when the adjective modifies a mass term in predicate position, it modifies a complex general term.

One of the fortunate aspects of Parsons' presentation is the explicitness with which certain types of inferences are shown to come out as valid according to the proposal. For example, inferences of the type: 'all blue water is water' comes out as valid on Parsons' interpretation since it is construed to be about bits of matter and quantities. Our sample sentence is reinterpreted as 'everything that is blue and is a quantity of water, is a quantity of water'. The symbolization of this and similar sentences is obvious. Other types of complexes such as 'muddy water is widespread' (Parsons, 1970, p. 373ff.) are analyzed in terms of complex substance names and adjectives construed as general terms. The subject expression of our sample sentence would have to be 'the substance constituted by bits of matter that are muddy and are quantities of water'.

It must be obvious by now that the main burden of this analysis rests on the introduction of the primitive 'is a quantity of'. The explanation

that we are given is said to be only rough and in need of qualifications
(Parsons, 1970, p. 367). It is stated that to be a quantity of gold is to be a
bit of matter that makes up the substance *gold* that is scattered around the
universe. We are also told that "if it is true to say of a physical object that
it 'is gold', then the matter making it up will be a quantity of gold." This
account is qualified so as to rule out cases in which we describe something
as gold only in view of its color or other perceptual quality, or something
that is only partly gold, etc., and we are told that not all parts of matter
that are quantities of gold are themselves gold – in accordance with the
principle Quine already stated.

Parsons' proposal can be summarized by comparing it with the scheme
in terms of which Quine's proposal was presented.

(1)   NP (N) + VP = Nabstr. sing. (In the subject position a mass
        term behaves like an abstract singular term, naming a sub-
        stance.)

(2)   . . . + VP (. . . + N) = is a quantity of N (where 'quantity of'
        is a primitive general term).

(3)   No adjective is treated as a mass term.

(4)   NP (Demonstr. + N) = is a quantity of N. (like (2) above.)

(5)   Identical with Quine's treatment.

(6)   Parsons' treatment leaves it an open question whether we can
        have a well-formed combination of a mass noun and a count
        adjective.

(7)   An adjective modifying a mass noun is interpreted as a general
        term modifying an abstract singular term.

(8)   Quantifier + N = Quantifier + quantity of X. (With the
        quantifiers we reinterpret mass nouns as elliptical for a complex
        general term: 'quantity of F'.)

(9)   See under (3).

(10)   Def. Descr. (the + Nmass) = the + quantity of F.

(11)   The 'is' of predication always stands for class-membership.
        (Or class-subsumption.)

From this survey we can see that Parsons' treatment differs from Quine's
in the following respects. Parsons makes some of the consequences of his
proposal in terms of different syntactic configurations and inference-
patterns more explicit. He treats mass nouns in the subject position

unlike Quine, for while Quine treats them as mereologically interpretable within the actual world, Parsons treats them as abstract singular terms. Another important difference is that many of Parsons' solutions depend on the introduction of the primitive 'quantity of'. Finally, Parsons has no suggestions concerning the possible division of adjectival denoting terms into count and mass.

We shall now consider several criticisms of the two proposals summarized above. As mentioned earlier, there may be good reasons for wanting to restrict the count vs. mass distinction to nouns, but in any case, it does not seem that Parsons' account can reveal any of the striking semantic similarities between 'iron', 'water', etc., and 'red', 'sweet', 'heavy', etc. A uniform treatment of all adjectives from the semantic point of view requires some justification; yet none is given in this paper.

There are several questions concerning Parsons' treatment of substances. It is not clear that the Platonistic treatment that is recommended is really necessary. For though in the examples considered by Parsons two substances are contained in the same spatio-temporal region in the actual world, there are spatio-temporal parts of one that are not spatio-temporal parts of the other. Thus one possible alternative to Parsons' proposal is to regard as the criterion of identity of substance s' and s'' that any parts of s' that is s' should be also a part of s'' that is s'' and also the other way around. There may be independent reasons for wanting not to construe substances in Parsons' way, for it seems odd to have adjectives like 'red', 'heavy', etc., modify, or be predicated of substances that are construed Platonistically. To be sure, these uses are cases of the so-called generic use, and there are general problems concerning the semantic interpretation of sentences with terms used generically as subjects. For example, 'the tiger is striped'; this is not equivalent to a statement about all tigers, or about most tigers. It is also not a statement about an abstract tiger, or tigerhood. It is, somehow, about the typical tiger, or about what tigers are under natural circumstances, etc. In any case, Quine's treatment of mass nouns as singular terms referring mereologically leaves the interpretation of adjectives intuitively clearer. It also allows us to treat some substances as parts of others, while in Parsons' framework we would have to express this indirectly, by talking about all of the quantities of one and then all of the quantities of the other.

The main difficulty seems to involve the introduction of the primitive 'quantity of'. First, about the terms of the relation. We saw already that one of these, i.e., substances as Parsons interprets them, may need to be given a different analysis. The other is introduced as 'bits of matter'. It seems that bits of matter should not be regarded as the ultimate subjects of propositions. For what are criteria of identity and individuation for bits of matter? How are we to identify bits of matter 'qua bits of matter' across possible worlds? From this point of view the proposition that this ring is made of gold, seems clearer than the proposition that the bit of matter making up this ring is a quantity of gold. From the point of view of individuation it is desirable to have rings, crowns, etc., as subjects of propositions rather than bits of matter. Needless to say, these considerations will not carry weight with those who are not concerned with questions of individuation and cross-world identification.

Apart from qualms about the relata, what about the relation itself? We are told at one point that wherever gold occurs we will have a bit of matter that is a quantity, and then again that matter making up a golden object is a quantity of gold. How are these statements related? Why is it that only bits of matter can be quantities? Are quantities of F simply a restricted collection of parts of F? If not, why not? Quine is driven to make use of a whole collection of predicates like 'batch of', 'bit of', etc., in view of the fact that there is no general condition in terms of which one could explain what the minimal parts of each substance-stuff are. Is the introduction of Parsons' primitive anything but a notational variant to Quine's? In comparison with Quine's proposal it seems that all of the difficulties that arise in connection with explaining how complex noun phrases can be built up semantically from different types of components are swept under the rug by the introduction of the primitive 'quantity of'.

Needless to say, all systems must have primitives, and one cannot fault Parsons for introducing some. But some primitives are intuitively clearer than others, and some are tied clearer to the rest of the system than others. Parsons' primitive does not seem to fare well by these criteria. Finally, as it was remarked above, a proposal has to show what is unique about mass terms. But it is not clear that the burden of showing this is taken up by anything in Parsons' proposal except the newly introduced primitive. Pending further information about quantities, this seems not to be an illuminating way of indicating something unique about mass terms.

Quine's proposal seems to encounter three difficulties. The first one concerns the relationship between Quine's semantic proposal and a plausible grammar. Part of a plausible grammatical proposal would be the claim that the combinations N + VP (be + Adj) and NP (N + Adj) are transformationally related in that we would derive the latter from the former. Let us now consider the role of 'red' in the following sentences:

(i)   this red ink is hard to read.
(ii)   this ink is red.
(iii)   ink is red.
(iv)   red ink is hard to read.

According to Quine 'red' in (i), (ii) and (iii) has the same semantic interpretation while it has a different one in (iv). Transformationally, however, (i) and (ii) are related, and again (iii) and (iv). The latter two sentences exemplify – as Mrs. E. Traugott pointed out to me – what linguists call the generic use. It seems intuitively that 'red' should have the same semantic interpretation in all four sentences. But even if this is disputed, at least it should receive the same interpretation between pairs. This argument does not assume that transformations should be meaning preserving, since no really sound argument has been advanced so far for that general thesis. It seems, however, that at least in this context, we should get uniform interpretations of 'red' among the transformationally related sentences. The condition of meaning preservation on the sentential level creates problems for pairs like (iii) and (iv) in any case, since on any reasonable interpretation (iii) and the noun phrase of (iv) do not have the same cognitive significance. Item (iii) seems to be a sentence about ink in general – a false one at that and (iv) contains the complex name of what might be regarded as a species of ink. To sum up, viewed in this context, the dual role of mass terms that Quine introduces seems to be of dubious value.

Another difficulty arises when we consider the introduction of mass terms as general terms, or parts of complexes of general terms. It is not easy to present a clear and rigorous argument concerning these matters, since there is no general agreement on the question of what exactly a genuine general term must be. This survey is written from the point of view that assumes that a genuine general term allows constructions such as 'a so-and-so', 'the same so-and-so', 'one so-and-so', and 'the so-and-so'. For example, 'is a star', 'is the same star', 'is one star', 'is the star . . .'. Indeed, Quine himself emphasizes this feature of general terms. Now if we construe mass terms as general terms, the conditions do not seem to fit. Locutions like 'a water', 'one water', 'the same water' do not make sense unless we interpret them generically, and construe them to be about a kind or kinds of water. Interestingly enough, locutions forming definite descriptions with mass terms do make sense; e.g., 'the ice melted'. This suggests that perhaps within such locutions the mass term is elliptical, and this brings us to the alternate interpretation of Quine's proposal. The difficulty is, however, elliptical for what? For when one considers the building blocks of the complex general terms that Quine builds up with the help of mass terms, we get complexes that seem grammatical but have no clear semantic interpretations. That is to say, phrases like 'bit of', 'batch of', etc., do fit the locutions 'a', 'one', and 'the same', but if we ask for criteria of individuation or conditions for cross-world identification, no clear answers are available.[2] How many bits of water do we have here? Under what conditions does a bit of water remain the same bit of water? Unless answers can be provided to these questions, Quine's introduction of a whole group of new complex general terms remains somewhat problematic. Needless to say, one might complain that we set too stringent conditions for genuine general terms. This matter will be taken up again below.

The third difficulty in Quine's proposal concerns the internal structure of sentences like 'red ink is ink'. It seems that under an adequate interpretation this should come out as a tautology, but it is not clear that Quine's proposal provides such an interpretation. For on his account 'red ink' in subject position functions as a singular term, say a, while 'ink' in predicate position functions as a general term, say R. Thus the whole sentence has the structure of 'Ra', and that does not have the form of a tautology. Alternately, one could construe this as a generic statement, thus interpreting 'is ink' as 'is a kind of ink'. Under that interpretation one might describe the sentence as expressing something that is necessary, but if it is, it is necessary by definition, not by the truths of logic. Parsons' account would interpret the sentence as 'every quantity of ink that is red, is a quantity of ink', and this form, yielding the formula (x) (Ix . Rx. – Ix) does reveal the appropriate logical structure. One could write something similar in Quine's terminology, such as 'all bits of red ink are bits of ink' but this requires interpreting a mass term in subject position in a way in which Quine's proposal in general would not allow us.

Before we turn to constructive suggestions, let us summarize the conditions that an adequate proposal must meet. First, it has to provide interpretations for the eleven schemes in terms of which the various proposals were summarized. Secondly, the analysis should reflect the deep semantic differences between mass terms and count terms in some revealing way; differences that show why the reference of one is cumulative and the other divisive or individuative, and why the former and not the latter allows quantitative analysis. Third, the proposed semantic analysis should link up in some natural way with transformational grammar. Fourth, the analysis should reveal the structure of valid inferences involving mass terms, and should show how we can compute the denotation ranges of complex elements from the denotation ranges of simples.

The key to the proposal to be outlined is the attempt to do away with ad hoc general terms manufactured solely for the purpose of helping out with mass predicates, to capture the mass vs. count difference as a deep semantic difference, and to give a uniform mereological treatment to mass terms. The main obstacle to such a uniform treatment is summed up by Quine's argument in which he shows that though 'x is water' entails 'x is a part of the individual Water', the entailment does not work the other way around since not every part of the Water is water.

Let us first consider the mass terms as names of substances. In each world – the actual and the possible ones – a substance such as water is that spatio-temporally scattered individual whose parts are all the water that was, is, and will be in that world. Contrary to Parsons' proposal, one can treat substances in each world as mereological units and still end up with a satisfactory way of individuating them. For two substances F and G are distinct if and only if there is a part of one, say F, that is an F-part but though it may be a part of G it is not a G-part. Thus, e.g., in Parsons' hypothetical case Wood and Furniture can be distinguished since there will be a wood-part of Wood that – though it may be a part of Furniture – is not a furniture-part of Furniture. The meaning of a mass term will be the function that picks out the right mereological units from all those worlds in which there are such units. (Much of what follows was inspired by the early versions of Montague's work on English as a formal language, though he would not approve of what is proposed here.) Given this characterization, we have two choices for the denotation of a mass term. It is either the class whose members are the mereological units from each possible world, or the mereological unit ('superindividual') that is made up of all of the mereological units from the various possible worlds. If one could opt for the latter, then all statements about substances can be interpreted as being about a mereological unit. There are difficulties, however, facing such an option. For one thing, one would have to interpret each possible world in such a way that it contains a distinct set of individuals with various relations binding these across worlds. This would run against much of what has been said about general terms above. The other alternative still leaves one the mereological interpretation of substances within each world; this leaves us with a mereological interpretation of all nonnecessary statements – in other words, all of the empirical ones. This proposal still leaves us with a treatment of mass terms that is different from the one according to which the denotation is a completely set-theoretical entity across possible worlds. It is not clear how on that interpretation one can distinguish mass terms from count terms. Furthermore, according to the interpretation proposed one can distinguish two possible substances even if neither has any instances in the actual world.[3] For the two substances will be different as long as in some possible world their mereological units do not coincide in the way specified above.

Let us see now how one might give a uniform interpretation to mass terms so that they designate mereological units even when in predicate position. In view of Quine's argument and others supplied by members of the workshop the following appears to be the case. If we consider the actual world and wish to characterize 'x is water' mereologically, we must face the following conditions: 'x is water' if and only if (i) x is a part of the individual Water; (ii) x is a part of this individual such that it is water (not all parts of water are water); (iii) the conditions governing the issue of which part of a mass term M is itself m vary from term to term, and further-more with respect to one term they may vary from one possible world to another. That is to say, some mass terms, like water, may have parts too small to count as water, while others, e.g., 'long', may not have such minimal parts. Furthermore, the same mass term may designate something, e.g., water, that has minimal parts in some possible worlds but not in others.

What emerges from these considerations is that a substance with minimal parts is a mereological unit such that not all parts count as proper m-parts. Thus, e.g., some water is a part of that part of the individual Water that has certain structural properties P where P varies from mass term to mass term and may vary across possible worlds with respect to the same mass term. It seems that this could be captured by a mereological interpretation of the following sort:

For any mass term 'F', to say that 'x is F' is to say that x is a part of that part of F that has structural properties P where P varies from term to term and may vary with regard to any F across possible worlds.

According to this interpretation we can represent the copula when mass terms function as predicates as the 'part of' relation. To be sure, the complex predicates we get in this manner have to be spelled out case by case, and thus we get a wide variety of different mereological units from mass term to mass term and across possible worlds. As a defense of this proposal one might compare the semantics of mass terms as construed here with the semantics of functional terms like 'chair', or 'house'. With respect to these too, the structural properties defining each set in each possible world will vary widely; what counts as a house in one possible world may be very different from what counts as a house in the actual world; what they have to have in common is their usability as a place of shelter.

If this proposal turns out, on further consideration, to be unacceptable, an alternative that would still capture the same spirit would be to construe the copula to be standing in these contexts for a whole collection of mereological connectives, one corresponding to each mass term in predicate position.

This proposal can also handle sentences in which the subject term is a mass term that fails to denote in the actual world. Let us consider the sentence 'unicorn stuff is organic'. According to the analysis proposed this will be equivalent to 'there exist the individual Unicorn-stuff and it has the property of being organic'. Since the existential assertion made here is false, the whole conjunction comes out as false. Definitional statements can be interpreted as true or false, since these can be construed as being about the denotation of mass terms in all possible worlds.

Let us now summarize this proposal in terms of the same scheme that we employed for the other proposals.

(1)   NP (N) + VP = Nmass. (Mass terms in subject position are interpreted mereologically.)

(2)   ... + VP (... + N) = Nmass. (Mass terms in predicate position are interpreted mereologically with qualifications that vary from term to term and may vary for one term across possible worlds.)

(3)   ... + VP (... + Adj) = Adjmass. (Mass adjectives are interpreted mereologically when in predicate position, with restrictions as on mass nouns.)

(4)   NP (Demonstr. + N) = Nmass. (E.g., 'this iron' becomes 'this part of that part of Iron that has the required structural properties P'.)

(5)   NP (Ncount + Adj) = NPcount. (When what could be a mass adjective modifies a count noun, then it is part of a complex count term).

(6)   Identical with Quine's condition.

(7)   NP (Nmass + Adjmass) = NPmass. (A combination of a mass noun and an adjective that is mass modifying it is interpreted mereologically, in terms of the 'overlap' relation.)

(8)   Quantifier + Nmass = e.g., 'some water is drinkable' is interpreted as 'some parts of the Water that are also parts of that part of the Water that has structural property P have the property of being drinkable'.

(9)   Same as Quine's.

(10)   Def. Descr. (the + Nmass) = e.g., 'the water that ...' is interpreted as 'the part of that part of the Water that ... is so-and-so.

(11)   The 'is' of predication when the predicate is a mass term stands for the 'part of' relation.

Given this proposal one can interpret the semantics of NP's without considering the higher nodes that dominate them, and no problem arises in connection with the linking to a transformational grammar. Since in

(11) we have a revealing way of showing what is unique in mass terms, and the semantics of complexes is determined by the semantics of parts, the four conditions of adequacy stated at the beginning are met.

Someone might object that the proposal meets the condition of construing mass terms as unique only too well, for our formulation makes it impossible to interpret all of the semantics of a natural language within set-theoretic notions. It seems, however, that formal uniformity should not be the last standard by which to judge proposals of this type. With regard to those mass terms the elements of the denotation of which has minimal parts, a set-theoretic interpretation may seem natural. But we saw above that not all mass terms have minimal parts and that such a condition may vary from possible world to possible world. Someone might, of course, reject the implicit condition that only where there are minimal parts is the set-theoretic interpretation natural. This brings us, however, to the key problem with interpretations that take the denotation of mass terms in predicate position to be sets. How can one show on that account in some formal way the uniqueness of the semantics of mass terms? In general, if the semantics of all of the nouns and adjectives is expressed in terms of functions and sets, what is it that distinguishes count+ from count− in a formal and philosophically revealing way? Future research may bring answers to this question. If so, then the present attempt served at least as a clarification of the problems and work done on this problem, and hopefully serves as a catalyst for future work in this area.

Stanford University

NOTES

[1] Quine (1960, pp. 90–91). Also leading up to these ideas Quine (1953, Essay 4).

[2] For a different view, see Cartwright (1970).

[3] The remainder of this paper benefited from critical comments made by John Dolan, Richard Grandy, David Kaplan, Richard Montague, and Barbara Hall Partee.

CHUNG-YING CHENG

COMMENTS ON MORAVCSIK'S PAPER

1

It seems to me that mass terms are general terms which have no contrasting singular terms, because there is no intrinsic individuative principle in the language to give divided reference to these terms. In other words, mass terms are general terms without commonly agreed or linguistically articulated individuating instances. As general terms, mass terms can be either concrete (or observational) or abstract (or nonobservational). The concrete mass terms depend upon observational classifiers (e.g., a part of [beef], a glass of [milk], an acre of [land]) for individuation, whereas the abstract mass term depends upon nonobservational units of measurement or quantification (e.g., 3 watts of [electricity], 100 degrees of [temperature], 5 joules of [heat]) for individuation.

2

Mass terms seem to be dispositional as they are associated with different adjective terms under different conditions, e.g., water freezes in very cold weather. Because of this, they, as a rule, satisfy certain lawlike statements.

3

There are many kinds of mass terms, and they can be distinguished only by different linguistic contexts. But we can also formulate a general defining condition for mass terms. Before we do this, we should make clear the general nature of the object to which mass terms apply.

4

We call the object to which a mass term applies a mass object. I think that what characterizes mass object is the internal uniformity of its discernible composition. Informally speaking, a mass object has a homogeneity of distribution of composing elements which enables us to identify the whole

Hintikka et al. (eds.), Approaches to Natural Language, 286–288. *All rights reserved.*

thing by identifying part of the thing or to identify the part by identifying the whole as well as to identify one part by identifying another part. Formally and without reference to our ability of identification, we may define and describe mass object in the following fashion.

(1)   Given a part of the mass object to be w, then any part of the mass object is w.

(2)   The sum (or the whole) of parts of mass object which are w is itself w (Quine's condition).

(3)   Any part of the whole of the mass object which is w is w (call it Cheng's condition).

Now it is not clear whether these three conditions are equivalent and therefore individually necessary; one has to look for examples to prove their dependence. I am inclined to take them as collectively necessary conditions for being a mass object, that is, any mass object must satisfy all of them. But, of course, theoretically speaking, one could have an object which satisfied all of these conditions, but still not be a mass object. This means that mass object could be an open category and no complete definition (necessary and sufficient conditions) is possible. To support my view regarding (1), (2), and (3) as collectively necessary conditions for being mass objects, we may point out that Quine's condition (2) is certainly justified by a mass object such as 'water'. But satisfaction of it by the object 'class' does not decide class as an *abstract mass object*. For it is clear that any sum of parts of a class which are classes is a class. As it stands, *class* has identity conditions by axiom of identity of class. Thus, class is an individual of a certain order, but no mass object. In light of this violation of (2) by our notion of class, and because (3) perhaps cannot be violated by the notion of class, we can regard (3) as a *better* condition for determining an object to be a mass object. Now a mass term is a term purported to refer to mass object described by the conditions (1), (2), and (3). An alternative definition of mass term is that a mass term is one which by itself does not satisfy the axioms of identity.

5

Physical mass objects are made of molecules in terms of modern physical science. Thus, water is made of water-molecules. By the above condition (3), a water-molecule as a part of water is water. This, no doubt, makes scientific sense. Someday we may be able to *distinguish* one water-molecule from another or find it useful to do so. Then we shall speak of water-molecules, instead of waters or when we do speak of waters, we would mean water-molecules (apart from the present meaning of rivers, lakes and oceans). We note that water-molecules are not mass objects as they have no part which is a water-molecule. Similarly, an organism of type (α) has no part which is (α) and this makes organisms individuals, not mass objects. My point here is that the concept of mass term or mass object can have an epistemological and practical dimension in that it is determined relative to our abilities of individuating identification and needs for employing individuating identification.

Thus, in regard to abstract mass terms, there must be a period when individuation (in terms of individuating identification) was difficult or felt unnecessary, e.g., 'science' was not an abstract general term which could take plurals before it was made one when sciences are more developed. Therefore, Moravcsik's point on page 265 seems to be dubious. The difference between qualitative and quantitative analysis does not suggest any real difference between mass terms and nonmass terms. For in science, when individuation is not otherwise possible, we use measurement and quantification for individuating identification. In elementary particle physics we do *count* electrons.

6

I believe that we must have a clear understanding of epistemology of mass terms as mass terms and ontology of mass objects as mass objects before we can have a clear understanding of semantics and syntax of 'mass terms'. To talk about semantics and syntax of 'mass terms' without a grasp of the epistemology of mass terms and the ontology of mass objects will not lead to a complete elucidation and explanation of behaviors of 'mass terms' in a particular language or in any language. In light of our epistemological and ontological remarks on mass terms and mass objects, we can expect a clear explanation and elucidation of behaviors of 'mass terms', not only in a particular natural language such as English, but in any natural language which lacks some of the syntactic or grammatical devices for the marking of mass terms.

University of Hawaii

COMMENTS ON
MORAVCSIK'S PAPER

The basic problem is to determine what concrete mass nouns denote and how one is to give truth conditions for sentences containing them. I ignore for the most part 'abstract mass nouns' and 'mass adjectives', but see below.

I speak within the normal intuitive framework, according to which ordinary proper nouns denote individuals, ordinary common nouns and intransitive verbs denote sets of individuals, infinitives of ordinary intransitive verbs denote properties of individuals (that is, functions from possible worlds to sets of individuals), and so on; and not within the elaborately inflated framework of my paper at the present workshop. The more elaborate framework is introduced in order to accommodate intensional verbs and the like. The present proposal could be made to fit in with that development by a rather obvious inflation in type, but for clarity it is better to avoid such complications and accordingly to renounce intensional verbs here.

Moravcsik has very usefully set out the main proposals so far advanced, and has presented arguments and examples sufficient to show all but one of them inadequate; the single exception is not his own but Parsons'. Thus I need not consider alternative proposals (apart from Parsons'; see below) but simply give the one that appears to me right.

Concrete mass nouns should basically be taken as denoting properties of individuals. For instance, **water** should denote the property of being a body of water, and **iron** the property of being a piece of iron. In general, a mass term will denote that function on possible worlds which takes as its value for a given world the set of all samples (or, to give synonyms, portions or quantities (in the sense ascribed to Parsons) or "parts with the correct structural properties") of the substance in question in that world. (It would be irrelevant to object that there may be no *minimal* portions;

Hintikka et al. (eds.), Approaches to Natural Language, 289–294. *All rights reserved.*
Copyright © 1973 *by D. Reidel Publishing Company, Dordrecht-Holland.*

the proposal applies equally to the unusual case in which every part of a portion of the substance is itself a portion of the substance.)

This much is sufficient to account for occurrences of mass nouns standing alone in normal substantive positions – for instance, in **portion of** α, which should clearly denote the extension (in the actual world) of the property denoted by the mass noun α, or in α **is a liquid**. (**Liquid** should clearly be taken as a higher-order common noun, that is, as denoting a set of properties of individuals.) Other contexts, however, must also be explained. A mass noun α standing alone in predicative position should be regarded as synonymous with **a portion of** α. If a quantifier (for example, **some**, **all**), a demonstrative, or an adjective phrase accompanies a mass noun, then the mass noun should in that occurrence be taken as denoting the extension of the property usually denoted. (In this connection notice that **water is wet** should be taken as elliptical for **all water is wet**; notice that this sentence is quite different from **water is a liquid**.)[1] In those exceptional cases in which a mass noun is used as an adjective (as in **iron bed**) the denotation of the adjective (which must as always be a function) can be easily obtained in terms of the extension of the property denoted by the mass term. (To be more explicit, if ζ is a common noun phrase and hence denotes a set A, then **iron** ζ denotes the intersection of A with the extension of the property denoted by **iron**.)

Notice that it would not be good to treat a mass noun as denoting the **set** of portions of the substance in question. For consider the example brought up in the September workshop session of two never-to-be-realized (but describable and realizable) substances called Kaplanite and Suppesite. The two sets in question would then be identical, but **Kaplanite is a liquid** might be true and **Suppesite is a liquid** false.[2]

So far I have said nothing about such phrases as **the gold in Smith's ring**. Let me give what now appears to me the best treatment, though I may be on shakier ground here than in the foregoing. In the first place, **in Smith's ring** is an adjective phrase; hence, in accordance with what was said above, **gold** should here be taken as denoting the set of portions of gold, and it would be natural to take **gold in Smith's ring** as denoting the set of portions of gold that are 'in' Smith's ring. In the second place, I would take **the** in **the gold in Smith's ring** as the ordinary singular definite article, so that **the** ζ has a denotation if and only if ζ denotes a unit set, and in that case **the** ζ denotes the only element of that set.[3] But is there not a conflict here? It would seem that there are many portions of gold in Smith's ring. For while not all parts of portions of gold are portions of gold, still many are; and these would appear to be in Smith's ring. Yet for **the gold in Smith's ring** to denote, it is necessary for **gold in Smith's ring** to denote a unit set.

The solution is I think to regard **in** as in one sense (and indeed the prevailing though not altogether unique sense when accompanying mass nouns) amounting to **occupying** or **constituting**. Then **gold in Smith's ring** comes to **gold constituting Smith's ring**, denotes the set of maximal portions of gold that are 'in' (in the more inclusive sense) Smith's ring, and hence denotes a unit set.

It seems more or less arbitrary whether to assume that the set of portions of a given substance is always closed under physical composition, but I prefer to make this assumption, inasmuch as it appears to simplify the treatment of such compounds as **much** α and **more** α, where α is a mass noun. Then, for instance, it is not unreasonable to treat **much** α **F's** as synonymous with **some large portion of** α **F's**, and **more** α **F's than G's** as synonymous with **there is a portion of** α **that F's and is larger than any portion of** α **that G's**. (The word **larger** is of course ambiguous, and the linguistic or extralinguistic content must be considered to determine whether it is to mean **greater in volume**, **greater in weight**, or something else. **Large**, besides sharing the ambiguity of **larger**, is in addition vague; but the vagueness and ambiguity of these two words is fairly accurately reflected in **much** and **more**.)

The question naturally arises whether portions of substances are full-fledged physical objects like tables and rings (together with physical compositions of these). Perhaps. At least, I see no clear-cut argument to the contrary. If this is so, then under appropriate conditions (for instance, that Smith's ring is made entirely of gold) the sentence **Smith's ring is the same as the gold constituting Smith's ring** could very well be true. This may appear strange, and indeed seems to contradict the intuitions of Cartwright (1970, especially the first sentence on p. 28); but I cannot find any good argument for rejecting it.

There is, however, a *bad* argument. Suppose that Jones had an all-gold ring, but that it was melted down and made into a ring for Smith. Then, given our understanding that portions of gold are full-fledged physical objects, it would be reasonable to assert the following:

(1)   **Smith's ring is the same as the gold that constitutes Smith's ring,**
(2)   **Jones' ring was the same as the gold that constituted Jones' ring,**
(3)   **the gold that constitutes Smith's ring is the same as the gold that constituted Jones' ring.**

At first glance these three sentences might appear to imply the rather clearly false conclusion,

(4)   **Smith's ring is Jones' ring;**

but the appearance would be deceptive. The supposed inference would amount to one involving substitution on the basis of an identity sentence within the scope of a tense operator; and as everyone knows (cf. Cocchiarella's UCLA dissertation), that is invalid. (Of course,

Smith's ring is the same as the gold that constituted Jones's ring

does follow from (1) and (3), but this is unobjectionable. And if we were to change *was* to *is* in (2), (4) would follow from (1)–(3); but then (2) would be false.)

At the moment, then, I should recommend regarding portions of substances as full-fledged physical objects, or physical compositions of these. But if some strong argument were found for not doing this, and indeed for distinguishing between Smith's ring and the gold constituting Smith's ring, my general proposal for treating mass terms would not thereby be overturned. It is perfectly possible to construct an ontology allowing for physical objects of different sorts, objects that may coincide without being identical. The construction was sketched in a letter I wrote in June 1968 to Dana Scott, and corresponds, I believe, to Hume's outlook. Let us for present purposes suppose that our *basic objects* have no temporal duration, each of them existing only for a moment; they are accordingly what we might regard as temporal slices of 'ordinary objects', and might include such physical slices as heaps of molecules at a moment, and possibly such additional objects as instantaneous mental states. Then *ordinary objects* or *continuants* (for instance, physical objects, persons) would be constructs obtained by 'stringing together' various basic objects – or, more exactly, certain functions from moments of time to basic objects. Two continuants f and g may be said to *coincide* at a moment i just in case the function values $f(i)$ and $g(i)$ are the same.

To quote from my letter:

Now most pairs of ordinary objects are such that if they coincide at one moment, then they do so always . . . . But this is not true of all pairs of ordinary objects. There *are* different ways of stringing basic objects together.

For instance, we are told that we change our bodies completely every so often. It follows that some living organisms 'correspond' at different times to two or more different heaps of molecules. Yet suppose we are materialists and do not believe in 'souls' or 'transcendent unities' or 'entelechies'. We should seem to be faced with an identity crisis.

The solution is of course obvious. Both heaps of molecules and organisms are continuants made out of heaps-of-molecules-at-a-moment (Homaams). But they are pieced together in different ways: each heap of molecules consists of Homaams related in simple ways describable in physics, while organisms consist of Homaams related in certain functional or biological ways. Thus it may well be that no organism is a heap of molecules, but that materialism is nevertheless true in the sense that every organism coincides with a heap of molecules . . . . It may also be (though butterflies, caterpillars, and divisions of protozoa give one pause) that whenever two *organisms* or two *physical objects* coincide, they are also identical. And indeed this may give some clue to *natural kinds*. For a set (or property) to be a natural kind it is probably necessary (though not sufficient) that for any two of its members, if they coincide, then they are identical.

Full-fledged physical objects and substance-portions could be similarly distinguished, though I do not at the moment recommend it. For instance, Jones' ring might be identified with a certain function defined just for that interval of time I_1 during which Jones' ring existed, and having as its value for a moment i in I_1 the Homaam which is its temporal slice at i; Smith's ring might be identified with a similar function defined for the later interval I_2 during which that ring exists; and the gold-portion constituting Jones' ring during I_1 and Smith's ring during I_2 might be identified with a function defined over a much longer interval of time (including both I_1 and I_2), always having Homaams as its values, and coinciding with Jones' ring and Smith's ring throughout I_1 and I_2, respectively.

Abstract mass nouns (correctly delimited; some of Moravcsik's examples, like **vagueness,** are unfortunate) would be treated in exactly the same way as concrete mass nouns. For instance, **information** would basically denote the property of being a piece of (that is, portion of) information. Of course, this leaves much unsettled: what sort of object is a piece of information? But that is a problem independent of the analysis of mass nouns and would arise even if we were to renounce mass nouns, treat **piece of information** as an unanalyzed common noun, and avoid using **information** in any other context. Such problems must be solved before we can expect a completely definite treatment of 'abstract mass nouns'.

Now some words that are *basically* adjectives (primarily and perhaps exclusively color words) have a derivative use in substantive positions; and in those positions they should be taken, like concrete mass nouns, as denoting properties of individuals. For instance, **red** in **red is a color** should denote the property of being red (or of being a red object). One could, if one liked, call such adjectives mass adjectives; but observe that there are few of them and that they definitely do not include Moravcsik's examples **sweet** and **heavy**.

I promised to say something about Parsons' treatment of mass nouns. It appears to be completely correct as far as it goes, and is I think completely compatible with my treatment. In fact, my treatment can be regarded simply as an amplification of Parsons', consisting mostly in saying what sort of thing 'substances' are (properties of individuals) and in consequence giving an analysis of Parsons' **quantity of** (that is, **portion of**).

University of California, Los Angeles

NOTES

[1] It should also be pointed out that **blue water is a liquid** turns out meaningless, but I think that on reflection this will be found compatible with intuition. ("How many liquids are there, and how many metals?" "Umpteen and phumpteen." "Did you count water?" "Yes." "How about blue water?" "Oh, I forgot." "And red water, and green water, and...") Of course **heavy water** is different; **heavy** is here syncategorematic and **heavy water** an unanalyzed mass noun.

[2] It would not be good to maintain that **Kaplanite is a liquid** might involve a nonextensional context and for that reason might not, together with **Kaplanite is the same as Suppesite**, imply **Suppesite is a liquid**. No context is more paradigmatically extensional than those of the form **is a** ζ, and to rule such contexts nonextensional would require supplying a meaning for them other than the obvious and natural one.

[3] In a comprehensive treatment it is perhaps best never to assign a denotation (or at least one that is an individual) to a phrase of the form **the** ζ, but rather to treat such phrases syncategorematically; see Montague (1970a) and my paper in the present volume. Nevertheless, it will cause no harm to speak, for intuitive purposes, of such phrases as sometimes denoting; then the 'intuitive denotation' of the phrase will be genuinely involved in arriving at the 'real denotations' of longer expressions containing the phrase.

RICHARD E. GRANDY

COMMENTS ON
MORAVCSIK'S PAPER*

The problem of finding a satisfactory analysis of sentences containing mass
terms has attracted an increasing amount of attention in the past few
years.[1] Most of the recent literature springs from dissatisfaction with the
account offered by Quine (1960). More specifically, the uneasiness stems
from the fact that Quine treats mass terms as singular terms when they
occur before the copula and as general terms when they occur after. Thus
'Snow is white' is regimented into the form 'White(s)', while 'The stuff in
the yard is snow' is regimented into 'Snow ($\iota x(x$ is in the yard))'.

In the remainder of this paper I shall argue that

(a) treatment of mass terms as singular terms in occurrences before the
copula and as general terms in occurrences after the copula has unacceptable defects,

(b) treatment of all occurrences of mass terms treated as singular terms
has the defect of requiring new, primitive (i.e., not explicitly definable)
technical terms,

(c) one can treat almost all occurrences of mass terms as general terms

(d) mass terms need not be treated differently from count terms, and
finally,

(e) treatment of mass terms in the same way as count terms seems to be
the correct analysis.

A. Various examples have been suggested to show the defect of Quine's
analysis. All appeal to the failure of regimentation à la Quine to preserve
obvious equivalence of truth value, but this is a criterion which Quine
seems quite willing to accept. If one accepts Quine's regimentation of
'Snow is white' as 'White(s)' and of 'The stuff in the yard is snow' as
'Snow ($\iota x(x$ is the stuff in the yard))', the inference from those two sentences to 'The stuff in the yard is white' is not the simple logical inference

Hintikka et al. (eds.), Approaches to Natural Language, 295–300. All rights reserved.
Copyright © 1973 by D. Reidel Publishing Company, Dordrecht-Holland.

which it appears to be in ordinary English. The inference will be sanc-
tioned only on the basis of some additional nonobvious principles.
Another example that expresses the same discontent is 'Blue water is
blue', an obvious truth, which is regimented into a sentence that may be
true, but is certainly not obvious. Thus it would appear desirable to seek
an analysis of mass terms that gives a uniform treatment regardless of
where the mass term occurs in a sentence.

B.   The strategy of Moravcsik and Parsons has been to attempt to give a
uniform treatment of mass terms by treating them as names also when
they occur after the copula. To see the difficulty in this approach, consider
the task one sets for oneself when attempting to treat 'snow' in 'x is snow'
as a singular term. In order to end with a well-formed sentence, one must
construct a predicate that contains the singular term. That is, the logical
form of the sentence must ultimately turn out to be something like $\phi(s)$,
where ϕs is a complex predicate containing the singular term 'snow',
which is co-extensive with 'is snow'. Parsons' analysis requires the predicate '$xC\sigma y(S(y))$', to be read as 'x is composed of the substance snow', or
'x is snow'; Moravcsik's analysis involves the predicate 'x is part of that
part of snow which has structural properties P', where the 'P' is to be
filled in variously in particular cases. Both treatments run afoul of the fact
that the singular term and the part relation cannot be treated as in the
calculus of individuals because not every part, in that technical sense of
'part', of snow is snow.[2] Thus both authors not only introduce technical
terms that have no obvious counterpart in the English sentence, but these
technical terms are new notions which require explication.

C.   I would suggest that we can give an analysis of mass terms which is
parallel to that of count terms in that almost all occurrences are treated as
general terms. On this view, 'Snow is white' is regimented as '$(x)(S(x)$
$\supset W(x))$' and 'Blue water is water' is regimented as '$(x)(B(x)\&W(x)$
$\supset W(x))$'; these analyses seem to preserve the obvious connections which
Quine's treatment severed.

D.   The reader may recall that the reason Quine chose to treat occurrences
of mass terms before a copula as singular terms was that in some sentences
such as 'Gold is an element' or 'Water is widespread', the form of the

sentence cannot be that of a disguised universal conditional. Thus we must either treat mass terms differently in occurrences before and after the copula or else distinguish various kinds of occurrences before the copula. The latter treatment would be exactly parallel to the situation for nonmass terms, for there are sentences such as 'Lions are a species' and 'Lions are widespread', in which 'lions' must be a singular term denoting the class of lions. (One misunderstanding which must be warned against is the following: it is not the case that the claim, that in the sentence 'Lions are widespread' one is predicating a property of a set, entails that the sentence is equivalent to 'The set of lions is widespread'. This misinterpretation is parallel to a fallacious argument against Frege's analysis of belief sentences; the argument is that if in the sentence 'John believes Plato is wise' the term 'Plato' refers to the sense of 'Plato' rather than Plato, then the sentence is equivalent to 'John believes that the sense of "Plato" is wise'.)

There is no need to introduce individuals into the analysis of mass terms for we can simply view 'Water is widespread' as the predication of a property of the class of objects which are water. The problem still remains of sorting out systematically which predicates apply to bits of water and which apply to the class of all bits of water, but this problem must equally be solved in order to have an adequate analysis of count terms. Similarly, identity statements such as 'Gold is the element with atomic number 79' will have the form $\{x: \text{gold}(x)\} = \{x: x \text{ has atomic number 79}\}$. This analysis of singular-term occurrences of mass terms as names of sets is preferable to the treatment as names of spatio-temporally discontinuous individuals because the individuals prove to have the wrong conditions of identity for substances (Parsons, 1970, pp. 376–78). Thus, as Parsons notes, even if all wood were made into furniture and all furniture were made only of wood, we would not want to assert the identity of the substances furniture and wood.[3] This creates problems for Parsons and Moravcsik, because they would prefer to treat the substances as individuals, but individuals are identical when they occupy the same space-time regions. When treated as sets, however, furniture and wood turn out to be nonidentical even under the hypothesis above, for there are members of the set $\{x: \text{wood}(x)\}$ which are not members of the set $\{x: \text{furniture}(x)\}$, e.g., arms of chairs.

E.   To recapitulate briefly the theory and its advantages thus far, mass terms are treated exactly like nonmass terms. They function in general as predicates, except in a few sentences where the predicate requires that they be singular terms naming the sets consisting of all the things which they are true of in their other occurrences. The advantages of the theory are that it gives a uniform treatment of mass and nonmass terms that requires no new technical devices and that preserves obvious connections between sentences.

Of course the very simplicity of the theory and its similarity to the treatment of count terms might be taken as a disadvantage. For example, one might object that the theory sketched above does not give any indication why it is that mass nouns resist pluralization, or why mass terms, unlike count terms, may be prefixed by 'How much . . .?' while count nouns must be prefixed by 'How many . . .?' Nor does the theory give any indication that, in Quine's (1960, p. 91) phrase, "mass terms refer cumulatively." To begin with the last point, it appears to me that since the relevant fact – that the sum of any two F's is itself F, when F is a mass term – can be stated in nonsemantical terms there is no reason to regard it as a *semantic* fact. Hence there is no reason to expect the fact to be reflected in our semantics. An analogous case is the fact that the union of any two sets is itself a set, which has prompted no one to suggest that this should be reflected in the semantics of the term 'set'.

The issue of pluralization is related to the 'how many – how much' distinction, but appears not to be of any systematic interest in itself. 'Groceries' is a mass term that is always pluralized, while count nouns such as 'deer' and 'sheep' resist pluralization. But, these seem to be mere grammatical quirks. Also, a host of complex terms have the feature that the sum of F's is F, but when they are pluralized they take 'how many' rather than 'how much'. These are locutions of the form 'bit of gold weighing more than n pounds'.

The fact that mass terms are prefixable by 'How much . . .?' but not 'How many . . .?' is possibly of more importance. Nevertheless, in the absence of arguments to the contrary, it seems reasonable to attribute this difference to the empirical facts about the objects to which mass terms apply. That is, for most mass terms 'F' and most bits of F, the bit can be divided into two bits of F. This is not true for all bits, such as molecules of water, but it is true of most bits of most substances encountered in every-day life. For the exceptional mass terms, such as 'furniture', 'jewelry', and 'apparel', the question 'How much F?' has an acceptable answer in count terms, viz., 'Seven pieces of furniture'.[4] Thus there seems to be no reason not to attribute the grammatical differences between mass and count terms to these empirical factors plus our sensible propensity for asking only interesting questions. The relevance of the difficulty or ease of physical fission and fusion of the objects may be indicated by such count nouns as 'rock' and 'stone'; these seem more like substances than typical count nouns, but are easily individuated by spatio-temporal properties.

In conclusion, I should like to mention one other advantage of not appealing to individuals as the reference of mass terms and to a problem which parallels that of count terms.[5] It sometimes appears that there is an implicit claim that the above grammatical distinctions are accounted for by the fact that in the theories proposed mass terms are names of individuals. This seems to be an unnecessary addition to both one's ontology and axioms. That is, one must add principles that guarantee the existence of the individual, which is the sum of any two individuals, and the sum must be among the values of the variables of the theory in order for the theory to be true. In addition to the Occamite motivation of avoiding any unnecessary entities (and the general need for the sum of individuals seems to be avoided by the theory proposed here), there seems to be some evidence in ordinary usage that indicates individuals should not be included in the ontology of one's regimented theory.

Quine (1960, p. 116) notes that although Heraclitus bathes in the same river twice and that all rivers are water, Heraclitus does not therefore bathe in the same water twice. Part of the puzzle that arises from these facts is alleviated by making temporal distinctions, i.e., the water which the river is today is different from the water which the river was yesterday. But the example points to the fact that the criteria of individuation for the entities rivers and waters are quite different. To eliminate the temporal dimension, consider an occasion on which Heraclitus and Parmenides both bathe at the same time, though not in the same place. Since there is an individual which is the sum of waters they separately bathed in, there is an individual which is water and in which they both bathe. Yet we would not say that they bathed in the same water. The problem of setting out the individuating conditions for 'same water' will likely be nontrivial, but it is not obviously different from the kinds of problems that arise when we attempt the parallel task for such count nouns as 'man' or 'ship'. What the example does seem to show, however, is that ordinary usage does not sanction the inference to the conclusion that there is an individual in which Heraclitus and Parmenides both bathed, and thus it casts further doubt on the reasonableness of having the axioms of individuals as part of the regimented theory.

Princeton University

NOTES

* This note was written while the author was an NSF Fellow. David Rosenthal and Tyler Burge have helped to clarify my view by attempting to change it. I am also indebted to Burge for the opportunity to read an unpublished paper of his which helped to stimulate this note.
[1] Parsons (1970, pp. 363–88), Moravcsik (this volume pp. 263–85); Cartwright (1965, 1970, in press). An extended and systematic critique of Parsons and Quine, and a theory somewhere between that of Parsons and the one suggested below is in Burge's Ph.D. dissertation (1971).
[2] See Goodman and Leonard (1940) for details; I shall use 'individual', 'sum' and 'part only in this technical sense.
[3] The example is Parsons (1970, p. 377); I have reservations, to be noted later, concerning whether furniture is a paradigmatic mass term.
[4] Discussion with Susan Sherwin of an earlier draft of this note was helpful in clarifying this point.
[5] The reader should, to avoid confusion, recall that 'individual' is being used in the technical sense noted earlier.

JULIUS MORAVCSIK

REPLY TO COMMENTS

A number of comments, written and verbal, made since the completion of my paper have made me reflect further on the problems that I tried to deal with; what follows is the result of these reflections. The first three points were stimulated by conversations with Professor R. Grandy.

1. THE STATUS OF MY 'INDIVIDUALS'

An illustration of my final account of mass terms would be the following: 'x is snow' $\equiv$ 'x is part of that part of Snow that has the required SP'. Given this definition it follows that there might be parts of some snow in the sense of spatio-temporal parts such that they are not parts of Snow – the individual that includes all of the scattered things that are snow. This, in turn, means that for this explication of the logic of individuals – part relations, etc. – the principle of transitivity has to be given up. The individual Snow, on my account, does not have as its parts everything that is a spatio-temporal part of some part of Snow. One important consequence of this view is that it allows for the possibility of two individuals being contained in the same spatio-temporal region.

These consequences render my conception of 'individuals' rather different from the one worked out by Goodman (1951) and others. One might say that my individuals are less concrete than those of the more standard type. This in itself does not seem to me to be a serious objection. It becomes one, however, when it is pressed that one of the fundamental motivations for my proposal – which is admittedly less elegant formally than the others – was the insistence that the semantics must provide an illuminating way of marking the deep difference between count terms and mass terms. But perhaps my conception of individuals loses some of the intuitive explanatory force when we give up the transitivity of the 'part of' relation; indeed, it is worth asking the question: how do my individuals differ from sets?

Hintikka et al. (eds.), Approaches to Natural Language, 301–308. *All rights reserved.*
Copyright © 1973 *by D. Reidel Publishing Company, Dordrecht-Holland.*

2. SETS AND INDIVIDUALS

It seems to me that as long as I can show important differences between sets and my individuals, I can defend the account against the charges considered in the paragraph above. One such difference, of course, is the fact that my individuals are still concrete in the sense that they have spatio-temporal location – though not uniquely so – and that they have the so-called secondary qualities attached to them that we ordinarily use to characterize concrete things. But more importantly, even if one abandons the transitivity principle one can show how the two concepts are different by contrasting the 'set of' and 'sum of' relations. For it is still true on my account that while the set of all men is not itself a man, the sum of all snows is itself snow. In general terms: the set of all w's is not itself a w, while the sum of all w's is itself a w. This helps also to see why 'union of sets' is different from 'sum of w's'. The union of two sets of men is itself a set of men, but the set itself is not a man, while the sum of two parts of Water is not only itself containing individuals that are water, but the sum itself is part of Water. So we see that the relation between set and a member is different from the relation between a sum and one of its parts. The only sense in which sets might be regarded as having parts is when one considers the relation between set and subset.

3. THE STATUS OF SP'S

It has been pointed out that it is not a necessary truth that all mass terms should carry 'built-in' SP's – why could not some refer to individuals that are such that for an individual W, all spatio-temporal parts are W? (Perhaps space and time could be treated as such individuals?) And certainly, it could be the case that in some possible world what is referred to by a mass term M cumulatively has no SP, while in the actual world it does. It seems to me that my scheme can take care of these cases by regarding the set of SP's when this is in fact the zero set, as a limiting case. And it is a natural consequence of this view that those mass terms that have no SP's distinguishing the genuine parts of the respective individuals can be on my account to be having the same SP.

The following four remarks were stimulated by a correspondence with Professor Quine; though, needless to say, he might not approve at all of the ways in which I try here to defend my suggestions and elaborate on some of these.

4. REGIMENTATION AND LINGUISTIC ANALYSIS

Professor Quine might say that it is not quite appropriate to compare his account with mine, or some of the others proposed, since the purposes may be different. As he would say, his purpose is that of regimentation leading to the formulation of acceptable logical form, while several other proposals seek the best linguistic analysis. The contrast invoked here is a topic of lively debate among philosophers of language today. His most extensive treatment of the distinction is to be found in Quine (1970b). In the context of these remarks this distinction cannot be treated adequately. In my remarks on the papers concerning belief-sentences I urged that syntactic deep structure and logical form are not identical. It is gratifying to find Quine coming to the same conclusion. Nevertheless, it seems to me that within semantics, something important is lost if one paraphrases away mass terms. It is fair to say, however, that in terms of the goals of regimentation by a logician, I have not spelled out what this important loss is.

5. AMBIGUITY OR ELLIPSIS

Instead of adopting my proposed explanation in terms of ellipsis, Professor Quine might opt for treating a term like 'water' in a straightforward manner as ambiguous; the ambiguity being between its use as a singular term and as a general term. The price one would pay is partly that this view invokes a most curious ambiguity; one that does not have typical analogues among the phenomena commonly labelled as ambiguity; and partly that such ambiguity would not be based on empirical data drawn from the speakers of the language. It should be said, however, that this price would be gladly paid by someone whose sole aim is regimentation and moving to canonical notation.

6. THE ALLEGED PROBLEM OF INDIVIDUATING THE PARTS OF WATER, SUGAR, ETC.

In my paper I suggest strongly that the ultimate vehicles of reference must be expressions that involve count + nouns (or verbs, adjectives), and that this is partly a matter of what kinds of things have clear principles of individuation. Thus: "How many lakes?" is a clear question, but "How many water-parts?" is not. Quine would not agree. His answer to the question: "How many water-parts in that puddle?" would be: "Countless," and I can hardly object to this answer, since there are many types of entity with clear principles of individuation such that to various "how many . . .?" questions, the answers about these entities will be: "Countless." (Obvious example: numbers.) Given my views about reference and the basic objects of our conceptual scheme, one could show that the spatiotemporal parts of water as such would not qualify. This, however, involves the condition that what we basically refer to must be cross-identifiable from possible world to possible world. This involves essentialism, and Quine will have none of it. In the context of this paper I can only say that different philosophers will adopt different principles of individuation with differing 'strengths', one might say. I cannot deny that in a way the parts of Water can be individuated, but it is an open issue as to what the role of this sort of individuation is in the general conceptual framework that – I think – underlies our ability to use language and articulate thoughts. Even apart from the questions of essentialism, however, one can point to one intuitively clear difference between the individuation of the parts of Water, and that of other terms that are count +. For when one considers two lakes, one cannot describe these equally well as one lake, or three lakes, etc. – they are simply two lakes. But when one considers a part of Water that is the sum of various water-parts, one can describe it equally correctly as one water-part, or two, or three, etc. In other words, the 'arithmetic' attached to count + terms is fixed in a way in which the arithmetic of mass terms is not. Again, whether this is a significant point depends on whether one's purpose is solely that of regimentation, or that of accounting for other aspects of understanding.

7. ALTERNATIVE READINGS FOR 'INK IS RED'

According to the interpretation proposed in my paper Quine would interpret in (iii) ink is red, 'red' as a general term, or as an ellipsis for a more complex general term. This interpretation might saddle him with some difficulties concerning the grammatical relation between 'red' in that sentence, and 'red ink' when the latter is in subject position. As an alternate reading one might propose that Quine could read 'red' in (iii) as a singular term naming the red part of the world, with the 'is' in (iii) signifying a mereological relation. This reading would thus preserve the. close semantic connection between 'ink is red' and 'red ink . . .'. What prevented me from considering this reading is that one must – on Quine's view – interpret a mass term behind the 'is' of predication as a general term. The proposed alternative, however, does not violate that dictum, since it does not construe the 'is' in question (i.e., in (iii)) as the 'is' of predication. In short, my interpretation of Quine did not allow for the possibility that he might construe some occurrences of 'is' as mereological, and not as the 'is' of predication. Such an alternative is certainly possible; one would then have to spell out within which configurations 'is' is to be taken predicatively, and within which configurations mereologically.

The following remarks are prompted by written comments of Dr. C. Cheng.

8. MASS TERMS AND DISPOSITIONS

I find it difficult to see why mass terms should be regarded as typically dispositional any more than count terms. To be sure, the same stuff can be water or ice, under different circumstances, but this is also true of what is designated by count terms. The same object can be now a church and then later a warehouse, under different circumstances. Both mass terms and count terms can figure equally in lawlike statements explicating various dispositions.

9. WHY WE SHOULD NOT TALK ABOUT 'MASS OBJECTS'

It is a mistake, or at best misleading, to talk about 'mass objects'. Quine (1960, p. 91) put it very well in the course of explaining the difference between count+ and −, "The contrast lies in the terms and not in the stuff they name . . . consider 'shoe', 'pair of shoes', and 'footwear': all three range over exactly the same scattered stuff, and differ from one another solely in that two of them divide their reference differently and the third not at all." In other words the same thing can be viewed either as something of which a count term is true, or as a part of an individual designated by a mass term. Quine says that the difference lies in the terms; those of us with a more Platonistic, or Fregean ontology would say that the difference lies in the concepts associated with the respective terms. Of course, we are left with some interesting questions, first posed by Aristotle, of how to characterize the 'sameness' of a bit of matter and the substance that is made of it. But this difficult issue lies beyond my paper or Dr. Cheng's comments; I attempt to deal with it elsewhere. (Some papers on essentialism; forthcoming.) Internal uniformity of discernible composition can mark something referred to both by a mass term and by a count term. For example, a chunk of ice has the required uniformity and it is both a mereological part of the individual Ice, as well as an instance of the property of being a chunk of ice (clearly count +).

For this reason I doubt very much that Professor Quine would be happy with Dr. Cheng's attempted reconstruction of criteria for being a mass term; what is called 'Quine's condition' contains the phrase 'mass object'; something that I think Quine would no more want in the statement of the criterion that I do.

10. CLASSES AS ABSTRACT MASS OBJECTS

Rephrasing the matter slightly, the issue is: are we to treat 'class' as an abstract mass term? The argument behind the affirmative answer is that "any sum of parts of a class which are classes is a class." The problem is, of course, how shall we construe the relations of 'sum of' and 'part of' with regard to entities like classes? As suggested above, we might construe the 'parts' of a class its subclasses. Then in order for the claim to go through, one would have to consider the 'sum of' relation as exemplified by the notion of union. But it was pointed out already, in connection with (2) that 'union' cannot be a case of 'sum of'. It simply is not clear what 'sums of classes' (or sets) could mean. Intuitively, however, it is clear that 'class' or 'set' are not abstract mass terms; for the latter refer cumulatively and thus in connection with the latter Russell's paradox could not arise, nor could they be then organized hierarchically, the way classes – at least on some accounts – are. Sums as well as parts of stuff remain always on the same ontological level, while elements, sets, and sets of sets do not. Anything that can be arranged in such a hierarchical order cannot be referred to by a mass term. However, Dr. Cheng is right in claiming that this has not been spelled out so far in my treatment of these matters.

11. MASS TERMS AND QUANTITATIVE ANALYSIS

In my paper I tried to show why the count + − distinction should be regarded as deep, fundamental, and probably running through all of the syntactic categories. The main importance of the distinction is that it helps to lay the foundation for the difference between quantitative and qualitative analysis of the external world, and thus helps to explain the foundations of scientific thought. The point is simply that an effort toward quantitative descriptions and eventually measurement can only come about once we have two sets of count − terms in our language. One set is the set of 'true mass terms', i.e., terms like 'snow', 'iron', 'water', 'earth', etc., terms that Aristotle would have called 'matter terms'. Without such terms, or in case we have such terms but they are construed as representing anthropomorphic deities as it seems to have been the case in Homeric Greek, we have no concepts in terms of which questions about matter such as mass, area, changes in material, etc., can be raised. In a culture which lacks a clear understanding of mass terms, explanations of the world in terms of material constituents and their causal connections are absent and we find in their place mythological or partly mythological and partly genetic modes of explanations. The heavy emphasis in Ionian thought on mass terms is the result of – or partly cause of? – the effort to change the explanation of the material world from the genetic-mythological model to a model that searches for basic constituents, and laws of transforming one kind of stuff into another. The atomic theory came only after this general framework was laid out by the Ionians. The other set of count − terms we need are those that designate dimensions, e.g., 'length', 'weight', 'volume'. Of course, we turn these into complex count + terms once we apply concepts of measurement to these dimensions.

At no point have I argued that mass terms can replace the need for count + terms. Roughly speaking, count + terms allow us to characterize entities for which we have principles of individuation, and mass terms give us the concepts in terms of which – together with the application of mathematics – we can invent explanations for natural phenomena that are quantitative in nature. Thus both types of terms are essential for a natural language in which we recognize objects and then compare these in terms of their different dimensions.

12. SEMANTICS AND EPISTEMOLOGY

In the case of some family of terms, e.g., intensional verbs, there is indeed a strong connection between semantics and epistemology. But I fail to see what an epistemology of mass terms would be; and I already indicated why it is a mistake to talk about an ontology of mass objects. Perhaps there may be some interesting questions concerning our perceptual apparatus and the recognition of dimensions of objects. For example, what is it to perceive length, volume, etc.? However, work on the semantics of mass terms is by and large independent of such issues and can thus proceed without waiting for results in neighboring fields.

Stanford University

BARBARA HALL PARTEE

THE SEMANTICS OF BELIEF-SENTENCES

1. INTRODUCTION

Bar-Hillel in 1954 suggested that formal semantics as developed by such logicians as Tarski and Carnap had achieved insights and developed approaches which linguists might profitably make use of for the analysis of natural language. The long delay in taking up Bar-Hillel's suggestion has stemmed in part from the rejection by some linguists (notably Chomsky, 1955) of the claimed relevance of formal to natural semantics, and in part from the preoccupation of linguists with the more tractable syntax and phonology of natural language to the almost total exclusion of serious attention to semantics. Within the last few years, however, linguists have begun to be more concerned with semantics, and to give more than lip service to the principle that semantic considerations should have equal weight with syntactic ones in evaluating competing theories of grammars.[1] The present study is a preliminary investigation into the mutual relevance of some formal semantical notions developed by Carnap and the natural-language syntactic theory developed by Chomsky.

The problem around which this study revolves is the analysis of sentences whose main verbs take as objects or complements (a linguists' distinction) sentences or propositions (a philosophers' distinction), and in particular, the question of how closely the meaning of such a sentence is tied to the linguistic form of the embedded clause. The verb *believe* is of central historical importance for such an investigation, because it was the analysis of belief-sentences that led Carnap to the important notion of intensional isomorphism, but it seems worthwhile to investigate as wide a range of such verbs as possible, because they show great variation in relevant semantic behavior.

I will begin with Carnap's notion of intensional isomorphism, and then discuss belief-sentences in the light of his proposals. Then I will back-track to make some informal remarks about the Chomskyan notion of

Hintikka et al. (eds.), Approaches to Natural Language, 309–336. All rights reserved.
Copyright © 1973 by D. Reidel Publishing Company, Dordrecht-Holland.

deep structure, and to suggest how it might be applied to such sentences. Since it will be readily apparent that neither intensional isomorphism nor deep structure provides satisfactory notions of equivalence for belief-sentences, the problem will then be to suggest alternatives. A number of other predicates will be examined before any generalizations are suggested.

2. CARNAP'S NOTION OF INTENSIONAL ISOMORPHISM

The notion of *intensional isomorphism* was introduced by Carnap in *Meaning and Necessity* (1947) in an attempt to handle some problematical aspects of the semantics of belief-sentences. In this section, with apologies to philosophers and logicians, I will recapitulate some preliminary features of Carnap's semantical systems, leading up to his statement of the problem of belief-sentences and his suggested approach to its solution.

2.1. *Equivalence and L-Equivalence*

For Carnap, the specification of a semantical system S typically includes syntactic rules of formation, semantical rules of designation for the descriptive constants of the system, and semantical rules of truth for sentences. In Carnap's examples the metalanguage is English, and the rules of designation for the individual constants and predicates are translations into English; likewise the sample rule of truth for atomic sentences simply requires that "the individual to which the individual constant refers possesses the property to which the predicate refers." The fact that English is taken as the metalanguage, with its own semantics presupposed, raises immediately the question of the relevance of this kind of semantics to the analysis of natural language, but for the moment we will brush this problem under the rug.

Two sentences A and B are said to be *equivalent* in a semantical system S if they are both true or both false in S, i.e., if $A \equiv B$ is true in S. Two sentences A and B are *L-equivalent* in a semantical system S if $A \equiv B$ is *L-true* in S, i.e., $A \equiv B$ holds in every state description (possible world) in S. The notion of *L*-truth (in S), intended as an explication of necessary or analytic truth, amounts to truth which can be established on the basis of the semantical rules (of S) alone. The concepts of equivalence and *L*-equivalence are extended in a natural way from sentences to other designators such as predicates and individual expressions.

2.2. *Extension and Intension*

Two designators are said to have the *same extension* in a semantical system S if they are equivalent in S. Two designators *have the same intension* in S if they are *L*-equivalent in S.

The extension of a sentence is taken to be its truth-value; of a predicate, the class it designates; and of an individual expression, the individual to which it refers (taken as a special individual such as the null set or the number zero in case the individual expression is a description whose uniqueness condition fails to hold).

The *intension* of a sentence is taken to be the proposition expressed by it; the intension of a predicate is the property it designates; the intension of an individual expression is what Carnap calls an "individual concept." These terms are made precise by the condition for sameness stated above.

2.3. *Extensional and Intensional Context*

Two expressions occurring within a sentence are said to be *interchangeable* if substitution of one for the other preserves the truth-value of the sentence. If substitution moreover preserves the intension of the sentence, the two expressions are said to be *L-interchangeable*.

A sentence A is called *extensional with respect to a certain occurrence* of B within it if the occurrence of B_1 in A is interchangeable with any expression B_2 which is equivalent to B_1. B_1 is then said to occur in A in an *extensional context*.

A sentence is *intensional with respect to a certain occurrence* of a sub-expression if (a) the sentence is not extensional with respect to the sub-expression and (b) the subexpression is *L*-interchangeable with any *L*-equivalent expression. The subexpression is then said to occur in an *intensional context*.

For example, a sentence constructed with any of the standard connectives $\sim$, $\vee$, $\supset$, etc., is extensional with respect to its components. A sentence constructed of a predicate letter and an individual constant is extensional with respect to both the predicate and the individual constant.

On the other hand, a sentence constructed with a modal operator such as the necessity operator is not extensional, but is intensional, with respect to the expression within the scope of the modal operator.

2.4. *Belief-Sentences and Intensional Isomorphism*

In first-order predicate logic, all sentences are extensional with respect to all their subparts; when the modal operator for necessity is added, all sentences are either extensional or intensional with respect to their subparts. But not all contexts are either extensional or intensional, and among the important exceptions are sentences about beliefs. Carnap's argument for the nonintensionality of belief-sentences leads from a consideration of examples like the following:

(1)   John believes that D
(2)   John believes that D'.

Carnap invites us to take as object language S a part of English that includes the predicator *believes that* and some mathematical terms, and to take John's responses to questions about his beliefs as acceptable evidence for his beliefs. Then one can find some L-true sentence for which John professes belief, which can be taken as D (e.g., "Scott is either human or not human"). On the other hand, as Carnap says, "Since John is a creature with limited abilities, we shall find some L-true sentences in S for which John cannot profess belief." Then we take as D' some such sentence. Then D and D', both being L-true, are equivalent and L-equivalent; yet since (1) is true and (2) is false, D and D' are neither interchangeable nor L-interchangeable in the context of (1). Hence the belief-sentence is neither extensional nor intensional with respect to its subsentence D.

Carnap proposes the notion of "intensional isomorphism" as a possible way to capture a relation sufficiently much stronger than L-equivalence to guarantee interchangeability in belief contexts. Two sentences are *intensionally isomorphic* if they are constructed in the same way out of elements that are L-equivalent down to the smallest units. (Carnap gives a fuller definition though not an exact one, since an exact one would require a fully specified semantical system or systems within or between which isomorphism could be defined.) Carnap then suggests that the sentence 'John believes that D' in S can be interpreted by the following semantical sentence:

(3)   [15-1]. "There is a sentence S_i in a semantical system S'

such that (a) S_i in S′ is intensionally isomorphic to 'D' in S and (b) John is disposed to an affirmative response to S_i as a sentence of S′." (1947, p. 62.)

Then if D and D' are two intensionally isomorphic sentences, (1) and (2) are equivalent in S and furthermore L-equivalent in S since their equivalence follows from [15-1], which is a rule of S.

Carnap suggests that his analysis of belief-sentences might be regarded as a first step in the logical analysis of propositional attitudes. To extend the analysis to include terms about doubt, hope, fear, surprise, etc., would simply require the development and refinement of other dispositional notions analogous to the notion of "disposition to assent to a sentence" suggested for belief-sentences.

3. PROBLEMS ABOUT BELIEF-SENTENCES

A number of distinct though interconnected problems arise in the analysis of belief-sentences and other sentences about propositional attitudes. The one I take as fundamental to the semantics of belief-sentences is the question of what kind of equivalence between two sentences will suffice to make them L-interchangeable in a belief-context. The question is fundamental in that an answer to it would provide an important step toward the specification of conditions for the synonymy of two belief-sentences. An examination of some objections to Carnap's solution will lead us to the question of what counts as evidence for the truth of a belief-sentence and the question of whether the object of *believe* should be construed as a sentence or a proposition.

3.1. *The Substitution Problem*

Mates (1950) constructed a counterexample to Carnap's analysis, using an argument quite similar to Carnap's argument (stated above, 2.4) for the nonintensionality of belief-contexts. Mates considers sentences like the following:

(4)   Whoever believes that D, believes that D.
(5)   Whoever believes that D, believes that D'.

where D and D' are abbreviations for two different sentences which are intensionally isomorphic (or synonymous by any other explication). According to Carnap's account, if D and D' are intensionally isomorphic, then so are (4) and (5). Hence (4) and (5) would be L-equivalent. But as Carnap (1954) acknowledges, "However, while [4] is certainly true and beyond doubt, [5] may be false, or, at least, it is conceivable that somebody may doubt it." The argument holds for any relation between D and D' short of inscriptional identity, so it is not simply a matter of looking for a relation a little stronger than intensional isomorphism.

But Carnap (1954) gets out of Mates's trap by a ploy he attributes to Church, namely, by revoking his earlier stipulation that we take a person's disposition to assent to a sentence as definitive evidence for his belief. If that assumption is abandoned, and belief taken instead as a theoretical construct for which many kinds of evidence may offer inductive support, one can simply *require* (5) to be true for intensionally isomorphic D and D', and discount any apparent evidence to the contrary. The question of what constitutes evidence for belief is therefore of fundamental importance, and will be taken up in the next section.

3.2 *Evidence for Belief*

3.2.1. *Assent to sentences.* Carnap's assumption in *Meaning and Necessity* (1947) that a person's beliefs can be inferred directly from his dispositions to affirmative responses to presented sentences is not quite the same as equating what a person believes with what he says he believes, since the subject's understanding of the predicate 'believes that' is not brought into the matter at all on Carnap's analysis. But in addition to letting in Mates's problem, Carnap's assumption has other undesirable consequences, which also need to be avoided by an adequate theory of belief-sentences.

(a) *Nonreductionism.* One kind of objection to the assumption is voiced by Carnap (1954), namely, that a term like 'believes' cannot be reduced to any equivalent expression in the language of observables. This is, I suppose, an aspect of the general inadequacies of logical positivism, and is related to Chomsky's insistence on linguistic competence (a theoretical construct) as opposed to performance (directly observable data) as the basis for linguistic theory.

One example of the possible misleadingness of disposition to assent as criterial for belief would be the chronic liar. (If his dispositions to assent really reflected his beliefs, he should presumably be called not a liar, but a fool.) For another example, consider the sentence "John believes that a stalagmite is always larger than the corresponding stalactite." Assume that John and his interlocutor, to all appearances, speak the same language, namely, standard English, and that John is disposed to assent to the embedded sentence. It may nevertheless be false that John believes that a stalagmite is . . . , because of the (nonobservable) fact that John has unwittingly mixed up the terms *stalagmite* and *stalactite*. Perhaps it could be argued that such differences in language are always potentially observable, but it seems clear that at the very last, a person's language would have to be determinable on the basis of purely observational data in order for a person's beliefs to be so determinable.

(b) *Dogs*. If "John believes that *D*" means that John is disposed to assent to a certain sentence, then we would never be allowed to assert of a dog, at least of a nontalking dog, "Alf believes that his mistress is in this building." This might not be too consequential a limitation, since I for one would be willing to be limited to assertions like "that dog is acting as if he believed that . . . ." But even that sentence does not represent anything I would want to assert under Carnap's explication, since it would mean "that dog is acting as if he were disposed to an affirmative response to . . . ," which is not at all what I have in mind if I say that that dog is acting as if he believed such-and-such. The things that I take as evidence for what a dog believes (or for thinking that he believes anything) include only marginally his responses to presented linguistic stimuli – a much more typical bit of evidence for the example cited would be his refusal to be budged from the doorway until his mistress emerged. An adequate theory of evidence for beliefs must at least allow someone to be able to claim that dogs have beliefs without thereby ascribing to them any linguistic competence.

(c) *Transparency*. The assent criterion is manifestly inadequate for examples like the following, which exhibit what Russell and Quine call the transparent reading of the verb.

(6)   The students believe that the chancellor has more power than he really does.

(7)   Tom believes that you and I are sisters.

(8)   Jones believes that that new mistress of Smith's is Smith's
             wife.

In such cases the belief-sentence does not provide an extractable embedded
sentence appropriate for presentation to the alleged believer, nor does
there seem to be any uniformly effective procedure for reconstructing an
appropriate presentation sentence. Hence any account of belief-sentences
that attempts to include the transparent cases (which are in other respects
considered logically simpler than the opaque cases) is doomed if it requires
belief to involve assent to the actual embedded sentence (or a sentence
intensionally isomorphic to it).

3.2.2. *Belief as a theoretical construct.* Carnap's later position (1954) is
that belief is a theoretical construct for which evidence such as disposition
to assent offers inductive support but not conclusive indication. He there
leaves open the question of what other evidence counts as relevant, and
appears to leave room for a reasonable account of liars, dogs, and those of
us who tend to confuse *stalagmite* and *stalactite*. He also, and explicitly,
leaves open the question of whether a proposition or a sentence is the
more appropriate object of belief. The main condition he imposes on the
notion of belief in the later article is that the problematical Mates sentence,

(5)   Whoever believes that D, believes that D',

should count as logically true when D and D' are synonymous. Any
psychological evidence to the contrary would ipso facto be untrustworthy
evidence.

Such a stipulation is quite appropriate for the philosopher engaged in
rational reconstruction. But the linguist, although he may agree whole-
heartedly that 'believes' is a term for whose correct application no single
kind of observational evidence is criterial, is not thereby free to discount
a priori whatever observational evidence happens to conflict with his
favorite hypothesis. Hence as a linguist I am simply unable to accept
Carnap's way out of Mates's problem, since I am unable to dismiss the
apparent counterevidence (Putnam, 1954) that not everyone who believes,
for instance, that all Greeks are Greeks believes that all Greeks are
Hellenes. (It may be possible to argue one's way out of such counterevidence, as Sellars, 1955, attempts to do, but I cannot simply discount it
as Carnap is prepared to do.)

3.3. *Inconsistent Beliefs*

Carnap's approach allows the possibility of a person's holding inconsistent beliefs. This comes out in his discussion of the example of John believing that D but not believing that D' for various sentences D' L-equivalent to D, when he says, "This does not necessarily mean that he commits the error of believing their negations."[2] (That is, from *not necessarily* I am (pragmatically) inferring *possibly*.)

Some logicians (e.g., Hintikka, 1962; Montague,1970b) would prefer to narrow the concept of belief by putting a requirement of consistency on a person's beliefs. This is natural from a logician's viewpoint, since it would be much more difficult, if not impossible, to construct a formal system which allowed a person to hold inconsistent beliefs without thereby believing everything.[3] But a formal system which disallows inconsistent beliefs, no matter how elegant it may be, is of dubious value as an explication of the meaning of belief-sentences in ordinary language unless it can be argued that all purported attributions of inconsistent beliefs to a person are necessarily in error.

There seem to be arguments for both sides of this last question. On the one hand, we do not normally countenance flat contradictions. If someone makes a statement like (9) or (10), we would be inclined to question his sincerity, his sobriety, or perhaps his understanding of the word *believe*; I find it quite implausible that we could ever be led to accept (9) or (10) as true.

(9)   John believes that Scott is the author of Waverley and that Scott is not the author of Waverley.

(10)   I believe that 2 is not equal to 2.

On the other hand, it is not so difficult to imagine a person sanely and sincerely asserting something like (11), and what is more important, it seems to me that (11) as normally understood could be true.[4]

(11)   Smith believed that all the women at the party were accompanied by their (monogamous) husbands, and that there were more women at the party than men.

The most natural explanation of a case where (11) is true is that Smith simply failed to draw a connection between the two beliefs. Thus this situation is a result of the fact that the logical consequences of a person's beliefs are not automatically also beliefs of his – certainly at least not consciously so. But are a person's beliefs only his conscious beliefs, and if not, can unconscious beliefs be inconsistent? What are we to make of (12) as a possible response to (11)?

(12)   Smith couldn't *really* believe both of those things, because they're incompatible.

We are back to the evidence question by another route. What would constitute evidence for the truth of (11)? One piece of evidence might be Smith's first-person declaration of belief, but such assertions, like dispositions to assent, ought not to be accorded the status of conclusive evidence. I can imagine other more indirect sorts of evidence, most of them verbal – that is, remarks made by him and responses to remarks made by others. But there is possible nonverbal evidence as well, pointing to the conclusion that beliefs can be inconsistent even at a nonverbal level, and that (12) simply expresses an unjustifiable faith in human rationality. The sorts of nonverbal evidence I can imagine include: (i) Smith is helping in the kitchen and gets out more pink napkins than blue ones, (ii) Smith is helping with coats and takes the women's coats to the larger of the two closets, (iii) Smith doesn't ask any of the women to dance although at all other parties he has always asked all women not accompanied by their husbands to dance.

In a case where a person holds inconsistent beliefs, it may not be difficult to get him to *give up* one of his beliefs, but that very phraseology supports the contention that it was previously indeed a belief of his. Hence I think we are forced on all counts to conclude that a person can hold inconsistent beliefs without thereby believing everything, and that a sentence which asserts that someone holds inconsistent beliefs (without believing everything) must therefore not be counted as necessarily false.

This conclusion may be strengthened further by showing that even dogs could conceivably hold inconsistent beliefs. (I am still not arguing that dogs *do* have beliefs, only that various kinds of sentences ascribing beliefs to dogs are not *necessarily* false.) For example, (13) is perfectly analogous to (11) above, and could have similar (though probably much less clear) kinds of evidence:

(13)   My dog believed (saw, noticed) that every dog who came to the dog show brought his own person with him, but he believed that there were many more dogs there than people.

It seems to me that (13) could be made plausible (though this would not be actual evidence for it) by considering a dog who is used to seeing crowds of people but not used to seeing crowds of dogs and therefore the number of dogs present seems larger to him than it actually is, even though he noticed the one-to-one correlation of dogs and people as they entered.

The consequence of this requirement that at least some inconsistent beliefs must be allowed for is that logical equivalence cannot be a sufficient condition for interchangeability in belief-contexts. This principle was already asserted in Carnap (1947), but it still needs to be argued for, because the method Carnap (1954) used to get out of Mates's trap can be extended to the case of logical equivalence, as it is, for instance, in Montague (1970b). If the only argument in favor of allowing inconsistent beliefs were the argument that people sometimes claim that they (or others) hold beliefs which in fact are inconsistent, then the insistence on excluding inconsistent beliefs in principle would be a valid case of rational reconstruction (much like Chomsky's competence/performance distinction). The argument advanced here, like much of the argument of Hintikka (1970a), is intended to show that such a limitation would not be an idealization but a distortion.

3.4. *Sentences or Propositions*

The question of whether belief is a relation between a person and a sentence or between a person and a proposition is fundamental for the substitution problem and has ramifications far beyond it besides. A review of the distinction is in order.

By a *sentence* we mean a linguistic object, a certain form of words. There is general agreement among linguists and philosophers on this point. The term *proposition* is used somewhat less uniformly. Intuitively it is generally taken as that which is expressed by a sentence, that which can be said to be true or false. Formally it has been defined as the intension of a sentence (Carnap, 1947) and as a function from possible worlds to truth-values (Kripke, 1963). All these definitions have in common the important property that logically equivalent propositions count as identical.

The relation of sentences to propositions is many-to-many. One sentence corresponds to many propositions if the sentence is noneternal (Quine, 1960), i.e., if it contains indexical terms like *I*, *here*, *yesterday*, etc. On the other hand one proposition always corresponds to many sentences, in particular to a whole equivalence class of logically equivalent sentences. The relation of *eternal* sentences (in Quine's sense) to propositions is many-to-one.

If belief is construed as a relation between a person and a *proposition*, then logical equivalence should guarantee interchangeability, and beliefs would have to be consistent. Carnap (1954) appears in his discussion of Church to be claiming otherwise, but I cannot understand the argument.

If belief is construed as a relation between a person and a *sentence*, then problems arise with regard to noneternal sentences. For example, in sentences like (14) and (15), as well as (6)–(8) above, the question arises as to what sentence, if any, is being asserted to be in the belief-relation with some believer.

(14)   John believed that he was already here.

(15)   Mary believes that she saw you yesterday.

Linguistically, the problem can be described by saying that if belief is a relation between a person and a sentence, then it ought to be expressed by direct quotation, and yet in fact the only linguistically possible form is indirect quotation. And there is no general way to recover a unique direct quotation form from a given indirect quotation.

If we limit our attention to *that*-clauses which contain eternal sentences, we can at least temporarily avoid the problem just mentioned. In that case, construing belief as a relation between a person and a sentence allows us to make interchangeability conditions as strong as we like, since we can define them in terms of both the form of the sentence and of the unique proposition the sentence expresses.

Note that such a view of sentence as object of belief does not commit one to a view that believers must have any linguistic capabilities. We can assert that a dog stands in a certain relation to a certain sentence of English, and if we have abandoned the assent-definition of belief, we are quite free to adduce all sorts of nonverbal behavior as evidence for such an assertion (as exemplified above in the discussion of evidence for (11)).

It is possible in the sentence-object view of belief to claim that *no* two sentences are interchangeable in a belief context. It is also possible to argue for a criterion stronger than logical equivalence but less strong than total identity. Carnap's intensional isomorphism is such a criterion, involving the linguistic form of a sentence plus the semantic interpretation of its smallest units. Hintikka (1970a) discusses another proposal, one which involves the logical form of a sentence rather than its purely linguistic form. Hintikka's proposal looks very promising to my untutored eye; Carnap's does not, and it may be worthwhile to examine why.

At first glance, the notion of intensional isomorphism would seem to capture a relation of just about the right sort of strength: excluding arbitrary logical equivalence, but allowing interchange of very close paraphrases. But on closer inspection it can be seen to lead to a kind of accidental language-dependence in the ascription of belief. Take a sentence like "Jones believes that Smith is hungry": this could be true if Jones is an English-speaker, but not if Jones speaks, say, Spanish or French or German, where the noun for 'hunger' is used with the verb for 'have'. The same sorts of nonisomorphism crop up with many other expressions which have no morpheme-by-morpheme translations between various pairs of languages. In fact if 'be' and 'have' are taken as primitives in English, and their nearest equivalents in other languages are also taken as primitives, their designation rules would undoubtedly be different in every language. Then no belief-sentence involving 'be' or 'have', including the classic "Jones believes that the earth is round," would be true if the believer's language was different from the language in which the belief-sentence was stated.

At least a partial solution to this problem would be to say that terms like 'be' and 'have' which have a wide range of use are actually multiply ambiguous, with the number of distinct subterms to be determined by inter-linguistic comparisons. Most prepositions and the most common verbs would no doubt have to be split up into many subterms if there was to be any hope of achieving real universality; and even then it is only cases like "the earth is round" which would be handled, not those like "Smith is hungry." The suggested partial solution is unsatisfactory on linguistic grounds as well. It is artificial to determine ambiguity within a language on the basis of cross-language comparisons, since a naive language-

learner (e.g., a child) has in general no access to data from outside his own
language, and his internally constructed system therefore takes no account
of such data (except for linguistic universals which can be regarded as in
some sense 'programmed' into his innate competence.)

An argument of this sort is a fortiori an argument against the claim that
no two sentences are interchangeable in a belief-context, for that would be
to say that belief-sentences can never be translated from one language to
another. What is needed is some semantic relation, one which hugs the
surface of syntactic form so as to disallow arbitrary logical operations, but
which is at the same time independent of particular languages (assuming
that it is correct that belief-sentences *can* in fact often be translated from
one language to another). Hintikka's proposal appears to be of just this
sort.

At this point we should return to the problem of how to analyze belief-
sentences whose *that*-clauses contain noneternal sentences. Here it seems
to me is a place where formal logic can come to the linguist's rescue. Since
we have argued above that the relation governing interchangeability is a
semantic one, and since the semantics of natural languages must in some
sense include quantificational logic even though their syntax is very different from the syntax of logic, a deeper *semantic* analysis of these sentences is
in order. Take for example a case like that of Hintikka's cited in footnote
4, and add indexical terms:

(16)   John believes that my father was an only child, and that you
        are my first cousin on my father's side.

The pronouns in the embedded sentence are clearly not to be taken as part
of John's belief in their occurring form; the relevant semantic structure
can be shown by (17):

(17) $(\exists x)\,(\exists y)$ (I am x and you are y and John believes: x's father
        was an only child, and y is x's first cousin on x's father's side.)

We have thus removed the indexical terms to a purely referential position,
but have not altered the *structure* of the sentence expressing John's
belief – in particular, the contradiction in his beliefs is no harder and no
easier to spot in (17) than in (16).

There are many problems remaining, but it seems to me that the way toward a solution must be to take the object of belief as a sentence, with appropriate quantificational extraction of all indexical terms (and in fact of any other terms that are to be taken in a transparent or *de re* sense), and then to try to formulate strong principles of interchangeability based on the semantic structure of the sentence. By semantic structure I mean something which is indeed rather close to the spirit of Carnap's intensional isomorphism, and rather far removed from the model theoretic "function from possible worlds to truth-values." But I am not sure that there exists any independent definition of the sort of structure I have in mind. If the Katz-Postal (1964) hypothesis that transformations preserve meaning had held up, syntactic 'deep structure' would have been a reasonable candidate. Perhaps the rather different sort of tree structures generated by a Montague-grammar will turn out to be appropriate.

4. OTHER PREDICATES

Verbs and other predicates which take sentences or propositions as one of their arguments exhibit a wide range of behavior with respect to the kinds of matters examined above in connection with 'believes'. We will examine here for a number of predicates whether the wording of the embedded sentence is taken to reflect the actual wording of some prior discourse; whether the predicate can be applied to dogs and other non-linguistic species; what kinds of substitutions preserve truth; and whether the predicate seems to have two or more well-defined senses (or perhaps uses).

4.1. *Emotives*

Certain verbs and adjectives express a relation between an animate being and what certainly appears to be a proposition rather than a sentence. The Kiparskys (1968) call these "emotives" and point out that the embedded sentence is always presupposed to be a fact. Examples of emotive predicates, all taking *that*-clauses, include *regret, hate, be surprised, be amazed, be sad, be glad, be upset, be delighted.* (These predicates also take infinitival complements, and some of them also take gerundives, but we will be concerned only with *that*-clauses.) The emotives all seem to be clearly at the propositional-object end of the scale, since logical equivalence seems to be quite sufficient for interchangeability.

4.2. *Verbs of Inference*

At the other end of the scale, though not quite so clear-cut, are verbs like *deduce, prove, establish, show, discover*, which we might call 'verbs of inference'.

(18)   John proved in 3 lines that all left-inverses in a group are right-inverses.

Here the embedded sentence is virtually a direct quotation (although the pronoun-shifts and other transformations associated with indirect discourse do apply), and the evidence for the truth of the whole sentence crucially involves an overt occurrence of (something very close to) the embedded sentence.[5] For truth-preserving substitution, logical equivalence is blatantly too weak. This is a case where intensional isomorphism might be the right strength, although the allowable differences due to 'merely syntactic devices' would have to be restricted to those syntactic differences which did not count as differences within any formal system.

Some verbs of inference can take as subject a noun phrase denoting some kind of evidence as an alternative to a subject which, as in (18), denotes the agent of the inference.

(19)   The fact that the bullets pierced the door shows that the police couldn't see who they were shooting.

In Fillmore's case grammar terms, we can say that such verbs take a sentential object and either an agent or an instrument (perhaps stretching that term slightly), and either of the latter two can be the subject. In some sentences like (20) below, an animate subject may in fact seem more an 'instrument' than an agent.

(20)   Sam proved that he was involved when he referred to Miss Faust as 'Maizie'.

In (19) and (20) the sentential objects of the verbs of inference are not understood as related to any overt occurrence of related sentences, as was the case in (18). The uses of *show* and *prove* in (19) and (20) seem to appeal to a commonsensical notion of what follows from what, rather than to a formal system of deduction as in (18). It is hard to formulate reasonable candidates for substitutional criteria for cases like (19) and (20). Perhaps logical equivalence might do, but it is hard to be certain, since common-sensical analogues of formal notions like deducibility tend to break down when confronted with nonstandard cases. For example, I am not sure whether (21) should count as equivalent to (20) or not:

(21)   Sam proved that he was involved and (that) Bill either was or was not at the scene the previous day, when he referred to Miss Faust as 'Maizie'.

Perhaps the clearest verb of the class is *deduce*, which always requires an agentive subject and for which logical equivalence is definitely too weak to guarantee substitutivity. *Infer*, surprisingly, cannot be included in this class, because its object-clauses seem to be propositions rather than sentences. Thus (22) is ambiguous, but if *infer* were replaced by *deduce*, *establish*, or the like, only the self-contradictory sense of the embedded clause would be possible.

(22)   Jones inferred that your yacht was longer than it was.

It is interesting that *infer* is nonfactive, while all the verbs that I have called 'verbs of inference' are factive; *infer* seems to denote a more subjec-tive process of inference than the others. Compare the normalcy of (23a) with the oddity of (23b).

(23)   Because he considered only Mary's remarks, he incorrectly
$\begin{cases} \text{(a) inferred} \\ \text{(b) established} \end{cases}$ that Sam was to blame.

An incorrect inference (in the subjective sense) is an inference; an incorrect proof is not a proof.

In sum, then, the verbs of inference (excluding *infer*) in their strictest use take sentences as object and have very strong substitutivity require-ments; they thus occupy the opposite pole from the emotives.

4.3. *Verbs of Communication*

One would expect that a verb like *say* or *tell* would be even more literally quotative than a verb like *deduce*, but that is not the case when the verbs are used with *that*-clauses, or what is normally called indirect quotation. All of the verbs *say, assert, report, allege, tell, suggest, hint, imply* can fit

naturally into the frame of example (22) above without forcing the contradictory reading of the embedded clause. In fact, while for *say* and most
of the others the embedded clause can be a quotation except for mandatory shifts in indexicals, for *hint* and *imply*, such a near-quotative reading
seems to be impossible. For example, a sentence like (24) would be
regarded as false, or at least misleading, if what Nixon actually said was
"the new South Vietnamese government will include Communists."

(24)   Nixon hinted that the new South Vietnamese government
        would include Communists.

(The situation is complicated by the fact, pointed out to me by Larry
Horn, that if the embedded clause has *might* in it, the hint can be a near-
quotation.)

It appears that these verbs, when used with a *that*-clause, are used to
report the content of a communication, and not its verbatim form. But
there are other verbs of communication, which could be called 'manner-
verbs of communication', which take *that*-clauses that seem to be what I
have been calling 'near-quotes', i.e., quotations except for shifts in
indexicals. Sentences (25) and (26) exemplify this class, which includes
shout, whisper, scream, hiss, hoot, giggle, bark, etc.

(25)   Jed hollered that them brown cows was back in the corn
        patch again.
(26)   She giggled that she would feel just too, too liberated if she
        drank another of those naughty martinis.

Since these verbs emphasize the manner of the communication, it is not
surprising that the form as well as the content of the embedded clause
is significant. Note that the verbs cannot be analyzed as 'communicate
by giggling', etc., since (27) and the like are quite odd, unless the dog is
assumed to have a bark-language:

(27)   Fido barked that someone was in the front yard.

All of the verbs of communication refer, by virtue of their central meaning,
to some overt utterance or other overt communication; but only for the
manner-verbs of communication is it the case that the embedded *that*-
clause must be a near-quotation of the overt utterance. Thus it would

seem that the normal verbs of communication take propositions as objects, but the manner-verbs of communication sentential ones.

4.4. *Epistemic Predicates*

Believe shares important semantic properties with *know, realize, forget, remember, be certain, think, suppose, doubt, be aware*. Chomsky (1969) cites examples with *realize* that fit Mates's schema for nonsubstitutivity of synonyms, and *realize* also passes the dog-test:

(28)   Fido finally realized that the children were nowhere around the house.

And although (29) is odd, unlike (6)–(8), the oddness is due simply to the factivity of *realize*. Hence (30), which avoids purporting as factive a falsity, is perfectly acceptable.

(29)   I realized that your yacht was longer than it is.
(30)   I didn't realize that your yacht was as long as it is.

With this brief attempt to put *believes* into perspective among verbs that take *that*-clauses, let us turn to the question of the linguistic 'deep structure' for such constructions.

5. DEEP STRUCTURE

In Chomsky's earliest formulations of transformational grammar, e.g., Chomsky (1957), it was emphasized that in postulating underlying representations and transformations, the justification must always be purely syntactic. Examples abound of resulting syntactic analyses that are quite unwieldy as bases for semantic interpretation. For example: (a) Syntactically, the contrast between definite and indefinite noun phrases was always regarded as simply a minimal contrast in the article position. (b) Quantifiers, demonstratives like *this* and *that*, the articles, and words like *only* and *other*, were all simply introduced by phrase structure rules as components of the 'determiner' of a noun phrase. (c) All adjectives were introduced in predicate position, so that the attributive use in (31) would be derived from (32):

(31)   Small elephants are big.
(32)   Elephants which are small are big.

Furthermore, since the formation of relative pronouns was assumed to involve deletion of a noun identical to the head noun, (32) would itself be derived from the semantically inappropriate pair of sentences (33):

(33)   Elephants are small.
          Elephants are big.

(d) In the earliest treatments, negative sentences were optional transforms of positive ones. Klima (1964) showed purely syntactic motivation for postulating a deep structure NEG morpheme for negative sentences, but his system included an optional *some-any* suppletion transformation (limited primarily to negative contexts) which allowed (34) and (35) to be derived from the same underlying representation:

(34)   John couldn't solve some of the problems.
(35)   John couldn't solve any of the problems.

5.1. *Deep Structure Semantics*

The arguments of Katz and Postal (1964) convinced Chomsky (1965) that deep structure as established by "purely syntactic motivations" would turn out to be the only level of syntactic structure relevant to semantic interpretation. That hypothesis rapidly gained favor to the point of becoming widely regarded as criterial rather than empirical, so that transformations like Klima's *some-any* rule came to be regarded as untenable.

Although semantically inappropriate analyses like those mentioned above were not immediately replaced, the general notion of deep structure did and does look basically quite promising as a way of coming close in many cases to the spirit of Carnap's "merely syntactic devices." Thus if one considers the problem of defining intensional isomorphism for natural languages, deep structure would be the appropriate level on which to require sameness of structure. The following pairs are typical cases of superficially distinct structures with identical underlying representations:

(36) (a)   That Mary wore a wig surprised Timothy.
     (b)   It surprised Timothy that Mary wore a wig.
(37) (a)   Sam turned out the light.
     (b)   Sam turned the light out.

But it has been widely disputed of late whether the Katz-Postal hypothesis really holds (for a survey of some of the arguments see Partee 1971). The following sets, which would classically be regarded as transformationally related, illustrate the problem:

(38) (a) Few rules are explicit and few rules are easy to read.
(b) Few rules are both explicit and easy to read.
(39) (a) It is particularly easy to get this baby into these overalls.
(b) This baby is particularly easy to get into these overalls.
(c) These overalls are particularly easy to get this baby into.

Sentences with *believe* in fact offer an interesting case in point. There is a (disputed) transformation familiarly known as 'subject-raising' which would transform (40a) into (40b).

(40) (a) Tom believes that Cicero denounced Catiline.
(b) Tom believes Cicero to have denounced Catiline.

But Quine (1960, pp. 145–50) argues that (40a) and (40b) are not synonymous, in particular that only in (40b) is *Cicero* in purely referential position. Yet the syntactic evidence for subject-raising is strong; among other things, it provides the only reasonable account for sentences like (41) and (42).

(41) Tom believes there to have been an earthquake recently.
(42) Susan believes it to be likely that no one will show up.

Sentences like those two simultaneously suggest that Quine's semantic intuition may be wrong, since *there* and *it* certainly cannot be taken as referential. My own feelings about (40b) are not strong, though I am inclined to regard it as ambiguous, with a slightly greater tendency for *Cicero* to be regarded as referential there than in (40a). But (43) below seems to me definitely ambiguous, which again argues against Quine's interpretation.

(43) John believes a Communist to have been at the heart of the plot.

5.2. *Generative Semantics*

The theoretical approach which is associated with the names of McCawley,

Lakoff, Ross, Postal, and Bach, and which often goes under the name of 'generative semantics', can be thought of as a deep structure semantics pushed to deeper structures. Within the framework of model theoretic semantics it makes no sense to call those deeper structures 'semantic'; that terminology is probably just a carryover from Katz-type semantics. At any rate, the proponents of the generative semantics approach suggest, among other things, having very different deep structures for definite and indefinite noun phrases, assigning the same deep structure to syntactically disparate (putative) paraphrases such as "Seymour sliced the salami with a knife" and "Seymour used a knife to slice the salami"; assigning appropriately different deep structures to sets like (38) and (39); etc. One of the key differences between Chomskyan deep structure and Lakovian abstract structure is that Chomsky regards deep structure as the level at which virtually all actual lexical items are inserted, but the corresponding terminal elements in Lakoff's system are abstract semantic primitives, with lexical insertion a complex transformational process. Actual lexical items are thus part of relatively superficial structure in Lakoff's system. Since the notion of 'intensional isomorphism' is relative to the smallest units of a system, it would have quite different interpretations in the two systems.

It is impossible to do justice in a short space to the prolific and stimulating flow of ideas that has resulted from the generative semantics approach. Let me then overgeneralize and say that it looked most plausible when it presented 'semantic-looking' abstract deep structures for classically difficult cases, accompanied by arguments for independent syntactic justification of those semantically appropriate structures. Some basic problems arose in attempting to solve the problem of how the syntactic transformations would be restricted to guarantee that a given abstract deep structure would be mapped *only* onto the right surface structure. For instance, sentences (38a–b) would have a single deep structure in the 'classical' theory; it was suggested in Partee (1970) that if a generative semanticist assigned them different deep structures, he would still have to separately prevent the usual conjunction-reduction transformation from mapping (38a) onto (38b). Lakoff's response (1970a) was in part to add the notion of 'global constraint' to his system, so that certain aspects of the 'semantic' deep structure could in effect control the subsequent syntactic processes. Whether and how the resulting system differs from alternative theories is debatable and debated.

5.3. *Interpretive Semantics*

Again oversimplifying, one might describe the 'interpretive semantics' approach of Jackendoff, recent Chomsky, and others as an attempt to rectify the deficiencies of the Katz-Postal type of deep-structure semantics, not by pushing the syntactic deep structure deeper, but by letting semantic rules take account of surface structure as well as deep structure, with the latter determined on the basis of 'purely syntactic arguments' as in the earlier theory. Then sets like (38a–b) and (39a–c) could still have single deep structures, but those structures would no longer be purported to be the sole determinants of meaning. Interpretive semantics, or the 'surfacist' approach, does not mean using *only* surface structure; and on some accounts it may allow all levels of structure to be involved – e.g., some semantic rules might operate in the transformational cycle. It is partly for this reason that it is difficult to establish whether generative semantics (with global constraints) and interpretive semantics might be different.

5.4. *Application to Verbs of Propositional Attitude*

The semantic problem to which linguists have given the most attention is the problem of how to show 'underlying' or 'deep' semantic similarities among sentences which have 'superficially' dissimilar forms. I think the reason for this has been that this is the kind of regularity transformational grammar is particularly adept at capturing, as has been emphasized repeatedly with examples like "John is easy to please" vs. "John is eager to please," etc.

Linguists have also accepted the tenet that the meaning of a sentence should be a function of the meanings of its parts, and have, I think, tended to construe that tenet rather narrowly. In particular, the notion of semantics as a 'deep level' has led to a conception of semantic structure as a combinatorial function of 'deep' structures of component parts of a sentence.

The interpretivists have been arguing against such a view, and I think that my arguments to the effect that the object of *believe* is a sentence rather than a proposition tend in the same direction. This alternative view may perhaps be represented by the tenet that the meaning of a sentence is a function of *the form and* the meanings of its parts. (I believe that the earlier formulation could be read this way, but sometimes is not.) Chomsky (1969) illustrates this principle with the verb *realize*, and it is further exemplified above by the indirect quotation construction with manner-verbs like *holler* and *giggle*, and by the verbs of inference.

Perhaps the clearest cases of the relevance of ('surface') form to meaning are cases with explicit quotation. Consider, for example, a sentence like (44):

(44)   'Slurp' is an onomatopoeic word.

Such sentences are not novel to philosophers (cf. "Giorgione was so-called because of his size," Quine, 1960, p. 153), but I do not believe that linguists have given much thought to how to represent them. Clearly the meaning of the subject of sentence (44) is not just a combination of the 'meaning' of *slurp* with the 'meaning' of quotation marks, or the meaning would be the same with any synonym substituted. The form, in this case the phonetic form, of the word *slurp* must be included in the meaning of the result. In some cases, such as (45) below, it might be argued that *only* the phonetic form is involved, so that one could consider representing the quoted material simply as a syntactically unanalyzed phonological string.

(45)   The little engine went, "Puff-puff, chug-chug, toot-toot."[6]

But in a sentence like (44), the meaning of the whole clearly involves both the phonetic form and the meaning of the word *slurp*; the predicate *onomatopoeic* explicitly concerns a relation between the two.

If the meaning of a quoted word is to be constant, and independent of the context, then it must always be taken to include all aspects of its form as well as its 'meaning' in the narrower sense. Different predicates may ignore different aspects of this total meaning, i.e., may allow inter-changeability under different sorts of conditions. Consider the following contexts, all of which can take quoted words:

(46) (a) "Burp" rhymes with ——.
   (b) "Myrrh" has as many letters as ——.
   (c) The Oxford Universal Dictionary does not contain words like ——.
   (d) "Squuck" does not mean quite the same as ——.

If we fit *slurp* into these contexts, its meaning does not change, but different aspects of its meaning contribute to the meaning of the whole. Sentence (46a) involves only the phonological structure of the part of the word including and following the last stressed vowel (*urp* in the case of *slurp*); (46b) only the spelling; (46c) is perhaps vague, but may be taken to involve something like standards of usage; (46d) involves 'meaning' in the narrow sense. The fact that (44) involves both sound and meaning underscores the impossibility of trying to regard a quoted word as perhaps just ambiguous between pure form and pure meaning.

The same argument extends to quoted sentences. For instance, suppose one were to try to represent the deep structure of (47a) as (47b), in order to indicate that the meaning of the whole involves the surface form of the quoted sentence.

(47) (a)   Ray said, "Seymour sliced the salami with a knife."

(b)

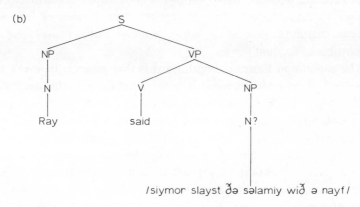

/siymor slayst ðə səlamiy wið ə nayf/

I have no idea what category could be suggested for the quotation; the essential feature is the hypothesis that there is no internal syntactic structure. Such a proposal may be appropriate for sentences like (45), but when the quotation is of an English sentence, the syntactic and semantic content of the quoted sentence is also relevant to the meaning of the total sentence. Consider, for instance, how we understand *she* in (48a), *one* in (48b), the ellipsis in (48c), and the word *opposite* in (48d).

(48) (a)   When the surgeon shouted, "I need the nurse!", *she* came right in.

(b)   When the surgeon said, "Give me the scalpel," she handed
      him the wrong *one*.

(c)   When he said, "Leave!", she wouldn't (———).

(d)   When he said, "Turn right," she did the *opposite*.

Hence a structure in the style of (47b) is inadequate for lack of internal
structure; but clearly the phonological string is an indispensable part of
the total meaning, since substitution of a synonymous but nonhomoph-
onous sentence can lead to a change in the meaning of the whole.

I have gone on at length about quotation because I think it is simply
a clearer case of the sentential-object use of verbs like *believe*, also exemplified by indirect quotation with verbs like *shout*, and by the verbs of inference. I think that the generative semantics approach has shed interesting
light on some aspects of the semantics of the propositional-object cases,
which seemed from the viewpoint of the classical linguistic theory much
harder to give semantically appropriate deep structures for. But it
appears that in the process the 'easier' sentential-object cases were made
impossible to account for.

The conclusion I am heading toward is that potentially, every aspect
of an embedded sentence, from the most 'superficial' to the 'deepest', can
be relevant to the contribution that sentence makes to the meaning of the
whole of which it is a part. When a sentence is embedded as a relative
clause, it may be only its meaning in the narrow sense that contributes to
the meaning of the resulting nominal. But when it is embedded into a quote
context as in (47) or (48), the form of the sentence is a crucial component
of the total meaning. And the same holds for the verbs like *holler* even
without direct quotation. Furthermore, constructions which may not
ordinarily involve the superficial form of an embedded sentence in
determining the meaning of the whole may do so when a modifier like 'in
so many words' or 'in his usual verbose way' is added.

It follows that no two distinct sentences have exactly the same semantic
potential or potential meaning, if by that we mean all those aspects of a
sentence which could contribute to the meaning of a larger whole. Katz-
Postal or Lakoff-type 'semantic representations' should be viewed as
offering additional structural information about a sentence beyond its
superficial form, but not the whole semantic story.

I would therefore recast the distinction drawn above between verbs which take propositions as objects and those which take sentences. I would say instead that an embedded *that*-clause always contains a whole sentence, but that different contexts require different aspects of the semantic potential (or 'total meaning' or 'form plus meaning') of the sentence to be taken into account. For some verbs, the only relevant part of the meaning of an embedded sentence may be the proposition it expresses; for others, various aspects of the form of the sentence may be relevant as well (or instead). What we mean when we say that a certain verb 'takes a propositional object', then, is simply that the meaning of the total sentence is invariant under substitutions of different sentences expressing the same proposition.

A given sentence will participate in a great many relations with innumerable other sentences; all of these relations are part of our understanding of a sentence, as are the truth-conditions for the sentence. To look for '*the* semantic representation' of a sentence seems to me misguided; contexts like belief-sentences and quotation-sentences require a much richer notion of semantics, one in which semantic structure includes syntactic and phonological structure rather than existing as a parallel but distinct level.[7]

University of California, Los Angeles

NOTES

[1] A linguist would, however, take issue with Montague's opinion that syntax is of no great interest except as a preliminary to semantics (Montague, 1970a). In spite of the notorious difficulty of making the notion of 'well-formed sentence' precise for natural languages, it is a striking and well-confirmed fact that all natural languages share many highly specific syntactic properties that lead the linguist toward the postulation of a notion of 'possible natural language' that is much narrower and more highly structured than the general notion of 'possible language'. I would not as a linguist argue against the complaint voiced by Montague and by Dana Scott among others that transformational linguists have not made much progress toward a rigorous formalization of their theories of grammar; there are still too many unresolved problems at a preformal level. I would only argue against drawing an inference therefrom that the aims and methods of linguistics are misguided and have been unfruitful.

[2] Note that Carnap is thereby rejecting the claim put forward by some linguists that sentences of the form (2-1) and (2-2) are synonymous, a claim which is used as one argument for a rule of 'NEG-raising':

(2-1)   A believes that not-S
(2-2)   A doesn't believe that S.

More recently the claim has been weakened to the following: that (2-2) is ambiguous, and on one of its readings is synonymous with (2-1). As a *semantic* claim, I believe it is indistinguishable from the claim that (2-1) entails (2-2) and not conversely.

On the other hand, sentences like (2-2) do seem to be used to assert something stronger than the absence of belief, at least in their most normal usage. Thus if I open a discourse with (2-3),

(2-3)   My three-year-old son doesn't believe that storks bring babies.

it is likely to be assumed by my hearers that my son has entertained the embedded proposition and rejected it. Yet if I am asked (2-4) and answer (2-5), which is presumably simply an elliptical form of (2-3), there will be no such assumption.

(2-4)   Does your three-year-old son believe that storks bring babies?
(2-5)   No, he doesn't.

The issues involved are not simple, since there are some very persuasive purely syntactic arguments for NEG-raising. There is also the complication that first-person belief sentences seem to behave quite differently from third-person ones; i.e., first-person cases of (2-2) seem much more nearly synonymous to (2-1) than third-person cases. Perhaps there is a pragmatic explanation for the difference.

Kimball (1970) discusses belief-sentences using mostly first-person examples, and comes to rather different conclusions from those reached here. I am excluding what he calls the 'expressive' sense of belief from the ensuing discussion.

[3] Hintikka (1970a) describes a way of carrying out such a project, and has some very interesting suggestions to make concerning possible factors involved in the failure to draw correct inferences.

[4] Hintikka (1970a) offers a similar example of someone's believing that *a*'s father was an only child and that *a* has first cousins on the father's side.

[5] John Searle has pointed out to me that this claim is too strong as it stands, because of sentences like (5-1), and that in any case it has as much to do with the phrase *in 3 lines* as with the choice of verb.

(5-1)   John proved in 3 lines that arithmetic is consistent.

Nevertheless, it is worth noting that not all verbs permit modification by phrases like *in 3 lines* and the even more restrictive 'in so many words'. It seems to me that any verb which can be modified by such a phrase cannot simply be taking a proposition as its object.

[6] It is sentences like these that can make first-grade readers and the like very difficult to analyze syntactically. Joyce Friedman and I noticed, when she was starting to write a transformational grammar for Yngve's sample text *Engineer Small*, that the verb *go* as used in (45) seems to allow as its complement any phonetic sequence that is not an ordinary sentence of English; it is hard, if not impossible, to characterize that restriction in a grammar of English. (Many teenagers now speak a dialect without that restriction on *go*; for them *go* can be used just like *say* with direct quotation.)

[7] I received many helpful comments and suggestions on an earlier draft of this paper, which was presented at the conference at Stanford and also to linguistics colloquia at the University of California at Berkeley and at San Diego. For helping me out of many philosophical muddles I am grateful to Julius Moravcsik and David Kaplan. I am also indebted to Jaakko Hintikka, who I think has already solved a great many problems whose existence I am just beginning to appreciate. Other useful comments came from John Kimball, John Searle, Chung-Ying Cheng, and Pieter Seuren.

CHUNG-YING CHENG

COMMENTS ON
PROFESSOR PARTEE'S PAPER

Partee has effectively shown in her paper that formal analysis of semantical notions and problems can be of great interest to linguists. The contributions of logicians in the field of semantics, as Hintikka pointed out, have not yet been fully noted and utilized by linguists in their studies of semantics of natural languages. Though we are not quite clear about what exact factors prompt linguists of recent times to devote more attention to the studies of semantics, we can with confidence say that this new development of linguistic studies would be impossible without a positive realization of the relevance of semantic analysis for synthetical and grammatical theorizing. Perhaps it is increasingly recognized by both linguists and logicians that syntax and semantics of a language can be only relatively separated and distinguished, but not absolutely bifurcated and abstracted from each other. For it seems clear that every semantic distinction *can be* given a synthetic marking in a language system and every synthetic form *can be* given a semantic interpretation, be it direct or indirect.

Partee is again right in focusing on the analysis of belief-sentences as a profound example of how logician's work can lead to the development of semantics of natural languages. The problem itself is intrinsically intriguing and interesting by itself, and its analysis, as Partee demonstrated, can be only revealing about basic problems now confronted by semantic studies of both logicians and up-to-date linguists. Let us formulate the problem of analysis of belief-sentences more carefully and we can see what results of reflection and investigation can turn up in light of Partee's paper.

In the first place, it seems to me that the problem of analysis of belief-sentences is a problem of understanding the *logical, semantic* and *referential* structures of belief-sentences of the form '*A* believes that *P*', where *P* is a sentence or a proposition which is an object of belief or other verbs of

Hintikka et al. (eds.), Approaches to Natural Language, 337–348. *All rights reserved.*
Copyright © 1973 *by D. Reidel Publishing Company, Dordrecht-Holland.*

propositional attitude. The logical structure problem of belief-sentences concerns clarification and elucidation of the structure of belief-sentences in expressing meaning and reference of belief-sentences. The semantic structure problem of belief-sentences deals with the relation of the meanings of belief-sentences to the objects of beliefs and how such meanings can be explained both generatively and theoretically. Finally, the referential structure problem is the most serious of all the problems. It concerns to what extent and in what sense a *belief-clause P* refers to an object and in what fashion it can be explained in case it does not succeed in referring.

1. There seem to be two major classes of specification for a semantical system as has been made clear by Frege, Carnap, Quine and others in the construction of formal semantics. There are specifications of designation conditions for singular terms and predicate terms and there are specifications for truth conditions for open sentences and closed sentences. In natural language cases, how to formulate these specifications are fundamental questions. There seem to be two different approaches in the logician's views of these specifications. Partee only mentioned Carnap's approach in terms of his theory of extension and intension for descriptive terms, predicates and closed sentences.

According to Carnap's approach, equivalence and logical equivalence are well defined in terms of semantical rules governing designation and truth conditions of terms, predicates and sentences, whereas extensions and intensions are definable in terms of concepts of equivalence and *L*-equivalence. This last point is very important, for it enables one to see where divergences can develop.[1] For if one does not take for granted that one can explain equivalence and *L*-equivalence in different senses, there cannot be identity conditions for the intended extensions and intensions of the Carnapian semantics.

An alternative approach in question is Quine's view that there are no logical equivalences beyond truth-functional tautologies and thus it follows that one cannot posit intensions on the basis of a general semantical concept of *L*-equivalence. An open question is therefore whether this approach and subsequent developments of ideas as applicable to belief-sentences may also shed light on and point to a way of understanding of belief-sentences in a way fundamentally different from the Carnapian approach, for example, the question of the distinction between sentential and propositional objects of belief and the answers according to different approaches of Carnap and Quine.

2.   Because of the distinction between equivalence and L-equivalence there is the distinction between interchangeability and L-interchangeability in extensional context and intensional context. From Quine's view, preservation of truth values of a sentence is intelligible, but preservation of intensions (propositionality of a sentence) is not intelligible, because he questions the assumption of intensions for sentences in the first place. Sentences can be grouped in a class because of their synonomy or near-synonomy on verbal behavioral basis. To assume that synonymous or near-synonymous expressions are intended expressions of a separate entity (called meaning or proposition) is not necessary. If Quine's view is correct, we like to ask what consequences will follow in regard to Carnap's problem of intensional isomorphism of belief-sentences.

In the first place the paradox of belief-sentences as being neither extensional nor intensional with respect to their components need not arise. For granted Carnap's distinction between extensional and intensional contexts and his distinction between equivalence and L-equivalence then it appears that, when

(1)   John believes that D,
it should be true that
(2)   John believes that D',
if D and D' are logically true and L-equivalent.

The reason is that by the definition of L-equivalence D and D' as being L-equivalent must be true in all possible worlds, including those compatible with John's belief. This case seems to be parallel to the argument for establishing the intensionality of the modal context of necessity in the following fashion:

(1)   Necessarily $9 > 7$
(2)   '9' and '3^3' are L-equivalent
(3)   Necessarily $3^3 > 7$.

The actual example of a case where John believes that D, but does not believe that D', where D and D' are L-equivalent, shows that D and D'

are not taken in the intended sense of L-equivalence, and shows that the intended sense of L-equivalence is not a clearly elucidated one. For one thing, it shows that we are not clear about how two sentences or two propositions are equivalent in a belief or in a possible world compatible with belief. It seems that unless we know all possible worlds in various intensional contexts, we cannot claim to know possible worlds or to speak of logical truth and L-equivalence in all possible worlds. We can perhaps speak of truth and equivalence in different intensional contexts. My point is that instead of saying that one needs to explain the nonintensionality of belief-sentences as in the above case, we can simply point to the obtaining of the above case as an indication that D and D' are not L-equivalent in the intended sense of Carnap. Logical truths are logically equivalent because they are true simultaneously by logic. In this way, we can still speak of intensionality of belief-sentences, because they do not always preserve truth value under substitution and account for the discrepancy of belief and nonbelief in terms of other conditions.

In this connection I see that Carnap has made constructive steps which Quine could agree with:

(1)   The doctrine of intensional isomorphism as a means of establishing interchangeability in the belief-sentence;
(2)   The interpretation of belief as a dispositional response to a form of sentence.

Of course, Quine would hasten to add that we should not presuppose L-equivalence in the definition of intensional isomorphism. Intensional isomorphism perhaps can be regarded as a type of synonomy or near-synonomy of two sentences based on behavioral and extensional considerations. Because of uncertainty of translation, belief-sentences can be explained without demanding or requesting that beliefs can be always absolutely scrutable. For Quine, there are double uncertainties to the analysis of belief-sentences:

(1)   The inductive uncertainty of disposition to assent to a sentence;
(2)   The deductive uncertainty of translation of the embedded sentence in belief-sentence.

3. The three questions concerning belief-sentences mentioned by Partee are well taken. The first question is a question of elucidating possible worlds of beliefs. Perhaps we can speak of belief-equivalence, knowledge-equivalence, etc., in regard to interchangeability in contexts of beliefs, knowledge, etc. The second question on the evidence for truth of a belief-sentence could be enlarged to include considerations of conditions of both truth and use of belief-sentences. That beliefs can be attributed to persons and higher species of animals seems to indicate a problem of use of belief-sentences, instead of problem of truth of a self-articulated belief-sentence. The third problem on the object of belief perhaps should be considered in an account of the logical semantic and referential features of belief sentences in its variety of *uses*. (Are there other problems of beliefs?)

4. Concerning the problem of belief-equivalence, various conditions of interchangeability of sentences can be suggested. Carnap provided the disposition to assent to a *sentence* as a basis of judging or deciding on interchangeability. I agree that Carnap's criterion of disposition to assent faces difficulties such as that of the chronic liar as well as that of mistaken belief. But the problem cannot be completely avoided short of a purely a priori theory of belief. These cases merely serve to suggest that beliefs are perhaps theoretical and explanatory in nature as pointed out by Partee. Carnap asserted later (1954) that belief is a theoretical construct for which disposition to assent does not offer conclusive indication. This means that belief-sentences are deduced on the basis of *proper* evidence statements and can be used to explain actual *behaviors* of certain characteristics. On this basis one may indeed regard beliefs as purely attributive and not a matter of expressive psychological experience.

Perhaps one can distinguish between first-person belief-sentences and nonfirst-person belief-sentences. For in the first-person belief-sentences, there would be an expressive meaning indicating a psychological experience, but in the nonfirst-person belief-sentences, there cannot be expressive meaning of any kind and must be understood as attributions of theoretical kind. Apart from the question of what constitutes *proper* evidence statements for belief constructions, which has significance for general discovery procedure problems of scientific theories, there is one more point regarding the distinction between first-person belief-sentences, and nonfirst-person belief-sentences. On observation it seems to be the case that for the first-person belief-sentences, opacity of reference in the belief-sentences would occur more frequently than in the case of nonfirst-person belief-sentences. In light of the fact that we are inclined to follow a principle of clear identification and simplicity, we can construe the nonfirst-person belief-sentences as basically transparent, while we cannot but reserve ambiguity as between opaque and transparent reference for belief-sentences of the first-person report, for there may not be immediate objective evidence statements for first-person belief-sentences.

5.   Now given the above view on belief as a theoretical construct, we can remark on Partee's dog test for determining the object of the belief to be a sentence or a proposition. It is clear that for a dog to believe that P this cannot mean that the dog is disposed to assent to a certain sentence. But if a dog is said to believe that P, say "His master is home," what we could mean is that the dog's behavior suggests to us that the dog believes his master is home is a proper description and explanation of his behavior. In order to make the proper description and explanation of the dog's behavior in terms of beliefs, however, we have to develop a total theory of dog's beliefs. Short of such a theory, we cannot attribute beliefs to dogs with justification. If we have such a theory, then the question of whether beliefs have a sentence or a proposition as its *object* of reference is not significantly decidable. It could be consistently held that sentences are objects of beliefs of dogs in the sense that given evidence E sentences of certain forms are related to beliefs of dogs which have explanatory *values* in the total theory. Quine's view on sentences as objects of *beliefs* cannot be ruled out in a theory of dog's belief. Another observation is that in attributing beliefs to dogs or what not, the objects of reference in the belief-sentences are normally directly referred to and are assumed to exist. Though there could be reasonable ground for saying that a dog believes that his master is home without believing that Smith is home, where his master is in fact Smith, because his beliefs are tied to his perceptions and impressions, we do not normally find ourselves to attribute chimerical nonexistent objects to terms of reference in the belief-sentences of dogs and for that matter of any other nonfirst-person individuals.

6.   By considering beliefs as theoretical constructs which are used to

account for behaviors of certain characteristics, the transparency problem as raised by Partee in regard to the sentence assent criterion of Carnap will cease to be a problem, for beliefs in the transparent case become relations involving actual existing referents to be determined on empirical observations and need not produce a sentence for registering assent, nor do we need thereby to regard the construction of a belief-sentence as referring to a proposition. In other words, that we cannot produce a sentence for registering assent does not entail reference to propositions in belief-sentences. We can regard sentences as objects of beliefs without requesting these sentences to register assent of the subjects of beliefs, but on the contrary, on the basis of assent of the scientific investigator or the belief-sentences in the whole theory.

7. What are defining conditions of beliefs? What is the logic of belief-sentences? These are questions which are not yet fully answered. Though logicians may specify what normative conditions a belief-sentence must satisfy in order to constitute a belief-sentence, one can, however, engage in empirical examination of cases of uses of belief-sentences in one language or in more than one language for an appreciation of the structure of belief-sentences and their relations to other forms of sentences. Without a wide investigation of *grammars* of belief-sentences, an a priori specification of logical conditions of belief-sentences is certainly questionable. Thus Partee's doubt of Carnap's requirement that belief-sentences should conform to the condition: "Whoever believes that D believes that D'" is fully justified, when D and D' are synonymous. For it is clear that by adding an assumption that John does not believe that D and D' are synonymous, the assumed consequence that John believes that D' will not follow. Thus it is difficult to require that *beliefs are transparent with regard to synonymy or for that matter with regard to inference.* For given the following statements, (1) John believes that $P \supset Q$; (2) P; one does not expect that John normally believes that Q, even though there is a sense of 'should' or 'compulsion' which enables one to say: (3) John *should* believe that Q by considering (1) and (2). Do we not have a natural tendency to expect that (3) follows? Though John may on psychological considerations hold that John believes that $\sim Q$, and thus the inference from (1) and (2) to (3) does not hold, we may conceive a perfectly rational believer to be such that he

can infer all consequences and preserve consistency of inference that (1) and (2) would lead to (3). But this case is still different from Carnap's requirement that (1) John believes that D; (2) D and D' are synonymous (3) John believes that D'. For even if John is a perfect reasoner, he could not utilize (2) as a premise for substituting D' for D. We as outsiders are privileged to see the discrepancy and draw different inference.

At this point we may say that there are two factors which contribute to the existence of inconsistent beliefs which Partee speaks of as possible. First, there is the failure of the subject of the belief as a perfect reasoner; second, there are *independent* beliefs for a person: even if the objects of these beliefs are not independent of each other, they are known to be so or believed to be so by the subject of the belief. This is a source of inconsistency of beliefs for a person.

8.   Partee has carefully shown that there are verbs which take propositions as objects and there are other verbs which take sentences as objects. Emotive verbs like *regret, hate, be surprised, be amazed, be sad, be glad, be upset, be delighted* and verbs of communication like *say, assert, report, allege, tell, suggest, hint, imply* belong to the first category, while verbs of inference such as *prove, establish, deduce, show* (except *infer*) and manner-verbs of communication like *shout, whisper, scream, hiss, hoot, giggle, bark,* etc., belong to the second category. I am not convinced, however, that this distinction is exact or feasible. One difficulty is the well-known one of providing identity criteria for propositions as distinguishing from that for *sentences*. Similar difficulty exists for verbs which are assumed to take as objects *sentences*. What are the identity criteria for embedded sentences of such verbs as *show* or *shout*? This similarity seems to indicate that the distinction claim does not carry much weight. The real ground of distinction and difference seems to lie in another direction. Verbs of inference and manner-verbs of communication show a dependence on a specific language, because the subjects of these verbs must involve a *specific* linguistic *act* or performance in a specific language. On the other hand, emotive verbs and verbs of communication do not show a dependence on a specific language, because the subjects of these verbs do not have to perform a linguistic act in a specific language known to the describer of the mental states corresponding to these verbs. For emotive

verbs, their objects can be regarded as sentences of the *describer's* language; for verbs of communication, their objects are sentences of the language known to the subjects of these verbs. But for verbs of inference, the subjects are required to know and refer to a specific language (not merely to use it), for manner-verbs of communication, the subjects of sentences must use the language or linguistic expressions of their familiarity. Insofar as we need not adopt a position of propositional realism of theory construction, there is no general reason why objects of emotive verbs and manner-verbs of communication and other related verbs cannot be regarded as taking sentences (of the *describer's*) as objects by way of attribution.

9. The above, of course, does not present any solution to the inter-changeability conditions problem for belief sentences and any other related propositional attitudes. Perhaps the interchangeability conditions should be relativized to specific beliefs or propositional attitudes. By this, I mean that unless an equivalence between two expressions or two sentences in a belief-sentence or in similar constructions is *believed* by and known to the subjects of belief-sentences or a sentence of propositional attitude, the *equivalence* cannot be valid for interchangeability in the construction of propositional attitude. Compare the following results:

(A)   John believes that 2 is a prime number. John does not believe that $2 = 1 + 1$. It is necessary that $2 = 1 + 1$ $\therefore$ John believes that $(1 + 1)$ is a prime number.

(B)   John believes that 2 is a prime number. It is necessary that $2 = 1 + 1$ and John believes that $2 = 1 + 1$ $\therefore$ John believes that $(1 + 1)$ is a prime number.

It is clear that (A) seems to be invalid and (B) seems to be valid. The point brought out in the comparison is that one cannot speak of meaningful exchange of equivalent or *L*-equivalent terms without requiring that equivalence and *L*-equivalence be transparent relative to the subject of the propositional attitude in question. To generalize, a construction of propositional attitude of any kind depends upon obtaining transparency of identity or implication, synonymy or equivalence in whatever sense toward a belief, a perception and a knowledge of the subject of the propositional verb for substitution or consequence-drawing in the context of propositional attitude.

10. In light of the above, there seem to follow three important points regarding characterization of belief constructions. First, for a non-transparent and therefore opaque (in Quine's sense) interpretation of propositional attitudes, substitution and consequence-drawing within the scope of propositional attitude must depend on satisfaction of belief conditions regarding identity for substitution, and regarding implication for consequence-drawing. Thus if,

(1)   John is surprised that Smith was elected as the commissioner,

then

(2)   John is surprised that his cousin was elected as the commissioner,

if

(3)   He believes that Smith = John's cousin.

In the case of emotive verbs like *being surprised*, consequence-drawing may not always preserve the truth value of the whole sentence.

This shows that belief condition is a universal requirement for substitution in construction of propositional attitudes insofar as these are interpreted in a nontransparent sense. This, of course, applies to a non-transparent interpretation of belief-sentences. Thus we cannot explain belief away in explaining the substitution problem of beliefs.

Second, it is correct to observe that beliefs are ambiguous as between a transparent interpretation and an opaque one. But this does not mean that beliefs can be taken to have as their objects sometimes sentences, sometimes propositions. They can consistently be considered as taking sentences as their objects depending on an expressive or a theoretical (attributional) interpretation of belief. For an opaque and expressive interpretation of beliefs, one cannot secure substitution without positing opaque belief of the substitution. Thus, to specify the conditions of substitution, one has to know what is in the content of beliefs of subjects of belief and what is excluded from there. Individual constructions of propositional attitudes will have individual or individual types of substitution conditions, and they cannot be *generalized* a priori. The possible-worlds approach to elucidation of semantical conditions is relevant here. Different possible

worlds are relative to different contents of beliefs. In different constructions of propositional attitudes, there are bound to be different equivalence
relationships. Therefore, there cannot be a uniform statement of substitution conditions for beliefs or other propositional attitudes insofar as
beliefs are inevitably presupposed in them.

Finally, because of the disuniformity of substitution conditions for belief
constructions and propositional attitudes, we may perhaps suggest that
the deep structure of a belief-sentence or other propositional-attitude
constructions must be relative to these constructions. This note on
relative deep structure can be elaborated for its usefulness. The assumption
of a universal general deep structure for all forms of constructions must
be abolished. This may be regarded as a reason for not requesting uniform
representation of deep structures in a generative semantic or an inter-
pretative semantic framework as mentioned by Partee.

11.   On the question of the deep structure of quotation and quoted
sentences, I think that we should distinguish between two kinds of
quotations. The first kind of quotation is quotations which are not
intended for contributing to the meaning of a discourse and are described
in terms of linguistic categories such as words, sentences, etc. Examples
are:

(1)   'Boston' is a six-letter word.
(2)   'I am a student' is an English sentence.

What is the interchangeability condition for such quotations? Apparently,
the context in which they occur specifies explicitly such conditions. Thus,
since 'Newton' is a six-letter word, its substitution for 'Boston' would
preserve the truth value of (1) and similarly 'I am not a student' is an
English sentence, its substitution for 'I am a student' also preserves the
truth value of (2). For this kind of quotation, no internal structure obtains
in the deep structure of the whole sentences containing the quotation. The
second kind of quotations are directly quoted speeches intended for contributing to the meaningfulness of a discourse and are not explicitly
described as a form of linguistic expression. Quotations of this kind do
have internal structures relevant for the understanding of the meaning of
the whole speech containing the quotation, as Partee clearly pointed out.

In principle, these kinds of quotations are capable of being transformed into indirect discourse and this shows why they can contribute to the meaning of the whole speech. The problem about direct quotations is one related to propositional attitude in general: namely, that of providing adequate substitution conditions for equivalent expressions. There is no reason why the deep structure of quotations of this kind should not be described in indirect discourse with strong substitution conditions specified.

12.   There seems to exist a general syntactic criterion for distinguishing between sentential that-clause of subjects of the whole constructions and what Partee calls 'propositional that-clause' or sentential that-clause of speakers of the whole constructions. While the so-called propositional verbs like emotive verbs and verbs of communication cannot take direct quotations as their objects, the sentential verbs like verbs of inference and manner-verbs of communications can as a rule take direct quotations as their objects. Example: John suggests, "The war should be ended." Mary shouts, "Don't shoot." The dog barks, "Bark, bark."

13.   We can suggest in this connection a syntactic criterion for distinguishing transparent sense of belief from opaque sense of belief over a large discourse. The criterion consists in identifying the embedded sentence of a belief construction as transparent if referring terms appear in other places of the connected discourse earlier or later independent of or free from propositional attitude constructions. If, on the other hand, there cannot be or is no direct referring in the connected discourse, the embedded sentence should be treated as opaque construction.

University of Hawaii

NOTE

[1] Two expressions are said to have the *same* extension in a semantic system S if they are equivalent in S; two expressions have the *same* intensions in S if they are L-equivalent in S. The extensions of an expression can be therefore defined as the object referred to by the expression and its logical equivalents in S; similarly, the intension of an expression can be defined as the object referred to by the expression and its L-equivalents in S.

JULIUS MORAVCSIK

COMMENTS ON PARTEE'S PAPER

In this paper I shall place some of the points made by Partee and Hintikka into perspective, and then draw some morals from these both for linguists and for philosophers.

1. FREGEAN THOUGHTS

Frege (1967, p. 19) wrote: "What does one call a sentence? A series of sounds; but only when it has a sense, by which is not meant that every series of sounds that has sense is a sentence. And when we call a sentence true we really mean its sense is. From which it follows that it is for the sense of a sentence that the question of truth arises in general."

Frege (1952, p. 52) called the sense of a sentence a thought, and re-marked: "By a thought I understand not the subjective performance of thinking, but its objective content, which is capable of being the common property of several thinkers."

Fregean thoughts (from now on Thoughts) are what is true or false. There are many ways of showing why this must be so. For one thing, a spoken sentence is a series of sounds, and whatever it is that we judge to be true or false, it is not the series of sounds but what these sounds express. Frege, like the linguists and philosophers of today, was interested in characterizing and understanding a family of mental processes; beliefs, inferences, deductions, etc., and he took it to be fundamental that these processes do not deal simply with sounds or markings on a piece of paper, but with Thoughts, i.e., with that which, under the proper circumstances, sounds and marks can express. One might say that the human mind operates with symbols, but it does so in view of the senses that these symbols express. Another way to approach the point is to see that a number of different sentences may express the same truth or falsehood, and that these sentences may even come from different languages, while the same sentence, such as 'it is raining now' may express different truths or falsehoods on different occasions. Frege would characterize the situa-

Hintikka et al. (eds.), Approaches to Natural Language, 349–369. *All rights reserved.*
Copyright © 1973 *by D. Reidel Publishing Company, Dordrecht-Holland.*

tion by saying that different sentences, also across languages, may express the same Thought, and that the same sentence may express on different occasions different Thoughts.

Sentences then, and some of their components, have senses. What can we say about Frege's notion of a sense? Briefly – and ignoring distinctions between sense and concept – one can say that a Fregean sense is some sort of procedure[1] by which one can tell, under ideal conditions, whether a given entity does or does not fall within the denotation range of a given word or expression. Intuitively this is easiest to see in the case of the concepts of arithmetic. There are certain procedures to figure out what is and is not an even number, and there are certain procedures to find out what number is designated by '127'. Analogously, there are certain procedures, one would say calculations, that enable us to grasp the sense of '3 + 2 = 5'. If we make the assumption that ideally one would understand the senses of nonarithmetical expressions and sentences in ways analogous to the ways in which we understand arithmetic, then we can extend the notion of a procedure or calculation to these other spheres of language. Thus the procedure contained in the sense of 'the first president of the USA' enables one, ideally, to tell which entity is referred to by this expression and which entities are not. Likewise, the understanding of a sentence is an operation on the senses of its components that enables us to grasp that which we can judge to be true or false. From this cursory characterization it is clear that Frege's notion of sense is fundamental for the characterization of the intellectual operations of understanding and reasoning.

Our final question about senses, and in particular about Thoughts, is how to individuate them. That is to say, by what criteria can we tell whether a collection of sentences express one or many Thoughts? It is obvious that if two senses are attached to two terms, such as 'evening star' and 'morning star', that have the same referent, this does not show the identity of the senses. On the level of sentences, the pair: 'the current president of the USA lives in Washington' and 'Richard Nixon lives in Washington' may be such that they correspond to the same state of affairs; they nevertheless express different Thoughts. It is equally easy to see that the mere fact that two sentences express what is logically equivalent does not guarantee that they express the same Thought. For example, all analytic truths are logically equivalent, since they are necessarily true, or true in all possible worlds. Nevertheless there are a number of different Thoughts that are analytically true. 'All men are rational animals' and 'all brothers are male siblings' are both analytically true and thus logically equivalent; but they clearly express different Thoughts. For the intellectual operations required to grasp the two are distinct – different groups of senses need to be 'computed'. Again, if all of simple arithmetic is analytic, then all of its truths are analytic. But clearly '2 + 2 = 4' and '4 + 5 = 9' express different Thoughts, for different calculations are required in order to grasp the senses of the two sentences. These negative remarks, however, do not lead us very far, for it is also obvious that we cannot associate a distinct calculation or procedure with each distinct analytic sentence or truth of arithmetic. The fundamental difficulty is, of course, that we know very little about the mental operations that go into the grasping of Thoughts expressed by sentences. Whatever the units and individuation of these operations are, those will individuate Thoughts, and – as we shall see – certain types of beliefs.

Hopefully, it needs no argument to show that the notion of a Thought is of fundamental importance for the understanding of the nature of sentences expressing beliefs. Roughly, certain types of beliefs are the fundamental units of reasoning, and Thoughts are the objects of these units. Thus it is unfortunate that Partee did not introduce or deal with these deep Fregean insights. To be sure, she rightly distinguished sentences from propositions, but she used only that sense of 'proposition' in which logically equivalent propositions count as identical. Whatever interest this notion of a proposition may have to logicians, since it cannot distinguish analytic beliefs and the many beliefs of arithmetic and thus cannot deal with notions like logical deduction, etc., it is of no interest to linguists or philosophers. In the rest of this paper I shall ignore that sense of the term 'proposition', and – in accordance with the usage employed in most of the useful philosophic literature – reserve the word 'proposition' to mean Fregean Thought.

2. PHILOSOPHICAL DEBATES ABOUT THE OBJECT OF BELIEF

Let us start by recalling the usual distinction between sentence types and sentence tokens, the latter being either a series of sounds or inscriptions.

Thus in the lines below:

(1)   The cat is on the mat.
(2)   The cat is on the mat.
(3)   The dog is on the mat.

We have three sentence tokens but only two sentence types, with (1) and (2) being tokens of the same type. We must distinguish from both token and type the occasion or event of someone producing a token. Such events are called by some speech acts. If we add to the collection propositions, as defined in the previous section, we get the following list of candidates for object of belief:

   (a) sentence types
   (b) sentence tokens
   (c) speech acts
   (d) propositions.

The interesting and perplexing fact is that at one time or another each of these candidates has been declared as the winner by some philosopher or logician. This circumstance hopefully justifies a brief excursion into the question of exactly what philosophers meant by characterizing something as the object of belief. There seems to be agreement on the point that whatever is the object of belief is also that which is true or false. There have been, however, equally sharp disagreements concerning the matter of what it is that is true or false. Tarski's famous truth definition is designed to hold for sentences, indeed to be precise, sentences within some given language (with certain specifiable properties). The success of this definition made it plausible to regard sentences as true or false, and thus also as the objects of belief. Further reflection on the nature of so-called indexical expressions ('I', 'you', 'here', 'now', etc.) and the sentences containing them suggested to some that the unit of truth and falsity is the sentence token, and thus the token recommended itself as the object of belief. Finally, reflections on the variety of speech acts that can be performed, such as promising, warning, commanding, etc., and the ways in which these can be criticized, suggested to some that perhaps this is the proper object for beliefs. Some of these alternatives have been suggested partly also because one hopes eventually to build an adequate analysis of belief into a framework of empirical psychological explanations, and it is said at times that within such a framework one has to treat the object of belief also as a causal condition, and for this purpose such spatio-temporal entities as sentence tokens or speech acts seem more plausible candidates than sentence types or propositions.

Before launching a defense of propositions as the objects of thought, it should be pointed out that the problem of giving truth definitions by itself does not favor one alternative over the other, since with some additional technical apparatus one can give analogous truth definitions for propositions (Fregean Thoughts) as well.

The defense should be fairly obvious from the way in which Thoughts were introduced. Even a cursory glance at ordinary language shows that propositions, in this sense, are regarded as that which we believe, doubt, entertain, question, etc. Consider locutions like: 'I don't believe it', 'I believe that too', etc. Or consider answers to the request to state your beliefs on a certain topic. The 'it' and 'that' do not refer to sentences; further explanations backing up the locutions considered can restate what it is that is believed or not believed without using the same sentence as the one used by the speaker who posed the original issue. Again, two people can restate the same set of beliefs concerning a topic, without using the same sentences. Disregarding sentences with indexical expressions, one can say that there is a one-many correlation between propositions and sentences; or – as Cartwright (1962) put it so felicitously – "sentences and statements differ in their arithmetics." All one needs to add is that the latter are the sort of thing that is said ordinarily to be believed, disbelieved, questioned, etc.

To sum up, the philosophical debates about the so-called objects of belief centered around the following issues: (a) What is it that is true or false? Answers to this question involve attempts to define truth, and the attempts fall within the field of logic. (b) What should be taken as the object of belief in a scientific framework within which we give a causal account of belief? This is a conceptual question within the field of psychology; one might say that it is a question discussed in so-called philosophical psychology. (c) In order to account for the semantics of a natural language like English that includes verbs like 'believe', what sort of thing should be regarded as the object of such a verb? Answers to this question must include an account of sentences like: 'what he believes can be expressed in different ways', and an account of the oddness of 'what he believes is made up of 16 letters'. Some philosophers think that a general constraint on answers to these questions should be some ontological principles; e.g., some that tend to minimize commitment to abstract entities. I shall ignore such ontological prejudices since no good ground has ever been stated for them. It is more worthwhile to reflect on whether it is reasonable to suppose that answers to the three questions will coincide. The main tension is between the logician's question and that of the psychologist. Anything that might do as a causally relevant factor to the psychological event of a belief is unlikely to be fit as the bearer of truth value as the logician conceives of this, and vice versa. This tension was seen clearly by Frege who then added that Thoughts must be conceived of as occupying a curious third realm, neither psychological nor physical. Admittedly, this is to pose the question rather than to solve it; but most other philosophers do not even see the question as clearly as Frege did. Solutions, as of now, have not been forthcoming. It is also debatable whether one should expect answers to either (a) or (b) to coincide with answers to (c) unless one assumes that there is a correct or at least plausible logical or psychological theory built into ordinary English. The fact that some of English behaves according to logical rules does not guarantee that there is a good theory about this logic built into the semantics of English.

3. THE INDIVIDUATION OF BELIEFS

The main question that occupies a dominant place in the writings on the semantics of belief sentences is that of individuating beliefs. In other words, what are the varieties of conditions under which one can express the same belief? This question is best attacked by considering a sentence that expresses a belief and then investigating the varieties of possible substitutions within the original sentence that will still enable us to express the same belief and to delineate those types of substitutions that produce a sentence no longer expressing the same belief. For example, one can consider

(1)   Sam believes that his best friend is the victim.

and then ask what can be substituted for 'his best friend', or 'the victim' and still have a sentence that expresses the same belief. Needless to say, one has to consider different types of sentences that can occur within the 'believes that . . .' context, and within these sentences different types of expressions such as general terms, singular terms, etc.

The standard treatment of this question is best stated by Quine (1960). He distinguished between transparent and opaque constructions. These constructions contain embedded sentences. A transparent construction creates a complex sentence whose truth value remains the same when we substitute within the embedded sentence singular expressions that are co-extensive, i.e., have the same referent. Thus if we assume that (1) contains a transparent construction, then on the assumption

(2)   Sam's best friend is the owner of the store.

we should be able to conclude

(3)   Sam believes that the owner of the store is the victim.

On the other hand, an opaque construction creates a context for an embedded sentence such that substituting co-extensive terms does not preserve truth-value. Thus if we interpret (1) as containing an opaque construction, then from (1) and (2) we cannot infer (3). Some contexts, such as 'it is the case that . . .' always create transparent constructions, while others such as 'de dicto' logical modal contexts always create opaque constructions. Quine's claim about belief-sentences is that they can be interpreted both ways. In order to keep within the terminology adopted by Partee, let us distinguish extensional and intensional beliefs. An extensional belief is one that can be expressed by a class of sentences the members of which are related via the co-extensionality of their replaceable parts (singular terms). An intensional belief is one which can be expressed only by a narrower class of sentences. Quine thinks that there are both kinds of beliefs, indeed that these are the only kinds of belief. Furthermore, there are no syntactic criteria by which we could distinguish belief-sentences that carry normally only one of these interpretations in contrast with the other. Partee's paper helps to bring out this point, by showing that constructions such as

(4)   Sam believes of the owner that he is the victim.

and

(5)   Sam believes the owner to be the victim.

have syntactic structures that do lend themselves in general to both types
of interpretations.

In order to complete this brief sketch of what I called the standard
theory – which will be related in the next section to more recent developments – we should add that according to Quine one must not refer or
quantify across opaque constructions. That is to say, if we interpret a
sentence like

(6)   The owner came in and Sam believed that he was the victim.

as involving co-reference between 'the owner' and 'he', then we must
interpret the belief-construction in (6) as transparent; in other words,
Sam's belief has to be construed as extensional.

Some of Partee's remarks lead me to think that it might not be un-
profitable to delineate the extent to which questions about the objects and
individuation of beliefs are empirical, and the extent to which these are
conceptual (nonempirical? definitional?). Considerations of the nature of
linguistic competence as well as some of the facts surveyed in our discussion
of the object of belief establish it that a belief is a theoretical construct,
an unobservable state or process for which we have a variety of indirect
evidence.[2] Thus to ask: "how many beliefs does Jones express in these
sentences?" is not like asking: "how many dimes are there in my pocket
right now?" In order to answer the second question all we have to do is to
look. But answers to the first question require conceptual decisions about
the objects and individuation of beliefs. Needless to say, however, that
like any definition that is couched within the framework of an empirical
science, the definitions under consideration too may turn out to be better
or worse, depending on how well they help to explain observations and
formulate predictions when joined with other definitions and hypotheses.
Perhaps the main reason for the relative obscurity of our notions and the
lack of general consensus in this area is the variety of theories within
which our notion of a belief will have to play important roles. As we saw,
these theories include theories of truth within logic, psychological theories,
and theories explaining the semantics of ordinary English. The theories
about English have to explain the inferences that one can draw from a
statement ascribing a belief to a person and the inferences that our
linguistic intuitions show to be invalid. This is the most obvious empirical

constraint on our theories; but there are other, so far less carefully worked out, constraints from psychological observations. All of this is supposed to be in harmony with the conceptual constraints imposed by whatever may turn out to be the most adequate account of truth.

I attempted here to contrast the discussions about the object of belief with the discussions of the individuation problem. The relationship between these topics does not come out quite clearly in Partee's paper. This, however, is not her fault. Unfortunately, the philosophical literature is simply unclear on how these topics should be related. Partee's demand seems to be that theories about one should be related to theories about the other, i.e., theories about what is the object of belief should be related to theories about the individuation of belief. This is an eminently reasonable request. For example, Quine's view of the two kinds of belief goes with his view that the objects of belief are sentences. This requires some explanation, especially if we shall try to cross-fertilize linguistics and philosophy. I hope that the remarks above concerning the variety of questions to which the philosophic constructs are supposed to help to find answers will provide at least some excuse for the obscurity surrounding these matters.

One position is clearly consistent and easy to explicate. This is the position that identifies the objects of belief as Fregean propositions, and then individuates beliefs accordingly. Thus the object of Sam's belief may be the Thought that all men are rational animals, and correspondingly, the only sentences that can express this belief are those of the same syntactic form and contain either the same words or the synonyms for 'men' and 'rational animals'. We saw already why logical equivalence is a useless notion here, since if we adopted that notion for individuation, then one would be able to substitute 'all brothers are male siblings' into the above and end up claiming that the resulting sentence expresses the same belief as the original. Thus we shall assume from here on that what we called intensional beliefs have as their objects Thoughts, and are individuated accordingly.

Perhaps the best way to characterize extensional beliefs is to say that these have as their objects expected states of affairs, where the latter notion can be explicated as specifiable by a set of sentences that differ only in the referring expressions that they contain, and these have to be co-extensive. There are certain formal difficulties with the notion of an extensional

belief that we shall disregard here. The considerations here and elsewhere
in this paper concern only the co-extensiveness of singular terms when
we talk of extensional belief. Thus, e.g., 'Richard Nixon lives in the White
House' and 'the current president of the USA lives in the White House'
describe the same state of affairs, and some of our beliefs can be best
characterized as expectation of certain states of affairs. In these cases the
belief that 'a is F' together with the true statement that $a = b$, gives us
ground for inferring that 'b is F' is believed. If some philosophers want to
go on to say that in these cases the object of the belief is a sentence (or
rather sentences), this should be construed as their proposed answer to the
logical and psychological questions mentioned in the previous section.
Such a position is certainly consistent, even if it requires a more cumbersome characterization within the framework of our approach. Thus from
here on we shall talk about intensional and extensional beliefs, with
propositions (in the Fregean sense) and expected states of affairs as the
corresponding objects. This account could accommodate – with some
additional clauses – those who think that sentence tokens are the objects
of belief. It is difficult to see how it could accommodate those who think
that the objects of belief are speech acts, but this position hardly merits
that much attention in any case.

4. RECENT CONTRIBUTIONS TO THE SEMANTICS OF BELIEF

It is important to understand the more recent contributions to the analysis
of belief-sentences – primarily those of Hintikka – with what was called
above as the standard theory as the background. Let us first consider
beliefs that have as their objects general propositions (of the 'all A's are
B's' form), and let us consider in particular the conditions for substituting
for general terms within a sentence that expresses a belief. The view
represented by Frege and Carnap is that the only adequate condition for
such substitution is synonymy. We shall consider exceptions to this below.
First, this view should be defended against the kind of objection that is
exemplified by Putnam, as mentioned by Partee. Putnam points out that
not everyone who believes that all Greeks are Greeks believes that all
Greeks are Hellenes. Cases of this sort, however, should not lead us to
abandon the Frege view; they point, rather, to the need for an interesting
qualification. For beliefs of certain level of complexity must be expressed

in language. Given beliefs of this complexity, the question of what terms can be substituted in order to preserve expression of the same belief must be made relative to the languages and parts of languages that the believer in question has mastered. The person who does not believe that all Greeks are Hellenes is not someone who believes that some Greeks are not Hellenes, but rather someone who does not know what 'Hellenes' means. This dependency on language should be of interest both to linguists and philosophers. For it is not obvious what the level of complexity is at which the dependency becomes necessary. One plausible criterion is logical complexity, quantificational structure as well as complex truth-functional structure. But it is plausible to argue that in addition to this, there is also a semantic criterion, i.e., that beliefs involving some concepts – such as certain functional ones, those of lawyer, doctor, prime minister – can be entertained and expressed only by creatures that possess a language, and the expression must be within language. (Some beliefs, e.g., that danger is near, can be expressed obviously without the use of language.)

Thus with the qualification of language-dependency the Frege-Carnap criterion seems to fit most general terms that occur in sentences expressing beliefs. But not all such terms. There are expressions of general scope that can be interpreted extensionally within a belief-context. Thus let us contrast

(1)   Sam believes that all men are mortal.

with

(2)   Sam believes that all of the students in this room are intelligent.

The first type of general belief can be given only an intensional interpretation, and thus substitution is governed by synonymy. The second type of general belief, however, can be given both an intensional and an extensional reading. On the second reading then, any term or expression co-extensive with 'all of the students in this room' can be substituted. The difference between the two types of general beliefs is that the first one is 'global' in scope; 'all men' includes the members of the human race, all over the globe and all through history, past, present, and future. The second belief has as the subject a 'localized' class. It is conceivable that someone should be personally acquainted with all of the students in the room, and thus holds a belief about those individuals no matter what true descriptions they are represented by. So 'global' general beliefs can be interpreted only intensionally, while 'local' general beliefs admit of both extensional and intensional interpretation. In the intensional cases the substitution criterion for general terms is synonymy (relative to the linguistic data of the believer) and in the extensional cases the criterion is co-extensiveness – L-equivalence is irrelevant to both types of cases. This interpretation of general terms is also applicable to instances in which the general terms appear within sentences that have singular terms as their subject and express belief.

The fact that L-equivalence is irrelevant to the analysis of general beliefs raises an interesting question for those who wish to abandon the notion of synonymy in favor of less intensional notions. Given that the objects of global general beliefs have internal structure and that they are intensional, I see no way of adequately representing the semantics of such beliefs without the notion of synonymy.

This brief survey of general beliefs suggests that an extensional interpretation of terms in belief contexts is linked to the possibility of the believer having acquaintance or indirect knowledge of each of the bearers of such terms. This point comes up again in the case of singular terms, and suggests that the way in which we learn terms that figure in belief may not be irrelevant to the interpretation and substitution criteria that apply to these.[3]

Turning to the analysis of beliefs with singular terms as subjects, we note that some of these can be given only intensional interpretation. These are beliefs about abstract entities like numbers, shapes, etc. Thus

(3)   Sam believes that 8 is an even number.

cannot be interpreted extensionally. If

(4)   8 is the number thought of by Jones now.

is also true, then we can only conclude that

(5)   Sam believes that the number that is in fact the number thought of by Jones now is even.

And this is a different kind of claim from the ones we encountered when considering extensional beliefs. This again suggests that the possibility of empirical acquaintance with the referent or denotation range is perhaps a necessary condition for interpreting a term, singular or general, extensionally.

Although philosophers consider almost exclusively those singular terms within a belief that occur in subject position, we should realize – as Hintikka among philosophers and Fillmore among linguists would remind us – that in a full analysis of a sentence expressing a belief we must consider all of the singular terms, regardless of whether they occur as subject, or object, or place, etc.

Singular terms are either proper names or definite descriptions. The semantics of these types of expressions is one of the most controversial topics in the philosophy of language; thus it is not surprising that the semantics of singular beliefs should be also the subject of much debate and little agreement.

In his new analysis of singular beliefs Hintikka (1962, 1969a) utilizes the kind of semantics that can account for the internal structure of a sentence like (5). Roughly, this amounts to considering classes of possible worlds and tracing individuals within and across these worlds that can be viewed as specified by sets of descriptions. With regard to belief, Hintikka considers not the alternative possible worlds, but the alternative doxastic worlds; with respect to any belief that set of doxastic worlds that is compatible with what the belief contains. This approach helps to shed new light on what Quine described as quantifying across belief contexts. The new semantics illuminates such quantification by representing the problem simply as identifying the individual referred to outside the belief context with the individual in question across the doxastic worlds compatible with what the believer believes.

With respect to singular beliefs Hintikka introduced a new distinction. A sentence like

(6)   Sam believes that the innkeeper is clever.

will have different interpretations depending on whether Sam knows who the innkeeper is. One could interpret – though Hintikka would not necessarily want to put it that way – 'knowing who X is' or 'knowing (believing) what X is' as having knowledge – or belief – concerning the essential

characteristics of *X*, whether *X* is a human or a building like the Notre
Dame of Paris, or for that matter a mountain like the Matterhorn. If
Sam knows or has a belief about who the innkeeper is, then in his belief he
ascribes cleverness to that individual, while if he does not have any beliefs
concerning who the innkeeper is, then he is ascribing cleverness to whoever happens to be the innkeeper under the various circumstances that are
compatible with his beliefs.

In addition to accounting for a larger variety of cases, Hintikka's
analysis is also valuable because it sheds additional light on the individuation of beliefs. For with regard to the substitution problem Hintikka
proposed as one possible criterion to see if given any of the co-extensive
expressions, does the believer accept the sentence as expressing a belief
of his? Thus according to this proposal, the syntax and the semantics of
singular beliefs by themselves – at least when the subject is not abstract –
do not settle the individuation problem. This depends on individual cases
and the ranges of beliefs and empirical information (acquaintance) of
various believers. With regard to the substitution problem this is a more
realistic proposal than the ones available under the standard theory.

There is, however, a general principle of individuation that Hintikka
(1970a) proposed with regard to beliefs that are expressed with complex
quantificational structure. The proposal is that belief is preserved so long
as quantificational depth (number of layers of quantifiers) is preserved
when proving the consequence in question. When quantificational depth
is increased as a result of drawing entailments from the proposition
that is alleged to be believed, then belief can no longer be expected to be
preserved.

We see once more that *L*-equivalence does not figure in any of these
valuable proposals that differ in four crucial ways from what was called
above the standard theory. First they separate the question of existential
import from the issues of substitutivity; secondly, they account for a
greater variety of beliefs than the standard theory. Furthermore, they
allow for a more flexible and realistic set of proposals for substitution,
and lastly, by relying on the new kind of semantics of possible worlds
and cross-identifiable individuals they can shed new light on the problem
of cross-reference from outside of a belief-context to within, and propose
new criteria for the kinds of entailments that having a belief carries with it.

5. FREGEAN THOUGHTS AND FREGEAN DEEP STRUCTURE

In discussing different types of beliefs we noted above that in order to have beliefs of a certain degree of complexity, language is necessary. This means that syntactic structure is necessary in order to express certain beliefs. The question then arises to what extent the expression of thoughts is independent of syntax? That two sentences with different syntactic forms can express the same Thought was noticed by Frege. In connection with interrogatives that require only a "yes or no" answer Frege (1967) remarked:

An interrogative sentence and an indicative one contain the same thought; but the indicative contains something else as well, namely, the assertion. The interrogative sentence contains something more too, namely a request [p. 21].

The ideas suggested here for semantic analysis are extremely interesting and need further exploration; but equally interesting is the suggestion about the relatedness of the two sentences and their syntactic form. Frege followed this up with the suggestion:

The word 'but' differs from 'and' in that with it one intimates that what follows is in contrast with what would be expected from what preceded it. Such suggestions in speech make no difference to the thought [p. 23].

Finally, in a passage that anticipates to a striking extent Chomsky's conception of deep structure and transformation (Frege wrote this in 1918!) he said:

A sentence can be transformed by changing the verb from active to passive and making the object the subject at the same time. . . . Naturally such transformations are not indifferent in every respect; but they do not touch the thought, they do not touch what is true or false [p. 23].

Apart from the remarkable evidence of how far Frege was ahead of his time, these passages give interesting suggestion about the level at which syntactically different sentences have nevertheless enough structure in common that they can express the same Thought. Of course, these suggestions work best when applied to singular propositions; as we saw in recent work on transformational grammar, it is far from clear at what level we can also capture the syntactic form that allows sentences with somewhat different structure to express the same Thought where this involves quantification or its natural language equivalents.

Perhaps this is the appropriate point at which this discussion can tie up with a few points made about intensional verbs and substitutivity by Urmson (1968). One of Urmson's valuable points is that not all intensional verbs take a sentential or propositional unit as their object, and that the objects of some of these could hardly be described a concept, idea, etc. For example, 'he is building a house' where, as Urmson remarked, the house cannot yet exist if the building is still going on, and yet the reference to the house in question is hardly like the reference, or purported reference to unicorns in 'he is hunting for unicorns'. Urmson's example also shows the importance of subject-predicate form for certain type of sentences.

Urmson also introduced the notion of aptness of reference, and remarked correctly that one's report about what someone said or believed will depend in its form partly also on the issue of whom one is reporting to. For example, if someone said that the manager just parked his car, one might report this appropriately to his wife as a remark to the extent that her husband just parked the car. The same form of report will not do for just any addressee. This point, however – so it seems to me – should not be taken as showing something about the criteria for expressing a belief, and thus for individuation. It is one thing to deal with the question of how we individuate beliefs and another to discuss aptness of reporting about such belief to various types of audiences.

6. THE VARIETY OF INTENSIONAL VERBS; AN ATTEMPTED RECONSTRUCTION OF PARTEE'S RESULTS

Partee's most valuable survey of the variety of intensional verbs contains results that are of interest both to linguists and to philosophers. The distinctions she draws are valuable, but are not always expressed in felicitous ways. In what follows I shall try to restate the distinctions in terms of the conceptual framework developed in this paper.

One family of verbs singled out in her survey includes 'regret', 'hate', 'be sad', 'be glad', and 'be delighted'. These are described as emotives – perhaps verbs of attitude might be more appropriate. It is pointed out correctly that these verbs take that-clauses. In an earlier paper the Kiparskys stated that the embedded sentence is always presupposed to be a fact. This is simply false. For

(1)   Sam is delighted that the guest will come.

does not presuppose anything about the guest actually coming. It does, however, entail

(2)   Sam believes that the guest will come.

In short, the semantics of these constructions do not link the attitudes in question to facts, but rather to beliefs.

Partee sees rightly that in terms of substitution conditions the members of this family have something in common, and that the common criterion is a rather wide one. It is unfortunate, however, to say that they can take only one kind of object, and especially that this object is a proposition in the sense determined by L-equivalence. What one should say is that characteristically these verbs create constructions such that the substitution criterion is wide, indeed, it is simple co-extensiveness and not L-equivalence. (I am not claiming that this is always the object, but that it is typically, or in most cases so.)

In order to see this, let us consider

(3)   Sam is sad that the girl he loves does not love him.

By substituting for 'the girl he loves' definite descriptions that happen to have the same referent, we still preserve truth. E.g., from (3) and

(4)   The girl he loves = the girl next door.

it follows that

(5)   Sam is sad that the girl next door does not love him.

There may be cases in which some substitutions of this sort do not work. But typically emotions and attitudes are directed towards persons or objects that we are acquainted with, and in these cases the substitution criterion is simply that of co-extensiveness, and thus in our terminology the object is an expected state of affairs. Without wishing to enter upon a discussion whether our canine friends and other animals are capable of extended reasoning, it is sufficient to point out that in the case of the typical attitude or emotion ascribed to dogs, cats, etc., the co-extensiveness criterion works. Thus

(6)   Fido is glad that his master came home.

under the normal interpretation will be truth-preserving as long as we substitute for 'his master' singular terms that are co-extensive with that one.

This family contrasts sharply with what Partee calls the family of verbs of inference, such as 'deduce', 'prove', 'establish', etc. Here the substitution criterion is obviously not co-existensiveness or L-equivalence, but in the typical cases at least something as stringent as Thoughts. It is worth emphasizing the 'at least' here, because some of Partee's examples show convincingly that in some typical uses of 'deduce' the substitution criterion might involve reference to the syntactic form of the sentence, or indeed an almost quotative reference. Thus the interest of these cases is twofold. On the one hand we get an interesting contrast between verbs of attitude and verbs of inference. To put it in a nutshell, true sadness (and other attitudes) is extensional, while true deduction is intensional; indeed – and this is the second interest of these cases – its individuation may involve reference to syntactic structure as well as semantic elements. This gives the linguist a nice problem: what level of syntax is involved in this sort of substitution condition? I hope that it is clear from the discussion developed so far why it is better to describe the objects of these verbs as Thoughts or an even more narrow set of objects than to say that the object is a sentence. The latter, given the philosophical usage of that phrase, might have misleading connotations for the reader.

Further interesting facts are unearthed by Partee when she considers verbs like 'say', 'report', 'tell', 'hint', etc. Some of these, like 'say', or 'tell', admit both the extensional and the intensional interpretation. E.g.,

(7a)   Sam said about his neighbor that he is a nice person.

(7b)   Sam said that 2 is an even number.

Although – expectedly – all verbs of communication can admit the intensional interpretation, in which case the objects are Thoughts, it is not clear that all can admit the extensional interpretation. E.g., 'scream', 'giggle', do not seem to admit such an interpretation. Furthermore, the object of these two, as well as some other verbs that Partee calls "manner-verbs of communication" have what she calls "near-quotative" criteria of substitutivity; in other words, objects even more stringently defined –

and even more language (syntax) dependent – than Thoughts.

The last family mentioned is that of epistemic verbs. These seem all to admit both the extensional and the intensional interpretations, as well as the varieties that Hintikka pointed out. (With the beliefs of dogs presumably extensional?)

Thus the moral of this story is that not all intensional verbs have the same substitution conditions, and that not all of the substitution conditions fit into the extensional-intensional dichotomy. Not because there is *L*-equivalence 'in between', since this notion does not seem to enter into the substitution conditions of any of the families of verbs; but because in the case of some verbs we require something even more narrowly conceived and more syntax-dependent than Fregean propositions.

It should be mentioned here also that Partee's examples involving quotations show once again that what needs to be preserved is on the one hand not just verbal form, on the other hand not just content either, but some sort of a combination of both. In this area we are still in need of more precise characterizations.

7. THE RELATION BETWEEN THE SYNTAX AND SEMANTICS OF BELIEF-SENTENCES

The consideration of belief-sentences and other sentences with intensional constructions is very important for the assessment of the relation between syntactic structure and semantics. Given the general, formal, constraints on transformational grammar – the only grammar that has promised so far to be at least on the right track towards being adequate for the various aspects of natural languages – its rules must operate on sentences in 'molecular' fashion. That is to say, the analysis is piecemeal, with the final product simply the function of its parts (categorial). In the case of multiply embedded sentences the transformations apply cyclically and in order for them to function as filtering elements, it is essential that the analysis should start with the innermost embedded sentence and then work 'inside out'. In an attempt to achieve one-to-one correspondence between the syntactic and the semantic components, the semantic theories of the linguists (Katz, Fodor, and Lakoff, as well as the so-called componential analysis), also operate on the molecular model. In this respect

they are fundamentally different from the formal semantics of the
philosophers, and consequently cannot deal with some of the phenomena
that the philosophers are able to analyze. For the semantics of Frege,
Russell, etc., is with regard to certain phenomena *contextual*. That is to
say, an unambiguous expression that receives a certain semantic analysis
when taken by itself becomes ambiguous when placed in certain contexts.
The clearest example for this is the analysis of contexts involving logical
modalities or intensional verbs. Thus in these cases, in sharp contrast to
the syntactic analysis, the semantic analysis works 'outside in'; i.e., we
start with the outermost sentence and consider its semantics, and interpret
the semantics of the embedded sentence in light of this, previously given
information. This fact has not been noticed by linguists, and this helps to
explain the 'fallacy' that Hintikka (this volume, p. 205) discovered in the
works of both Partee and Lakoff. For both of these linguists have – in some
of their works – interpreted certain singular sentences that become ambiguous when placed in a belief-context as ambiguous when considered in
isolation. In his criticism Hintikka says rightly: ". . . from the fact that an
expression exhibits an ambiguity when embedded in a certain kind of context it does not follow that it is ambiguous when considered alone." I tried
to show that this is not simply a matter of an accidental fallacy, but that it
involves the essential contextualism of an adequate semantics, it involves
the fact that none of the semantic models of the linguists are sufficiently
contextual, and most importantly it involves the fact that the insight to be
gained here can be used to see why syntactic deep structure cannot be
identical with logical form, and the syntactic analysis does not correspond
to the semantic one. This last theoretical point is not in any way inconsistent with Partee's work, but it does clash with Lakoff's work and the
associated notion of 'generative semantics'. From the point of view of
generative semantics, it is essential to be able to give two different deep
structures for the two readings of a belief-sentence (the extensional and the
intensional), but it is not at all clear how one could give two different derivations unless one could also give two different derivations for the embedded
sentence. But we have seen already that the embedded sentence is not
semantically ambiguous and cannot be regarded as having two different
derivations. Thus, it seems, generative semantics cannot deal adequately
with the facts involving the semantics and syntax of belief-sentences.

8. SOME CONCLUSIONS

Having placed some of the results of Partee and Hintikka in what seems to me the proper conceptual context, let me attempt to draw conclusions that seem to follow from their interesting results.

For the philosophers, the following lessons are to be learned. First, the questions surrounding the issues of the object of belief and the questions of substitution – which are really questions about the individuation of belief – need to be related to each other and to be tied together conceptually much closer than these have been in the philosophical literature. A modest beginning toward this goal was attempted in my comments.

Secondly, the choices with regard to substitution are not simply those mentioned in the standard theory. Hintikka's work already showed that greater sensitivity to these issues is needed, and Partee's work showed how 'quasi-quotative' criteria of substitution need to be invoked in some cases.

Finally, we should note that not all types of intensional verbs carry with them the same substitutivity conditions. The differences also provide us with a basis for further insights into the semantics of different kinds of verbs.

For linguists the following lessons can be drawn. First, that there is the deep difference of contextualism between the more adequate philosophical semantic theories and the theories of the linguists such as Katz, Fodor, and Lakoff.

Secondly, that the study of belief-sentences and other sentences involving intensional verbs provides a basis for seeing some of the fundamental differences between syntactic and semantic structure.

Finally, the differences between families of verbs with respect to substitutivity requirements should spur the linguists to look for various syntactic criteria that might correlate with these semantic differences.

Stanford University

NOTES

[1] The following remarks were stimulated partly by suggestions from Mr. Fred Goldstein.
[2] This is also argued in Moravcsik (1969).
[3] This is also brought out with regard to singular terms in Kaplan (1969).

PATRICK SUPPES

SEMANTICS OF CONTEXT-FREE FRAGMENTS OF NATURAL LANGUAGES*

1. INTRODUCTION

The search for a rigorous and explicit semantics of any significant portion of a natural language is now intensive and far-flung – far-flung in the sense that wide varieties of approaches are being taken. Yet almost everyone agrees that at the present time the semantics of natural languages are less satisfactorily formulated than the grammars, even though a complete grammar for any significant fragment of natural language is yet to be written.

A line of thought especially popular in the last couple of years is that the semantics of a natural language can be reduced to the semantics of first-order logic. One way of fitting this scheme into the general approach of generative grammars is to think of the deep structure as being essentially identical with the structure of first-order logic. The central difficulty with this approach is that now as before how the semantics of the surface grammar is to be formulated is still unclear. In other words, how can explicit formal relations be established between first-order logic and the structure of natural languages? Without the outlines of a formal theory, this line of approach has moved no further than the classical stance of introductory teaching in logic, which for many years has concentrated on the translation of English sentences into first-order logical notation. The method of translation, of course, is left at an intuitive and ill-defined level.

The strength of the first-order logic approach is that it represents essentially the only semantical theory with any systematic or deep development, namely, model-theoretic semantics as developed in mathematical logic since the early 1930's, especially since the appearance of Tarski (1935). The semantical approaches developed by linguists or others whose viewpoint is that of generative grammar have been lacking in the formal precision and depth of model-theoretic semantics. Indeed, some of the most important and significant results in the foundations of mathematics belong to the general theory of models. I shall not attempt to review the approaches to semantics that start from a generative-grammar viewpoint, but I have in mind the work of Fodor, Katz, Lakoff, McCawley and others.

My objective is to combine the viewpoint of model-theoretic semantics and generative grammar, to define semantics for context-free languages and to apply the results to some fragments of natural language. The ideas contained in this paper were developed while I was working with Hélène Bestougeff on the semantical theory of question-answering systems. Later I came across some earlier similar work by Knuth (1968). My developments are rather different from those of Knuth, especially because my objective is to provide tools for the analysis of fragments of natural languages, whereas Knuth was concerned with programming languages.

Although on the surface the viewpoint seems different, I also benefited from a study of Montague's interesting and important work (1970a) on the analysis of English as a formal language. My purely extensional line of attack is simpler than Montague's. I adopted it for reasons of expediency, not correctness. I wanted an apparatus that could be applied in a fairly direct way to empirical analysis of a corpus. As in my work on probabilistic grammars (Suppes, 1970), I began with the speech of a young child, but without doubt, many of the semantical problems that are the center of Montague's concern must be dealt with in analyzing slightly more complex speech. Indeed, some of these problems already arise in the corpus studied here. As in the case of my earlier work on probabilistic grammars, I have found a full-scale analytic attack on a corpus of speech a humbling and bedeviling experience. The results reported here hopefully chart one possible course; in no sense are they more than preliminary.

This paper is organized in the following fashion. In Section 2, I describe a simple artificial example to illustrate how a semantic valuation function is added to the generative mechanisms of a context-free grammar. The relevant formal definitions are given in Section 3. The reader who wants a quick survey of what can be done with the methods, but who is not really interested in formal matters, may skip ahead to Section 4, which contains the detailed empirical results. On the other hand, it will probably be somewhat difficult to comprehend fully the machinery used in the empirical analysis without some perusal of Section 3, unless the reader is already quite familiar with model-theoretic semantics. How the results of this paper and the earlier one on probabilistic grammars are meant to form the beginnings of a theory of performance is sketched in Section 5.

2. A SIMPLE EXAMPLE

To illustrate the semantic methods described formally below, I use as an example the same simple language I used in Suppes (1970). As remarked there, this example is not meant to be complex enough to fit any actual corpus; its context-free grammar can easily be rewritten as a regular grammar. The five syntactic categories are IV, TV, Adj, PN and N, where IV is the class of intransitive verbs, TV the class of transitive verbs or two-place predicates, Adj the class of adjectives, PN the class of proper nouns and N the class of common nouns. Additional nonterminal vocabulary consists of the symbols S, NP, VP and AdjP. The set P of production rules consists of the following seven rules, plus the rewrite rules for terminal vocabulary belonging to one of the five categories.

Production Rule	Semantic Function
1. $S \rightarrow NP + VP$	Truth-function
2. $VP \rightarrow IV$	Identity
3. $VP \rightarrow TV + NP$	Image under the converse relation
4. $NP \rightarrow PN$	Identity
5. $NP \rightarrow AdjP + N$	Intersection
6. $AdjP \rightarrow AdjP + Adj$	Intersection
7. $AdjP \rightarrow Adj$	Identity

If Adj^n is understood to denote a string of n adjectives, then the possible grammatical types (infinite in number) all fall under one of the following schemes.

Grammatical Type
1. $PN + IV$
2. $PN + TV + PN$
3. $Adj^n + N + IV$
4. $PN + TV + Adj^n + N$
5. $Adj^n + N + TV + PN$
6. $Adj^m + N + TV + Adj^n + N$

What needs explaining are the semantic functions to the right of each production rule. For this purpose it is desirable to look at an example of a sentence generated by this grammar. The intuitive idea is that we define a valuation function v over the terminal vocabulary, and as is standard in model-theoretic semantics, v takes values in some relational structure.

Suppose a speaker wants to say 'John hit Mary'. The valuation function needs to be defined for the three terminal words 'John', 'hit' and 'Mary'. We then recursively define the denotation of each labeled node of the derivation tree of the sentence. In this example, I number the nodes, so that the denotation function ψ is defined for pairs (n, α), where n is a node of the tree and α is a word in the vocabulary. The tree looks like this.

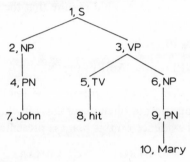

Let I be the identity function, $\check{A}$ the converse of A, i.e.,

$$\check{A} = \{\langle x, y \rangle : \langle y, x \rangle \in A\},$$

and $f''A$ the image of A under f, i.e., the range of f restricted to the domain A, and let T be truth and F falsity. Then the denotation of each labeled node of the tree is found by working from the bottom up:[1]

$$\psi(10, \text{Mary}) = v(\text{Mary})$$
$$\psi(9, \text{PN}) = I(v(\text{Mary}))$$
$$\psi(8, \text{hit}) = v(\text{hit})$$
$$\psi(7, \text{John}) = v(\text{John})$$
$$\psi(6, \text{NP}) = I(v(\text{Mary}))$$
$$\psi(5, \text{TV}) = I(v(\text{hit}))$$
$$\psi(4, \text{PN}) = I(v(\text{John}))$$
$$\psi(3, \text{VP}) = \overline{I(v(\text{hit}))}''Iv(\text{Mary})$$
$$\psi(2, \text{NP}) = II(v(\text{John}))$$
$$\psi(1, \text{S}) = f(\psi(2, \text{NP}), \psi(3, \text{VP})) = \begin{cases} T \text{ if } \psi(2, \text{NP}) \subseteq \psi(3, \text{VP}) \\ F \text{ otherwise.} \end{cases}$$

Clearly, the functions used above are just the semantic functions associated with the productions. In particular, the production rules for the direct descendants of nodes 2, 4, 5 and 6 all have the identity function as their semantic function.

One point should be emphasized. I do not claim that the set-theoretical semantic functions of actual speech are as simple as those associated with the production rules given in this section. Consider Rule 5, for instance. Intersection is fine for *old dictators*, but not for *alleged dictators*. One standard mathematical approach to this kind of difficulty is to generalize the semantic function to cover the meaning of both sorts of cases. In the present case of adjectives, we could require that the semantic function be one that maps sets of objects into sets of objects. In this vein, Rule 5 would now be represented by

$$\psi(n_1, \text{NP}) = \psi(n_2, \text{AdjP})''\psi(n_3, \text{N}).$$

Fortunately, generalizations that rule out the familiar simple functions as semantic functions do not often occur early in children's speech. Some tentative empirical evidence on this point is presented in Section 4.

3. DENOTING GRAMMARS

I turn now to formal developments. Some standard grammatical concepts are defined in the interest of completeness. First, if V is a set, V^* is the set of all finite sequences whose elements are members of V. I shall often refer to these finite sequences as *strings*. The empty sequence, 0, is in V^*; we define $V^+ = V^* - \{0\}$. A structure $G = \langle V, V_N, P, S \rangle$ is a *phrase-structure grammar* if and only if V and P are finite, nonempty sets, V_N is a subset of V, S is in V_N and $P \subseteq V_N^* \times V^+$. Following the usual terminology, V_N is the nonterminal vocabulary and $V_T = V - V_N$ the terminal vocabulary. S is the start symbol or the single axiom from which we derive strings or words in the language generated by G. The set P is the set of production or rewrite rules. If $\langle \alpha, \beta \rangle \in P$, we write $\alpha \to \beta$, which we read: from α we may produce or derive β (immediately).

A phrase-structure grammar $G = \langle V, V_N, P, S \rangle$ is *context-free* if and only if $P \subseteq V_N \times V^+$, i.e., if $\alpha \to \beta$ is in P then $\alpha \in V_N$ and $\beta \in V^+$.[2] These ideas may be illustrated by considering the simple language of the previous section. Although it is intended that N, PN, Adj, IV, and TV be nonterminals in any application, we can treat them as terminals for purposes of illustration, for they do not occur on the left of any of the seven production rules. With this understanding

$$V_N = \{S, NP, VP, \ AdjP\}$$
$$V_T = \{N, PN, Adj, IV, TV\}$$

and P is defined by the production rules already given. It is obvious from looking at the production rules that the grammar is context-free, for only elements of V_N appear on the left-hand side of any of the seven production rules.

The standard definition of derivations is as follows. Let $G = \langle V, V_N, P, S \rangle$ be a phrase-structure grammar. First, if $\alpha \to \beta$ is a production of P, and γ and δ are strings in V^*, then $\gamma\alpha\delta \underset{G}{\Rightarrow} \gamma\beta\delta$. We say that β is *derivable* from α in G, in symbols, $\alpha \underset{G}{\overset{*}{\Rightarrow}} \beta$ if there are strings $\alpha_1, \ldots, \alpha_n$ in V^* such that $\alpha = \alpha_1, \ \alpha_1 \underset{G}{\Rightarrow} \alpha_2, \ldots, \ \alpha_{n-1} \underset{G}{\Rightarrow} \alpha_n = \beta$. The sequence $\Delta = \langle \alpha_1, \ldots, \alpha_n \rangle$ is a *derivation* in G. The language $L(G)$ generated by G is $\{\alpha : \alpha \in V_T^* \ \& \ S \underset{G}{\overset{*}{\Rightarrow}} \alpha\}$. In other words, $L(G)$ is the set of all strings made up of terminal vocabulary and derived from S.

The semantic concepts developed also require use of the concept of a derivation tree of a grammar. The relevant notions are set forth in a series of definitions. Certain familiar set-theoretical notions about relations are also needed. To begin with, a *binary structure* is an ordered pair $\langle T, R \rangle$ such that T is a nonempty set and R is a binary relation on T, i.e., $R \subseteq T \times T$. R is a *partial ordering* of T if and only if R is reflexive, antisymmetric and transitive on T. R is a *strict simple ordering* of T if and only if R is asymmetric, transitive and connected on T. We also need the concept of R-immediate predecessor. For x and y in T, xJy if and only if xRy, not yRx and for every z if $z \neq y$ and zRy then zRx. In the language of formal grammars, we say that if xJy then x *directly dominates* y, or y is the *direct descendant* of x.

Using these notions, we define in succession *tree*, *ordered tree* and *labeled ordered tree*. A binary structure $\langle T, R \rangle$ is a *tree* if and only if (i) T is finite, (ii) R is a partial ordering of T, (iii) there is an R-first element of T, i.e., there is an x such that for every y, xRy, and (iv) if xJz and yJz then $x = y$. If xRy in a tree, we say that y is a *descendant* of x. Also the R-first element of a tree is called the *root* of the tree, and an element of T that has no descendants is called a *leaf*. We call any element of T a *node*, and we shall sometimes refer to leaves as *terminal nodes*.

A ternary structure $\langle T, R, L \rangle$ is an *ordered tree* if and only if (i) L is a binary relation on T, (ii) $\langle T, R \rangle$ is a tree, (iii) for each x in T, L is a strict simple ordering of $\{y : xJy\}$, (iv) if xLy and yRz then xLz, and (v) if xLy and xRz then zLy. It is customary to read xLy as 'x is to the *left* of y'. Having this ordering is fundamental to generating terminal strings and not just sets of terminal words. The *terminal string* of an ordered labeled tree is just the sequence of labels $\langle f(x_1), \ldots, f(x_n) \rangle$ of the leaves of the tree as ordered by L. Formally, a quinary structure $\langle T, V, R, L, f \rangle$ is a *labeled ordered tree* if and only if (i) V is a nonempty set, (ii) $\langle T, R, L \rangle$ is an ordered tree, and (iii) f is a function from T into V. The function f is the labeling function and $f(x)$ is the *label* of node x.

The definition of a derivation tree is relative to a given context-free grammar.

DEFINITION 1. *Let $G = \langle V, V_N, P, S \rangle$ be a context-free grammar and let $\mathcal{T} = \langle T, V, R, L, f \rangle$ be a labeled ordered tree. $\mathcal{T}$ is a derivation tree of G if and only if*

(i)   *If x is the root of $\mathcal{T}$, $f(x) = S$;*
(ii)   *If xRy and $x \neq y$ then $f(x)$ is in V_N;*
(iii)   *If $y_1, \ldots, y_n$ are all the direct descendants of x, i.e.,*

$$\bigcup_{i=1}^{n} \{y_i\} = \{y : xJy\} \neq \emptyset, \text{ and } y_i L y_j \text{ if } i < j,$$

then $\langle f(x), \langle f(y_1), \ldots, f(y_n) \rangle \rangle$

is a production in P.

We now turn to semantics proper by introducing the set Φ of set-theoretical functions. We shall let the domains of these functions be n-tuples of any sets (with some appropriate restriction understood to avoid set-theoretical paradoxes).

DEFINITION 2. *Let $\langle V, V_N, P, S \rangle$ be a context-free grammar. Let Φ be a function defined on P which assigns to each production p in P a finite, possibly empty set of set-theoretical functions subject to the restriction that if the right member of production p has n terms of V, then any function* *of* $\Phi(p)$ *has n arguments. Then* $G = \langle V, V_N, P, S, \Phi \rangle$ *is a* potentially denoting context-free grammar. *If for each p in* $P, \Phi(p)$ *has exactly one member then G is said to be* simple.

The simplicity and abstractness of the definition may be misleading. In the case of a formal language, e.g., a context-free programming language, the creators of the language specify the semantics by defining Φ. Matters are more complicated in applying the same idea of capturing the semantics by such a function for fragments of a natural language. Perhaps the most difficult problem is that of giving a straightforward set-theoretical interpretation of intensional contexts, especially to those generated by the expression of propositional attitudes of believing, wanting, seeking and so forth. I shall not attempt to deal with these matters in the present paper.

How the set-theoretical functions in $\Phi(p)$ work was illustrated in the preceding section; some empirical examples follow in the next section. The problems of identifying and verifying Φ even in the simplest sort of context are discussed there. In one sense the definition should be strengthened to permit only one function in $\Phi(p)$ of a given number of arguments. The intuitive idea behind the restriction is clear. In a given application we try first to assign denotations at the individual word level, and we proceed to two- and three-word phrases only when necessary. The concept of such hierarchical parsing is familiar in computer programming, and a detailed example in the context of a question-answering program is worked out in a joint paper with Hélène Bestougeff. However, as the examples in the next section show, this restriction seems to be too severe for natural languages.

A clear separation of the generality of Φ and an evaluation function v is intended. The functions in Φ should be constant over many different uses of a word, phrase or statement. The valuation v, on the other hand, can change sharply from one occasion of use to the next. To provide for any finite composition of functions, or other ascensions in the natural hierarchy of sets and functions built up from a domain of individuals, the family $\mathcal{H}'(D)$ of sets with closure properties stronger than needed in any particular application is defined. The abstract objects T (for truth) and F (for falsity) are excluded as elements of $\mathcal{H}'(D)$. In this definition $\mathcal{P}A$ is the power set of A, i.e., the set of all subsets of A.

DEFINITION 3. *Let D be a nonempty set. Then $\mathcal{H}'(D)$ is the smallest family of sets such that*

(i) $D \in \mathcal{H}'(D)$,
(ii)   *if* $A, B \in \mathcal{H}'(D)$ *then* $A \cup B \in \mathcal{H}'(D)$,
(iii)   *if* $A \in \mathcal{H}'(D)$ *then* $\mathcal{P}A \in \mathcal{H}'(D)$,
(iv)   *if* $A \in \mathcal{H}'(D)$ *and* $B \subseteq A$ *then* $B \in \mathcal{H}'(D)$.

We define $\mathcal{H}(D) = \mathcal{H}'(D) \cup \{T, F\}$, *with* $T \notin \mathcal{H}'(D)$, $F \notin \mathcal{H}'(D)$ *and* $T \neq F$.

A model structure for G is defined just for terminal words and phrases. The meaning or denotation of nonterminal symbols changes from one derivation or derivation tree to another.

DEFINITION 4. *Let D be a nonempty set, let* $G = \langle V, V_N, P, S \rangle$ *be a phrase-structure grammar, and let v be a partial function on* V_T^+ *to* $\mathcal{H}(D)$ *such that if v is defined for* α *in* V_T^+ *and if* γ *is a subsequence of* α, *then v is not defined for* γ. *Then* $\mathcal{D} = \langle D, v \rangle$ *is a* model structure *for G. If the domain of v is exactly* V_T, *then* $\mathcal{D}$ *is* simple.

We also refer to v as a *valuation function* for G.

I now define semantic trees that assign denotations to nonterminal symbols in a derivation tree. The definition is for simple potentially denoting grammars and for simple model structures. In other words, there is a unique semantic function for each production, and the valuation function is defined just on V_T, and not on phrases of V_T^+.

DEFINITION 5. *Let* $G = \langle V, V_N, P, S, \Phi \rangle$ *be a simple, potentially denoting context-free grammar, let* $\mathcal{D} = \langle D, v \rangle$ *be a simple model structure for G, let* $\mathcal{T}' = \langle T, V, R, L, f \rangle$ *be a derivation tree of* $\langle V, V_N, P, S \rangle$ *such that if x is a terminal node then* $f(x) \in V_T$ *and let* ψ *be a function from f to* $\mathcal{H}(D)$ *such that*

(i)   *if* $\langle x, f(x) \rangle \in f$ *and* $f(x) \in V_T$ *then* $\psi(x, f(x)) = v(f(x))$,
(ii)   *if* $\langle x, f(x) \rangle \in f$, $f(x) \in V_N$, *and* $y_1, \ldots, y_n$ *are all the direct descendants of x with* $y_i L y_j$ *if* $i < j$, *then* $\psi(x, f(x)) = \varphi(\psi(y_1, f(y_1)))$, $\ldots, \psi(y_n, f(y_n))$, *where* $\varphi = \Phi(p)$ *and p is the production* $\langle f(x), \langle f(y_1), \ldots, f(y_n) \rangle \rangle$.
        Then $\mathcal{T} = \langle T, V, R, L, f, \psi \rangle$ *is a* simple semantic tree *of G and* $\mathcal{D}$.

The extension of Definition 5 to semantic trees that are not simple is relatively straightforward, but is not given explicitly here in the interest of restricting the formal parts of the paper. The empirical examples considered in the next section implicitly assume this extension, but the simplicity of the corpus makes the several set-theoretical functions φ attached to a given production easy to interpret.

The function ψ assigns a denotation to each node of a semantic tree. The resulting structural analysis can be used to define a concept of meaning or sense for each node. Perhaps the most natural intuitive idea is this. Extend the concept of a model structure by introducing a set of *situations*. For each situation σ, $\langle D_\sigma, v_\sigma \rangle$ is a model structure. The meaning or sense of an utterance is then the function ψ of the root of the tree of the utterance. For example, using the analysis of *John hit Mary* from Section 3, dropping the redundant notation for the identity function and using the ordinary lambda notation for function abstraction, we obtain as the meaning of the sentence

$$\psi(1, S) = (\lambda \sigma) f(v_\sigma(John), \overline{v_\sigma(hit)}'' \, v_\sigma(Mary)),$$

but this idea will not be developed further here. Its affinity to Kripke-type semantics is clear.

4. NOUN-PHRASE SEMANTICS OF ADAM I

In Suppes (1970), I proposed and tested a probabilistic noun-phrase grammar for Adam I, a well-known corpus of the speech of a young boy (about 26 months old) collected by Roger Brown and his associates – and once again I wish to record my indebtedness to Roger Brown for generously making his transcribed records available for analysis. Eliminating immediate repetitions of utterances, we have a corpus of 6109 word occurrences with a vocabulary of 673 different words and 3497 utterances. Noun phrases dominate the corpus. Of the 3497 utterances, I have classified 936 as single occurrences of nouns, another 192 as occurrences of two nouns in sequence, 147 as adjective followed by noun, and 138 as adjectives alone. The context-free grammar for the noun phrases of Adam I has seven production rules, and the theoretical probability of using each rule in a derivation is also shown for purposes of later discussion. From a probabilistic standpoint, the grammar has five free parameters: the sum of the a_i's is one, so the a_i's contribute four parameters and $b_1 + b_2 = 1$, whence the b_i's contribute one more parameter. To the right are also shown the main set-theoretical functions that make the grammar potentially denoting. These semantic functions, as it is convenient to call them in the present context, are subsequently discussed extensively. I especially call attention to the semantic function for Rule 5, which is formally defined below.

Noun-phrase grammar for Adam I

Production rule	Probability	Semantic function
1. $NP \rightarrow N$	a_1	Identity
2. $NP \rightarrow AdjP$	a_2	Identity
3. $NP \rightarrow AdjP + N$	a_3	Intersection
4. $NP \rightarrow Pro$	a_4	Identity
5. $NP \rightarrow NP + NP$	a_5	Choice function
6. $AdjP \rightarrow AdjP + Adj$	b_1	Intersection
7. $AdjP \rightarrow Adj$	b_2	Identity

As I remarked in the earlier article, except for Rule 5, the production rules seem standard and an expected part of a noun-phrase grammar for standard English. The new symbol introduced in V_N beyond those introduced already in Section 2 is Pro for pronoun; inflection of pronouns is ignored. On the other hand, the special category, PN, for proper nouns is not used in the grammar of Adam I.

The basic grammatical data are shown in Table I. The first column gives the types of noun phrases actually occurring in the corpus in decreasing order of frequency. Some obvious abbreviations are used to shorten notation: A for Adj, P for Pro. The grammar defined generates an infinite number of types of utterances, but, of course, all except a small finite number have a small probability of being generated. The second column lists the numerical observed frequencies of the utterances (with immediate repetition of utterances deleted from the frequency count). The third column lists the theoretical or predicted frequencies when a maximum-likelihood estimate of the five parameters is made (for details on this see the earlier article). The impact of semantics on these theoretical frequencies is discussed later.

The fourth column lists the observed frequency with which the 'standard' semantic function shown above seems to provide the correct interpreta-

TABLE I

Probabilistic noun-phrase grammar for Adam I

Noun phrase	Observed frequency	Theoretical frequency	Stand. semantic function
N	1445	1555.6	1445
P	388	350.1	388
NN	231	113.7	154
AN	135	114.0	91
A	114	121.3	114
PN	31	25.6	
NA	19	8.9	
NNN	12	8.3	
AA	10	7.1	
NAN	8	8.3	
AP	6	2.0	
PPN	6	.4	
ANN	5	8.3	
AAN	4	6.6	
PA	4	2.0	
ANA	3	.7	
APN	3	.1	
AAA	2	.4	
APA	2	.0	
NPP	2	.4	
PAA	2	.1	
PAN	2	1.9	

tion for the five most frequent types. Of course, in the case of the identity function, there is not much to dispute, and so I concentrate entirely on the other two cases. First of all, if the derivation uses more than one rule, then by *standard interpretation* I mean the derivation that only uses Rule 5 if it is necessary and that interprets each production rule used in terms of its standard semantic function. Since none of the derivations is very complex, I shall not spend much time on this point.

The fundamental ideas of denoting grammars as defined in the preceding section come naturally into play when a detailed analysis is undertaken of the data summarized in Table I. The most important step is to identify the additional semantic functions if any in $\Phi(p)$ for each of the seven production rules. A simple way to look at this is to examine the various types of utterances listed in Table I, summarize the production rules and semantic functions used for each type, and then collect all of this evidence in a new summary table for the production rules.

Therefore I now discuss the types of noun phrases listed in Table I and consider in detail the data for the five most frequently listed.

Types N and P, the first two, need little comment. The identity function, and no other function, serves for them. It should be clearly understood, of course, that the nouns and pronouns listed in these first two lines – a total of 1833 without immediate repetition – do not occur as parts of a larger noun phrase. The derivation of N uses only P1 (Production Rule 1), and the derivation of P uses only P4.

The data on type NN are much richer and more complex. The derivation is unique; it uses P5 then P1 twice, as shown in the tree. As before, the semantic function for P1 is just the identity function, so all the analysis of type NN centers around the interpretation of P5. To begin with, I must

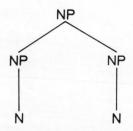

explain what I mean by the choice function shown above as the standard semantic function of P5. This is a set-theoretical function of A and B that for each A is a function selecting an element of B when B is the argument of f. Thus

$$\varphi(A, B) = f_A(B) \in B.$$

I used 'A' rather than an individual variable to make the notation general, but in all standard cases, A is a unit set. (I emphasize again, I do not distinguish unit sets from their members.) A standard set-theoretical choice function, i.e., a function f such that if B is in the domain of f and B is nonempty then $f(B) \in B$, is a natural device for expressing possession. Intuitively, each of the possessors named by Adam has such a function and the function selects his (or hers or its) object from the class of like objects. Thus *Daddy chair* denotes that chair in the class of chairs within Adam's purview that belongs to or is used especially by Daddy. If we restrict our possessors to individuals, then in terms of the model structure $\mathcal{D} = \langle D, v \rangle$, $\varphi(A, B)$ is just a partial function from $D \times \mathcal{P}(D)$ to $\mathcal{D}$, where $\mathcal{P}(D)$ is the power set of D.[3]

The complete classification of all noun phrases of type NN is given in Table II. (I emphasize that this classification must be regarded as tentative at this early stage of investigation.) As the data in Table II show, the choice function is justly labeled the standard semantic function for P5, but at least four other semantic functions belong in $\Phi(P5)$. One of these is the converse of $\varphi(A, B)$ as defined above, i.e.,

$$\breve{\varphi}(A, B) = f_B(A),$$

which means the possessor is named after the thing possessed. Here are examples from Adam I for which this interpretation seems correct: *part trailer* (meaning *part of trailer*), *part towtruck, book boy, name man, ladder firetruck, taperecorder Ursula*. The complete list is given in Table II.

The third semantic function is a choice function on the Cartesian product of two sets, often the sets' being unit sets as in the case of *Mommy Daddy*. Formally, we have

$$\varphi(A, B) = f(A \times B),$$

and $f(A \times B) \in A \times B$. Other examples are *Daddy Adam* and *pencil paper*. The frequency of use of this function is low, however – only 12 out of 230 instances according to the classification shown in Table II.

The fourth semantic function proposed for $\Phi(P5)$ is the intersection function,

$$\varphi(A, B) = A \cap B.$$

Examples are *lady elephant* and *lady Ursula*. Here the first noun is functioning like an adjective.

The fifth semantic function, following in frequency the choice function and its converse, is the identity function. It seems clear from the transcription that some pairs of nouns are used as a proper name or a simple description, even though each noun is used in other combinations. (By a *simple description* I mean a phrase such that no subsequence of it denotes (see Definition 4).) Some examples are *pin game* and *Daddy Cromer*.

TABLE II

Semantic classification of noun phrases of type NN[a]

Choice function

Adam checker	Adam horn
Adam hat	Adam hat
Adam bike	Adam pillow
Moocow tractor	Moocow truck
Catherine dinner	Car mosquito
Newmi book	Newmi bulldozer
Daddy briefcase	Adam book
Adam book	Adam paper
Daddy chair	Daddy tea
Mommy tea	Tuffy boat
Tuffy boat	Adam pencil
Adam tractor	Tuffy boat
Judy buzz	Judy buzz
Ursula pocketbook	Ursula pocket
Daddy name	Daddy name
Daddy Bozo	Daddy Johnbuzzhart
Daddy name	Adam light
Catherine Bozo	Monroe suitcase
Adam glove	Adam ball
Adam locomotive	Daddy racket
Daddy racket	Adam racket
Adam pencil	Joshua shirt
Joshua foot	Adam busybulldozer
Robie nail	Adam busybulldozer
Train track	Adam Daddy
Daddy suitcase	Cromer suitcase
Adam suitcase	Daddy suitcase
Adam doggie	Adam doggie
Choochoo track	Daddy Adam
Adam water	Ursula water
Ursula car	Adam house
Hobo truck	Doctordan circus
Doctordan circus	Joshua book
Daddy paper	Adam Cromer
Cromer coat	Adam pencil
Adam pillow	Mommy pillow
Adam pillow	Daddy pillow
Dan circus	Doctordan circus
Adam ladder	Adam mouth
Adam mouth	Daddy desk
Doctordan circus	Adam sky
Adam horn	Adam baby

Table II (Continued)

Adam piece	Adam candy
Adam playtoy	Kitchen playtoy
Doggie car	Man Texacostar (?)
Adam book	Adam paper
Adam shirt	Adam pocketbook
Adam ball	Daddy suitcase
Cromer suitcase	Adam suitcase
Adam letter	Adam pencil
Adam firetruck	Adam firetruck
Bambi wagon	See Daddy car
Like Adam bookshelf	Give doggie paper
Pull Adam bike	Read Doctor circus
Write Daddy name	Write Daddy name
Hit Mommy wall	Hit Mommy rug
Hit Adam roadgrader (?)	See Adam ball
Spill Mommy face	Bite Mommy mouth
Bite Cromer mouth	Bite Ursula mouth
Hit Mommy ball	Take Adam car
Get Adam ball	Sit Adam chair
Write Cromer shoe	Sit Monroe car
Sit Missmonroe car	Walk Adam Bambi
Walk Adam Bambi	Going Cromer suitcase
Adam Panda march (?)	Doggies tummy hurt
Oh Adam belt	Yeah locomotive caboose
Adam bite rightthere (?)	Adam shoe rightthere
Fish water inhere	Take lion nose off
Put Adam bandaid on	Pick roadgrader dirt (?)
Put Missmonroe towtruck (?)	Put Adam boot
Mommy tea yeah	Adam pencil yeah
Adam school tomorrow	Becky star tonight
Daddy suitcase goget it	Adam pocket no
Take off Adam paper	Big towtruck pick Joshua dirt up
No Adam Bambi	Look Bambi Adam pencil
That Adam baby	Break Cromer suitcase Mommy
Powershovel pick Adam dirt up	Where record folder go

Converse of choice function

Part trailer	Part towtruck
Book boy	Name man
Ladder firetruck	Record Daddy
Part head	Part game
Foot Adam	Track train
Car train	Part broom
Taperecorder Ursula	Circus Dan
Speghetti Cromer	Part apple
Part basket	Piece candy

Table II (Continued)

Game Adam   Time bed (?)
Take piece candy   Paper kitty open
Excuseme Ursula part broom

Choice function on Cartesian product

Pencil paper   Paper pencil
Mommy Daddy   Towtruck fire
Mommy Daddy   Record taperecorder
Pencil roadgrader (?)   Jack Jill
Busybulldozer truck (?)   Give paper pencil
Jack Jill come   Adam wipeoff Cromer Ursula

Intersection

Lady elephant   Lady Ursula
Lady Ursula   Lady elephant
Toy train   Record box

Identity

Pin Game   Babar Pig
Daddy Cromer (?)   Mommy Cromer (?)
Doctor Doctordan

Unclassified

Joshua home   Pencil doggie
Train train (Repetition?)   Adam Adam (Repetition?)
Dog pepper   Kangaroo bear
Suitcase water   Doggie doggie (Repetition?)
Doggie pepper   Kangaroo marchingbear
Daddy home (S)   Ball playtoy (?)
Door book   Pumpkin tomato
Pumpkin tomato   Put truck window (2)
Chew apple mouth (2)   Hit towtruck knee (2)
Hit door head (2)   Make Cromer Doctordan (2)
Hit head trash (2)   Hurt knee chair (2)
Show Ursula Bambi (2)   Show Ursula Bambi (2)
Look car mosquito (2)   Daddy Daddy work (Repetition?)
Pick dirt shovel up (2)   Mommy time bed
Ohno put hand glove (2)   Time bed Mommy

---

[a] Whenever the type NN appeared in the context of a longer utterance, the entire utterance is printed.

Note: 230 utterances of type NN are shown instead of the 231 shown in Table I, because one of the 231 was incorrectly classified as NN.

I do not consider in the same detail the next two most frequent types shown in Table I, namely, AN and A. The latter, as in the case of N and P, is served without complications by the identity function. As would be expected, the picture is more complicated for the type AN. Column 4 of Table I indicates that 91 of the 135 instances of AN can be interpreted as using intersection as the semantic function. Typical examples are these: *big drum, big horn, my shadow, my paper, my tea, my comb, oldtime train, that knee, green rug, that man, poor doggie, pretty flower.* The main exceptions to the intersection rule are found in the use of numerical or comparative adjectives like *two* or *more.* Among the 116 AN phrases standing alone, i.e., not occurring as part of a longer utterance, 19 have *two* as the adjective; for example, *two checkers, two light, two sock, two men, two boot, two rug.* No numerical adjective other than *two* is used in the 116 phrases.

I terminate at this point the detailed analysis of the Adam I corpus, but some computations concerning the length of noun phrases in Adam I are considered in the next section.

5. TOWARDS A THEORY OF PERFORMANCE

The ideas developed in this paper and in my earlier paper on probabilistic grammars are meant to be steps toward a theory of performance. In discussing the kind of theories of language wanted by linguists, philosophers or psychologists, I have become increasingly aware of the real differences in the objectives of those who want a theory of ideal competence and those who are concerned with performance. Contrary to the opinions expressed by some linguists, I would not concede for a moment that a theory of competence must precede in time the development of a theory of performance. I do recognize, on the other hand, the clear differences of objectives in the two kinds of theories. The linguistic and philosophical tradition of considering elaborate and subtle examples of sentences that express propositional attitudes is very much in the spirit of a theory of competence. The subtlety of many of these examples is far beyond the bulk of sentences used in everyday discourse by everyday folk. The kind of corpus considered in the preceding section is a far cry from most of these subtle examples.

The probabilistic grammars discussed in the preceding section, and elaborated upon more thoroughly in the earlier paper, clearly belong to a theory of performance. Almost all of the linguists or philosophers interested in theories of competence would probably reject probabilistic grammars as being of any interest to such theories. On the other hand, from the standpoint of a theory of performance, such grammars immediately bring to hand a detailed analysis of actual speech as well as a number of predictions about central characteristics of actual speech that are not a part of a theory of competence. Perhaps the simplest and clearest example is predictions about the distribution of length of utterances. One of the most striking features of actual speech is that most utterances are of short duration, and no utterances are of length greater than 10^4 even though in the usual theories of competence there is no way of predicting the distribution of length of utterance and no mechanism for providing it. A probabilistic grammar immediately supplies such a mechanism, and I would take it to be a prime responsibility of a theory of performance to predict the distribution of utterances from the estimation of a few parameters.

Here, for example, are the theoretical predictions of utterance length in terms of the parameters a_i and b_j assigned to the production rules for Adam I noun phrases. In order to write a simple recursive expression for the probability of a noun phrase of length n, I use ℓ_i for the probability of an utterance of length $i < n$. Thus, for example, one of the terms in the expression for the probability of a noun phrase of length 3 is $2a_5\ell_1\ell_2$. By first using Rule 5 (with probability a_5) and then generating for one NP a noun phrase of length 1, which starting from NP has probability ℓ_1, and generating for the other NP a noun phrase of length 2 with probability ℓ_2, we obtain $2a_5\ell_1\ell_2$, since this can happen in two ways. We have in general the following:

Length of noun phrase	Probability of this length
1	$a_1 + a_2b_2 + a_4$
2	$a_2b_1b_2 + a_3b_2 + a_5(a_1 + a_2b_2 + a_4)^2$
3	$a_2b_1^2b_2 + a_3b_1b_2 + 2a_5\ell_1\ell_2$
$\vdots$	$\vdots$
n	$a_2b_1^{n-1}b_2 + a_3b_1^{n-2}b_2 + a_5\sum_{\substack{1 \le i,j < n \\ i+j=n}} \ell_i\ell_j$

Using the maximum-likelihood estimates of the parameters a_i and b_j obtained to make the theoretical predictions of Table I, we can compare theoretical and observed distributions of noun-phrase length for Adam I. The results are shown in Table III for lengths up to 3.

TABLE III

Prediction of length of noun phrases for
Adam I

Length	Observed frequency	Theoretical frequency
1	1947	2027.1
2	436	314.1
3	51	66.9
>3	0	25.9
	2434	2434.0

Because this paper is mainly concerned with semantics, I shall not pursue these grammatical matters further, but turn to the way in which the theory of semantics developed here is meant to contribute to a theory of performance. From a behavioral standpoint it is much easier to describe the objective methods used in constructing a probabilistic grammar, because the corpus of sentences and the classification of individual words into given syntactic categories can be objectively described and verified by any interested person. The application of the theory, in other words, has an objective character that is on the surface. Matters are different when we turn to semantics. For example, it does not seem possible to state directly objective criteria by which the classification of semantic functions as described in the preceding section are made. Clearly I have taken advantage of my own intuitive knowledge of the language in an inexplicit way to interpret Adam's intended meaning in using a particular utterance. If the methodology for applying semantics to actual speech had to be left at the level of analysis of the preceding section, objections could certainly be made that the promise of such a semantics for a theory of performance was very limited.

A first naive approach to applying semantics to the development of a more complete theory of performance might have as an objective the prediction of the actual sentences uttered by a speaker. Everyone to whom this proposal is made instantly recognizes the difficulty, if not the impossibility, of predicting the actual utterance made once the structure of the utterance goes beyond something like a simple affirmation or denial. Frequently the next step is to use this common recognition of difficulty as an argument for the practical impossibility of applying any concepts of probability in analyzing actual speech behavior. This skeptical attitude has been expressed recently by Chomsky (1969b, p. 57) in the following passage:

... If we return to the definition of 'language' as a "complex of dispositions to verbal behavior", we reach a similar conclusion, at least if this notion is intended to have empirical content. Presumably, a complex of dispositions is a structure that can be represented as a set of probabilities for utterances in certain definable 'circumstances' or 'situations'. But it must be recognized that the notion 'probability of a sentence' is an entirely useless one, under any known interpretation of this term. On empirical grounds, the probability of my producing some given sentence of English – say, this sentence, or the sentence "birds fly" or "Tuesday follows Monday", or whatever – is indistinguishable from the probability of my producing a given sentence of Japanese. Introduction of the notion of 'probability relative to a situation' changes nothing, at least if 'situations' are characterized on any known objective grounds (we can, of course, raise the conditional probability of any sentence as high as we like, say to unity, relative to 'situations' specified on *ad hoc*, invented grounds).

One can agree with much of what Chomsky says in this passage, but also recognize that it is written without familiarity with the way in which probability concepts are actually used in science. What is said here applies almost without change to the study of the simplest probabilistic phenomenon, e.g., the flipping of a coin. If we construct a probability space for a thousand flips of a coin, and if the coin is approximately a fair one, then the actual probability of any observed sequence is almost zero, namely, approximately 2^{-1000}. If we use a representation that is often used for theoretical purposes and take the number of trials to be infinite, then the probability of any possible outcome of the experiment in this theoretical representation is strictly zero. It in no sense follows that the concept of probability cannot be applied in a meaningful way to the flipping of a coin. A response may be that a single flip has a high probability and that this is not the case for a single utterance, but corresponding to utterances, we can talk about sequences of flips and once again we have extraordinarily low probabilities attached to any actual sequence of flips of length greater than, say, a hundred. What Chomsky does not seem to be aware of is that in most sophisticated applications of probability theory the situation is the same as what he has described for sentences. The basic objects of investigation have either extremely small probabilities or strictly zero probabilities. The test of the theory then depends upon studying various features of the observed outcome. In the case of the coin the single most interesting feature is the relative frequency of heads, but if we are suspicious of the mechanism being used to toss the coin we may also want to investigate the independence of trials.

To make the comparison still more explicit, Chomsky's remarks about the equal probability of uttering an English or Japanese sentence can be mimicked in discussing the outcomes of flipping a coin. The probability of a thousand successive heads in flipping a fair coin is 2^{-1000}, just the probability of any other sequence of this length. Does this equal probability mean that we should accept the same odds in betting that the relative frequency of heads will be less than 0.6, and betting that it will be greater than 0.99? Certainly not. In a similar way there are many probabilistic predictions about verbal behavior that can be made, ranging from trivial predictions about whether a given speaker will utter an English or Japanese sentence to detailed predictions about grammatical or semantic structure. Our inability to predict the unique flow of discourse no more invalidates a definition of language as a "complex of dispositions to verbal behavior" than our inability to predict the trajectory of a single free electron for some short period of time invalidates quantum mechanics – even in a short period of time any possible trajectory has strictly zero probability of being realized on the continuity assumptions ordinarily made.

Paradoxically, linguists like Chomsky resist so strongly the use of probability notions in language analysis just when these are the very concepts that are most suited to such complex phenomena. The systematic use of probability is to be justified in most applications in science because of our inability to develop an adequate deterministic theory.

In the applications of probability theory one of the most important techniques for testing a theory is to investigate the theoretical predictions for a variety of conditional probabilities. The concept of conditional probability and the related concept of independence are the central concepts of probability theory. It is my own belief that we shall be able to apply these concepts to show the usefulness of semantics at a surface behavioral level. Beginning with a probabilistic grammar, we want to improve the probabilistic predictions by taking into account the postulated semantic structure. The test of the correctness of the semantic structure is then in terms of the additional predictions we can make. By taking account of the semantic structure, we can make differential probabilistic predictions and thereby show the behavioral relevance of semantics. Without entering into the kind of detailed data analysis of the preceding section, let me try to indicate in more concrete fashion how such an application of semantics is to be made.

I have reported previously the analysis of the corpus of Adam I. We have also been collecting data of our own at Stanford, and we have at hand a corpus of some 20 hours of Erica, a rather talkative 30-month-old girl.[4] We have been concerned to write a probabilistic grammar for Erica of the same sort we have tried to develop for Adam I. The way in which a semantic structure can be used to improve the predictions of a probabilistic grammar can be illustrated by considering Erica's answers to the many questions asked her by adults. For the purposes of this sketch, let me concentrate on some of the data in the first hour of the Erica corpus. According to one straightforward classification, 169 questions were addressed to Erica by an adult during the first hour of the corpus. These 169 questions may be fairly directly classified in the following types: *what*-questions, *yes-no*-questions, *where*-questions, *who*-questions, etc. The frequency of each type of question is as follows:

What-questions	79
Yes-no-questions	60
Where-questions	12
Who-questions	9
Why-questions	4
How-many-questions	3
Or-questions	1
How-do-you-know-questions	1.

By taking account of the most obvious semantic features of these different types of questions, we can improve the probabilistic predictions of the kind of responses Erica makes without claiming that we can make an exact prediction of her actual utterances. Moreover, the semantic classification of the questions does not depend on any simple invariant features of the surface grammar. For example, some typical *yes-no*-questions, with Erica's answers in parentheses, are these: *Can you sit on your seat please?* *(O.K.)*, *You don't touch those, do you?* *(No)*, *Aren't they?* *(Uh huh. That Arlene's too)*, *He isn't old enough is he?* *(No. Just Martin's old enough.)*

It is an obvious point that the apparatus of model-theoretic semantics is not sufficient to predict the choice of a particular description of an object from among many semantically suitable ones. Suppose John and Mary are walking, and John notices a spider close to Mary's shoulder. He says, "Watch out for that spider." He does not say, "Watch out for the black, half-inch long spider that has a green dot in its center and is about six inches from your left shoulder at a vertical angle of about sixty degrees." The principle that selects the first utterance and not the second I call a *principle of minimal discrimination*. A description is selected that is just adequate to the perceptual or cognitive task. Sometimes, of course, a full sentence rather than a noun phrase is used in response to a *what*-question, the sort of question whose answer most naturally exemplifies a minimal principle. Here is an example from Erica: *What do you want for lunch?* *(Peanut butter and jelly)*, *What do you want to drink?* *(I want to drink peanut butter)*. In answering *what*-questions by naming or describing an object, Erica uses adjectives only sparingly, and then mainly in a highly relevant way. Here are a couple of examples: *What are you going to ride on?* *(On a big towel)*, *What are those?* *(Oboe and clarinet. And a flute. Little bitty flute called a piccolo.)*. Preliminary analysis of the Erica corpus indicates that even a relatively crude probabilistic application of the principle of minimal discrimination can significantly improve predictions about Erica's answers. Presentation of systematic data on this point must be left for another occasion.

I want to finish by stressing that I do not have the kind of imperialistic ambitions for a theory of performance that many linguists seem to have for a theory of competence. I do not think a theory of performance need precede a theory of competence. I wish only to claim that the two can proceed independently – they have sufficiently different objectives and different methods of analysis so that their independence, I would venture to suggest, will become increasingly apparent. A probabilistic account of main features of actual speech is a different thing from a theory-of-competence analysis of the kind of subtle examples found in the literature on propositional attitudes. The investigation of these complicated examples certainly should not cease, but at the present time they have little relevance to the development of a theory of performance. The tools for the development of a theory of performance, applied within the standard scientific theory of probability processes, are already at hand in the concepts of a probabilistic grammar and semantics. Unfortunately, many linguists dismiss probabilistic notions out of hand and without serious familiarity with their use in any domain of science.

Quine ended a recent article (1970b) with a plea against absolutism in linguistic theory and methodology. It is a plea that we all should heed.

Stanford University

NOTES

* This research has been supported by the National Science Foundation under grant NSFGJ-443X. I am indebted to Pentti Kanerva for help in the computer analysis and organization of the data presented in Section 4, and I am indebted to Elizabeth Gammon for several useful ideas in connection with the analysis in Section 4. D. M. Gabbay and George Huff have made a number of penetrating comments on Section 3, and Richard Montague trenchantly criticized an unsatisfactory preliminary version.
[1] I have let the words of V serve as names of themselves to simplify the notation.
[2] As Richard Montague pointed out to me, to make context-free grammars a special case of phrase-structure grammars, as defined here, the first members of P should be not elements of V_N, but one-place sequences whose terms are elements of V_N. This same problem arises later in referring to elements of V^*, but treating elements of V as belonging to V^*. Consequently, to avoid notational complexities, I treat elements, their unit sets and one-place sequences whose terms are the elements, as identical.
[3] Other possibilities exist for the set-theoretical characterization of possession. In fact, there is an undesirable asymmetry between the choice function for *Adam hat* and the intersection function for *my hat*, but it is also clear that $v(my)$ can in a straightforward sense be the set of Adam's possessions but $v(Adam)$ is Adam, not the set of Adam's possessions.
[4] The corpus was taped and edited by Arlene Moskowitz.

DOV M. GABBAY

REPRESENTATION OF THE MONTAGUE SEMANTICS AS A FORM OF THE SUPPES SEMANTICS WITH APPLICATIONS TO THE PROBLEM OF THE INTRODUCTION OF THE PASSIVE VOICE, THE TENSES, AND NEGATION AS TRANSFORMATIONS*

1. OUR PURPOSE

In this paper we shall represent the Montague (this vol., pp. 221–42) semantics as a homomorphic image of the Suppes (this vol., pp. 370–94) semantics. For this purpose we shall construct a Suppes-type syntax and semantics SMG that will essentially enlarge the Montague semantics M and that will contain passives and allow deletion. SMG will also have the advantage of correlating with each sentence a semantical object that can be taken to be its meaning. This is not possible in M as the semantical object associated with sentences is only a truth function.

Towards the construction of SMG we shall present two intermediate systems SG and G, which will serve to illustrate our ideas. In fact the main part of the work will be concerned with SG and G, as they incorporate all the typical problems. M was constructed with such elegance that it is not easy to see which of its features are conceptually essential and which are technical options. The presentation of SG and G will follow the lines traditionally used in modal logics and will be concerned mainly with conceptual features. We shall indicate what kind of technical changes would lead to Montague's formulation. Thus the reader could gain insight into M (see Partee, this vol., pp. 243–58 concerning M grammar).

Before we introduce SG and G let us remark that although the grammar of M is not context free (because of problems of agreement, for example), the semantics is not affected by this fact. One can give a context-free grammar suitable for the semantics and then add the necessary modifying transformations without affecting the semantics. Our own grammars shall therefore be context free. The reader interested in the semantics may wish to go to Section 4.

Hintikka et al. (eds.), Approaches to Natural Language, 395–409. All rights reserved.
Copyright © 1973 by D. Reidel Publishing Company, Dordrecht-Holland.

2. SYNTAX OF SG AND G

SG contains essentially all the categories of M. For semantical reasons that will be evident later, we split some categories into several categories. We do not bother with agreement as the rules of SG are context free.

SG has only one tense – the present – and contains no negation. We shall discuss later how one can add negation and the tenses to the system. We shall argue that these are *not* transformations.

In order to incorporate the passive as transformation in SG, we enlarge SG to a system G by adding more categories.

We shall then indicate how the tenses and negation can be added as categories.

The basic categories of SG are the following.

$$
\begin{aligned}
\text{IV} \quad &= \{\text{run, walk, talk, rise, change}\} \\
\text{T}_1 \quad &= \{\text{John, Mary, ninety}\} \\
\text{T}_2 \quad &= \{\text{he}_0, \text{he}_1, \text{he}_2, \ldots\} \\
\text{TV}_1 \quad &= \{\text{find, hit, lose, eat, love, date, seek, conceive}\} \\
\text{Adv} \quad &= \{\text{rapidly, slowly, voluntarily, allegedly}\} \\
\text{CN}_1 \quad &= \{\text{man, woman, price, fish, park, unicorn, temperature}\} \\
\text{SC}_1 \quad &= \{\text{necessarily}\} \\
\text{SC}_2 \quad &= \{\text{believe that, assert that, deny that}\} \\
\text{OA} \quad &= \{\text{try to, wish to}\} \\
\text{Prep} \quad &= \{\text{in, about}\} \\
\text{Con}_1 \quad &= \{\text{and}\} \\
\text{Con}_2 \quad &= \{\text{or}\} \\
\text{Q}_1 \quad &= \{\text{every}\} \\
\text{Q}_2 \quad &= \{\text{some (or equivalently a)}\} \\
\text{Q}_3 \quad &= \{\text{the}\}
\end{aligned}
$$

The derived categories shall be denoted by IV^*, S^*, T_1^*, etc. There will be more derived categories than the basic ones. The rules are given below and the numberings show to what rule of Montague's paper they correspond. The rules are written as derivation rules of a context-free grammar but they should be understood as an inductive definition of the elements of the derived categories. For example: $X^* \rightarrow Y^* + Z^*$ means that if $a \in Y^*$ and $b \in Z^*$ then (ab) is in X^*; e.g., $\text{hit} \in \text{TV}^*$ and $\text{Mary} \in \text{T}^*$, and so hit Mary $\in \text{IV}^*$.

S1 : $A^* \to A$ for any basic category.

S2: $T_3^* \to Q_i^* + CN_i^*$, $i = 1, 2, 3$

    (T_3^* is a new derived category.)

S4: (a) $S^* \to T_1^* + IV^*$

    (b) $S^* \to T_2^* + IV^*$

    (c) $S^* \to T_3^* + IV^*$

S5: (a) $IV^* \to TV_1^* + T_1^*$

    (b) $IV^* \to TV_1^* + T_2^*$

    (c) $IV^* \to TV_1^* + T_3^*$

S6: (a) $Adv^* \to Prep^* + T_1^*$

    (b) $Adv^* \to Prep^* + T_2^*$

       (We do not allow T_3^* here in order to keep our semantic functions simple, but this can be done.)

S7: $IV^* \to SC_2 + S*$

S8: $IV^* \to OA^* + IV^*$

S9: $S^* \to SC_1^* + S^*$

S10: $IV^* \to IV^* + Adv^*$

S11: $S^* \to S^* + Con_i^* + S^*$, $i = 1, 2$

S12: $IV^* \to IV^* + Con_i^* + IV^*$, $i = 1, 2$

S13: (a) $T_i^* \to T_i^* + Con_2^* + T_i^*$, $i = 1, 2$

     (b) $T_3^* \to T_3^* + Con_2^* + T_3^*$

The system G has the following additional categories and rules which allow us to have the passive voice.

S30: (a) $VI^* \to T_1^* + TV_1^*$

     (b) $VI^* \to T_2^* + TV_1^*$

     (c) $VI^* \to T_3^* + TV_1^*$

S31: $VI^* \to VI^* + Adv^*$

S32: $VI^* \to S^* + SC_2^*$

S33: (a) $S^* \to VI^* + T_1^*$

     (b) $S^* \to VI^* + T_2^*$

     (c) $S^* \to VI^* + T_3^*$

Let us now give some examples and remarks:

(a) T_2 is a category of variables. It allows us to form, e.g., Mary hit he$_0$ (i.e., Mary hit herself).

(b) The category VI^* of S30 and S31 will enable us to deal with passive sentences. We need this category for the following reason. In SG we can form 'hit Mary'. The passive of this is 'Mary is hit', but this is an element of VI*. Rule S31 takes care of cases like 'Mary is hit rapidly'. We do not employ the word 'by' (Mary is hit by———) because we want to keep our grammar context free. So we form 'Mary is hit John' and then use a transformation to put the 'by' in. Otherwise S31 would not be sufficient since we have to go from 'Mary is hit by' to 'Mary is hit rapidly by'.

We shall have other means of dealing with the passive, using a suggestion of Partee.

3. THE PROBLEM OF INTRODUCING THE PASSIVE, THE TENSES AND NEGATION AS TRANSFORMATIONS

We first need some preliminary remarks.

In SG there is essentially no ambiguity while in G ambiguity exists. This is a necessary concession that we have to make, if we want to introduce the passive as a transformation. The ambiguity is, however, of the same kind that arises in natural language, and has, as we shall see, a very clear and intuitive semantical manifestation.

As for negation and the tenses, one cannot introduce them as transformations, which have the correct semantical meaning. We shall deal with this after we introduce some necessary basic definitions.

A derivation (or construction) tree of an element a of a category X^* is a finite labeled binary tree with 'a' labeling the top with the following properties (see Suppes, this volume, pp. 375–6 for the precise definitions; we expect the reader to have some idea of these matters):

(a) For any labeled subtree of the form

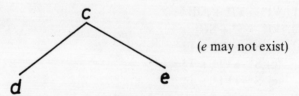

(e may not exist)

such that $c \in X^*$, $d \in Y^*$, and $e \in Z^*$ then $X^* \to Y^* + Z^*$ is one of our S rules and $c = de$.

(b) The bottom (terminal) nodes of the tree are labeled with elements of one of the basic categories.

Let us give some examples and remarks:

(i) The absence of ambiguity in SG means that every element of any category has a unique construction tree. (Of course, one can construct 'he runs quickly rapidly', which means the same as 'he runs quickly and rapidly' and 'he runs rapidly and quickly'. The *real* ambiguity occurs only in G.)

(ii) The sentence 'every man hits some man' is ambiguous in G. It has two construction trees.

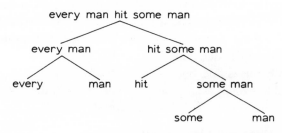

Fig. 1.

Semantically, as we shall see later, this construction tree gives the meaning: For all x there is a y; while the tree below gives the meaning: There is a y such that for all x

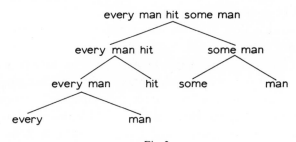

Fig. 2.

The reader will see later that sentences of the form 'John hit Mary' do not become ambiguous in G although they have two possible construction trees, because they do not contain quantifiers.

We are now ready to discuss the introduction of negation, tenses, and the passive as transformations. Of course, we want to introduce them as transformations that have a corresponding semantical meaning. In other words, if we transform a construction tree of a sentence to that of its passive or future form, then a corresponding transformation exists on the semantics that yields the *expected intuitive* semantics of the passive or future form of the sentence. This is possible only for the passive; it is not possible for the future, past, or negation. (It is therefore not surprising that Montague did not take the tenses and negation as transformations.)

The reason why we cannot introduce the future, for example, as a semantically meaningful transformation can be explained even without introducing the formal semantics. (After all, the formal semantics, as you will see, is very intuitive!) The syntactical transformation one may have in mind is to replace the verb in the derivation tree by its future form. This will yield a perfect derivation tree of the future form of the sentence. Syntactically this is fine, but not semantically. In fact, it is not correct in any plausible semantics, not only the one given in the next section. The trouble can be seen in the following example:

'John will allegedly run'.

This means that in the future, it will be the case that 'John runs allegedly' is true. Semantically the meaning we get is that it is now alleged that John will run. Another example is 'John did not die tragically'. Semantically we get (if we take negation as transformation) that the meaning is: it is tragic that John did not die.

How do we treat, then, negation and the tenses? The way to do that is to add the words 'will', 'did', and 'not' to the category SC_1 (besides necessarily). Thus syntactically we derive, for example, 'Not John run' and then using transformations of agreement obtain 'John does not run'. Transformations of agreement do not affect the semantical meaning. This treatment of the tenses and negation was also adopted by Montague. It is not, however, entirely satisfactory. Take, for example, 'John will pay promptly'. Here the meaning (or at least the ambiguity) is that 'promptly' applies to mean 'soon'. So in this case 'will' plays the role of a transformation, doing exactly what the semantics did to 'John will run allegedly'.

There is another problem connected with negation as a transformation which Partee told me about. The negation of 'John gave some books to some of his friends', according to the rules of our system as well as of M, is 'John did not give any books to any of his friends', but if we apply syntactical transformation we get 'John did not give some books to any of his friends'.

The role that negation and 'some', 'none', and 'any' play is *not* context free and we *cannot* account for it here.

In order to introduce the passive we need some more definitions.

Let τ be a construction tree. Let t be a point in τ. Then there exists a unique path of points beginning with t and leading to the top. The point t is said to be *undominated* if for no point t' on this path (except possibly to the top point of τ) do we have the following diagram:

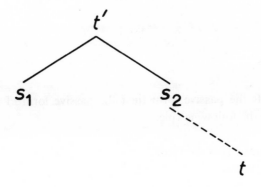

For example,

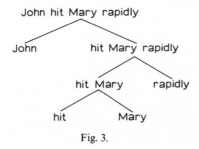

Fig. 3.

The points labeled with 'Mary' and 'rapidly' are dominated.

A tree τ is said to accept the passive form if there exists an undominated point t in τ labeled with an element of TV_1 or SC_2. The tree in the example above accepts the passive form because of the point labeled with 'hit'. The tree below does not accept the passive form.

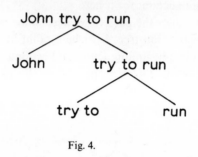

Fig. 4.

If τ accepts the passive form then the passive form of τ is obtained according to the following rule.

By definition τ is of the form:

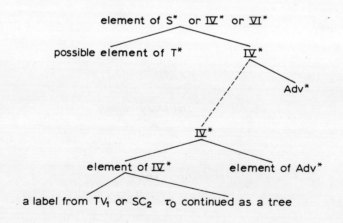

Fig. 5.

Let the transformation be:

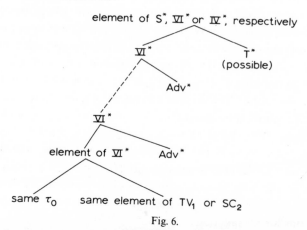

Fig. 6.

This is the construction tree of the passive form. If we look at the semantics (next section) we get the intuitively expected semantical object. This way, for example, we can obtain 'John tries to be hit by Mary'.

4. SEMANTICS FOR SG AND G (WITH THE TENSES AND NEGATION)

Let us now turn to the Suppes semantics for SG and G.

Consider a set of possible worlds of the form $I \times J$. J is the set of real numbers; each number corresponds to a moment of time. (We need this since we have the tenses.) I is a set of possible worlds. (We need I because we have words like 'necessarily' and 'believe'.) All the words (i, j) have the same domain D of individuals or of 'people' living in that world. We shall correlate with the elements of the basic categories semantical objects or operations which are meaningful in each world and which approximate their meaning. For example, 'John' is a name of a person and so we correlate with 'John' an element of the domain $\|John\| \in D$. 'Run' is a property of people. Some run, some do not. So $\|run\|$ is a function that gives for each world (i, j) those people that run, that is, $\|run\|_{i,j} \subseteq D$. Similarly, $\|hit\|_{i,j} \subseteq D \times D$, that is, it is a list of who hits whom at the world (i, j).

Even as early as this, our semantics differs from Montague's in an inessential way. Look at 'John runs'. An elegant way of understanding this is that 'John' *operates* on 'run' to yield a sentence. In other words, T* operates on IV* to yield S*. Montague therefore would make $\|\text{John}\|$ not an object of D but a function that yields truth values from every $\|\text{IV*}\|$ (i.e., from every subset of D). So $\|\text{John}\| \in 2^{2^D}$. We do not do that because we can use the object 'John' itself to define the operation, namely, the value is truth if $\text{John} \in \|\text{IV}\|$. For reasons that have to do with rule S13(b), we shall not take $\|\text{John}\| \in D$ but $\|\text{John}\| \subseteq D$, a subset that has one element, namely, 'John'. This way we can take 'John and Mary' as $\{\text{John}, \text{Mary}\} \subseteq D$. To gain further insight into Montague's functions, look at the rule for forming IV*: $\text{IV*} \to \text{TV}_1^* + \text{T*}$, for example, 'hit John'. So 'hit' operates on 'John' to yield IV. So Montague would then take $\|\text{hit}\|_{i,j} \in (2^D)^{2^{2^D}}$, and not a subset of $D \times D$ as we did. However, this is only a matter of elegance. By the way, Montague does not do *exactly* as we described, because some further modifications become necessary, but essentially these are the reasons for his functions.

Let us now turn to a more formal description of our semantics. It is conceptually the same as that of Montague. It will be given in the style of Suppes (i.e., related to the construction tree).

A semantical structure is a system $(\bar{D}, I \times J, A, \| \ \|)$, where $\bar{D}$ is the set of individuals, $I \times J$ is the set of possible worlds, and A is a function assigning to each he_n an element of the form $\{x\} \subseteq \bar{D}$. In the sequel $\bar{D}$ and $I \times J$ are fixed (though A may change values) and all the definitions are relative to $\bar{D}$ and $I \times J$. Let D be the set of all finite nonempty subsets of $\bar{D}$.

$\| \ \|$ is the function that gives values (semantical objects) to each element of the basic categories in each world (i, j). The properties of $\| \ \|$ are the following:

(1) $x \in \text{IV} \Rightarrow \|x\|_{i,j} \subseteq D$.

(2) $x \in T_1 \Rightarrow \|x\|_{i,j}$ is the same one-element subset of D for all (i, j).

(3) $\|\text{he}_n\|_{i,j} = A(\text{he}_n)$.

(4) $x \in \text{Adv} \Rightarrow \|x\|_{i,j} \in (2^D)^{2^D}$ (i.e., Adv transforms IV into another IV.)

(5) $x \in \text{CN}_1 \Rightarrow \|x\|_{i,j} \subseteq D$.

(6) $x \in \text{SC}_1 \Rightarrow \|x\|_{i,j}$ is a function such that it operates on subsets of $I \times J$ and yields 1 if they are equal to $I \times J$ and 0 otherwise.

(7) $x \in \text{SC}_2 \Rightarrow \|x\|_{i,j} \in (2^D)^{2^{I \times J}}$.

(8) $x \in \text{OA} \Rightarrow \|x\|_{i,j} \in (2^D)^{2^D}$.

(9) $x \in \text{Prep} \Rightarrow \|x\|_{i,j} \in ((2^D)^{2^D})^D$.

(10) $\|\text{and}\|$ and $\|\text{or}\|$ are intersection and union operators when they

operate on S or IV but $\|\text{and}\|$ is union when operating on terms (if you insist on set-theoretical object make $\|\text{or}\|$ and $\|\text{and}\|$ to be the empty set).

(11) $\|\text{every}\|$ operates on subsets of D. If $D_0 \subseteq D$ then $\|\text{every}\|(D_0) = \{E | E \supseteq D_0\}$. Similarly: $\|\text{some}\|(D_0) = \{E | E \cap D_0 \neq \Phi\}$ $\|\text{the}\|(D_0) = \{E | E \cap D_0$ is a one-element set$\}$.

We need the above definitions since, for example, 'every man' is a noun phrase.

Given the labeled construction tree τ, we associate with it another labeled tree, denoted by $\|\tau\|$, which is actually the same tree τ but with more labels on it. We do this 'the Suppes way', that is, label the terminal points of τ and then 'climb' up the tree according to the rules below.

(1) The terminal points of τ are labeled, by definition, with elements x of one of the basic categories. We add $\|x\|$ as a further label.

(2) Assume that we labeled the points t and s of τ with the further labels K^t and K^s. Let r be the immediate point on top.

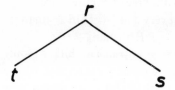

We want to label r with a further label. We know that r is already labeled with some element of a derived category. This label was put according to some rule. Our additional label depends on that rule. So all we need to do now is to list the rules and say for each case what K^r is. (The reader should verify that we do not contradict ourselves.)

S1: t does not exist. Let $K^r = K^s$.

S2: Let $K^r_{i,j}$ be $K^t_{i,j}(K^s_{i,j})$. (Notice that $K^t_{i,j}$ is assumed to be a function that yields a family of subsets; see (11) in the definition of $\|\ \|$ above. $K^r_{i,j}$ is then this family for the case of $K^s_{i,j}$.

S4(a) or S4(b): $K^r_{i,j}$ is 1 iff $K^t_{i,j} \subseteq K^s_{i,j}$, otherwise it is 0.

S4(c): $K^r_{i,j}$ is 1 iff $K^s_{i,j} \in K^t_{i,j}$, otherwise it is 0.

S5(a) or S5(b): $K^r_{i,j} = \{a \in D | (a, K^s_{i,j}) \in K^t_{i,j}\}$.

S5(c): $K^r_{i,j} = \{a \in D | \{r | (a, r) \in K^s_{i,j}\} \in K^t_{i,j}\}$.

S6(a) or (b): $K^r_{i,j} = K^t_{i,j}(K^s_{i,j})$.

S7: $K_{i,j}^r = K_{i,j}^t(K^s)$.

S8: $K_{i,j}^r = K_{i,j}^t(K_{i,j}^s)$.

S9: $K_{i,j}^r = 1$ iff $K_{i,j}^t(K^s) = 1$.

S10: $K_{i,j}^r = K_{i,j}^s(K_{i,j}^t)$. (Notice that the order is reversed here.)

S11–S12: Either intersection or union depending on whether we have 'and' or 'or'.

S13: $K^r = K^t \cup K^s$.

S30: Like S5 but with the converse relations everywhere.

S31: Like S10, with VI* playing the part of IV*.

S32: Like S7, with VI* playing the part of IV*.

S33: Like S4, with VI* replacing IV*.

The reader can now understand why Montague gains elegance, because for the M semantics $K^r = K^t(K^s)$ for all the rules.

Let us now illustrate the ambiguity, in the system G, of 'every man hit some man'.

(a) The labels for the tree of Figure 1 are:

$\|\text{man}\| \subseteq D$, $\|\text{every man}\| = \{E | E \supseteq \|\text{man}\|\}$

$\|\text{some man}\| = \{E | E \cap \|\text{man}\| \neq 0\}$

$\|\text{hit some man}\| = \{a | \{r | (a, r) \in \|\text{hit}\|\} \in \|\text{some}\|\}$, that is, all elements x such that there exists a y such that x hit y.

$\|\text{sentence}\| = \text{truth iff } \|\text{hit some man}\| \in \|\text{every man}\|$, that is, the sentence is true iff for every man x there exists a y such that x hit y.

(b) The labels for the tree of Figure 2 are:

$\|\text{every man}\|$, $\|\text{some man}\|$, as before. The value of $\|\text{every man hit}\|$ is computed exactly like the case of $\|\text{hit every man}\|$ except that we take the converse of the relations involved.

That is, $\|\text{every man hit}\| = \{a | \{r | (r, a) \in \|\text{hit}\|\} \in \|\text{every man}\|$.

That is, all elements y that are hit by every x.

$\|\text{sentence}\|$ is 'truth' iff $\|\text{every man hit}\| \in \|\text{some man}\|$.

That is, the sentence is true if there exists a y such that every man hits y.

In view of the above examples and the semantic constructions it is natural to define the *meaning of a sentence* to be its construction tree. Thus 'every man hit some man' has two different meanings. Other sentences (like 'John hit Mary') that do not contain quantifiers *are not ambiguous*, although they may have more than one construction tree. *This correspondence between the formal results and the known linguistic results should be taken as evidence of the success of the Suppes semantics.*[1]

It would be appropriate to add here that the semantics is limited. Take 'John seeks advice', for example. It is not clear what semantical object to associate with 'advice' (i.e., what $\|advice\|$ should be). But let us hope that further investigation will clarify this and similar points.

Deletion is also possible; it means chopping the construction tree.

We conclude this section with a remark on the semantics of the passive form of a construction tree. If the tree accepts the passive form then there exists a node labeled with an $x \in TV^*$ which is undominated with $\|x\|$ $\subseteq D \times D$. In the semantics of the passive, take the converse of $\|x\|$. That is, in 'John hit Mary' $\|hit\| \subseteq D \times D$, $\|is\ hit\|$ is the converse. This way the operations on the semantics parallel those on the tree.

5. SMG AND ITS RELATION TO M

In this section we want to justify the title of this paper. We shall be brief, since all the methods were already employed in connection with G.

The system SMG will be essentially Montague with some modifications that we need in order to have the passive. This was suggested by Partee and it is not too different from the way passive was introduced in G.

The semantics shall be described in Suppes style and thus we obtain the result of the title of the paper (see Suppes, this volume, pp. 370–94).

Let us first represent Montague syntax (without agreement) as a context-free syntax. The reader is urged to look at Montague's paper and compare.

M rules as context-free rules

(i) Rules S1, S2, S4–S13 of Montague were already represented in Section 2 as the context-free rules of SG.

(ii) In order to account for the other rules we need more categories.

$$Ab = \{s_1, s_2, s_3, \ldots\}$$

s_n is to be read *such-that$_n$*. Example: 'Every man such that Mary likes he$_n$' is written 'every man s_n Mary likes he$_n$'. Rule S3 of Montague becomes
S3: $CN^* \to CN^* + Ab^* + S^*$.

(iii) To cope with S14 we add another category
Sub $= \{b_1, b_2, b_3, \ldots\}$.

b_n means 'substitute a name for he_n'. We thus get

S14: $S^* \rightarrow T_1^* + Sub^* + S^*$.

(Of course, we do not worry about agreement.)

S15: $CN^* \rightarrow T_1^* + Sub^* + CN^*$

S16: $IV^* \rightarrow T^* + Sub^* + IV^*$

The rule S17 need not be dealt with since we put the tenses in the category SC_1 and so S17 is redundant in view of S9.

Now to show that Montague's semantics is a form of Suppes', define the notion of a construction tree of a sentence and define, for elements x of the basic categories $\|x\|$ to be what Montague assigns to $\|x\|$ in his paper. The operation mentioned in T3 is $\|s_n\|$ and $\|b_n\|$ is a suitable λ abstraction operator. In fact, we can assign anything we want to s_n and b_n, e.g., Φ if you insist on a set-theoretical object.

Now to define $\|\tau\|$ we follow the construction of τ, as we did in the case of G, but use with each rule S the Montague-T instructions.

We are not dwelling on this because the interest in fact that Montague's semantics can be represented as a Suppes semantics lies in the possibility of formulating systems like G, which are very natural, and not in the mere fact of the representation.

The passive can be incorporated as an operator π operating on sentences. It is best explained by an example.

Form: he_n hit Mary.

Apply π: Mary is hit by he_n.

Apply substitution: Mary is hit by John.

This is not essentially different from the passive in G. In G what we do is:

Form: hit Mary

Apply π (here we needed
a new category but we
do not need Sub*):   Mary is hit by

Add John: Mary is hit by John.

APPENDIX

We could have added to SG the category of adjectives. We could divide the adjectives into two kinds: $Adj_1 = \{red\}$, those adjectives that divide the entire universe D into two subsets, like red, triangular, etc., and those who divide any CN into two classes but not the universe. For example, Adj_2 = {big}. We can say big lizard but small animal. The rules are, for example, $CN^* \rightarrow Adj_i^* + CN^*$ and some other rules if we want. The semantical function $\|Adj_1\|$ is a subset of D and $\|Adj_2\|$ is a mapping that gives for each $E \subseteq D$ a subset $\|Adj_2\|(E) \subseteq E$. This conforms with Strawson's view. I am grateful to Julius Moravcsik for helpful discussion about Adj.Suppes uses Adj_1.

REMARK: In our system SG we do have semantics for 'John seeks a unicorn', but the sentence is always false (if they do not exist). This is just an accident. We could have put seek in a different category and managed the proper semantical meaning.

Stanford University

NOTES

* This research has been supported in part by the National Science Foundation under grant NSFGJ-443X. I am greatly indebted to F. Goldstein, Julius Moravcsik, Barbara Partee, and P. Suppes for many conversations out of which this paper has evolved.
[1] The semantic functions of Section 2 of Suppes' paper are identical with the intuitive functions that we gave above for rules that Suppes considers. The reader should note that Suppes obtained these r-functions on the basis of the empirical evidence.

PART III

SPECIAL TOPICS

CHUNG-YING CHENG

ON THE PROBLEM OF SUBJECT STRUCTURE IN LANGUAGE WITH APPLICATION TO LATE ARCHAIC CHINESE

In current research on the grammatical structure of classical Chinese, efforts have been made to describe elementary constituents and their types and levels in reference to specifically chosen data (Dobson, 1959, 1962, 1964; Chou, 1961; Wang, 1962, 1964). Unfortunately there appear to be two basic defects in this approach. First, the usefulness and adequacy of the categories that characterize the language are not independently justified. Second, this approach seems to lend itself only to syntactical-formal considerations of the surface data, and fails to bring out the properties of the language as a system for communicating knowledge, information or meaning.[1]

To overcome the basic defects mentioned above, first of all, we should posit an overall theory in which grammatical categories are well defined. Second, we should treat sentences not simply as isolated items in a discourse, but instead as well-defined parts whose meanings and forms have an organic relation to other parts of the discourse. Third, we should consider sentences as having more than one dimension of structure, namely, that of the surface syntax.

In the analysis of the subject-predicate structure of classical Chinese there is want for adequate and well-defined criteria for determining the various types of subject-predicate structures. This is due to the absence of a general theory to explain the purposes of the analysis.

In this paper I shall start with general consideration of the distinction between subject and predicate and proceed to a relevant application of such distinction to any language. Once we have made this clear, it is only a corollary to show that subject-predicate structures in Late Archaic Chinese[2] may be systematically illustrated and logically explained. Specifically, I shall confine myself to the analysis of the subject structure in language while leaving the treatment of the predicate structure to a separate article.

1. PHILOSOPHICAL DISTINCTION BETWEEN SUBJECT
AND PREDICATE

Linguistic forms cannot be separated from all the uses to which they can be put. Among all the uses of linguistic forms, the most important and basic one is that for saying (or stating) how things are. For this purpose, linguistic forms are capable of being asserted – which means that we are able to make reference to things or processes in the world we live in and we are able to say things about them. Our ability to refer to things depends on our ability to identify particular things as well as the general types of things, and our ability to make statements about things depends upon our ability to recognize the properties, general and particular, of things and the relations of things to other things including ourselves.[3] The transference between the particular and the general is exactly how the assertive and communicative function of language is achieved.

As noted by Strawson (1967, p. 4) among others (Quine, 1960) a certain asymmetry essentially characterizes the referential and predicative functions of the linguistic form. In predications we attach some selected characteristics to a particular thing (referent), thereby excluding all other possible characteristics that may be used to describe that particular thing. The reason is that the stock of all possible characteristics may contain some mutually incompatible elements which cannot be used at the same time to characterize a particular thing. While we cannot always include all possible predicates (characteristics) of one thing at the same time, we can always refer to many things under a single predicate (characteristic) at the same time. This asymmetry is a logical criterion by which we can distinguish a thing from a characteristic and hence between reference and predication. Because we are able to refer to many things under a single predicate, we can make not only particular statements, but also general statements of either universal quantification or existential quantification. Because we are able to attach certain characteristics to a particular thing, we can make informative statements and conceive our linguistic forms as a potential device for understanding the world.[4]

The above account provides a ground for us to distinguish two basic functions of linguistic forms, namely, the referential function and the predicative function.[5] The linguistic form with the referential function may be called a logical subject, and the linguistic form with the predicative function may be called a logical predicate. The object which a logical subject stands for, i.e., the object to which a linguistic form is referentially directed, may be called the ontic subject, whereas the characteristic or characteristics of the ontic subject which is predicated in the linguistic form, may be called the ontic predicate. Several things may be noted in regard to this distinction.

First, the referring expression of our sentence in general may not merely refer, but also contribute to the characterization of the types of situations ostensibly identified. Similarly, the predicative expression of our sentence may not merely predicate or ascribe characteristics to the referents, but also include referential elements designating the temporal and spatial location of things. For general purposes we do not need to consider referring expressions as purely referential, for that means that they must be considered as variables of quantification. They may be considered as referring to individuals or particulars understood or specified in a particular universe represented or presupposed in the discourse.

Second, referring expressions such as proper names and definite descriptions may be considered semantically meaningful, even though they are referential. They are referential and their predicative features need not concern us if these are understood in relation to either extralinguistic or linguistic contexts or both, the linguistic context being the discourse in which they occur. The extralinguistic context involves such things as the intentions and assumptions to which the speech or writing is intended to apply.[6] In other words, referring expressions are referential insofar as they relate to a semantically specifiable discourse and context. Consequently, the referents (or the ontic subjects) of referring expressions are always categorized according to the discourse and context.[7]

Third, even though we can identify ontic subjects with actual or presupposed things and facts in the world, we do not have to assume existence of another kind for predicative expressions, namely, things or facts other than the objects of referring expressions. Since controversies and technical difficulties are involved in developing a full theory of this, we simply maintain, along with Quine, but generally in opposition to Frege and Church, that ontic predicates are ontic subjects characterized in certain ways. Therefore at the lowest level the logical predicates can be said to have a divided reference (in Quine's terminology), because they can be applied to many individuals. The ontic predicates, in contrast to ontic subjects, are therefore ways in which things are understood once these things are identified as ontic subjects in a discourse.

2. DEEP STRUCTURE AND SURFACE STRUCTURE
OF A LANGUAGE

If we assume that an ideal linguistic form is logically simple (in whatever logical sense of simplicity) for performing the functions of reference and predication, then we have good reason as well as good motivation to distinguish between the deep structure and the surface structure of a language. The deep structure of a language may be said to consist of those ideal linguistic forms which can perform functions of reference and predication with greatest logical simplicity.[8] The surface structure, on the other hand, consists of linguistic expressions (phonological or morphological) which exhibit the deep structure forms that often result from various combinations of the deep structure forms for pragmatic considerations. In this sense the surface structure of a language is logically more complicated, even though pragmatically more facile, than the deep structure, and it is derived from the deep structure by way of transformations.

Methodologically, we need transformations (or rules of transformation) if we want to preserve the correlation between a surface structure sentence and the corresponding constituent deep structure sentence or sentences. For in the surface structure a given actualized sentence produced in the learning or use situation does not exactly correspond *simpliciter* to idealized linguistic forms which exhibit the functions of reference and predication and their interconnections in the deep structure.[9] This distinction between deep structure and surface structure of a language has been made quite clear in Chomsky (1965). See also Katz (1966, pp. 131ff., 138ff.; Postal, 1964). Chomsky posits the deep structure of a language for the purpose of accounting for real structural differences of sentences with apparent structural similarity such as found in the pair:

I persuaded John to leave.
I expected John to leave.

or for uniquely determining the meaning of structurally ambiguous sentences such as:

> Flying planes can be dangerous.
> I learned the shooting of lions.[10]

Deep structure is also used to account for structural relations such as those between passive voice and active voice and between questions and statements.

Although the above are valid reasons for making a distinction between the deep structure and the surface structure of a language, it is to be noted that our reason for such a distinction is a more fundamental one. For us the deep structure is a logical structure which fulfills an ontological purpose and therefore is not merely part of a formal scheme. It is in fact an interpreted scheme, interpreted in terms of things and their characteristics with full consideration for reference and predication underlying every linguistic expression.

Specifically, our scheme differs from Chomsky's in two respects: (1) The semantic component in Chomsky's scheme is separated from the syntactic base component, whereas in our scheme they are intimately integrated. (2) As we shall see, even though a sentence in its deep structure may differ from its derived counterpart in the surface structure, they share in common the same ontological significance. Because of this, the linguistic forms in the deep structure are intimately related to their uses in the surface structure. They are therefore not to be correlated merely by logically simple rules of transformation. In fact, they are correlated by transference of the ontological significance of the deep structure sentence which is preserved after the application of transformations. Rules of transformation apply only to the syntactic component or form, while they leave the semantic component or meaning intact.

With the referential and predicative functions properly assigned to the ontic subject and ontic predicate, respectively, we can adopt Chomsky's NP and VP to respectively designate our purely formal logical subject and logical predicate. According to Chomsky (1965, p. 71), a formal definition of logical subject and predicate is as follows:

(1) Subject of: [NP, S]

(2) Predicate of: [VP, S].

In order to apply these definitions of the logical subject and logical predicate to our case, we must formulate a principle governing the context of the deep structure with respect to the whole discourse. The principle is this. The NP occupying the position of a logical subject in the deep structure must appear at least once in the surface structure as exhibited by a well-defined discourse. The same holds for VP which occupies the position of a logical predicate. We can call this principle the verification principle for the deep structure.[11] Chomsky does not seem to have ever made explicit such a principle.

In terms of the verification principle for the deep structure, as well as the basic considerations for the communicative, i.e., referential and predicative functions of language, the deep structure may be conceived as an ideal form-meaning composite underlying the actual expressions in the surface structure. This concept of deep structure represents a deviation from Chomsky's original formulation of deep structure with some significant consequences. Clearly one consequence, *inter alia*, is that syntax is no longer separated from the semantics of reference and predication in the deep structure of a language. In this sense this deviation is in fact an improvement.

Now let us proceed to characterize the content of the surface structure. In the first place, remember that a sentence in the surface structure, like one in the deep structure, is only part of a discourse, related to linguistic and extralinguistic contexts. In other words, sentences are used to perform certain various functions in the surface structure on the basis of the referential and predicative functions.[12] We shall confine ourselves to the fact that a sentence in the surface structure may differ structurally from its corresponding sentence in the deep structures. These differences arise primarily as a result of expressing our thought under various pragmatic considerations. For example, we use sentences in the passive voice for accentuating the reverse relation of action, or for describing actions without presupposing knowledge of or reference to their agents. Furthermore, we use impersonal pronouns, such as 'it' in English, as dummy grammatical subjects to indicate something which we are familiar with, but which we cannot definitely and precisely specify, or to represent a state of affairs which can be or will be specified in another context, temporally or logically prior to the given one. We make deletions or subjects or predicates in a discourse or linguistic and/or extralinguistic contexts when there is no practical risk of confusion and/or there is a gain in simplicity.

In our present discussion we cannot give explanation for all the grammatical and syntactic features of sentences in the surface structure. Suffice it be recognized that all the grammatical paraphernalia in the surface structure are either pragmatically or contextually justified or both. This implies that when there are more or fewer items in the surface structure than in the corresponding deep structure, it is assumed that they are added or subtracted for pragmatic reasons, but not for logical or ontological reasons. The size of these discrepancies and the extent to which they develop between the deep structure and the surface structure depend on individual languages. One can of course always assume a universal or very general deep structure for all languages, as Chomsky appears to do. If we adopt this assumption, we can perhaps compare different surface languages in terms of the underlying universal deep structure. Thus, perhaps one may say that whereas the surface structure of English appears to add more than necessary in the corresponding deep structure, the classical Chinese (wen yen in general) tends to reduce what is needed in an adequate description of the deep structure by way of deletions and so on.

3. TWO CHARACTERISTICS OF SENTENCES IN THE SURFACE STRUCTURE

If we can grasp the distinction between the deep structure and the surface structure of a language in the sense we have intended above, we may now proceed to make distinctions in regard to the surface structure alone. These are the distinctions between a grammatical subject and a grammatical predicate on the one hand and the distinction between topic and comment on the other.

A good way to explain the distinction between a grammatical subject and a grammatical predicate is in terms of the phrase-structure markers NP and VP. The NP in a surface structure sentence of the form NP + VP is always a grammatical subject, whereas the related VP is always a grammatical predicate. Whether this corresponds to a deep structure distinction is another question. It is not necessary that it does. In other words, we assume that we can identify the $S = NP + VP$ construction in the surface structure without assuming that the NP is in fact logically referential or that the VP is in fact logically predicative. For NP and VP in the surface structure can be related in all sorts of ways. In general, perhaps we have to assume certain formal criteria for making the grammatical distinction in question. These formal criteria will make reference to the transformation rules by which they can be shown to be formally related to the underlying logical structure. For example, one formal criterion for a full sentence in Chinese (ancient as well as modern) is that the only noun phrase which physically precedes the verb phrase is always the grammatical subject.

Now as to the topic-comment distinction, Chao Yuan-ren has drawn a distinction between the subject-matter to talk about and the remarks said about the subject-matter.[13] In these general terms, the topic and comment distinction seems to correspond to the distinction between reference and predication. But in fact, a topic is more broadly conceived than a reference: any expression, complete or incomplete, can be a topic, but not every expression in fact is referential, nor is any comment in fact predicative with respect to a given topic in the sentence. The distinction between topic and comment however brings out some surface connections between linguistic items in sentences. These various surface connections remain to be analyzed in terms of different categories.

At this point, one might wonder what purpose is served in drawing a distinction between topic and comment apart from providing a basis for further analysis. However, in order to give full significance to the distinction in question, we may suggest that the comment represents the focus of attention or an act of knowing and the topic represents the background in which the focus is related to other things (points) of interest. Construed in this way, the distinction between topic and comment therefore pertains to sentences (or language) in actual use, and consequently, is closely linked to extralinguistic factors such as the awareness of the speaker or the listener. In the consideration of the context of use, the topic can suggest, even though it does not fully symbolize, the grammatical or logical subject of the sentences for which the comment is grammatically or logically relevant (MacIver, 1954).

Insofar as a topic suggests the logical subject and/or the grammatical subject, and the comment on the topic serves as the center of interest or focus of attention in the speech situation, a topic may be called a psychological or epistemological subject, and relative to this, a comment may be called a psychological or epistemological predicate, i.e., that part of speech on which the point of message or information falls.[14]

According to a suggestion by Chao (1965, p. 103) the psychological or epistemological predicate in a sentence may be brought into a prominent place in the sentence by 'contrastive prosodic stress', or by magnified length and pitch range. Indeed the psychological or epistemological predicate may be indicated also by acts of nonspeech such as gestures or other tokens. This indicates that topic and comment in the sense of psychological or epistemological subjects and predicates sometimes may be revealed only in actual speech situations. But since ancient Chinese, which we are going to deal with, is codified in nonphonetic script, we might adopt the convention that (1) the beginning position of a sentence is always reserved for the topic of the sentence and the rest for the comment, and (2) in case of a minor sentence,[15] the whole sentence is a comment.[16]

4. FOUR LEVELS OF ANALYSIS OF THE SUBJECT STRUCTURE

In the above we have seen that a language has two levels – the deep structure and the surface structure. The deep structure sentence is an idealized reconstruction of a corresponding surface structure sentence in the light of the consideration of the whole discourse and in accordance with the linguistic functions of reference and predication preserved in a logically simple form. It contains therefore the ontic subject and the ontic predicate on the one hand, and the logical subject and the logical predicate on the other. The surface structure sentence is a natural language sentence in its actual use conforming to a pragmatically oriented grammar. In terms of its use for communication, it may have a topic and a comment (the psychological/epistemological subject and predicate).

It is clear that these four levels of the subject and predicate structure distinguished above are interrelated and interdependent. We must realize that the answer to the question as to exactly how these four levels are related completely depends upon individual languages. In English writing (not in speech), for example, the grammatical subject is almost a must and can be always identified in the relevant linguistic discourse or context. On the other hand, in Chinese, the grammatical subject is not necessarily identifiable in the context. In other words, it is logically (not just pragmatically) dispensable, and this is the basis of the classification of what I call *essentially subjectless* sentences.[17] Of course, I must point out that in the analysis of the subject structure in any language, the ontic subject and the ontic predicate are always presupposed. They are to be determined through consideration of the whole discourse and possible extralinguistic factors under which the language was or possibly was used.

Now once we have determined the ontic subject and the predicate, we can determine, on the evidence of the given discourse, the logical subject and logical predicate, i.e., those linguistic expressions (or forms) which stand for (or symbolize) the ontic subject and the logical predicate. In this sense, the logical subject and the logical predicate coincide with the ontic subject and the ontic predicate by the semantical relation of 'designating' and 'being true of'. Given the determination of these we can of course ask whether a given surface sentence in the discourse coincides with a deep structure sentence. The answer is that the logical subject and the logical predicate need not be the same as the grammatical subject and the grammatical predicate. This means that the logical subject-expression and the logical predicate-expression need not be the same as the grammatical subject-expression and the grammatical predicate-expression. One has to inquire how the surface sentence is derived from the deep structure sentence by transformation rules.

Just as the logical subject and predicate need not be the same as the surface grammatical subject and predicate, one can see that the grammatical subject and predicate need not be the same as the topic and comment or psychological/epistemological subject and predicate. Since each pair is specified according to a different and distinctive criterion, there is no contradiction or incompatibility in their being different. This only shows how the various aspects of a sentence must be revealed in a rich theory.

In the light of the above analysis, it is clear that for a full understanding of a sentence, it is necessary that we should look into its subject-predicate structure on these four levels: the ontic and the logical in the deep structure and the grammatical and psychological/epistemological in the surface structure. To analyze this structure one can begin with the surface structure distinctions and work into the deep structure distinctions, or one can proceed reversely. A linguistic specification of a sentence in regard to its subject-predicate structure must be therefore four-valued in terms of: the values of the ontic subject and predicate, the values of the logical subject and predicate, the values of the grammatical subject and predicate, and the values of the psychological/epistemological subject and predicate. The values of the ontic subject and predicate are the actual objects and attributes determined by the discourse. The values of the logical subject and predicate are the subject-expressions and predicate-expressions standing for the predetermined ontic subjects and predicates; the values of the grammatical subject and predicate are the subject-expressions and predicate-expressions introduced by transformation rules; finally the values of the psychological/epistemological subject and predicate are the linguistic expressions which serve to provide a background of knowledge and at the same time to introduce new items of information as the focuses of attention.

An important point about the four-level characterization of the subject-predicate structure is this. Whereas the ontic subject and predicate in the deep structure are always present (this is due to our assumption of the basic assertive or communicative functions of our language), and the psychological/epistemological subject and predicate in the surface structure are also always present (this is due to the fact that the topic-comment structure is a necessary condition for the actual use of a sentence), the logical subject and predicate in the deep structure and the grammatical subject and predicate in the surface structure are not always present. In other words, a sentence must be analyzable with regard to a pair of specifiable ontic subject and predicate on the one hand and a pair of specifiable topic and comment on the other. It need not be analyzable with regard to a pair of specifiable logical subject and predicate and/or a pair of specifiable grammatical subject and predicate.

The foregoing point may appear to be surprising. But in the light of the following facts, our surprise need not prevent us from perceiving the truth of the foregoing point: (1) the topic and comment need not coincide with the grammatical subject and predicate or the logical subject and predicate and vice versa. (2) The ontic subject and predicate are different in kind from the logical subject and predicate. (3) The logical subject and predicate need not coincide with the grammatical subject and predicate. (4) No logical subject-expression and logical predicate-expression need be evidenced in the given discourse, even though they can be suggested. (5) The grammatical subject and predicate can be deleted or added through certain transformation rules. On the basis of these facts, it is natural to expect that either the logical subject and predicate or the grammatical subject and predicate or both may be missing (and therefore theoretically dispensable) from the given sentence. On (4) alone, due to considerations of the verification principle, the logical subject could be absent. On (5) alone, due to considerations of transformation, the grammatical subject could be absent. On both (4) and (5), both the logical subject and the grammatical subject could be absent. To say this however is not to say that language activity may not fulfill its intended purpose of communication. The reason why it does not consists in the fact that the deep level of the deep structure and the surface level of the surface structure of a language always provide a framework in terms of which reference, predication, and therefore communication, can be understood and indeed reconstructed.

Because of the possible absence of the logical or grammatical subjects or both from a given sentence, we can generally describe the subject structure of a sentence in terms of the four levels and by noting whether or not it has a logical or grammatical subject, or has both or neither.

Summarizing the above, our scheme of four levels of analysis of the subject structure of a sentence can be represented as follows in Table I.

TABLE I

Levels / Cases	Deep structure		Surface structure	
	ontic subject	logical subject	grammatical subject	topic or comment
Case I	+	+	+	+
Case II	+	+	−	+
Case III	+	−	+	+
Case IV	+	−	−	+

Given the case that the logical subject and the grammatical subject are present in the analysis of a sentence, we face another question the answer to which is essential for specifying the subject structure of the sentence. The question is whether the existent logical subject coincides with the grammatical subject, whether it coincides with the topic, and finally whether grammatical subject in fact coincides with topic? If we let L stand for the presence of the logical subject, $\overline{L}$ for the absence of the logical subject, G the presence of the grammatical subject, $\overline{G}$ the absence of the grammatical subject, T the presence of topic or comment, we have the following eight possible cases in the analysis of the subject structure of a sentence:

Case I: (L, G, T)
   subcase (i): $L = G = T$
   subcase (ii): $L = G \neq T$
   subcase (iii): $L \neq G = T$
   subcase (iv): $G \neq T, T \neq L, L \neq G$
Case II: (L, $\overline{G}$, T)
Case III: ($\overline{L}$, G, T) subcase (i): $G = T$; subcase (ii): $G \neq T$
Case IV: ($\overline{L}$, $\overline{G}$, T).

The question may be raised as to why Case II does not admit of subcases (i) $L = T$, (ii) $L \neq T$. The reason for this is that in the absence of the grammatical subject, T will always be identical with the grammatical predicate and hence will not serve the purpose of reference. This means that it cannot coincide with L. One may also note the rarity of Case I, subcase (iv), i.e., the case of (L, G, T) where $G \neq T, T \neq L, L \neq G$. This rarity may be explained as a result of the presence of very strong transformation restrictions.

Since the classical Chinese, particularly Late Archaic Chinese, to which we shall apply our analysis, is rich with the subjectless sentences, we shall note a distinction between the relatively subjectless sentences on the one hand and the essentially subjectless sentences on the other:

(1) Relatively subjectless sentences are those whose grammatical subjects are suppressed in a linguistic context and those that are normally identifiable in preceding sentences in a connected discourse. The grammatical subjects are deleted by a deletion rule. They do not lack logical subjects, for, on the verification principle, the deleted grammatical subjects may be regarded as being present in the deep structure as logical subjects.

(2) Essentially subjectless sentences are those that have no grammatical subjects or logical subjects, but whose ontic subjects may be identified in the immediate extralinguistic contexts of their use. There are no certain definite terms or definite descriptions in the preceding or succeeding linguistic contexts to identify their logical subjects. Yet one may 'recon-

struct' their logical subjects as terms or expressions referring to something
or everything or anything of certain categories. Hence the essentially
subjectless sentences are of two kinds:

(i) Their ontic subjects are 'something' of a certain category and hence
are equivalent to referents of indefinite descriptions or ranges of values of
variables of existential quantification.

(ii) Their ontic subjects are 'everything' or 'anything' of a certain category and hence are equivalent to ranges of values of variables of implicit
universal quantification of various scopes. It is clear that the relatively
subjectless sentences belong to Case II, whereas the essentially subjectless
sentences belong to Case IV. These two kinds of the subjectless sentences
have not been distinguished in studies on the grammar of the classical
Chinese.[18]

Perhaps we can elucidate the ontic subject of sentences of the form
It is raining or *It rains* (in classical Chinese *raining* or *rains*) in a little detail. This form of sentence may be said to have an unarticulated logical
subject *rain* or *snow* or *frost*, etc., so that it may be construed as *rain rains* or
snow snows and *frost frosts*. We may treat *rain, snow, frost*, etc., as mass
terms which do not have divided reference. Thus the original sentence *It
rains* simply means that rain has a certain property, say of falling down as
indicated by the verb *rains*. To quantify such a sentence, we need classifiers
(such as *'a glass of'*, *'a liter of'* or *'a drop of'*) as we need these for any of
the mass terms in sentences involving them. By using a classifier to *rain*,
It rains may be construed as saying the same thing as

For [some] drops of rain x, x falls down.

The ontic subject of *It rains* therefore is the referent of the mass term *rain*
or more specifically the referent of *'drops of rain'* of which certain properties as indicated by the verb *rains* is true. Finally, it perhaps can be hypothesized that if we cannot observationally identify an individuative subject
for an event-phenomenon, we tend to use an essentially subjectless sentence
such as *it rains* to 'express' that event-phenomenon.

5. APPLICATION TO LATE ARCHAIC CHINESE

We will now apply the above theory of the subject-structure to the analysis
of the subject structure in the Late Archaic Chinese. This will serve not only

to clarify the subject-structure of Late Archaic Chinese, but it also will illustrate the usefulness of the general theory presented above.

In all the following examples, we shall note stylistic eccentricities, their semantical characteristics as well as their general frequencies in the classical texts.

Case I (L, G, T),

Subcase (i): $L = G = T$, most frequently instantiated.

(1)   Chün tzu pu yu pu chü
Superior man not worry not fear.
The superior man does not worry nor fear. (*The Analects*, 12.4)
Chün tzu (the superior man) = $L = G = T$

(2)   Meng tzu chien Liang Hui wang
Meng tzu see Liang Hui King
Meng tzu saw King Hui of Liang. (*The Mencius*, 1.2)
Meng Tzu = $L = G = T$

(3)   Jen, nei yeh, fei wai yeh; yi, wai yeh
Benevolence, internal, not external; righteousness, external.
Benevolence is internal not external; righteousness is external.
fei nei yeh
not internal
external, but not internal. (*The Mencius*, 11.4)
Jen (benevolence) = $L = G = T$
yi (righteousness) = $L = G = T$

Subcase (ii): $L = G \neq T$, frequently instantiated.

(1)   Shui huo, wu chien tao erh ssu che yi, wei chien tao
Water fire, I see step and die, not see step
I have seen men stepping on water and fire to die, but
jen erh ssu che yi
benevolence and die
have not seen men stepping on benevolence to die. (*The Analects*, 15.35)
(water and fire) = T
(I) = $L = G$

(2)   Wan ch'eng chih huo, shih chi chün che,
        Ten thousand carriages state (kingdom), kill its ruler,
        In the case of a state of ten thousand carriages, the one
        pi ch'ien ch'eng chih chia.
        must ten hundred carriage family
        who will kill his ruler must be [from] a family of ten hundred
        carriages. (*The Mencius*, 1.1)
        (a state of ten hundred carriages) = T
        (the one who will kill his ruler) = L = G

(3)   Yeh tsai Yu yeh
        Rude Yu
        Yu is rude. (*The Analects*, 13.3)
        (rude) = T
        (Yu) = L = G

Subcase (iii): $L \neq G = T$, not frequently instantiated.

(1)   Tao shu chiang wei tien hsia lieh
        The art of Tao will be the world break (destroy)
        The art of Tao will be broken by the world. (Chuang-Tzu,
        On the World)
        (the world) = L
        (the art of Tao) = G = T

(2)   Wu ch'ang chien hsiao yu ta fang chih chia
        I always see laugh at great way masters
        I should always have been laughed at the Masters of the Great
        Way. (Chuang Tzu, *The Autumn Flood*)
        (the Masters of the Great Way) = L
        (I) = G = T

(3)   Lao li che ch'ih yu jen
        Labor force persons govern at men
        The bodily workers are governed by others. (*The Mencius*,
        5.4)
        ([some] men) = L
        (the bodily workers) = G = T

Subcase (iv): $G \neq T$, $T \neq L$, $L \neq G$, rarely instantiated.

This case is very rare in Late Archaic Chinese, and perhaps rare in any language, as we have pointed out earlier. The reason for this is that the existence of an instance of the case depends upon the reversion of a passive of the voice which is already indirect. But conceivably we could have a sentence of the form *Chin Pen Cheng-kua wei chi wang so sha*. (Now Pen Cheng-kua was killed by the King of Chi) where Ching (now) = T, (The King of Chi) = L, (Pen Ch'eng-kua) = G. The closest actual example which I have found in the classical texts is the following: *Hsi che, Lung Feng chan, Pi Kan po, Chang Hung?, Tzu Hsü fei*. (In the past, Lung Feng was beheaded; [the heart of] Pi Kan was cut open, [the bowels of] Ch'ang Hung was cut open; [the body of] Tzu Hsü was made to rot. Chuang Tzu, *Opening Brief*), where the logical subject in each constituent sentence has to be supplied on the basis of the verification principle for the deep structure.

Case II (L, $\bar{G}$, T), frequently instantiated.

Consider the sentences taken from *The Mencius*, 3.2

       [1'] fei chi chün pu shih
          not his ruler not serve

If [any ruler] is not his type of ruler, [Pei Yi] will not serve [him].

       [1''] fei chi min pu shih
          not his people not command

If [any people] is not his type of people, [Pei Yi] will not command [them].

       [2'] ch'ih [2] yi chin
          well-governed too advance

If [a state] is well-governed, [Yi Yin] will advance [himself to an office.]

       [2'] Tuan [2] yi chin
          out of order too advance

If [a state] is out of order, [Yi Yin] will too advance [himself to an office].

       [3] k'o yi shih [3] tse shih
          can become an official then become an official

When [Kung Tzu] found it possible to become an official, [Kung Tzu] would become an official.

> [3] k'o yi chiu [3] tse chiu
>   can stay long then stay long
> If [Kung Tzu] found it possible to stay long, he would stay long.
> [4] chieh ku sheng jen yeh
>   all ancient sage
> [Pei Yi, Yi Yin, and Kung Tzu] were all ancient sages.
> [5] Nai so yuan, [5] tse hsüeh Kung Tzu yeh
> As to what is wished, then learn Kung Tzu
> As to what I wish to be, I wish to follow Kung Tzu.

The brackets [1], [2], [3], [4], [5] in these sentences without grammatical subjects indicate the presence of logical subjects which can be located in the immediate or immediately enlarged contexts of the discourse. In fact they are explicitly identified by Mencius. Thus these sentences are relatively subjectless and have the type of subject structure $(L, \bar{G}, T)$, whereby [1] = Pei Yi = L, [2] = Yi Yin = L, [3] = Kung Tzu = L, [4] = Pei Yi, Yi Yin, Kung Tzu = L, [5] = Wu (I = Meng Tzu) = L.

Case III $(\bar{L}, G, T)$
   Subcase (i): G = T, frequently instantiated.

(1)   Yu p'eng chih yuan fang lai, pu yi lo fu?
         Have friend from distance come, not also delightful
         If a friend comes from afar, is that not a delightful thing?
         (*The Analects*, 1.1)

Here the sentence is of the form $(S + P_1) = P_2$ or $(S = NP + VP_1) + VP_2$. Hence it does not have the logical subject in the defined sense, but it has the grammatical subject and the topic which is *Yu p'eng chih yuan fung lai* (there is a friend coming from afar).

(2)   Fu wei ping ping shih yi pu ping
         Only sick sick thus not sick
         Only when one is sick of [one's] sickness is [one] not sick.
         (Lao Tzu: *Tao Te Ching*, 59)

Fu wei ping ping (Only [when one is] sick of [one's] sickness) is not the logical subject of the whole sentence, but the grammatical subject and the topic of the sentence.

(3)   Kuo erh pu kai shih wei kuo yi
         Fault and not correct, this called fault
         If one has faults and does not correct them, this is then called a
         [real] fault. (*The Analects*, 15.30)

Shih (this) is a grammatical subject as well as a topic. It is not a logical
subject, nor is its referent *kuo erh pu kai* (having faults without correcting
them) the logical subject of the sentence in the defined sense.

   Subcase (ii): $G \neq T$, not frequently instantiated.

(1)   Ta tsai Yao chih wei chün yeh
         Great Yao's act as ruler
         Great is [the way in which] Yao acted as a ruler. (*The Analects*,
         8.19)

Yao chih wei chün yeh ([the way in which] Yao acted as a ruler) = G
Ta tsai (great) = T

(2)   Chiu yi wu pu fu mêng chien Chou kung
         Long I not again dream-see Chou duke
         For long I have not dreamed of Duke Chou. (*The Analects*, 7.5)

Wu pu fu meng chien Chou kung ching (that I have not dreamed of Duke
Chou) = G.

   Both examples are of the sentence form $P_1 + (S + P_2)$ or $VP_1 + (NP + VP_2)$ where $(S + P_2)$ or $(NP + VP_2)$ is the grammatical subject and
P_1 or VP_1 is the topic.

   Case IV ($\overline{L}, \overline{G}, T$), frequently instantiated.

   In Case II we have dealt with the relatively subjectless sentences. In
the present case (Case IV) we will deal with essentially subjectless sentences. In connection with the examples of Case II, we can see that the
brackets [1'], [1"], [2'] which represent the missing grammatical subjects
are not to be located in the immediate or immediately enlarged contexts
of the discourse. Hence the related subsentences are essentially subjectless. These sentences are understood in the context to refer to something
or some class of things of a certain category. Thus, [1'] = any ruler,
[1"] = any people, [2'] = any state or the world.

Other types of examples of Case IV are the following:

(1)   Yü wo kung t'ien, sui chi wo ssu
Rain I public field, and reach I private
Rain over my public field, and so over my private one. (*The
Book of Poetry, Smaller Odes*, 'Large Field')
Yü (rain over) = T
wo kung t'ien (my public field) = locomotive

(2)   Keng ch'en, ta yü hsüeh
Keng-ch'en big rain snow
In the year of Keng-ch'en, [there was] a big snowstorm. (*The
Annals of Spring and Autumn*, 'Duke Yin', Ninth Year)
Keng ch'eng (in Keng Ch'en year) = T
Ta yü hsüeh ([there was] a big snow-storm) = comment

(3)   Yu peng chih yuang fang lai
Have friend from afar
There is a friend coming from afar. (*The Analects*, 1.1)

Yu has the function of changing a definite term such as *peng* into an indefinite term. But this transformation does not determine a grammatical subject for the sentence to which it belongs. For apparently neither *peng* nor *yu p'eng* nor *yu* can be considered the grammatical subject of the sentence. One might argue that *yu p'eng* determines a logical subject. But then the difficulty is that this apparent logical subject is not 'realized' in any grammatical subject. Here we simply decide that sentences of *yu/wu* type simply are essentially subjectless. Their ontic subjects are to be referred by indefinite descriptions such as *yu p'eng*.

The topic as well as the comment of (3) is the whole sentence as it stands.

Instances similar to (3) can be multiplied, for examples:

(4)   Wei yu jen erh yi chi ch'in che yeh
Not have benevolence and forget his parents.
There is no person who is benevolent but who forgets his
parents. (*The Mencius*, 1.1)
Wei yu jen (no person who is benevolent) = T

(5)   Wei neng shih hen, yen neng shih kuei
Not able serve man, how can serve ghosts

If [one] is not able to serve man, how can one serve ghosts?
(*The Analects*, 11.12)
Wei neng shih jen ([one] is not able to serve man) = T
(6)   Fei fu jen chih wei t'ung erh shui wei
Not that man grieve who should
If [I] do not grieve for that man, for whom should I grieve?
(*The Analects*, 11.12)
Fei fu jen chih wei t'ung (if [I] do not grieve for that man) = T

Of course, in this instance one might consider *I* (referring to Kung Tzu himself) as understood in the context of saying and thus there is an implicit logical subject of the sentence. The possibility of this interpretation applies to the following instance:

(7)   Yu yeh ch'ien ch'eng chih kuo, k'o shih ch'ih
Yu one thousand carriages state, may govern
Yu [is such a person that] a state of a thousand carriages may
put him in charge of its military system. (*The Analects*, 5.8)
chi fu yeh
its military system.

Both *Yu yeh* (*Yu*) and *ch'ien ch'eng chih kuo* (a state of a thousand carriages) can be regarded as topics.

University of Hawaii

NOTES

[1] Indeed it is true that in the study of classical Chinese, as in the study of other classical languages, we are dealing with a body of codified documents, with no immediate living speech corresponding to its content. Yet, this does not mean that we should not analyze the structure of the given data with a view to their actual function and use in communicating a subject matter.

[2] The use of the term is due to W. A. C. H. Dobson (1959).

[3] Austin (1961) prescribes that two types of convention are necessary to the possibility of our saying things about the world: *descriptive conventions* correlating words with general types of things and *demonstrative conventions* correlating words as uttered on particular occasions with particular situations to be found in the world.

[4] It is in this sense that our statement can be true and false and our language is basically referentially involved.

[5] There are other criteria for separating the referential from the predicative parts of a sentence. They are all related to this one and in fact equivalent to it. Frege (1952) has indicated that

subjects are complete or saturated in a certain sense, i.e., in the sense that the thought of it is completely sensible. On the other hand, the predicates are incomplete or unsaturated in the sense that they will not indicate anything about the world unless they are 'filled' with (and therefore are used to say about) things in the world. Compare Frege (1952) with Geach (1962, Chapter 2; 1965). Geach (1965) points out that we can negate a singular proposition by negating its predicate but not by negating its subject. The reason clearly is simple and related to the asymmetry noted here: i.e., whereas predicates have complementaries and contradictions, subjects do not have these at all.

[6] Cf. Austin (1965) regarding the conditions of successful use of a sentence.

[7] It is the same with the pure quantificational variables to be defined in a discourse. In other words, for ordinary language, we can regard proper names as equivalent to quantificational variables of many sorts. This, however, will not prejudice our attitude toward the issues of eliminability of singular terms between Quine (1960) and Strawson (1963).

[8] Perhaps Quine's system of canonical notation in his book *Word and Object* (1960) in first-order logic with identity can be taken as providing an example of this logical deep structure. Recently Quine (1970a, Chapter 2) discusses explicitly the notion of grammar of a language in this logical sense. Modern linguistic studies tend to recognize the possibility of formulating the base component of a language in similarity to logical systems of Carnap and others. Cf. Bach (1968).

[9] The rules of transformations are logical possibilities, not real laws, which we can adopt to analyze the surface structure sentences to make their functions of reference and predication explicit and clear under considerations of simplicity. In other words, the deep structure is the simplest model of a language whose surface structure can be derived through a simple set of rules of transformation.

[10] The first three are taken from Chomsky (1965, pp. 21–22).

[11] We may also title the principle the manifestation principle for the deep structure of a language.

[12] Here we shall not enumerate such functions. See Austin (1965).

[13] See Chao (1965). Chao contrasts the distinction between topic and comment on the one hand and actor-action distinction on the other.

[14] In this regard, we note that Chao Yuan-ren distinguishes topic from the 'logical subject' in the sense of our psychological or epistemological subject. On the other hand, we do not make such distinction, but instead we define implicitly topic in terms of psychological or epistemological subject, and distinguish it from the logical subject in the deep structure of a language. Chao's characterization of the 'logical subject' corresponds to Cook Wilson's characterization of the same. Cf. Wilson (1926, 119 ff.); also Chao (1965).

[15] A minor sentence is not of the subject-predicate form in the surface structure; cf. Chao (1965, p. 77 and Section 5).

[16] By the very nature of a comment, a comment demands attention and therefore exposition. A topic, on the other hand, is often suppressed in known linguistic contexts or extralinguistic situations in which knowledge of the topic is presupposed or the topic is in fact strongly suggested.

[17] For clarification of this, see later discussion.

[18] E.g., Chou (1961, 6ff) and Dobson (1959) in his *Late Archaic Chinese* fail to make this distinction and therefore fail to appreciate the intricacy and significance of the distinction. The reason is simple, they do not have a sufficiently rich theory to characterize the various aspects of the subject-structure of a sentence in the classical Chinese.

TERESA M. CHENG

COMMENTS ON CHENG'S PAPER

This paper as I understand it tries to set up four levels of linguistic representation in accordance with semantic interpretation. I shall go directly to p. 424 where an outline is given as Table I.

TABLE I

Levels / Cases	Deep structure		Surface structure	
	ontic subject	logical subject	grammatical subject	topic`
I	+	+	+	+
II	+	+	−	+
III	+	−	+	+
IV	+	−	−	+

At one glance we notice that the so-called ontic subject and topic play no role in distinguishing the four cases. In all cases the ontic subject and the topic are always present. Theoretically it takes n features to distinguish 2^n cases. Now that there are four cases, $n = 2$. Hence, in terms of formal characterization and systematic distinction, the levels of ontic subject and topic are to be considered superfluous hypo-constructs.

Now let us turn to the definitions and examples to see if conceptually we have anything to gain by positing the four levels of subject structure. We shall start with the shallow surface and move toward the unfathomable deep structure. In the surface we find the topic. Here Cheng's remark in Note 13 regarding Y. R. Chao's distinction between 'logical subject' and 'topic' may be unclear to a nonlinguist reader. My interpretation of this remark is that Cheng considers topic as something within the sentence immediately perceivable or recognizable as a piece of information where attention is focused by the speaker.

Hintikka et al. (eds.), Approaches to Natural Language, 435–438. All rights reserved.
Copyright © 1973 by D. Reidel Publishing Company, Dordrecht-Holland.

While Cheng did not mention it, I shall add that the recognition of a topic is often facilitated by some explicit form or patterning in the surface structure. For example, a topic in Chinese is formed by preposing the constituent in focus to sentence initial position, as in:

(1)   *ji   bù   chi lè*
         chicken not eat
         As for chicken, (I) don't eat any more.

(2)   *jintian bú   qù   lè*
         today   not go
         As for today, (we are) not going.

In English, a topic is often marked by such phonological features as pitch and stress, as in the sentence:

(3)   John loves Máry.

While *Mary* receives a primary (or ultra-primary) stress, it is understood that it is Mary and not Jane, or Betty, or any other woman that John loves. By employing such formal techniques, the user of the language is able to draw special attention to a particular constituent, and hence, its information content. This is probably the reason why Cheng defines topic as the psychological or epistemological subject, with the psychological or the epistemological equated to the perceptual.

One point worth mentioning about the topic is that while other deeper levels of subject structure refer to objects (or NP's), a topic may refer to a noun, a verb, an adjective, an adverb, or an embedded sentence, whichever is the focus of attention for the utterance. Consider Cheng's examples:

(4)   *Yeh tsai* Yu yeh (p. 428)
         rude   Yu
         Yu is rude. (*The Analects*, 13.3)

(5)   *Kuo erh pu kai*   shih wei   Kuo yi (p. 431)
         fault and not correct this called fault
         If one has faults and does not correct them, this is then called a (real) fault. (*The Analects*, 15.30)

(6)   *Chiu yi* wu pu fu   meng chien Chou Kung
         long   I   not again dream see   Chou duke
         For long I have not dreamed of Duke Chou. (*The Analects*, 7.5)

(7)   *Yü* wo kung t'ien, sui chi   wo ssu (p. 432)
          rain I   public field and reach I   private
          Rain over my public field, and so over my private one. (*The Book of Poetry, Smaller Odes*, 'Large Field')

(8)   *Keng ch'en* ta yü   hsueh (p. 432)
          Keng-ch'en big rain snow
          In the year of Keng-ch'en, (there was) a big snow-storm. (*The Annals of Spring and Autumn*, 'Duke Yin, Ninth Year')

From these examples and the identification of topics in these examples, we notice that Cheng analyzed written sentences of Classical Chinese pretty much after Chao's fashion. The unfortunate fact is that, whereas Chao dealt with spoken Chinese, Cheng is dealing with written documents. The identification of topics depends largely on situational and/or linguistic (especially phonological) contexts. Taken out of context, example (1) can also mean "The hens are not eating any more" while in example (2), *jintian* may just be a sentence adverbial in the periphery. Since it is possible for a constituent to occupy a sentence-initial position without being the focus of attention, whether or not *jintian* 'today' receives more attention than *bú qù lè* 'not going' is debatable. When such subtle ambiguities arise, the context is a major deciding factor. Classical Chinese, like all other written documents, lacks some of the necessary contextual information. As a result, when no empirical supports can be found, the decision has to be arbitrary.

If Cheng is making his decision on the basis of constituent structure of the sentence, it would be necessary for him to set up a norm for untopicalized forms in order to recognize any change of position or deviation from the noun as an indication of topicalization. In other words, the identification of topics in terms of linguistic features presupposes a grammar for the language.

While the choice of topic is particular to situation and context, the formation of grammatical subject is particular to language. This is reflected in what is commonly called the 'voice' of the verb. For English we have the active and the passive voices, but for Tagalog, Bloomfield reported four 'voices'. This kind of interaction between the choice of grammatical subject and 'voice' is further examined by Fillmore in his study of 'case' relations between the verb and its NP complements. For Classical Chinese

Cheng recognized two voices, namely, the active and the passive, and hence two types of grammatical subjects according to the absence and presence of the passive particle 為 *wei*. Though other kinds of case relations can be held between the predicate and the reference, for instance, a locative relation holds between *yü* 'rain' and *wo kung t'ien* 'my public field' in example (7), such relations are not overtly marked by the linguistic structure and there is no way of making these relations explicit in the surface structure.

As for the logical subject, it is the favorite of logicians and linguistic philosophers but not necessarily of a structural linguist because it is doing away with syntactic structures and proposes logical propositions in its place. Logicians may claim that it would yield a better (or logically simple) representation for languages in general, but linguists are after a level of representation that is structurally linked to the surface realization. In other words, there are empirical considerations which logicians tend to ignore and linguists want to incorporate in their theory.

Cheng's proposal of ontic subject as a separate level of subject structure has both philosophical and linguistic grounds. Consider the sentences:

(9)　It snows.
(10)　It rains.

Cheng is correct in saying that they are essentially subjectless despite the presence of a grammatical subject. Likewise, sentences like:

(11)　Ghosts exist.
(12)　God exists.

may be considered 'essentially predicateless' in the sense that in a quantificational theory, they are interpreted as

$$\exists x$$

which is a referential statement, and by definition, a subject.

So far linguists have not been able to agree whether to call sentences like (9), (10), (11), and (12) predicative statements or referential statements, because in each case we will end up with a contradiction in term. The proposal of an ontic level may solve such problems by getting around the definitions of reference and predicate as commonly used by logicians.

University of Hawaii

TERESA M. CHENG

SOME CONSIDERATIONS FOR THE PROCESS OF TOPICALIZATION

The present paper has grown out of ideas conceived before, during, and after the Workshop on Syntax and Semantics. In this paper I have incorporated the original workshop paper in my preliminary discussions which lead up to my proposal concerning question words. The major points in the proposal are:

(1) While questions are known to be related to their corresponding affirmative and negative counterparts, question words are also used in nonquestion constructions in a related manner.

(2) Relatedness mentioned in (1) can be accounted for by the similarity in underlying structure while differences in meaning, use, and surface forms can be attributed to differences in feature specification.

(3) The range of 'questioned' constituent corresponds to the range of focus in a declarative statement.

(4) Closed-class morphemes like prepositions and question words are selected in the base component and not introduced by transformations.

1. PRELIMINARY DISCUSSIONS

In the past few decades we have witnessed the development of an approach to linguistics which aims at a linguistic theory adequate to account for the data on observational, descriptive, and explanatory levels. As early as 1957, Chomsky made the claim that transformational grammars can explain the relations among sentences. This remains one of the important claims about the explanatory power of transformational grammars. Relations among sentences, as the statements and examples go, cannot be characterized by constituent analysis alone, though there is observable similarity among the sentences. Yet, in any event, the sentence has always been the basic unit for analysis. In the following section I would like to examine the role of a sentence in linguistic studies and raise doubts about

Hintikka et al. (eds.), Approaches to Natural Language, 439–456. All rights reserved.
Copyright © 1973 by D. Reidel Publishing Company, Dordrecht-Holland.

the assumed completeness and autonomy of a sentence as commonly held
by structural linguists.

Katz and Postal (1964) claimed that sentences are related because their
underlying P-markers are similar. We now raise the question of how to
characterize 'similarity' and 'difference' which underlie the intuition of
semantic and syntactic relatedness. That is to ask: How can we state in a
simple and explicit manner the conditions under which various related
sentences can be realized from similar underlying P-markers? And, if rule
operations are involved in such realization, what are the factors that motivate and constrain these operations? I shall attempt to answer these
questions in connection with the study of question words. 'Similarity'
would be explained in terms of categorial features, relational features, and
selectional features; whereas 'difference' among intuitively recognized
related sentences would be explained as difference in rule features,
derivational or transformational.

1.1. *The Role of a Sentence in Linguistic Studies*

Lyons (1969) summarized Bloomfield's definition of the sentence as
follows: "the sentence is the maximum unit of grammatical description
to which the structuralist's notion of distribution is not applicable." In
other words, a sentence is distributionally independent except for some
"practical connexion" with other parts of the discourse. What exactly is
this "practical connexion"? Would a theory that claims to account for
sentence relatedness admit "practical connexion" as an explanation for
sentence relations? Certainly not. It is obvious that in proposing similar
underlying P-markers as a solution, generative transformationalists seek
a formal, rather than intuitive or practical, explanation for sentence relations in their model.

With this orientation in mind, let us examine some 'intuitively recognized' related sentences and try to account for their relatedness. First of
all, we shall consider the sentences involving the use of pronouns. The
understanding of these sentences depends on the hearer's ability to associate
the pronouns with their correct referents, given, explicitly or implicitly, in
the context. Associated with each pronominal sentence, one may say, is
a related sentence in which names of the referents appear in the place of the
pronouns.

One may even say that pronominal sentences are 'derived' from under-lying sentences where the referents are explicit. On the other hand, how-ever, one may argue that sentences consisting of pronouns are complete in themselves, provided pronouns are regarded as constituting a formal category or a closed class of lexical items which can participate in sentence generation regardless of their referents and without involving the use of transformations. The latter is in fact the practice found in Chomsky (1957) and other earlier works of the generative-transformationalist school. The notion of completeness is to be understood as completeness in formal characterization. Hence, sentences generated by the grammar are formally complete though they may be in want of additional information from the context in order to be completely meaningful.

Second, we shall examine the so-called 'minor' or 'elliptical' sentences. It is not uncommon in language use to find utterances like *John's* given in response to the question *Whose car are you going in?* In fact, this kind of 'minor' sentence constitutes a good portion of our everyday speech. One may say that minor sentences are 'derived' from an underlying 'full' sentence through anaphoric processes that trim off contextual redundant elements. The natural consequence of such operations is that minor sen-tences lose their autonomy and become apparently dependent on the con-text for their completeness in meaning and form. Redundancy of form and meaning, therefore, can be regarded as the distributional constraint that operates beyond the boundaries of an otherwise 'autonomous' sentence. To return to our cited definition of a sentence, we find that the structuralist's notion of distribution is not only inadequate, but also irrelevant to the explanation of sentence relatedness. The study of conjunction, relativiza-tion, pronominalization, and other forms of sentence embedding in English clearly indicates that the true unit of communication is something larger than a 'sentence' as defined by the structuralist.

Thus we come to the conclusion that sentences are independent only by their formal definition within the theory and that in actual practice sentence boundaries are crossed over and sentences are not self-sufficient for either formal characterization or semantic interpretation. $\#S\#$ is to be understood as a convenient formal unit which is defined for the system. It does not necessarily correspond to a complete message or an autonomous piece of information.

Would such a formal definition really free syntax from semantics and
grant it autonomy? In connection with such processes as conjoining,
relativization, pronominalization, and ellipsis, we notice that the practice
of the generative transformationalists has been such that whenever structural or semantic information is lacking in the surface data, 'dummies' or
'fillers' are used to fill in the gap between what is ideal and what actually
occurs. It would be interesting to ask where and how one obtains the information which justifies the use of dummies. It would be contradictory to
say that dummies are provided on the basis of semantic considerations
and that syntactic autonomy can be claimed on the basis of these 'dummi-
fied' structures. Even Chomsky's later proposal (1970b) concerning 'intended referent' and the use of 'index' does not seem to have freed syntax
from the clutches of semantic considerations. A formal system and a
competence model certainly has its limitations. It may be very powerful,
but it is not omnipotent. There are areas of performance that a model
cannot and should not even attempt to account for if it is to be consistent
with its assumptions and claims. Otherwise, its basic assumptions and
claims would have to be drastically revised. This is exactly what the generative semanticists did to the generative transformational theory when
McCawley (1968) proclaimed the downfall of autonomous syntax. In order
to give $\#S\#$ both syntactic and semantic completeness, generative
semanticists have invented ways of including presuppositions and other
contextual and semantic considerations into the underlying structure. It
seems that within their theoretical framework the underlying form is always richer and more uniform than its surface realization. It is by such
semantic deep structure that surface forms are paraphrased and interpreted, and it is from this semantic deep structure that surface forms can be
systematically derived. One may say that the generative-semanticist's
model consists of an ideal base component which has a claim to universality
besides a power for semantic interpretation and disambiguation. Somehow
in actual speech events this ideal structure becomes degenerated and loses
its independence.

I would like to further raise the question whether sentences are truly
self-sufficient and complete even in the base component of a generative-
semanticist's model. Semantic interpretations are conditioned by external
nonlinguistic situational elements. Deictic forms like 'here', 'now', 'this',

and 'that' change their information content according to the situation. Without a real situation, an expression like *Now he is here* would be completely meaningless. Sooner or later a linguist would have to draw a line on how far he would go in including semantic consideration and specification in his deep structure. It is linguistically irrelevant to pursue presuppositions that cannot be defined in terms of some formal characterization of the linguistic context. If one should pursue indefinitely the line of presuppositions, one would ultimately deduce that interpretation of sentences is dependent on one's ontological commitments and the whole reservoir of human experience.

It may be true that semantic deep structure facilitates semantic interpretation to a certain extent, but the burden of proof is laid upon the generative semanticist to prove that universal semantic features are not postulated in an *ad hoc* manner without any empirical grounds.

In the preceding elaboration, I have pointed out the polarized positions taken by the formal lexicalists and the generative semanticists. At this point I tend to agree with Fillmore that it is doubtful whether there is a 'level' of syntactic description discoverable in one language at a time on the basis of purely syntactic criteria. Take the case of structural indices, for example. It seems that while they act as formal constraints on transformational operations they are actually semantically and situationally motivated. By the simple law of transitivity one can say that the application of transformational rules is also semantically and situationally motivated. It would be sheer ostrich-like obstinacy for a structuralist to refuse to see that the assumed sentence autonomy and syntactic autonomy are only smoke-screens created to protect himself from confronting the nebulous areas of discourse analysis and semantics. In an attempt to present an integrated theory of syntax and semantics within the generative transformational framework, Katz and Postal (1964) postulated the universality of syntactic elements such as Q, I, *wh*, Negative, etc., on semantic grounds, primarily on the fact that each of these elements has the same meaning in every language in which it occurs.

In so doing, Katz and Postal (1964) implicitly provided a definition of language universals as well as a guideline that restricts one's freedom in introducing semantically motivated elements into the description of language. First of all, attempts should be made to discover a set of basic

categories of language by examining languages of the world. This set of
basic categories is the set of 'language universals'. Corresponding to each
category is a function and overt forms in some, if not all, languages. Moreover, each of these language universals has the same meaning or function
in every language in which it occurs. Hence, language universals may be
regarded as universal syntactic categories motivated by function and form.
Language universals have empirical grounds for their existence and should
not be confused with vague intuitive conjectures on meaning alone. For
example, the feature [±animate] has both syntactic form and function
within the grammar as well as a plausible semantic interpretation, but it is
the syntactic considerations that count in our formal system. Furthermore,
it is important that grammatical subcategorization is matched by lexical
subcategorization. Whereas syntactic matters are included in the grammar,
semantic elements may be kept in the lexicon till they are introduced into
the system through lexical insertion and selection.

1.2. *Similarity and Difference and Sentence Relations*

To recapitulate Katz and Postal's claim that sentences are related because
their underlying *P*-markers are similar, I would like to make precise this
notion of similarity and examine the differences which differentiate the
meaning and surface forms of these 'related' sentences. Such considerations
lead to a more fundamental issue in generative grammar, namely, the
problem of derivational and transformational constraints.

With a belief that the need for communication is basically the same for
all human beings and that meaning can to a certain extent be formulated
into a formal system, we require the set of grammatical rules for each
individual language to perform the function of deriving the more particular
from the more general underlying structure which may be compared with a
formal logical system. However, where there is great resemblance in their
formal characterization, their power of explanation, disambiguation, and
paraphrasing the surface phenomena, a fundamental difference nonetheless exists between the two kinds of formal systems. The postulation of
grammatical deep structure must have empirical justification from
linguistic data, synchronic or comparative, while a formal logical system
based primarily on philosophical speculation does not necessarily have
any overt linguistic justifications.

Thus we are faced with the problem of explicit characterization of the motivations and constraints which govern the grammatical operations that give us the superficial forms found in actual speech. Transformational rules are either obligatory or optional. When its turn comes in a transformational cycle, an optional transformation can either be by-passed or taken up. The decision of choice is made on the basis of situation or stylistic preference. By allowing optionality for the application of transformational rules we allow alternative ways of expressing similar or related ideas. It is also assumed for all transformations, optional or obligatory, that no change of meaning occurs after the operation. It would follow from this assumption that all semantic characterizations of an utterance should be completed before the application of transformational rules.

The term 'optional' may be quite misleading. It seems to imply that structures generated by optional transformations are only stylistic variations of the more basic form called the 'kernel sentence'. Chomsky (1965) already abandoned this idea of kernel sentences as related to sentence relation and optional transformation. Moreover, Fillmore has successfully demonstrated with his study of case relations that the traditional active voice is not any more basic than the passive. The traditional notion of a 'subject' is to be interpreted as an aspect of the surface structure. In the deep structure there are only 'case relations'. A case relation is a relation held between the verb and one of its several NP-complements. A case relation, according to Fillmore, may get focused upon and the NP-complement holding such relationship with the verb then becomes marked as the subject of a sentence. This idea of focus can be likened to the figure against the ground but should be differentiated from emphasis. This process of bringing out the 'figure' relationship is called topicalization or subject formation. The most unmarked choice would be the agent as subject, which gives us the active voice in English. Theoretically, all case relations should have a chance of being focused upon and any NP-complement of the verb may be cast as the subject of a sentence. Since the surface structure requires a subject, we are obliged to choose among these possibilities when we produce an utterance. In this context the keyword is not 'optionality'; rather, it is 'selection'. Statistically, some case relations are more readily cast in focus than others. The marking convention can probably help provide a cue for our selection.

We may ask the related question of whether the results of these alternative selections are indeed synonymous. From my knowledge of the use of passive forms in Chinese, English, and Japanese – to name just three common languages – the passive structure seems to carry with it some connotations not conveyed by the active form. For example, the passive marker *bèi* and its variants *gěi* and *ái* of Mandarin Chinese always co-occurs with verbs which imply undesirable consequences. In Chinese we would say *Ta ái dǎ lè* (He was beaten up) but not *Ta ái shǎng lè* (He was rewarded). Similarly, the English 'get' co-occurs with a class of verbs implying adversity or undesirable events as in *get killed, get blamed, get fired, get broken.* As for passive forms in Japanese, they convey the feeling of submissiveness, passivity, and even an intended evasion of responsibility. In a report given by Niyakawa-Howard (1968) the so-called Japanese passive is indeed an adversitive passive. When a person makes the statement *X ga kita* (X visited me) he might be neutral or favorable to X's visit, but when he says *X ni korareta* (I was visited by X) he implies that X's visit is not welcome. When combined with the causative, the passive seems to indicate passivity and freedom from responsibility. This is well illustrated by the favorite expression used by husbands going home late to their wives: *nomasareta* (I was made to drink [against my will]).

With these examples in mind, we now return to the problem of focus selection or subject selection. One may argue that focusing is only a matter of attention shifting, a difference in the choice of figure and ground. However, a shift of attention often reduces the background. As a result, the distribution of information becomes essentially different. The bits of information carried by these related sentences do not match one another. The structural configuration is different; the Gestalt is different; the information conveyed and eventually the meaning perceived are different. Hence, there is more to it than a random selection of focuses. It seems that we will have to eliminate 'optional' transformation and place the burden of choice or selection on the base component. Motivations for a certain choice would also have to be built into the base component. These may be primarily semantic and situational motivations. Once some generalizations are made on these motivations, such as the expression of adversity, we can devise a finite set of semantically motivated rule features which would instruct us to apply certain transformational rules to achieve certain purposes in communication.

The production and perception of sentences involve at least two parameters, namely, the structural parameter and the situational parameter. One may wish to add a statistical parameter in order to mark the frequencies of occurrences of the various related forms. Some forms are indeed 'favored' over the others and this favoritism differs from language to language. For example, given the choice of agent-focus (active) and object-focus (passive) constructions, Chinese favor the use of the former and use the latter only with adversitive verbs, whereas in Amis, a Formosan aboriginal language, and Tagalog object-focused constructions are more frequently used and are not limited to verbs implying undesirable consequences. Nominalization of verbs is very frequent in Amis and Tagalog. Utterances like *ira tukur* ‖ KU *sapay-ala nira tamdaw tia nani (The ladder*
$$1 \qquad 2 \quad 3 \ 4 \qquad 5 \qquad 1$$
is what *the man used* to *rescue the cat)* constitute approximately 30 percent
$$4 \quad 2 \quad 3 \quad 5$$
of Amis sentences involving verbal constructions. Such constructions are structurally similar to equational constructions involving two NP's. Consider the equational expression *u ina nira* ‖ KU *matu? asay(The elderly*
$$1 \quad 2 \qquad 3 \qquad 3$$
person is *his mother).* That *sapay-ala* is a derived noun marked by *ku,*
$$2 \quad 1$$
the particle used to introduce a focused NP. The place where a copula is expected in view of the English translation is marked by double-bars. In English, verbal nouns or gerunds are used much less frequently than in Amis. In Chinese, such constructions are not used at all except in some *tour de force* translations of Western texts. A word-for-word translation of the English gerundial expression such as *his leaving (*ta dè lí-kai)* or *my typing (*wǒ dè dǎ-zì)* are terribly awkward if not unacceptable expressions in Chinese. How we can express this sort of linguistic favoritism is beyond the scope of the present study. For the time being we shall restrict our attention to the structural and situational parameters.

1.3. *Transformational Constraints*

Katz and Postal (1964), in connection with pronominalization and other transformations involving deletion or substitution, state the structural constraint on transformational derivations as follows:

A transformation T whose elementary transformations include a deletion or substitution affecting the ith term of T's structure index applies to a P-marker PM bracketed in terms of the structure index of T just in case one of the following conditions is met:

   (i) The ith term of the structure index of T is a string of terminal symbols.

  (ii) The string of terminal symbols of the ith term of the bracketing of PM is necessarily identical with a different string of terminal symbols also occurring in PM.

 (iii) The string of terminal symbols of the ith term of the bracketing of PM is dominated by Pro.

On examining this statement we notice that the formal elements involved in specification of structural constraints are:

   (i) *P*-marker

  (ii) labeled bracketing

 (iii) structure index

 (iv) terms or constituents

  (v) strings of terminal symbols

 (vi) node domination

(vii) relation between the constituents

(viii) feature specification of the constituents.

These formal elements are given as constraints or conditions for every transformation in the name of structural description (SD). Since the derivational history and node domination of the constituents play an important role in characterizing the structure of the terminal string, the terminal string is given in the stratified form of labeled bracketing. Structure indices are used to identify the terms and their positions for structural reference and for indicating the structural change (SC) that will take place upon application of the transformation under consideration.

Last, but not the least, is the feature specification of the constituents. Feature specifications require special attention here because they contribute to the semantic interpretation of the underlying *P*-marker. They constitute a formal machinery for expressing certain semantically motivated factors in the base component. These factors serve to condition transformation on the one hand while they subcategorize the syntactic constituents and prepare them for lexical matching and insertion on the other. Feature specifications may appear to be semantically motivated, but in general there should be empirical grounds for their postulation. Among them output consideration and language universals are two primary factors.

We also notice that relatedness and redundancy of the constituents, the primary motivation for processes like pronominalization, deletion or substitution, cannot be expressed by the formal machinery of SD. Consequently, a separate list of conditions has to be enumerated in longhand at the end of SD and SC statements. For the purpose of illustration, I shall cite Ross' statement of transformational constraints for pronominalization, which is a modified version of the formulation of Katz and Postal cited above:

Given the following SD:

$$X - \begin{bmatrix} NP \\ -PRO \end{bmatrix} - Y - \begin{bmatrix} NP \\ -PRO \end{bmatrix} - Z \quad \overset{\text{OBLIG}}{=\!=\!=\!=\!=\!=\!\Rightarrow}$$

$$1 \qquad 2 \qquad 3 \qquad 4 \qquad 5$$

A. 1 2 3 $\begin{bmatrix} 4 \\ +PRO \end{bmatrix}$ 5 *or*

B. 1 $\begin{bmatrix} 2 \\ +PRO \end{bmatrix}$ 3 4 5

The following conditions apply:

(i) $2 = 4$

(ii) That the structural change in (A) is subject to no conditions

(iii) That backward pronominalization is *only* permissible if the NP in term 2 is a part of the subordinate clause which does not contain the NP in term 4.

This presentation, accurate as it may be, is rather cumbersome. What happens is that in an effort to simplify the base component, the transformational device inevitably becomes more and more complicated in order to make the right transitions and to yield the varied surface output. One way to remedy this is to have a more specific SD input, not only with labeled bracketing and structure indices, but also with every relevant constituent marked for its macro- and microstructures – 'macro-' in the sense of node domination and 'micro-' in the sense of feature specification.

In connection with my study of question words, I shall elaborate on the microstructural description of syntactic categories without making any attempts to improve upon the present convention for expressing structural constraints on transformations.

Our next concern is the situational parameter for sentence production and perception. This is the most difficult parameter to enumerate, exhaust, and express in formal terms. In order to incorporate linguistic context, we find ourselves in the area of discourse analysis faced with the problem of presupposition and reference. If we are to imitate communication in action, our model would have to have a memory to hold the previous linguistic context as well as some vital information about the persons and situation involved. There seems to be no upper limit for the situational context since it encompasses the whole of human knowledge and experience. However, we may limit ourselves to one subject matter at a time and consider a more immediate context. Yet, it is still questionable whether one can handle this much in a model of communication. Let us just assume that we can. During a communicative process the memory is constantly scanned for gaps in information which would motivate the speech act. It is true that an utterance can be made without giving any new information, but our primary concern is in the interaction of stimulus and response and not in a reiteration of information already stored in the memory. When a situation arises and the related memory is scanned, we search for gaps of information to be filled by new lexical entries and their semantic and relational contents. Messages are generated when the gaps of information are filled for a certain syntactic frame with substantial lexical items. When a slot is filled by an unknown, we have a question instead. We shall see in connection with our study of question words that there are at least three types of information we can expect as the response to our stimulus, i.e., the information gap. The information can be given as definite, indefinite, or unknown.

When a situation arises, we may ask the question:

> Who does what to whom, with what instrument, for the benefit of whom, in the company of whom, when, where, how, and why?

This question can be regarded as an explicit formulation of the situation. It serves as a frame of reference in which old information can be displayed and new information can be inserted. In the use of language it is expected that an explicit question like this would condition the content and structure of the answer.

When the situation requires that a certain piece of information be given special attention, this part of the answer becomes the 'topic' or the focus of attention. Questions are goal-oriented. Question words like 'who', 'what', 'when', etc., should obtain for us the desired pieces of information. Structurally the topic of a sentence is always marked for attention and is associated with explicit syntactic and/or phonological forms in the surface.

When several pieces of information are introduced simultaneously, the sentence usually takes on the form most unmarked for focus or attention. When this is the case, the subject of a sentence is not to be considered a topic because it is not a figure that stands out against the ground. It is neutral to focus or attention. That is to say, a subject is only a slot to be filled in according to surface structural requirement. If special attention should be given to the subject or any nonsubject constituent, this particular constituent would have to be topicalized. Then it would be specifically marked for focus or attention at the expense of the other constituents within the same utterance. If anaphoric processes are applied to a topicalized structure, the topic, i.e., the part directly responding to the attention-getting question word, is always preserved while other parts may be deleted. Hence, subject formation and topicalization are two separate processes, the application of which is motivated by situation. Situational requirement places a constraint on the application or nonapplication of the topicalization process. In other words, the selection of rule application is situationally motivated. The selection itself is recorded in the form of a T-marker or of a rule feature in the base component. Once a selection is made, each of the related structures begins to take its separate course toward a separate destiny according to the T-marker or rule feature specification. In the process of its realization, elements that differentiate the functions and forms of the related sentences which share similar P-markers in the base are duly introduced.

2. QUESTIONS AND THEIR RELATED STRUCTURES

Katz and Postal (1964) observed that, like imperative and negative sentences, questions seem to have the same sequence of underlying P-markers as their corresponding declaratives, yet they clearly do not have the same meaning. If we recall our interpretation of sentence relatedness, it is clear that questions are related to their corresponding declaratives, and by transitivity, to their corresponding imperative and negative sentences as well. Through cross-linguistic observation of the forms and uses of question words, we also find that other nonquestion constructions are related to questions.

Occurrences of question words are found not only in structures underlying questions but also in those underlying relative phrases. In declarative sentences or imperative sentences containing embedded questions as their nominalized object, question words perform the function of subordinate conjunctions. Moreover, in some languages indefinite pronouns or other proforms resemble question words in both function and form. We can say that all these structures are paraphrastically related to questions. In the following section we shall use English examples in connection with our attempt to characterize such paraphrastic relations in terms of similarity and difference.

2.1. *Feature Characterization of Question and Topic*

Traditionally, questions are divided into two types, namely, the yes-no questions and the wh-questions. In English, the first type is characterized by the use of auxiliary verbs and the anticipated answer of either 'yes' or 'no'. The second type is characterized by the use of question words like 'who', 'what', 'when', 'where', etc., and an anticipated answer which provides the specific information requested by the question words. Katz and Postal, by introducing 'whether' as the question word associated with the yes-no type questions, reduced the difference between the two types to a difference between simple and disjunctive structures of the form A versus $A \ or - A$.

One way to paraphrase the question is to change it into an imperative sentence beginning with *Tell me* ... Given a set of English questions

(1) will you come
(2) does John love Mary
(3) who killed the mockingbird
(4) who(m) did John see
(5) which man did John see
(6) when did John see Charles.

They may be paraphrased as

(1') Tell me whether you will come or not
(2') Tell me whether John loves Mary or not
(3') Tell me who killed the mockingbird
(4') Tell me who(m) did John see
(5') Tell me which man did John see
(6') Tell me when did John see Charles.

The use of *whether* makes the type of yes-no questions a subtype of wh-questions. Still there is a fundamental difference between them. While the information specifically requested by question words like 'who', 'what', 'when', etc., range over an NP, the information requested by *whether* is a truth value of the statement A. We may also request information on the verb in questions like *What did Mary do?* In order to handle the problem of information range, Katz and Postal proposed using the features ±Q and ±wh in a combinatorial way. The feature +wh may be dominated by an NP, by a VP, or by a sentence adverbial. Together with the presence of the feature +Q, +wh dominated by an NP yields a regular wh-question, while it yields a yes-no question when dominated by the sentence adverbial 'yes or no', and a question which requests specific information that ranges over the verb when it is dominated by a VP.

When combined with the feature −Q, +wh yields the proforms that are used as subordinating conjunctions in indirect, embedded questions. *Whether* has the feature specification of −Q and +wh while other question words are specified ±Q and +wh, +Q for direct questions and −Q for indirect questions.

Yet there is a class of morphemes closely related to question words that can also be characterized by the features −Q and +wh. This class consists of indefinite nonspecific pronouns like 'someone', 'somebody', 'sometime', 'somewhere', etc., which are used in simple declarative sentences. Consider the following set of sentences:

(a) *Where* is the book?
(b) Tell me *where* I can find him.
(c) The key is *somewhere* in this room.

Where in (a) is marked $+Q$ and $+wh$; *where* in (b) is marked $-Q$ and $+wh$; and *somewhere* in (c) is also marked $-Q$ and $+wh$. How, then, can we differentiate between indefinite, nonspecific pronouns and the question words used as relative pronouns? We know that questions are goal-oriented. Whether asked directly or indirectly, a question asks for specific information. While Katz and Postal have already used the feature $\pm$ definite to distinguish 'which' from 'what', I propose to use the feature $\pm$ specific to distinguish 'what' from 'somebody' or 'something'. Hence we have the following morphemes with different use and feature specifications:

Class A

Feature specification: $\begin{bmatrix} +Q \\ +wh \\ +spec \end{bmatrix}$

Function: To ask for specific information in the form of direct questions.

Membership: {who, what, where, when, how, why, (which)}.

Class B

Feature specification: $\begin{bmatrix} -Q \\ +wh \\ +spec \end{bmatrix}$

Function: To ask for specific information in the form of indirect questions. (Since the sentence with a question embedded in it is either imperative or declarative, we mark the relative clause with the feature $-Q$).

Membership: {who, what, where, when, how, why, whether, which (that)}.

Class C

Feature specification: $\begin{bmatrix} -Q \\ +wh \\ -spec \end{bmatrix}$

Function: Used as indefinite, nonspecific pronouns in simple declarative sentences. It does not expect any response that will provide specific new informations.

Membership: {some, somebody, someone, somewhere, sometime}.

In English, the three classes do not have a one-to-one correspondence
among their one-word members. However, if we should extend the membership to include NP's as Katz and Postal did, we shall have a more uniform
correspondence. As a matter of fact, this generalization is necessary since
not all languages have one-word morphemes for these concepts. Chinese,
for example, uses *shémmè* (what) + *dìfang* (place) as well as *nǎr* (where) for
translating the English 'where', and uses *shémmè* (what) + *shíhòu* (time) to
translate the English 'when'. There is no one-word morpheme in Chinese
to correspond with the English 'when'.

Paraphrasing all one-word morphemes into a prepositional phrase is a
relatively easy process for all languages. With their generalization, Katz
and Postal reassigned the feature +wh that ranges over an NP in both
direct and indirect question to the determiner in the NP. Since the determiner can be marked +definite or −definite, we have subclasses of
question words or question expressions differentiated by the feature
±definite. The definite class is expressed by the determiner 'which' in
English and *nǎ* + *NC* in Chinese (NC stands for noun-classifier, sometimes
called measure-words MW). The indefinite class is expressed by the determiner 'what' in English and *shémmè* in Chinese.

Previously, in our discussion of situational constraints for transformations, we noted that the choice of focus is situationally motivated. And
since the situation can be formulated into a question with the feature +wh
ranging over any constituent or combination of constituents, we can claim
that the choice of focus is motivated by the feature specifications of the
NP's. An intended focus may be marked among other specifications by
the features −Q, −wh, and +spec to indicate that it is a response to an
underlying question or to a question in the preceding linguistic context.
Whereas +wh marks the request for information, −wh is used to indicate
the response.

Since these closed-class morpheme categories and their feature specifications are used as part of the transformational constraint, it is necessary
that these categories are selected and specified in the base component
prior to the application of transformational rules. In so doing, we can
tighten our constraint on transformations by making all transformational
operations obligatory whenever the structural descriptions are matched
and the stated conditions are met. At the same time, the inclusion of these
categories and their feature specifications in the base component will
facilitate the explanation for sentence relations and hence gain explanatory
power for our theory.

University of Hawaii

W. C. WATT

LATE LEXICALIZATIONS*

1. INTRODUCTION

1.1.   This paper, whose alternate title is 'On the Surface Verb "Bottle"',
presents facts about some English words which, on the whole, support
the view that these words are more naturally treated in a 'transformational'
than in a 'lexical' fashion. These words appear to be derived, like phrases
or clauses, through the operation of transformations upon underlying or
more abstract material: from which it follows that these words cannot be
inserted, pretransformationally, as atomic units. Basically, the argument
takes the form of showing that the syntactic structures that would underlie
such words in a 'transformational' account, do in fact underlie them,
because they are needed to play other syntactic roles. The particular role
examined here is that of providing antecedents and anaphors for anaphora.
Apart from showing that the words in question should not be inserted
pretransformationally, I do not take up the issue of just where they *are*
inserted, except to present internal evidence that suggests that their
insertion is late in the sentential derivation and to cite some relevant
external evidence which, if correct, strongly upholds that position and
moreover sites the insertion more exactly. Thus the main burden of the
paper is to show that (for at least some words) lexicalization is not early;
but the evidence presented here is compatible with the view that what is
really at issue is the 'late lexicalizations' of the title.

The paper has an extrapolation to the English lexicon as a whole, for
having argued that *some* words are best not introduced pretransformationally I note that the lexicalization rules needed to introduce those words
will also serve, appropriately extended, to introduce others; in all, it
appears that once the grammar contains lexicalization transformations
of the sort specifically indicated, it may easily generalize those rules for
lexicalization (lexical insertion) as a whole. I provide a reason for thinking
this tactic nonartificial when I show, finally, that even so ordinary a word

Hintikka et al. (eds.), *Approaches to Natural Language*, 457–489. *All rights reserved.*
Copyright © 1973 by *D. Reidel Publishing Company, Dordrecht-Holland.*

as 'father' must seemingly be underlaid by a syntactic phrase on the order of 'one who has sired a child'.

Above, I used the terms 'transformational' and 'lexical' in order to sidestep for a moment the broader issue of what general theory of grammar this paper supports. It is obvious that the 'Transformationalist' theory and (in one version) the 'Lexicalist' theory outlined by Noam Chomsky in a recent paper (1970b) are not, either of them, much affected by the argument at hand. In Chomsky's 1970 use of these terms the first applies to a theory in which, for example, 'acceleration' is to be derived transformationally from 'accelerate' during the derivation of the sentence, with 'accelerate' introduced from the lexicon; while the second (in one version) applies to a theory in which what is introduced from the lexicon is an abstract entity which is neither word but which is converted by rules to whichever word (verb or noun) is appropriate. But even in the 'Lexicalist' account, apparently, some words may be derived or partially derived transformationally: for example, the causal verb *grow* of "John grows marijuana" may be generated transformationally as part of a derivation of the just-quoted sentence from an underlying structure on the order of "John makes marijuana grow." Indeed, the need for some such derivation is very convenient to the 'Lexicalist' argument, so it seems: for a nominalization can occur in place of the corresponding verb only where the verb is not transformationally derived (hence where the position in question could have been filled, indifferently, by either nominalization or verb, from the lexicon). Evidence: "John accelerated the process" and "John's acceleration of the process . . ." are both grammatical because both verb and nominal are directly from the lexicon; while "John grows marijuana" contrasts with the ungrammatical "*John's growth of marijuana . . ." precisely because the *grows* of the first sentence did *not* come directly from the lexicon, and so neither could *growth* have had that origin. That is, *grow* in its causative meaning appears in sentences after the point at which *grow* alternates with *growth*.[1] In short, then, the present paper, which holds that some words are to be derived transformationally, is scarcely in direct conflict with either of the theories just indicated, though of course it might argue against particular grammars constructed on those theories. Rather, the argument before us discriminates between *extensions* of these theories. The first such extension, which I will call the 'New

Lexicalist' theory (NL) for want of a better name, holds essentially that *no* words are derived in the 'transformational' fashion just outlined, except in very mild cases where for example 'the ones' can be collapsed into 'those'. The second extension, which I will call 'New Transformationalist' (NT), holds that typically *all* words are derived transformationally. It is of course perfectly clear that the present argument is very prejudicial against the first or NL extension, and insofar as the NL extension is identified as a cardinal tenet of 'Interpretivism' and the NT extension is identified as a tenet of 'Generative Semantics', the latter is here upheld over the former.[2]

The present argument favors the NT view in holding that the syntactic underlying structure that the NT theory produces is needed for anaphora in any case; but it must be admitted that a quite different conclusion might be drawn from the same evidence. The underlying elements that anaphora demand could be said to reside, not in a subcutaneous level of the syntax, but rather *in the lexicon*: the process of tying together antecedent and anaphor, on this view, must sometimes refer to abstract elements that are to be found only in the lexical definitions of the words that appear on the surface. The claimed underlying syntactic structure would not be needed, and so the claimed rebuff to the NL theory would be without foundation. Since this alternative is 'descriptively adequate' the ultimate appeal of the present argument is necessarily to an 'explanatory' notion of economy; since the needed underlying elements could, grossly, be either syntactic or lexical, to justify choosing the first possibility over the second it must be shown that the first is largely a required part of the grammar in any case, and then that: "It is necessary that the grammar be empowered to perform anaphora upon elements of the syntax; such an anaphoric operation suffices to treat those cases which might have been claimed to compel recourse to the lexicon; therefore recourse to the lexicon is superfluous." This statement does obscure some necessary qualifications, since after all if words are formed in (or at the end of) the syntax then word-formation rules must be present; but the basis of the comparison is tolerably clear. It will be a question of comparing the added burden of word-formation rules against the added burden of having two distinct ways (syntactic and lexical) of tying anaphors to antecedents.

The term 'anaphora', used several times above, will not be determined

with any greater precision in this paper than is usual; and far from reducing the number of open questions about anaphora, I will actually add to
that number. Where appropriate I will allude to one or another of these
open questions; but mostly I will rely on the likelihood that the arguments
to be presented will apply to *any* notion of anaphora as that term may
come to be defined more precisely. For further discussion of this point
see, e.g., Postal (1969). For the moment it will suffice to say that the
anaphoric relationship is one that obtains between two sentential elements
(words, say) that are identical in some (much-brooded) sense, and that
binds them together in such a way that the sentence is understood as if the
anaphor were replaced by a copy of the antecedent.[3] (Because I am not
treating them here I can afford to ignore the many cases where the anaphor
itself has been omitted ('zeroed', in Harris' term, 1968), as from the
bracketed part of the sentence "Nixon upbraided the students and Agnew
[   ] the professors").

1.2. The phenomena we are chiefly concerned with here are similar to,
indeed mainly identical with, those that Postal (1969) recently analyzed
under the heading 'Anaphoric Islands'. Postal observes that some lexical
items (like 'New Yorker') incorporate as constituents other words ('New
York') to which anaphoric reference, though possible when those constituents occur as words in their own right, is nevertheless forbidden when
they are incorporated. He illustrates the contrast with examples like these:

(1)   + Harry is from New York, but I wouldn't want to open a store
         there.

as against:

(1a)   *Harry is a New Yorker, but I wouldn't want to open a store
         there.[4]

The word *New York* is the antecedent of *there* in (1), but cannot be so
in (1a), even though the *New Yorker* of (1a) not only overtly contains
'New York' but also, and presumably more pointfully, subsumes 'New
York' in its meaning, 'from New York'.[5] From this and from many other
examples (some, as we will see, quite different from the one just cited)
Postal concludes that in general words that are incorporated into other

words are not available as anaphoric antecedents. Or, put the other way around, words do not allow anaphora to penetrate their boundaries to find antecedents like 'New York' inside them: words, in Postal's term, are 'anaphoric islands'.[6] Postal also notes islands that are even less breachable than 'New Yorker' was: for example the word 'father' directly implies the word 'child' in some way, yet 'child' seems to be totally occulted by 'father', as witness:

(2)   *Harry is a father, but no one has ever seen it.

as against:

(2a)   +Harry is someone who has sired a child, but no one has ever seen it.

There are various ramifications of Postal's argument at this point, but one's attention is first drawn to his consideration of exceptions, cases where an 'interior' word *is* accessible to anaphoric reference. In an NL grammar, the English words that are clearly 'derived' in a simple sense – compounds like 'self-taught', for instance – might in any case be given a source other than a listing (as a holophrase) in a lexicon; if actually 'derived' in some sense than they would yield fairly naturally to anaphoric penetration to a contained antecedent or anaphor. Thus if all noninsular exceptions turned out to be compounds then an NL grammar would have a motivated reason to treat them as 'derived' exceptions, retaining however all of the insular and non-'derived' words as lexical items. Thus we note with interest the nature of Postal's exceptions. His clearest cases involve exception to a kind of anaphoric island not yet mentioned here, namely, the kind where anaphora demands, not that the *antecedent* be found within another word, but that the *anaphor* be. That is, instead of having *there* outside and *New York* inside, the reverse would hold true, as in:

(1b)   *Harry is a [There]er, but I wouldn't want to open a store in New York.

As we see, in general this sort of 'inbound' anaphora, to use Postal's term, plainly results in sentences that are ungrammatical, incomprehensible, and abominations to the mind. Still, Postal found exceptions. They involve the prefix 'self', as in:

(3)   +Origen was self-emasculated.

It is clear that (3) can only mean 'Origen was emasculated by Origen', and that therefore the anaphoric relationship 'Origen . . . self' is present in (3). Thus inbound anaphora can invade words. Moreover, words prefixed by the Greek synonym of 'self-', namely, 'auto-', act just like the 'self-' compounds:

(4)   + W. C. Fields was an autodidact.

where (4) has only the reading that Fields was taught by himself, so that 'auto-' is also an exception to the insularity of inbound anaphora.

Compounds like 'self-emasculated' and 'autodidact', then, show that some strings conventionally called 'words' allow a constituent to serve as an anaphor; but since almost any NL grammar might well find independent reason for deriving such words in any case (in whatever way, and where-ever), these exceptions are not very telling. Postal also cites a couple of noncompound (simplex) exceptions to insularity, of which to me the only convincing one is 'cannibal':

(5)   + On the Nobile expedition to the North Pole, one man turned cannibal.

In (5), *cannibal* might be seen as containing an anaphor similar to 'self-', as in the synonymous phrase 'eater of own [= self's] kind'; and if this is so there must be a few other examples of like character. Still, a few such examples are not overwhelmingly convincing. In fine, Postal's argument from the anaphoric islands confronts any NL theory with problems, but with problems not impossible to sidestep.

1. 3.   I can now lay out my intentions. First, I will retraverse some of Postal's material, considering a set of idiolects in which some of his islands prove not to be islands. Then I will expand the scope of the inquiry beyond the sort of example taken up by Postal (though the widened set is directly inspired by his paper); in the expansion set I will focus on the numbers of words that 'should' be islands but that in fact seem to be altogether penetrable, for most speakers. I will consider, in this set of 'penetrable reefs', both compound words and simple words. I will then examine, and refute, the claim that there *is* no such evidence (that there are no penetrable reefs). After this I will consider some implications, and conclude.

2. EVIDENCE

2.1. *Anaphoric Islands and Anaphoric Insularity*

First, it is to be noted that many of the examples cited as anaphoric islands by Postal are, to many Americans, in fact penetrable. One such example is the very one we have used above, 'New Yorker': I find that a majority of speakers easily accept sentences like:

(6)   +Conrad is a confirmed New Yorker now, but I wouldn't live there on a bet.

Most of the speakers who accept (6), however, reject Postal's example (1a). Without going into the matter at length, I think it safe to say that the main reasons for this differential behavior are two: (i) it is clearer in (6) what *New Yorker* means; and (ii) the *but* . . . clause in (6) jibes with the main clause and is consonant with the reading of *New Yorker* forced by the main clause of (6) (whereas the *but* . . . clause in (1a) conflicts with the main clause of (1a), so that (1a) is for many no worse than (1) itself). Sentence (6) makes *New Yorker* more specific because it modifies that word with *confirmed*, and this reduces the polysemy of *New Yorker* because, while *New Yorker*, alone means 'citizen of New York', 'resident of New York', or any of several other things, the impossibility of '*confirmed native of New York' reminds us that *confirmed New Yorker* can really only mean 'confirmed *resident* of New York' or the like ('inhabitant', 'denizen'). By univocalizing *New Yorker* we make it possible to design a *but* . . . clause consonant with the one possible reading, so that the sentence is no longer rejected for irrelevant reasons. In short, (6) is accepted because, unlike (1a), it excludes the reading:

(1b)   *Conrad is a native of New York, but I wouldn't live there on a bet.

To emphasize this point I now list a few other sentences in which compound words (not containing 'self-' or whatever) seem to most speakers to be penetrable by anaphoric reference:

(7)   +Most native Philadelphians would rather live there than in New York.

(8)   + Most longtime Philadelphians would never even consider
        living anywhere else.

(9)   + Dognog is the only Scotsman I know who has lived there all
        his life without tasting porridge.

(10)   + If Jan had been only a naturalized Dutchman he would never
        have gone back there after the War.

(11)   + If Baron Geauxbois had been only a naturalized Froggie he
        might not have built his new château there.

(12)   + All native Hoosiers who have moved away make every effort
        to go back there for the Feast of St. Anna Electra.

Example (7) is much like the 'New Yorker' sentences, and (8) is too except
that the anaphor is *where* rather than *there*. In (9) we see that the country
to which *there* refers need not ('Scotland') be incorporated bodily in the
provenience-term (*Scotsman*) into which anaphoric penetration is necessary; this point is even more ineluctable in (10). In (11) and (12) we see the
extreme of this case, for in the latter sentences the provenience-terms
Froggie and *Hoosier*, which are pejorative and diminutive, respectively,
do not even contain a (surface) hint of the underlying localities (respectively, 'France' and 'Indiana') to which, nevertheless, anaphoric penetration is possible. On the whole, then, the preceding examples show
conclusively that anaphoric penetration to an underlying (or 'implied')
locality-antecedent is *in no way* contingent upon the overlying provenience-
term's yielding up the locality-name in an obvious or overt way.

   There are ways of making such sentences still more acceptable. One
way we have already seen: for some reason 'there' is a more penetrating
anaphor than is 'it'; compare:

(13)   + When two Australians entered the room Max claimed he
        wished he lived there himself.

Vs.:

(14)   ?When two Australians entered the room Max claimed it was
        the last place on earth he would like to live in.

Nor is 'there' the only anaphor more penetrating than 'it':

(14a)   + When two Australians entered the room Max claimed that
        that was the last place on earth he would like to live in.

Also, on another facet, compare:

(15)   +I will certainly take out Canadian citizenship if I ever go there
        to live.

Vs.:

(15a)   +If I ever go there to live I will certainly take out Canadian
        citizenship.

The acceptability difference between (15) and (15a) and the larger such
difference between (14) and (13) show that the property of anaphoric
insularity is not at all a property solely of the antecedent, for just as some
antecedents are more penetrable so are some anaphors more penetrating;
what is more, anaphor-antecedent order (15a) allows penetration more
easily than does the reverse order (15). Insularity is a property of the
anaphoric bond taken as a whole; and insularity, in some instances at
least, proves surprisingly evanescent.

2.2. *But Some Insularity Is Unyielding*

Most of the cases where anaphoric insularity turns out to be 'soft' have
been cases where a segment of a word can be regarded as representing the
antecedent or anaphor, either directly ('[New York]er', '[self-]emasculate')
or indirectly ('[*Dutch*]man'). The only exceptions are the words like
Froggie and *Hoosier* as in (11) and (12), and these instances are so peculiar
that they might well be discounted.[7] That is, it appears so far that accessible contained antecedents or anaphors must be 'represented' segmentally
on the surface, however covertly. Contrariwise, simplex words (or
apparent simplexes) are not penetrable, on the evidence so far presented,
and so in general are like the word *father* of (2), repeated:

(2)   *Harry is a father, but no one has ever seen it.

Or to cite another example, from Postal, a "blonde" is "someone who has
blonde (capital) hair," but while the word *hair* is accessible in the phrase
it is not so in the simplex *blonde,* as witness:

(19)   *Marlene is a blonde and Frank the Fetishist loves to caress it.

In other words, the revision to the NL theory adumbrated above, in which
compounds are somehow derived but simplexes are imported bodily

from the lexicon, must seem so far to be very much borne out, even when the set of penetrated insularities is extended. And this must remain true until it is demonstrated that paradigms of simplexes are penetrable.

2.3. *Penetrable Reefs*

2.3.1. The addition of contrastive stress to a word results, for almost all speakers in my experience, in a dramatic increase in penetrability: rather than being totally penetrable only with the 'right' anaphor and under ideal (e.g., cataphoric) conditions, many words become wholly penetrable under any and all conditions. Illustrating this first with compounds, the point is easily made:

> (20)   + Girls with LONG legs are more likely to succeed as strippers than girls with SHORT ones are.

(I use upper-case letters to indicate contrastive stress.) The preceding sentence is to be compared with:

> (20a)   + LONGlegged girls are more likely to succeed as strippers than girls with SHORT ones are.

The great majority of American speakers of English find nothing whatsoever wrong with [20a] – presumably the reader agrees with this consensus, for it is overwhelming – and, much more significantly, they do not volunteer or agree to downgrade (20a) as compared with (20). Nor can it be argued that (20) and (20a) are not paraphrases, since the only plausible alternative reading would have (20a) mean "Girls with long legs are more likely to succeed as strippers than girls with short long legs are," which (if a sentence) is patently not the correct reading. Then the anaphor *ones* in (20a) has *legs* as its antecedent, and so *longlegged*, when contrastively stressed, is eminently penetrable. Of course *longlegged* is a compound.[8] However, there are simplex words that behave just like 'longlegged'.

Consider this sentence:

> (21)   + Dognog wanted to NAIL the boards together, but Gripsnake made him do it with TAPE.

If *do it* is an anaphor then in (21) it has for its antecedent something that is missing from the surface altogether. The antecedent is clearly not the most obvious surface candidate, the verb [*to*] *nail*, since this would have Gripsnake wanting to 'nail the boards together with tape', which (if from a possible sentence) is not the way (21) is understood at all. Plainly, the antecedent is something like 'fasten (together)', a verb that is not present in (21) but which might be thought to underlie, or be implied by, the verb *nail*. In short, *do it* has the same antecedent in (21) that it has in the synonymous:

(21a)   + Dognog wanted to fasten the boards together with NAILS, but Gripsnake made him do it with TAPE.

Words like *nail* in (21) are the primary examples of what I will call 'penetrable reefs': they are words that 'should' be anaphoric islands but that, in most idiolects, turn out to be penetrable. Further examples will be exhibited later; a more pressing task is showing that (21) really does display anaphoric penetration, hence a penetrated reef.

2.3.2.   Counterarguments to the reefs' existence
2.3.2.1.   A first possible counterargument is that 'do it' is not an anaphor; it is to claim that we can sort of interpret 'do it with TAPE' because we know what one does with tape, not because 'do it' has a grammatical antecedent. However, this counterargument is easily refuted, it seems to me, on two independent grounds.

First, the argument ignores the fact that for many people (though not really for me) 'do it' has a twin anaphor, 'do so', where there can be no doubt that 'do so' is *essentially* an anaphor, since 'do so' can occur *only* as an anaphor. One can conceivably inaugurate and conclude a discourse with the single sentence "John did it," but to try this with "John did so," would be to betray the most grievous ignorance of English. But 'do so', for people who use it as the twin of *do it*, operates with complete success in sentences like (21):

(22)   + Stilton wanted to fasten the boards together with NAILS, but Cheshire made him do so with TAPE.

(22a)   + Stilton wanted to NAIL the boards together, but Cheshire made him do so with TAPE.

Thus if *do so* is obligatorily an anaphor and if (22a) does not mean that Cheshire made Stilton nail the boards together with tape, then in (22a) *do so* must have 'fasten' (or the like) as its antecedent.

The second means of refuting the counterargument is to examine it more closely. What it must claim is, presumably, that *do so* and *do it* are verbs of very vague or even empty meaning which we 'know how to interpret' by examining their contexts: in the context '——— with TAPE', if '——— with TAPE' is under contrast with either 'fasten with NAILS' or 'NAIL' we know that *do it* or *do so* must mean 'fasten'. *Do it* and *do so* function as independent verb phrases, then. For this line of argument to hold, the only grammatical or syntactic properties of *do it* and *do so* must be their own intrinsic properties; they can have no extrinsic properties acquired from antecedents, since they have no antecedents. Let us see if this is so.

(23)   + Dognog wanted to make love to Mae West in sardine-vats, but Matutinal hoped to do it in pickle-barrels.

(23a)   + Dognog wanted to make love to Mae West in sardine-vats, but Matutinal hoped to do so in pickle-barrels.

On the grounds that (23) and (23a) are exactly equal in acceptability and on the grounds that (23) and (23a) are typical sentences of their type, we can conclude I think that *do it* and *do so* easily occur with Locative phrases. On the nonanaphor argument, of course, *do it in pickle-barrels* and *do so in pickle-barrels* are both interpreted in some way other than by grammatically relating *do it/do so* to the antecedent [*to*] *make love to Mae West*.

(24)   *Dognog wanted to put the home-brew in BOTTLES, but Sodak wanted to do it in pickle-barrels.

(24a)   *Dognog wanted to put the home-brew in BOTTLES, but Sodak wanted to do so in pickle-barrels.

As we see, . . . *do it (do so) in pickle-barrels* are '*' in (24) and (24a), though they were '+' in (23) and (23a). Why is this? Why are there *some* Locative expressions from construction with which 'do it'/'do so' are excluded: namely, those which Chomsky (1965, p. 71) identified as being inside the (surface) Verb Phrase? But how could *in pickle-barrels* be inside the VP in (24) and (24a) but *out*side the VP in (23) and (23a)?

Answer: in (24) and (24a) the main verb of the previous clause was *put,* whose Locative ... *in BOTTLES* was inside rather than outside the VP; no other explanation seems possible. But what could possibly explain the fact that *do it/do so* take as their Locative precisely the sort of Locative that is taken by, crudely, the main verb of the previous clause? Answer: *nothing* can explain this bizarre phenomenon unless *do it* and *do so* are bound so tightly to the main verb as perforce to mirror that verb's syntactic properties. But, as respects syntactic properties, that is 'anaphora'.

Now look at these sentences:

(25)   *Dognog wanted to BOTTLE the home-brew, but Deadwood wanted to do it in pickle-barrels.

(25a)   *Dognog wanted to BOTTLE the home-brew, but Deadwood wanted to do so in pickle-barrels.

The '*' qualities of (25) and (25a) exactly mirror those of their synonyms (24) and (24a), and this, plus all of the other arguments already presented on this point, strongly implies that *do it* and *do so* fail in (25) and (25a) for the same reason they fail in (24) and (24a), namely, their attempting to anaphorize a verb while contrasting their 'close' (inside VP) Locative with the antecedent's. But 'put' does not appear in (25) or (25a). It seems fair to say that 'put' (or the like) must lie somewhere under the surface of (25) and (25a) and that it is this underlying 'put' that is the antecedent of the anaphors *do so* and *do it*. (The point that 'put' is the antecedent is, of course, distinct from the point that *do so/do it* are anaphors and thus *have* an antecedent.)

I have argued the case for the anaphoricity of 'do so'/'do it' first because it seemed the harder to establish, hence perhaps the more persuasive; but in fact with some other putative anaphors, including some that penetrate reefs, I fail to see how there can be any serious doubt as to their status. Consider (20a), for example: I submit that either *ones* is an anaphor in (20a), with *legs* as its antecedent, or else English has no anaphors and the whole notion of 'anaphora' has simply been a popular fallacy.

We turn now to the nature of the contrast that is set by the contrastive stress in (21) and (21a), again in (22) and (22a). Take just the first half of (21) and (21a):

(23)   Dognog wanted to NAIL the boards together ...

(23a)   Dognog wanted to fasten the boards together with NAILS ...

What can follow? Contrastive stress, in both sentences, falls on the instrumentality with which the boards are to be fastened: in fact, in whatever grammar, on an Instrumental. Not on the entire VP, certainly, for then the contrastive stress would fall on *boards*, as in:

(24) +Dognog wanted to nail the BOARDS together, but Baron Geauxbois made him clean the stables instead.

(25) +Dognog wanted to nail the BOARDS together, but his girlfriend Lou Garou reminded him of a previous engagement.

The initial clauses (to *but*) of both sentences are of course ambiguous, since the contrastive stress in both cases could be taken as falling just on the word *boards* rather than on the whole VP *hence* on the superficial object *boards*. This is clear enough from, e.g.:

(26) +Dognog wanted to nail the BOARDS together, but his frigid wife made him nail the SHEETS together instead.

but this is not the point. The point is that on one reading when contrastive stress falls on *boards* the contrast is on the entire VP, which may not be the case when the stress falls on *nail(s)*; in the latter instance only the instrumental is in contrast. (And this is the classical sort of instrumental on Lakoff's criteria, 1968a, and so matched with the paraphrase in:

[21b] +Dognog wanted to use NAILS to fasten the boards together, but Gripsnake made him use TAPE.

And also in:

[21c] +Dognog wanted to NAIL the boards together, but Gripsnake made him use TAPE.)

If placing contrastive stress on *NAIL* entails that the instrumental be put into contrast with something else, generally of course another instrumental, then these ought to be ungrammatical:

(27) *Dognog wanted to NAIL the boards together, but Quilty reminded him of his boast that he could drink a gallon of Iron City beer.

(28) *Dognog wanted to NAIL the boards together, but Mrs. Hemoglobin reminded him of a dinner engagement.

(29)   *Dognog wanted to NAIL the boards together, but his frigid wife made him nail the SHEETS together instead.

But of course (27)–(29) are plainly ungrammatical, as in any sentence, apparently, in which *NAIL* is not contrasted with another instrumental. More than this, the contrasted phrases (containing *NAIL* and the other instrumental) must in all other pertinent respects be synonymous; thus, in (21a), *do so with TAPE* must be synonymous, except for *TAPE*, with *fasten the boards together with NAILS*. This additional fact is neatly accommodated if we assume that *NAIL the boards together* is underlaid by a phrase on the order of 'fasten the boards together with NAILS', since on that analysis the two contrasted phrases are indeed, once 'NAILS' and 'TAPE' are disregarded (being the terms in contrast), identical.
   In all, I conclude that:

(a)   'do so' and 'do it' are actually anaphors;
(b)   *do it* in (21a) means 'fasten the boards together';
(c)   *do it* in (21a) has 'fasten the boards together' as antecedent.

2.3.2.2.   However, while the above reasoning may perhaps be found persuasive on the anaphoric nature of 'do so'/'do it', there is a fall-back counterargument, and a serious one. For one might argue that sentences containing penetrated reefs do indeed contain an anaphor 'do so'/'do it' and a covert antecedent – *but that by virtue of precisely that fact they are ungrammatical*. In this way the sentences would be admitted to have the structures and meanings I have claimed them to have, but at the same time the requirement that the grammar therefore account for those structures and meanings would be adroitly vitiated. Moreover it might seem at first that this counterargument is especially telling because it is notoriously hard to win any argument of the 'X is ungrammatical'/'No it isn't' variety. Actually I think that this impression is ill-founded, because the vagueness of such arguments is just what ails them, since they trade on the irreducible vagueness of any 'intuitive' (i.e., unverified) notion of 'ungrammaticality'. Even so, the argument has a more serious side, since if we cannot decide definitely whether or not such sentences are grammatical then we put them under the shadow of the notion, advanced long ago by Chomsky (1957), that in any such doubtful cases the grammar must judge for itself. Thus if we must abide by the grammar's arbitration, and if an NL grammar seems correct except for its ability to accommodate penetrated reef sentences, then if the penetrated reef sentences are dubious they can be rejected from the set of grammatical sentences *because* the NL grammar does not readily accept them.

Such a claim is complicated, in the case of the reefs, by the fact that 'do it' and 'do so' are not of equal interidiolectal status. Many Americans cannot use 'do so' with any facility unless 'do so' has the entire VP as its antecedent, which means that such speakers cannot use 'do so' with facility in sentences like (22) *or* (22a). ('Do it' is less restrictive in this regard, it seems.) This means that for 'do so', the most anaphoric of the anaphors, one is obliged to investigate the *joint* grammaticality (or 'dubiety') of both sorts of sentence, those in which the antecedent is overt and those in which it is covert. If a speaker has (22), does he also have (22a)?

Of 109 speakers tested in a recent experiment 83 percent found one or both of the 'do so' types acceptable. Of those who accepted 'do so' in either type, a minority (42 per cent) accepted *only* the overt-antecedent sort while rejecting the penetrated-reef sort: so a majority (58 per cent) who accept either, accept both.[9] It is certainly reasonable to say that some speakers have mental grammars whose rules do not generate 'do so' sentences of either type at issue here; but that for the other speakers the necessity of penetrating a reef impairs grammaticality for only a minority. I am not sure that the phrase 'complete grammaticality' has any significance, but if it did it would be worth noting that of the 90 speakers who accepted either 'do so' at all, about one in four found both overt and covert sentences to be of total acceptability.[10] It is certainly worth noting that the closeness in acceptability of both sorts of sentence, for many speakers, directly conflicts with the fact that reef sentences must require a little more processing effort; furthermore, according to the comments of some of my subjects, some secondary school teachers of prescriptive (proscriptive) grammar enjoin their charges to avoid any sentence in which a surface 'parallelism of structure' is not maintained.

With 'do it' the case is even clearer, and many speakers, especially if they hear 'do it' reef sentences instead of reading them, are prone to ask the interrogator what the point of his question can be. In all, the argument that all penetrated reef sentences are ungrammatical is, for many speakers and apparently a majority even with 'do so', overturned. The fact that some theory cannot handle the reef sentences in a satisfactory manner means that the theory is jeopardized, not that the sentences can be dispatched.

But perhaps the experiment may be found unpersuasive. No matter; for the thesis that the reef sentences are 'dubious' on some general principle is itself highly questionable. The most obvious such principle, indeed the only one that I can see, is this: that penetration of, e.g., 'nail' by a subsequent anaphor requires that the first or antecedent clause be processed (at least to the point where '[to] nail' is comprehended to mean 'fasten with nails' or the like) before the second or anaphor clause is, and that such a mandatory order-of-processing is somehow beyond the scope of what is ordinarily or properly required, hence beyond the pale of performances required by grammatical sentences. But this more general basis has no plausibility at all, simply because there are many sentences that would have to be ejected from the grammar on the same grounds. Consider:

(30)   + The Canadian decision to prohibit other nations from dumping crude-oil in Hudson Bay was protested by the Eskimos, who claimed that the oil was good for their complexions.

Who are the *other nations* of this sentence? Clearly, 'other than Canada'. But then to make any sense of *other nations* at the point of reaching that phrase one must already have realized that 'Canada' is a 'nation' and that *Canadian* means 'of Canada'. (So 'Catholic' will not do because there is no political entity '*Cathol' and 'Haligonian' will not do because 'Halifax' is not a 'nation'.) Furthermore there are actually sentences that demand, not just that the first part be parsed before the second can be understood, but that the parse of the first part be revised or amplified to accord with the understanding of the second part. Consider:

(31)   + Respighi's *The Fountains of Rome,* which tone-poem has now had its logical sequel in *The Pissoirs of Paris,* inaugurated a new era in patriotic program-music.

In (31), anyone who had not known *The Fountains of Rome* or who had thought it an opera would obviously have to absorb the intelligence that it is in fact a tone poem just in order to understand, and traverse, the relative *which tone poem*. Otherwise *which tone poem* has nothing to relate to. Since (31) seems to be an English sentence, I conclude that there is no principle barring 'later revision' or 'prior understanding' from English sentences. Hence this most obvious and appealing candidate for a principled means of stigmatizing penetrated reef sentences is apparently not available. It seems unlikely, then, that reef sentences can be ejected from the language either on grounds of widespread unacceptability or on grounds that their acceptability is due only to their having some hidden flaw that escapes the naive speaker's attention.

If the reader is still troubled by residual qualms, however, I should like to assure him that, in fact, the question of the absolute grammaticality of the reef sentences is immaterial; we return to this point in (3).

2.4. *Sum of the Evidence*

This has been only an introductory coverage of the anaphoric phenomena under view, but even so it suffices, I think, to suggest that the English language contains penetrable reefs. The English of almost all speakers (perhaps all) contains compound words that are penetrable reefs; the speech of the majority includes simplex reefs as well. Moreover this inclusion is not just of isolated words, it is of paradigms: this claim, so far upheld only by stray remarks about 'instrumentals' and by the cohesion among my examples, will be further defended in the next section. The need for the grammar to give an account of the reefs is concomitantly more unarguable.

This section ought ideally to conclude by offering a comparison between anaphoric island and penetrable reef that would neatly dichotomize the two and provide a means of distinguishing between them in the instance. This I will refrain from doing, however, since to my mind there is no such dichotomy, as see below. It should be noted at this point that for many speakers the presence or absence of contrastive stress is not critical for the acceptance or rejection of penetrated reefs: the stress seems aidful in such cases as '[to] nail' more than in the compound cases, but even so no dichotomy seems justified. It might also be noted that the set of penetrable compounds is by no means restricted to provenience terms as in (1), (7)–(10), (13)–(15a), and so on; consider:

(32)   + All the Nixonites I know say they wish he would abdicate and
        make off with Mrs. Simpson.

In all, the evidence is fairly general and seemingly unimpeachable; and it
remains chiefly to see what implications this evidence has for theories of
grammar.

3. LEXICALIZATIONS: EARLY, LATE, AND LAGGARD

3.1.   To rephrase an earlier remark, there are broadly speaking two
extremes of current views on the role of words in grammar. (i) The NL
view holds basically that words are of markedly different character from
phrases and clauses and that all words (revised, all simplex words at least)
have a markedly different history, having been inserted at some point
directly from the lexicon rather than having been, like a phrase, built up
and altered generatively. (ii) The opposing NT view, which had its origins
in Gruber's work (1965) and in Postal (1966), holds that words occupy no
special place in the grammar and that they are essentially a type of phrase
except in being more compact, more rigidly ordered as to constituents,
and in many cases more insular. An NT grammar would presumably
produce the verb '[to] nail' only as a result of transformations operating
upon a moderately late phrase on the order of '[to] fasten with nails'; but
a more NL grammar would probably claim, instead, that '[to] nail' enters
a sentence's derivation in the form, precisely, of the verb '[to] nail',
with 'fasten' present nowhere in the syntactic derivation at all. 'Fasten'
would appear, if anywhere, as part of the definition, in the lexicon, of the
verb '[to] nail'. Or, in a hybrid NT/NL scheme, leaning heavily toward
NL however, '[to] nail' might be derived from '[to] fasten with nails', but
derived outside of the syntax somewhere, say in a generative lexical
subcomponent. The hybrid scheme – call it (iii) – would contain '[to]
nail' rules much like those that an NT grammar would have (indeed, it is
hard to see what the difference might be), but in the (iii) version these rules
would be placed in the lexicon (or in some lexico-syntactic subcomponent).

    (As is plain, I am discussing NL vs. NT implications without direct
reference to specific implementations of these proposals, since the reefs
have not been treated at all by anyone working in NL theory and the

previous treatment within NT theory (Postal, 1969) is directed against the
reefs rather than in their favor. Equally plain is the fact that many further
'hybrid' views are possible beyond the single one I have considered here;
and perhaps a more imaginative NL theorist might find other NL adapta-
tions to accommodate the reefs. But those sketched above appear to be
the fundamental differences and basic approaches; and by mostly ignoring
hybrids and ancillary concerns we will find it a little easier to articulate the
main issues.) The essential difference between an NL-like treatment and
an NT-like treatment can be expressed as a difference between ways of
binding the 'do so' or 'do it' anaphors to a covert 'fasten': and that difference boils down to whether 'fasten' is to be located in the lexicon somewhere or in the sentence's (syntactic) derivation.

3.2.   I now give three sets of sentences whose phrases and words will be
useful in following discussion:

(33)   + Swinburne wanted to tie himself up with ROPE, but Watts-
Dunton made him do so with CHAINS.

(33c)   + Swinburne wanted to ROPE-tie himself, but Watts-Dunton
made him do so with CHAINS.

Also:

(34)   + Bride bingo was played, and those who won prizes presented
them to Miss Cowan.

(34a)   + Bride bingo was played, and the winners of prizes presented
them to Miss Cowan.

(34b)   + Bride bingo was played, and the prize winners . . . presented
them to Miss Cowan.[11]

Also:

(35)   + All those I know who follow Nixon say they wish he would
abdicate.

(35a)   + All the followers of Nixon I know say they wish he would
abdicate.

(35b)   + All the Nixon-followers I know say they wish he would
abdicate.

(35c)   + All the Nixonites I know say they wish he would abdicate.[12]

For ease of reference I list and label separately the phrases and words of interest here:

(33)	*tie . . . with ROPE*
(33c)	*ROPE-tie*
(34)	*win . . . prizes*
(34a)	*winners of prizes*
(34b)	*prize winners*
(35)	*follow . . . Nixon*
(35a)	*followers of Nixon*
(35b)	*Nixon-followers*
(35c)	*Nixonites.*

3.3. Each set of forms given in the section just above is tied together by these two criteria: within each set the words/phrases are (i) paraphrastic, hence each subject to exactly the same subcategorizational restrictions; and (ii) penetrable, with degree of penetrability decreasing toward the (c) forms, in other words with the degree of insularity decreasing backwards toward the (a) forms.

3.3.1. The implication of these forms' synonymy is presumptively that first marked by Chomsky (1957) in his initial elaboration of the reason for merging at some underlying abstract level the Active and Passive transforms of English; this argument, which is too well known to bear extended comment, is that subcategorization (co-occurrence) restrictions must be stated for the Active's Subject-Verb and Verb-Object constructions and also for the Passive's Subject-Verb and Verb-Agent constructions; but the former's first and second constructions have the same restrictions as the latter's second and first, respectively; and so a diseconomy can be averted only by stating, at a level underlying both Active and Passive, two restrictions instead of four. Such notions are somewhat more controversial nowadays than they were in earlier times, but without going into that issue we can here consider the question of how this sort of economy argument, for any who accept such, bears on the matter at hand. We see that in the set (33), the sequence *tie . . . with ROPE* is exactly as natural as 'ROPE-tie' and any verb + instrumental is exactly as natural as the corresponding 'instrumental + verb' *if* the latter exists in the language. By the same token, if '?tie . . . with a spoon' is not natural then '?spoon-tie' will not be either: cf. '+spoon-feed' and '?rope-feed'. The restrictions on what instrumental can occur with 'tie' must be stated identically for 'tie . . . with instrumental' and for 'instrumental-tie'. Again, *won . . . prizes*, *winners of prizes*, and *prize(-)winners* have the same property, as do the members of set (35). In short, if the argument from paraphrase does have any viability at all then it must and does apply in these cases, and on that basis the sets (33), (34), and (35) must each have a single underlying source if they are to avoid being responsible for a diseconomy. If this is so the grammar is forbidden to derive *follow . . . Nixon* in the syntax and *Nixonites* or 'Nixonite' as a monolithic word in the lexicon.

Paraphrases aside, the grammar must somehow provide an account of the meaning of 'follow . . . Nixon' and 'Nixonite'; but in an account where the former is generated in the syntax but the latter in the lexicon the fact that 'Nixonite' means 'one who follows Nixon' (or the like) is available only in the lexical definition of 'Nixonite'; the interpretation of 'follow . . . Nixon' must be made on a syntactic construction when 'follow . . . Nixon' actually occurs in the syntax, but on a part of a lexical definition when 'Nixonite' is accessed in the lexicon. No such interpretation can as economically be based on 'Nixonite' itself: indeed, there is some doubt that it can be so based at all. The meaning 'follow' cannot correctly be assigned just to '-ite', to force 'Nixonite' artificially closer to 'follow . . . Nixon'. First, the meanings (the segments) of the two strings would even so be in different orders, and without further operation reversed orders are not identical environments.[13] Secondly, notice that the English '-ite' does not uniformly translate as '-follower' or the like, as see 'New Jerseyite' ('*follower of New Jersey'); 'Janeite' (= 'enthusiast of Jane [Austen]', not 'Jane-follower'); not to mention 'Woolite'.[14] In short, either 'follow . . . Nixon' and 'Nixonite' are derived from sources differing only in irrelevancies (where order is a relevancy), or else the same meaning must be recovered in two different ways, with the consequent diseconomy.

Against this it might be argued that the semantic interpretation of 'Nixonite' could be divided into two parts, one pushing 'Nixonite' back to 'ite of Nixon', the other recovering the meaning of 'ite' (i.e., 'follow') and then the meaning of the sequence as a whole. Only the first part of the interpretation would be done in the lexicon itself; the rules for interpreting 'follower of Nixon' would however apply, as indicated above, both to syntactic constructions and to the same constructions when recovered from lexical words. Certainly such a division of labor is possible; but is it plausible? For what of 'Nixon-follower'? Suppose that the latter form is generated in the syntax, perhaps as a late form of 'follower of Nixon', in turn perhaps an intermediate form from 'follow . . . Nixon'. As we see, 'Nixon-follower' has as part of its syntactic derivation all of the information that in the case of 'Nixonite' was derived partly from the operation, on lexical information, of rules which in essence exploit syntactic structure. Surely 'Nixon-follower' *is* generated in the syntax and not listed as a monolithic word in the lexicon. But the argument for deriving 'Nixonite' differently from 'Nixon-follower' is, to say the least, not convincing: such derivation insists that 'follower of Nixon' be recovered from 'Nixonite' (via 'ite of Nixon'?) by a special lexical rule, which rule is quite needless in the case of 'Nixon-follower' because 'Nixon-follower' *derives from* 'follower of Nixon'. Given the fact that in both 'Nixon-follower' and 'Nixonite' the segment meaning 'follow' follows, it might be very natural to have 'Nixonite' interpreted *via* 'Nixon-follower', on the way to the interpretation 'follower of Nixon', on the way to '[one who] follows Nixon'. But this scheme of interpretation is, reversed, the most plausible path of derivation, and so consists of a process of 'recovering' information which, in the derivational scheme, is there anyway, in *any* grammar down at least to 'Nixon-follower'. This being so, the burden of supporting any syntax-independent source for 'Nixonite' becomes very heavy. The same comment holds true, it seems to me, of other and more imaginative NL treatments of 'Nixonites' and like reefs; it holds true, for example, for a treatment casually propounded by R. S. Jackendoff (personal communication to Peter Culicover, 1971) in which the meaning of 'Nixonite' would be imported from the lexicon *into* the syntactic account of the containing sentence, in the form of something like 'follower of Nixon': notice however that the rules for interpreting 'follower of Nixon' would in this scheme still operate in two different ways since when 'follower of Nixon' is generated directly in the syntax there is no need to actuate rules for importing 'follower of Nixon' from the lexicon.

In fine, 'Nixonite' is best handled as being as close to 'Nixon-follower' as possible and this maximal propinquity is attainable when both forms are derived in the syntax; lodging both as monoliths in the lexicon is completely implausible. The syntactic rules needed to form the 'word' from the 'phrase' – to form 'Nixonite' from 'Nixon-follower' – may seem a bit unusual at first, but they seem a lot less so once one realizes that very similar rules are clearly needed *in any case* to form the word 'Nixon-follower' itself.

3.3.2.   As I said in introducing (3.3.1) there is some controversy nowa-days over how much one should lean on the notion of economy, and so it is nice that the argument given above has additional corroboration. One piece of corroborating evidence comes from the facts about antecedents. For anyone who accepts all of the sentences of set (35), all members of that set permit *Nixon* to serve as antecedent of *he*; and the argument for per-mitting the operation of tying anaphor to antecedent to be a wholly syntactic one, as far as possible, seems beyond question. Then the same syntactic derivation motivated on diseconomy grounds is – with no changes at all – the syntactic derivation adequate for providing antecedents in the syntax for any and all anaphors. Since the arguments are quite independent of each other, they are mutually corroborating.

Similarly, we might note the possible claim that *Nixonite* is different from (say) *follow . . . Nixon* with respect to penetrability. Granted. There is no question that with most speakers (35c) is slightly less acceptable than (35). But it turns out that this is no argument for the separate (lexical) derivation for *Nixonite*: in fact, quite the contrary. For notice that though (35c) is indeed less penetrable than (35), so also is (35b); for some, so also is (35a). Over-all, there is a slight but steady decline in penetrability from (35) through (35c). Then to argue that the increased insularity of (35c) forces separate derivation for *Nixonite* is to ignore the plain fact that, though to a lesser extent, the increased insularity of (35b), say, ought to force the same treatment. On this, the counterargument from insularity evaporates. Worse: it becomes an argument on the other side, for now clearly the grammar will be obliged to mark *Nixonite* for insularity, *Nixon-follower* for insularity in some weaker degree, and so on. That is, a property hitherto associated just with 'words' – insularity – turns out to be associated also with phrases, and, at that, increasingly with phrases as they get closer to 'words'. Some unified way of assigning insularity must be made available: and, clearly, this is possible only when the path of increasing insularity is an accompaniment of some other path. But what path can this be other than the path of derivation? Again we have an independent, and therefore corroborating, argument.

3.3.3.   What I have tried to do in the preceding paragraphs is progressively to divest *Nixonite* of any special status and to show that there is much to be gained from giving such 'words' a treatment maximally uniform with that given to other members of the set (35). In the sets (33)–(35), *Nixonite* was the most word-like element; and so without further ado we may say that the same arguments that applied for the set (35) apply also for sets (33) and (34): for example what applied to *Nixon-follower* applies to *prize*(-)*winner*. In all, for both hyphenated and suffixal forms of all sets, syntactic derivation seems moderately well motivated, with the only argument for independent or lexical derivation being, apparently, completely outside our present concerns.

3.4.   But what of '[to] nail'? Relating this verb to '[to] fasten with nails', we then relate these two forms to those of sets (33)–(35), in what appears to be a straightforward way:

(33) *tie . . . with rope*; (34) *win . . . prizes*; (35) *follow . . . Nixon*; (36) 'fasten . . . with nails'.

(33a) [vacant]; (34a) *winner of prizes*; (35a) *follower of Nixon*; (36a) [vacant].

(33b) [vacant]; (34b) *prize*(-)*winner*; (35b) *Nixon-follower*; (36b) 'nail-fastener'.

(33c) *rope-tie*; (34c) [vacant]; (35c) *Nixonite*; (36c) [vacant] [cf. '*nail-fasten'].

(33d) [vacant]; (34d) [vacant]; (35d) [vacant]; (36d) '[to] nail'.

Some of the possible forms are absent, or in some cases have only a shadowy existence that I have ignored; but generally the sets are fuller than their superficially disparate natures might have suggested. I have added a new subset of forms, in (d), in which only (36) is represented; but only (36) and (33) are verbs in any case, so that only the failure of (33) to have a (d) form can be accounted as very significant. And even this significance drops away when we note how many forms like (36d) there are in English and, above all, how very uniform in meaning and predictable in function they are.

As is almost self-evident, the arguments that were applied above to sets (33)–(35) apply with equal force to the new set (36): the paraphrase argument from (3.3.1.), the antecedence argument from earlier and as summarized in (3.3.2.), and the insularity argument from (3.3.3.). The only surprises are the vacancy in (36c), '*nail-fasten', and the presence of the striking (36d), '[to] nail'. But there is little in these ancillary facts that looks threatening. As we see illustratively by comparing *tie . . . with ropes* and 'fasten . . . with nails', 'instrumental verbs' in English seem to have as their most condensed ('word'-like) manifestation *either* a (c) form like *rope-tie or* a (d) form like '[to] nail'. This is an interesting fact but not, apparently, a fact of importance to the main argument, which argument now rests on the additional conclusion, reachable without repeating points previously made for similar cases, that '[to] nail' is generated in the syntax as a late derivative of 'fasten . . . with nail'.

This being so it seems obvious that the term 'word', as applied to '[to] nail', to 'Nixonite', and to countless other strings, is as to formal considerations but a snare and a delusion. I drop the term forthwith; needing a label-of-convenience, however, and at the same time wanting to capture these strings' most defining characteristic, their likelihood of appearing in a conventional dictionary, I will hereafter term such strings 'websters'. It is to be noted that websters are *not* formal entities (like 'sentences' or 'nouns') – indeed, they are so defined.

3.5. *General Counterarguments*

The most general rejoinder possible, which is that reefs like 'Nixonite' or '[to] nail' are simply exceptions, hence in no need of uniform treatment, is perhaps worth passing attention at this juncture. It does seem worth no more. The reefs we have been examining do not on even the most casual glance seem to be just a group of exceptions. First, some sets of reefs are of infinite size, since the processes for forming them are regular and they are formed from other sets which are in principle infinite. Thus, 'Nixonite' is scarcely a nonce-coinage, since by adding '-ite' (or some more euphonious allomorph) one can form a 'NAME-follower' reef from any imaginable surname. The process of forming such reefs as 'New Yorker' and 'Philadelphian' is also quite regular (with the same qualification), and extends to almost every political-entity proper noun in English (including Englished foreign nouns): again, a set of terms in principle of infinite size. Even the reefs less blessed in unboundedness are still very numerous and fairly regular as a set, with qualifications: any noun in English that can be an Instrumental is more or less amenable to the process, and the process is so regular that to add a new such Instrumental is very possibly to add a new reef automatically. For instance just as 'flavor with salt' yields the verb '[to] salt', so 'flavor with sugar' yields '[to] sugar', 'flavor with pepper' yields '[to] pepper', 'flavor with salt and pepper' yields '[to] salt-and-pepper'; and 'to flavor with basil' almost yields '[to] basil'. Just as 'fasten with nails' yields '[to] nail', so 'fasten with tenons' yields '[to] tenon', 'fasten with glue' yields '[to] glue', 'fasten with paste' yields '[to] paste', 'fasten with mortar (cement)' yields '[to] mortar (cement)'; and so on. If a normally *non*-Instrumental is made an Instrumental, then the corresponding nonce-reef may prove almost as comprehensible and, to that degree, natural:

(37)   +Chthonic III wants to plant the Cathedral grounds with TREES, but Matutinal wants to do so with POISON-IVY.

(37a)   ?Chthonic III wants to TREE the Cathedral grounds, but Matutinal wants to do so with POISON-IVY.

To the extent that the classes of reefs under consideration are highly productive, there is simply no substance whatever to any claim that the reefs are individual exceptions in no need of grammatical accommodation: indeed, productive processes are the paradigm case of phenomena that must be treated generatively.

The only possibility of breathing new life into this rejected rejoinder, I think, is to generalize it still further, to claim that *other* websters merit an NL treatment even if reefs do not. However, I mean in my conclusion to make the (obvious) point that what is sauce for the goose is sauce for the gander.

3.6. Grammaticality Revisited

Above, in (3.3.2.) I touched on the fact that there appear to be no 'plateaux' separating 'those who follow Nixon' from 'followers of Nixon' or the latter phrase from 'Nixon-followers' or the latter from 'Nixonites'; all of these forms seem to be about equidistant on a cline of decreasing penetrability, hence, for most, a cline of decreasingly easy acceptance. The force of this comment would be blunted but little by holding that every penetrated reef is a 'mistake' of some sort, a form existing perhaps only by 'analogy' with such highly penetrable words as 'our'. The grammar is indirectly responsible for accommodating 'mistakes', by showing how serious they are; and so any claim that the reefs are mistakes leads directly to the question of how serious such mistakes are. Since according to the behavior of speakers the mistakes are venial, we seem to be led immediately back to the familiar cline of increasing insularity, where 'Nixonites' is more insular than 'Nixon-followers' which in turn is more insular than 'followers of Nixon', and where the two increases in insularity seem about equal. The only difference, on the argument as to 'mistakes', is that now 'Nixonites' is *too* insular, because penetrating that webster is a 'mistake'. So, on the NT treatment that establishes this cline of insularity, the view that penetrating 'Nixonites' is a mistake involves no more than setting the 'ungrammaticality' threshold a little higher than I did in the earlier discussion. No more is involved, surely. But it is hard to see how an NL treatment, where websters receive markedly different treatment, could be reconciled with the only possible view of the 'mistakenness' of penetrating 'Nixonites'; it is hard to see how a major difference with respect to the grammar can be judged a minor difference just because a putative 'ungrammaticality' threshold is crossed. Thus the argument from 'mistakes' seems to be only a version of the argument from insularity, and so seems to favor the NT treatment over the NL one.

Of course it is just as plausible to maintain that penetrating 'Nixonites' does not cross the threshold at all; indeed, to my mind it is just as plausible to maintain, in the light of present knowledge, that a threshold of the sort cited here is just a fiction. Once degrees of grammaticality are admitted *within the generatum of the grammar*, as I simply assumed to be the case in my discussion of the cline of insularity, the firmness of any meaningful threshold as such becomes extremely dubious, to my mind. In sum, then, the argument that it is a mistake to penetrate reefs is either inconcinnous or empty.

4. CONCLUSIONS[15]

We have considered a set of arguments for the position that penetrable reefs are generated in the syntax and do not originate as holophrases in the lexicon. We looked at sets of strings like (a) 'those who follow Nixon'/ 'those who win prizes'; (b) 'followers of Nixon'/'winners of prizes'; (c) 'Nixon-followers'/'prize-winners'; and (d) 'Nixonites'. Also, (e) 'fasten with nails'/'feed with a spoon'; (f) '*nail-fasten'/'spoon-feed'; and (g) '[to] nail'/'[to] bottle'. The forms are given in, roughly, their order of increasing compression, with conventional 'phrases' at the beginning and conventional 'words' – i.e., websters – at the end. This is also, roughly, their order of increasing insularity. The forms (a) through (d) are more regular (the paradigm is fuller) than the forms (e) through (g), and this for reasons not fully understood; but on the other hand within the limits described above the occurrence of either (f) or (g) is fairly predictable if the English word for the instrumentality is short and common. Beside the less-complete (f) and (g), in any case, we can set exceptions within the other sets, too. For instance there is the occasional (c) form ('wage-earners', 'price-fixers') for which the putatively prior (b) is not available (never reaches surface): '??earners of wages', '?fixers of prices'. Cf. (c) 'bread-winners' against (b) '*winners of bread' (in the intended sense.) Again, English has (g) '[to] type' and (f) 'typewrite', but scarcely (e) '*write with type' (in the intended sense). Yet again, English has (b) 'proponents of *Pax Nixonica*' but no (a) '*those who propone *Pax Nixonica*'; these examples are like those covered long ago by Lakoff (1965). Sometimes only the most insular form is found, as in (g) '[to] bottle' but (f) '?bottle-containerize', (e) '?containerize with bottles'. For quite a few items, then, the rules that take (a) through to (d) or (e) through to (f) or (g) must for one or more steps be obligatory: but the reefs are scarcely more demanding in this respect than are verbs like '*propone'.

The NT treatment sketched above, in which phrases are compressed into websters as a late syntactic step, must of course be outfitted with rules to accomplish that objective. These rules of late compression – we might call them 'sphincter' rules – have had their functions roughly outlined above, and their nature and even their approximate ordering is more or less obvious. On the other hand their formal statement, due to some minor problems that yet remain, cannot be made with any assurance at this time, and so will be omitted.

Given the character of the 'sphincter' rules argued to be necessary for the reefs, however, even without knowing the formal expression of those rules we may ask whether it seems likely that they apply *only* to the reefs. Weakly, can other websters (even all other websters) be generated through applying the same sphincter rules or those rules trivially extended; more strongly, is the efficiency of those rules reduced *unless* they automatically generate many other (or most other) kinds of webster also? That is, can the sphincter rules already envisaged be restricted to just the reefs already covered without penalties in additional complexity in the statement of those rules? The answer to the stronger question is not at all certain at present; but the answer to the weaker is in a way preempted by an additional piece of evidence. For the need to extend the sphincter rules to cover new sorts of websters becomes independently motivated from a familiar direction if it should turn out that new sorts of websters are also reefs. In fact should enough new kinds of reef turn up even the stronger question would begin to be preemptively answered, since to carve out greater and greater parts from the set of nonreef websters is to leave those remaining increasingly exceptional. It is fitting, then, to conclude with an example in which the word 'father', earlier (1.2.) cited as the archetype of impenetrability, appears to many speakers to be penetrable, hence a reef:

(38)   + Flywheel is already a father THREE TIMES OVER, but
         Firefly hasn't even had ONE yet.

University of California, Irvine

NOTES

* Some of the material of the present paper was discussed as part of 'Anaphoric Islands and Penetrable Reefs', presented at the Seminar on the Construction of Complex Grammars, convened by Jane J. Robinson in Cambridge, Massachusetts, for the Center for Advanced Study in the Behavioral Sciences, June, 1970. Under the same title I expect to publish a fuller coverage of insularity phenomena in the near future. At the seminar I benefited from discussions of the arguments with John Robert Ross and Guy Carden, and was relieved there when Paul Postal found plausible some of the acceptances of penetrated reefs. I have also benefited from discussions with Herbert H. Clark and Eve V. Clark, to whom I am very grateful for providing numerous instances (and for providing no counterinstances). I have discussed

many of the NL ramifications of the argument with Peter Culicover, with great profit to me and I hope no onus on him. I have also profited from some unpublished notes of the nineteenth-century English philologist H. Dumpty.

[1] Actually, 'accelerate'/'acceleration' appears to be an interesting (because central) *exception* to the specific hypothesis in question, because "John's acceleration of the process had his nervous co-workers worried" ought on the hypothesis to be ungrammatical: but clearly the facts are otherwise. For a brief discussion, see Watt (1970). It may be added that the 'acceleration' example is equally a central exception to the alternative analysis of causal *grow* and like verbs in which causal *grow* has a source on the order of [+cause]/[Grow].

[2] For a survey of these competing theories see Chomsky (1970a).

[3] I am aware that the 'as if' of this statement is a live issue: Bach (1970), Carden and Miller (1970), Chapin (1970), Karttunen (1969), Watt (1971a), Watt (1971b).

[4] I will use the symbols '+' and '*' to contrast 'more grammatical' and 'less grammatical', respectively; '?' will mean 'doubtful'. As here, synonymous sentences will bear the same number, with letters distinguishing the synonyms.

[5] In all cases I have omitted, for readability, any explicit or formal indication of the anaphoric bond by which, e.g., the anaphor *there* has *New York* as its antecedent; throughout, I have used only sentences where the intended bond will be obvious to the reader.

[6] As Postal makes clear, the items in question here are not uniformly identifiable as 'words' in the conventional sense: for instance in the usual sense 'our' is a word but there has never been any question about the penetrability of 'our': "+Our wives don't understand us." Still, many of the items of present interest are words, and I will use that term as long as it is not confusing. Later, when I will be trying to stress the ephemeral quality of the 'word', I will adopt a facetious synonym.

[7] The difficulty is precisely the nature of the words 'pejorative' or 'diminutive': if *Froggie* means 'Frenchman, pejoratively' and not 'someone from France, pejoratively' then *Froggie* is presumably underlaid by 'Frenchman' itself. Such an underlay cannot really be urged seriously at this time, but it is certainly worth noting that pejoratives are morphologically formed like diminutives – e.g., by adding the suffix '-y' – and that what is morphologically transformed in this way does appear to be the provenience-term, not the political-entity-name itself: cf. 'Dutchie' from *Dutchman*, and notice that 'Kanuck' has an unusual stress-pattern and that this is the stress-pattern of 'Canadian', not of 'Canada'.

[8] Note, however, that *longlegged* is not compounded by adding 'long' to 'legged'; there is no such word as '*legged' and there is presumably no such constituent either. *Longlegged*, then, must be 'longleg' plus '-ed' (cf. 'greyhair + ed'), and so the process of finding the antecedent of *ones*, in (20a), must track back through *longlegged* to 'longleg' and thence to 'leg'. Not a particularly favorable instance, perhaps.

[9] Subjects were undergraduates at the University of California, Irvine, in their initial linguistics course. Participating in the experiment was part of the course work. Subjects were tested individually but in class; the experiment was conducted during the first hour of the term. Subjects were given cards each of which contained one sentence. Only two of the sentences contained 'do so'; these were:

(i) Gripsnake wanted to fasten the boards together with NAILS, but Dognog made him do so with *adhesive-tape*.

(ii) Dognog wanted to NAIL the boards together, but Gripsnake made him do so with *adhesive-tape*.

The other three sentences were: (iii) The law requires that all bottles or cans containing alcoholic beverages which are open or the seal is broken must be kept in the trunk of the car; (iv) Nixon wants to admit South Vietnam as the 51st State, but Agnew wants it to be part of

Maryland; and (v) Dick, Pat, Spiro, and Judy had a taco and a burrito, respectively. The five sentences were presented in 109 of the 120 possible different orders; there was no correlation between the performances of subjects and the order in which the 'do so' sentences occurred relative to any of the other three sentences, and so I have regarded those three as 'dummy' sentences of equal weight, ignoring their order relative to the two of interest. Of the 'do so' sentences the second presented was generally ranked higher, whichever was second; I have merged all results. Subjects were instructed to examine only one sentence at a time (to turn up one card at a time). They were to rank each sentence on a 'grammaticality scale' from 0 to 9, and it was explained that 'grammaticality' meant 'acceptability to you as a speaker of English'. I have thought it appropriate to judge a given sentence 'more or less acceptable/grammatical' to a given speaker if he ranked it at 5 or above, but of course the figures given for those who assigned a higher ranking (7,8,9) must be accorded greater importance, as see Note 11.

[10] Twenty-four per cent assigned *both* sentences a rank of 9. An additional 17 per cent ranked one sentence 7 and the other 8 or ranked both either 7 or 8; in all, 41 per cent of those who accepted 'do so' sentences at all assigned both 'do so' sentences ranks of 7 or above.

[11] From the Deadwood (S. Dak.) *Pioneer-Times*, July 31, 1970, p. 4.

[12] The assumption that 'Nixonite' and 'Nixon-follower' (&c) are strictly synonymous is not essential, as see Note 15.

[13] This, however, is to ignore Langacker (1969a).

[14] Even when the stem is a human proper name, as in 'Nixon' and 'Jane', interpreting '-ite' as having a uniform meaning like '-enthusiast' does not seem correct, since it appears that in the former case one is an enthusiast of the person himself, in the latter of the person's (literary) productions. In view of the uncertainty of attaching the right NT derivation to *Nixonite* and the like it must be noted that *Nixon-follower*, whatever is wrong with it, is in the last analysis more accurate than *Nixon-enthusiast*, in view of: (i) +Twitford is an unenthusiastic Nixon-follower; (ii) +Twitford is an unenthusiastic Nixonite; but (iii) *Twitford is an unenthusiastic Nixon-enthusiast.

[15] These will be just the local conclusions that can be based on the brief treatment here accorded the reefs; broader implications will not be taken further than the assertion, which the whole of this paper has been directed at upholding, that the reefs appear to yield more naturally to an NT treatment than to an NL one. For example, though in such a treatment the reefs are formed late in the derivation, just *how* late they are to be inserted is not elaborated beyond the (obvious) point that since reef-formation entails transformational sphincter rules, reef-formation cannot precede actuation of the transformational component. Postal (1969) has of course argued that some webster-formation must follow application of Complement-NP-Deletion, since that transformation applies to structures which word-formation spoils. For instance "The American decision to liberate South Yemen and the South Shetlands" is underlaid by "The American decision *for America* to liberate ..." on his analysis; but deletion of [*for*] *America* is more simply done when 'America' is identical with some other NP, which is possible only if such an NP lies behind *American* (in the form '[of] America'). In other words, possible only if *American* represents a derivational stage subsequent to that at which, given the structure '... [of] America ... [for] America ...', the second 'America', with its preposition, was deleted on conditions of identity. *If* lexicalization (webster-formation) happens uniformly (an issue in itself) then the sphincter rules that form reefs would also have to follow Complement-NP-Deletion.

Postal's remarks have recently been directly challenged by Chomsky (1970a). Chomsky argues (p. 32) that Postal's instances are perfectly compatible with the Lexicalist (or NL) hypotheses, since on the latter arguments the notion 'subject-verb relation' is 'generalized' so as to hold for "America, attempt," "America's, attempt," and – "perhaps" – "even of the same pair in the phrase 'the American attempt'." Ignoring the crucial "perhaps," I admit that this is true; but this remark is meaningful only if the Complement-NP-Deletion transformation is reformulated so as to deal, not with identical NP anymore, but with identical 'subjects'. Nor, obviously, will the old *Aspects* (Chomsky, 1965) definition of 'subject' ('[NP, S]') suffice here. Moreover it is not clear to me how the notion of 'subject' *can* be broadened to cover the pair (American, attempt) without (a) broadening it too far, by letting the notion cover cases of (adjective, attempt) where the adjective is no subject at all – e.g., ('recent, attempt') – or else (b) barring such false subjects by specifying that any adjectival subject must be Noun-derived or consist of some Noun plus some morphological alteration: which begs the question.

But notice that, in any case, Chomsky's counterargument to the late formation of 'American' and the like has *no bearing whatever* on the question of late formation of reefs like '[to] nail', since the latter case is partly based on the fact that anaphora can penetrate to an underlying antecedent 'fasten', which is not present or available in the syntax on any imaginable strictly-NL treatment. There is no (verb, instrumental) generalization available within NL because within NL there is nothing syntactically for (verb) to correspond to: nothing at all.

Parenthetically, the notion that Complement-NL-Deletion takes place in an environment of 'identical' NP is not quite right. If subjectless complements always got that way through deleting a subject NP 'identical' with (roughly) the matrix subject NP, then it would be true that complement and matrix would contain the same subject and so it could not be that one had a verb that demanded a different kind of subject from the subject that the other had. But notice: "John wanted to adjourn." This cannot come from "John wanted for John to adjourn," since 'adjourn' does not accept a singular subject like 'John'; so the complement has a verb whose subject cannot have been the same as the subject of the matrix. Yet notice that the only possible understanding of "John wanted to adjourn" is "John wanted for *the group of which he was a member* to adjourn," so that 'John' and the italicized subject NP of the complement do have a fixed relation: John is one of the group. This suggests that the actual relation between NP amenable to Complement-NP-Deletion is not identity, but neither is it 'sloppy': the relation is that of *inclusion*, including proper inclusion.

Among the many further steps the present paper can be taken in future work are these: (a) the comments on insularity and penetration can be related more closely to actually worked-out NL treatments for other anaphoric problems, and perhaps more imaginative NL solutions could be worked out that would be more satisfactory yet well within reasonable extensions from Jackendoff's classic NL treatment of like problems (1969). (b) Some of the subsidiary questions raised along the way could be returned to, in relation to reefs and related issues; for example, the whole notion of what a linguistic 'mistake' is deserves treatment. (c) Chomsky has rightly pointed out (1970a) that webster-forming sphincter rules in some cases demand the prior application of other rules whose sole raison-d'être is to serve the sphincter rules. Thus adopting the NT position for the reefs, though to my mind completely motivated so long as one restricts oneself to the reefs themselves and like forms, does force alterations elsewhere in the grammar, and so the 'diseconomies' in the NL treatment of the reefs are perhaps counterbalanced by the diseconomies elsewhere in the NT treatment. This final note leaves us in a difficult position, but it is not the same position that Chomsky (1970a) leaves us in, since he argues that the diseconomies of the NT treatment have no justification (he rejects the NT analyses that supported the diseconomies). In the present paper I have tried to restore justification, and so make rejection of the NT version find new support, if it can.

BOB AND CAROL AND TED AND ALICE

1. THE PROBLEM

Consider the following:

(1)   The last word of (1) is obscene.
(2)   The last word of (1) is obscene.

It would appear that (1) cannot be turned into a truth by addition of quotation marks, but that (2) can be so changed – namely, by putting quotation marks around its last word. Yet it would also appear that (1) = (2); and if this is so, then by Leibniz' Law whatever is true of (2) is also true of (1). How is this apparent contradiction to be resolved?[1]

2. PRELIMINARIES

Call the sentence token which occurs in the line indexed above by '(1)', 'Bob'. Call the sentence token which occurs in the line indexed by '(2)', 'Carol'. Bob and Carol are twins. Using 'T' to abbreviate 'the type of', we can express this as follows:

$$\text{Bob} \neq \text{Carol, but } T(\text{Bob}) = T(\text{Carol}).$$

Suppose that next Sunday morning I add quotation marks to Carol's last word (token), and the following Monday morning I do the same to Bob. By the following Tuesday morning, they would both look like this:

The last word of (1) is 'obscene'.

Call Bob's descendent 'Ted', and Carol's descendent 'Alice'. Ted and Alice are also twins.

$$\text{Ted} \neq \text{Alice, but } T(\text{Ted}) = T(\text{Alice}).$$

In order to decide whether Bob and Carol and Ted and Alice are true we must know to whom they are referring. Clearly the Great Designer,

Hintikka et al. (eds.), Approaches to Natural Language, 490–518. All rights reserved.
Copyright © 1973 by David Kaplan, Los Angeles.

Professor Cartwright, designed them to use '(1)' to refer to the individual dubbed '(1)' by the '(1)' which occurs to the left of Bob. Call that token of '(1)', 'Index-1'. *Our* use of '(1)' is governed by the use of Index-1. A point of the problem is to make *their* use of '(1)' co-referential with ours.[2]

Index-1 occurs as part of an act of dubbing in which what is displayed to the right of Index-1 is dubbed '(1)'. Our dubbings, of Bob and Carol and Ted and Alice and Index-1, have all been by description – "Call the blah blah blah, 'Bob'." But the dubbing which occurs in the line containing Index-1 is a dubbing by demonstration – "Call this: _ _ _ '(1)'." So, Index-1 must refer to whatever is displayed to its right.

Bob is certainly displayed there, but it seems equally appropriate to claim that T(Bob) is displayed there.

3. THE OBVIOUS SOLUTION

For this solution we assume that it is always a sentence *type* that is displayed in dubbings of the kind in question. Thus:

$$(1) = T(\text{Bob}) = T(\text{Carol}) = (2).$$

Is it true that in violation of Leibniz' Law (2) can be changed into a truth by the addition of quotation marks but (1) cannot?

Let us begin by discussing (2) in both its actual form, T(Carol), and its potential form, T(Alice). T(Carol) is not true[3] because the last word of (1), namely, the word 'obscene', is not itself obscene. However, T(Alice) is true (allowing for a tacit shift from the 'is' of predication to the 'is' of identity) because the last word of (1) is the word 'obscene'.

But wait a minute! On Sunday morning, when Alice first appears, she (or, if you prefer, her type) is true. However by Monday afternoon, when Ted has replaced Bob, the last word of (1), i.e., the last word of the referent of Index-1, seems to be the word ' 'obscene' '. Thus at that time Alice degenerates to falsity.

Alice's apparent instability is illusory. On Monday morning, when we replace Bob with Ted, we replace the display in a dubbing. Since we neglect to simultaneously replace the name being bestowed, distinct entities are given the same name. Horrors! There is the old (1), T(Bob); and there is (1) Jr., T(Ted).

If at her birth on Sunday, Alice uses '(1)' to refer to T(Bob), then there is no reason to believe that Bob's replacement by Ted should cause her to forget Bob and begin using '(1)' to refer to T(Ted). Indeed, her type and that of her mother are both named '(2)', but this has not caused her to forget her own mother, nor to confuse their differently truth valued types. Alice may continue to refer to whichever (1) she referred to on Sunday. This allows that she may – presciently – have referred to T(Ted) all along.

Alice's constancy aside, the conclusion is that so long as the twins refer to the same (1) they have the same truth value.[4]

When (2) is changed, it is changed into a truth with respect to (1), but a falsehood with respect to (1) Jr. *Exactly the same holds when* (1) *is changed!* Thus Leibniz' Law applies without contradiction.

The puzzle was generated by thinking that both (2) and (2) Jr. must refer to (1); whereas both (1) and (1) Jr. must be self-referential. Thus (2) Jr. and (1) Jr. would refer to different sentences. The puzzle is resolved by recognizing that there are two (1)'s and keeping track of which (1) is under discussion.

4. A MORE INTERESTING SOLUTION

There is a grave difficulty in the obvious solution. The problem speaks the language of 'turn into' and 'change into', but the solution is couched in a metaphysics of replacement.[5]

We did not *change* the false Carol into the true Alice, we *replaced* the false Carol with the true Alice. Or did we? What really happens when I take my pen to Carol next Sunday morning? Could it be that Alice and Carol, like Hesperus and Phosphorus, are one?

There is every reason to think so. Sentence tokens are physical objects and macro-objects at that. They are created, wear down, fade, are touched up, and sometimes are distorted. Neon sentence tokens frequently malfunction and thereby change type. If sufficiently comical, such transformations are enshrined in *The Reader's Digest*.

I conclude that:

Carol = Alice and Bob = Ted.

This not only accounts for the critical use of 'changed' in the formulation of the problem, but as we shall see, it also illuminates the respect in which Carol *can* be changed into a truth by the addition of quotation marks while Bob cannot.

Our bookkeeping simplifies. We can make the natural assumption that only two tokens are involved, Bob-Ted and Carol-Alice, and also that only two dubbings are involved, one incorporating Index-1 and one incorporating its colleague, Index-2. Index-1 stands beside the same token, Bob-Ted, throughout the period of interest. In the problem it is (1) and (2) that are 'changed'. So it must be intended that:

$$(1) = \text{Bob-Ted, and } (2) = \text{Carol-Alice.}$$

With only one (1) to contend with, we can make the natural assumption that throughout the period of interest both Bob-Ted and Carol-Alice use '(1)' to refer to Bob-Ted.

Both (1) and (2) are false at the present time. But their potentialities differ.

(2) *can* be transformed into a truth by putting quotation marks around her last word. In fact, next Sunday morning she *will* be so transformed. Note that this possibility depends on the possibility of making no earlier transformation in (1). When quotation marks are put around the last word in (1), on Monday morning, (2) will again change in truth value. This time not because *she* has changed, but because the world has changed around her and she has viewed it as unchanged.

In contrast, (1) *cannot* be transformed into a truth simply by the addition of quotation marks to his last word. In particular, when those quotation marks are added next Monday morning, his revised self-analysis is true only of his unrevised self. Thus he continues to dissemble. In order to change (1) into a truth, a second change must be made so that (1) looks like this:

The last word in (1) was 'obscene'.

5. A COMPLETE SOLUTION

The preceding solution, though it adequately accounts for the critical elements of *change* and *self-reference*, is yet only a partial solution to the original problem. A complete solution must, in addition, satisfy all three of the following paradoxical conditions:

(1) cannot be changed into a truth by addition of quotation marks to its last word,

(2) can be changed into a truth by addition of quotation marks to its last word,

(1) = (2).

According to the preceding solution, (1) = Bob-Ted ≠ Carol-Alice = (2). Thus the preceding solution clearly fails to satisfy the third condition. This is a cheap avoidance of paradox, no more subtle in this respect than the obvious solution, which simply fails to satisfy the first condition.

In order to obtain a complete solution we must abandon our preliminary claim that Index-1 is used to dub some individual displayed to its right. In a dubbing, a proper name is introduced. But treating Index-1 as a proper name, whether of Bob-Ted or Bob-Ted's current type, is what led to the incompleteness of the previous solutions.

Thus, what is required is an analysis which treats Index-1 as semantically complex. Index-1 must refer to a type, but not by naming it as in the obvious solution. Instead Index-1 should be thought of as *describing* its referent, in the manner of the functional expression, 'the type of *this*'. The only *naming* involved is that of the component demonstrative 'this', which names what is displayed – in the present case, the token Bob-Ted. Since we never replace the display, the demonstrative 'this' always refers to Bob-Ted. If we assume that a proper name functions rather like a demonstrative with a fixed demonstratum, we might describe Index-1 as semantically equivalent to 'T(Bob-Ted)'. When Bob-Ted changes, 'T(Bob-Ted)' takes on a new referent.

The treatment of Index-2 clearly should parallel that of Index-1. We can express the strong equivalence of 'T(Bob-Ted)' with the use of '(1)' introduced by Index-1, and of 'T(Carol-Alice)' with the use of '(2)' introduced by Index-2, roughly as follows:

(a)   Necessarily $((1) = T(\text{Bob-Ted}))$, and
           necessarily $((2) = T(\text{Carol-Alice}))$.

If the third condition on a complete solution is to be satisfied, Index-1 and Index-2 must refer to types as in the obvious solution. But if the first two conditions are to be satisfied, Index-1 must reflect the self-referential element represented in the more interesting solution. The present treatment is simply the natural way to combine the advantages of each of the previous solutions.

Given this interpretation of '(1)', how shall we treat the predicate "can be changed into a truth by addition of quotation marks"? This too has a simple and natural interpretation.

Consider first an analogous predicate. Let M be a metal bar exactly one meter long. A typical claim for a potential of change is:

(b) M's length can be changed to more than a meter by heating it to 200°.

Change is mentioned, and change is indeed involved. But a change in M, not a change in the length: *one meter*. M, not M's length, is heated; as a consequence, M's former length, one meter, is replaced by a new length, 1.001 meters. Ignoring the subtleties involved in the use of 'can' as opposed to 'would', and also ignoring the presupposition that M's length is not now more than one meter, an approximate equivalent to (b) is:

(c)   If M were heated to 200°, then M's length would be more than one meter.

The purpose of this example is to point out the *intensional context* involved in (b).[6]

Returning to the present interpretation of '(1)', we expand the first condition for a complete solution in the style of (c):

(d)   It is not the case that, if quotation marks were put around Bob-Ted's last word, then T(Bob-Ted) would be true.

To establish that (d) holds, suppose that quotation marks *were* put around Bob-Ted's last word. Bob-Ted would then look like this:

The last word of (1) is 'obscene'.

Recalling that it is an assumption of the problem that both Bob-Ted and Carol-Alice always use '(1)' as we do, we see, by (a), that T(Bob-Ted) would then be true if and only if the last word of what would then be T(Bob-Ted) were the word 'obscene'. But the last word of what would then be T(Bob-Ted) would be ' 'obscene' ' not 'obscene'. Hence T(Bob-Ted) would not be true. Hence the subjunctive conditional in (d) does not hold. Hence (d), and thereby the first condition for a complete solution, is satisfied.

The second condition for a complete solution expands as follows:

(e)   If quotation marks were put around Carol-Alice's last word,
           then T(Carol-Alice) would be true.

Arguing as above, we see that (e) is satisfied if and only if the placing of
quotation marks around Carol-Alice's last word would leave the last
word of T(Bob-Ted) (currently the word 'obscene') unaffected. Since the
stability of Bob-Ted surely *is* one of the background conditions to be
assumed in evaluating a subjunctive conditional like (e), it follows that (e),
and thereby the second condition for a complete solution, is satisfied.

Bob-Ted and Carol-Alice *currently* have the same type. Thus, by (a),
the third condition is also satisfied.

Our solution is therefore complete.

APPENDIX I: THE ADDITION OF QUOTATION MARKS

In the preliminaries, quotation marks were added directly to the token
Bob, and T(Ted) was taken to be the type so tokened. An alternative is to
treat the addition of quotation marks as an operation applied directly to
the type T(Bob), and yielding the type T(Ted).

Homework Problem # 1. The alternative treatment leads to a solution even less interesting
than the obvious solution. What is it?

Homework Problem # 2. Can the three solutions given above be reconstructed using the
alternative treatment of quotation marks?

APPENDIX II: TYPES, TOKENS, AND REFERENCE

Although in the obvious solution T(Bob) = T(Carol), it did not immediately follow that Bob and Carol share a truth value. Tokens of 'Ari is
so clever' in the mouths of Plato and Jackie could differ in truth value.
Tokens of 'I am so clever' in the mouths of Plato's Aristotle and Jackie's
Aristotle could differ in truth value.

Homework Problem # 3. Do the two pairs of twins (of the types 'Ari is so clever' and
'I am so clever') differ in the same way?

APPENDIX III: A NONSOLUTION

It might be thought that the original problem could be dissolved simply by claiming that (1) = Bob and (2) = Carol. Then (1) ≠ (2). Hence no application of Leibniz' Law is possible. Hence no paradox. But this leaves unexplained how twins can differ in truth value when they do not differ in the ways discussed in Appendix II. The use of twins to construct the puzzle is, in fact, inessential.

Homework Problem # 4.   Reconstruct the original problem and discuss its solution using the following:
   (Dick)   My last word is obscene.
   (Helen)   Your last word is obscene.

APPENDIX IV: TRUTH AND CONTENT

It may be thought that another plausible candidate for the referent of Index-1 is the *content* of Bob – the proposition expressed by *T*(Bob) in the context in which Bob occurs. Indeed, the problem uses language of the form:
>   (1) is not true.

How can truth or falsity be predicated directly of either a token or a type? (1) must be a proposition. But the same proposition is expressed by each of the following:

>   The last word of (1) is obscene.
>   An obscene word is the last word of (1).

So if (1) is a proposition, how can the function *the last word of* be applied directly to (1)?

   To make sense of the conditions of the problem, both of the following must be meaningful:

(i)   the last word of (1)
(ii)   (1) is false.

We have chosen to interpret '(1)' in such a way that (i) has an obvious meaning. (ii) is then accommodated by implicit (and sometimes, explicit) relativization to features which fix the content of a fugitive sentence. Among the features implicitly taken into account are that the language is English. Among the features explicitly accounted for are the referent of the '(1)' contained in (1) (see note 3). In the obvious solution we spoke of (1)

Jr. being *true with respect to* (1) but *false with respect to* (1) Jr. Similarly, in the more interesting solution when the tense of (1) became relevant, the notion of truth used was that of (1) being *true on Tuesday morning*.

Homework Problem # 5. Construct a solution in which the referent of '(1)' is such that truth is not relativized as above. That is, construct a solution in which the content is built into (1).

APPENDIX V: THE INDIVIDUATION OF TYPES

I have suggested that the most natural notion of a token allows a token to change its type – in the sense that a token can be so changed that a new type will replace its former type. What principle of individuation should we use for types? It is not really necessary that homographous words should share a type. If a useful notion of type can grant the tokens:

> homographous
> *homographous*

the same type, why should it deny 'yellow' (a color) and 'yellow' (a character) distinct types?

Homework Problem # 6. Do the verb 'paint' and the noun 'paint' have distinct types?

APPENDIX VI: CONGRUENCE AND IDENTITY

We might have said that although Bob-Ted ≠ Carol-Alice, there are times at which Bob-Ted *is congruent with* Carol-Alice. We could have symbolized this with an explicit three-place predicate:

> Cong(Bob-Ted, Carol-Alice, *t*)

or with a tensed two-place predicate:

> Bob-Ted ≈ Carol-Alice
> Next Sunday morning (Bob-Ted ≉ Carol-Alice)

where 'next Sunday morning' is a temporal operator treated in the standard way.

Instead, in order to achieve a real identity between (1) and (2), we introduced a tensed functor: '*T*'. Thus '*T*(Bob-Ted) = *T*(Carol-Alice)', with tenseless '=', is true at the same times as 'Bob-Ted ≈ Carol-Alice'.

Homework Problem # 7. Under what conditions on the three-place congruence relation can the tensed predicate '≈' be traded off for a tensed functor and real (i.e., tenseless) identity?

A dubbing by demonstration takes the form:

> Let us call this: _ _ _ 'McBlank'.

A dubbing by description takes the form:

> Let us call α 'McAlpha',

where the blank is replaced by the individual being dubbed, and 'α' is replaced by a description of the individual being dubbed.

It would be good if dubbings by demonstration and dubbings by description were to correspond respectively to dubbings with the subject present and dubbings in absentia.[7] But first some problems concerning display potentials must be resolved.

Some individuals, like the universe, are hard to display all at one place because they are difficult to gather up. Some individuals, like Quine, are hard to display all at once because, as he would protest, "of my hence and ago." Other individuals, like 'Quine' and red are hard to display because they themselves are not within space-time, though their manifestations are. Still other individuals, like nine and the null set, neither are, nor have manifestations, within space-time.

Nine and null can probably only be dubbed by description. But things like Quine, 'Quine', red, and the universe, which have locally presentable aspects or manifestations might be deemed demonstrable in themselves.

There are epistemological reasons for coming to think, as Russell did, that only completely local beings can be demonstrated directly. On this view when I point to Venus and say 'this planet', I am giving a *description* of Venus which incorporates a *demonstration* of one aspect of Venus. Such a treatment provides a Fregean explanation of how a long slow utterance of:

> This planet [pointing to Venus in the morning] = this planet [pointing to Venus in the evening]

can be both informative and true. The denoting phrases are thought of as stylistic variants of 'the planet of which *this* is an aspect'.

On the other hand it seems more natural to think of nice solid continuous four dimensional objects as typical of the kind of thing we point at (directly), and to think of their aspects and stages as somehow derived and abstracted (by description).

Homework Problem # 8. Can Quine be demonstrated or only described?

Homework Problem # 9. Are Quine's aspects and stages like 'Quine's manifestations'?

Homework Problem # 10. Are 'Quine's manifestations' like red's?

Homework Problem # 11. How do we dub nine and null?

Only on a view such as Russell's is it at all reasonable to make it a prerequisite for a dubbing that the dubbor *know*, or stand in some other special epistemological relationship to, the dubbee. Though most pointings are *teleological* (the finger is aimed at a preconceived individual), *blind demonstrations* (as in spin-the-bottle) are also possible and provide an equally satisfactory basis for a dubbing. Descriptions also may be either teleological or blind. A description like 'the first child to be born in the twenty-second century' is near-blind.

Homework Problem # 12. How much was known of Jack the Ripper when he was so dubbed?

APPENDIX VIII: THE AMBIGUITY OF DEMONSTRATIONS

There are conventions governing what is demonstrated when I point. I cannot aim my finger at you and thereby refer to myself. Even though you and the rest of my auditors know that I have mistaken you for your twin, I cannot aim my finger at you and thereby refer to your twin. But in cases like that of Index-1 and cases where my finger is genuinely aimed at a boy, his jacket, and its zipper the conventions are not completely determinative. The only further resource available to resolve the issue seems to be my intentions, taken in a broad sense to include that which guided my pointing. If we wish to avoid introducing an intentional element into the truth conditions for assertions in which 'this' is completed by a pointing, we might require that 'this' always be accompanied by a common noun phrase – 'this boy', 'this zipper', 'this momentary stage of a rabbit surface'. When my finger aims at more (or less) than one such, the demonstrative phrase could be treated in the manner of an improper description. The more general commoun noun phrases, 'physical object', 'entity', would invariably produce improper demonstrations.

Homework Problem # 13. If one points at the center of a pool of blood, is the demonstrative phrase 'this blood' proper or improper?

Homework Problem # 14. Does the correct solution to the problem – and in particular to the question of what is displayed to the right of Index-1 – depend on what Cartwright had in mind?

Homework Problem # 15. Donnellan's account (1966, 1968, 1970) of the referential use of a description is more along intentional lines. If he were to adapt his account to pointings, what would he say about the mistaken pointing at a twin?

APPENDIX IX: RIGID DESIGNATORS

The introduction of an expression which is a simple name syntactically, but a compound description semantically, I call an *abbreviation* – to contrast with the more common form of introduction, a *dubbing*. Proper names are, or at least purport to have been, introduced by dubbings. Since the introduction of a syntactically simple expression, like Index-1, is almost invariably a dubbing, I took special care to point out that in the complete solution I was interpreting the introduction of Index-1 as an abbreviation.

The semantical differences between descriptions like 'the number of planets' and proper names like '9' are already familiar. The description may denote different numbers under different circumstances, but the name always denotes the same number. It has been less widely noticed that in this respect all proper names are like '9'. In fact, the very purpose of introducing a proper name is often to provide an expression free from the vagaries of 'the number of planets'. Kripke (1972) has remarked that proper names are *rigid designators* – the same name designates the same individual in all circumstances. I add that the introduction of a proper name may as well be occasioned by frustration over the flaccidity of a description as by frustration over its length. Discussion of an individual's potentiality to fail to fulfill the description by which he is known, will almost always be facilitated by the introduction of a proper name. The yacht owner's guest who is reported by Russell to have become entangled in "I thought that your yacht was longer than it is" should have said, "Look, let's call the length of your yacht a 'russell'. What I was trying to say is that I thought that your yacht was longer than a russell." If the result of such a dubbing were the introduction of 'russell' as a mere abbreviation for 'the length of your yacht', the whole performance would have been in vain.

Through its use in a dubbing by description, an arbitrary description can produce a name which *rigidly* designates whatever the description *happens* to describe in the context of the dubbing.

Homework Problem # 16 (adopted from Kripke). '100° Centigrade' is *defined* as 'the temperature at which water boils at sea level'. Are such definitions dubbings or abbreviations?

Homework Problem # 17. The insertion of words like 'present' and 'actual' in a description – 'the *present* Queen of England', 'the *actual* length of your yacht' – cause the description to take the referent it would have if it were not within the scope of any temporal, modal, epistemological, or other intensional operators. In Russell's language, they give the description *primary scope.* Thus the insertion of such words fixes the referent independently of any intensional operators within whose scope the description lies. Do such words convert the description into a rigid designator?

Others, before Kripke, had recognized the rigidity of proper names. His notable contribution has been to indicate a technique for *finding* the referent of a proper name, on a particular occasion of use, which is independent of the knowledge and belief of the user. The technique consists in tracing the history of acquisition of the name from use back to bestowal. It is based on the exceedingly plausible assumption that if a name enters your vocabulary from hearing me use it (you learn the name from me), then your utterances of the name have the same referent as mine. Kripke's technique for finding the referent frees proper names from their supposed dependence on currently associated descriptions[8] and thus eases the way for recognition of their rigidity.

I have attempted to supplement the view by emphasizing the techniques for bestowing a proper name and thus *fixing* reference. I call such acts of bestowal 'dubbings'. (Other terms are available, but they tend to carry a sectarian bias.) The resulting view of the reference of proper names can be encapsulated as follows:

If α is the proper name used on some particular occasion, then
  (i) α denotes x iff α originated in a dubbing of x, and
  (ii) for all possible circumstances w, α denotes x with respect to w iff α denotes x.

It is a corollary that if α did not originate in a successful dubbing (one which is a dubbing of *some x*), α nowhere denotes anything.

This view of the reference of proper names is anti-intentional. It says what the *name* (in use) refers to, not what a *user* refers to, or intends to refer to, or is most plausibly taken to be talking about, in *using* the name. The latter (user's reference) is an important, but different, sense of 'refer'. Suppose the name 'Jaakko Hintikka' is introduced to me by having Julius Moravcsik introduced to me with the lie "This is Jaakko Hintikka." When I later remark, "Hintikka's Finnish accent is a very unusual one," I, no doubt, am talking about Moravcsik. I may even be said to have referred to him. But my *utterance* of the name refers to Hintikka. Thus the sentence token I have uttered is false. (There may be other Hintikka's with unusual Finnish accents, but the Finnish accent of the Hintikka referred to in the lie is usual. Remember it was a lie, so the 'this' and the 'Jaakko Hintikka' could not be co-referential.) I see no way, other than speaking carefully, of avoiding the ambiguating effects of this distasteful dualism.

Homework Problem # 18.   Kaplan (1968, especially §IX) has introduced a peculiar relation between an occurrence of a name and an individual, which he expresses with an italicized '*of*'. To which of the following does his notion correspond: the name's reference, the user's reference, some confused combination of the two, none of the above?

APPENDIX X: DENOTATION AND EXISTENCE

Some have claimed that though a proper name might denote the same individual with respect to any possible world (or, more generally, possible circumstance) in which he exists, it certainly cannot denote him with respect to a possible world in which he does not exist. With respect to such a world there must be a gap in the name's designation, it designates nothing. This is a mistake.[9] There are worlds in which Quine does not exist. It does not follow that there are worlds with respect to which 'Quine' does not denote. What follows is that with respect to such a world 'Quine' denotes something which does not exist in that world. Indeed, Aristotle no longer exists, but 'Aristotle' continues to denote (him).

The view that no expression could name Quine with respect to a possible world in which he does not exist seems to be based on one of two ideas. The first is usually expressed with respect to possible worlds, but I will caricature it with respect to the moments of time.

Individuals are taken to be specific to their moment, thus they are momentary stages of what *we* would call individuals. Variables and constants, when evaluated with respect to a moment *t*, take as values stages occurrent at *t*. *Our* individuals can be constructed from these individuals (which were sliced out of our individuals in the first place) by assembly (or, perhaps, reassembly). The assemblages of stages are used to evaluate quantification into and out of temporal operators. Although you cannot literally step in the same river twice, you can step in two stages of the same assemblage. A variable which recurs within and without a temporal operator will take different values in its different occurrences, but its values will be from the same assemblage.[10] Note that though each stage belongs to one or more assemblages, the values of the variables are not assemblages but stages. The individuals are stages. Genidentity, as determined by the assemblages, holds between distinct stages.[11]

Homework Problem # 19. Let **T** be the set of moments of time ordered by $<$. The present time is 0. Let $S(t)$, for $t \in \mathbf{T}$, be the set of stages occurrent at t; let $F(t)$, for $t \in \mathbf{T}$, be the subset of $\mathbf{S}(t)$ of which 'F' is true at t; let **A** be the set of assemblages f, where the domain of f is included in **T** and for each t in the domain of f, $f(t) \in \mathbf{S}(T)$. The operator 'P' is read 'at some earlier time'. Translate the following sentence, involving a quantification out of a temporal operator, into the metalanguage:

$$P[\forall x(Fx] \to Fx)$$

(In English: There is a certain time in the past such that all individuals, of that time, who were then female still are.)[12]

According to the foregoing view, at each moment of his lifetime 'Aristotle' denoted a different entity, the Aristotle of the moment. Thus, at the present moment, when no current entity is sufficiently well connected to the other Aristotle stages to be an Aristotle stage, 'Aristotle' denotes nothing. What should it denote, a stage of Quine?[13] But according to this view, there is no real Aristotle to be denoted, only the Aristotles of each moment, so this view, in its pure form, is too bizarre to support the mistake.

A compromise is proposed. Continue to think of things as before, but take the assemblages themselves as the values of the variables and constants. Whenever a term denoted a stage, let it now denote that stage's assemblage (or one of them). Whenever a term denoted nothing (i.e., at those times not in the domain of a relevant assemblage), let it still denote nothing. Here is the mistake in full bloom.

The original view may have been bizarre, but it had its uses in explicating bizarre notions, for example that I might change into twins or that twins might have changed into me.[14] The compromise view does not have one becoming two, instead it has two coincident assemblages diverging. An unusual situation, but one not violative of Leibniz' Law. As individuals, assemblages are quite well behaved. Thus no reason remains not to take them as values of their proper names with respect to moments when they do not exist.[15] If, on the compromise, 'Quine' denotes the same thing yesterday and today, why not let 'Aristotle' denote the same thing 2300 years ago and today? After all, it does.

The second idea that might lead one to doubt that 'Quine' could denote where Quine does not exist is a simple confusion between our language and theirs. For reasons to be adumbrated shortly, ever-unactualized possibilia are extraordinarily difficult to dub. Thus the inhabitants of a world in which Quine never exists would likely have no name for him.[16] So what! He exists here. *We* have a name for him, namely, 'Quine'. It is *our* terms and formulas whose denotation and truth value are being assessed with respect to the possible world in question.

Homework Problem # 20. If a horse's tail were called a 'leg', horses would have five appendages called 'legs'. How many legs would a horse have?

Homework Problem # 21. Does 'Quine' denote Quine with respect to the time of Aristotle's birth? Who was then called 'Quine'?

APPENDIX XI: NAMES FROM FICTION

I have argued that 'Aristotle' denotes something which, at the present time, does not exist. I could now argue that 'Pegasus' denotes something which, in the actual world, does not exist. I shall not. Pegasus does not exist, and 'Pegasus' does not denote. Not here; not anywhere. What makes 'Aristotle' more perfect than 'Pegasus'?

The 'Aristotle' we most commonly use originated in a dubbing of some-one,[17] our 'Pegasus' did not. Some rascal just *made up* the name 'Pegasus',[18] and he then pretended, in what he told us, that the name really referred to something. But it did not. Maybe he even told us a story about how this so-called Pegasus was dubbed 'Pegasus'. But it was not true.

Maybe he proceeded as follows. First, he made up his story in Ramsified form: as a single, existentially quantified sentence with the made up proper names ('Pegasus', 'Bellerophon', 'Chimaera', etc.) replaced by variables bound to the prefixed existential quantifiers; second, he realized that the result was possible, and that therefore it held in some possible world, and that therefore there was at least one possible individual who played the winged horse in at least one possible world; and third, he tried to dub one of those possible individuals 'Pegasus'. But he would not succeed. How would he pick out just one of the millions of such possible individuals?

Homework Problem # 22. Suppose that Quine and Kripke both might have been winged horses of the kind described in the story. Which one, if either, is Pegasus? (Hint: remember that 'Pegasus' is a rigid designator, so whoever might be Pegasus *is* Pegasus.)

I do not assume that there are no proper names which succeed in naming ever-unactualized possibilia (be they individuals, worlds, or circumstances). But the dubbing problem raises serious questions about the content of discourse using such putative proper names. I fear that those who would so speak have adopted the logician's *existential instantiation* as a form of dubbing:

> There is at least one cow in yonder barn. Let's call one of them 'Bossie'. Now, how much do you think she weighs?

I am skeptical of such dubbings. The logician is very cautious in *his* use of the names so derived.[19]

The requirement for a successful dubbing is not that the dubbor know who the dubbee is. As remarked in Appendix VII, the dubbor can point with his eyes closed or use a description like 'the first child to be born in the twenty-second century'. The requirement is simply that the dubbee be, somehow, uniquely specified. This our story teller has not succeeded in doing. Probably he did not even try.

Perhaps I am being too harsh on 'Pegasus'. I have treated a myth as if it were pseudo-science, and dismissed it for failure of factuality. Even pseudo-science may have something to offer other than factuality.

Suppose we start out by acknowledging that the Pegasus-myth is FICTION.[20] Still it is, in a sense, possible. Should we not take 'Pegasus' to denote what it denotes in *the world of the myth*? We must be very careful now.

If 'the world of the myth' is meant to refer to the (or even, *a*) possible world with respect to which the myth – taken as pseudo-science – is true, there is an immediate objection. As given, the myth uses the name 'Pegasus'. Thus its truth with respect to a possible world requires a *prior* determination of what, if anything, 'Pegasus' names with respect to the possible world. Suppose we turn, then, to the Ramsified myth. Although it will be true in millions of possible worlds, Ramsification eliminates the very name whose denotatum we seek.

An alternative strategy arises in connection with the Ramsified myth. Wherever it is true, *something* plays Pegasus. If we limit attention to those cases where exactly one thing plays Pegasus, we can refer to it by means of the description ⌐the x $\mathcal{M}$⌐, where $\mathcal{M}$ is the Ramsified myth without the existential quantifier which binds the variable 'x' which replaced all occurrences of 'Pegasus' in the myth as given. Why not take 'Pegasus' to *abbreviate* ⌐the x $\mathcal{M}$⌐?[21] The objection to this wonderfully candid proposal is that the Friend of Fiction is unlikely to accept it. First, 'Pegasus' loses the status which allowed it to function so smoothly in 'Bellerophon hoped that Pegasus...' contexts. The expansion of such declarations is awkward at best. Second, there is no fixed individual, Pegasus, denoted by 'Pegasus' with respect to all possible worlds in which he exists. Third, 'Pegasus' still denotes nothing. When the presumed dubbing is disregarded and 'Pegasus' ceases to be a rigid designator, the world of the myth ceases to be of interest.

There is another interpretation of 'the world of the myth' which, I believe, better represents the position of those who take the view that 'Pegasus' finds its denotatum in the world of the myth.[22] The myth is possible in the sense that there is a possible world in which it is truthfully *told*. Furthermore, there are such worlds in which the language, with the exception of the proper names in question, is semantically and syntactically identical with our own. Let us call such possible worlds of the myth, 'M worlds'. In each M world, the name 'Pegasus' will have originated in a dubbing of a winged horse. The Friend of Fiction, who would not have anyone believe the myth (even Ramsified), but yet talks of Pegasus, pretends to be in an M world and speaks its language.

But beware the confusion of our language with theirs! If w is an M world, then *their* name 'Pegasus' will denote something with respect to w, and *our* description 'the x such that x is called 'Pegasus'' will denote the same thing with respect to w, but *our* name 'Pegasus' will still denote nothing with respect to w. Also, in different M worlds, different possible individuals may have been dubbed 'Pegasus'; to put it another way, *our* description 'the x such that x is called 'Pegasus'' may denote different possible individuals with respect to different M worlds.

I do not object to the inhabitants of one of the M worlds remarking that their name 'Pegasus' denotes something with respect to *our* world that does not exist in our world. But I reserve the right to retort that *our* name 'Pegasus' does not even denote with respect to their world.

To summarize. It has been thought that proper names like 'Pegasus' and 'Hamlet' were like 'Aristotle' and 'Newman 1', except that the individuals denoted by the former were more remote. But regarded as names of *our* language – introduced by successful or unsuccessful dubbings, or just made up – the latter denote and the former do not.

Homework Problem # 23.   Is the foregoing account of proper names deriving from fiction correct? If so, how could its fourth sentence be true?

APPENDIX XII: THE UNIVERSE OF DISCOURSE

At the present time, the techniques are available to produce a completely axiomatized formal theory of definite descriptions to fit almost any specification. We should now more carefully distinguish that part of the metalinguistic apparatus which consists of logicians' tricks, adopted for purely instrumental reasons and devoid of philosophical import, from that part which directly realizes the intended interpretation of the object language.

It may be technically convenient to introduce an entity, † , completely alien to the universe of discourse of the object language and to adjust slightly our use of 'denotes' so that we can say that a singular term α does *not* denote, in the following odd way:

$$\alpha \text{ so-to-speak-denotes } \dagger.$$

We have not lost sight of the fact that α does not really denote, *denotation* and *so-to-speak-denotation* are interdefinable. The use of the latter is fairly described as a logician's trick for smoothing some definitions in the metalanguage. Though it seems unlikely, it may even turn out to be useful to introduce more than one such way of saying that α does not denote.

Definite descriptions are rather special kinds of terms. A definite description ⌐the x ϕ⌐ is proper if among the values of 'x' there is a unique individual satisfying ϕ. As ordinarily conceived, a proper definite description denotes one of the values of the variables, and an improper definite description does not denote at all (though of course it may so-to-speak-denote something). Thus a definite description can denote an individual who fails to exist only if among the values of the variables are things which do not (in the appropriate sense) exist. For example, if among the values of the variable 'x' are all persons who ever lived, and if 'exists' is taken to apply to those persons who are yet alive, then 'the x such that x wrote *Meaning and Necessity*' denotes someone who fails to exist and 'the x such that x wrote *Principia Mathematica*' fails to denote. If the values of the variables are limited to persons now alive, then neither description denotes.

The universe of discourse of a theory need not be limited to the values of the variables. There may well be entities which are not among the values of the variables but which are related to those values in various natural and interesting ways, as books are related to their authors, sets to their members, and ancestors to their surviving descendents. A theory may afford recognition to such entities by mentioning them individually, by name or singular term, without quantifying over them. Much that would otherwise be artificially constrained can thus be treated easily and naturally.

Though our variable binding discourse be limited to natural numbers, we may wish to drop in occasional reference to an unnatural rational, perhaps via the functional expression '$x/2$'. When the values of the variables are so restricted, the following are all true. Why deny them?

$$\exists x \, \forall y \; y \neq x/2$$
$$\forall x \; 2(x/2) = x$$
$$\forall x \, \forall y \, (y = x/2 \leftrightarrow 2y = x)$$

Must '$x/2$' fail to denote when 'x' takes the value 3? Of course not. The reasonable course is to let it then denote 1-1/2. Must 'the y such that $2y = x$' fail to denote when 'x' takes the value 3? Yes.

Homework Problem # 24. In Zermelo-Fraenkel set theory the set of all values of the variables is not among those values. This can be expressed as follows:
$$\sim\exists x \; x = \{y : y = y\}$$
Must '$\{y : y = y\}$' fail to denote? Must 'the x such that $\forall y \, (y \in x \leftrightarrow y = y)$' fail to denote?[23]

Usually it is most convenient to allow the values of the variables to comprehend the entire universe of discourse, marking realms of special interest with predicates. Expressibility increases at no apparent cost. Such motivations lead modal logicians to take as values of their variables all *possible* individuals and to add a predicate of actuality. Similar motivations lead logicians of tense to range their variables over past, present, and future

individuals, and to add a predicate of occurrence. But this strategy may
entail hidden costs. The systematization of a theory that comes with
axiomatization may be lost or compromised. Increased expressibility
may open the door to the discussion of issues we shun. In addition, a
wider range for the variables may engender talk of new entities in a still
wider universe of discourse, with the result that the universe of discourse
does not yet close with the domain of values of the variables.

Homework Problem # 25. What happens if the strategy of expanding the domain of
values of the variables to meet the universe of discourse is applied to a set theory with ab-
stracts, $\ulcorner\{x:\phi\}\urcorner$, some of which denote sets not among the values of the variables?

We have seen that although our choice of values for the bound variables
will restrict the possible values of definite descriptions, there is no sound
reason to restrict the values of all terms in the same way. Thus, putting
aside the bizarre view of Appendix X, there is nothing to prevent us from
treating proper names which denote with respect to some circumstance as
denoting the same entity with respect to all possible circumstances,
including those in which the entity is not among the values of the variables
or, in some other sense, does not exist. The analysis of proper names taken
from fiction does not motivate any departure from this practice. I conclude
that a proper name either denotes the same individual with respect to every
possible circumstance or else denotes nothing with respect to any possible
circumstance.

APPENDIX XIII: THE EXCLUSION OF NONDENOTING TERMS

There is an alternative to so-to-speak-denotation which is equally smooth.
We can use so-to-speak definite descriptions. An entity, ∗, is chosen from,
or added to, the universe of discourse of the language. A slight alteration
is made in the definite description operator; now written 'the∗'. $\ulcorner$the∗ x $\phi\urcorner$
is translated as 'the unique entity among the values of the variable 'x'
which satisfies ϕ; or, if there is none, ∗'.[24] It is clear that 'the∗$x(x \neq x)$' denotes ∗. Whatever ease of semantical formulation resulted from the adop-
tion of so-to-speak-denotation also accrues to the adoption of 'the∗',
provided that a similar alteration is made in the meaning of *all* nondenoting terms.[25]

Let α^* be the altered version of α. It is conceptually important to distinguish the following:

$\alpha*$ denotes $*$
α so-to-speak-denotes †.

The latter is equivalent to saying that α does not denote; the former holds when α does not denote, but also holds when α denotes $*$. Another aspect of the difference comes out when we ask what considerations are relevant to determining the truth values of atomic sentences. When α does not denote, the considerations relevant to determining the truth value of $\ulcorner \Pi\alpha \urcorner$ (for extensional atomic predicates Π) are very different from those relevant to determining the truth value of $\ulcorner \Pi\alpha* \urcorner$. The truth value of $\ulcorner \Pi\alpha* \urcorner$ is fixed by the choice of $*$ and its properties. Determination of the truth value of $\ulcorner \Pi\alpha \urcorner$, and even whether it has one, suffers no such constraints. Since † is alien to the universe of discourse of the object language, its properties are irrelevant. If identity is given its standard interpretation, $\ulcorner \alpha* = \beta* \urcorner$ *must* be true when neither α nor β denote, since in that case both $\alpha*$ and $\beta*$ denote the same element of the universe of discourse. But the mere interpretation of identity does not yet determine the truth value of $\ulcorner \alpha = \beta \urcorner$ when neither α nor β denotes. Adoption of so-to-speak-denotation may be a consequence of the decision to call $\ulcorner \alpha = \beta \urcorner$ true, but so-to-speak-denotation also has its uses when $\ulcorner \alpha = \beta \urcorner$ is to be neither true nor false.

It is clear from the interdefinability of 'denotes' and 'so-to-speak-denotes' that the use of the latter for the formulation of the semantical rules does not limit the semantical alternatives for treating nondenoting terms. On the other hand, the use of $\alpha*$ rather than α, *avoids* the problem of nondenoting terms by confining the object language to terms whose denotation is guaranteed.

Within the systems which exclude nondenoting terms, a variety of altered definite description operators are available. Among those of the form 'the*' some choose $*$ within the values of the variables, some without. An inner choice of $*$ yields a simpler axiomatization of the resulting logic. But it has turned out that the logic resulting from an outer choice of $*$ is much more smoothly axiomatizable than was thought possible twenty years ago. An outer choice of $*$ allows $\alpha*$ to better simulate α. But the improvement is only to the extent that nondenoting terms are clearly distinguished from terms which denote elements of the domain of values of the variables. The formula $\ulcorner\alpha* = \text{the*}x\ x \neq x\urcorner$ does not differentiate non-denoting terms α from those which naturally denote $*$.

There is no general way, within a theory, to absolutely determine whether a term α for which $\ulcorner\sim\exists x\ x = \alpha\urcorner$ is true denotes an element of the universe of discourse or only so-to-speak-denotes $\dagger$. The distinction is not in general expressible within the language.[26] Even the difference between a choice of $*$ within or without the domain of values of the variables may be disguised by interdefinable alterations of notation which extend or restrict the range of quantification by just that one element. But the intended semantics may often be inferred from theorems of the form $\ulcorner\alpha = \Delta\urcorner$, where Δ is a term which 'naturally' denotes. For example, within a theory of virtual classes, 'the $x(x \neq x) = \{x : x = x\}$' suggests that 'the $x(x \neq x)$' denotes an element of the universe of discourse, whereas such tantalizing assertions as '$\{$the $x(x \neq x)\} = \{x : x \neq x\}$' suggest that 'the $x(x \neq x)$' denotes nothing.

The important question is whether we accept the outer entities (those in the universe of discourse but not in the domain of values of the variables) as *real*, as entering into properties and relations of interest to the object language with as much vigor and independence as do the inner entities, lacking only the characteristic property of the inner entities. If we do, then the choice of $*$ as inner or outer seems of secondary importance. If we do not, then there seems no need for more than one outer entity, and its choice as $*$ amounts to identifying it with $\dagger$.

Homework Problem # 26. Dana Scott has proposed a theory of descriptions according to which the value of an improper description is not an element of the domain of values of the variables.[27] Is he recommending the adoption of so-to-speak-denotation or just an outer choice of $*$?

Homework Problem # 27. 'the $x\ Fx$' denotes the unique inner entity satisfying 'Fx'. If more than one entity satisfies 'Fx', there may still be a unique common value for the functional expression '$g(x)$' whenever the value of 'x' satisfies 'Fx'. Thus in a generalized theory of definite descriptions we may wish an operator of the form 'the $x(g(x):Fx)$'. So long as the value of '$g(x)$' is an inner entity, this operator is expressed by 'the $y\exists x(Fx \wedge y = g(x))$'. But if the language includes terms such as '$x/2$', which carry inner entities to outer ones, a new operator must be introduced. We write $\ulcorner$the $x_0 \ldots x_n (\alpha:\phi)\urcorner$ for the generalized definite description. The variables $x_0 \ldots x_n$ are bound by the operator. It is permitted that the value of α may be an outer entity. The familiar $\ulcorner$the $x\ \phi\urcorner$ is definable by $\ulcorner$the $x(x:\phi)\urcorner$. A single schema characterizes the generalized definite description:

(L) $\quad \beta \neq$ the $x(x:x \neq x) \rightarrow$
$[\beta =$ the $x_0 \ldots x_n (\alpha:\phi) \leftrightarrow \exists x_0 \ldots x_n [\forall y_0 \ldots y_n (\exists x_0 \ldots x_n (\phi \wedge \alpha = \alpha_x^y) \leftrightarrow \alpha = \alpha_x^y) \wedge \alpha = \beta]]$

where α_x^y is the proper substitution of $y_0 \ldots y_n$ for $x_0 \ldots x_n$ in α. Call the schema which results from (L) by restricting attention to the familiar case of the form ⌐the $x(x:\phi)$⌐ ⌐(D)⌐. Give a simple characterization of the theory of descriptions which results from (D) by adding:

(I) $\exists x(x = \text{the } x(x : x \neq x))$.

Give a simple characterization of the theory which results from adding the negation of (I) to (D). Show that (D) is equipolent to the disjunction of the two theories as you have characterized them. Is any alteration in (L) called for if 'the $x(x:x \neq x)$' is taken as so-to-speak-denoting †?

APPENDIX XIV: A LAST SOLUTION

Take the changing tokens of the more interesting solution and slice them up as in the bizarre view of Appendix X. Now ignore all properties of the slices but their time and type (ignore, for example, their location). We can then reassemble the tokens as in the compromise view of Appendix X. A token can now be thought of as a function which assigns to each moment in its lifetime, its type at that moment. Under this interpretation two tokens with the same type at a given time literally coincide at that time. These tokens are idealized versions of the real tokens (the physical objects afflicted with location and all that) with which we usually deal. To each such real token there corresponds, in the obvious way, an ideal token. Using ideal tokens we can construct a variant of the more interesting solution which is slightly less natural but which may come closer to meeting the adequacy condition: (1) = (2). Treat Index-1 as naming the ideal token which corresponds to Bob-Ted, and similarly for Index-2. The addition of quotation marks becomes an operation directly on the types which constitute the slices of (1) and (2). Otherwise, the argument proceeds as in the more interesting solution. We do not quite achieve the identity of (1) and (2), but almost. At the present time, (1) *coincides* with (2).[28]

Compared to the more interesting solution this solution has the drawback of standing the relation between tokens and types on its head. A consequence of the upside down perspective is that when two real tokens are congruent, their idealizations are coincident. If congruence is as close to identity as coincidence is, then the last solution is no improvement over the more interesting one. From a methodological point of view, however, the last solution is very interesting. Let us look at it as a variant of the complete solution. There, '(2)' was regarded as abbreviating a description which denoted different sentence types at different times. Since applicability of the predicate 'can be changed . . .' depends on the referent of the abbreviated description at times other than the time of utterance (at which time $(1) = (2)$), it was not surprising that the substitution of '(1)' for '(2)' in this context did not preserve truth. The now common diagnosis of such failures of substitutivity is that substitution in *intensional* contexts like those produced by the 'can be changed...' predicate requires that '(1)' and '(2)' have, not only the same referent, but the same sense.[29] Frege (1952) would agree and go further; within such contexts, '(1)' and '(2)' *refer* to their ordinary sense. When '(1)' and '(2)' are given the interpretation appropriate to their occurrence as subjects of the 'can be changed...' predicate, it will be discovered that the purported identity, $(1) = (2)$, is not a true identity but only a matter of coincidence.[30] Thus we see that the interpretation of Index-1 proposed in the last solution accords exactly with the method of Frege, made explicit by Church, for *completing* the complete solution.

Frege exports intensionality by reinterpreting the expressions which lie within an intensional context. Those which would ordinarily be taken to designate different things with respect to different possible circumstances are reinterpreted to take a fixed designatum, the sense, which by itself determines the entire spectrum of former designata. To put it Kripke's way, a flaccid designator is transformed into a rigid one. But in a way very different from the introduction of a proper name through a dubbing by description. A dubbing by the description α introduces a new expression which rigidly designates the same entity as that which happens to be designated by α with respect to the context of the dubbing. Frege's reinterpretation of α has α itself rigidly designating a new entity of a higher level than any of those which it formerly designated.[31] According to Frege, even an expression in an oblique context is open to substitution by an expression whose entire spectrum is determined by means of the same higher level entity (the same sense). Thus the reinterpretation allows free substitution of expressions whose *reinterpreted* designata are the same. But very few pairs of expressions will pass *that* test.

The process of Fregean ascent can be reversed to import intensionality where none is apparent. Any continuant with different stages in different circumstances, can be sliced into its stages. Any rigid designator of such a continuant can be deinterpreted to designate, with respect to a circumstance, only the then occurrent *stage* of the continuant it formerly designated.[32] The unity of the continuant is dissipated, perhaps irretrievably. It survives primarily in the spectra of the vestigial, no longer rigid, designators. Identity becomes a subject demanding serious attention. Distinct things can be 'the same individual'! Coincidence degenerates to identity. Intensionality runs rampant.

> Although I *am identical with* my body, one of us will survive the other.

Thus begins the long process of Darwinian descent.[33]

University of California, Los Angeles

NOTES

[1] The problem is stated thus in *The Journal of Philosophy* **68** (1971), p. 86, where it is attributed to Professor Richard Cartwright. Solutions follow. Certain collateral issues are discussed in a series of appendices of varying interest. Suggestions for further study are given in the homework problems. An Instructor's Manual is in preparation. All of this has been supported by the National Science Foundation.

[2] I shall use 'refers to', 'denotes', 'designates', 'takes as value', etc., indifferently for the standard notion. Though my way of talking may suggest it, Donnellan's *referential use* is not here applicable.

[3] There is an ellipsis here. The truth of T(Carol) depends on the reference made by T(Carol)'s '(1)'. (Carol may have a remote twin whose '(1)' token is not co-referential with Carol's.) A more explicit form is:

T(Carol) is not true when T(Bob) is taken as referent of '(1)'.

Or, since T(Carol)'s '(1)' is the only word in T(Carol) whose reference is under examination:

T(Carol) is not true with respect to T(Bob).

Or since we have fixed *our* use of '(1)' by means of Index-1:

T(Carol) is not true with respect to (1).

Or, since, as remarked in the preliminaries, it is an assumption of the problem that Carol's use of '(1)' is co-referential with ours:

T(Carol) is not true.

[4] I waver between Alice and T(Alice) as vehicle of truth. The ambivalence is not critical. The truth value of T(Alice) should, for this problem, be evaluated with respect to the individual referred to by Alice.

[5] Surely on a distinction of such fundamental metaphysical importance, the choice of language in framing the problem was no accident.

[6] The *subjunctive* conditional is not critical to this example or to the following analysis of the problem. We may suppose that M *will* be heated to 200°, and thereby shift to the simple future tense.

When M is heated to 200°, M's length will be more than one meter. The occurrence of 'M's length' remains oblique; it cannot be replaced by its co-designator, 'one meter'. A similar shift from the subjunctive or modal to the future tense would also not affect the following analysis of the problem. It is interesting to note, in comparison, that no intensional context of any form was involved in the preceding solution to the problem. According to that analysis, it is the *present* referent of Index-1, Bob-Ted himself not one of his types or stages, that becomes true.

[7] Anything of which we can frame a definite description can be dubbed by description including, for example, Newman 1 (the first child to be born in the twenty-second century). Thus we might dub by description even when the subject is present, if we are unaware of the fact, or if he is not appropriately 'available', or if we have an ulterior motive.

[8] There was always something implausible about the idea that the referent of a proper name is determined by the currently associated descriptions. For example, the entry under 'Rameses VIII' in the *Concise Biographical Dictionary* (Concise Publications: Walla, Washington) is 'One of a number of ancient pharaohs about whom nothing is known'.

[9] An explicit perpetration occurs in Kaplan (1968, p. 196). But he has not erred alone.

[10] To interpret this theory within a normal one, take the stages to be ordered couples consisting of a moment of time and the coincidence class of one of the normal (continuant) individuals at that time. The coincidence class of a given continuant at a given time is the class of all those continuants which coincide with the given continuant at the given time. The assemblages are determined by the normal individuals. The assemblage corresponding to a normal individual a is that function which assigns to each moment of time at which a occurs the coincidence class of a at that time. Though the value of each occurrence of a variable is a stage, these stages are coordinated by means of assemblages determined by the quantifiers. An existentially quantified formula holds at a given moment if there is an assemblage which has a stage at that moment and which is such that the formula is satisfied by taking as value of each occurrence of the quantified variable the relevant stage of the assemblage. The universal quantifier is, as usual, the dual of the existential. Atomic predicates must also be reinterpreted to apply to the coincidence classes of the continuants to which they originally applied.

[11] See Carnap, (1958, esp. §48) for further discussion of genidentity and its topology.

[12] Since the problem of quantifying out has only recently been solved, the solution to Homework Problem No. 19 is given here, but in a form intended to discourage peeking.

$$\exists t \llcorner \mathsf{T} \; [\imath > 0 \lor \wedge \int \! \forall \, \mathsf{V} \; [\int(\imath)\mathsf{S}\mathsf{e}(\imath)] \leftarrow (\imath)\mathsf{S}\mathsf{e}(\imath)\int) \leftarrow (\imath)\mathsf{H}\mathsf{e}(\imath)\int]\mathsf{H}\mathsf{e}(0)\int\mathsf{H}\mathsf{e}(0)]]$$

[13] There is a tacit prejudice in this argument. Namely, that the value of a constant with respect to a given moment must be among the values of the variables in variable binding operators evaluated with respect to that moment. I shall attempt to exorcise this prejudice in Appendix XII. Even then, what stage of Aristotle should 'Aristotle' now denote? His birthstage? His deathstage? A triumphant middle-age stage?

[14] The bizarre view is adopted in Kaplan (forthcoming) and Lewis (1968), in neither of which, I fear, is the relation to normal theories correctly seen.

[15] No reason remains other than the prejudice alluded to in note 13, and even given the prejudice, why not let the variables themselves take nonoccurrent assemblages as values? How else to express the fact that I now remember someone who is no longer alive?

[16] Hence, 'the person who both is Quine and is named 'Quine'' would not denote anything with respect to such a world.

[17] Like the token Bob-Ted, the name 'Aristotle' may have been somewhat changed in the course of its travels.

[18] I am not sure that this is how our 'Pegasus' originated but let us assume it so.

[19] Suppose, for the moment, that we take possible individuals, both actualized and unactualized, seriously enough to quantify over them (thus validating $\lceil \Diamond \exists x \phi \rightarrow \exists x \Diamond \phi \rceil$). It still does

not follow from the fact that if the Ramsified myth had been true there would have been an actualized winged horse, that there is some possible individual such that if the Ramsified myth had been true *he* would have been an actualized winged horse. There are simply too many ways (possible worlds) in which the Ramsified myth might have been true. (The critical invalidity is $[(\phi \Rightarrow (\psi \vee \chi)) \rightarrow ((\phi \Rightarrow \psi) \vee (\phi \Rightarrow \chi))]$ where '$\Rightarrow$' symbolizes the subjunctive conditional.) Much less does it follow that we could properly speak of *the* possible individual who would have been an actualized winged horse had the Ramsified myth been true. But some such descriptions may be proper. In the most plausible cases we speak of the unique possible individual that would have resulted had a certain closed, developing, deterministic system not been externally aborted. (The possibility of externally induced abortion implies that the system is not completely closed.) Consider, for example, the completely automated automobile assembly line. In full operation, it is, at each moment, pregnant with its next product. Each component: body, frame, motor, etc., lies at the head of its own subassembly line, awaiting only Final Assembly. Can we not speak of the very automobile that would have been produced had the Ecologists Revolution been delayed another 47 seconds?

[20] I will ignore the immediate conjecture that Pegasus symbolizes, and thus 'Pegasus' denotes, *that which man strives for but never fully attains*. Such symbolizations are not reserved to fictional entities; Carnap symbolized the same.

[21] Lewis (1970) would so define theoretical terms of science.

[22] A conversation with my colleague John Bennett caused me to believe this.

[23] Hint: re-read Scott (1967). But see Appendix XIII regarding his answer to the second question.

[24] Note that '*' is a symbol of the metalanguage, and 'the*' is an operator of the object language.

[25] In a generalized theory of descriptions (see Homework Problem # 27) this can be accomplished by treating each term α as semantically equivalent to $\ulcorner$the x $(\alpha : x = x)\urcorner$ where 'x' is not free in α.

[26] The problem is that a formal isomorphism can be constructed between a model using † and one in which the universe of discourse is enlarged to include a new element *. (Barring, of course, the possible decision to treat $\ulcorner \alpha = \alpha \urcorner$ as false, or at least not true, for nondenoting α.) *Given* that the definite description operator of a theory is 'the' not 'the*', the formula $\ulcorner \alpha = $ the $x(x \neq x)\urcorner$, which holds only for nondenoting α, can be used. But lacking some notational sign to distinguish the two operators they are in general indiscernable.

[27] Dana Scott (1967). Also see references to other authors therein.

[28] My attention was drawn to this solution by Richard Montague's solution (in 'The Proper Treatment of Quantification in Ordinary English', this volume) to Partee's paradox: from the premises 'the temperature is ninety' and 'the temperature is rising', the conclusion 'ninety is rising' would appear to follow by normal principles of logic; yet there are occasions on which both premises are true, but none on which the conclusion is. Montague has 'the temperature' denote the function which assigns to each moment the temperature at that moment, 'ninety' denote the constant function to ninety, and the putative 'is' of identity (in the first premise) denote the relation of coincidence.

. An alternative to Montague's solution, in the style of the complete solution, would take 'the temperature' and 'ninety' both to designate a number (the unit, degrees Fahrenheit, is tacit in the terms); the name rigidly and the description flaccidly. The 'is' of the first premise then *is* the 'is' of identity. The predicate 'is rising' must be regarded as producing an intensional context, but it receives the now standard treatment.

The availability of, and some of the consequences of, certain trade-offs between the reference of terms, the intensionality of contexts, and the like is the subject of this appendix.

[29] Here I take the sense of an expression to be its *intension* in the sense of Carnap (1947), namely that function which assigns to each possible circumstance the denotatum (called, by Carnap, the *extension*) of the expression with respect to that circumstance. Strictly speaking the sense *determines* the intension. The same intension may be determined (in different ways) by different senses.

[30] If f and g are functions, they coincide at a point if their values are the same at that point. If α and β are terms such that $\ulcorner \alpha = \beta \urcorner$ is true with respect to a given possible world, then the intension of α and the intension of β will coincide at that world. A predicate expressing coincidence is easily definable in Church's (1951) formalization of Frege's semantics.

[31] To regard an expression other than a proper name as a rigid designator need not entail any unwillingness to recognize the distinctive *syntactical* role played by expressions of differing syntactical categories. Not all rigid designators are, prima facie, proper names; not all are, prima facie, names. Designators like the 'red' in 'Your eye is red' and the 'penguin' in 'Peter is a penguin', which would not ordinarily be regarded as proper names, may yet be rigid if regarded as designating the appropriate entities. If 'red' designates the property of being red, it is probably rigid. If it designates the class of red things, it is certainly not rigid. In my own esoteric doctrines, 'red' rigidly designates a third entity, the color red. Similarly, 'penguin' rigidly designates the species penguin (almost all single words other than particles seem to me to be rigid designators). For Frege, even 'the class of red things' and 'the class of penguins', when located within an oblique context, are rigid designators (though not of classes of red things and penguins).

[32] Just such a process will transform the last solution back into the complete one.

[33] Sam Darwin is the widely acclaimed ontologist and delicatessen operator who once remarked, "Balonies? I don't believe in them. All there is are *slices* arranged in different ways. They come arranged in one way; my job is to rearrange them in tastier ways." The Sam Darwin Fund supports research on the principle of individuation for balonies (what properties of slices determine them as coming from 'the same baloney'). The Fund reports that a breakthrough may be near based on discoveries made with the help of a recently acquired electron microscope. Related investigations, not sponsored by the Darwin Fund, are reported in Geach (1967b), Perry (1970), Lewis (1971), and Perry (forthcoming).

BIBLIOGRAPHY

Ajdukiewicz, K., *Język i Poznanie*, Warsaw 1960.

Austin, J. L., 'Truth' in *Philosophical Papers* (ed. by J. O. Urmson and G. J. Warnock), Oxford 1961.

Austin, J. L., *How To Do Things With Words*, New York 1965.

Bach, E., 'Nouns and Noun Phrases' in *Universals in Linguistic Theory* (ed. by E. Bach and R. Harms), New York 1968.

Bach, E., 'Problominalization', *Linguistic Inquiry* **1** (1970) 121–2.

Bach, E. and Harms, R. (eds.), *Universals in Linguistic Theory*, New York 1968.

Bar-Hillel, Y., 'Logical Syntax and Semantics', *Language* **30** (1954) 230–7.

Bar-Hillel, Y., Gaifman, C., and Shamir, E., 'On Categorial and Phrase-Structure Grammars', *Bulletin of Research on the Council of Israel* **9F** (1960) 1–16.

Becker, E., *An Analysis of Thirty-One Primers*, Unpublished master's thesis, University of Pittsburgh, 1936.

Bell, A., *A State-Process Approach to Syllabicity and Syllable Structure*, Unpublished doctoral dissertation, Stanford University, 1971.

Berman, A., 'Abstract and Agentive Sentences', Unpublished manuscript, Harvard University, 1970.

Bierwisch, M., 'Two Critical Problems in Accent Rules', *Journal of Linguistics* **4** (1968) 173–9.

Binnick, R., Morgan, J., and Greene, G., 'Camelot, 1968', Mimeographed manuscript, 1968.

Bolinger, D., 'Stress and Information' in *Forms of English* (ed. by I. Abe and T. Kanekiyo), Cambridge, Mass., 1958.

Bormuth, J. R., 'Readability: A New Approach', *Reading Research Quarterly* **1** (1966) 79–132.

Braine, M. D. S., 'On Two Types of Models of the Internalization of Grammars' (1971).

Bresnan, J., 'An Argument Against Pronominalization', *Linguistic Inquiry* **1** (1970a) 122–3.

Bresnan, J., 'On Complementizers: Toward a Syntactic Theory of Complement Types', *Foundations of Language* **6** (1970b) 297–321.

Bresnan, J., 'Sentence Stress and Syntactic Transformations', this volume, pp. 3–47.

Bresnan, J., 'The Theory of Complementation in English Syntax', 1971 (in preparation).

Brown, R. and Hanlon, C., 'Derivational Complexity and the Order of Acquisition', in *Cognition and The Development of Language* (ed. by J. R. Hayes), New York 1970.

Burge, T., *Truth and Some Referential Devices*, Unpublished doctoral dissertation, Princeton University, 1971.

Burling, R., 'Language Development of a Garo and English-Speaking Child', *Word* **15** (1959) 45–68.

Carden, G. and Miller, A. G., 'More Problominalizations', *Linguistic Inquiry* **1** (1970) 555–6.

Carnap, R., *Meaning and Necessity*, Chicago 1947. (Enlarged edition 1956).

Carnap, R., 'On Belief Sentences' in *Philosophy and Analysis* (ed. by M. Macdonald), Oxford 1954. Also Appendix C in Carnap (1956).

Hintikka et al. (eds.), Approaches to Natural Language, 519–526. *All rights reserved.*
Copyright © 1973 by D. Reidel Publishing Company, Dordrecht-Holland.

Carnap, R., *Introduction to Symbolic Logic and Its Applications*, New York 1958 (transl. by W. H. Meyers).

Cartwright, H. M., 'Heraclitus and the Bath Water', *Philosophical Review* **74** (1965) 466–85.

Cartwright, H. M., 'Quantities', *Philosophical Review* **79** (1970) 25–42.

Cartwright, H. M., 'Chappell on Stuff and Things', *Nous* (1971, in press).

Cartwright, R., 'Propositions' in *Analytical Philosophy* (ed. by R. J. Butler), New York, 1962.

Chall, J. S., *Readability, An Appraisal of Research and Application*, Columbus, Ohio, 1958.

Chao, Y. R., *A Grammar of Spoken Chinese*, Berkeley 1968. (Preliminary edition, 1965).

Chapin, P. G., 'Samoan Pronominalization', *Language* **46** (1970) 366–78.

Chomsky, N., 'Logical Syntax and Semantics; Their Linguistic Relevance', *Language* **31** (1955) 36–45.

Chomsky, N., *Syntactic Structures*, The Hague 1957.

Chomsky, N., *Aspects of the Theory of Syntax*, Cambridge, Mass., 1965.

Chomsky, N., 'Linguistics and Philosophy' in *Language and Philosophy: A Symposium*, part II (ed. by S. Hook), New York 1969a.

Chomsky, N., 'Quine's Empirical Assumptions' in *Words and Objections, Essays on the Work of W. V. Quine* (ed. by D. Davidson and K. J. Hintikka), Dordrecht 1969b.

Chomsky, N., 'Some Empirical Issues in the Theory of Transformational Grammar', Indiana University Linguistics Club, 1970a.

Chomsky, N., 'Remarks on Nominalization' in *Readings in English Transformational Grammar* (ed. by R. A. Jacobs and P. S. Rosenbaum), New York 1970b.

Chomsky, N., 'Deep Structure, Surface Structure, and Semantic Interpretation' in *Semantics: An Interdisciplinary Reader* (ed. by D. D. Steinberg and L. A. Jakobovits), Cambridge 1971.

Chomsky, N. and Halle, M., *The Sound Pattern of English*, New York 1968.

Chou, F., *Chung kuo ku-tai yu-fa, Ch'ao chu pien, (A Historical Grammar of Ancient Chinese, Part I, Syntax)*, Taipei 1961.

Church, A., 'On Carnap's Analysis of Statements of Assertion and Belief', *Analysis* **10** (1950) 97–9.

Church, A., 'A Formulation of the Logic of Sense and Denotation' in *Structure, Method, and Meaning* (ed. by P. Henle, H. Kallen, and S. Langer), New York 1951.

Church, A., 'Intensional Isomorphism and Identity of Belief', *Philosophical Studies* **5** (1954) 65–73.

Dobson, W. A. C. H., *Late Archaic Chinese*, Toronto 1959.

Dobson, W. A. C. H., *Early Archaic Chinese*, Toronto 1962.

Dobson, W. A. C. H., *Late Han Chinese*, Toronto 1964.

Donnellan, K., 'Reference and Definite Descriptions', *Philosophical Review* **75** (1966) 281–304.

Donnellan, K., 'Putting Humpty Dumpty Together Again', *The Philosophical Review* **77** (1968) 203–15.

Donnellan, K., 'Proper Names and Identifying Descriptions', *Synthese* **21** (1970) 335–58.

Dougherty, R., 'An Interpretive Theory of Pronominal Reference', *Foundations of Language* **5** (1969) 488–519.

Emonds, J., *Root and Structure Preserving Transformations*, Unpublished doctoral dissertation, Massachusetts Institute of Technology, 1970.

Feldman, J., 'Some Decidability Results on Grammatical Inference and Complexity', Memo AI–93, 1969, Stanford University, Artificial Intelligence Project.

Feldman, J., Gips, J., Horning, J., and Reder, S., 'Grammatical Complexity and Inference',

Technical Report N. CS 125, 1969, Stanford University, Department of Computer Science.

Fillmore, C., 'Toward a Modern Theory of Case', *Project on Linguistic Analysis* **13** (1965) 1–24.

Fillmore, C., 'The Case for Case' in *Universals in Linguistic Theory* (ed. by E. Bach and R. Harms), New York 1968.

Fodor, J. D., 'Whose Description?', Unpublished manuscript, Harvard University, 1968.

Frege, G., 'On Sense and Reference' in *Translations from the Philosophical Writings of Gottlob Frege* (ed. by P. T. Geach and M. Black), Oxford 1952.

Frege, G., 'The Thought: A Logical Inquiry' in *Philosophical Logic* (ed. by P. F. Strawson) Oxford 1967.

Friedman, J., 'A Computer System for Transformational Grammar', *Communications of the ACM* **12** (1969) 341–8.

Friedman, J., Bredt, T. H., Doran, R. W., Martner, T. S. and Pollack, B. W., *A Computer Model of Transformational Grammar*, New York 1971.

Friedman, J. and Myslenski, P., *Computer Experiments in Transformational Grammar: The UCLA English Grammar*, Ann Arbor, Michigan, 1970 (multilith).

Fromkin, V., 'The Non-Anomalous Nature of Anomalous Utterances', *Language* **47** (1971) 27–52.

Gammon, E., *A Syntactical Analysis of Some First-Grade Readers*, Unpublished doctoral dissertation, Stanford University, 1969.

Gates, A. I., *Interest and Ability in Reading*, New York 1930.

Geach, P. T., *Reference and Generality*, Ithaca 1962.

Geach, P. T., 'Assertion', *Philosophical Review* **74** (1965) 449–65.

Geach, P. T., 'Intentional Identity', *Journal of Philosophy* **64** (1967a) 627–32.

Geach, P. T., 'Identity', *The Review of Metaphysics* **21** (1967b) 3–12.

Ginsburg, S. and Partee, B., 'A Mathematical Model of Transformational Grammars', *Information and Control* **15** (1969) 297–334.

Gleitman, L. and Gleitman, H., *Phrase and Paraphrase*, New York 1971.

Gold, E. M., 'Language Identification in the Limit', *Information and Control* **10** (1967) 447–74.

Goodman, N., *The Structure of Appearance*, Cambridge, Mass., 1951.

Goodman, N. and Leonard, H. S., 'The Calculus of Individuals and Its Uses', *Journal of Symbolic Logic* **5** (1940) 45–55.

Gruber, J. S., *Studies in Lexical Relations*, Unpublished doctoral dissertation, Massachusetts Institute of Technology, 1965.

Hamburger, H., *On the Learning of Three Classes of Transformational Components,* doctoral dissertation, University of Michigan, Ann Arbor, 1971.

Hamburger, H. and Wexler, K., 'Identifiability of a Class of Transformational Grammars', this volume, pp. 153–66.

Harris, Z. S., *Mathematical Structures of Language* (Interscience Tracts in Pure and Applied Mathematics, 21), New York 1968.

Hasegawa, K., 'The Passive Construction in English', *Language* **44** (1968) 230–43.

Hilbert, D. and Bernays, P., *Grundlagen der Mathematik*, I–II, Berlin 1934, 1939.

Hintikka, K. J., *Knowledge and Belief*, Ithaca 1962.

Hintikka, K. J., *Models for Modalities: Selected Essays*, Dordrecht 1969a.

Hintikka, K. J., 'Partially Transparent Senses of Knowing', *Philosophical Studies* **20** (1969b) 5–8.

Hintikka, K. J., 'Knowledge, Belief, and Logical Consequence', *Ajatus* **32** (1970a) 32–47.

Hintikka, K. J., 'Surface Information and Depth Information', in *Information and Inference* (ed. by K. J. Hintikka and P. Suppes), Dordrecht 1970b.

Hintikka, K. J., 'Objects of Knowledge and Belief: Acquaintances and Public Figures', *Journal of Philosophy* **67** (1970c) 869–83.

Hintikka, K. J., 'The Semantics of Modal Notions and the Indeterminacy of Ontology', *Synthese* **21** (1970d) 408–24.

Hintikka, K. J., 'Knowledge by Acquaintance–Individuation by Acquaintance' in *Bertrand Russell* (*Modern Studies in Philosophy*) (ed. by D. Pears), Garden City, N.Y., 1972a.

Hintikka, K. J., 'On the Different Constructions in Terms of the Basic Epistemological Concepts: A Survey of Some Problems and Proposals' in *Contemporary Philosophy in Scandinavia* (ed. by R. E. Olson and A. M. Paul), Baltimore, 1972b.

Hintikka, K. J., 'Grammar and Logic', this volume, pp. 197–214.

Hockett, J. A., *The Vocabulary and Content of Elementary School Readers*, Sacramento, Calif., 1938.

Hopcroft, J. and Ullman, J., *Formal Languages and Their Relation to Automata*, Reading, Mass., 1969.

Jackendoff, R., *Some Rules of Semantic Interpretation for English*, Unpublished doctoral dissertation, Massachusetts Institute of Technology, 1969.

Jakobson, R., *Child Language, Aphasia, and Phonological Universals*, The Hague 1968.

Jakobson, R., 'Why "Mamma" and "Papa"?' in *Selected Writings of Roman Jakobson*, The Hague 1939. Reprinted in *Child Language: A Book of Readings* (ed. by A. Bar-adon and W. F. Leopold), Englewood Cliffs, N.J., 1970.

Kanger, S., *Provability in Logic*, Stockholm Studies in Philosophy, vol. 1, Stockholm 1957.

Kaplan, D., 'Trans-World Heir Lines', Unpublished manuscript of an address presented to a joint Meeting of the Association for Symbolic Logic and the American Philosophical Association, May 1967.

Kaplan, D., 'Quantifying In', in *Words and Objections: Essays on the Work of W. V. Quine* (ed. by D. Davidson and K. J. Hintikka), Dordrecht 1969. Reprinted from *Synthese* **19** (1968) 178–214.

Karttunen, L., 'Co-Reference and Discourse', presented to the Winter Meeting of the Linguistic Society of America, 1968.

Karttunen, L., 'Pronouns and Variables' in *Papers from the Fifth Regional Meeting, Chicago Linguistic Society*, 1969.

Katz, J. J., *The Philosophy of Language*, New York 1966.

Katz, J. and Postal, P., *An Integrated Theory of Linguistic Descriptions*, Cambridge, Mass., 1964.

Kimball, J. P., 'Predicates Definable over Transformational Derivations by Intersection with Regular Languages', *Information and Control* **11** (1967) 177–95.

Kimball, J. P., 'The Semantic Content of Transformations', *Linguistic Inquiry* (to appear).

Kiparsky, R. P. V. and Kiparsky, C. A. S., 'Fact', in *Recent Advances in Linguistics* (ed. by M. Bierwisch and K.-H. Heidolph) (forthcoming).

Kleene, S. C., *Introduction to Metamathematics*, Princeton 1952.

Klima, E. S., 'Negation in English', in *The Structure of Language* (ed. by J. Fodor and J. Katz), Englewood Cliffs, N.J., 1964.

Klima, E. S. and Bellugi, U., 'Syntactic Regularities in the Speech of Children' in *Psycholinguistics Papers* (ed. by J. Lyons and R. Wales), Edinburgh 1966.

Knuth, D. E., 'Semantics of Context-Free Languages', *Mathematical Systems Theory* **2** (1968) 127–31.

Kripke, S. A., 'Semantical Considerations on Modal Logic', *Acta Philosophica Fennica* **16** (1963a) 83–94.

Kripke, S. A., 'Semantical Analysis of Modal Logic: I, Normal Modal Propositional Calculi', *Zeitschrift für mathematische Logik und Grundlagen der Mathematik* **9** (1963b) 67–96.

Kripke, S. A., 'Semantical Analysis of Modal Logic: II, Non-Normal Modal Propositional Calculi', in *The Theory of Models* (ed. by J. W. Addison, L. Henkin, and A. Tarski), Amsterdam 1965.

Kripke, S. A., 'Naming and Necessity' in *Semantics of Natural Language* (ed. by D. Davidson and G. Harman), Dordrecht 1972.

Kuno, S., 'Some Properties of Non-Referential Noun Phrases' in *Studies in Oriental and General Linguistics* (ed. by R. Jakobson), Tokyo (to appear).

Lakoff, G., *On the Nature of Syntactic Irregularity*, NSF-16, 1965, Indiana University, Mathematical Linguistics and Automatic Translation Report.

Lakoff, G., 'Pronominalization, Negation, and the Analysis of Adverbs', Mimeographed manuscript, 1967.

Lakoff, G., 'Instrumental Adverbs and the Concept of Deep Structure', *Foundations of Language* **4** (1968a) 4–29.

Lakoff, G., 'Counterparts, or the Problem of Reference in Transformational Grammar', presented (under a different title) to the Summer Meeting of the Linguistics Society of America in 1968, 1968b.

Lakoff, G., 'On Derivational Constraints' in *Papers from the Fifth Regional Meeting of the Chicago Linguistics Society* (ed. by R. Binnick *et al.*), Chicago 1969.

Lakoff, G., 'Repartee', *Foundations of Language* **6** (1970a) 389–422.

Lakoff, G., *Linguistics and Natural Logic*. Studies in Generative Semantics, vol. 1., Ann Arbor, Mich., 1970b. (Also appeared in a modified form in *Synthese* **22** (1970–71) 151–271. References in the text pertain to the earlier version whose relevant theoretical theses have been somewhat modified and weakened in the newer version.)

Lakoff, R., 'A Syntactic Argument for Negative Transportation' in *Papers from the Fifth Regional Meeting of the Chicago Linguistics Society* (ed. by R. Binnick *et al.*), Chicago 1969.

Langacker, R., 'Semantic Theory and the Problem of Supposition', Mimeographed manuscript, 1966.

Langacker, R. W., 'Mirror Image Rules', *Language* **45** (1969a) 575–98, 844–62.

Langacker, R. W., 'On Pronominalization and the Chain of Command' in *Modern Studies in English* (ed. by S. A. Schane and D. A. Reibel), Englewood Cliffs, N.J., 1969b.

Leech, G. N., *Towards a Semantic Description of English*, Bloomington 1969.

Lees, R., 'A Multiply Ambiguous Adjectival Construction in English', *Language* **36** (1960) 207–21.

Leopold, W. F., *Speech Development of a Bilingual Child*, vol. 1, Evanston 1939.

Lewis, C. I., 'The Modes of Meaning' in *Semantics and the Philosophy of Language* (ed. by L. Linsky), Urbana 1952.

Lewis, D., 'Counterpart Theory and Quantified Modal Logic', *The Journal of Philosophy* **65** (1968) 113–26.

Lewis, D., 'How to Define Theoretical Terms', *The Journal of Philosophy* **67** (1970) 427–46.

Lewis, D., 'Counterparts of Persons and Their Bodies', *The Journal of Philosophy* **68** (1971) 203–11.

Lewis, D., 'General Semantics', in *Semantics of Natural Language* (ed. by D. Davidson and G. Harman), Dordrecht 1972.

Lyons, J., *Introduction to Theoretical Linguistics*, Cambridge 1969.

McCawley, J., 'Concerning the Base Component of a Transformational Grammar', *Foundations of Languages* **4** (1968) 243–69.

McCawley, J., 'English as a VSO Language', *Language* **46** (1970) 286–99.

MacIver. A. M., 'Demonstratives and Proper Names' in *Philosophy and Analysis* (ed. by M. Macdonald), Oxford 1954.

McKaughan, H., 'Topicalization in Maranao – An Addendum', in *Pacific Linguistic Studies in Honor of Arthur Capell* (ed. by S. A. Wurm and D. C. Laycock), Canberra A.C.T. Australia, 1970.

Marsh, W. and Ritchie, R. W., 'Predictably Enumerable Sets' (to appear).

Mates, B., 'Synonymity' in *Meaning and Interpretation*, Univ. of Calif. Publications in Philosophy **25** (1950) 201–26. Also in *Semantics and the Philosophy of Language* (ed. by L. Linsky), Urbana 1952.

Mehl, M. A., *A Vocabulary Study of First Grade Readers*, Unpublished master's thesis, University of Colorado, 1931.

Montague, R., 'Pragmatics' in *Contemporary Philosophy – La Philosophie Contemporaine*, vol. 1 (ed. by R. Klibansky), Florence 1968.

Montague, R., 'On the Nature of Certain Philosophical Entities', *The Monist* **53** (1969) 161–94.

Montague, R., 'English as a Formal Language' in *Linguaggi nella Società e nella Tecnica* (ed. by B. Visentini *et al.*), Milan 1970a.

Montague, R., 'Pragmatics and Intensional Logic', *Synthese* **22** (1970b), 68–94.

Montague, R., 'The Proper Treatment of Quantification in Ordinary English', this volume, pp. 221–42.

Montague, R., 'Universal Grammar', *Theoria* **36** (1970, published 1971), 373–98.

Moravcsik, J. M. E., 'Competence, Creativity, and Innateness', *Philosophical Forum* **1** (1969) 407–37.

Moravcsik, J. M. E., 'Subcategorization and Abstract Terms', *Foundations of Language* **6** (1970) 473–87.

Moravcsik, J. M. E., 'Mass Terms in English', this volume, pp. 263–85.

Moskowitz, A. I., 'The Two-Year-Old Stage in the Acquisition of English Phonology', *Language* **46** (1970) 426–41.

Newman, S., 'On the Stress System of English', *Word* **2** (1946) 171–87.

Niyakawa-Howard, A., 'A Psycholinguistic Study: The Whorfian Hypothesis Based on the Japanese Passive', Paper presented to the 13th Annual National Conference in Linguistics, New York, March 1968.

Ousley, O. and Russell, D., *The Pre-Primer Program*: *My Little Red Story Book*, *My Little Green Story Book*, *My Little Blue Story Book*, Boston, Mass., 1957.

Ousley, O. and Russell, D., *The Little White House*, Boston, Mass., 1961.

Pap, A., 'Belief, Synonymity, and Analysis', *Philosophical Studies* **6** (1955) 11–5.

Pap, A., 'Belief and Propositions', *Philosophy of Science* **24** (1957) 123–36.

Parsons, T., 'An Analysis of Mass Terms and Amount Terms', *Foundations of Language* **6** (1970) 363–88.

Partee, B. H., 'Negation, Conjunction, and Quantifiers: Syntax vs. Semantics', *Foundations of Language* **6** (1970a) 153–65.

Partee, B. H., 'Opacity, Coreference, and Pronouns', *Synthese* **21** (1970b) 359–85.

Partee, B. H., 'On the Requirement that Transformations Preserve Meaning' in *Studies in Linguistic Semantics* (ed. by C. J. Fillmore and D. T. Langendoen), New York 1971.

Partee, B. H., 'The Semantics of Belief-Sentences', this volume, pp. 309–36.

Perlmutter, D., *Deep and Surface Structure Constraints in Syntax*, New York 1970a.

Perlmutter, D., 'Surface Structure Constraints in Syntax', *Linguistic Inquiry* **2** (1970b) 187–255.

Perry, J., 'The Same F', *The Philosophical Review* **79** (1970) 181–200.

Perry, J., 'Can the Self Divide?' (forthcoming).

Peters, S. and Ritchie, R. W., 'On Restricting the Base Component of Transformational Grammars', *Information and Control* **18** (1971) 483–501.

Peters, S. and Ritchie, R. W., 'On the Generative Power of Transformational Grammars', *Information Sciences* (1972) (to appear).

Peters, P. S., Jr., and Ritchie, R. W., 'Nonfiltering and Local-Filtering Transformational Grammars', this volume, pp. 180–93.

Postal, P., 'Underlying and Superficial Linguistic Structures', *Harvard Educational Review* **34** (1964) 246–66.

Postal, P. M., 'On So-Called "Pronouns" in English', *Monograph Series on Languages and Linguistics* **19** (1966). Reprinted in *Modern Studies in English* (ed. by D. A. Reibel and S. A. Schane), Englewood Cliffs, N.J., 1969.

Postal, P. M., 'Cross-Over Phenomena' in *Specification and Utilization of a Transformational Grammar*, Yorktown Heights, N.Y., 1968a.

Postal, P. M., *On Coreferential Complement Subject Deletion*, Yorktown Heights, N.Y., 1968b.

Postal, P. M., 'Anaphoric Islands' in *Papers from the Fifth Regional Meeting, Chicago Linguistic Society*, 1969.

Putnam, H., 'Synonymity and the Analysis of Belief-Sentences', *Analysis* **14** (1954) 114–22.

Quine, W. V. O., *From a Logical Point of View*, Cambridge, Mass., 1953.

Quine, W. V. O., *Word and Object*, Cambridge, Mass., 1960.

Quine, W. V. O., 'Quantifiers and Propositional Attitudes', *Journal of Philosophy* **53** (1956) 177–87; reprinted in W. V. O. Quine, *The Ways of Paradox and Other Essays*, New York 1966.

Quine, W. V. O., *Philosophy of Logic*, Englewood Cliffs, N.J., 1970a.

Quine, W. V. O., 'Methodological Reflections on Current Linguistic Theory', *Synthese* **21** (1970b) 386–98.

Ritchie, R. W., 'Classes of Predictably Computable Functions', *Transactions of American Mathematical Society* **106** (1963) 139–73.

Robinson, H. M., Monroe, M., and Artley, A. S., *Sally Dick and Jane*. Chicago 1962a.

Robinson, H. M., Monroe, M., and Artley, A. S., *Second and Third Pre-Primers*, Chicago 1962b.

Robinson, H. M., Monroe, M., and Artley, A. S., *Fun with our Friends*, Chicago 1962c.

Robinson, H. M., Monroe, M., and Artley, A. S., *More Fun with our Friends*, Chicago 1962d.

Ross, J., 'On the Cyclic Nature of English Pronominalization', Unpublished manuscript, 1966.

Ross, J., *Constraints on Variables in Syntax*, Unpublished doctoral dissertation, Massachusetts Institute of Technology, 1967.

Ruddell, R. B., 'The Effect of the Similarity of Oral and Written Patterns of Language Structure on Reading Comprehension', *Elementary English* **42** (1964) 403–10.

Ruddell, R. B., *The Effect of Four Programs of Reading Instruction with Varying Emphasis on the Regularity of Grapheme-Phoneme Correspondences and the Relation of Language Structure to Meaning on Achievement in First Grade Reading*, Berkeley, Calif., 1965.

Russell, D. and Ousley, O., *On Cherry Street*, Boston 1957.

Scheffler, I., 'On Synonymy and Indirect Discourse', *Philosophy of Science* **22** (1955) 39–44.

Scott, D., 'Existence and Description in Formal Logic' in *Bertrand Russell: Philosopher of the Century* (ed. by R. Schoenman), London 1967.

Sellars, W., 'Putnam on Synonymity and Belief', *Analysis* **15** (1955) 117–20.

Shvachkin, N., 'The Development of Phonemic Speech Perception in Early Childhood' in *Studies of Child Language* (ed. by D. I. Slobin and C. A. Ferguson), New York (to appear).

Slobin, D. I. and Welsh, C. A., 'Elicited Imitation as a Research Tool in Developmental Psycholinguistics', Working Paper No. 10, University of California, Berkeley, 1968, Language Behavior Research Laboratory.

Spache, G., 'Problems in Primary Book Selection: The Selection of Pre-Primers . . . Supplementary Pre-Primers . . . Primers and Supplementary Primers . . . First and Second Readers', *Elementary English Review* **18** (1941) 5–12, 52–9, 139–48, 175–81.

Stockwell, R. P., Schachter, P., and Partee, B. H., *Integration of Transformational Theories on English Syntax*, Los Angeles 1968–1969, Multilith paper, 1969.

Strawson, P. F., *Individuals*, New York 1963.

Strawson, P. F. (ed.), *Philosophical Logic*, Oxford 1967.

Strickland, R. G., 'The Language of Elementary School Children: Its Relationship to the Language of Reading Textbooks and the Quality of Reading of Selected Children', *Bulletin of the School of Education*, Indiana University **38** (1962) 1–131.

Suppes, P., 'Probabilistic Grammars for Natural Languages', *Synthese* **22** (1970) 95–116.

Suppes, P., 'Semantics of Context-Free Fragments of Natural Languages', this volume, pp. 370–94.

Tarski, A., 'Der Wahrheitsbegriff in den formalisierten Sprachen', *Studia Philosophica* **1** (1935) 261–405.

Urmson, J. O., 'Criteria of Intensionality', *Proceedings of the Aristotelian Society, Supplementary Volume* **42** (1968) 107–22.

Wang, L. (ed.), *Ku-tai han-yu* (*The Ancient Chinese*), vol. 1, part I, Peking 1962.

Wang, L. (ed.), *Ku-tai han-yu* (*The Ancient Chinese*), vol.1, part II, Peking 1964.

Watt, W. C., '*Review, Aspects of the Theory of Syntax* (2nd ed.), by N. Chomsky', *College Composition and Communication* **21** (1970) 75–81.

Watt, W. C., 'Paradox Lost', Manuscript, 1971a.

Watt, W. C., 'Paradox Regained', Manuscript, 1971b.

Wilson, C., *Statement and Inference*, vol. 1, Oxford 1926.

SYNTHESE LIBRARY

Monographs on Epistemology, Logic, Methodology,
Philosophy of Science, Sociology of Science and of Knowledge, and on the
Mathematical Methods of Social and Behavioral Sciences

Editors:

DONALD DAVIDSON (Rockefeller University and Princeton University)
JAAKKO HINTIKKA (Academy of Finland and Stanford University)
GABRIËL NUCHELMANS (University of Leyden)
WESLEY C. SALMON (Indiana University)

‡JAAKKO HINTIKKA and PATRICK SUPPES, *Information and Inference.* 1970, X + 336 pp.
Dfl. 60,—

‡KAREL LAMBERT, *Philosophical Problems in Logic. Some Recent Developments.* 1970, VII + 176 pp.
Dfl. 38,—

‡P. V. TAVANEC (ed.), *Problems of the Logic of Scientific Knowledge.* 1969, XII + 429 pp.
Dfl. 95,—

‡ROBERT S. COHEN and RAYMOND J. SEEGER (eds.), *Boston Studies in the Philosophy of Science.* Volume VI: *Ernst Mach: Physicist and Philosopher.* 1970, VIII + 295 pp.
Dfl. 38,—

‡MARSHALL SWAIN (ed.), *Induction, Acceptance, and Rational Belief.* 1970, VII + 232 pp.
Dfl. 40,—

‡NICHOLAS RESCHER *et al.* (eds.), *Essays in Honor of Carl G. Hempel. A Tribute on the Occasion of his Sixty-Fifth Birthday.* 1969, VII + 272 pp.
Dfl. 50,—

‡PATRICK SUPPES, *Studies in the Methodology and Foundations of Science. Selected Papers from 1911 to 1969.* 1969, XII + 473 pp.
Dfl. 72,—

‡JAAKKO HINTIKKA, *Models for Modalities. Selected Essays.* 1969, IX + 220 pp.
Dfl. 34,—

‡D. DAVIDSON and J. HINTIKKA (eds.), *Words and Objections: Essays on the Work of W. V. Quine.* 1969, VIII + 366 pp.
Dfl. 48,—

‡J. W. DAVIS, D. J. HOCKNEY and W. K. WILSON (eds.), *Philosophical Logic.* 1969, VIII + 277 pp.
Dfl. 45,—

‡ROBERT S. COHEN and MARX W. WARTOFSKY (eds.), *Boston Studies in the Philosophy of Science*, Volume V: *Proceedings of the Boston Colloquium for the Philosophy of Science 1966/1968*, VIII + 482 pp.
Dfl. 60,—

‡ROBERT S. COHEN and MARX W. WARTOFSKY (eds.), *Boston Studies in the Philosophy of Science*, Volume IV: *Proceedings of the Boston Colloquium for the Philosophy of Science 1966/1968.* 1969, VIII + 537 pp.
Dfl. 72,—

‡NICOLAS RESCHER, *Topics in Philosophical Logic.* 1968, XIV + 347 pp.   Dfl. 70,—

‡GÜNTHER PATZIG, *Aristotle's Theory of the Syllogism. A Logical-Philological Study of Book A of the Prior Analytics.* 1968, XVII + 215 pp.
Dfl. 48,—

‡C. D. BROAD, *Induction, Probability, and Causation. Selected Papers.* 1968, XI + 296 pp.
Dfl. 54,—

‡ROBERT S. COHEN and MARX W. WARTOFSKY (eds.), *Boston Studies in the Philosophy of Science.* Volume III: *Proceedings of the Boston Colloquium for the Philosophy of Science 1964/1966.* 1967, XLIX + 489 pp.
Dfl. 70,—

‡GUIDO KÜNG, *Ontology and the Logistic Analysis of Language. An Enquiry into the Contemporary Views on Universals.* 1967, XI + 210 pp.
Dfl. 41,—

*EVERT W. BETH and JEAN PIAGET, *Mathematical Epistemology and Psychology.* 1966, XXII + 326 pp.
Dfl. 63,—

*EVERT W. BETH, *Mathematical Thought. An Introduction to the Philosophy of Mathematics.* 1965, XII + 208 pp.
Dfl. 37,—

‡Paul Lorenzen, *Formal Logic*. 1965, VIII + 123 pp.   Dfl. 26,—

‡Georges Gurvitch, *The Spectrum of Social Time*. 1964, XXVI + 152 pp.
                                                                     Dfl. 25,—

‡A. A. Zinov'ev, *Philosophical Problems of Many-Valued Logic*. 1963, XIV + 155 pp.
                                                                     Dfl. 32,—

‡Marx W. Wartofsky (ed.), *Boston Studies in the Philosophy of Science*. Volume I:
Proceedings of the Boston Colloquium for the Philosophy of Science, 1961–1962.
1963, VIII + 212 pp.   Dfl. 26,50

‡B. H. Kazemier and D. Vuysje (eds.), *Logic and Language. Studies dedicated to
Professor Rudolf Carnap on the Occasion of his Seventieth Birthday*. 1962, VI +
256 pp.   Dfl. 35,—

*Evert W. Beth, *Formal Methods. An Introduction to Symbolic Logic and to the Study
of Effective Operations in Arithmetic and Logic*. 1962, XIV + 170 pp.   Dfl. 35,—

*Hans Freudenthal (ed.), *The Concept and the Role of the Model in Mathematics
and Natural and Social Sciences. Proceedings of a Colloquium held at Utrecht, The
Netherlands, January 1960*. 1961, VI + 194 pp.   Dfl. 34,—

‡P. L. Guiraud, *Problèmes et méthodes de la statistique linguistique*. 1960, VI +
146 pp.   Dfl. 28,—

*J. M. Bocheński, *A Precis of Mathematical Logic*. 1959, X + 100 pp.   Dfl. 23,—

SYNTHESE HISTORICAL LIBRARY

Texts and Studies
in the History of Logic and Philosophy

Editors:

N. KRETZMANN (Cornell University)
G. NUCHELMANS (University of Leyden)
L. M. DE RIJK (University of Leyden)

LEWIS WHITE BECK (ed.), *Proceedings of the Third International Kant Congress.* 1972, XI + 718 pp.   Dfl. 160,—

‡KARL WOLF and PAUL WEINGARTNER (eds.), *Ernst Mally: Logische Schriften.* 1971, X + 340 pp.   Dfl. 80,—

‡LEROY E. LOEMKER (ed.), *Gottfried Wilhelm Leibnitz: Philosophical Papers and Letters.* A Selection Translated and Edited, with an Introduction. 1969, XII + 736 pp.
                                                                                Dfl. 125,—

‡M. T. BEONIO-BROCCHIERI FUMAGALLI, *The Logic of Abelard.* Translated from the Italian. 1969, IX + 101 pp.   Dfl. 27,—

Sole Distributors in the U.S.A. and Canada:
*GORDON & BREACH, INC., 440 Park Avenue South, New York, N.Y. 10016
‡HUMANITIES PRESS, INC., 303 Park Avenue South, New York, N.Y. 10010